Super VGA Graphics

Graphics

Programming Secrets

This one's for Megan as well.

Super VGA Graphics

Graphics

Programming Secrets

Steve Rimmer

Windcrest®/ McGraw-Hill
New York   San Francisco   Washington, D.C.   Auckland   Bogotá
Caracas   Lisbon   London   Madrid   Mexico City   Milan
Montreal   New Delhi   San Juan   Singapore
Sydney   Tokyo   Toronto

FIRST EDITION
FIRST PRINTING

© 1993 by **Windcrest Books**, an imprint of TAB Books.
TAB Books is a division of McGraw-Hill, Inc.
The name "Windcrest" is a registered trademark of TAB Books.

Library of Congress Cataloging-in-Publication Data
Rimmer, Steve.
     Super VGA graphics: programming secrets / by Steve Rimmer.; aa13
12-18-92
       p.   cm.
     Includes index.
     ISBN 0-8306-4427-X (h)   ISBN 0-8306-4428-8 (p)
     1. Computer graphics.   2. Expansion cards (Microcomputers)
I. Title.
T385.R5537   1993
006.6'765—dc20   92-38282
                                                                        CIP

Acquisitions editor: Brad Schepp
Editorial team: Robert Ostrander, Executive Editor
                David M. McCandless, Book Editor
                Jodi L. Tyler, Indexer
Production team: Katherine G. Brown, Director of Production
                Tina M. Sourbier, Coding
                Wanda S. Ditch, Layout
                Linda L. King, Proofreading
Design team: Jaclyn J. Boone, Designer
                Brian Allison, Associate Designer
Cover Design and Illustration: Sandra Blair, Harrisburg, Pa.   WC-1

If you have bought this book, you have bought the following rights to use the code herein for your applications.

You're free to abstract code fragments from this book as you require and incorporate them into programs that you write. You can distribute these programs freely in their executable form, such that they can be run by other users but not readily decompiled, disassembled or linked into other applications.

You cannot distribute any of the source code from this book as source code, in either human or machine readable form.

In distributing executable application files that contain functions or variations on function from this book, you are not required to pay any additional royalties, nor do you require explicit written permission. No credit need be given to this book.

You are free to distribute the font resources found on the companion disk to this book as part of your own applications, subject to applicable laws. See Chapter 6 for clarification of this.

You cannot distribute any of the applications, utilities, documentation or complete packages on the companion disk for this book without explicit written permission from Alchemy Mindworks Inc.

In short, you can use the source code in any way that would not allow someone who has not bought this book to use the source.

Contents

Preface

"There are three kinds of people in the world—those who can count, and those who can't."
  — Graffiti

There's a human quality to graphical computer applications that's missing from software that runs in text mode. Even fairly serious packages such as Microsoft Windows seem to take on the apprehension of being amusing. Windows not only allows for questionable pictures and obtuse icons to be affixed to its desktop—it positively cries out for them. I think the most salient description of Windows I can recall is that it's more entertaining than a bug zapper and a six-pack of beer.

To some extent this quality can manifest itself in any graphical application. It might be simply that, after years of looking at screens troweled together from the IBM text mode block graphics characters, most computer users are taken by anything that looks different. For whatever reason, you can make people like your applications a lot more if they draw pictures rather than display text. If you can allow your users to add questionable pictures to the applications they boot up as well, you'll probably be hailed as some manner of low-rent god.

While a bit awkward in years gone by, PC-based graphics have coalesced to some extent of late. Everyone seems to have settled on VGA cards. In fact, as you'll probably appreciate once you've gotten through the first chapter of this book, the VGA standard isn't much of a standard at all. The first thing that most VGA card manufacturers set out to do is violate it. While not as unworkable as the generations of display adapters preceding it, the multiple VGA standards take a bit of understanding to fully implement.

It's probably a useful rule that whenever any prefix appears before an acronym associated with computers, at least half of the software written prior to its introduction will no longer function. Of all the offending prefixes used in this respect, "super" is arguably among the most dreaded.

Super VGA Graphics will allow you to write graphic-based software that will astound your users. Even fairly inexpensive super VGA cards have facilities to do things far more interesting than most conventional software typically asks of them. The complexity involved in using these resources has kept a lot of applications from implementing them.

This book will provide you with the tools you need to make super VGA graphic modes work for you. With very little unpleasant math, indirect addressing, or exponential notation, the examples herein will let you access the super VGA graphics modes of most of the popular display cards, display pictures, print graphics, manage a mouse, use clickable buttons, draw graphic primitives and quite a bit more.

This book will also give you a leg up on writing what might be the most interesting sort of graphical application—a VGA arcade game. In most cases, this will not be a good thing to try on company time, but writing games is among the most engaging flights of imagination you can undertake with a personal computer.

Figure P-1 illustrates a screen from *Alice*, the sample game from Chapter 8 of this book.

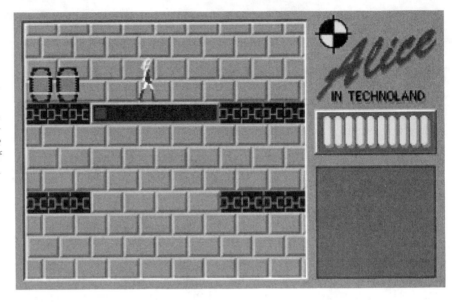

P-1

*Alice in TechnologyLand—
a graphic adventure game
from the far-off lands of
Chapter 8.*

If you've had a look through this book you'll have noticed that it contains a lot of source code. It also contains a disk at the back that has all the source code in machine readable form. You won't have to erode your fingerprints typing in voluminous listings to use the functions this book provides you with.

The companion disk for this book also includes two versions of the executable files for Desktop Paint, a shareware paint program. Desktop Paint uses much the same code as appears in this book. It will provide you with a way to create images for use in your own applications, as well as a source of font resources. Fonts will turn up later.

Super VGA Graphics has not been written to be an exhaustive reference about VGA cards. There are dozens of obscure VGA registers it doesn't even mention, write modes it only alludes to, and whole chapters worth of hardware timing diagrams and chip pinouts it never gets within a light year of. There are several really ponderous books available to provide you with this information if you really want to stare at it for a while.

The information in *Super VGA Graphics* is intended to be immediately useful. If you're writing graphical applications on a PC, you can lift the code from this book, pour it into your own software, and quickly move on to the functional parts of your project. Unless you particularly want to immerse yourself in VGA lore, you can create complex applications without even knowing what a write mode is.

I hope that *Super VGA Graphics* proves to be as much fun to use as it has been to write. At the very least, it should be more engaging than a bug zapper and a six-pack of beer.

Steve Rimmer
BBS: (416) 729-4609
CIS: 70451,2734

1 *Birds, martians, & flying pigs*

"You can marry more money in five minutes than you can make in a lifetime."
 —Murphy's Law

There are a lot of peculiar-looking birds about. You can see them in zoos, on public television and, if you live in a part of the world where the acid rain and the weekend warriors haven't decimated them, you might even see one in its natural habitat. We had an influx of eagles this year. By the middle of the summer, they'd become so commonplace that no one even noticed them unless a few swooped down and carried off an unsuspecting Toyota.

Figure 1-1 illustrates a pair of suitably peculiar-looking birds. Printed on a sheet of paper, as they are here, you'd probably not notice them unless someone specifically drew your attention to them.

If you've done any desktop publishing, you'll probably appreciate that FIG. 1-1 isn't a photograph. It's a scanned image derived from a photograph. While this doesn't really matter to either the birds or to what they look like on paper, it does offer a third medium upon which to reproduce them: You can display them on a monitor.

Now, looking out at you from a computer monitor, these two birds probably won't be quite as unexciting as they might have been on paper. For one thing, they'll be in color. In fact, they'll be in rich, luminous colors, because that's what computer monitors do. Finally, they'll appear in the context of one of the most unsensual devices yet devised by human beings, a personal computer. The juxtaposition is extremely effective.

It is perhaps worth noting that these birds displayed on a monitor would have a fraction of the image resolution and color depth of a 35 millimeter slide—on its best day, microcomputer digital imaging displayed on a tube would make a toy camera from Sears laugh out loud, if cameras could laugh at all. However, the effect of computer graphics—especially graphics that successfully emulate our perception of reality—are startling and eye-catching none the less.

In addition, computer graphics hold the possibility of stumbling into the unexplored dark corners of reality, places where cameras aren't allowed. Figure 1-2 illustrates one example of this. This image didn't start out as a photograph at all—it's a ray-traced graphic, created wholly by mathematics. In a sense, it's "realer" than reality. It offers a convincing impression of reality without any of the nasty restrictions of images seen in the real world.

Perhaps the best thing about computer graphics is not what they can do—they can do just about anything—but rather the number of people who can use them. Graphic display hardware that cost more than the computers that drove it a few years ago is pretty well standard now. You can buy the sorts of display adapters to be examined in this book starting at under a hundred dollars.

Admittedly, though, they don't stop until they're well above this figure.

A brief history of PC displays

With the advent of the IBM PC systems in the early eighties, PC display adapters took on their present characteristics, a situation that has not changed in over a decade. They started out chaotic, poorly standardized, and designed by punch-drunk, prematurely-bald Martians, and so they have remained. As you will better appreciate by the end of this chapter, the display cards you'll be working with throughout the course of this book do work, and work well, but they are anything but easy to understand.

This isn't as bad as it sounds, of course. Consider it a challenge. Alternately, consider that if your graphic programs work, they'll have relatively little competition.

The first PC display adapters were the CGA and MDA cards—the *color graphics adapter* and *monochrome display adapter* respectively. The former had graphics so ugly as to frighten slugs into immediate suicide rather than live with the memory of what they'd seen. The latter had no graphics at all.

Hot on the virtual heels of these first-generation cards, the third party Hercules graphics adapters offered better graphics—the slugs that survived their first glimpse of CGA graphics could usually deal with Hercules cards—but Hercules cards only worked with two colors. They were also monumentally unpleasant to write programs for.

The first generation of display adapters to use large scale integration and hence a manageable software interface were EGA cards, or *enhanced graphic adapters*. They offered a glowing sixteen colors, but at awkward screen dimensions.

The current generation of popular display cards are generically called VGA cards, for *video graphics array*. The original IBM VGA card was a real dog's breakfast of hardware—a full-size card with a daughter board clamped onto it to hold all the chips it required. More recent, third-party cards have improved on this to some extent. A straight VGA-compatible card can occupy less space than a mouse.

1-3

Several popular super VGA cards.

Figure 1-3 illustrates several contemporary VGA cards.

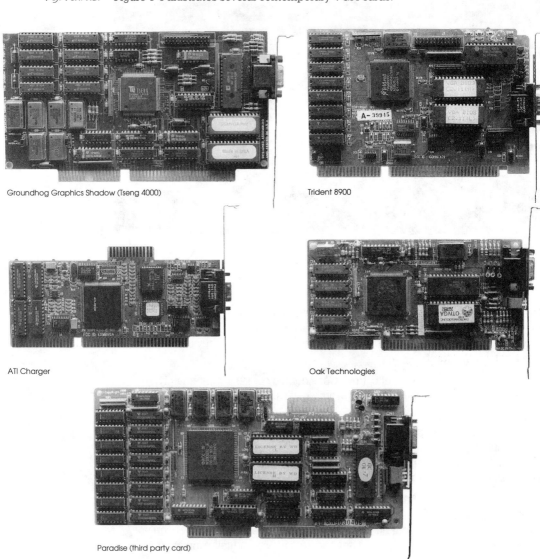

Groundhog Graphics Shadow (Tseng 4000)

Trident 8900

ATI Charger

Oak Technologies

Paradise (third party card)

Birds, martians, & flying pigs

The original IBM VGA card had all sorts of graphic modes; among other things, it could emulate all the questionable graphic facilities of its predecessors. There were two modes that are of interest to this book. The first, the "business graphics" mode, offered sixteen colors drawn from a palette of a quarter of a million at a resolution of 640 by 480 pixels. The second, the "multiple color graphics array" mode, offered 256 colors drawn from a palette of a quarter of a million at a resolution of 320 by 200. This latter mode makes it possible to display convincing digitized color photographs, albeit at a very coarse resolution.

For reasons best understood by punch-drunk, prematurely-bald Martians, most of the hardware that IBM designs is somewhat conservative. This might explain, for example, why the maximum amount of conventional memory a PC will support is just over half a megabyte and why a stock VGA card has relatively low resolution graphic modes. It's likely that the 256-color graphics mode of the original VGA specification was regarded as little more than a curiosity.

Shortly after its introduction, the IBM VGA card was copied by some of the hardware manufacturers that had done so well copying EGA cards a few years earlier. As is usually the case when third-party manufacturers clone hardware, these knock-off VGA cards worked better, cost a lot less, and used a lot less silicon than the original IBM card. One of the first things to appear plastered across the backs of the boxes in which third-party VGA cards were sold were pronouncements to the effect that these cards had more and better graphics modes than a real IBM VGA card.

These super set modes typically offered business graphics out to 800 by 600 pixels at sixteen colors and 256-color modes to at least 640 by 400 pixels. At present, it's not uncommon to find the higher-end third-party cards with sixteen-color graphics out to 1024 by 768 or 1280 by 960 pixels and 256-color graphics out to 1024 by 768 pixels.

These superset cards are often referred to as super VGA cards—hence the title of this book.

There are two catches to all this expansion. The first one is that graphics require memory to store them, and more pixels entail that you have more memory on board. An old-style IBM VGA card could get by with about 150 kilobytes. A contemporary high- end super VGA card requires a megabyte. As catches go, this is a pretty minimal one because memory is fairly cheap.

The second catch is rather more nettlesome. The IBM VGA card defined a standard, at least for the graphic modes it supported. Super VGA cards support this standard for the original IBM VGA modes that they emulate, but they implement their superset modes in whatever way their creators thought might work well. This means that no two super VGA card manufacturers have created hardware that can be driven the same way in their non-IBM modes.

In addition to the aforementioned modes, a growing number of super VGA cards also support "high-color" modes. This is a radical departure in VGA card technology that allows you to display up to 32,768 distinct colors at a resolution of 640 by 480 or 800 by 600 pixels. These modes have no equivalent in a standard IBM VGA card. More will be said about them later.

A lot of what this book is about consists of ways to deal with this incredible profusion of super VGA standards.

It's worth noting that VGA cards support all the modes of the earlier IBM display cards that preceded them. Super VGA cards can usually manage all this as well as Hercules graphics, should you want them. As such, the standard IBM VGA graphics modes are available even on the most sophisticated super VGA cards.

In writing software that is to be run in the graphic modes of a VGA card, you will have two choices in dealing with the lack of super VGA standards. You can either restrict your applications to using the standard VGA modes, which are available on all VGA and super VGA cards, or you can arrange to provide drivers for most or all of the available super VGA cards. This latter undertaking can be a bit hairy if you intend to do it as completely as possible. There are well over a dozen VGA card manufacturers; and most of them have produced several generations of hardware, not all of which are backwards compatible. New manufacturers turn up periodically.

One potential way out of all this confusion is the introduction of the VESA standard—that's Video Electronics Standards Association. On display cards that support VESA, it's possible to use a standardized interface to drive the super VGA modes of any card. There are, in turn, two catches to this. The first is that not all cards support VESA, although many that do not have resident VESA interpreters available for them, which might allow you to cheat around this limitation. This, in effect, will retrofit many older super VGA cards to support VESA by loading a small TSR. The second catch is that not all implementations of VESA are particularly well done. Some of the problems are fairly subtle—a few, such as the early implementations of the Orchid Fahrenheit 1280° VESA BIOS, are truly unworkable.

If your heart sank when you read this mention of the Orchid Fahrenheit cards, it's worth noting that Orchid can supply you with a BIOS upgrade that more or less fixes the Fahrenheit's VESA problems.

Some driver philosophy

I've written numerous applications which use VGA and super VGA graphics—two of them, Desktop Paint 16 and Desktop Paint 256, are on the companion disk for this book. Others, such as Graphics Workshop, are available as shareware.

Graphic Workshop uses super VGA graphics to display images for viewing and interactive manipulation. It can sneak past the super VGA driver problem fairly easily. It supports the most popular super VGA cards with dedicated drivers. Users who have unsupported cards can fall back to the standard IBM VGA modes. These aren't as attractive or as flexible, and Graphic Workshop has to include ways to deal with this: for example, it must dither pictures that would require a high-color card if a user of a card without high-color facilities attempts to view one. However, for the most part anyone can use the software even if his or her particular super VGA card isn't explicitly supported by the current drivers.

Desktop Paint 256 is a 256-color paint program (see FIG. 1-4). Because the 320 by 200 pixel 256-color IBM VGA mode is too coarse to allow for the menus and toolbox and such of the program and still leave enough room to do anything useful with a picture, Desktop Paint 256 requires a super VGA card. It can't fall back to the standard IBM graphic modes. As such, users without one of the display cards that Desktop Paint 256 supports can't use the software at all.

Desk   File   Edit   Extra   Fonts   Text   Colour   Tools

1-4
Desktop Paint 256, now playing on the disk in the back of this book.

To further complicate this situation, Desktop Paint 256 makes such complex use of super VGA graphics as to get it into trouble with most of the early generations of the contemporary cards it does work with.

People who don't understand the distinction between VGA cards and super VGA cards occasionally buy Desktop Paint 256 to run it on a standard VGA system and then can't understand why it doesn't work. This also happens to owners of unsupported super VGA cards. Scaring up and writing drivers for some of the more obscure super VGA cards would be a major undertaking and would ultimately support relatively few potential users of Desktop Paint 256.

I've done several other graphics applications, such as Desktop Paint 16—a sixteen-color paint package—that have deliberately avoided the super VGA issue for just this reason. While the 800 by 600 pixel graphic modes of super VGA cards might arguably be useful in Desktop Paint 16, the potential confusion represented by writing dozens of drivers to support them arguably overwhelms its potential utility.

One prevalent attitude among many software users is that they won't buy software that doesn't "fully support" their systems. It seems to be much more acceptable to buy software that only supports standard VGA 640 by 480 pixel graphics, for example, than software that supports both 640 by 480 pixels graphics and some 800 by 600 pixel modes if one's card is not among those supported in the higher resolution mode. This is another bit of driver philosophy to keep in mind.

This book will deal specifically with the IBM VGA graphics modes—as they're a good place to start and something you'll probably want to support in your

Hardware supported

software—as well as a number of the popular super VGA cards. Here's a complete list:

❏ Paradise
❏ ATI VGA Wonder
❏ Tseng Labs 4000
❏ Trident 8900
❏ Oak Technologies
❏ VESA

This list probably deserves some elaboration.

To begin with, just because there are super VGA cards around doesn't mean that all the standard VGA cards have been recycled as cat toys. Aside from whatever original IBM VGA cards are still lurking about, there are PS/2 displays, which are essentially standard VGA cards and a number of "basic" third-party VGA displays. These latter cards are very low cost display adapters that will drive equally low-cost monitors. While made by some of the super VGA card manufacturers, such as ATI and Paradise, they don't offer any of the super VGA modes.

A super VGA card consists of a VGA chip and some glue hardware to make it work. The VGA chip is what handles all the hard work, and in speaking of a Paradise card, for example, one is really speaking of the Paradise chip or "chip set". Super VGA chips are square and usually located in the middle of the cards they live on. Figure 1-5 illustrates some super VGA cards and their VGA chips.

In most cases, the manufacturers of super VGA chips will sell the raw chips to other companies that want to build super VGA cards. As such, you can buy Paradise-compatible super VGA cards that consist of real Paradise chips on generic cards. Such cards are every bit as functional as a comparable "real" Paradise card, save that they don't come in the attractive Paradise boxes painted with tropical birds. You might want to consider this in light of the discussion of birds earlier in this chapter.

It's worth noting that a super VGA chip is of little use without a VGA extension BIOS to support it. As such, if one were to buy the Paradise VGA chip set with the intent of manufacturing super VGA cards, for example, one would also buy the Paradise BIOS to go with it. In speaking of a particular chip set, we'll also be speaking about the BIOS that goes with it.

The propensity of chip manufacturers to spread their chips around, however, can make the task of knowing what sort of card one is using a bit tricky. If you're not quite sure what chip set's in use on your card, you can either look at the BIOS copyright message when your system boots up or at the markings on your VGA chip. Figure 1-6 (on page 10) illustrates the super VGA chips of the cards to be examined in this book.

The markings on your chips might vary a bit.

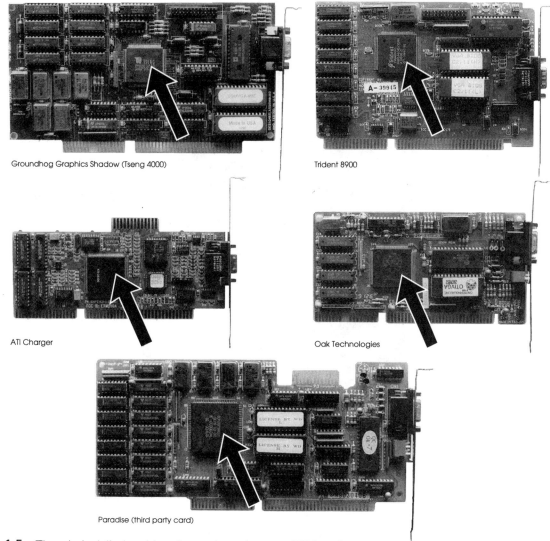

Groundhog Graphics Shadow (Tseng 4000)

Trident 8900

ATI Charger

Oak Technologies

Paradise (third party card)

1-5   *The principal display chips of several popular super VGA cards.*

Here's another useful way to see what sort of card you have in your system. Run the DEBUG program that comes with MS-DOS and issue the command:

```
DC000:0000
```

This will dump the data at the beginning of the VGA BIOS area. Most VGA BIOSs put their copyright messages at the beginning of the VGA BIOS area. Figure 1-7 illustrates the one for a Paradise card. Note the text along the right side of the DEBUG listing. You may have to hit D and then enter a few more times if the message is somewhat verbose.

1-6
A layperson's guide to the markings on super VGA chips.

I mentioned that most super VGA cards will display their parentage in their BIOS copyright messages when you first boot up your system. This is not always true, however; in some cases, you'll find that display cards bundled with computers will display the name of the manufacturer of the computer. In addition, as it's the first thing on the screen, you might find that the BIOS copyright notice vanishes pretty quickly as your system boots up.

The next section is a quick overview of the cards and chips created by the manufacturers in the foregoing list.

Paradise   The Paradise cards are a product of Western Digital Imaging. The markings on Paradise chips include the letters WD for this reason. In addition to making super VGA cards, Paradise also makes a basic VGA card, with no super VGA modes.

There are three generations of Paradise super VGA chip sets as of this writing:

❑ 90C00 or revision B
❑ 90C11 or revision C
❑ 90C30 or revision D

```
H>debug
-dc000:0000
C000:0000   55 AA 40 EB 15 37 34 30-30 31 30 2F 32 32 2F 39   U.@..740010/22/9
C000:0010   31 2D 31 30 3A 32 35 3A-30 30 E9 35 01 02 49 42   1-10:25:00.5..IB
C000:0020   4D 20 43 4F 4D 50 41 54-49 42 4C 45 20 50 41 52   M COMPATIBLE PAR
C000:0030   41 44 49 53 45 30 30 33-32 33 34 2D 35 31 37 43   ADISE003234-517C
C000:0040   4F 50 59 52 49 47 48 54-20 57 45 53 54 45 52 4E   OPYRIGHT WESTERN
C000:0050   20 44 49 47 49 54 41 4C-20 49 4E 43 2E 20 31 39    DIGITAL INC. 19
C000:0060   38 37 2C 31 39 39 31 2C-20 41 4C 4C 20 52 49 47   87,1991, ALL RIG
C000:0070   48 54 53 20 52 45 53 45-52 56 45 44 00 56 47 41   HTS RESERVED.VGA
-d
C000:0080   3D 45 00 00 00 00 00 FF-0F 00 00 00 00 02 00 00   =E..............
C000:0090   00 00 00 00 42 00 00 C5-E1 6D 04 00 00 C7 00 C0   ....B....m......
C000:00A0   02 F0 FF 00 80 00 00 01-00 00 00 00 00 00 00 00   ................
C000:00B0   00 00 00 00 00 00 00 00-00 00 00 00 00 00 00 82   ................
C000:00C0   48 DC 48 D0 44 56 73 46-08 9B 03 D0 44 EC 44 08   H.H.DVsF....D.D.
C000:00D0   45 3E 45 58 45 24 45 00-00 00 00 00 00 AE 80 46   E>EXE$E........F
C000:00E0   00 90 44 00 00 00 00 00-00 00 00 00 00 00 00 00   ..D.............
C000:00F0   00 00 F0 65 F0 7E 00 01-00 04 0E 04 12 04 16 E0   ...e.~..........
—
```

1-7 *Using DEBUG to find the VGA BIOS copyright message.*

The B series chips support sixteen-color graphics to 1024 by 768 pixels and 256-color graphics to 640 by 480 pixels. The C series chips support sixteen-color graphics to 1024 by 768 pixels and 256-color graphics to 800 by 600 pixels. The D series chips support sixteen-color graphics to 1024 by 768 pixels and 256-color graphics to 1024 by 768 pixels. They also support high-color graphics to 800 by 600 pixels if you have a megabyte of memory on your card and a RAMDAC chip.

The Paradise-specific code in this book was developed using a Paradise 90C30-based card.

There's a profusion of ATI VGA cards. The basic ATI VGA Wonder card, essentially the early forbearer of the brood, has spawned the ATI Charger, the ATI Ultra, the ATI XL and so on. There is also the very low cost ATI Basic 16, a VGA-only card that does not support super VGA graphics.

ATI

The ATI Charger is a low-cost super VGA card. The ATI Ultra adds Windows acceleration, something which isn't really relevant to the code in this book. The ATI XL adds high-color support, among other things.

Fortunately, the core chip set of the plethora of ATI cards is fairly standard, and for the purposes of this book one ATI super VGA card is pretty much like another. The ATI-specific code in this book was developed using an ATI Charger.

The Tseng Labs ET4000 super VGA chip set is found in numerous third-party cards, among them the popular Orchid Prodesigners. It's a relatively basic super VGA chip. It's also available as the ET4000X, which adds support for an off-board Sierra DAC, giving the card high-color facilities.

Tseng Labs

Prior to the introduction of the ET4000 chips there were ET3000 chips, which still lurk about on older boards. The ET4000 doesn't maintain the finest backwards compatibility with its ancestor, and code to drive the ET4000 very often will send the ET3000 into paroxysms of screen gyrations.

The Tseng-specific code in this book was developed using a Groundhog Graphics Shadow card.

Trident micrososystems

The Trident 8900 super VGA chip set is comparable to the Tseng Labs ET4000, although as of this writing Trident-based cards do not support high-color graphics. One of the salient aspects of the Trident 8900 chips is that they're particularly inexpensive and as such are found on a lot of very low cost cards.

The BIOS that supports the Trident 8900 chips has appeared in four revisions as of this writing—the 8900, 8900A, 8900B and 8900C. Rumor has it that the B series BIOSs are particularly twitchy, and some code that behaves itself under other BIOS revisions does not get along with the B BIOS. No details of what the B BIOS does to make it such a reprobate seem to be available.

The 8900-series chips were preceded by the 8800 chips. As with the Tseng Labs chips, the earlier Trident chips are only semi-compatible with their current descendants.

The Trident-specific code in this book was developed with a generic Trident 8900-series card with an 8900-series BIOS.

Oak Technologies

There appears to be but a single generation of Oak Technologies chips available as of this writing. The Oak chips are inexpensive and require fairly little additional hardware, making them the basis of some very low cost super VGA display adapters.

The Oak-specific code in this book was developed using a generic Oak Technologies super VGA card.

VESA

As was touched on earlier in this chapter, the VESA standard was devised as a path to sneak around the chaotic non-standardization of the super VGA cards that appeared in the wake of the original IBM VGA adapter. When it works, VESA is superb. You can quickly determine whether a VESA card is present in your system, work out which modes it supports, and drive it without even knowing who actually made the hardware. As an aside, it will tell you who the manufacturer was too, if you're curious.

The drawback to VESA is that it's a fairly open-ended standard, and one that has been through several revisions as of this writing. It's a bit ambiguously worded in some areas too. This has left numerous VESA BIOS implementations with somewhat dodgy VESA support. While the majority of cards that support VESA do so quite well, it would be unwise to write a VESA driver and assume that absolutely every card with the word VESA printed somewhere on its box will be comfortable with it.

A VESA BIOS is really a sort of command translator. It uses a dedicated software interrupt and translates calls made through this interrupt to whatever BIOS or hardware functions are required by the card it supports. For example, in order to switch a Paradise card into its 640 by 480 pixel, 256-color graphics mode, you would do this:

```
MOV AX,005FH
INT 10H
```

You could achieve the same results on a late-model Paradise card with a VESA BIOS like this:

```
MOV AX,4F02H
MOV BX,0101H
INT 10H
```

This is a standard VESA BIOS call to switch modes—mode 0101H is the 640 by 480 pixel, 256-color mode. In effect, what the VESA part of the Paradise BIOS does is to translate the VESA call into a normal Paradise call.

Some of this will become a bit clearer in the detailed discussion of driving a VESA card, later in this book.

Most of the popular super VGA cards that don't support VESA directly have TSRs available to bolt VESA support onto them. A VESA TSR simply traps VESA calls, such as the one in the second example here, and translates them into whatever would be the equivalent BIOS calls for the card it's designed to support. The only drawbacks to this approach to VESA support is that the VESA TSRs take up some DOS memory when they're loaded, and they tend to be a bit version-dependent.

If you'd like to experiment with VESA and don't have a VESA BIOS, you can find most of the popular VESA TSRs on the bulletin board mentioned at the end of the preface to this book.

Before you can properly understand why super VGA cards represent such a box of snakes—and rather evil-tempered, highly venomous snakes at that—you'll probably need to understand how display cards work in general. This will also prepare you for the rest of this book, which will undertake to de-toxify the snakes in question, or at least to improve their disposition.

A display card overview

A PC display card is a memory mapped device. It looks like regular system memory, and you can address it as such. A VGA card in one of its graphics mode has its display memory beginning at location A000:0000H. This means that if you write something to this area of memory while your card's in graphics mode, the contents of your screen will change.

Let's begin with a simple example. The display modes of a VGA card are usually referred to by hexadecimal numbers—the use of these numbers will become apparent later in this book. This discussion will begin with mode 12H. Under mode 12H, a VGA card initially behaves as a monochrome bitmapped graphics display. In fact, there's a lot more to this mode, but we won't get into it for a while yet. This mode has the dimensions 640 by 480 pixels.

As a monochrome display, each line of your screen corresponds to an array of bytes. Each byte represents eight bits, so one 640-pixel line would require 640 bits or 80 bytes to store its bits. A full screen would require 38,400 bytes.

In the default configuration for mode 12H, any bits that are set in the video buffer will display as white pixels. Any bits that are unset will display as black pixels. Initially, all the bits are unset, and the screen will be black. Here's how you would turn on the very first pixel on the screen:

```
char *p;
```

```
p=MK_FP(0×a000,0×0000);
*p=0×01;
```

There's a fair bit going on in this code. To begin with, it assumes that p is a far pointer; as will be covered later in this chapter, all the pointers in the code in this book live with this assumption. The MK_FP macro will create a far pointer that points to a specific segment and offset in memory, in this case to A000:0000H, the base of the graphics buffer for a VGA card. The value 0×01 represents a byte with its first bit set.

Here's how you would draw a white line down the left side of your screen:

```
char *p;
int n;

for(n=0;n<480;++n) {
        p=MK_FP(0×a000,n*80);
        *p=0×01;
}
```

As each line on the screen requires 80 bytes, you can address line n as being n*80 bytes from the base of the graphics buffer. This is actually a seriously ineffective way to handle addressing pixels on the screen; a great deal more will be said about all this later in this book.

Figure 1-8 illustrates the relationship between pixels and bytes on a monochrome screen.

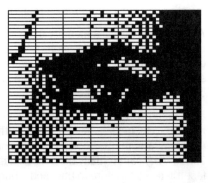

1-8
Pixels and bytes in a monochrome bitmapped image.

You might want to think of a monochrome graphics display mode as having a *palette*. A palette is a list of colors. In a monochrome mode such as the one we've been examining here, each pixel can have one of two states, and as such the palette can only have two colors. The two colors are typically black and white.

On a palette-driven display—which is what mode 12H of a VGA card really is—there is a lookup table of color values, and each pixel in the display defines an index into the table. This means that the unset bits in mode 12H address color zero and the set bits address color one. This might seem a bit elaborate for a two-color display, but it's what a VGA card is really doing behind your back in this mode.

We'll be back to mode 12H presently, because in reality everything in the discussion of it thus far is only true if you want it to be. Mode 12H is really a sixteen-color mode.

The picture in FIG. 1-9 is a 320 by 200 pixel, 256-color image suitable for display on a super VGA card. The display mode that corresponds to these dimensions, the multiple color graphics array mode touched on earlier, is called mode 13H.

Real color

1-9
A 320 by 200 pixel, 256-color graphic—in black and white. Downloaded from Rose Media, (416) 733-2285.

Color on a monitor is defined using *additive synthesis*, which is a very erudite sounding way of saying that all colors on a monitor are either black or they're not. In order to make color appear on an initially black monitor, colored light must be added to the blackness. There are three primary colors in additive synthesis, these being red, green, and blue. You can create any color you like from pure black to pure white by combining suitable percentages of red, green, and blue light.

When it turns up in conjunction with monitors, additive synthesis is usually called *RGB color*, based on the three colors of light involved.

As an aside, you might well ask if additive color implies the existence of subtractive color. It does—subtractive color defines colors that are either white or they're not. It applies to printing on white paper, for example. It will turn up later in this book when we examine color printing.

For the purposes of this text, we'll define an RGB color as being three numbers ranging from zero through 255. This means that one RGB color definition can be stored in three bytes. By convention, the first byte holds the red value, the second the green value and the third the blue value. Increasing the value of one component of an RGB color will make the corresponding percentage of its primary color brighter.

Here are some color definitions based on RGB colors:

Color	Red	Green	Blue
Black	0	0	0
Bright red	255	0	0
Dark red	128	0	0
Bright Green	0	255	0
Bright Blue	0	0	255
Cyan	0	255	255
White	255	255	255

The ideal sort of color display card would be one that actually structured its display memory this way, that is, with three bytes for each visible pixel. Under such a card, it would be possible to have as many different colors on the screen at once as there were pixels. Unfortunately, such a card would require rather a lot of memory—about 190K for a coarse 320 by 200 pixel screen, and 900K for a 640 by 480 pixel screen. While the former value is actually in keeping with the maximum amount of memory available on a stock VGA card, the original designers of the card had reasons to want to keep the mode 13H display buffer down to less than 64K of memory.

This type of color is called "true color." It's actually available on some high-end display adapters, but not in anything that will turn up in this book.

The way around using all this memory for an RGB display buffer is to make one's display palette-driven instead. A palette driven display only requires one value per pixel, rather than three.

A 256-color palette consists of a lookup table with 256 RGB colors in it. While you can set each color entry to whatever color you like, a maximum of 256 distinct colors can be stored in the table at once. The screen buffer, then, rather than having an RGB color for each pixel, represents each pixel as a number from zero through 255—that is, as an index into the lookup table.

If color number 37 in the table was green and you wanted to plot a green pixel at location (122,81) on the screen, you would place the number 37 in this location.

Under mode 13H, the screen is "byte-mapped" because there are 256 colors available under this mode and, as a byte can hold numbers from zero through 255, mode 13H assigns one byte per pixel. There are 320 pixels per line and 200 lines, for a total of 64,000 bytes in the mode 13H graphics buffer.

Here's how you would set the pixel at x,y to color n in mode 13H.

```
char *p;
p=MK_FP(0xa000,0000);
p[x+y*320]=n;
```

In mode 13H, the screen buffer again begins at location A000:0000H. Each line is 320 bytes long.

In fact, despite its having a lot of colors to work with, mode 13H is dead easy to program for because of its unusually simple screen buffer structure.

There is one nominal catch to working with mode 13H—and, in fact, with all VGA card modes that use palettes. It's usually the case that RGB colors are defined as three 8-bit bytes, for a total of 24 bits of color. This provides for a range of about sixteen-million distinct colors. A VGA card's palette registers are actually only six bits wide, rather than eight. This provides for a range of about a quarter of a million colors.

Converting standard 24-bit RGB colors to 18-bit VGA colors isn't at all difficult—simply divide each color value by four, or shift it right by two bits. However, if you neglect to do this, your pictures will look very strange indeed, with random colors scattered throughout.

The relatively coarse display of mode 13H makes it suitable for looking at small graphics in a pinch, but it's hardly the basis for sophisticated graphic-based software. The super VGA 256-color modes, which start at a resolution of 640 by 400 pixels, are decidedly better. They're also decidedly more complex to work with. While they behave just like mode 13H in some respects, mapping one byte to each pixel, they're immeasurably complicated by the segmented memory structure of the processors that make PCs go.

Super VGA 256-color modes

In addition to whatever system memory is in your computer, your display card will have some memory of its own. Until now, we have been discussing graphic modes with relatively little memory. High end super VGA cards can come with as much as a megabyte of display memory. None of this is useful as program memory; it's only used to store graphics in when they're visible on your screen.

For the purpose of this discussion, we'll allow that the addressable part of the video memory of a VGA card can only be 64 kilobytes long. The addressable part is the part you can actually read and write to. In fact, there are instances in which you can cheat on this somewhat, but not sufficiently to obviate the problem inherent in super VGA 256-color graphics. As with the mode 13H video buffer, the display memory lives at A000:0000H and runs to A000:FFFFH.

This 64K video address space at location A000:0000H is just sufficient to hold the 64,000 bytes of memory required by mode 13H, but it clearly can't address all the memory required by a higher resolution mode. The coarsest of the popular super VGA 256-color modes, at 640 by 480 pixels, requires 300 kilobytes. Initially, only the first 64K of this would be accessible in the video address space at A000:0000H.

There are several instances in which PC systems have to address large chunks of memory with relatively little address space—this problem turns up in working with expanded memory as well. Super VGA cards solve it in the same way, too. They use memory paging.

One line of a 640 by 480 pixel, 256-color graphics screen requires 640 bytes, so the 64K video buffer will allow you to directly address a little over 102 lines. In order to get at the 103rd line, you would tell the display card to *page* its memory— that is, to hide the first 64K of video memory and to make the second 64K visible at

A000:0000H. You can access all the memory on a one megabyte card this way, one 64K page at a time.

There are several problems in implementing super VGA page switching. The first one can be easily understood with nothing more than a calculator. You will note that in none of the standard super VGA 256-color graphics modes do the lines end on a 64K boundary. For example, at a resolution of 640 by 480 pixels, the transition between the first and second pages of display memory occurs about a third of the way along the 103rd line.

This makes devising a high speed screen driver for these modes somewhat challenging. You can write data to the screen quickly by using the 8086 string move instructions, but these most certainly do not take into account super VGA card page changes part way through a move. Writing bytes to the screen one pixel at a time and checking for a page switch after each would make for dreadfully slow screen updates.

In practice, there are ways to cheat around this problem. They'll be explained later in this book.

The second and perhaps more vexing problem is logistical. While all super VGA cards can bank their pages in 64K chunks, as we've seen, there are two salient details that are unique to each manufacturer of super VGA hardware. The first is the code to actually put the card in question into a super VGA graphics mode. The second is the code to tickle the card's registers, and so to make it change pages.

This book will deal with these elements for the cards it supports, but if you find yourself confronted with writing a driver for a card that isn't examined herein, you'll have to scare these things up yourself.

With a suitable driver, it's possible to treat the super VGA 256-color graphics modes much as you would mode 13H. However, it's worth noting that in updating a 640 by 480 pixel, 256-color screen you will have to move about four times as much data from your computer's memory to the display card memory, and under somewhat less alacritous circumstances—the code that does the move will have to take into account the page changes.

As will be dealt with in detail later in this book, when we come to write an arcade game, mode 13H allows you to create some pretty speedy graphics routines. The same cannot be said for the super VGA 256-color modes.

Sixteen-color graphics
The sixteen-color graphics modes of a super VGA card are to programming what a sack of enraged polecats are to a crowded shopping center on a hot Saturday afternoon in August. You might have to read this section over a few times to fully understand it—and you might have to actually see some of the code involved later in this book to completely wrestle the beast to the ground. When it's all over with, you might decide that you'd rather deal with the polecats instead.

We'll examine mode 12H in this section—it provides for sixteen colors at a resolution of 640 by 480 pixels. Most super VGA cards have additional sixteen-color modes that allow for at least 800 by 600 pixels as well. They work the same way as mode 12H, save for their different screen dimensions.

As was dealt with earlier in this chapter, mode 12H behaves like a monochrome mode by default. With a bit of register tickling, however, it will be found to be a sixteen-color mode in disguise. It arrives at this duality of character through some of the most peculiar memory management one might imagine.

The mode 12H screen buffer lives at A000:0000H. In treating it as a monochrome display, it was observed that this entailed about 38K of memory. In fact, there is actually 150K of memory at this location. It's arranged in a rather diabolical way, though: it's split into four pages, or *planes*, all of which exist overlayed at A000:0000H. As the story opens, if you write to this location, you will actually write to all four pages at once.

It's possible to make one or more of the pages vanish from the address bus. For example, if you were to make all but the first page vanish—called "banking out" the unwanted pages—writing to the video memory space would only result in data being written to the first page.

Pages that have been banked out can't be written to, but they remain visible on your monitor. As such, if you were to write something to page zero, and then something different to page one, both objects would be visible on your screen.

In practice, one updates a sixteen-color screen by writing to one page at a time.

The four pages of display memory have four "weights," as follows:

Page	Weight
0	1
1	2
2	4
4	8

Another way to look at this is that the weight page n is $1<<n$. The weight is used in working out how colors will appear on a sixteen-color screen. This is where the theory of display technology really takes a giant leap into hyperspace.

Figure 1-10 illustrates a sixteen-color picture and its palette. In this case, it's actually a sixteen-level grey scale picture—this book being printed in black and white—but you can regard the grey levels as colors. The sixteen colors in the palette correspond to sixteen RGB colors stored in a VGA card's palette registers. Color 0 is black, color 7 is medium grey, and color 15 is white.

As with the 256-color modes, to plot a pixel in, say, color 7 at location (211,52), you would set the number at this location to 7. This would cause the hardware of your VGA card to look up its table of colors, find out what the color value for color 7 was, and to then display that color at this location. What might be a bit less than clear is how you store 7 in the display memory of a sixteen-color mode, which has four pages and no obvious relationship between the bytes in the display memory and the pixels on your screen.

The binary representation of the number seven is 0111. Each digit in a binary number starting from the rightmost one represents a weight of $1<<n$, where n is the digit position. As such, the binary value of 7 can be worked out as

$$(0<<3) + (1<<2) + (1<<1) + (1<<0)$$

which works out to

$$0 + 4 + 2 + 1$$

This looks suspiciously like the weights assigned to the pages of memory in the mode 12H display buffer.

In order to store the number seven at location (211,52), you would do the following:

❏ Make only the first page addressable. It has a weight of one. Because the first digit in the binary representation of 7 is 1, locate the pixel at (211,52) and turn it on.
❏ Make only the second page addressable. It has a weight of two. Because the second digit in the binary representation of 7 is 1, locate the pixel at (211,52) and turn it on.
❏ Make only the third page addressable. It has a weight of four. Because the third digit in the binary representation of 7 is 1, locate the pixel at (211,52) and turn it on.

❏ Make only the fourth page addressable. It has a weight of eight. Because the fourth digit in the binary representation of 7 is 0, locate the pixel at (211,52) and turn it off.

This is quite the dancing pig show for setting the value of one pixel, and in fact there are more efficient ways of doing so in real software. It does illustrate how the display memory in a sixteen-color screen buffer works, though. Figure 1-11 might further clarify it.

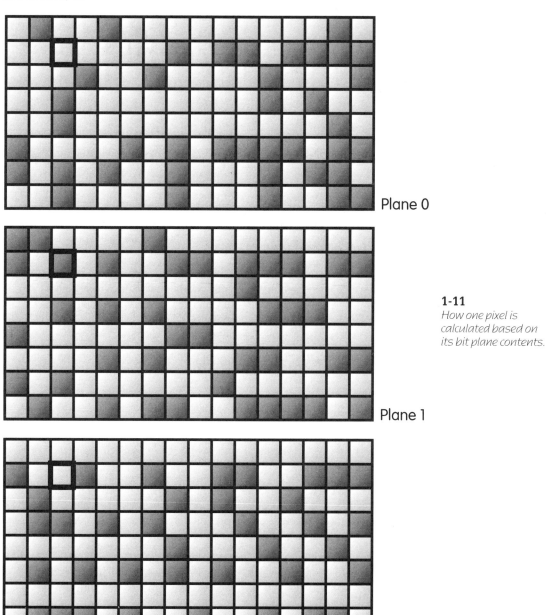

Plane 0

Plane 1

Plane 2

1-11
How one pixel is calculated based on its bit plane contents.

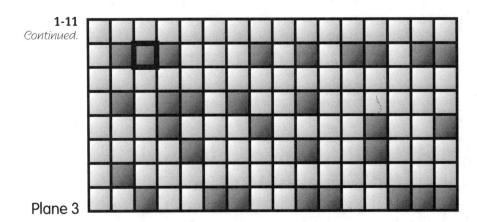

1-11
Continued.

Plane 3

$$= 1 \times 2^3 + 0 \times 2^2 + 1 \times 2^1 + 0 \times 2^0 = 8 + 4 = 12$$

In practice, knowing how to actually set pixels on and off, as well as how to page the display banks on and off the PC's address bus, will be of no small importance in making this procedure work, of course. These things will be dealt with in detail later in this book.

None of this has actually explained why mode 12H so conveniently behaves like a monochrome display mode until one starts meddling with its display planes. You can probably work this out for yourself if you observe that when you first enable mode 12H, all four planes will have been paged onto the address bus, and they'll remain there until you explicitly page one or more of them off.

With all four pages on the bus, any pixels that are turned on will have the value

$(1<<3) + (1<<2) + (1<<1) + (1<<0)$

or

$8 + 4 + 2 + 1$

or fifteen. Any pixels that are turned off will have the value of

$(0<<3) + (0<<2) + (0<<1) + (0<<0)$

or just plain 0. As the card is first configured upon enabling mode 12H, color 0 is black and color 15 is white. Because it's impossible to write pixel values of other than 0 or 15 with all four planes on the bus, all the pixels on the screen will be either black or white, and the display will appear to be in a monochrome mode.

High-color graphics   Several high end super VGA cards have appeared supporting "high color." This is a display mode that has no equivalent in the IBM VGA standard. It's exceedingly useful for sophisticated imaging applications, although it comes with several uncomfortably large numbers associated with it.

It was noted earlier in this chapter that a display card capable of representing each pixel on your screen as a true RGB color would be very useful, but somewhat memory hungry, as it would entail having three bytes of display memory for each pixel. A high-color super VGA card actually approaches this function, and it gets around the extreme memory requirements simply by having lots of memory. You will need a megabyte of display memory on a high-color card.

In fact, a high-color card is something of a compromise. It doesn't display true 24-bit color because the underlying display hardware can only handle six-bit color registers. In fact, in the high-color modes it's only called upon to deal with five bits of color information. Three five-bit values, for a total of fifteen bits, can be stored in one sixteen-bit word with one bit left over. As such, in high-color graphics each pixel requires two bytes, rather than the three that would be needed for true 24-bit color.

Losing three bits of color information per color value doesn't actually alter the colors in an image *per se*—rather, it reduces the degree of color resolution. A 15-bit image can define colors less precisely than a 24-bit image can. In fairness, it usually requires a pretty serious effort to be able to spot the effects of this. By comparison, reducing a 24-bit image down to 256 colors can introduce some noticeable aberrations into your pictures.

Figure 1-12 illustrates the relationship between one 24-bit pixel and the two bytes of a 15-bit high-color pixel.

There are several decided advantages to high-color graphics. Unlike as with the 256-color modes, you can see a scanned image using a high-color mode pretty much as it really appears. The only loss is the slight loss in color resolution involved in reducing 24-bit color to 15 bits. This amounts to a maximum theoretical shift in color or brightness of under three percent.

The drawbacks to high color tend to be tied up with the amount of data an RGB image represents. At 640 by 480 pixels, you must move 600K of screen data from wherever it's initially stored to a high-color display card's screen buffer. As with the 256-color super VGA modes, this involves swapping memory pages in the middle of some lines. As such, high-color graphics are wont to be a bit slow to update.

As with the 256-color super VGA graphics modes, there is no standard for high-color support. The high-color cards to be described later in this book each implement mode and page switching differently.

Using this book

Graphics programming is among the more challenging things you can do with a computer—it requires a substantial degree of insight into how the hardware and formats involved work, something this book will go a long way toward providing you with. It also requires a fair to middling understanding of how to write programs, something this book really won't handle.

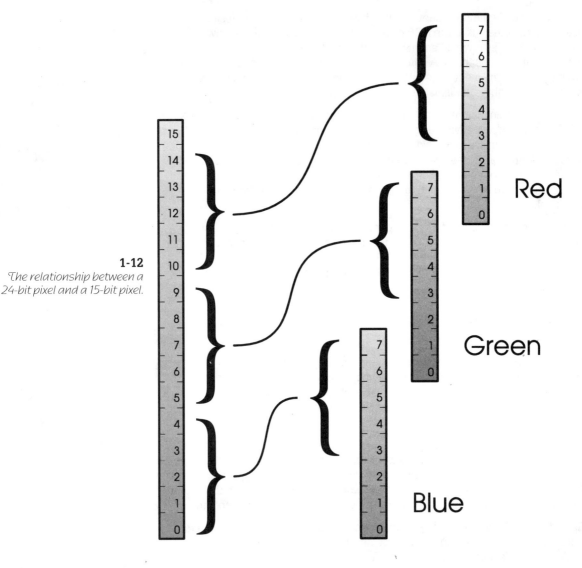

1-12
The relationship between a 24-bit pixel and a 15-bit pixel.

In order to make the code in this book do anything worthwhile, you should be reasonably familiar with the C language. Some understanding of assembler will provide useful as well. Attempting to learn to work with graphics at the same time as you learn C may prove a bit daunting.

The code in this book has been written using Borland's Turbo C language. One of the things that proponents of C like to cite as being among its virtues is its legendary portability. Programs written in C on one system or under one development environment can easily be moved to other platforms or other compilers. Under the currently available DOS C compilers, this is about as likely to happen as pigs are to fly.

If you're working with something other than Turbo C—Microsoft C, for example—you can still use the code in this book, but you should be prepared to fine-tune it a bit. In order to do this, you'll really need to understand what it's up to. Once again, this isn't something to attempt if you're relatively new to C language programming.

One of the unfortunate aspects of graphics programming is that graphics are a bit inscrutable, and relatively hard to debug. If you tickle what you think is the appropriate register of a VGA card to make it perform one of its tricks and no trick proves to be forthcoming, it's frequently difficult to ascertain exactly what has gone amiss. This is often further compounded by the minutia and subtleties of C compilers.

While it's arguably impossible to cover all the problems you might run into when working with the code in this book and applying it to your own applications, a bit of insight into how C and assembly language work—as they pertain to the programs to be dealt with in the chapters following this one—will probably give you the resources to avoid several teeming phyla of bugs.

The 8086 series of processors upon which PC systems are based are somewhat peculiar things, and they deal with their memory in a way that you or I probably wouldn't have come up with. This unusual approach to handling memory has several decided advantages, as well as a few catches that are likely to sneak up behind you and bite your ankles if you're unaware of their presence.

Memory & memory models

Back in the early days of personal computers, processors were designed to have memory addresses that ran from zero to the top of memory using linear addressing. Linear addressing simply means that one uses a number to address memory and that the number gets bigger to deal with higher addresses. It's elegantly simple. The important thing to keep in mind about this, however, is that back then the top of memory was at 64K, and the number that handled memory addressing could fit in sixteen bits.

With the advent of the first 8086 series processors, capable of addressing a megabyte of memory, linear addressing proved to have some arguable drawbacks. A megabyte of memory could be addressed linearly using a 24-bit number, but this would have proven awkward to work with on a processor that only supported 16-bit registers. It would have required that every address be handled this way, slowing down the processor considerably. Keep in mind, too, that those first generation 8086 chips were pretty slow at the best of times.

In order to get around the problem of efficiently addressing a megabyte of memory with 16-bit numbers, the designers of the 8086 processor came up with segmented memory. In a segmented processor, a complete memory address consists of a 16-bit offset and a 16-bit segment. The offset specifies single-byte increments. The segment specifies 16-byte paragraphs.

In discussing an absolute memory address on a PC, such as the VGA screen buffer at A000:0000H, we are actually defining a number of 16-byte paragraphs from the base of memory and then a number of bytes above the beginning of paragraph in question. In this case, the address is

A000H * 10H + 0

The value 10H is sixteen in decimal. This works out to

40960 * 16 + 0

or 655,360 bytes above the base of memory. In fact, this number is relatively useless—you should never have cause to do linear addressing on a PC running in real mode.

Segmented memory allows programs to run faster. Unless it's necessary to specifically address something outside the current 64K segment, code running on a PC can ignore the whole issue of segments and just work with offset values. As such, an 8086-series processor can use fast 16-bit addressing much of the time.

There are several catches inherent in segmented memory as well. The one that will be most relevant to the code in this book is that of memory models. It's fairly important to understand what these mean to a C compiler.

If you write a very small program, it's likely that all its code and data will fit in less than 64K. In this case, it will be possible to simply ignore the whole issue of segments and address everything in the program with 16-bit offset numbers. This is called the *small* memory model. It makes for fast code, but restricts the size of the program you can write using it.

There is also a "tiny" memory model, which is like the small model but is structured so as to allow programs written in it to be converted to DOS COM files, which load and execute even more quickly.

Under the small memory model, a pointer is a 16-bit entity. It always references things in the current data segment, and as such it only consists of an offset value. The segment value is implied.

If you require more than 64K of code or your program must address more than 64K of data, you'll have to work in the "large" memory model. Large model programs use complete pointers to address things. Each pointer consists of a segment and an offset value. Large model pointers are 32-bit entities.

Under the small model, then, the expression `sizeof(char *)` would return two, while under the large model it would return four.

Large model pointers have several important characteristics. They can be set up to point to anywhere in the first megabyte of memory in a PC. Turbo C provides a convenient macro to create a pointer to an absolute address in memory, `MK_FP`, which has been used informally earlier in this chapter. As such, you can address the video buffer of a VGA card, for example, by simply creating a pointer to it.

Should you intend to use the code in this book with another compiler—one that doesn't include a definition for `MK_FP`—here's what it looks like:

```
#define MK_FP(segment,offset) ((void far *) \
    (((unsigned long)(segment) << 16) | (unsigned)(offset)))
```

It's extremely important to note that you can create several different pointers to the same absolute location in memory by fiddling their offset and segment values. For example, the addresses 0000:0010H and 0001:0000H both point to the same place in memory. In the first case it's the sixteenth byte in the zero'th paragraph and in the second it's the zero'th byte in the first paragraph.

The C language allows you to compare pointers; this is not a particularly reliable operation in some cases under the large model. Consider the following example:

```
char *p1,*p2;
p1=MK_FP(0x0000,0x0010);
p2=MK_FP(0x0001,0x0000);
if(p1 == p2) {
        /* some code goes here */
}
```

In this case, the two pointers point to the same location in memory, but the comparison would fail. In comparing these two pointers under the large memory model, C simply checks to see if their offset and segment values are equal—which they're not.

The C language allows you to add offsets to a pointer, but pure C does not define what pointers and integers really are; these are matters best left to the environment in which C is to be used. Under the large memory model, you can only add pointers and integers, not pointers and longs. In fact, what happens when you do this is that the integer in question is added to the offset of the pointer. This can lead to some pretty ghastly problems, as you might well imagine, when you start working with large objects.

Here's an example of what can happen if you try to use large memory model pointers to deal with single memory objects which approach or exceed 64K of memory. Let's begin by creating a large object in memory:

```
char *p;
p=farmalloc(131072L);
```

The value 131072 is, in fact, 128K of memory. The farmalloc function accepts long integers for its size argument, allowing it to allocate blocks of memory larger than 64K. This example assumes that p is a large model, or far, pointer.

In this case, the segment portion of p would represent the actual segment of the allocated memory. The offset would be some small value—usually four or eight, depending on the version of Turbo C you're using.

If you do this:

```
p+=0x8000;
```

the location pointed to by p will be 32K from the base of the buffer. If you do it again,

```
p+=0x8000;
```

you might well think that p would point to the location 64K from the base of the buffer, but it wouldn't. If you add 8000H and 8000H, you will wind up with 10000H, a number one too large to fit in sixteen bits. Adding an integer to a large model pointer doesn't involve any consideration of overflow or carry. The offset value will simply wrap around, and the result will be to have p pointing back to the base of the buffer again.

This doesn't mean that you can't work with buffers larger than 64K, of course—it just requires that you go at the problem of addressing them a little differently. The most effective way to do this is to create a function that will add long integers to large model pointers, fiddling the offset and segment values appropriately. Here it is:

```
char *farPtr(p,l)
        char *p;
        long l;
{
            unsigned int seg,off;
        seg = FP_SEG(p);
        off = FP_OFF(p);
        seg += (off / 16);
        off &= 0x000f;
        off += (unsigned int)(l & 0x000fL);
        seg += (l / 16L);
        p = MK_FP(seg,off);
        return(p);
}
```

This function will not only return the value of p+1, but it will *normalize* the resulting pointer. This means that it will adjust the segment and offset values of the pointer such that the offset is as small as it can be, allowing you to add fairly large integers to it without running into trouble. The offset of a pointer returned by farPtr will never be larger than fifteen, allowing unsigned integers up to 65520 to be added to one safely using simple addition.

The farPtr function will turn up occasionally in this book.

There is one drawback to using farPtr: it's not terribly portable. It works well enough in Turbo C but gets into trouble under Microsoft C, which objects to having its pointers fiddled like this.

The accepted way to deal with objects larger than 64K is to change memory models—again. You can address them with "huge" pointers. In the huge model, you can add pointers and long integers. Each time you do so, the pointer will be converted to a linear memory address, adjusted with the long integer being added to it and then normalized back to a segment and offset value. This gets comfortably around the problem of an offset value wrapping.

The drawback to using the huge model is that it makes for very much larger, slower applications, as every pointer in a huge model program will be treated this way. In most cases, simple large model pointers would do—you only need true huge pointers for those objects are likely to exceed 64K in size.

Turbo C allows for "mixed model" programming, which addresses this problem. Under a large model program, if you declare a pointer like this:

```
char *p;
```

it will be treated as a normal large model pointer, as we have said. If you declare it like this:

```
char huge *p;
```

it will be treated as a huge pointer, even though it's part of an otherwise large memory model program. While—for the sorts of applications you're likely to write with the code in this book—using the `farPtr` function represents a faster way to handle huge pointer arithmetic, doing so with genuine huge model pointers is more portable.

As an aside, if you happen to port anything in this book to Windows, keep in mind that Windows will absolutely not tolerate programs that do pointer arithmetic, such as that performed by `farPtr`. In a Windows environment, you would always use huge pointers in this application. If you're interested in working with graphic code and Windows, you might want to look at my book *Bitmapped Graphics for Windows*, also published by Windcrest.

All the programs in this book have been written with the assumption that they'll be compiled under the large memory model. It's absolutely critical that your compiler be set up this way, or dire things may happen. Be aware that Turbo C doesn't do much toward checking for memory model problems.

Here are a few examples. This is a function that will fill the mode 12H VGA graphics screen with white:

```
FillWithWhite()
{
    char *p;
    int i;

    for(i=0;i<480;++i)
        memset(MK_FP(0xa000,i*80),255,80);
}
```

By now you'll probably have no difficulty understanding what it's up to. The important thing to keep in mind about this is that it will work properly if it's compiled under the large memory model. In this case, the pointer created by `MK_FP` will consist of the segment A000H and an offset. If you compile it under the small memory model, the pointer will consist of the segment value of your current data segment—as this is where all small model pointers point—and an offset. Rather than fill your screen with white, it will write about 38K of 255-bytes over your program data—an almost certain system crash.

Depending on how your compiler is configured, Turbo C probably will not catch this potential mishap.

As will be dealt with in a moment, your choice of memory models will also affect how assembly language functions work.

There was a time—quite some while ago, when the world was a younger and simpler place—when the C language was a fairly integral thing and supported few dialects or variations. No longer the case, C has become as complicated as you want to make it.

Of ANSI, objects, & other paraphernalia

This code in this book has been written in somewhat pure C, without the extensions that have been grafted onto the language of late. It's very likely that you will not wish to use it as such, and it's relatively easy to change it if you like. This section will discuss exactly what all the extra bits of C might mean to the code in this book.

Under C, everything is regarded as being a signed integer unless you explicitly declare it otherwise. This, for example, is an acceptable C language function declaration:

```
PigsCanFly(n)
{

}
```

In this case, n is assumed to be an integer. This is a fairly sloppy way to declare a function—you should specify the types of all arguments.

You might want to specifically declare another type:

```
PigsCanFly(n)
        unsigned long n;
{
```

At this point, all the code that might come to exist between the curly brackets of the function PigsCanFly will know that n is an unsigned long integer and will treat it as such. Attempts to use it otherwise will be noted by your compiler and complained about in warning messages.

Code outside the confines of the PigsCanFly function will have no idea what the argument to this function should be. As such, the following function call will not offend your compiler one bit:

```
PigsCanFly("Pigs can fly!");
```

It probably need not be said that if the PigsCanFly function was expecting a long integer, passing it a pointer to a string is not likely to provoke any meaningful results from it.

You would not normally pass illogical arguments to a function on purpose; but in a large program with a lot of functions you aren't completely familiar with, it's pretty easy to do so accidentally. Even passing an integer where you meant to pass a long integer can often conjure some pretty strange results, especially if it's one argument of several, and as such confuses the other arguments as well. Some of this will become a bit more apparent in a moment when we deal with assembly language and the true operation of function arguments under C.

You can avoid this sort of problem by using prototypes. A prototype is a declaration that tells your C compiler what sort of arguments to expect for the functions you'll be using. A compiler that accepts prototypes—as Turbo C and most other contemporary implementations of the language do—will complain if you attempt to pass the wrong arguments to a prototyped function.

Here's a prototype for PigsCanFly:

```
void PigsCanFly(unsigned long n);
```

This tells your compiler that PigsCanFly expects to be passed a long integer. It also specifies that you should not use the value that PigsCanFly returns, as it's meaningless. That's what the void keyword indicates. If you don't declare a function void, C will assume that it returns a signed integer.

Birds, martians, & flying pigs

In most cases, such as this one, prototypes are optional. You must have them, however, for functions that return something other than a signed integer so that C will know how to treat the returned values. For example, the farPtr function mentioned earlier in this chapter would require the following prototype:

```
char *farPtr(char *p, long l);
```

Without a prototype, C would assume that farPtr returned an integer, and any attempt to assign its value to a pointer or pass it as an argument to a function expecting a pointer would arouse your compiler's error messages. Note that under Turbo C, the headers that you include to support the library functions provided with the compiler have prototypes for all the functions in question.

You can switch off some or all of the prototype checking that your compiler undertakes. In some cases you'll probably want to do so, as a compiler that wants to use all the ANSI extensions to C is exceedingly rigid and will check your code to an extent that will often genuinely restrict what you can do. One such case that will come up if you try to compile the code in this book as it stands with all the ANSI features of Turbo C switched on is that of the "Function should return a value" warning.

Here's an example of this problem. The following is a perfectly acceptable function declaration:

```
PigsCanFly(n)
        int n;
{
        if(n > 10) puts("The pigs are airborne.");
        else puts("Pigs are pigs are grounded due to fog.");
}
```

At least, it's acceptable under conventional C. With the ANSI extensions enabled, your compiler would note that this function ostensibly returns an integer value—as it has not been declared void—but that it lacks a return statement. With all the ANSI warnings enabled, it would complain about this, as it means that were you to use the return value from this function, it would be meaningless.

You can deal with this problem in one of two ways as you apply the source code in this book. The first is simply to switch off the "Function should return a value" warning of your compiler—which is, incidentally, how I handle it. The second is to explicitly declare all the functions that don't return a value as being void, like this:

```
void PigsCanFly(n)
        int n;
{
        if(n > 10) puts("The pigs are airborne.");
        else puts("Pigs are grounded due to fog.");
}
```

Note, however, that because C assumes that functions return integers unless you specifically tell it otherwise, there will be a difference of opinion between its assumption of the return value of PigsCanFly and what you've declared it as. You must iron out these differences by providing a prototype for any function that doesn't return an integer, as was discussed previously. As such, leaving the "Function should return a value" warning enabled and declaring functions that don't return things as void also requires that you create a prototype for every such function. This isn't too onerous if you like the error trapping features of prototyping, but it's quite cumbersome if you would not normally prototype things.

The issue of prototypes also involves that of the style you use to declare functions. The C language currently offers you two distinct choices in this. You can declare functions using the classic C notation:

```
void PigsCanFly(n,p)
        int n;
        char *p;
    {

    }
```

or you can use the more contemporary Pascal-style notation:

```
void PigsCanFly(int n,char *p)
    {

    }
```

If you use the former, you will be troubled by "Obsolete declaration style" warnings from Turbo C unless you switch this warning off.

The code generated by the foregoing two examples will be identical, and the declaration style you use can be left to your own judgment. It might be argued that the classical notation is easier to read, and less likely to present you with function declarations that run off the right edge of your screen, or wrap for three lines if you write functions with lots of arguments. The Pascal-style notation makes it easier to create prototypes.

Finally, it's worth observing that the code in this book is written in C, rather than the more recent extension to the C language, C++. There are types of applications for which C++ is decidedly superior to C, but moderately low-level graphics applications to be handled by a single programmer are arguably not among them. The C++ extensions are a great advantage to projects that will be worked on by teams of programmers.

The current implementation of Turbo C is, in fact, Turbo C++. Keep in mind that C++ is a superset of C--if you compile C language code with a C++ compiler, the compiler will simply not use any of the C++ extensions. You can, of course, modify the code in this book to use C++ notation, or you can mix it with C++ functions if you like. The resulting executable programs won't really care.

Setting up your compiler The actual setup of your C compiler to work with the code in this book will vary a bit with the version of Turbo C or Borland C you use. It will vary a lot more if you have chosen to use these programs with a different C compiler. Here are a few guidelines to help your compiler and these programs get along:

❏ Use the large memory model.
❏ Switch register variables off.
❏ Set the default char type to unsigned.
❏ Switch the ANSI warnings off.
❏ Switch the C++ extensions off.
❏ Switch case-sensitive linking off.
❏ Switch the default graphics library off.

All the programs in this book have been compiled and run without any warnings or errors. If you attempt to compile them and find that your compiler is complaining, recheck the way it's set up.

Many accomplished C language programmers never learn to work with assembly language and still have rich, rewarding lives and a fairly comfortable relationship with the rest of the universe. A great deal of the code in this book will allow you to carry on with this tradition and ignore the rather intimidating discipline of assembly language as well. There are, however, a few places where assembly language functions are all but inevitable if you want to be able to create graphics applications that get the most out of the hardware they run on.

The awesome fear of assembly language

Assembly language functions are used in C programming for one of several reasons. To begin with, there are some things that you just can't do in C, or can't do very well. Typically this involves low-level hardware matters—of which graphics programming is unfortunately fairly well-infested—and odd code structures, such as drivers and resident programs. In fact, you can handle drivers and resident programs in C, but the results are often less than impressive.

Secondly, assembly language functions offer the potential for doing things very much more rapidly than comparable C code. It's common to use assembly language to optimize the time-critical functions of a program. This is where it will turn up in this book for the most part.

Thirdly, assembly language usually results in code that is much smaller than comparable C language functions.

The drawbacks to assembly language are substantial, however. In a sense, a C compiler gives you a way to express your ideas in a human-readable form, which is then translated into machine-readable instructions by the compiler. Assembly language requires that you express your ideas in a form that's almost the language of the microprocessor in your system. At this level, it will become apparent that human beings and computers do not think in anything like the same ways.

In addition, in order to program in assembly language, you'll need a substantial amount of low-level knowledge about the workings of DOS, your system BIOS, and the hardware of your computer—things that C insulates you from. You'll also have to understand the actual language of an 8086-series microprocessor, which is considerably more daunting than C.

Finally, whereas the C language includes substantial facilities to trap errors in your source code, assembly language will let you get away with just about anything—no matter how nasty it might actually be.

Writing assembly language functions implies a considerable level of skill and expertise. Even applying previously written functions can be a bit challenging, as you will frequently have to fine tune things a bit for compiler variations and such.

This section will help you to understand a bit about how assembly language works when it finds itself bolted onto a C language program. It will assume that you have at least some familiarity with assembly language programming. If some of the following examples seem a bit like two Martians discussing the weather, you might want to consult a basic book on assembly language.

Alternately, you might just want to ignore the assembly language issue entirely—which you can can do for most of the code in this book.

Arguments Writing an assembly language function to be called from a C program actually breaks down into two distinct problems—to wit, writing the actual function, and knowing how to interface it to your program. The latter issue is easily the most awkward, and one that isn't usually very well-documented.

The first thing to know about writing assembly language functions is that your C compiler expects them to behave just like its own functions do. In a sense, an assembly language should do what a C function might have done but do so in a more tightly coded, effective way.

Most of the interface questions surrounding assembly language functions involve passing arguments to your function, retrieving return values from it, and preserving the machine state while it's working, such that your program doesn't return from the assembly language function and promptly crash. Most of this involves understanding a bit about what a C language program does behind your back. This, in turn, involves understanding its use of stacks and registers.

Under the C language, arguments passed to a function are passed on the stack and returned in registers. This is something you needn't know just to write in C, but it's pretty well essential in assembly language. Let's begin with passing arguments to a function. Here's a typical C function:

```
putch('A');
```

This line of code really means to push 'A' onto the stack and call the function `putch`. Knowing that it's intended to fetch an argument from the stack, `putch` will peek back up the stack and see what's there. Here's what this call would look like in assembly language:

```
MOV   AX,0041H
PUSH  AX
CALL  _putch
ADD   SP,2
```

To begin with, the stack always works in 16-bit objects—the `PUSH` instruction will always push one word onto the stack, and a `POP` will pop one word off it. The value 0041H has the ASCII code for the letter A in its low order byte and nothing in its high order byte. The `putch` function only wants to deal with a 1-byte object, but on a PC everything must be rounded up to the nearest word.

The current stack position is defined by the SP register, the stack pointer. The stack always grows downwards in absolute memory. As such, if the SP register starts off at 0FFFEH, executing a `PUSH` instruction will cause whatever has been pushed to be written to where SP points and SP to subsequently be decremented by 2. Executing a `POP` instruction will increment SP by 2 and copy the contents of where it points to whatever is being popped.

In calling a function like `putch`, then, arguments must be pushed onto the stack and then popped off afterwards. Especially for functions with lots of arguments, it's much quicker to simply add the requisite value to the SP register than it is to execute a `POP` instruction for each PUSH.

In a large model program, executing a far `CALL` instruction will cause the current code segment value and the current instruction pointer value to be pushed onto the stack, such that when the function being called returns, the processor can pop them off the stack and get back to what it was doing prior to the call. As such, in the call to `putch` there will be three words—or six bytes—on the stack. The latter two words will be removed from the stack by the processor when `putch` returns.

In fact, there will be eight words. For reasons that will be dealt with in a moment, every function that uses arguments must preserve the BP register as well.

Note that there are two words pushed onto the stack for a large memory model CALL—there's only one word pushed if you're writing in the small memory model. This is one of the reasons why the programs in this book that use assembly language absolutely must be compiled in the large memory model.

The problem of looking back up the stack to retrieve function arguments is one that complicates the workings of assembly language functions. Knowing that there will be six words on the stack ahead of the first argument, it would seem to be possible to find the first argument like this:

```
MOV AX,[SP + 6]
```

In fact, this has several problems inherent in it, not the least of which is that the 8086 doesn't allow you to index off the stack pointer. Instead, it provides a special register to handle this particular situation: the base pointer or BP register. The BP register implicitly addresses the stack segment, in the same way that the SI register implicitly addresses the data segment. To fetch an argument, then, you would do this:

```
MOV BP,SP
MOV AX,[BP + 6]
```

The second argument, if there was one, would be

```
MOV AX,[BP + 8]
```

and so on. Because the stack offset for arguments will be constant, it will be represented by a symbol in this book:

```
_AOFF EQU     6
```

You would fetch the first argument, then, like this:

```
MOV AX,[BP + _AOFF + 0]
```

Note that passed integers and bytes live in one word; large model pointers live in two. While a large model pointer is passed as one argument under C, it turns out to be two arguments to an assembly language function. Here's how you would fetch a pointer passed as the first argument to an assembly language function:

```
MOV SI,[BP + _AOFF + 0]
MOV DS,[BP + _AOFF + 2]
```

Note that, once again, this only works properly in the large memory model. For example, in the small memory model, a pointer only requires one word for the offset; the segment will always be your program's data segment.

Arguments are returned from an assembly language function in the machine registers. Here's a typical C language call that returns something:

```
a=getch();
```

The getch function returns a byte value, but as everything will be rounded up to sixteen bits, it really returns a word with the upper byte set to zero. Objects of sixteen bits or less are always returned in the AX register, so what this code really means is to execute the function getch and then to place whatever happens to be in the AX register at its conclusion into a.

You can return 32-bit objects, such as long integers or pointers, in the DX and AX register, with the high order word in DX and the low order word in AX.

Finally, aside from the BP register, you must preserve registers that your C compiler might want to use in whatever functions will call your assembly language functions. At a minimum, you should preserve DS and ES. Turbo C uses the SI and DI registers as register variables—you must preserve these as well unless you make sure to switch the register variables off in your compiler setup.

Here, then, is a simple assembly language function to be linked with a C program:

```
             PUBLIC    _PigsCanFly
_PigsCanFly  PROC      FAR
             PUSH      BP
             MOV       BP,SP
             PUSH      DS
             PUSH      ES

             MOV       AX,[BP + _AOFF + 0]
             CMP       AX,10
             JG        PCF1

             MOV       AX,_DATA
             MOV       DS,AX
             MOV       DX,OFFSET PIGSNOFLY
             MOV       AH,9
             INT       21H
             MOV       AX,0000H
             JMP       PCF2

    PCF1:    MOV       AX,_DATA
             MOV       DS,AX
             MOV       DX,OFFSET PIGSCANFLY
             MOV       AH,9
             INT       21H
             MOV       AX,0001H
    PCF2:
             POP       ES
             POP       DS
             POP       BP
             RET
PigsCanFly   ENDP
```

This function is roughly the equivalent of the C language PigsCanFly function discussed earlier in this chapter. It will print a message about the aviatorial status of pigs in general, based on its argument. The pigs will be flying if the argument is over ten. It will return a true value if they're flying and a false one if they're grounded.

This function assumes that its two message strings will be available in the data segment for the program this function is linked to:

```
PIGSNOFLY    DB    'Pigs are grounded due to fog.$'
PIGSCANFLY   DB    'The pigs are airborne.$'
```

Let's have a look at what the foregoing pseudo-English is all about.

The first line of the assembly language function declares that this function is public, which means that it can be linked to and called by functions outside the module in which it resides. Unlike C, which assumes that all functions are public, assembly language requires that public functions be so declared. This means that you can have function names in an assembly language module that duplicate those in a C program or its libraries—unless they're explicitly declared as being public, they won't conflict.

Note that the function name for PigsCanFly is preceded by an underbar. This is a peculiarity of Turbo C. By default, it adds underbars to any external function name. As such, if you call PigsCanFly from within a C program, it will actually try to resolve a function named _PigsCanFly. In using other functions written in C, Turbo C keeps track of the underbars for you. In creating assembly language functions, however, you must handle this yourself, such that the Turbo C linker will find what it's looking for.

The actual PROC declaration for _PigsCanFly declares the function as being FAR, which affects what type of RET instruction will actually be used at its conclusion, among other things.

Note that BP, DS, and ES are pushed onto the stack and then popped off in the reverse order prior to returning.

The code that prints the appropriate message for _PigsCanFly uses a call to DOS. In this function, DOS will print a string pointed to by DS:DX if AH holds the value nine and INT 21H is executed. For historical reasons, DOS expects the string to be terminated by a dollar sign, rather than a zero byte. This makes printing strings with actual dollar signs in them a bit tricky using this function.

The one remaining peculiarity of this code is the symbol _DATA. In a complete assembly language module—several of which will appear in this book—this symbol represents the common data segment for the program into which the module will be linked. When the EXE file which contains _PigsCanFly is run, DOS will replace all the instances of _DATA with the actual common data segment value.

Note that you cannot move a fixed value into the DS register directly. As such, you must set AX to _DATA and then DS to AX.

As with many programming issues, assembly language functions can sound pretty daunting when they're discussed in abstract. They're a bit more manageable in real life. You'll probably find that you have no real need to modify the functions to be explored in this book, and you'll be able to use them as they stand. As such, you will be able to introduce yourself to assembly language for C a bit at a time if you've not done any of it before.

Bring on the graphics

The best way to deal with super VGA graphics is to warm up your compiler and dig into them. Having made it thus far you should have a pretty good idea as to how the relevant hardware works—at least in theory—and what's involved in making graphic-based programs work. The rest of this book will, in a sense, be involved with filling in the blanks with the grotty details that actually drive graphic software.

Grotty details are the things that keep programming such a black art, of course. If it was easy, everyone would be able to do it.

2 Graphic files

Visual fiction

"If it looks like a duck and walks like a duck and quacks like a duck, chances are it's a duck."

—Murphy's Laws

Books are one of the things that separates people from baboons, cocker spaniels, lawyers and other lower life forms. Aside from being able to merely figure things out, we've devised a way to preserve what we've learned and pass it on to other people. This is something that most of us take for granted, but writing was a very much larger leap of technology than wheels or fire.

It's a pity that whoever figured it out didn't think to copyright it.

Graphic files are a bit like books in this respect. They allow you to create graphics and store images, such that they can be viewed later on, passed along to someone else, or used as part of a larger application. In a real sense, a graphic file is a way to store the screen data that was described in Chapter 1 of this book. Having said this, it's worth noting that there's a lot more to graphic files than one might initially consider.

Bitmapped graphics can be seen as being a two-dimensional array of pixels. This analogy works best if you consider the 256-color VGA modes, in which each pixel is in fact one byte. As we'll deal with later in this chapter; however, all the techniques herein apply to other image formats, even the ones that are oriented as byte planes.

For reasons that will probably be apparent after the discussion of screen graphics in the previous chapter, image files store pictures as horizontal lines of bits, more or less like they're set up in a screen buffer. Each line, then, can be regarded as a string of bytes.

Figure 2-1 illustrates an example bitmapped graphic.

The salient point about the picture in FIG. 2-1 is that there's quite a bit of blank space in it. This is a picture with the mode 13H dimensions of 320 by 200 pixels. If it were to be written to a file as it stands, it would occupy 64,000 bytes of disk space, and a fair bit of that would be redundant data.

Recognizing that this situation is fairly common in working with bitmapped images, programmers have written most graphic file formats to compress their contents. The simplest sort of compression is what's called "run-length" compression. Here's an example of how it might work—note that every file format that uses run-length compression implements it slightly differently.

Image information is always compressed one line at a time. In this case, then, we'll be compressing a string of 320 bytes and then moving on to the next line and 320 more bytes. For reasons that will become apparent later in this chapter, compression functions don't compress across the boundaries between lines.

2-1
*An example bitmapped
graphic image.*

In compressing a line of bytes, then, you would begin by counting the number of identical adjacent bytes, beginning with the first byte in the line. The count would proceed, moving right along the line, until you encountered the first different byte. If the count is greater than zero, this portion of the line would be regarded as a "run of bytes" field. If the count was zero, the first two bytes in the line would be known to be different. The first byte would be added to a buffer, the pointer to the start of the line would be moved up by one and the process repeated.

The contents of the buffer are called a "string field." These are uncompressable bytes.

Figure 2-2 illustrates this process.

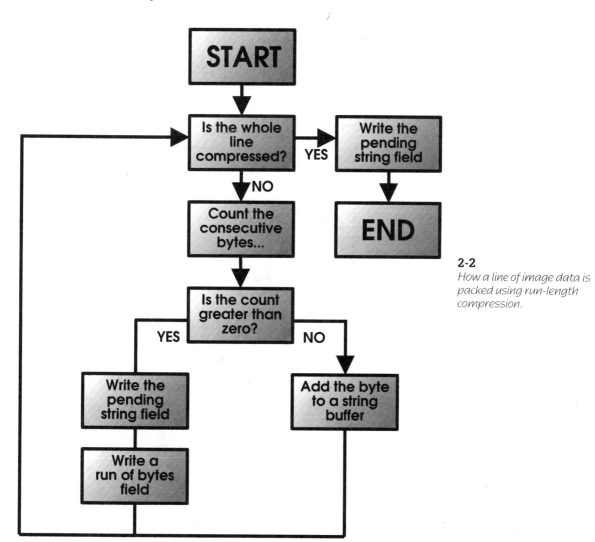

2-2
How a line of image data is packed using run-length compression.

In writing a compressed image to disk, each field will be preceded by a "key." A key is what will tell the uncompressing software that will ultimately read this image how to make sense of the compressed data. Let's allow that if a field is a run of bytes, the first byte of the field will be FFH, the second byte will be the length of the field, and the third byte will be the byte which gets repeated. If the field is a string, the first byte will be 00H, the second byte will be the length, and the number of bytes after the length byte specified as the length of the field will be the string data.

In this way, any image data with adjacent identical bytes can be compressed. In real-world image file compression systems, things would be handled a bit differently—the key byte and length byte can usually be compressed into a single byte, for example—but the principal is the same.

Now, this approach to image file compression has some holes in it. An image with no adjacent bytes would actually be bigger compressed than uncompressed, for example, as it would contain the key bytes and length bytes for each field as well as the actual image data. This is called "negative compression" and often takes place if you try to run-length compress scanned images. Scanned images typically exhibit no meaningful patterns.

Figure 2-3 illustrates a fragment of a screen dump from Microsoft Windows.

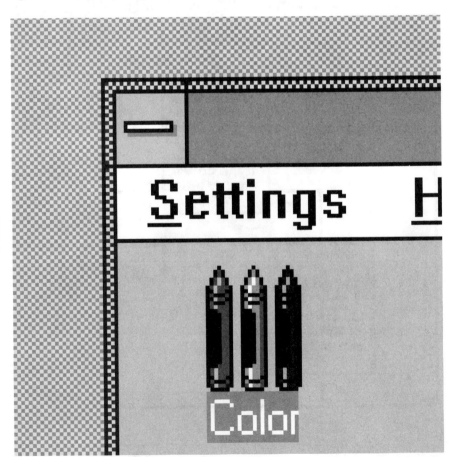

2-3
Part of a screen from Microsoft Windows.

The thing to note about FIG. 2-3 is that it does exhibit a meaningful pattern in many places. However, it won't compress very well using run-length compression because the pattern spans two bytes. There are lots of regular areas in the picture, but few adjacent identical bytes.

In a sense, a byte is a pattern of bits. In talking about compressing adjacent bytes, we're also talking about compressing strings of bits. The strings are fixed at 8-bit lengths, which is convenient, as this is a form in which a PC's processor can effectively work with data. However, as was illustrated by FIG. 2-3, this isn't always the most efficient string length for compressing image data.

In practice, the most effective string length varies between images. You could create a more efficient type of compression by compressing fields of bits, the length of which would be determined by the nature of the image being compressed. This is called "string table" compression. Compared to run-length compression, it's a real bear to implement; and, all other things being equal, a string table uncompression function will work much slower than a run-length uncompressor confronted with the same image. However, a string table compressed file will usually be a lot smaller, and string table compression is much less likely to result in negative compression for complex images.

There are about a dozen popular bitmapped image file formats in use at the moment. While they all do effectively the same thing—storing pictures—no two are compatible. There is no real standard for image file formats on a PC—the format you use will be determined by the software that's involved. You can find a thorough airing of the image file format issue in the books mentioned at the end of this chapter.

If one had to pick the nearest thing to a standard format for PC bitmapped graphics, it would probably be either PCX or GIF at the moment. The PCX format was created by Z-Soft, the authors of PC Paintbrush. However, they were so generous in handing out the details of its workings to anyone who asked that it has been adopted as an import option for virtually all desktop publishing packages and word processors that will accept graphics. It's probably the most widely used single bitmapped graphic format in PC circles.

In addition to being ubiquitous, the PCX format uses very simple run-length compression and is dead easy to work with. It will support images ranging from simple monochrome pictures to 24-bit true color graphics. Furthermore, its internal structure is usually more or less that of the various PC display modes that pictures are displayed in. For example, it stores 16-color images as interleaved planar lines, just like they appeared in the discussion of 16-color graphic modes in Chapter 1.

The only arguable drawback to PCX files is that their run-length compression method was really designed for graphics that had been drawn, rather than scanned. The PC Paintbrush software was, at least in its inception, primarily a drawing tool. As such, storing scanned images in PCX files is likely to leave you with pretty large files, frequently exhibiting alarming negative compression.

The GIF format was created by CompuServe as a medium to store public domain images and is only now turning up as a file format supported by commercial applications that read or write bitmapped graphics. Its primary feature of interest is that it uses string table compression and, as such, squeezes files down as much as they're likely to be squeezed. One of the reasons for the existence of the GIF format is to facilitate the exchange of files by modem, a situation in which file size is of considerable interest.

The useful thing about GIF files is that there are so many of them. Most bulletin boards—and, of course, CompuServe itself—can provide you with buckets of them.

There are a few limitations to the GIF format. The software to read and write GIF files is inherently more complex than that which would handle PCX files. It's also a lot slower; when we get down to looking at a GIF decoder, you'll probably appreciate that it has to do a lot more than the comparable function to read PCX files. The GIF format currently only supports images with up to 256 colors—it will not handle 24-bit files. Finally, in dealing with any image having fewer than 256 colors, the image data that emerges from a GIF decoder will probably not be in the form you'll need it if you're working with a VGA display, entailing some data swabbing before it can be used. This further increases the effective unpacking time for a GIF file.

Figure 2-4 illustrates a super-VGA image. It has the dimensions 640 by 400 at 256 colors, and occupies 256,000 bytes of memory unpacked. Stored as a GIF file, it requires 215,040 bytes of disk space. Stored as a PCX file, it requires 321,965 bytes of disk space. Despite its limitations and added complexity, the utility of the GIF format should be apparent.

2-4
A super VGA image.

Lute Players, by Maxfield Parrish

Working with PCX files

In addition to merely storing data, image files typically require "headers." A *header* is a data structure that will define things like the dimensions of a stored image, how many bits of color it has, and what the colors in its palette are, for those files that use palettes. A palette will be required for any file with more than 1 bit of color and less than 24 bits. In fact, there are exceptions to this: some formats allow for 16-bit RGB files, similar in structure to the high-color screen format explained in Chapter 1. Secondly, some formats allow for grey scale images, which don't require a palette *per se*. Neither of these options is supported by either the PCX or GIF formats, and they won't turn up here.

The PCX format has a very simple header structure. Expressed as a C language struct, it looks like this:

```
typedef struct    {
        char manufacturer;
        char version;
        char encoding;
        char bits_per_pixel;
        int xmin,ymin;
        int xmax,ymax;
        int hres;
        int vres;
        char palette[48];
        char reserved;
        char color_planes;
        int bytes_per_line;
        int palette_type;
        char filler[58];
        } PCXHEAD;
```

You can work out the characteristics of a PCX image by interpreting the fields of a PCXHEAD object as follows. The *manufacturer* field will always contain ten. This is how a PCX reader knows that what it's been asked to read is actually a PCX file. The version number defines which version of PC Paintbrush ostensibly created the file. In fact, what it really defines is how to handle the palette information. We'll look at PCX palettes in detail in a moment.

Here's what the values of the *version* field mean:

0   Version 2.5 of PC Paintbrush

2   Version 2.8 of PC Paintbrush, palette included

3   Version 2.8 of PC Paintbrush, use default palette

5   Version 3.0 of PC Paintbrush or better

The `encoding` field is always one, indicating run-length encoding. At present this is the only type of encoding PCX files support.

The `bits_per_pixel` field indicates the number of bits of color required by each pixel of the image in question.

The `xmin` and `ymin` elements specify the coordinates of the upper left corner of the image relative to the upper left corner of your screen. These will usually both be zero. The `xmax` and `ymax` elements specify the distance from the upper left corner to the lower right corner. As such, if `pcx` is an object of the type PCXHEAD that has been loaded with a PCX file header, you can calculate the actual dimensions of a PCX image like this:

```
int width,depth;

width=pcx.xmax-pcx.xmin+1;
depth=pcx.ymax-pcx.ymin+1;
```

The `hres` and `yres` elements of the header indicate the horizontal and vertical resolution respectively. These values aren't normally used.

The `palette` field of the header holds the color palette for the picture being unpacked—assuming, of course, that it has one. This also assumes that the image supports no more than sixteen colors. The next step up—256 colors—requires a palette that is added to the end of the image data, as will be discussed presently.

The `color_planes` field—perhaps not surprisingly—specifies the number of color planes in the image. In a 16-bit image, for example, this would be four. In a 24-bit image, it's three—once again, something to be discussed shortly.

The `bytes_per_line` field defines the number bytes in a compressed line of image information. The usefulness of this value will become apparent in a moment.

With the exception of image file formats that can only hold monochrome pictures— none of which will turn up in this book—and of those that hold 24-bit images, all image files will carry a palette definition of some sort. In the case of the PCX format, this is a bit fragmented. Pictures with up to sixteen colors can have their palettes stored in the `palette` field of the header. However, there isn't enough space in the header to hold all the color definitions for a 256-color image—the original designers of the PCX format don't appear to have envisioned the day when displays capable of handling more than sixteen colors might appear.

A PCX file with 256 colors has its palette stored at the end of the file, after the image data. A 256-color image requires 768 bytes to store its palette, with three bytes per RGB color definition. The palette is always preceded by a byte that holds the value 12. As such, the palette in a 256-color PCX file can be located by seeking to the end of the file, seeking back by 769 bytes and reading the value at the file pointer. If it's 12, read the following 768 bytes as the palette. It it's not, there's something amiss with the file being read.

Once you've read past the 128 bytes of a PCX file header, the next byte will be the first byte of the compressed image data. In essence, reading this is pretty elementary. A few things will crop up to confuse it in a moment.

The PCX format uses very simple run-length encoding—simpler even than the hypothetical run-length encoding method discussed earlier in this chapter. Each line in a PCX file will unpack to the number of bytes in the `bytes_per_line` field of its header. Here's a function to unpack one line:

```
readpcxline(p,fp,bytes)
        char *p;
        FILE *fp;
        int bytes;
{
        int n=0,c,i;

        do {
                c=fgetc(fp) & 0xff;
                if((c & 0xc0) == 0xc0) {
                        i=c & 0x3f;
                        c=fgetc(fp);
                        while(i--) p[n++]=c;
                }
```

```
            else p[n++]=c;
      } while(n < bytes);
      return(n);
}
```

In this example, p is a buffer large enough to hold the line, fp is a file pointer to the open PCX file, and bytes is the number of bytes in a line, as determined by the PCX file's header. In PCX run-length compression, if a byte has its two high order bits set, it's the key byte for a run of bytes field. In this case, the six low order bits represent the length of the field. This value can range from 0 through 63. The next byte in the file is the byte to be repeated this number of times.

If the two high order bits aren't set, the byte is read from the source PCX file and written to the uncompressed line as is. There is no string field in PCX compression.

You might well have noticed a catch in the aforementioned procedure: the format would seem to have a problem with bytes written "as is" if they happen to have their two high order bits set. In fact, the PCX format handles this in a particularly inelegant way—all such bytes are treated as one-byte runs. As such, each one takes two bytes to store compressed. This might help to explain why PCX files don't have the best compression ratios when they're confronted with complex images.

To uncompress a whole PCX image, you would call the foregoing function once for each line, storing the lines it unpacks somewhere between calls. The value it returns should be the same as the bytes argument passed to it for each call.

In a single plane image—that is, one with two colors—each line will be approximately width / 8 bytes wide. The width value will be pcx.xmax-pcx.xmin+1, as noted earlier. The approximation is a possible error of one. If width is evenly divisible by eight, this calculation will be correct. If it's not, the rounding inherent in integer arithmetic will make the number of bytes one too small. As such, you should always calculate the byte width of a bit field—the number of bytes in a line—using the macro pixels2bytes. Here it is:

```
#define pixels2bytes(n) ((n + 7) / 8)
```

In fact, the number of bytes in a PCX image line might not be pixels2bytes(pcx.xmax-pcx.xmin+1) in all cases, as some PCX writers pad the lines out by a byte or two in some cases. The correct value to unpack to will always be pcx.bytes_per_line, although you might want to use pixels2bytes(pcx.xmax-pcx.xmin+1) internally in your own software.

This will become more meaningful when we get into the unspeakable tangled morass of 16-color PCX files.

A 256-color PCX file is exceedingly easy to unpack. Image data appears from the PCX decoder in essentially the same form as a VGA card expects to see it, that is, with one byte per pixel. The width of each line in bytes is again defined by the bytes_per_line field of the header.

The 24-bit PCX format is also pretty easy to work with. Each line consists of three planes. Each plane is actually eight bits deep. The first plane consists of all the red values for the line. The second plane is all the green values, and the third plane is all the blue values. You must do a certain amount of data swabbing to arrange these into true RGB pixels.

Note that PCX files do not support color depth values of 32, 64, or 128 colors. Images with these color depths would be promoted to 256 colors to store them in a PCX file.

16-color PCX files

If the foregoing types of PCX files seemed relatively tame, the 16-color PCX format should go a long way toward reviving the mystique and legendary dread of the PCX format most programmers feel. A chaotic juggling act of standards, patches and flat-out lies, 16-color PCX files take some doing to work with.

The code to handle them in this chapter will manage all the types and mutations—it has taken years to perfect.

In its simplest form, a 16-color PCX file is very easy to understand. It has four bits of color, and each line consists of four color planes, just like the lines of a VGA card's screen buffer in its 16-color graphics mode. Each of these planes is the number of bytes specified by `pcx.bytes_per_line` long. It all sounds very simple.

It's not.

One of the things that helped to make the PCX format so commonplace in PC graphics circles was a pamphlet released by Z-Soft detailing its workings. It explained most of the forgoing, with the injunction that in compressing an image, one should be sure not to compress across line boundaries. Now, this was worded a bit ambiguously, and it wasn't clear whether it meant not to compress across the boundaries of lines or across the boundaries of the four planes in a line. In fact, it means the latter, but not all the third-party software developers who have used PCX interpreted it this way.

A 16-color PCX file that is compressed so that all four planes are handled as one single compressed line will usually uncompress properly, even if you uncompress it as four separate planes. It will only run into problems if the data at the end of one plane happens to be the same as that at the beginning of the next, such that a run of bytes field spans the gap between lines. In this case, the first plane will unpack to be a few bytes long and the next plane will come up a few bytes short. A PCX reader will interpret this as a corrupted file.

Astute programmers will look at this situation and observe that it can be dealt with by simply assuming that all 16-color PCX files are handled incorrectly, and unpacking them as single lines that are four times the value in `pcx.bytes_per_line`. This, too, almost works. The problem is that this value can be a byte or two longer than the actual length of the line, due to padding, causing each plane to be offset by eight or sixteen pixels. This looks very colorful—leaving multiple colored shadows to the left of the objects in affected pictures—but it's not at all desirable.

There is no obvious way to determine whether a 16-color PCX file has been packed correctly or not. There is, however, a way to sneak past this problem. Inasmuch as both types of PCX files will unpack correctly if you unpack all four planes as one object—at least, the unpacking function won't assume that the file has been corrupted—this is how a PCX reader should deal with 16-color files. It should then copy each plane out of the unpacked line into a new buffer. The length of the source planes must be `pcx.bytes_per_line` and the length of the destination planes must be `pixels2bytes(pcx.xmax-pcx.xmin+1)`. This will adjust the final plane width if there are padding bytes at the end of each plane in the unpacked lines.

A function that handles 16-color PCX files this way will deal with all the permutations of planar 16-color files currently extant. Note the use of the word "planar." This might seem like it implies the existence of still other types of 16-color PCX files—and so it does.

Microsoft Windows does not store 16-color bitmaps as planar lines. Its internal bitmap format—what it calls a "device independent bitmap"—uses stacked nybbles. A *nybble* is half a byte. In this format, each byte of a line would store two pixels, with the first pixel in the upper four bits and the second pixel in the lower four bits.

Windows manages to update a 16-color screen with these things fairly quickly, although they're pretty nasty to work with for any other application.

While it's not really documented anywhere, there is a third sort of 16-color PCX files that store their lines in this format. They're created, among other things, by several Windows screen capture programs. There's a fairly good reason for this, actually: in order to capture a screen or a portion thereof under Windows, one must ask Windows for a device-independent bitmap that represents the screen contents in question. This bitmap will be stored as stacked nybbles, rather than as planes, and converting it into the more common planar format to write it to a PCX file is time consuming. As it happens, the Windows Paintbrush application that accompanies Windows will read PCX files in this unusual format, although few DOS-based applications will.

The Desktop Paint packages on the companion disk for this book do handle these files correctly.

Obviously, attempting to unpack a stacked-nybble PCX line as if it were a planar line won't cut it—among other things, the number of bytes in a line might vary by one, depending on the image dimensions, and the data will prove meaningless if it's treated this way. You can work out whether you have a planar file or a stacked-nybble file, however, by having a peek at the header. In a stacked-nybble file, `pcx.bits_per_pixel` will be four and `pcx.color_planes` will be one, a condition that can't occur with any other permutation of color planes and color depth.

Converting stacked nybbles to planes is a bit processor intensive, but it's essentially pretty simple.

The Turbo C graphics library includes two useful functions for dealing with bitmaps: `getimage` and `putimage`. Given the rectangular coordinates of an area of your screen, the `getimage` function will copy the image therein into a buffer. The `putimage` function will accept a buffer previously loaded up by `getimage` and paint its contents anywhere else on your screen you like.

A digression on bitmap fragments

You can fool `putimage` into being eminently more useful by passing it buffers that you have set up to look like they've been created by `getimage`, even if they really haven't been. All this entails is a knowledge of how a Turbo C image fragment is structured, of course.

A putimage fragment in a monochrome screen mode consists of two integers followed by some image data. The first integer is one less than the number of pixels across the area represented by the image. The second integer is one less than the number of pixels down the area.

One can derive three very useful macros from this observation:

```
#define   ImageWidth(p)   (1+p[0]+(p[1] << 8))
#define   ImageDepth(p)   (1+p[2]+(p[3] << 8))
#define   ImageBytes(p)   (pixels2bytes((1+p[0]+(p[1] <<8))))
```

The ImageWidth macro will return the width of an image fragment in pixels. The ImageDepth macro will return its depth in pixels. The ImageBytes macro will return the number of bytes in one line of an image fragment.

In a 16-color screen mode, the internal structure of an image fragment is a bit different. Each line of the image actually consists of four planes. Each plane is ImageBytes(image) wide. Each line is four times this width in bytes.

The order of the planes is the reverse of the way you'd expect them to appear in the screen buffer of a 16-color display. The first plane in a line is actually the high-order plane in a display. This is something to keep in mind as you work with image fragments.

A second complication in using image fragments with the Turbo C putimage function is that putimage can only deal with images occupying less than 64K. A complete mode 12H screen occupies more than twice this amount of memory. This will be dealt with later in this book.

Finally, a 256-color image fragment consists of an array of bytes. The two integers at the start of an image fragment buffer will be the same, but each line will consist of ImageWidth(image) bytes. The ImageBytes macro is meaningless in 256-color modes.

Creating image fragments from PCX files

As will become apparent later in this book, being able to get bitmapped images into your programs as putimage fragments can be extremely useful. While uncompressed, and therefore a bit bulky compared to PCX files, simple image fragments can be displayed very quickly and used in all sorts of applications. They'll turn up extensively in writing arcade games toward the end of this book.

You can write the contents of an image fragment buffer out to a disk file, creating a sort of portable uncompressed image file. Compared to an accepted file format, like PCX, this lacks a number of important elements. Specifically, an application reading such a file would have no way of knowing if it was, in fact, an image fragment—there is no signature that will identify a putimage fragment as such. Secondly, a color putimage fragment doesn't include a palette. In using getimage and putimage as they were intended to be used, this doesn't matter, as image fragments captured from and painted to the same screen will always have the same palette. This might not be true if you save a fragment to a disk file and then read it into another application.

In fact, image fragments don't even include a way to specify the number of bits of color they represent—an important consideration, as each color format is handled decidedly differently.

The basic image fragment format would be a great deal more useful if it had a header preceding it, to turn it into a complete file format. Here's what such a header will look like in this book:

```
typedef struct {
        char sig[4];
        unsigned int width,depth,bits,bytes,planebytes;
        unsigned long palette;
        unsigned long image;
        } IMAGEHEAD;
```

The `sig` element of an `IMAGEHEAD` object will always contain the same four bytes, allowing a program reading one of these fragments to know what it has. This is the signature string:

```
#define IMAGESIG "IFRG"
```

The five integers in an `IMAGEHEAD` object are probably pretty well self-explanatory. The `width` and `depth` values are the dimensions of the image fragment—this information will, in fact, be duplicated in the first two integers in the fragment itself. The `bits` element specifies the color depth—it will be 1, 4, 8, or 16. For practical purposes, it's much more useful to store 24-bit images with only 16 bits of color, as was outlined in the discussion of high-color graphics in Chapter 1. The same pixel format will be used for these image fragment files. At present there is no Turbo C BGI driver capable of working with a 16-bit display, but you might find you want to use the image fragment format in these circumstances anyway.

Chapter 5 will include a synthetic `putimage` function for use with 16-bit image fragments, and an application for 16-bit image fragment files.

The `bytes` element specifies the number of bytes in a line and the `planebytes` element specifies the number of bytes in an image plane. The latter value will only differ from the former for 16-color image fragments.

The `palette` and `image` elements specify the offset from the start of the file to the palette color lookup table, if there is one, and to the start of the image fragment data. In the programs in this book, the palette will start immediately after the header, so this value will always be `(long)sizeof(IMAGEHEAD)`. The `image` will point to the position immediately after the palette. Note that one and 24-bit image fragments don't have palettes, in which case both these elements will point to the same place.

You might have cause to change these values if you wanted to put the palette after the image data, or if you wanted to put something between the header and the palette.

The data pointed to by `palette` will be three-byte RGB color definitions, one for each color in the image. The number of colors in the image will always be `1 << ih.bits`, where `ih` is an `IMAGEHEAD` object. The data pointed to by `image` will be a normal `putimage` buffer, as covered earlier in this chapter.

Figure 2-5 illustrates the structure of a complete fragment file. The example programs in this book use the extension FRG for these files. This stands for "fragment," of course, although it seems inevitable that they'll be referred to as "frog files" sooner or later.

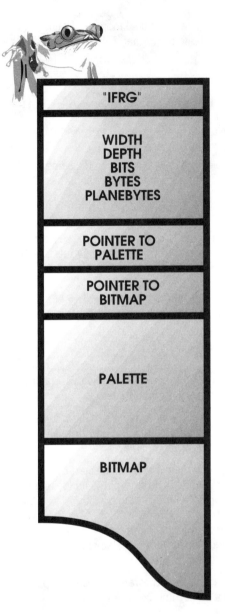

| "IFRG" |
| WIDTH
DEPTH
BITS
BYTES
PLANEBYTES |
| POINTER TO
PALETTE |
| POINTER TO
BITMAP |
| PALETTE |
| BITMAP |

2-5
How a FRG file is structured.
The amphibian is optional.

As will turn up later in this book, you can use FRG files by seeking to the data pointed to by the `image` element of the header, reading the remainder of the file into a suitable buffer and then passing the buffer to `putimage`.

The first program we'll look at to use FRG files will be `PCX2FRG`, which will translate PCX files to the FRG format. This will allow you to get create images with a paint program and then translate them into a form that's easy to incorporate into an application. The Desktop Paint applications on the companion disk for this book will provide you with the tools to create graphics suitable for use with PCX2FRG, as will PC Paintbrush, Windows Paintbrush, and Deluxe Paint, among others.

In essence, creating an FRG file from a PCX file involves unpacking the PCX file into memory and writing an IMAGEHEAD header, the palette information for the file if it's appropriate, and finally the uncompressed line data. In fact, the procedure can be handled even more efficiently by observing that the lines which emerge from a PCX decoder do so in exactly the order they would be written to a FRG file. As such, it's only necessary to buffer one line at a time, rather than a complete image.

As will be covered in the next section of this chapter in dealing with GIF files, buffering a whole image can leave you with some awkward memory requirements. The GIF format does not constrain image lines to appear in a convenient order.

Figure 2-6 is the source code for PCX2FRG.

```
/*
        PCX to image fragment translator

        Copyright (c) 1992 Alchemy Mindworks Inc.
*/

#include "stdio.h"
#include "alloc.h"

#define RGB_RED      0
#define RGB_GREEN    1
#define RGB_BLUE     2
#define RGB_SIZE     3

#define IMAGESIG     "IFRG"

#define pixels2bytes(n) ((n+7)/8)

#define HIGHCOLOUR(r,g,b)  (((((unsigned int)r >> 3) & 0x1f) << 10) + \
                           ((((unsigned int)g >> 3) & 0x1f) << 5) + \
                           (((unsigned int)b >> 3) & 0x1f))

typedef struct         {
        char manufacturer;
        char version;
        char encoding;
        char bits_per_pixel;
        int xmin,ymin;
        int xmax,ymax;
        int hres;
        int vres;
        char palette[48];
        char reserved;
        char colour_planes;
        int bytes_per_line;
        int palette_type;
        char filler[58];
        } PCXHEAD;

typedef struct {
        char sig[4];
```

2-6

The source code for PCX2FRG.C.

```
unsigned int width,depth,bits,bytes,planebytes;
unsigned long palette;
unsigned long image;
} IMAGEHEAD;

char pcxpalette[48]= {
        0x00,0x00,0x0E,0x00,0x52,0x07,0x2C,0x00,
        0x0E,0x00,0x00,0x00,0xF8,0x01,0x2C,0x00,
        0x85,0x0F,0x42,0x00,0x21,0x00,0x00,0x00,
        0x00,0x00,0x6A,0x24,0x9B,0x49,0xA1,0x5E,
        0x90,0x5E,0x18,0x5E,0x84,0x14,0xD9,0x95,
        0xA0,0x14,0x12,0x00,0x06,0x00,0x68,0x1F
        };

char palette[768];
char masktable[8]={0x80,0x40,0x20,0x10,0x08,0x04,0x02,0x01};
char bittable[8]= {0x01,0x02,0x04,0x08,0x10,0x20,0x40,0x80};

main(argc,argv)
        int argc;
        char *argv[];
{
        IMAGEHEAD ih;
        PCXHEAD pcx;
        FILE *source,*dest;
        char b[129],*linebuffer,*extrabuffer,*ps,*pd;
        unsigned int a,i,j,k,n,x,width,depth,bytes,wbytes,bits,*ip;

        puts("PCX2FRG version 1.0\r\n");

        if(argc <= 1)
            error("I need a path to a PCX file");

        /* make the argument upper case */
        strupr(argv[1]);

        /* open the source file */
        if((source=fopen(argv[1],"rb"))==NULL)
            error("Error opening the source file");

        /* create a path to the destination file */
        strmfe(b,argv[1],"FRG");

        /* create the destination file */
        if((dest=fopen(b,"wb"))==NULL)
            error("Error creating the destination file");

        /* read the source header */
        if(fread((char *)&pcx,1,sizeof(PCXHEAD),source) !=
            sizeof(PCXHEAD))
                error("Error reading header");

        /* check to make sure it's a PCX file */
        if(pcx.manufacturer != 10) error("This is not a PCX file");
```

```
/* read the header fields */
width=pcx.xmax-pcx.xmin+1;
depth=pcx.ymax-pcx.ymin+1;

if(pcx.bits_per_pixel==8 && pcx.colour_planes==3) bits=24;
else if(pcx.bits_per_pixel==1) bits=pcx.colour_planes;
else bits=pcx.bits_per_pixel;

/* get the palette */
if(bits==8 && pcx.version >= 5) {
        fseek(source,-769L,SEEK_END);
        if(fgetc(source)==12) {
                if(fread(palette,1,768,source) != 768)
                    error("Can't read palette");
        } else memcpy(palette,pcx.palette,48);
} else if(pcx.version == 3) memcpy(palette,pcxpalette,48);
else memcpy(palette,pcx.palette,48);

/* restore file position */
fseek(source,(unsigned long)sizeof(PCXHEAD),SEEK_SET);

/* say what the file is */
printf("%s (%u by %u) with %u bit(s) of colour\r\n",
    argv[1],width,depth,bits);

/* work out the line byte width */
if(bits > 1 && bits <= 4) {
        if(pcx.bits_per_pixel==4 && pcx.colour_planes==1)
            wbytes=bytes=pcx.bytes_per_line;
        else wbytes=bytes=pcx.bytes_per_line*bits;
}
else if(bits==24) {
        bytes=pcx.bytes_per_line*RGB_SIZE;
        wbytes=width*2;
}
else wbytes=bytes=pcx.bytes_per_line;

/* allocate some scratch buffers */
if((linebuffer=malloc(bytes)) == NULL)
    error("Can't allocate line buffer");

if((extrabuffer=malloc(bytes)) == NULL)
    error("Can't allocate extra buffer");

/* get the plane width */
n=pixels2bytes(width);

/* clear out the header */
memset((char *)&ih,0,sizeof(IMAGEHEAD));

/* install the identification string */
memcpy(ih.sig,IMAGESIG,4);

/* install the dimension values */
ih.width=width;
```

```
ih.depth=depth;
if(bits==24) ih.bits=16;
else ih.bits=bits;
ih.bytes=wbytes;
ih.planebytes=n;

/* point to the palette */
ih.palette=sizeof(IMAGEHEAD);

/* point to the image */
if(bits > 1 && bits <= 8)
    ih.image=sizeof(IMAGEHEAD)+RGB_SIZE*(1<<bits);
else
    ih.image=sizeof(IMAGEHEAD);

/* write the header */
if(fwrite((char *)&ih,1,sizeof(IMAGEHEAD),dest) !=
    sizeof(IMAGEHEAD))
        error("Error writing destination header");

/* write the palette */
if(bits > 1 && bits <= 8) fwrite(palette,RGB_SIZE,1<bits,dest);

/* write the dimension integers for the image */
i=width-1;
fwrite((char *)&i,1,sizeof(unsigned int),dest);
i=depth-1;
fwrite((char *)&i,1,sizeof(unsigned int),dest);

for(i=0;i<depth;++i) {

    /* read a PCX line */
    if(readpcxline(linebuffer,source,bytes) != bytes)
        error("Error reading line");

    if(bits == 1) {
            /* just write the line */
            if(fwrite(linebuffer,1,n,dest) != n)
                error("Error writing line");

    }
    else if(bits > 1 && bits <= 4) {
            if(pcx.bits_per_pixel == 4 &&
                pcx.colour_planes == 1) {
                    /* convert a stacked nybble line */
                    memset(extrabuffer,0,bytes);

                    pd=extrabuffer;
                    ps=linebuffer;
                    for(j=0;j<bits;++j) {
                        memcpy(pd,ps,pcx.bytes_per_line);
                        ps+=pcx.bytes_per_line;
                        pd+=n;
                    }
```

```c
                memset(linebuffer,0,bytes);
                for(j=x=0;j<width;) {
                        a=0;
                        ps=extrabuffer;
                        for(k=0;k<bits;++k) {
                            if(ps[j>>3] & masktable[j & 0x0007])
                                a |= bittable[k];
                            ps+=n;
                        }
                        linebuffer[x] = ((a & 0x0f) << 4);

                        ++j;

                        a=0;
                        ps=extrabuffer;
                        for(k=0;k<bits;++k) {
                                if(ps[j>>3] & masktable[j & 0x0007])
                                    a |= bittable[k];
                                ps+=n;
                        }
                        linebuffer[x] |= (a & 0x0f);
                        ++j;
                        ++x;
                    }
                }

                /* write the planes (in inverse order) */
                ps=linebuffer+pcx.bytes_per_line*bits;
                for(j=0;j<bits;++j) {
                        ps-=pcx.bytes_per_line;
                        if(fwrite(ps,1,n,dest) != n)
                            error("Error writing line");

                }
            }
        else if(bits==8) {
                /* eight-bit lines go as is */
                if(fwrite(linebuffer,1,width,dest) != width)
                    error("Error writing line");
        }
        else if(bits==24) {
                /* reorder the RGB pixels */
                ip=(unsigned int *)extrabuffer;
                ps=linebuffer;
                for(j=0;j<width;++j)
                    ip[j]=HIGHCOLOUR(ps[j],
                                ps[RGB_GREEN*pcx.bytes_per_line+j],
                                ps[RGB_BLUE*pcx.bytes_per_line+j]);

                if(fwrite(extrabuffer,1,wbytes,dest) != wbytes)
                        error("Error writing line");
        }
    }

    free(extrabuffer);
    free(linebuffer);
```

```
                    fclose(dest);
                    fclose(source);

                    puts("Ok");
            }

        error(s)
                    char *s;
            {
                    puts(s);
                    exit(1);
            }

        /* make file name with specific extension */
        strmfe(new,old,ext)
                    char *new,*old,*ext;
            {
                    while(*old != 0 && *old != '.') *new++=*old++;
                    *new++='.';
                    while(*ext) *new++=*ext++;
                    *new=0;
            }

        /* read one PCX line */
        readpcxline(p,fp,bytes)
                    char *p;
                    FILE *fp;
                    unsigned int bytes;
            {
                    int n=0,c,i;

                    do {
                        c=fgetc(fp) & 0xff;
                        if((c & 0xc0) == 0xc0) {
                                i=c & 0x3f;
                                c=fgetc(fp);
                                while(i--) p[n++]=c;
                        }
                        else p[n++]=c;
                    } while(n < bytes);
                    return(n);
            }
```

There's quite a lot happening in PCX2FRG—it's a good place to see how PCX decoding works, even if you don't have a requirement for image fragment files. You can excise the PCX-specific functions from this listing for your own applications if you like.

Most of the work of PCX2FRG is done in its main function, which is a bit larger than most. It sets up two file pointers, one to read the source PCX file and one to write the destination FRG file. It begins unpacking the PCX file it will be converting by reading its header into a PCXHEAD object, pcx.

Note that the error function simply returns to DOS with a message if it's called.

Having read a PCX header, the function checks to see that its `manufacturer` field does indeed contain ten and reads the image dimensions and color depth values. The latter is a bit tricky, as it can involve both the `bits_per_pixel` and `color_planes` elements of a PCX header. A 16-color file, for example, will have one bit per pixel in each of four planes. A 24-bit file will have eight bits per pixel in each of three planes.

If the program encounters an 8-bit PCX file, it must locate the palette at the end of the image data. Otherwise, the palette will be in the `palette` element of the header. One exception to this is in PCX files with a `version` value of three. These use a default fixed palette, which is stored in PCX2FRG as `pcxpalette`.

The program allocates two scratch buffers—one to actually read lines into and one to use for manipulating them.

The next portion of the `main` function of PCX2FRG creates the header and palette of the destination FRG file. It fills in an `IMAGEHEAD` object, `ih`, and writes it to the `dest` file pointer. It then writes the palette if one is applicable to the file being created.

Because the image data in a FRG file should look like a normal `putimage` buffer, it's preceded by the two dimension integers.

The rest of the code in `main` unpacks a PCX file and writes its lines out to the destination FRG file. This is a fairly complicated undertaking, as a PCX decoder must be able to deal with the various color depths involved and to handle the variations on 16-color PCX files, as dealt with earlier in this chapter.

The `readpcxline` function, called at the top of the main loop in `main`, will read the image data of one line from the source PCX file. This will be `pcx.bytes_per_line` long in most cases, save for that of some four and all 24-bit files. Planar 4-bit files will have `pcx.bytes_per_line * 4` bytes in a line—the four planes will be extracted after each line is read. The three "planes" of a 24-bit line will be swabbed into an array of high-color integers.

The really complex condition of the loop in `main` is the one that handles Windows-style stacked-nybble PCX files. It reads each stacked-nybble pixel from a line in `linebuffer` and sets the appropriate bits in `extrabuffer`. The mechanics of bitwise manipulation will be explored in detail in the next chapter.

Note that the order of the planes in a 16-color PCX line must be reversed for a FRG file, as this corresponds to the way `putimage` expects to see them.

Having compiled PCX2FRG.C, creating PCX2FRG.EXE, you can convert a PCX file to a FRG file by passing its name as the command line argument to PCX2FRG. For example, to convert PICTURE.PCX to PICTURE.FRG, you would type

```
PCX2FRG PICTURE.PCX
```

Note that PCX2FRG is quite capable of created image fragments that are too large for `putimage` to work with.

Having created a FRG file, the obvious way to look at it would be to load it into memory and pass its image as an argument to `putimage`. This will, in fact, only work under limited circumstances. Specifically, the image fragment must be suitable for your current display—in the case of a VGA card running in its 16-color

Viewing image fragments

graphics mode, it would have to be a 16-color fragment. It would have to be small enough to occupy less than 64K of memory and its color palette would have to match that of the display at the time of calling putimage, lest all the pixels turn up in seriously distorted colors.

We'll be looking at a variety of ways to get around the limitations of putimage, but for the moment it would be handy to have a way to look at FRG files without having to deal with putimage at all. The VIEWFRG program will do this. Passed the path to a FRG file that was created with PCX2FRG, it will read it and display it correctly on a VGA card. In fact, just as PCX2FRG avoided having to load an entire fragment into memory, so too will VIEWFRG only work with one line at a time.

There is one notable catch to the use of VIEWFRG. As was discussed in the first chapter, a standard VGA card can't display 16-bit or 24-bit pictures. At the moment VIEWFRG only works with the available standard VGA modes—if you find you're using FRG files a lot, you might want to modify it later on once we've had a look at how to drive super VGA hardware.

There are a number of approaches to dealing with displaying all the colors in a 16-bit file on a display card that can only manage 256 colors at best. One way is to algorithmically reduce the number of colors in the image, a process called quantization and remapping. Unfortunately, this takes a long time if it's to create attractive images. A second approach, and the one that's used in this version of VIEWFRG, is to reduce all the colors to corresponding levels of grey. A 256-level grey scale image *can* be displayed in mode 13H of a standard VGA card.

A color defined as RGB values can be converted to a grey level using the following formula:

```
grey = red * .30 + green * .59 + blue * .11
```

The VIEWFRG program converts each RGB color in a 16-bit fragment to a grey value and displays it in the 256-color mode.

In fact, because the image fragment format stores true color FRG files with only sixteen bits of color—in two bytes per pixel—it's handy to create some macros to get at the real RGB values:

```
#define    HIGHRED(c)      ((((c) >> 10) & 0x1f) << 3)
#define    HIGHGREEN(c)    ((((c) >> 5) & 0x1f) << 3)
#define    HIGHBLUE(c)     (((c) & 0x1f) << 3)
```

Figure 2-7 is the source code for VIEWFRG. Once you've compiled it, you can view an FRG file by passing a path to it to VIEWFRG as a command line argument.

The VIEWFRG program, like PCX2FRG, does most of its work in its main function. It opens the file passed to it and reads the IMAGEHEAD header, checking the sig field to make sure it's a read FRG file. If the file is of a color depth that requires a palette, it finds the palette be seeking to it; in the case of files created by PCX2FRG, the palette will be located immediately after the header. It then seeks past the two integers at the start of the image data and begins to read the image lines themselves.

```
/*
        Image fragment viewer

        Copyright (c) 1992 Alchemy Mindworks Inc.
*/

#include "stdio.h"
#include "dos.h"
#include "alloc.h"

#define RGB_RED      0
#define RGB_GREEN    1
#define RGB_BLUE     2
#define RGB_SIZE     3

#define IMAGESIG     "IFRG"

#define HIGHRED(c)          (((((c) >> 10) & 0x1f) << 3)
#define HIGHGREEN(c)        (((((c) >> 5) & 0x1f) << 3)
#define HIGHBLUE(c)         ((((c) & 0x1f) << 3)

#define pixels2bytes(n)             ((n+7)/8)
#define egawriteplane(n)    { outp(0x3c4,2); outp(0x3c5,n); }
#define greyvalue(r,g,b)            (((r*30)/100) + ((g*59)/100) + ((b*11)/100))

typedef struct {
        char sig[4];
        unsigned int width,depth,bits,bytes,planebytes;
        unsigned long palette;
        unsigned long image;
        } IMAGEHEAD;

char palette[768];
char masktable[8]={0x80,0x40,0x20,0x10,0x08,0x04,0x02,0x01};
char bittable[8]= {0x01,0x02,0x04,0x08,0x10,0x20,0x40,0x80};

unsigned int screenwide,screendeep,screenbytes;
char *screentable[480];

main(argc,argv)
        int argc;
        char *argv[];
{
        IMAGEHEAD ih;
        FILE *source;
        unsigned int c,i,j,n;
        int r,g,b;

        puts("VIEWFRG version 1.0\r\n");

        if(argc <= 1)
            error("I need a path to a FRG file");

        /* make the argument upper case */
        strupr(argv[1]);
```

```
/* open the source file */
if((source=fopen(argv[1],"rb"))==NULL)
    error("Error opening the source file");

/* read the source header */
if(fread((char *)&ih,1,sizeof(IMAGEHEAD),source) !=
    sizeof(IMAGEHEAD))
        error("Error reading header");

/* check to make sure it's a FRG file */
if(memcmp(ih.sig,IMAGESIG,4)) error("This is not a FRG file");

/* say what the file is */
printf("%s (%u by %u) with %u bit(s) of colour\r\n",
    argv[1],ih.width,ih.depth,ih.bits);

if(ih.bits > 1 && ih.bits <= 8) {
        fseek(source,(unsigned long)ih.palette,SEEK_SET);
        if(fread(palette,RGB_SIZE,1<<ih.bits,source) != (1<ih.bits))
            error("Error reading the palette");
}

fseek(source,(unsigned long)ih.image+4,SEEK_SET);

printf("Hit any key...");

getch();

graphics(ih.bits);

if(ih.bits > 1 && ih.bits <= 8) setvgapalette(palette,ih.bits);
else if(ih.bits > 8) setgreypalette();

if(ih.bits==1) {
        for(i=0;i<ih.depth;++i) {
                if(i >= screendeep) break;
                if(fread(screentable[i],1,ih.bytes,source) !=
                    ih.bytes) break;
        }
}
else if(ih.bits > 1 && ih.bits <= 4) {
        for(i=0;i<ih.depth;++i) {
                if(i >= screendeep) break;
                egawriteplane(8);
                if(fread(screentable[i],1,ih.planebytes,source) !=
                    ih.planebytes) break;
                egawriteplane(4);
                if(fread(screentable[i],1,ih.planebytes,source) !=
                    ih.planebytes) break;
                egawriteplane(2);
                if(fread(screentable[i],1,ih.planebytes,source) !=
                    ih.planebytes) break;
                egawriteplane(1);
                if(fread(screentable[i],1,ih.planebytes,source) !=
                    ih.planebytes) break;
```

```
                }
                egawriteplane(15);
        }
        else if(ih.bits > 4 && ih.bits <= 8) {
                for(i=0;i<ih.depth;++i) {
                        if(i >= screendeep) break;
                        if(fread(screentable[i],1,ih.bytes,source) !=
                            ih.bytes) break;
                }
        }
        else {
                n=ih.bytes/2;
                for(i=0;i<ih.depth;++i) {
                        if(i >= screendeep) break;
                        for(j=0;j<n;++j) {
                                c=fgetc(source)+(fgetc(source)<<8);
                                r=HIGHRED(c);
                                g=HIGHGREEN(c);
                                b=HIGHBLUE(c);
                                if(j < screenwide)
                                        screentable[i][j]=greyvalue(r,g,b);
                        }
                        if(c==0xffff) break;
                }
        }

        getch();
        text();

        fclose(source);

        puts("Ok");
}

text()
{
        union REGS r;

        r.x.ax=0x0003;
        int86(0x10,&r,&r);
}

graphics(bits)
        int bits;
{
        union REGS r;
        int i;

        if(bits <= 4) {
                r.x.ax=0x0012;
                screenwide=640;
                screendeep=480;
                screenbytes=80;
        }
        else {
```

```
                                        r.x.ax=0x0013;
                                        screenwide=320;
                                        screendeep=200;
                                        screenbytes=320;
                        }

                for(i=0;i<screendeep;++i)
                        screentable[i]=MK_FP(0xa000,i*screenbytes);

                int86(0x10,&r,&r);
        }

        error(s)
                char *s;
        {
                puts(s);
                exit(1);
        }

        setvgapalette(p,n)
                char *p;
                int n;
        {
                union REGS r;
                int i,j;

                j=1<<n;
                outp(0x3c6,0xff);
                for(i=0;i<j;++i) {
                        outp(0x3c8,i);
                        outp(0x3c9,(*p++) >> 2);
                        outp(0x3c9,(*p++) >> 2);
                        outp(0x3c9,(*p++) >> 2);
                }
                if(n <= 4) {
                        r.x.bx=0x0000;
                        for(i=0;i<j;++i) {
                                r.x.ax=0x1000;
                                int86(0x10,&r,&r);
                                r.x.bx+=0x0101;
                        }
                }
        }

        setgreypalette()
        {
                int i;

                outp(0x3c6,0xff);
                for(i=0;i<256;++i) {
                        outp(0x3c8,i);
                        outp(0x3c9,i >> 2);
                        outp(0x3c9,i >> 2);
                        outp(0x3c9,i >> 2);
                }
        }
```

Monochrome image lines can be read directly into the mode 12H screen buffer. This is also true of 16-color lines, save that they must be read one plane at a time, with a call to `egawriteplane` between each. The `egawriteplane` call—actually a macro— switches the appropriate page onto the memory bus for writing, as was discussed in Chapter 1. It will be dealt with in much greater detail later on.

The lines of a 256-color image fragment can be read directly into the mode 13H display buffer. In handling 16- bit lines, VIEWFRG reads each byte of the image data and converts the three-byte color pixels into grey levels using the `greyvalue` macro defined at the top of the program. This implements the grey scale formula discussed earlier, but it does so using integer arithmetic, which is quite a lot faster than handling the calculations in floating point. This also limits the accuracy of the conversion, but it's suitable for a conversion to 256-levels of grey.

In fact a VGA card displaying grey scale images in mode 13H can really only show you 64 distinct levels.

The `graphics` function in VIEWPRG illustrates how to initiate mode 12H and mode 13H graphics. This is another area that will become clearer later on.

As high speed graphics screen displays go, VIEWFRG is pretty rudimentary. For one thing, it can display image fragments no faster than it can read them from your disk. In real-world applications, graphics are typically buffered in memory.

The process of creating a PCX file isn't all that much more complicated than that of unpacking one. Because the run-length compression used by PCX files is so simple, it's relatively easy to write a function to compress lines of data.

Creating PCX files from image fragments

In creating a PCX file, you must fill in the appropriate fields of a PCXHEAD object and write the header to the disk. Having done so, you should write the compressed lines of image data, and finally, a 256-color palette if one is applicable.

As a rule, compressing image files is a lot less involved than uncompressing them, as you need not write code to discern between different file types or to deal with illegal files; it's probably safe to assume that your software can be trusted to handle PCX files correctly.

The program in FIG. 2-8 is FRG2PCX; perhaps predictably, it reverses the function of the PCX2FRG file, packing the contents of an image fragment into a PCX file. While it's unlikely that you'll have a requirement for it as it stands, it should serve to illustrate the process of creating a PCX file. You can lift the relevant parts of FRG2PCX for your own software.

A more useful application of the code to create PCX files—that of saving a graphic screen to a file—will turn up over the next three chapters.

If you've worked your way through VIEWFRG, you'll probably have found FRG2PCX to be at least partially familiar. Like the image fragment viewer, FRG2PCX opens a FRG file and reads its header. It locates the palette information if any exists and stores it in a buffer. Finally, it reads the image data one line at a time.

The one and eight-bit lines in an image fragment are stored exactly as they should be for compression in a PCX file. Four-bit lines are almost correct—the order of their image planes must be reversed. Lines of a 16-bit FRG file require extensive swabbing to separate the components of each high-color value into three planes.

```
/*
                    Image fragment to PCX

                    Copyright (c) 1992 Alchemy Mindworks Inc.
*/

#include "stdio.h"
#include "dos.h"
#include "alloc.h"

#define RGB_RED         0
#define RGB_GREEN       1
#define RGB_BLUE        2
#define RGB_SIZE        3

#define IMAGESIG        "IFRG"

#define HIGHRED(c)      (((((c) >> 10) & 0x1f) << 3)
#define HIGHGREEN(c)    (((((c) >> 5) & 0x1f) << 3)
#define HIGHBLUE(c)     ((((c) & 0x1f) << 3)

#define pixels2bytes(n)         ((n+7)/8)

typedef struct      {
        char manufacturer;
        char version;
        char encoding;
        char bits_per_pixel;
        int xmin,ymin;
        int xmax,ymax;
        int hres;
        int vres;
        char palette[48];
        char reserved;
        char colour_planes;
        int bytes_per_line;
        int palette_type;
        char filler[58];
        } PCXHEAD;

typedef struct {
        char sig[4];
        unsigned int width,depth,bits,bytes,planebytes;
        unsigned long palette;
        unsigned long image;
        } IMAGEHEAD;

char palette[768];
char masktable[8]={0x80,0x40,0x20,0x10,0x08,0x04,0x02,0x01};
char bittable[8]= {0x01,0x02,0x04,0x08,0x10,0x20,0x40,0x80};

main(argc,argv)
        int argc;
        char *argv[];
{
```

```
PCXHEAD pcx;
IMAGEHEAD ih;
FILE *source,*dest;
char s[129],*linebuffer,*extrabuffer,*pr;
unsigned int i,j,*ip;

puts("FRG2PCX version 1.0\r\n");

if(argc <= 1)
    error("I need a path to a FRG file");

/* make the argument upper case */
strupr(argv[1]);

/* open the source file */
if((source=fopen(argv[1],"rb"))==NULL)
    error("Error opening the source file");

/* read the source header */
if(fread((char *)&ih,1,sizeof(IMAGEHEAD),source) !=
    sizeof(IMAGEHEAD))
        error("Error reading header");

/* check to make sure it's a FRG file */
if(memcmp(ih.sig,IMAGESIG,4)) error("This is not a FRG file");

if((linebuffer=malloc(ih.bytes)) == NULL)
    error("Can't allocate memory");

if((extrabuffer=malloc(ih.bytes)) == NULL)
    error("Can't allocate memory");

/* create a path to the destination file */
strmfe(s,argv[1],"PCX");

/* create the destination file */
if((dest=fopen(s,"wb"))==NULL)
    error("Error creating the destination file");

/* say what the file is */
printf("%s (%u by %u) with %u bit(s) of colour\r\n",
    argv[1],ih.width,ih.depth,ih.bits);

if(ih.bits > 1 && ih.bits <= 8) {
        fseek(source,(unsigned long)ih.palette,SEEK_SET);
        if(fread(palette,RGB_SIZE,1<<ih.bits,source) != (1<<ih.bits))
            error("Error reading the palette");
}

memset((char *)&pcx,0,sizeof(PCXHEAD));
memcpy(pcx.palette,palette,48);

if(ih.bits==1) {
        pcx.manufacturer=10;
        pcx.encoding=1;
```

```
                pcx.xmin=pcx.ymin=0;
                pcx.xmax=ih.width-1;
                pcx.ymax=ih.depth-1;
                pcx.palette_type=1;
                pcx.bits_per_pixel=1;
                pcx.version=2;
                pcx.colour_planes=1;
                pcx.bytes_per_line=pixels2bytes(ih.width);
        }
        else if(ih.bits > 1 && ih.bits <=4) {
                pcx.manufacturer=10;
                pcx.encoding=1;
                pcx.xmin=pcx.ymin=0;
                pcx.xmax=ih.width-1;
                pcx.ymax=ih.depth-1;
                pcx.palette_type=1;
                pcx.bits_per_pixel=1;
                pcx.version=2;
                pcx.colour_planes=ih.bits;
                pcx.bytes_per_line=pixels2bytes(ih.width);
        }
        else if(ih.bits > 4 && ih.bits <=8) {
                pcx.manufacturer=10;
                pcx.encoding=1;
                pcx.xmin=pcx.ymin=0;
                pcx.xmax=ih.width-1;
                pcx.ymax=ih.depth-1;
                pcx.palette_type=1;
                pcx.bits_per_pixel=8;
                pcx.version=5;
                pcx.colour_planes=1;
                pcx.bytes_per_line=ih.width;
        }
        else {
                pcx.manufacturer=10;
                pcx.encoding=1;
                pcx.xmin=0;
                pcx.ymin=0;
                pcx.xmax=ih.width-1;
                pcx.ymax=ih.depth-1;
                pcx.colour_planes=3;
                pcx.bytes_per_line=ih.width;
                pcx.bits_per_pixel=8;
                pcx.version=5;
        }

        if(fwrite((char *)&pcx,1,sizeof(PCXHEAD),dest) != sizeof(PCXHEAD))
          error("Error writing header");

        fseek(source,(unsigned long)ih.image+4,SEEK_SET);

        for(i=0;i<ih.depth;++i) {
                if(fread(linebuffer,1,ih.bytes,source) != ih.bytes)
                    error("Error reading line");
```

```
                if(ih.bits==1) {
                        if(pcxwriteline(dest,linebuffer,pcx.bytes_per_line) !=
                            pcx.bytes_per_line)
                                error("Error writing line");
                }
                else if(ih.bits > 1 && ih.bits <= 4) {
                        pr=linebuffer+ih.planebytes*ih.bits;
                        for(j=0;j<ih.bits;++j) {
                                pr-=ih.planebytes;
                                if(pcxwriteline(dest,pr,pcx.bytes_per_line) !=
                                    pcx.bytes_per_line)
                                        error("Error writing line");
                        }
                }
                else if(ih.bits > 4 && ih.bits <= 8) {
                        if(pcxwriteline(dest,linebuffer,pcx.bytes_per_line) !=
                            pcx.bytes_per_line)
                                error("Error writing line");
                }
                else if(ih.bits == 16) {
                        ip=(unsigned int *)linebuffer;
                        for(j=0;j<ih.width;++j)
                            extrabuffer[j]=HIGHRED(ip[j]);
                            /* linebuffer[j*RGB_SIZE+RGB_RED];*/
                    if(pcxwriteline(dest,extrabuffer,pcx.bytes_per_line) !=
                        pcx.bytes_per_line)
                            error("Error writing line");

                        for(j=0;j<ih.width;++j)
                            extrabuffer[j]=HIGHGREEN(ip[j]);
                            /*linebuffer[j*RGB_SIZE+RGB_GREEN];*/
                        if(pcxwriteline(dest,extrabuffer,pcx.bytes_per_line) !=
                            pcx.bytes_per_line)
                                error("Error writing line");

                        for(j=0;j<ih.width;++j)
                            extrabuffer[j]=HIGHBLUE(ip[j]);
                            /*linebuffer[j*RGB_SIZE+RGB_BLUE];*/
                        if(pcxwriteline(dest,extrabuffer,pcx.bytes_per_line) !=
                            pcx.bytes_per_line)
                                error("Error writing line");
                }
        }

if(ih.bits > 4 && ih.bits <=8) {
        fputc(12,dest);
        if(fwrite(palette,1,768,dest) != 768)
            error("Error writing palette");
}

fclose(dest);
free(extrabuffer);
free(linebuffer);
fclose(source);

puts("Ok");
```

```
                    }
          error(s)
                    char *s;
          {
                    puts(s);
                    exit(1);
          }

          /* make file name with specific extension */
          strmfe(new,old,ext)
                    char *new,*old,*ext;
          {
                    while(*old != 0 && *old != '.') *new++=*old++;
                    *new++='.';
                    while(*ext) *new++=*ext++;
                    *new=0;
          }

          pcxwriteline(fp,p,n)
                    FILE *fp;
                    char *p;
                    unsigned int n;
          {
                    unsigned int i=0,j=0,t=0;

                    do {
                              i=0;
                              while((p[t+i]==p[t+i+1]) && ((t+i) < n) && (i < 63))++i;
                              if(i>0) {
                                        if(fputc(i | 0xc0,fp)==EOF) return(-1);
                                        if(fputc(p[t],fp)==EOF) return(-1);
                                        t+=i;
                                        j+=2;
                              }
                              else {
                                        if(((p[t]) & 0xc0)==0xc0) {
                                                  if(fputc(0xc1,fp)==EOF) return(-1);
                                                  ++j;
                                        }
                                        if(fputc(p[t++],fp)==EOF) return(-1);
                                        ++j;

                              }
                    } while(t<n);
                    return(n);
          }
```

Note that, as there is no 16-bit format defined for PCX files, the pixels of a 16-bit of
FRG file are promoted to 24-bits. As an aside, if you translate a complex 24-bit PCX
file to a 16-bit FRG file and then translate the FRG file back to a PCX file, you'll
probably find that the final image compresses a bit better than it did originally. This
is because the low-order three bits of color information have been removed from
each pixel, simplifying the image data slightly.

Having extracted the information from the IMAGEHEAD object at the start of a FRG file, FRG2PCX will set up a PCXHEAD based on it. When the header is complete, it can be written to the destination file.

The large loop at the end of the `main` function of FRG2PCX reads the lines from the source image fragment file and sends them to `pcxwriteline` to be compressed—after a bit of swabbing in some cases.

Finally, a 256-color palette is tacked onto the end of the image data for those files that require it.

The `pcxwriteline` function is mercifully simple as run-length compression procedures go. The lack of a true string field type in PCX compression makes this pretty easy to implement. The function begins by counting bytes in the line to be compressed until it either runs out of bytes, as indicated by the n argument to the function, finds two adjacent bytes that are not identical, or discovers that it has counted more than 63 bytes. Run of bytes fields are limited to 63 bytes per field in PCX compression because the upper two bits of a length byte serve as a flag for the following byte to be written as is. The remaining six bits can hold numbers ranging from zero through 63.

Longer runs of bytes would be compressed as multiple fields.

If the process of counting bytes turns up a count of zero—indicating that the first two bytes in a line are not identical—the first byte is written as is. If it's less than 64, it can be written directly. If it's 64 or greater, it must be written as a single byte field. The key byte to indicate a single byte run is C1H—that's the two high order bits set and the number one in the lower six bits.

The peculiar graphic in FIG. 2-9 is the work of the TESTFRG program. While not of any real use, TESTFRG illustrates how you would load the `putimage` fragment from a FRG file, use the palette information to set the system palette and then display the graphic. In this example, the program expects to be passed the path to a four-bit FRG file, and will as such use mode 12H. This example uses Turbo C's BGI calls to set the graphics mode, and then calls to `putimage` to actually paint the fragment on the screen.

Using image file fragments

You can use any 16-color FRG file with TESTFRG, although small fragments generally produce more interesting patterns. They also allow TESTFRG to run at a reasonable speed. The Turbo C `putimage` function is none too quick, and a large fragment can slow the whole process down considerably.

The patterns created by TESTFRG occur because the image fragment it's passed is repeatedly painted on the screen, with each iteration offset from the last by one pixel. When the image reaches one of the screen boundaries, it reverses direction—a bit like an old-style Pong game. Sounds effects and paddles might have made TESTFRG a bit more interactive.

Figure 2-10 is the source code for TESTFRG.C.

Note that even though the BGI functions are used to actually update the screen, the code in TESTFRG sneaks around them to set the palette. This approach to setting the mode 12H palette allows you greater control over the colors than the EGA color numbers that the BGI `setpalette` function accepts. This function will be dealt with in greater detail in later chapters.

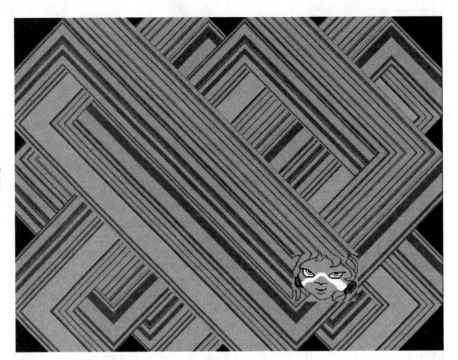

2-9
A graphic created with a JRG file and a bit of patience.

2-10
The source code for TESTJRG.C, a program to do something with JRG files

```
/*
            Image fragment test program —— bounces ´em off the walls

            Copyright (c) 1992 Alchemy Mindworks Inc.
*/

#include "stdio.h"
#include "dos.h"
#include "alloc.h"
#include "graphics.h"

#define RGB_RED        0
#define RGB_GREEN      1
#define RGB_BLUE       2
#define RGB_SIZE       3

#define IMAGESIG       "IFRG"

/*#define    pixels2bytes(n)          ((n+7)/8)*/
#define ImageWidth(p)  (1+p[0]+(p[1] << 8))
#define ImageDepth(p)  (1+p[2]+(p[3] << 8))

typedef struct {
        char sig[4];
        unsigned int width,depth,bits,bytes,planebytes;
        unsigned long palette;
        unsigned long image;
        } IMAGEHEAD;
```

```c
char palette[48];

main(argc,argv)
        int argc;
        char *argv[];
{
        IMAGEHEAD ih;
        FILE *source;
        char *p;
        unsigned int i;
        int x,y,xi=1,yi=1;

        puts("TESTFRG version 1.0\r\n");

        if(argc <= 1)
            error("I need a path to a FRG file");

        /* make the argument upper case */
        strupr(argv[1]);

        /* open the source file */
        if((source=fopen(argv[1],"rb"))==NULL)
            error("Error opening the source file");

        /* read the source header */
        if(fread((char *)&ih,1,sizeof(IMAGEHEAD),source) !=
            sizeof(IMAGEHEAD))
                error("Error reading header");

        /* check to make sure it's a FRG file */
        if(memcmp(ih.sig,IMAGESIG,4)) error("This is not a FRG file");

        /* check to see it's a suitable file */
        if(ih.bits != 4 || ((long)ih.bytes*(long)ih.width) > 0xfff0L)
            error("This image is unsuitable");

        fseek(source,(unsigned long)ih.palette,SEEK_SET);
        if(fread(palette,RGB_SIZE,1<<ih.bits,source) != (1<<ih.bits))
            error("Error reading the palette");

        fseek(source,(unsigned long)ih.image,SEEK_SET);

        i=ih.bytes*ih.depth+4;
        if((p=malloc(i))==NULL)
            error("Error allocating memory");

        if(fread(p,1,i,source) != i)
            error("Error reading image");

        graphics();

        setvgapalette(palette);

        x=(getmaxx()-ImageWidth(p))/2;
        y=(getmaxy()-ImageDepth(p))/2;
```

```
          do {
                  putimage(x,y,p,COPY_PUT);

                  if(x==0 || (x+ImageWidth(p)) >= getmaxx()) xi*=-1;
                  if(y==0 || (y+ImageDepth(p)) >= getmaxy()) yi*=-1;

                  x+=xi;
                  y+=yi;

          } while(!kbhit());

          text();

          fclose(source);

          puts("Ok");
  }

  setvgapalette(p)
          char *p;
  {
          union REGS r;
          int i;

          for(i=0;i<16;++i) {
                  r.h.dh=*p++>>2;
                  r.h.ch=*p++>>2;
                  r.h.cl=*p++>>2;
                  r.x.bx=i;
                  r.x.ax=0x1010;
                  int86(0x10,&r,&r);
          }

          r.x.bx=0x0000;
          for(i=0;i<16;++i) {
                  r.x.ax=0x1000;
                  int86(0x10,&r,&r);
                  r.x.bx+=0x0101;
          }
  }

  text()
  {
          closegraph();
  }

  graphics()
  {
          int d,m;

          detectgraph(&d,&m);

          if(d<0) return(0);
          initgraph(&d,&m,"");
          if(graphresult() < 0) return(0);
```

```
        return(1);
}

error(s)
        char *s;
{
        puts(s);
        exit(1);
}
```

The drawback to PCX files will become apparent if you create a few fairly complex ones. As was covered earlier in this chapter, PCX compression is acceptable for simple drawn images but starts to fall apparent and become very ineffective when it's confronted with a complex picture, such as a scanned image. This is particularly troublesome because of the way scanners create pictures.

A color flatbed scanner digitizes source graphics by ascertaining how much red, green, and blue light is reflected by the image being scanned. As such, scanners are wont to output graphic files in a format that corresponds to the way they view the world—the fundamental image format of a color scanner is a 24-bit RGB image. As has been touched on, you can't display a 24-bit image on a standard VGA card; only the higher end super VGA cards have a mode to accommodate them to some extent. In addition, RGB images take up a lot of disk space, require lots of memory to work with, and compress notoriously badly. In fact, most RGB images are stored uncompressed, as attempting to compress them only annoys them and makes them bigger still.

A 640 by 480 pixel RGB image would require 900K of storage.

Images with eight bits of color are a lot more workable—they can be displayed on a VGA card. They require substantially less memory and disk space and they're usually at least somewhat amenable to compression, if you choose the right sort of compression. The problem, then, is in translating a 24-bit RGB image into a respectable looking palette-driven image.

As was mentioned earlier in this chapter, the process for doing this translation is called *quantization*. It samples an RGB image and derives a palette of 256 colors that best represents the mix of colors in the source image. Having done this, software can "remap" all the source pixels to the new palette; that is, each source pixel can be replaced with the color from the quantized palette that it's closest to.

The only problem with all this is that it usually results in really ugly looking pictures. Figure 2-11 illustrates this.

The problem with remapping a picture is that 256 colors really aren't enough to create a convincing simulation of a scanned 24-bit image.

The solution to this is to "dither" the source image, rather than remapping it. Dithering is a bit tricky to implement code for, but it's easy to understand in theory. For example, if you wanted to display an orange area on a VGA screen that lacked anything like orange in its palette, you could create a pretty convincing simulation of orange by alternating pixels of red and yellow. In dithering an image, the software charged with reducing a 24-bit image to 256-colors creates the illusion of

Working with GIF files

2-11
Remapping a 24-bit scanned image to 256 colors.

colors that don't exist in the destination picture by alternating pixels of colors that do. The effect of dithering that's been done well can be extremely effective.

The drawback to dithered images is that they usually consist of large areas of alternating bytes, a condition calculated to totally fox simple run-length compression, such as that used by PCX files.

The GIF format uses string table compression to compress variable-length bit fields. While this doesn't totally overcome the tendency of scanned and dithered images to exhibit negative compression, it's pretty well the best approach available for image file compression that doesn't alter the image being compressed. The string table compression algorithm used by the GIF format is also called LZW compression, for Lempil-Ziv and Welch, who initially postulated it. This is essentially the same compression that's used by file archive programs such as PKZIP.

There are a number of things that serve to make the GIF format a bit tricky to work with. To begin with, simply writing functions to encode and decode GIF files is considerably more complex than the comparable functions to handle PCX files were. String table compression is fairly involved.

Secondly, in order for it to work efficiently, string table compression requires that each pixel be stored as one byte, no matter how many bits of color are actually involved. Because the compression algorithm only compresses those bits in each byte that are actually relevant, this doesn't waste any space in the compressed file. However, it does mean that the lines emerged from a GIF decoder will not be in the right format to be displayed if they're part of an image with four or fewer bits of color. Some bit swabbing will be in order.

Note that as of this writing, the GIF format can only store images with eight or fewer bits of color—there's no GIF equivalent to 24-bit PCX files.

Finally, the image lines in a GIF file are not constrained to appear in a linear order— the first line out of the file need not be the first line of the image. There's a permutation of the GIF format which allows for "interlaced" lines, in which the lines appear at intervals down your screen. While such a file will leave you with a complete image when it's fully unpacked, interlaced GIF files do preclude handling GIF images one line at a time, as was done in dealing with PCX files.

A GIF image must be buffered in memory before you can work with it.

If you want to store images on disk—or send them through a modem without winding up with a phone bill best expressed in exponential notation—the GIF format is a good choice. This is a well accepted sentiment, and GIF files appear on virtually every bulletin board and on-line network on the planet. They're a useful source of images, and a format well worth supporting in super VGA applications that import bitmapped graphics.

If you've dabbled in the culture of bulletin boards a bit, you'll probably have become at least somewhat familiar with the more sultry nature of GIF files; most of the images that ply the phone lines between modems as GIF files are nudes. This is the sort of thing to amuse the jaded and incense the unaware—and is precisely the place where most books that deal with graphics say something like "this subject is beyond the scope of this discussion to adequately explore."

2-12
Several more or less typical GIF files.

This subject is beyond the scope of this discussion to adequately explore.

Figure 2-12 illustrates several GIF files downloaded from a local bulletin board. These are arguably typical of the art form, save that the subjects have their clothes on.

It's worth noting that aside from merely storing images, as the PCX format did, GIF files can include a number of other bits of information. A GIF file can include a text description or copyright message for its image, secondary images, information to animate the display of an image and specialized, application specific data. These optional "extension blocks" allow the GIF format to be customized for applications beyond that of simply dealing with pictures. These features will not be dealt with in this chapter—the code herein will treat the GIF format much as PCX files were handled, that is, with one image per file.

Reading a GIF file

Unpacking a GIF file requires some fairly extensive code. There are two things that are wont to make a GIF decoder pretty complex. The first is the structure of GIF files themselves. Unlike as in the PCX format, where the header, image data, and palette were constrained to appear at fixed locations in a file, almost all the elements in a GIF file can appear wherever they want to be. A GIF file consists of a small file header and then one or more blocks. A block can be an image or one of several types of extensions. A file can contain multiple image blocks.

A GIF decoder has to be able to deal with whatever permutation of blocks it encounters. In the case of the code herein, we'll be ignoring the extension blocks entirely, and only dealing with the first image in multiple-image files.

The second complexity in a GIF file is its elaborate compression method. As you'll note in a moment, string table compression requires a lot of memory and a lot of code to unravel.

A GIF file always begins with a GIFHEADER struct. This is what it looks like:

```
typedef struct {
        char sig[6];
        unsigned int screenwidth,screendepth;
        unsigned char flags,background,aspect;
        } GIFHEADER;
```

The sig element of a GIFHEADER will contain the string "GIF" followed by either "87a" or "89a" as of this writing. These strings indicate revision levels of the GIF standard and are, in fact, the years when these revisions were introduced. For the most part, the GIF 89a standard is a superset of the GIF 87a standard and simply added things to the original format. While the code in this chapter will read both types of files, we'll really only be using the GIF 87a elements of GIF.

The screenwidth and screendepth elements of a GIFHEADER specify the dimensions of the display that was originally used to create the file. Note that this is not the same as the actual image dimensions, which will come later. These values are rarely used, although many GIF readers will get upset if they aren't sensible.

The flags element of a GIFHEADER holds a number of useful bits of information. If flags & 80H is true, the file has a global color map. This means that there's a table of RGB color values following the GIFHEADER. The number of colors in the table will be 1 << ((flags & 7) + 1).

If a global color map is present, it should be read after the GIFHEADER has been read and interpreted. It will require three bytes for each color.

The background value of a GIFHEADER is the entry in the color table that should be used to fill any areas of the screen not occupied by image data, and to set the overscan of a VGA card. This isn't relevant to image fragments.

The aspect value defines the aspect ratio of the image in GIF 89a files—it's set to zero in GIF 87a files—and can be safely ignored here.

Having read past a GIF file's header and global color map if there is one, the next byte will define the type of the first block. At present, there are three possibilities for block types. If the byte in question is a comma—the most likely occurrence—the block is an image. If it's an exclamation point the block is an extension. If it's a semicolon, the end of the file has been reached.

The applications for GIF files in this chapter need only concern themselves with image blocks. An image block always begins with an IMAGEBLOCK header, which looks like this:

```
typedef struct {
        unsigned int left,top,width,depth;
        unsigned char flags;
        } IMAGEBLOCK;
```

The left and top values of an IMAGEBLOCK object define the upper left corner of the rectangle where the image in the block wants to be displayed—assuming you care. They can be ignored, and usually are. The width and depth elements specify the actual image dimensions in pixels, which are very important values.

The flags element specifies a number of important things about this image. As with a GIFHEADER object, if flags & 80H is true, there's a color map after the IMAGEBLOCK object. This is called a local color map, and is assumed to override the global map if it exists. Most single-image GIF files don't have local color maps. The size of the color map is, again, 1 << (flags & 7) + 1).

If flags & 40H is true, the image in the block being read is interlaced, which means that its lines will not emerge from the decoder in a linear order. The order is, in fact, quite complicated—you'll be able to see how it works in the working GIF decoder, to be dealt with momentarily. Interlaced GIF files are intended for use with applications that allow them to be viewed as they're downloaded, such that you can see a coarse approximation of an image being downloaded even when only a relatively small part of it has been transmitted, and abort the transfer if you don't like what's being displayed.

Even if you have no interest in on-line viewing, a GIF decoder must be able to handle interlaced images, as quite a few of them exist. The only practical way to do this is to read an entire GIF image into memory in the order it's unpacked and then read it out of memory in the order you want it. A 640 by 480 pixel, 256-color GIF file requires 300K of memory to buffer, which should help explain why applications that work with GIF files tend to be pretty serious memory pigs.

Following the IMAGEHEADER object in an image block will be the local color map if one exists, followed by a byte that contains the initial number of bits of storage for the image. This is a value that's used by the string table decoder, to be dealt with in a moment. Following this byte is the first field of compressed image information.

The compressed data in an image block is stored in fields of up to 255 bytes each. Each field is preceded by a byte to indicate its length. The end of the image is reached when a zero-length field is reached. The following bit of code would step through all the fields in an image block. It assumes that `fp` is a file pointer that is initially pointing to the first byte of the first field.

```
int c;

while((c=getc(fp)) != 0 && c != EOF)
        fseek(fp,(unsigned long)c,SEEK_CUR);
```

When the `while` loop terminates, c will contain zero if the image block data was intact or EOF if the end of the file was reached prematurely.

Understanding how a GIF file is unpacked—that is, how string table decompression works—is a bit involved. It's worth noting that you don't need to understand it to work with GIF files; you can extract the code from the example GIF reader later in this chapter, pour it into your own application, and move on to more interesting things. If the following discussion isn't entirely lucid, you can easily get away with ignoring it.

A function to decode compressed GIF data operates on three objects—a `code stream`, a `code table`, and a `character stream`. The code stream is the data being read from the compressed file; in the example to be presented presently, it can be thought of as a FILE pointer. The character stream is the uncompressed data, which will go to wherever your uncompressed image data is bound. In this case, it's a pointer into memory where the unpacked pixels will be stored. The code table consists of a stack of entries in which codes from the file will be associated with strings of data. In a GIF file, the code table has 4096 entries. The image data in a GIF file can be compressed with up to twelve bits per code. Two raised to the power of twelve is 4096.

Keep in mind that these twelve bits refer to the maximum number of bits which the LZW compression function that originally created the GIF file in question was allowed to squeeze into a code for maximum compression efficiency. This is not the same as the number of bits of color the file might contain. Compression will always begin by assuming that there are no fewer than the number of bits of color in the picture being compressed, but it's allowed to increase the bit count to a maximum of twelve bits.

There are a number of other bits of information which are important to keep in mind before you start trying to fathom GIF decoding. Specifically, there are several special codes that are defined before the decoding process starts working. These are as follows:

```
#define CODESIZE      (1 << bits_per_pixel)
#define CLEAR_CODE    CODESIZE
#define END_OF_IMAGE  (CLEAR_CODE + 1)
#define FREE_CODE     (CLEAR_CODE + 2)
```

Before the decoding process gets under way, the string table must be partially initialized. Specifically, the first `CODESIZE` entries must be initialized with their positions in the table. Entry zero will contain zero, entry one will contain one and so on.

For an 8-bit picture—one with 256 colors—entries 0 through 255 will be initialized. Code 256 is the clear code, and code 257 is the end of image code. Code 258 is the first free code in the table. If a GIF decoder encounters CLEAR_CODE in the code stream, it will immediately re-initialize its string table. If it encounters END_OF_IMAGE in the code stream, it will shut down and go home.

The use of CLEAR_CODE might not be entirely clear. As an image is compressed, the string table of the compression function gradually gets full of strings. For as long as there are fewer than 4096 strings in it, it's free to use the existing strings, should it find duplicates of them in the data it's compressing, and to add new ones to it should it discover strings it has not previously encountered. If the string table becomes filled, it deals with this condition by throwing away all its strings and starting over. However, it must signal this event so that when the file is decoded, the decoding function will know to throw away its string table at the same time. The signal for this is CLEAR_CODE.

The program in FIG. 2-13 is a GIF decoder that will create the same FRG files that PCX2FRG did earlier in this chapter. Much of the code in its main function will probably be familiar, as it duplicates what PCX2FRG did. The principal distinction between GIF2FRG and PCX2FRG is that this program doesn't read one line at a time and then write it to a FRG file. Because it must deal with the possibility of interlaced source images, it buffers the whole works in memory.

This means that if you want to convert a 640 by 480 pixel, 256-color GIF file to a FRG image fragment file, you must have at least 300K of memory free after GIF2FRG has loaded. In fact, this program is a bit wasteful of memory, as it stores everything it reads as one byte per pixel, even if all the bits aren't used. If you're using the Borland integrated development environment to work with this program, you might find that there isn't enough memory to test GIF2FRG from within Turbo C, even though it will work correctly after you quit to DOS.

Note also that GIF2FRG doesn't use anything other than conventional DOS memory to store its images in as it stands. There's a decided upper limit to the dimensions of the image files it will work with. You might manage an 800 by 600 pixel image if you have nothing else installed in memory at the time, but that's about as good as it gets.

Converting GIF files to image fragments

```
/*
        GIF to image fragment translator

        Copyright (c) 1992 Alchemy Mindworks Inc.
*/

#include "stdio.h"
#include "alloc.h"
#include "dos.h"

#define RGB_RED          0
#define RGB_GREEN        1
#define RGB_BLUE         2
#define RGB_SIZE         3

#define GOOD_READ        0        /* return codes */
#define BAD_FILE         1
#define BAD_READ         2
#define UNEXPECTED_EOF   3
```

2-13
The source code for GIF2FRG.C.

```
#define BAD_CODE            4
#define BAD_FIRSTCODE       5
#define BAD_ALLOC           6
#define BAD_SYMBOLSIZE      7
#define NO_CODE             -1

#define IMAGESIG            "IFRG"

#define pixels2bytes(n)     ((n+7)/8)

typedef struct {
        char sig[4];
        unsigned int width,depth,bits,bytes,planebytes;
        unsigned long palette;
        unsigned long image;
        } IMAGEHEAD;

typedef struct {
        char sig[6];
        unsigned int screenwidth,screendepth;
        unsigned char flags,background,aspect;
        } GIFHEADER;

typedef struct {
        unsigned int left,top,width,depth;
        unsigned char flags;
        } IMAGEBLOCK;

typedef struct {
        char blocksize;
        char flags;
        unsigned int delay;
        char transparent_colour;
        char terminator;
        } CONTROLBLOCK;

typedef struct {
        char blocksize;
        unsigned int left,top;
        unsigned int gridwidth,gridheight;
        char cellwidth,cellheight;
        char forecolour,backcolour;
        } PLAINTEXT;

typedef struct {
        char blocksize;
        char applstring[8];
        char authentication[3];
        } APPLICATION;

typedef struct {
        unsigned int width,depth,bits,flags;
        char palette[768];
        } FILEINFO;
```

```
char *farPtr(char *p,long l);

char *buffer=NULL;
char masktable[8]={0x80,0x40,0x20,0x10,0x08,0x04,0x02,0x01};
char bittable[8]= {0x01,0x02,0x04,0x08,0x10,0x20,0x40,0x80};

main(argc,argv)
        int argc;
        char *argv[];
{
        static FILEINFO fi;
        IMAGEHEAD ih;
        FILE *source,*dest;
        char b[129],*linebuffer,*extrabuffer;
        int i,j,k,n,bytes;

        puts("GIF2FRG version 1.0\r\n");

        if(argc <= 1)
            error("I need a path to a GIF file");

        /* make the argument upper case */
        strupr(argv[1]);

        /* open the source file */
        if((source=fopen(argv[1],"rb"))==NULL)
            error("Error opening the source file");

        /* create a path to the destination file */
        strmfe(b,argv[1],"FRG");

        /* create the destination file */
        if((dest=fopen(b,"wb"))==NULL)
            error("Error creating the destination file");

        if(loadfile(source,&fi) != GOOD_READ)
            error("Error reading the source file");

        /* say what the file is */
        printf("%s (%u by %u) with %u bit(s) of colour\r\n",
            argv[1],fi.width,fi.depth,fi.bits);

        /* work out the line byte width */
        if(fi.bits <= 4) bytes=pixels2bytes(fi.width)*fi.bits;
        else bytes=fi.width;

        /* allocate a scratch buffer */
        if((extrabuffer=malloc(fi.width)) == NULL)
            error("Can't allocate extra buffer");

        /* get the plane width */
        n=pixels2bytes(fi.width);

        /* clear out the header */
        memset((char *)&ih,0,sizeof(IMAGEHEAD));
```

Working with GIF files **Working with GIF files**

```
/* install the identification string */
memcpy(ih.sig,IMAGESIG,4);

/* install the dimension values */
ih.width=fi.width;
ih.depth=fi.depth;
ih.bits=fi.bits;
ih.bytes=bytes;
ih.planebytes=n;

/* point to the palette */
ih.palette=sizeof(IMAGEHEAD);

/* point to the image */
if(fi.bits > 1 && fi.bits <= 8)
    ih.image=sizeof(IMAGEHEAD)+RGB_SIZE*(1<<fi.bits);
else
    ih.image=sizeof(IMAGEHEAD);

/* write the header */
if(fwrite((char *)&ih,1,sizeof(IMAGEHEAD),dest) !=
    sizeof(IMAGEHEAD))
        error("Error writing destination header");

/* write the palette */
if(fi.bits > 1 && fi.bits <= 8)
    fwrite(fi.palette,RGB_SIZE,1<<fi.bits,dest);

/* write the dimension integers for the image */
i=fi.width-1;
fwrite((char *)&i,1,sizeof(unsigned int),dest);
i=fi.depth-1;
fwrite((char *)&i,1,sizeof(unsigned int),dest);

for(i=0;i<fi.depth;++i) {
    linebuffer=farPtr(buffer,(long)i*(long)fi.width);

    if(fi.bits == 1) {
            memset(extrabuffer,0,n);

            for(j=0;j<fi.width;++j) {
                    if(linebuffer[j])
                            extrabuffer[j>>3] |= masktable[j & 0x0007];
            }

            if(fwrite(extrabuffer,1,n,dest) != n)
                error("Error writing line");
    }
    else if(fi.bits > 1 && fi.bits <= 4) {
            memset(extrabuffer,0,n);
            for(j=fi.bits-1;j>=0;--j) {
                    for(k=0;k<fi.width;++k) {
                            if(linebuffer[k] & bittable[j])
                                extrabuffer[k>>3] |=
            masktable[k & 0x0007];
```

```
                                else
                                        extrabuffer[k>>3] &= ~masktable[k & 0x0007];

                         }
                         if(fwrite(extrabuffer,1,n,dest) != n)
                                 error("Error writing line");
                 }
         }
         else {
                 /* eight-bit lines go as is */
                 if(fwrite(linebuffer,1,fi.width,dest) != fi.width)
                         error("Error writing line");
         }
 }

 free(extrabuffer);
 free(buffer);

 fclose(dest);
 fclose(source);

 puts("Ok");
}

error(s)
        char *s;
{

        puts(s);
        exit(1);
}

/* make file name with specific extension */
strmfe(new,old,ext)
        char *new,*old,*ext;
{

        while(*old != 0 && *old != '.') *new++=*old++;
        *new++='.';
        while(*ext) *new++=*ext++;
        *new=0;
}

/* unpack a GIF file */
loadfile(fp,fi)
        FILE *fp;
        FILEINFO *fi;
{

        GIFHEADER gh;
        IMAGEBLOCK iblk;
        int b,c;

        /* make sure it's a GIF file */
        if(fread((char *)&gh,1,sizeof(GIFHEADER),fp) != sizeof(GIFHEADER) ||
            memcmp(gh.sig, "GIF", 3)) return(BAD_FILE);

        /* get screen dimensions */
```

```
                fi->width=gh.screenwidth;
                fi->depth=gh.screendepth;
                fi->bits=(gh.flags & 0x0007) + 1;

                /* get colour map if there is one */
                if (gh.flags & 0x80) {
                        c = 3 * (1 << ((gh.flags & 7) + 1));
                        if(fread(fi->palette,1,c,fp) != c) return(BAD_READ);
                }

                /* step through the blocks */
                while((c=fgetc(fp))==´,´ || c==´!´ || c==0) {

                        /* if it's an image block... */
                        if (c == ´,´) {
                                /* get the start of the image block */
                                if(fread(&iblk,1,sizeof(IMAGEBLOCK),fp) !=
                                    sizeof(IMAGEBLOCK)) return(BAD_READ);

                                /* get the image dimensions */
                                fi->width=iblk.width;
                                fi->depth=iblk.depth;

                                /* get the local colour map if there is one */
                                if(iblk.flags & 0x80) {
                                        b = 3*(1<<((iblk.flags & 0x0007) + 1));
                                        if(fread(fi->palette,1,b,fp) != c) return(BAD_READ);
                                        fi->bits=(iblk.flags & 0x0007) + 1;
                                }

                                /* get the initial code size */
                                if((c=fgetc(fp))==EOF) return(BAD_FILE);

                                fi->flags=iblk.flags;

                                /* allocate a buffer */
                                if((buffer=farmalloc((long)fi->width *
                                                (long)fi->depth)) == NULL)
                                                return(BAD_ALLOC);

                                /* unpack the image */
                                return(unpackimage(fp,c,fi));
                        }
                        /* otherwise, it's an extension */
                        else if(c == ´!´) skipextension();
                }
                return(GOOD_READ);
        }

/* unpack an LZW compressed image */
unpackimage(fp,bits,fi)
        FILE *fp;
        int bits;
        FILEINFO *fi;
{
```

```
int bits2;              /* Bits plus 1 */
int codesize;           /* Current code size in bits */
int codesize2;          /* Next codesize */
int nextcode;           /* Next available table entry */
int thiscode;           /* Code being expanded */
int oldtoken;           /* Last symbol decoded */
int currentcode;        /* Code just read */
int oldcode;            /* Code read before this one */
int bitsleft;           /* Number of bits left in *p */
int blocksize;          /* Bytes in next block */
int line=0;             /* next line to write */
int byte=0;             /* next byte to write */
int pass=0;             /* pass number for interlaced pictures */

char *p;                /* Pointer to current byte in read buffer */
char *q;                /* Pointer past last byte in read buffer */
char b[255];            /* Read buffer */
char *u;                /* Stack pointer into firstcodestack */
char *linebuffer;       /* place to store the current line */

static char firstcodestack[4096];    /* Stack for first codes */
static char lastcodestack[4096];     /* Stack for previous code */
static int codestack[4096];          /* Stack for links */

static int wordmasktable[] = {  0x0000,0x0001,0x0003,0x0007,
                                0x000f,0x001f,0x003f,0x007f,
                                0x00ff,0x01ff,0x03ff,0x07ff,
                                0x0fff,0x1fff,0x3fff,0x7fff
                                };

static int inctable[] = { 8,8,4,2,0 }; /* interlace increments */
static int startable[] = { 0,4,2,1,0 };  /* interlace starts */

p=q=b;
bitsleft = 8;

if (bits < 2 || bits > 8) return(BAD_SYMBOLSIZE);
bits2 = 1 << bits;
nextcode = bits2 + 2;
codesize2 = 1 << (codesize = bits + 1);
oldcode=oldtoken=NO_CODE;

if((linebuffer=malloc(fi->width)) == NULL) return(BAD_ALLOC);

/* loop until something breaks */
for(;;) {
        if(bitsleft==8) {
                if(++p >= q &&
                (((blocksize = fgetc(fp)) < 1) ||
                (q=(p=b)+fread(b,1,blocksize,fp))< (b+blocksize))) {
                        free(linebuffer);
                        return(UNEXPECTED_EOF);
                }
                bitsleft = 0;
        }
}
```

```
thiscode = *p;
if ((currentcode=(codesize+bitsleft)) <= 8) {
        *p >>= codesize;
        bitsleft = currentcode;
}
else {
        if(++p >= q &&
          (((blocksize = fgetc(fp)) < 1) ||
          (q=(p=b)+fread(b,1,blocksize,fp)) < (b+blocksize))) {
                free(linebuffer);
                return(UNEXPECTED_EOF);
        }
        thiscode |= *p << (8 - bitsleft);
        if(currentcode <= 16) *p >>= (bitsleft=currentcode-8);
        else {
                if(++p >= q &&
                  (((blocksize = fgetc(fp)) < 1) ||
                  (q=(p=b) + fread(b,1,blocksize,fp)) < (b+blocksize))) {
                        free(linebuffer);
                        return(UNEXPECTED_EOF);
                }
                thiscode |= *p << (16 - bitsleft);
                *p >>= (bitsleft = currentcode - 16);
        }
}
thiscode &= wordmasktable[codesize];
currentcode = thiscode;

if(thiscode == (bits2+1)) break;          /* found EOI */
if(thiscode > nextcode) {
        free(linebuffer);
        return(BAD_CODE);
}

if(thiscode == bits2) {
        nextcode = bits2 + 2;
        codesize2 = 1 << (codesize = (bits + 1));
        oldtoken = oldcode = NO_CODE;
        continue;
}

u = firstcodestack;

if(thiscode==nextcode) {
        if(oldcode==NO_CODE) {
                free(linebuffer)
                return(BAD_FIRSTCODE);
        }
        *u++ = oldtoken;
        thiscode = oldcode;
}

while (thiscode >= bits2) {
        *u++ = lastcodestack[thiscode];
        thiscode = codestack[thiscode];
```

```
                }

        oldtoken = thiscode;
        do {
                linebuffer[byte++]=thiscode;
                if(byte >= fi->width) {
                                memcpy(farPtr(buffer,(long)line*(long)fi->width),
                                    linebuffer,fi->width);
                                byte=0;

                                /* check for interlaced image */
                                if(fi->flags & 0x40) {
                                        line+=inctable[pass];
                                        if(line >= fi->depth)
                                                line=startable[++pass];
                                } else ++line;
                        }

                        if (u <= firstcodestack) break;
                        thiscode = *-u;
                } while(1);

                if(nextcode < 4096 && oldcode != NO_CODE) {
                        codestack[nextcode] = oldcode;
                        lastcodestack[nextcode] = oldtoken;
                        if (++nextcode >= codesize2 && codesize < 12)
                            codesize2 = 1 << ++codesize;
                }
                oldcode = currentcode;
        }

        free(linebuffer);
        return(GOOD_READ);
}

char *farPtr(p,l)    /* return a far pointer p + l */
        char *p;
        long l;
{

        unsigned int seg,off;

        seg = FP_SEG(p);
        off = FP_OFF(p);
        seg += (off / 16);
        off &= 0x000f;
        off += (unsigned int)(l & 0x000fL);
        seg += (l / 16L);
        p = MK_FP(seg,off);
        return(p);
}

skipextension(fp)
        FILE *fp;
{

        PLAINTEXT pt;
```

```
                CONTROLBLOCK cb;
                APPLICATION ap;
                int n,i;

                clrscr();
                switch(fgetc(fp)) {
                        case 0x0001:            /* plain text descriptor */
                                if(fread((char *)&pt,1,sizeof(PLAINTEXT),fp)
                                    == sizeof(PLAINTEXT)) {

                                        do {
                                                if((n=fgetc(fp)) != EOF) {
                                                        for(i=0;i<n;++i) fgetc(fp);
                                                }
                                        } while(n > 0 && n != EOF);
                                } else puts("Error reading plain text block");
                                break;
                        case 0x00f9             /* graphic control block */
                                if(fread((char *)&cb,1,sizeof(CONTROLBLOCK),fp)
                                    != sizeof(CONTROLBLOCK))
                                        puts("Error reading control block");
                                break;
                        case 0x00fe:            /* comment extension */
                                do {
                                        if((n=fgetc(fp)) != EOF) {
                                                for(i=0;i<n;++i) fgetc(fp);
                                        }
                                } while(n > 0 && n != EOF);
                                break;
                        case 0x00ff:            /* application extension */
                                if(fread((char *)&ap,1,sizeof(APPLICATION),fp)
                                    == sizeof(APPLICATION)) {
                                        do {
                                                if((n=fgetc(fp)) != EOF) {
                                                        for(i=0;i<n;++i) fgetc(fp);
                                                }
                                        } while(n > 0 && n != EOF);
                                } else puts("Error reading application block");
                                break;
                        default:                /* something else */
                                n=fgetc(fp);
                                for(i=0;i<n;++i) fgetc(fp);
                                break;
                }
                getch();
        }
```

The element of GIF2FRG that distinguishes it from PCX2FRG is the function loadfile, which will unpack a GIF file into memory. This, in turn, will call unpackimage to do the actual image uncompression and skipextension to deal with any extension blocks it encounters. In a fully functional GIF decoder the main loop of this function would keep going until a block that started with a semicolon was reached. Because we're only interested in the first image in the file, the loop terminates after it has been read.

It's relatively rare that you'll encounter a GIF file with an extension block prior to the first image. One exception to this is files created by the GIFLITE program, which improves on the compression of GIF files by removing some image detail. It stores an extension block identifying the picture as having been compressed with GIFLITE as the first block in the file.

The unpackimage function implements the GIF decoding process, as described earlier. You can work your way through it if you like, but it's not really necessary to do so if you just want to work with GIF files in your own software.

The FRG2GIF program in FIG. 2-14 reverses the function of GIF2FRG. In fact, it will create GIF files from any FRG files, with one notable exception. The FRG format allows for up to 24 bits of color. The GIF format only handles a maximum of eight bits. As such, GIF2FRG will complain if it finds itself beset with a 24-bit source image.

Converting image fragments to GIF files

As with GIF2FRG, the FRG2GIF program buffers the entire source image in memory. It then calls writegif to pack the image. This, in turn, calls three functions to write the three elements of a basic GIF file. The writeScreenDesc call handles creating a GIFHEADER object at the start of the file. The writeImageDesc function stores everything associated with an image block except for the image itself. The compressImage function writes the actual image data. Finally, writegif writes a semicolon to the file just before it's closed, which serves as a final terminator block.

The compressImage function is passed a pointer to a function to fetch pixels from the source image. These must be GIF-style pixels—that is, with each pixel stored in one byte, no matter how many bits of color are involved. The function must return EOF when all the pixels in the source image have been read.

This arrangement allows compressImage to be easily customized to write GIF files from source images stored in any number of ways. The function used in this example is getpixel, down near the end of the listing in FIG. 2-14.

```
/*
        Image fragment to GIF

        Copyright (c) 1992 Alchemy Mindworks Inc.
*/

#include "stdio.h"
#include "dos.h"
#include "alloc.h"

#define RGB_RED         0
#define RGB_GREEN       1
#define RGB_BLUE        2
#define RGB_SIZE        3

#define IMAGESIG        "IFRG"

#define largest_code    4095    /* largest possible code */
#define table_size      5003    /* table dimensions */

#define pixels2bytes(n)    ((n+7)/8)
```

2-14
The source code for FRG2GIF.C.

2-14
Continued.

```
typedef struct {
        char sig[4];
        unsigned int width,depth,bits,bytes,planebytes;
        unsigned long palette;
        unsigned long image;
        } IMAGEHEAD;

typedef struct {
        char sig[6];
        unsigned int screenwidth,screendepth;
        unsigned char flags,background,aspect;
        } GIFHEADER;

typedef struct {
        unsigned int left,top,width,depth;
        unsigned char flags;
        } IMAGEBLOCK;


int getpixel();
char *farPtr(char *p,long l);

char *buffer=NULL;
char palette[768]="\000\000\000\377\377\377";
char masktable[8]={0x80,0x40,0x20,0x10,0x08,0x04,0x02,0x01};
char bittable[8]= {0x01,0x02,0x04,0x08,0x10,0x20,0x40,0x80};
unsigned int byteread=0,lineread=0;
IMAGEHEAD ih;

char code_buffer[259];              /* where the codes go */

int oldcode[table_size];            /* the table */
int currentcode[table_size];
char newcode[table_size];

int code_size;
int clear_code;
int eof_code;
int bit_offset;
int byte_offset;
int bits_left;
int max_code;
int free_code;

main(argc,argv)
        int argc;
        char *argv[];
{
        FILE *source,*dest;
        char s[129],*linebuffer,*p,*ps;
        int i,j,k;

        puts("FRG2GIF version 1.0\r\n");

        if(argc <= 1)
            error("I need a path to a FRG file");
```

```
/* make the argument upper case */
strupr(argv[1]);

/* open the source file */
if((source=fopen(argv[1],"rb"))==NULL)
    error("Error opening the source file");

/* read the source header */
if(fread((char *)&ih,1,sizeof(IMAGEHEAD),source) !=
    sizeof(IMAGEHEAD))
        error("Error reading header");

/* check to make sure it's a FRG file */
if(memcmp(ih.sig,IMAGESIG,4)) error("This is not a FRG file");

if(ih.bits > 8)
    error("Too many colours");

if((linebuffer=malloc(ih.bytes)) == NULL)
    error("Can't allocate memory");

if((buffer=farmalloc((long)ih.width*(long)ih.depth)) == NULL)
    error("Can't allocate memory");

/* create a path to the destination file */
strmfe(s,argv[1],"GIF");

/* create the destination file */
if((dest=fopen(s,"wb"))==NULL)
    error("Error creating the destination file");

/* say what the file is */
printf("%s (%u by %u) with %u bit(s) of colour\r\n",
    argv[1],ih.width,ih.depth,ih.bits);

if(ih.bits > 1 && ih.bits <= 8) {
    fseek(source,(unsigned long)ih.palette,SEEK_SET);
    if(fread(palette,RGB_SIZE,1<ih.bits,source) != (1<<ih.bits))
        error("Error reading the palette");
}

fseek (source, (unsigned long)ih.image+4< SEEK_SET);

for(i=0;i<ih.depth;++i) {

    if(ih.bits==1) {
            if(fread(linebuffer,1,ih.planebytes,source) !=
                ih.planebytes)
                    error("Error reading line");
            p=farPtr(buffer,(long)i*(long)ih.width);
            for(j=0;j<ih.width;++j) {
                    if(linebuffer[j>>3] & masktable[j & 0x0007])
                        p[j]=1;
                    else
                        p[j]=0;
```

```
                            }
                        }
                  else if(ih.bits > 1 && ih.bits <= 4) {
                        if(fread(linebuffer,1,ih.bytes,source) != ih.bytes)
                           error("Error reading line");

                        p=farPtr(buffer,(long)i*(long)ih.width);
                        memset(p,0,ih.width);

                        ps=linebuffer;
                        for(k=ih.bits-1;k>=0;--k) {
                              for(j=0;j<ih.width;++j) {
                                    if(ps[j>>3] & masktable[j & 0x0007])
                                          p[j] |= bittable[k];
                              }
                              ps+=ih.planebytes;
                        }
                  }
                  else if(ih.bits > 4 && ih.bits <= 8) {
                        if(fread(farPtr(buffer,(long)i*(long)ih.width),
                           1,ih.width,source) != ih.width)
                              error("Error reading line");
                  }
            }

            writegif(dest,getpixel,ih.width,ih.depth,ih.bits,palette);

            fclose(dest);
            free(linebuffer);
            free(buffer);
            fclose(source);

            puts("Ok");
      }

      error(s)
            char *s;
      {
            puts(s);
            exit(1);
      }

      /* make file name with specific extension */
      strmfe(new,old,ext)
            char *new,*old,*ext;
      {
            while(*old != 0 && *old != '.') *new++=*old++;
            *new++='.';
            while(*ext) *new++=*ext++;
            *new=0;
      }

      /* write a GIF file */
      writegif(fp,readpixel,width,depth,bits,palette)
            FILE *fp;
```

```
            int (readpixel)();
            unsigned int width,depth,bits;
            char *palette;
{

            /* write the header */
            if(writeScreenDesc(fp,width,depth,bits,0,palette)) return(1);

            /* write the image descriptor */
            if(writeImageDesc(fp,0,0,width,depth,bits,NULL)) return(2);

            /* write the image */
            if(compressImage(fp,readpixel,bits)) return(3);

            /* write the terminator */
            fputc(´;´,fp);
            return(ferror(fp));
}

/* write the header */
writeScreenDesc(fp,width,depth,bits,background,palette)
            FILE *fp;
            unsigned int width,depth,bits,background;
            char *palette;
{

            GIFHEADER gh;

            /* fill the header struct */
            memset((char *)&gh,0,sizeof(GIFHEADER));
            memcpy(gh.sig,"GIF87a",6);
            gh.screenwidth=width;
            gh.screendepth=depth;
            gh.background=background;
            gh.aspect=0;

            /* set up the global flags */
            if(palette == NULL) gh.flags=(((bits-1) & 0x07)<<4);
            else gh.flags = (0x80 | ((bits-1)<<4) | ((bits-1) & 0x07));

            /* write the header */
            fwrite((char *)&gh,1,sizeof(GIFHEADER),fp);

            /* write the colour map */
            if(palette != NULL) fwrite(palette,1,3*(1<<bits),fp);

            return(ferror(fp));
}

/* write an image descriptor block */
writeImageDesc(fp,left,top,width,depth,bits,palette)
            FILE *fp;
            unsigned int left,top,width,depth;
            char *palette;
{

            IMAGEBLOCK ib;

            memset((char *)&ib,0,sizeof(IMAGEBLOCK));
```

```
                    /* fill the image block struct */
                    fputc(´,´,fp);
                    ib.left=left;
                    ib.top=top;
                    ib.width=width;
                    ib.depth=depth;

                    /* set the local flags */
                    if(palette==NULL) ib.flags=bits-1;
                    else ib.flags=((bits-1) & 0x07) | 0x80;

                    /* write the block */
                    fwrite((char *)&ib,1,sizeof(IMAGEBLOCK),fp);

                    /* write the colour map */
                    if(palette != NULL) fwrite(palette,1,3*(1<<bits),fp);

                    return(ferror(fp));
        }

/* initialize the code table */
init_table(min_code_size)
        int min_code_size;
{
        int i;

        code_size=min_code_size+1;
        clear_code=(1<<min_code_size);
        eof_code=clear_code+1;
        free_code=clear_code+2;
        max_code=(1<<code_size);

        for(i=0;i<table_size;i++) currentcode[i]=0;
}

/* flush the code buffer */
flush(fp,n)
        FILE *fp;
        int n;
{
        fputc(n,fp);
        fwrite(code_buffer,1,n,fp);
}

/* write a code to the code buffer */
write_code(fp,code)
        FILE *fp;
        int code;
{
        long temp;

        byte_offset = bit_offset >> 3;
        bits_left = bit_offset & 7;

        if(byte_offset >= 254) {
                flush(fp,byte_offset);
```

```
                    code_buffer[0] = code_buffer[byte_offset];
                    bit_offset = bits_left;
                    byte_offset = 0;
            }

        if(bits_left > 0) {
                    temp = ((long) code << bits_left) | code_buffer[byte_offset];
                    code_buffer[byte_offset]=temp;
                    code_buffer[byte_offset+1]=(temp >> 8);
                    code_buffer[byte_offset+2]=(temp >> 16);
        }
        else {
                    code_buffer[byte_offset] = code;
                    code_buffer[byte_offset+1]=(code >> 8);
        }
        bit_offset += code_size;
}

/* compress an image */
compressImage(fp,readpixel,min_code_size)
        FILE *fp;
        int (*readpixel)();
        unsigned int min_code_size;
{
        int prefix_code;
        int suffix_char;
        int hx,d;

        /* make sure the initial code size is legal */
        if(min_code_size < 2 || min_code_size > 9) {
                    /* monochrome images have two bits in LZW compression */
                    if(min_code_size == 1) min_code_size = 2;
                    else return(EOF);
        }

        /* write initial code size */
        fputc(min_code_size,fp);

        /* initialize the encoder */
        bit_offset=0;
        init_table(min_code_size);
        write_code(fp,clear_code);
        if((suffix_char=(readpixel)())==EOF) return(suffix_char);

        /* initialize the prefix */
        prefix_code = suffix_char;

        /* get a character to compress */
        while((suffix_char=(readpixel)()) != EOF) {

                    /* derive an index into the code table */
                    hx=(prefix_code ^ (suffix_char << 5)) % table_size;
                    d=1;

                    for(;;) {
```

```
                                    /* see if the code is in the table */
                                    if(currentcode[hx] == 0) {

                                            /* if not, put it there */
                                            write_code(fp,prefix_code);
                                            d = free_code;

                                            /* find the next free code */
                                            if(free_code <= largest_code) {
                                                    oldcode[hx] = prefix_code;
                                                    newcode[hx] = suffix_char;
                                                    currentcode[hx] = free_code;
                                                    free_code++;
                                            }

                                            /* expand the code size or scrap the table */
                                            if(d == max_code) {
                                                    if(code_size < 12) {
                                                            code_size++;
                                                            max_code <<= 1;
                                                    }
                                                    else {
                                                            write_code(fp,clear_code);
                                                            init_table(min_code_size);
                                                    }
                                            }
                                            prefix_code = suffix_char;
                                            break;
                                    }
                                    if(oldcode[hx] == prefix_code &&
                                       newcode[hx] == suffix_char) {
                                            prefix_code = currentcode[hx];
                                            break;
                                    }
                                    hx += d;
                                    d += 2;
                                    if(hx >= table_size) hx -= table_size;
                            }
                    }

            /* write the prefix code */
            write_code(fp,prefix_code);

            /* and the end of file code */
            write_code(fp,eof_code);

            /* flush the buffer */
            if(bit_offset > 0) flush(fp,(bit_offset+7)/8);

            /* write a zero length block */
            flush(fp,0);

            return(ferror(fp));
    }
```

```
/* get one pixel from the source image */
getpixel()
{
        char *p;

        if(byteread >= ih.width) {
                byteread=0;
                ++lineread;
                if(lineread >= ih.depth) return(EOF);
        }

        p=farPtr(buffer,(long)byteread+(long)lineread*(long)ih.width);
        ++byteread;
        return(p[0] & 0x00ff);
}

char *farPtr(p,l)    /* return a far pointer p + l */
        char *p;
        long l;
{
        unsigned int seg,off;

        seg = FP_SEG(p);
        off = FP_OFF(p);
        seg += (off / 16);
        off &= 0x000f;
        off += (unsigned int)(l & 0x000fL);
        seg += (l / 16L);
        p = MK_FP(seg,off);
        return(p);
}
```

Despite its length and complexity, this chapter has really only begun to deal with the vagaries of commercial bitmapped graphics formats. The code examined herein will certainly give you enough command of them to deal with bitmapped images in the context of this book, but there's a lot more to them if you want to use them in more involved applications.

If you'd like to really wrestle the subject to the ground, you might want to consult several of my other books, *Bitmapped Graphics, second edition, Supercharged Bitmapped Graphics* and *Bitmapped Graphic for Windows.* All three are published by Windcrest.

More bitmapped images

16-Color graphics

The dark & brooding secrets of write mode two

"It's always darkest just before you step on the cat."
    —Murphy's Laws

The 16-color super VGA graphics modes aren't all that interesting for displaying scanned bitmapped images, but they're probably what you'll want to use to write interactive graphic-based software that doesn't involve displaying photographs. The 16-color modes require modest amounts of memory and offer a level of standardization that's only mildly chaotic—something the 256-color modes will not be able to claim when we deal with them in the next chapter.

All VGA cards have a standard 640 by 480 pixel, 16-color graphic mode. Pretty well all super VGA cards can manage an additional 800 by 600 pixel mode with this color depth, although as you'll see, they all implement these modes slightly differently.

Despite the differences in the 800 by 600 pixel modes, it's not at all difficult to write software that will support pretty well all the super VGA cards that implement them.

The planar nature of 16-color graphics, as dealt with in Chapter 1, makes writing to the super VGA video buffer in this mode a bit challenging. It will probably seem, at the outset, that drawing and painting in sixteen colors would be unworkably time-consuming. In fact, this is true as far as it goes, save that VGA cards have a number of really well hidden mysteries that will allow you to cheat like a bandit.

The various reading and writing modes of VGA cards will be discussed in this chapter—there's a lot more to 16-color graphics than you might imagine.

This chapter will deal with some fairly elemental graphic functions; you'll be able to expand on these quite a bit should you want to create a complete graphics library of your own. Specifically, it will present code to do the following:

❏ Initialize a super VGA graphics mode
❏ Clear the screen
❏ Set the VGA palette
❏ Set pixels
❏ Draw lines
❏ Draw rectangles
❏ Fill rectangles
❏ Draw text
❏ Get and put image fragments
❏ Animate a mouse cursor
❏ Create and manage three-dimensional buttons
❏ Save a graphic screen to a PCX file

Figure 3-1 illustrates the screen of the example program that will be created with the code in this chapter. While it's not enormously useful of itself, it does serve to illustrate most of what the functions in this chapter can do.

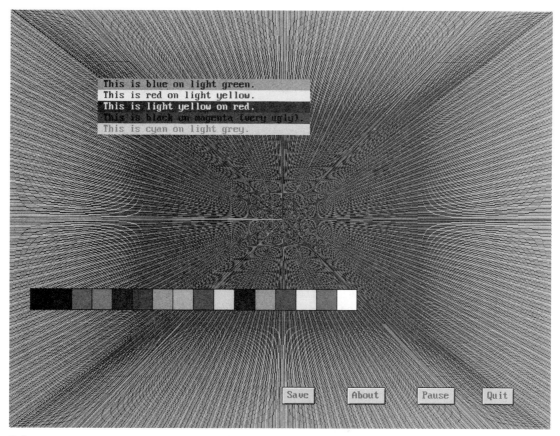

3-1 *The graphic created by the example program in this chapter.*

This chapter will also get into some serious use of the VESA BIOS extensions as well. There's a complete discussion of them at the end of the chapter; for the moment, we'll apply them informally, with a proper explanation to follow.

Finally, note that much of the code in this chapter will be handled in assembly language, both for reasons of speed and because there are a few elements of animating a super VGA mouse cursor that really can't be handled properly in C alone. The assembly language module will essentially add some additional functions to whatever C programs it's linked to. You'll need MASM or TASM to assemble it.

The first part of this chapter will examine the principals behind the code that will handle each of the foregoing functions. The code itself—an assembly language module to handle the mouse functions and selected graphics tools and a C language calling program—will be presented in its entirety toward the end of the chapter. Note that in order to keep the example code fragments in the first part of this chapter from becoming huge and awkward to understand, most of them are incomplete. The complete functions are in the code modules.

Selecting a 16-color graphic mode

Mode changes on a VGA card are always handled though calls to the BIOS—at least, this is true for all the standard VGA modes and for any defined modes available on super VGA cards. Real VGA gurus will tell you that there are additional, undocumented modes that can be had through careful manipulation of a VGA card's registers. We won't be dealing with them in this chapter; for the most part, these modes are undocumented for very good reasons.

Mode changes are handled by the INT 10H BIOS call. If the AH register is 0, the mode will be changed based on the contents of the AL register. On a standard VGA card, legal mode numbers range from zero through 13H. Mode three is normal 80 by 25 character text. Mode 12H is the 640 by 480 pixel, 16-color graphics mode.

Super VGA cards bolt "extensions" onto the standard BIOS. This allows the INT 10H call to correctly interpret other mode values—in this case, mode values that are peculiar to the specific VGA cards in question. For example, on a Paradise super VGA card, selecting mode 58H will enable 800 by 600 pixel, 16-color graphics. On an ATI card selecting mode 58H will do nothing at all: 58H is not a defined super VGA mode for an ATI card. The corresponding mode number for ATI is 54H.

Clearly, then, selecting the 800 by 600 pixel, 16-color graphics mode for any particular super VGA card is pretty easy. All you need is a list of the appropriate mode numbers.

Here's what the INT 10H call would look like from C:

```
union REGS r;

r.x.ax=MODENUMBER;
int86(0x10,&r,&r);
```

The following are the mode numbers that pertain to the super VGA cards being examined in this book.

```
#define PARADISE  0x58
#define ATI       0x54
#define TSENG     0x29
```

```
#define TRIDENT  0x5b
#define OAK      0x52
#define VESA     0x0102
```

Actually, the simple BIOS call to change modes is applicable in all cases save for a VESA BIOS, which requires some rather more involved manipulation. In dealing with a VESA display, you must first ascertain the existence of the VESA interpreter, make sure it supports the mode you're interested in, and finally do the actual mode change. The 800 by 600 pixel, 16-color graphics mode is mode 102H.

We'll deal with the complete saga of making VESA calls at the end of this chapter.

In addition to selecting the appropriate graphics mode, it's necessary to devise a way to effectively write graphics to the screen. The problem in this is that the screen dimensions use numbers that are comfortable for human users but less so for computers. At 800 by 600 pixels, each line will consists of four planes of 100 bytes each. As you'll recall from the first chapter of this book, the four planes need not be on the bus all at once; and for the purposes of working out the memory addressing you can consider that there's only one set of planes to deal with.

You can locate line n in the screen buffer with the following expression:

```
char *line;
line=MK_FP(0xa000,n*100);
```

This isn't quite as mysterious as it appears. The MK_FP macro returns a far pointer. The segment of the far pointer will be A000H, which is the base of the graphic mode VGA screen buffer. The offset will be the line number, n, multiplied by the number of bytes in an 800-pixel line—that is, 100 bytes.

The problem with this is the multiplication. While it can do integer multiplication, an 8086-series microprocessor takes a long time to perform a multiplication instruction, at least by computer standards. Addressing the screen this way would not produce the snappiest graphics.

It's possible to eliminate the multiplication. If we observe that there are only 600 possible results of the foregoing expression—there being only 600 lines on the screen—a program that required frequent access to the lines of its graphic buffer could set up a lookup table of pointers. If SCREENTBL is an array of integers such that each entry represents an offset into the screen buffer for its corresponding line, the previous expression could be rewritten using it.

```
char *line;
line=MK_FP(0xa000,SCREENTBL[n]);
```

The offending multiplication instruction has been excised. This approach requires about a dozen machine cycles to address a line, as opposed to well over a hundred for the one that used multiplication.

In fact, it's possible to have the contents of SCREENTBL initialized at compile time, so it's not even necessary to wait while the 600 offsets are initially calculated.

The code in this chapter will use five objects to deal with the screen:

SCREENWIDE	The width of the screen in pixels
SCREENDEEP	The depth of the screen in pixels
SCREENBYTES	The width of the screen in bytes
SCREENSEG	The segment of the screen buffer
SCREENTBL	An array of offsets into the screen buffer

The SCREENSEG value will always be A000H, of course, but it makes some of the code more efficient to deal with it this way.

As an aside—and as you'll see in the code to be dealt with later in this chapter— you can make the graphics functions work with a standard VGA card by simply manipulating these five objects, adjusting their values to suit the 640 by 480 pixel dimensions of mode 12H.

Setting the VGA palette

As was touched on in Chapter 1, colors are expressed as three-byte RGB values. It takes sixteen such colors to initialize the complete palette in the modes to be examined in this chapter.

When you first select a 16-color mode, the VGA palette is initialized to a standard set of colors. In this example, we'll use a somewhat different default palette; you are, of course, free to change it to support whatever colors you require. In this case, however, keep in mind that you'll have to keep track of which colors appear in which palette entries.

The 16-color VGA palette is complicated a bit by the existence of the earlier EGA cards, and the requirement that VGA hardware be backwards compatible with them. The EGA standard supported a singularly crude and inelegant way to specify color. The card allowed for only four gradations of each of its three primary colors— fully off, dim, bright, and fully on. The intensity of each primary color could be specified with two bits. All three primary color levels could be expressed with six bits, making it possible to define a color in one byte, rather than three, with two bits left over. Of course, this didn't provide for much color resolution; an EGA card can select its sixteen colors from a total palette of only 64, as opposed to the palette of a quarter of a million colors for a VGA card.

The bits are illustrated in FIG. 3-2. Setting these bits in various combinations results in numerical values of 0 through 63. These are called EGA color numbers.

You can set a VGA card's 16-color palette using the same BIOS calls that were used to set EGA color numbers, although there's little reason for doing so.

The hardware that translated color numbers into colors on an EGA card is not part of the architecture of a VGA card. Instead, VGA cards simulate the behavior of an EGA card in software. When you first select a 16-color VGA mode, the first 64 palette entries are set to the colors that would have been generated by the 64 permutations of bits in an EGA color number. There is a secondary lookup table of sixteen values that point into these first 64 palette entries. If you attempt to set the colors of a VGA card using EGA color numbers, the color numbers will in turn point into the first 64 entries of the color palette, and the VGA card will behave like an EGA card.

7	Unused
6	Unused
5	High intensity red
4	High intensity green
3	High intensity blue
2	Low intensity red
1	Low intensity green
0	Low intensity blue

3-2
The bits of an EGA color number.

In most cases, you'll be a lot happier if you can make a VGA card behave like a VGA card and have as little to do with EGA hardware as possible. This is pretty easy to do if you understand what a VGA card is up to behind your back. To set the sixteen colors of a VGA palette, you must first set the first sixteen palette registers to the RGB color values you want to use and then set the sixteen EGA color numbers to the values zero through fifteen. It doesn't matter what colors these color numbers would result in on an EGA card; on a VGA card, they'll point to the first sixteen colors in the VGA palette, which will have been set to the palette you want to use.

Maintaining backwards compatibility is one of the things that eventually crumbles empires and causes otherwise rational human beings to experiment with bungee jumping.

You can set both the VGA color palette and EGA color numbers with BIOS calls. The following function begins by setting up the VGA color palette; because the VGA registers are six bits wide, rather than eight, the RGB color values must be shifted right by two planes before they're used to set the color values. The second loop handles setting up the EGA color numbers.

```
SetVgaPalette(p,n)
        char *p;
        unsigned int n;
{
        union REGS r;
```

```
int i;
for(i=0;i<n;++i) {
        r.h.dh=*p++>>2;
        r.h.ch=*p++>>2;
        r.h.cl=*p++>>2;
        r.x.bx=i;
        r.x.ax=0x1010;
        int86(0x10,&r,&r);
}
r.x.bx=0x0000;
for(i=0;i<n;++i) {
        r.x.ax=0x1000;
        int86(0x10,&r,&r);
        r.x.bx+=0x0101;
}
}
```

The hitherto mentioned VGA gurus will tell you that the VGA palette can be set a lot more rapidly by directly fiddling the VGA registers. This is absolutely true, and for once the VGA gurus wouldn't be feeding you a lot of esoteric advice with no practical value outside of hyperspace. We'll look at how this is done in the next chapter when we come to deal with 256-color palettes.

To use this function, you'd pass a pointer to the color palette and the number of colors in it—usually sixteen—to the `SetVgaPalette` function. The following is the default palette for use in this chapter:

```
char palette[] = {
        0x00,0x00,0x00,
        0x00,0x00,0xaa,
        0x00,0xaa,0x00,
        0x00,0xaa,0xaa,
        0xaa,0x00,0x00,
        0xaa,0x00,0xaa,
        0xaa,0xaa,0x00,
        0xaa,0xaa,0xaa,
        0x55,0x55,0x55,
        0xcc,0xcc,0xcc,
        0x00,0x00,0xff,
        0x00,0xff,0x00,
        0xff,0x00,0x00,
        0xff,0xff,0x00,
        0xff,0x00,0xff,
        0xff,0xff,0xff
        };
```

Each line in this table represents one color, with the color values in the order red, green and blue. Here are what the colors actually look like. Note that this list of names is only useful for this palette—change the palette entries, and you'll want to change the name constants as well.

```
#define BLACK  0
#define BLUE   1
#define GREEN  2
```

```
#define CYAN          3
#define RED           4
#define MAGENTA       5
#define YELLOW        6
#define GREY          7
#define DARKGREY      8
#define LIGHTGREY     9
#define LIGHTBLUE     10
#define LIGHTGREEN    11
#define LIGHTRED      12
#define LIGHTYELLOW   13
#define LIGHTMAGENTA  14
#define WHITE         15
```

Note that some of these color names are defined in `graphics.h` and in `conio.h` for Turbo C. There's no reason to include these headers for the code in this chapter; make sure you don't, or Turbo C will complain about previously defined symbols.

It's very important to keep in mind that the color numbers defined by these constants aren't really colors—they're just references to the current VGA palette. As such, if you load RGB values that define a light yellow color into palette entry 13, setting pixels in the video buffer to 13 will cause light yellow dots to appear. If you load RGB values that define bright purple into palette entry 13, said dots will be bright purple—even if you've defined the constant as LIGHTYELLOW.

Clearing the screen

When a 16-color VGA mode is selected, the screen buffer is initially filled with zero bytes. This means, in effect, that all the pixels are set to color 0. In this palette, color 0 is black, so the screen will be black. If you define a different color for color 0, the screen will appear in that color.

Clearing screen to a defined color involves writing all the pixels on the screen with the color number in question. There are several ways to go about this, each one a bit sneakier than the last. The quickest one—and the one to be used in this chapter—gets into a bit of the lore of the alternate screen write modes of a VGA card.

Let's look at how you'd clear the screen to magenta using the palette defined in the previous section. This will be really ugly—magenta is a color only beloved by printing press operators and trendy imported car dealers—but it will serve as a workable example. Magenta is defined as color 5. In binary notation, this would be 0101.

To set the screen to magenta, then, you could use the following piece of code. This code assumes that the color to be used is stored in the value `color`.

```
char *p;
int i,j;

for(i=0;i<SCREENDEEP;++i) {
    p=MK_FP(SCREENSEG,SCREENTBL[i]);
    for(j=0;j<4;++j) {
        egawriteplane(1<<j);
        if(color & (1<<j))
            memset(p,255,SCREENBYTES);
        else
            memset(p,0,SCREENBYTES);
    }
}
```

This probably deserves a bit of explanation. To begin with, the egawriteplane macro will cause the planes specified in its argument to appear in the VGA graphics screen buffer for writing. There are four planes, and the first four bits in the argument correspond to them.

The four bits in the argument to egawriteplane correspond to the four bits in the color value to be used to clear the screen. Any plane whose corresponding bit is 1 should be filled with 255 bytes—the value 255 is a byte with all its bits on. Any plane whose corresponding bit is 0 should be filled with 0 bytes. As an aide, the plane switch macro is called egawriteplane rather than vgawriteplane for historical reasons. This screen architecture dates back to the old EGA cards.

This arrangement, while workable, is slow. It involves a lot of plane switching and writing to no fewer than 2400 individual planes to clear the entire screen.

This can be improved on a bit if you observe that the egawriteplane macro can accept arguments with more than one bit set and will set multiple planes onto the bus for writing if you like. As such, you could rewrite the function to write all the 0-byte planes and then all the 255-byte planes in a line at once.

```
char *p;
int i,j;

for(i=0;i<SCREENDEEP;++i) {
        p=MK_FP(SCREENSEG,SCREENTBL[i]);
        egawriteplane(color)
        memmset(p,255,SCREENBYTES);
        egawriteplane(~color);
        memset(p,0,SCREENBYTES);
}
```

This reduces the number of invocations of egawriteplane and the number of planes being written by half, resulting in a much faster screen clearing function.

The foregoing approaches to writing to the screen both use screen write mode zero, the default 16-color write mode. In this mode, the screen memory is just written to as you would any other memory, save that its planes can be paged in and out as you require.

The fastest screen clear can be handled using write mode two. It allows all four planes to be updated at once without any calls to egawriteplane. You can, in effect, write a color through all the planes at once in this mode. It allows a 600-line screen to be cleared by writing only 600 lines of data.

```
char *p;
int a,i,j;

for(i=0;i<SCREENDEEP;++i) {
        p=MK_FP(SCREENSEG,SCREENTBL[i]);
        outportb(0x3ce,5);
        outportb(0x3cf,2);

        for(j=0;j<SCREENBYTES;++j) {
                outportb(0x3ce,8);
                outportb(0x3cf,255);
```

```
                a=p[j];
                p[j]=color;
            }
    }
    outportb(0x3ce,5);
    outportb(0x3cf,0);
```

The `outportb` calls manipulate the VGA card registers to work in write mode two. The registers of interest are 03CEH and 03CFH, the graphics registers. You can access numerous functions of a VGA card through these registers. Register 03CEH handles the number of the function you're interested in and register 03CFH handles the value to be handed to that function. Function five allows you to select the write mode, among other things. The first pair of `outportb` calls select write mode two.

Note that some C compilers use the call `outp`, rather than `outportb`.

Function eight allows you to select which bits are to be updated in write mode two—this is called the "write mask." The value 255—all bits set—tells a VGA card that all the bits are to be written. Any byte written to the screen buffer in write mode two will be interpreted by the VGA hardware as a color number rather than as a literal byte, and will set the bit values in all four planes accordingly.

In write mode two, the color written to the screen buffer will appear in all the pixels of the byte being written that correspond to the bits in the write mask.

Actually, there's a really odd catch in this. You can only perform mode two writes like this if you read the byte to be written first. This is called a dummy read and is required to toggle some latches internal to a VGA card. This is a minor problem under C, as your compiler will warn you that the value `a` in the foregoing example is assigned a value that's never used. You can switch off this warning by preceding the function in question with the following pragma:

```
#pragma warn -aus
```

When the screen has been cleared, you should make sure to return the write mode to zero, as this is how most VGA graphics functions expect to find it. That's what the final two `outportb` calls do.

Applications of write mode two will turn up in several other places in this chapter.

Setting pixels

Setting individual screen pixels to specific colors is another instance of a fairly time consuming task in write mode zero that can be done very efficiently in write mode two. A function to set individual pixels to a specific color is the basis of a more complex function to draw lines.

In write mode zero, you would set a pixel by bringing each of the four memory planes onto the bus one at a time and setting the appropriate bits on or off, as determined by the number of the color to be set. As with the code to clear the screen, this would be fairly time consuming, entailing four calls to `egawriteplane` for each pixel to be set as well as some bitwise manipulation.

If you have a good understanding of how write mode two works, you'll realize that it's pretty easy to use it to set individual pixels. Rather than create a write mask with all the bits on, you could set one pixel by using a write mask with only one bit on.

To set a pixel at (x,y), then, you would locate the correct screen line by using the SCREENTBL array, like this:

```
char *line;
line=MK_FP(SCREENSEG,SCREENTBL[y]);
```

The byte that contains the pixel in question would be at `line[x / 8]`. Like multiplication, division is a procedure that takes an 8086 processor a relatively long time to perform. Division by eight can be simplified as shifting a value right by three places, and as such the calculation of the byte offset can be simplified to `line[x >> 3]`.

In write mask to be used to set the pixel at x will have one bit set. It can be calculated as 0×80 >> (x & 7). The values 0×80 is a byte with its high order bit set. It's shifted right by the value of the low order three bits of x, which is all that will be left when x is ANDed with seven.

This calculation can be further simplified as `masktable[x & 7]`. The `masktable` object turned up briefly in the last chapter. An explanation of its proper use will have to wait until nearer to the end of this one.

Here's a function to set pixels:

```
setpixel(x,y,c)
        int x,y,c;
{
        char *p;
        p=MK_FP(0xa000,SCREENTBL[y]+(x>>3));

        outportb(0x3ce,8);
        outportb(0x3cf,masktable[x & 0x0007]);

        outportb(0x3ce,5);
        outportb(0x3cf,2);

        *p=*p;
        *p=c;

        outportb(0x3ce,5);
        outportb(0x3cf,0);

        outportb(0x3ce,8);
        outportb(0x3cf,255);
}
```

By now you can probably walk through the workings of setpixel without much difficulty. Having derived a pointer to the screen line where the pixel to be set resides, the first pair of outportb calls set the write mask and the second pair set the VGA card up for write mode two. The following two lines do a dummy read and then the pixel write. Finally, the card is returned to write mode zero and the write mask is restored to all bits on, such that subsequent write operations aren't affected.

In real world applications, it's desirable to have `setpixel` operate as quickly as possible. For this reason, it's actually defined as a macro, rather than as a callable function, in the code to be presented later in this chapter.

Given two points on the screen, it should be possible to draw a line between them in any color you like. Clearly, this will entail multiple invocations of `setpixel`. Figuring out exactly where to set the pixels, however, is a little tricky. Allowing that line is not either perfectly horizontal or perfectly vertical, it might not be obvious how one would find all the points that lie along it without plotting numerous redundant points—that is, points that are mathematically different from each other but actually wind up as single pixels on your screen.

There is, in fact, an algorithm for drawing lines. It's called Bresenham's algorithm. It allows you to draw lines quickly and at any angle. It's also very easy to implement using nothing but integer math.

Bresenham's algorithm begins by calculating the slope of the line. In this example, we'll allow that the line to be drawn runs from (`left,top`) to (`right,bottom`)— that is, it's defined by the rectangular area that it crosses. We'll begin by figuring out which direction covers more distance:

```
x_delta=abs(right-left);
y_delta=abs(bottom-top);
```

Let's allow that `x_delta` is the larger of the two. In this case, the line is drawn by starting at the point (`left,top`) and incrementing `left` by one. There's a flag that will initially be positive—it's used to increment `top`. If the flag exceeds the change in the horizontal variable, it's made negative for the next iteration.

Clearly, this will create a line in which each successive point is an approximation of the accurate path of the line. However, because everything will be rounded to the nearest pixel, the result will be a drawn line in which all the points accurately track the theoretical path of the line.

Here's a `DrawLine` function based on Bresenham's algorithm. It calls `setpixel` to plot its points. Note that it also deals with lines that might be initially defined as having the wrong slope—lines that would in effect be plotted backwards. In these cases, rather than actually plotting backwards, it merely exchanges the start and end coordinates.

```
DrawLine(left,top,right,bottom,color)
        int left,top,right,bottom,color;
{
        int temp,dx,dy,x,y,x_sign,y_sign,flag;

        dx=abs(right - left);
        dy=abs(bottom - top);
        if(((dx >= dy) && (left > right)) ||
           ((dy > dx) && (top > bottom))) {
                temp=left;
                left=right;
                right=temp;
                temp=top;
                top=bottom;
                bottom=temp;
```

```
        }
        if((bottom - top) < 0) y_sign=-1;
        else y_sign=1;
        if((right - left) < 0) x_sign=-1;
        else x_sign=1;
        if (dx >= dy) {
                for(x=left,y=top,flag=0;x<=right;x++,
                                flag+=dy) {
                        if(flag>=dx) {
                                flag-=dx;
                                y+=y_sign;
                        }
                        setpixel(x,y,color);
                }
        }
        else {
                for(x=left,y=top,flag=0;y<=bottom;y++,
                                flag+=dx) {
                        if(flag>=dy) {
                                flag-=dy;
                                x+=x_sign;
                        }
                        setpixel(x,y,color);
                }
        }
}
```

More involved graphic libraries offer additional controls over line drawing—
allowing for lines of definable width, for example. You might want to see if you can
modify the DrawLine function to deal with this.

Drawing rectangles

Having created a function to draw lines, drawing rectangles is pretty easy. Here's
the function to handle it:

```
FrameRect(left,top,right,bottom,color)
        unsigned int left,top,right,bottom,color;
{
        DrawLine(left,top,right,top,color);
        DrawLine(left,bottom,right,bottom,color);
        DrawLine(left,top,left,bottom,color);
        DrawLine(right,top,right,bottom,color);
}
```

This is yet another one of those occasions wherein the oft' heard-from VGA gurus
will quite likely pipe up and wail about the incredible sloppiness of the foregoing
function. By making calls to DrawLine to draw lines that are constrained to be
either perfectly vertical or perfectly horizontal, a fair bit of time is wasted by
Bresenham's algorithm. None of those slope calculations and whatnot are really
called for in drawing a rectangle.

You can, in fact, write dedicated horizontal and vertical line drawing functions, and
if you do they will marginally improve the performance of FrameRect. The thing to
keep in mind, however, is that on all but the most barbaric first-generation, dust-
laden PCs, FrameRect can draw any rectangle you like pretty well instantaneously.
While it's possible to contrive a situation wherein lots of calls to FrameRect will

take a measurable amount of time—and in which a slightly faster `DrawRect` would be arguably desirable—these things rarely turn up in the real world.

The next chapter will illustrate an alternate approach to `FrameRect`.

If you really enjoyed the esoteric nature of write mode two when it turned up in some of the previous sections of this chapter, you'll probably be thoroughly delighted with this one. It uses write mode two to do in almost no time at all something that just seems to take forever in write mode zero.

Filling a rectangular area with a specific color is a lot like clearing the whole screen to a defined color, save that the left and right edges of the filled area aren't constrained to fall on convenient byte boundaries. This is the factor that really confuses the code. Now that I've said this, however, the solution to the problem turns out to fit in very well within the capabilities of write mode two.

One way to look at a filled rectangle is as a number of horizontal lines, one below the other. You could, as such, implement a function to fill rectangles very simply by drawing each line using calls to `setpixel`. While exceedingly easy to write, such a function would be pretty slow.

In fact, you can speed this up by drawing one line and then repeating it multiple times until the whole rectangular area had been filled. This is a lot faster and in fact results in a function that fills even large rectangles and runs pretty well instantly.

The `FillRect` function defines a mask that has set bits for all the pixels that will fall within the rectangle to be filled and unset bits outside it. The individual bytes of the mask can be used as write masks, just as the write masks in `ClearScreen` and `SetPixel` were. In this case, however, the write masks will represent set bits for all the points in the line that runs between the two extremes of the rectangular area to be filled.

The mask buffer will never require more than 100 bytes, as this is the maximum width of the screen. It can be set up using `masktable`. You might have to wait until the formal discussion of `masktable` later in this chapter to fully understand what it's up to.

Figure 3-3 illustrates how the mask is used to fill a rectangular area.

This, then, is `FillRect`. Squabbling VGA gurus probably won't have any complaints over this function—it uses all the underhanded techniques a VGA card can bring to bear on the problem, and runs at light speed.

```
FillRect(left,top,right,bottom,color)
        int left,top,right,bottom,color;
{
        char *p,bf[100];
        int a,i,j,width,depth,bleft,bytes;
        int xleft,xright,pleft,pright;

        xleft=left & 0xfff8;
        xright=right;
        if(xright & 0x0007) xright=(xright | 0x0007)+1;
        width=xright-xleft;
        depth=bottom-top;
        bleft=xleft>>3;
```

```
        pleft=left-xleft;
        pright=pleft+(right-left);
        bytes=pixels2bytes(width)+1;

          memset(bf,0,bytes);

          for(i=pleft;i<=pright;++i)
              bf[i>>3] |= masktable[i & 0x0007];

          for(i=0;i<=depth;++i) {
                  p=MK_FP(SCREENSEG,SCREENTBL[top+i]+bleft);
                  outportb(0x3ce,5);
                  outportb(0x3cf,2);

                  for(j=0;j<bytes;++j) {
                          outportb(0x3ce,8);
                          outportb(0x3cf,bf[j]);
                          a=p[j];
                          p[j]=color;
                  }
          }
          outportb(0x3ce,8);
          outportb(0x3cf,0xff);
          outportb(0x3ce,5);
          outportb(0x3cf,0);
    }
```

You'll note certain similarities between FillRect and ClearScreen. In
FillRect, the VGA card is placed in write mode two and each byte in the line
mask is in turn used to set the VGA write mask. The color value, as passed to the
function, is then written to the appropriate byte in the graphics screen buffer. Note
that here, too, a dummy read is required to correctly set up the VGA registers.

Mask

3-3
*Using a mask to fill a
rectangular area.*

Bitmap

When `FillRect` is complete, the card is returned to write mode zero and the write mask set with all its bits on, ready for whatever will come next.

Later on in this book we'll look at some very complex text drawing functions to handle proportionally spaced fonts and something approaching real typography. For the moment, though, it would be handy to be able to paint text on the screen. This is the sort of text that's used in menus and clickable buttons, among other things. Rather than looking elegant, such text should be quick to draw and easily readable.

In one sense, the code to draw text in super VGA graphics modes is already available; the system BIOS of most super VGA cards will paint crude text on the screen in any mode you select. This unquestionably has its limitations, however. At 800 by 600 pixels it's so small as to be almost unreadable. It can't be accurately positioned, nor will you have much control over the colors used to print it. Sophisticated, professional-looking graphics software must find better ways to handle this function.

The text used for menus and buttons and such is often referred to as "system" text, as opposed to the display text that a fancy word processor or desktop publishing package might draw on your screen. In this application, system text will be constrained to have certain useful characteristics. To begin with, it will be monospaced. This means that each character in the system text font will occupy the same number of pixels horizontally. This is as opposed to proportionally spaced text, such as the type you're reading now. Proportionally spaced screen text will have to wait for a few chapters.

Furthermore, the space that each character in the system text font will occupy will be constrained to be something convenient. Eight is the most convenient number a personal computer can imagine—eight it will be.

There's a rather obliging feature of the VGA BIOS that is rarely used. Correctly tickled, the VGA BIOS will return pointers to any of a number of system screen fonts. Two of these are of particular use. The first defines 256 characters that are eight pixels wide and eight pixels deep, while the second defines 256 characters that are eight pixels wide by sixteen pixels deep. It's the latter one that you'll probably find to be the most useful in 800 by 600 pixel graphics.

Here's how you would find a pointer to the eight by sixteen pixel screen found stored in your VGA BIOS.

```
struct REGPACK r;

r.r_ax=0x1130;
r.r_bx=0x0600;
intr(0x10,&r);

font=MK_FP(r.r_es,r.r_bp);
```

The `intr` function is an alternate Turbo C library call; it replaces the more familiar `int86`. It's used here because the data structure it calls for includes an element representing the value of the BP register, which this particular BIOS call requires. The value in the AX register when the call is made, 1130H, is the function and subfunction to return a pointer to a system font. The value in the BX register, 0600H, tells the BIOS that the eight by sixteen pixel font is being requested. Several other fonts are also on tap: using 0300H, for example, will return a pointer to the first 128 characters of the eight by eight pixel font.

Drawing a character in the eight by sixteen pixel system font is easy. In this example, we'll assume that the pointer font points to the eight by sixteen pixel font, as set by the foregoing call to the VGA BIOS. The following is some code to plot the character c at location (x,y) on the screen. This function is a bit simplistic, in that it will always plot characters in color 15 against a background of color 0.

```
char *p;
int i;

for(i=0;i<16;++i) {
        p=MK_FP(SCREENSEG,SCREENTBL[y+i]);
        p+=(x>>3);
        *p=font[(c<<4)+i];
}
```

You might find this a bit easier to understand if you consult FIG. 3-4. It illustrates how characters are set up in the eight by sixteen pixel system font.

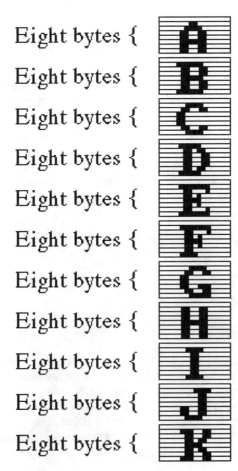

Eight bytes {

Eight bytes {

Eight bytes {

Eight bytes {

Eight bytes {

Eight bytes {

Eight bytes {

Eight bytes {

Eight bytes {

Eight bytes {

Eight bytes {

3-4
The monospaced system font structure.

In this example code to draw system text, the screen lines to receive the text are addressed by creating pointers from SCREENTBL, as has been done previously. The actual byte that the character to be drawn will occupy will live at x / 8 bytes along the line, or x >> 3. The character pattern will be c characters into the font. Because each character is sixteen bytes deep, character c will start c*16 bytes into the font. This can be written as c << 4.

There's a very important catch in all this. It's fast and easy to understand because it writes the bytes of the font data into bytes on the screen. This means that the horizontal position of text written this way must be evenly divisible by eight— or it will be rounded down to a value that is. This is, to be sure, a minor inconvenience in using system text. It's arguably compensated for by the speed at which even a lot of system text can be handled.

There are several things involved in creating a workable function to draw strings of text for real world software. It must be able to print strings, rather than individual characters, if it's to run at any reasonable speed. It must also be able to print text in any color against whatever background you like. While such a function could be written in C, it's fairly elemental in the creation of fast, workable graphic mode software. For this reason, the example function to be dealt with in this chapter, DrawString, will be handled in assembly language.

Here's what the equivalent C language function would look like. While not as fast as the assembly language version, it's considerably more lucid; if you understand what it's up to, you shouldn't have any difficulty seeing how the real DrawString works when it appears later in this chapter.

```
DrawString(x,y,s,color,background)
        unsigned int x,y;
        char *s;
        unsigned int color,background;
{
        char *p;
        int a,i,j,n;

        n=strlen(s);
        for(i=0;i<16++i) {
                p=MK_FP(SCREENSEG,SCREENTBL[y+i])+(x>>3);
                for(j=0;j<n;++j) {
                        outportb(0x3ce,5);
                        outportb(0x3cf,2);
                        outportb(0x3ce,8);
                        outportb(0x3cf,font[(c<<4)+i]);
                        a=*p;
                        *p=color;
                        outportb(0x3ce,5);
                        outportb(0x3cf,2);
                        outportb(0x3ce,8);
                        outportb(0x3cf,~font[(c<<4)+i]);
                        a=*p;
                        *p=background;
                        ++p;
                }
        }

                outportb(0x3ce,8);
```

```
                                          outportb(0x3cf,0xff);
                    outportb(0x3ce,5);
                    outportb(0x3cf,0);
            }
```

In this version of DrawString, the font is again assumed to be pointed to by font, and the font depth is assumed to be sixteen. Each byte of each character is actually written to the screen twice in write mode two. The first write paints all the bits that are set in the font in the foreground color. The second write NOTs the font data and paints all the bits that would normally be unset, this time in the background color.

Note that this code actually works by painting all the characters in a string one line at a time, rather than the whole first character, followed by the whole second character, and so on. Aside from looking better, this approach is actually genuinely faster.

As an aside, if you have cause to work with the Desktop Paint 16 package included on the companion disk for this book, you can see the assembly language version of DrawString in action. However, because Desktop Paint 16 runs in the standard VGA sixteen color mode, rather than in a super VGA 800 by 600 pixel mode, it uses an eight by eight pixel font. At the standard VGA resolution the size of the smaller font is acceptable, and it allows for still faster text drawing as there are fewer bytes per character to write to the screen.

The DrawString function in the assembly language module for this chapter can be set up to use either the eight by eight or eight by sixteen pixel VGA font. You can experiment with both, but you'll probably find that the larger font is pretty well mandatory for 800 by 600 pixel graphics.

Moving image fragments

The Borland BGI library functions getimage and putimage are among its more sophisticated inhabitants. Especially in dealing with 16-color graphics, they perform tasks that seem to be pretty remarkable. Despite the fact that graphics in a 16-color mode are bound up in byte orientations, getimage and putimage allow you to capture and paint image fragments regardless of where they fall in relation to the byte boundaries of your screen. More to the point, they do it fairly quickly.

There are two significant drawbacks to getimage and putimage in the context of this chapter. The first one is that the standard Borland BGI drivers don't support super VGA 800 by 600 pixel graphics as of this writing. Borland will provide you with tools to write your own custom BGI drivers, but using them is no simple undertaking. Secondly, because the BGI versions of these functions are constrained to work with image fragments no larger than 64K, there's a limit to the dimensions of the fragments they'll get and put.

There is a way around these problems, of course. You can write your own getimage and putimage functions. In fact, inasmuch as the code in this chapter doesn't use any of the BGI calls, doing so is pretty well essential if you want the facilities of moving image fragments around on your screen.

Let's begin the discussion of the problems of writing these functions with an understanding of what getimage is up to. In this simplified example, we'll deal with a monochrome getimage—the eventual 16-color version will work the same way, save that it will read each line four times, rather than just once.

It's probably worth noting that the hidden secrets of a VGA card offer almost no tricks to help `getimage` or `putimage`. Whatever works will have to be handled by raw animal cunning.

It would be pretty easy to copy an image fragment from a monochrome screen if the fragment could be constrained to rest between even byte boundaries, that is, if the left and right co-ordinates of the rectangle that enclosed it were evenly divisible by eight. You would just create a pointer to each line, count over by a suitable number of bytes and then copy the bytes within the area to be saved.

The restriction of having everything fall on 8-pixel boundaries would, of course, be a serious limitation.

Figure 3-5 illustrates the real problem.

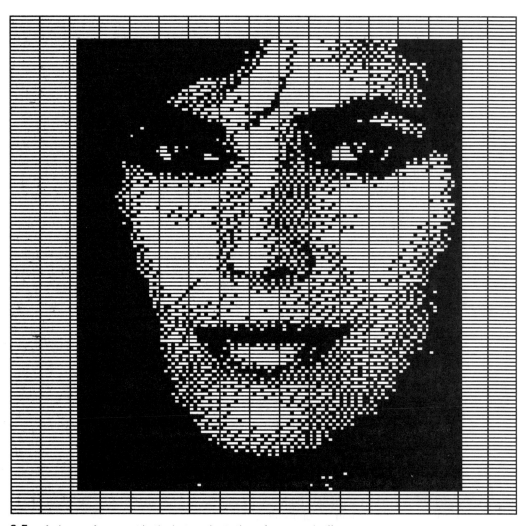

3-5 *An image fragment in the byte-orientation of a screen buffer.*

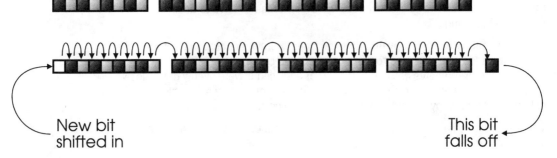

New bit
shifted in

This bit
falls off

3-6 *How a bit-field shift would work if one existed.*

In capturing a bitmap fragment that isn't byte-aligned, what we'd really like to do is to capture each line as if it were byte aligned and then somehow shift the bits to the left until all the bits between the byte boundary and the part of the bitmap we want had been shifted into oblivion. Sadly, the 8086 series of processors don't provide an instruction to shift whole bit fields; they only allow you to work on a byte or a word at a time.

The later 80286 and 80386 processors do include instructions that would be of some help in this, but using them to write a custom `getimage` function would make it unusable on machines with first-generation processors.

Figure 3-6 illustrates what a bit shift instruction would do to a line of image data if one did, in fact, exist.

In looking at FIG. 3-6—and keeping in mind the instructions that really do exist in an 8086-series processor—you can redefine the problem slightly. The difference between the portion of the image we'd like to capture and the actual byte alignment is three. There are, in fact, three bits hanging off the left edge of the picture. If we were to shift the first byte left by three places, those three bits would vanish and the first five pixels of the image would be correctly aligned.

If the second byte is shifted left by three places, its remaining five bits will be correctly aligned too. The problem with this is that the three bits that have been shifted out of the byte will have been lost, and there'd be a three pixel wide gap in the line. In fact, we don't really want to dispose of these bits; they should be used to fill the three pixel gap created by shifting the first byte left.

In reality, a function to shift a bit field left should catch the shifted-out bits of each byte and use them to fill in the gaps in the previous byte.

We can write a workable—and fairly fast—function to simulate this procedure using byte alignment. Here's what it looks like for a monochrome screen line. In this example, `ps` points to the screen—the source image line, which is probably not correctly byte aligned—and `pd` points to a line of the image fragment buffer where the image is to go. It will be correctly byte aligned in the image fragment buffer. The area to be captured is bounded by the values `left` and `right`. To begin with, we'll calculate a number of useful values:

```
width=pixels2bytes(right-left+1);
r=left & 7;
n-8-r;
start=left>>3
```

The value of width is the number of bytes contained between left and right. The value of r is the number of bits to shift each byte in the bit field left by to make it properly aligned in the destination image fragment. The value of n is the remaining number of bits in each byte. Finally, start is the offset from the left edge of the screen in bytes to the first byte of the source image data.

Here's how to do the copy and bit shift:

```
int a,i;

ps+=start;

for(i=0;i<width;++i) {
        a=ps[i+1] >> n;
        pd[i]=(ps[i] << r) | a;
}
```

This code is pretty fast, as it uses little more than addition and bitwise manipulation, two things an 8086-series processor is particularly good at.

As was noted in Chapter 2, a 16-color image fragment is structured as four planes for each line. To adapt the forgoing code to create 16-color image fragments, you would have to read the same area of the screen buffer four times for each line, having changed the planes between each read. The VGA card allows you to bring one plane at a time onto the bus for reading. Note that the state of the planes as they appear for writing has little to do with the state of the planes for reading.

The code in this chapter will use a macro called egareadplane to select which of the four planes is to be readable. Here it is:

```
#define egareadplane(n) \
     { outportb(0x3ce,4); outportb(0x3cf,(n)); }
```

The argument to egareadplane should be a value from 0 to 3, indicating which of the read planes you'd like to enable. Keep in mind that in creating an image fragment, the first plane in a line must be plane three in the screen buffer, not plane zero.

In creating a synthetic getimage function using the foregoing code, each plane will be width bytes apart, and each line width * 4 bytes apart. Because a 16-color image fragment can occupy more than 64K—and because one of the reasons for writing a new getimage function is to address this possibility—the pointer that addresses the image fragment buffer being filled must do so using farPtr, rather than simple pointer arithmetic. In fact, it's adequate to only call farPtr periodically, to normalize the pointer. It's called once per line, rather than at the end of every plane copy.

The complete GetImage16 function—our home made getimage—will appear in the example graphic program that created FIG. 3-1 later in this chapter.

If anything, the Turbo C putimage function is more useful than getimage. As was explored in detail in the previous chapter, you can create synthetic image fragments to use with `putimage`. Of course, the standard Turbo C `putimage` function suffers from the same limitations as `getimage` does. It's not much use in the super VGA graphics modes being dealt with in this chapter.

Writing a custom `putimage` function is a bit more involved than creating `GetImage16`. The example in this chapter will be inherently simpler than the Turbo C `putimage` function in that it will only perform the equivalent of the COPY_PUT option. It will place image fragments on your screen, but it will not be able to OR, XOR, AND or invert them.

The `putimage` function is passed an image fragment buffer that has been byte-aligned by `getimage` or by something pretending to be `getimage`. If it's asked to paint the image to your screen such that its left coordinate isn't evenly divisible by eight, it will have to do something like what `getimage` did, but in reverse. It will have to shift the bits of the image right until their position in the bytes which contain them matches that of the bytes in the screen buffer.

In fact, the procedure is a bit more complicated than this. Because it's constrained not to disturb any of the adjacent bits on the screen, `putimage` must place only the bits that are actually within the image being shifted. Some VGA card trickery will be called for to manage this.

The first thing we'll need to create `putimage` is a way to shift a field of bits right. In this example, `ps` will point to the line of an image fragment buffer to be copied to the screen and `pd` will point to the screen line, as derived from SCREENTBL. The objects `width`, `r`, `n` and `start` will be set up just as they were with `getimage`. Let's begin by seeing how the actual bit shift will work.

```
int a,i;

pd+=start;

a=0;
for(i=0;i<width;++i) {
        pd[i]=(ps[i] >> r) | a;
        a=ps[i] << n;
}
```

This fragment of code will place the source image in the correct position on your screen, but it will usually mangle the bits immediately adjacent to it.

The VGA write mask, hitherto only used in write mode two, is equally applicable to write mode zero. To make this code work properly, we must begin by creating a mask like the one used in `FillRect` and then use its bytes as write masks. We'll use a macro to set the bit mask:

```
#define setbitmask(n) \
    { outportb(0x3ce,8); outportb(0x3cf,(n)); }
```

Note that, as with write mode two, it's essential to perform a dummy read prior to each write. Here's the foregoing bit of code modified to correctly copy a line with a mask, such that the adjacent pixels are not disturbed. The mask is assumed to be in `mask`, an array of `chars`.

```
int a,i,nn;

pd+=start;
```

```
a=0;
for(i=0;i<width;++i) {
        setbitmask(mask[i]);
        nn=pd[i];
        pd[i]=(ps[i] >> r) | a;
        a=ps[i] << n;
}
```

Once again, you can find the complete PutImage16 function in the example
program later in this chapter.

It's probably worth noting that the Borland putimage and getimage functions
have been written in assembly language, rather than C, and are a good deal faster
than the ones in this chapter. You might want to try to transliterate these into
assembly language if you're ambitious—it's a bit of an undertaking, and not one
that will leave you with particularly lucid code. For most applications, you'll
probably find that the C language functions are quick enough.

If you understand how GetImage16 and PutImage16 work, you're probably ready
to tackle something truly nasty: that of making a mouse cursor work in an 800 by
600 pixel graphic mode. Alternately, if you really understand these functions, and
can imagine the potential complexity involved in making a mouse cursor move in
real time, you might just choose to use the code to be discussed here, and not
bother getting into the complexities of its workings.

There's a lot to be said for selective ignorance if you're chasing a deadline.

This section will assume that you have a Microsoft-compatible mouse in your
system, and that the mouse driver—usually MOUSE.COM—has been loaded.

The Microsoft mouse driver is a pretty clever little rodent and has all sorts of
hitherto unsuspected features. Among other things, it will animate a graphic cursor
for you in any of the standard PC display modes. You might want to try this little
program.

```
#include "stdio.h"
#include "dos.h"

main()
{
        union REGS r;
        int i,a=0x55;

        r.x.ax=0x0012;
        int86(0x10,&r,&r);

        for(i=0;i<480;++i)
            memset(MK_FP(0xa000,i*80),a ^= 0xff,80);

        r.x.ax=0x0000;
        int86(0x33,&r,&r);

        r.x.ax=0x0001;
        int86(0x33,&r,&r);
```

Animating a
mouse cursor

```
getch();

r.x.ax=0x0000;
int86(0x33,&r,&r);

r.x.ax=0x0003;
int86(0x10,&r,&r);
}
```

This program will put your VGA card in its standard 640 by 480 pixel, 16-color
graphics mode, and fill the screen with grey. It will then switch on the mouse
cursor and let it wander about the screen until you hit a key. Note that this program
will usually crash in some particularly nasty way if you don't have a mouse driver
loaded when you run it.

The INT 33H calls are hooks into the Microsoft mouse driver. We'll look at a few of
them in just a moment. In fact, for the standard VGA graphics modes, there are INT
33H calls to perform all sorts of useful mouse functions, such as turning the cursor
on and off, moving it, returning its position and button status, changing its
appearance, and so on. If you've begun to suspect that these won't be of much use
in a super VGA graphics mode, you're probably starting to get a good sense of
high-end graphics in general.

The graphic cursor that works so well in mode 12H, as in the foregoing example,
won't appear in one of the 800 by 600 pixel modes we've been using in this chapter.
If an application wants to use a mouse in one of these modes, it must animate the
cursor itself. The Microsoft mouse driver does provide hooks to help implement this,
but as you'll see in the code that handles it, doing so is not a trivial undertaking.

Specifically, you can pass a pointer to the Microsoft mouse driver through one of
the INT 33H functions such that the driver will call the function pointed to by the
pointer every time the mouse moves or one of its buttons is clicked. When it calls
your function, the driver will pass it the current mouse position and button status.
It's up to your function to actually move the cursor and put the button status
somewhere useful.

In a sense, animating a mouse cursor involves a specialized application of the
techniques explored in the previous section of this chapter. The cursor is a bitmap
of sorts, and it must be moved across the screen independent of its byte alignment.
In addition, however, the code to animate it must work very, very quickly. Some
substantial cheating is required.

A mouse cursor actually consists of two elements. The first is a "mask," which
knocks a black area out of whatever the cursor appears over. The second is the
cursor image itself, which will appear as a white area within the mask. Typically,
the mask will be one pixel larger than the cursor image, such that if the cursor
moves over a black area, you'll see the image, and if it moves over a white area,
you'll see the image surrounded by a thin black line.

Mouse cursors are constrained to have the dimensions sixteen by sixteen pixels. In
fact, this is a convention, and you're arguably free to change it if you have a good
reason for doing so. Keep in mind, however, that larger cursors will soak up more
processor time to animate.

Figure 3-7 illustrates the geography of the default arrow cursor and its mask. Note that as each line is sixteen pixels across, each line will fit in two bytes, or one word.

In moving a mouse cursor across your screen, the alignment of the bytes in the cursor bitmap will not match that of the bytes in the screen buffer for seven-eighths of the time. Figure 3-8 illustrates this. Note that even though the lines of the cursor only occupy two bytes, they can span up to three bytes of screen memory if the byte alignments don't match.

To draw the mouse cursor, then, it's necessary to shift the bits of each line of the original cursor mask and image right until it can be placed on the screen in the appropriate location. Unfortunately, although the source lines are really just one word wide—something that can be shifted pretty effortlessly by an 8086-series processor—the resulting object after the shift could occupy as many as three bytes. There are no 8086 machine instructions to deal with single objects larger than two bytes. As such, the code to animate a mouse cursor will have to simulate a bit shift pretty much like the code for putimage did. There will be two differences in this case, however. The first is that the whole works will be written in assembly language. The second is that in this case, the line lengths will always be the same.

As you will appreciate, there is no absolute black and white on a VGA card—color 0 is assumed to be the darkest one available and color 15 the lightest, but this will only be true if you set them as such. The mouse functions in this chapter assume that this will be so; if you set the extremes of the palette to similar colors, you might find the mouse cursor a bit hard to see.

As an aside, the Desktop Paint 16 package from the companion disk for this book is confronted with much the same problem and in an environment that will quite often present it with poor choices of colors for the extremes of the VGA palette. Its palette is set by whatever file it opens to edit. It gets around this by sorting the palettes of the files it opens such that the first color is always the darkest and the last one is always the lightest. This is something to consider if your applications will work with differing palettes.

3-7 *Two cursors and their masks.*

One Byte

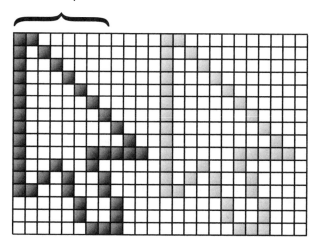

3-8
Animating a mouse cursor on a byte-oriented screen.

Once again, the work of animating a mouse cursor can be made a great deal simpler by using write mode two. In this case, the individual bytes of the cursor mask and image are read from the cursor pattern, shifted right by the appropriate number of bits and used as the write mask. This bit of code illustrates how the three bytes that make up one line of the cursor mask are handled. In this example, SI points to the cursor mask, DL contains the number of places to shift the cursor right, DH contains the number of places remaining, and DI points to the place on the current line where the cursor is to appear. The macro SETBITMASK, perhaps predictably, sets the write mask. The VGA card is assumed to be in write mode two.

```
MOV         AL,DS:[SI]
NOT         AL
MOV         CL,DL
SHR         AL,CL

SETBITMASK            AL
MOV         AL,ES:[DI]
MOV         BYTE PTR ES:[DI],00H

MOV         AH,DS:[SI]
NOT         AH
MOV         CL,DH
SHL         AH,CL
INC         SI
INC         DI

MOV         AL,DS:[SI]
NOT         AL
MOV         CL,DL
SHR         AL,CL
OR          AL,AH

SETBITMASK            AL
MOV         AL,ES:[DI]
MOV         BYTE PTR ES:[DI],00H

MOV         AH,DS:[SI]
NOT         AH
MOV         CL,DH
SHL         AH,CL
MOV         AL,AH
INC         SI
INC         DI

SETBITMASK            AL
MOV         AL,ES:[DI]
MOV         BYTE PTR ES:[DI],00H
```

If you work your way through this code, you'll find that it behaves very much like the putimage code discussed in the previous section did. It reads each of the bytes from the current line of the cursor mask—there are only two of them—and shifts them right by DL places. It then masks the screen with the resulting byte and writes zero to the appropriate byte of the screen buffer. This causes a black area to appear where the bits were set in the shifted mask byte. The remaining bits are shifted left by DH placed and OR'd with the next byte. The third byte is just whatever's left over in AH, shifted out from the second byte of the cursor mask.

The complete function to draw the two elements of a mouse cursor, DRAWCURSOR, will appear in the MOUSE16.ASM assembly language module to be presented later in this chapter.

In addition to being able to draw a mouse cursor, code that will animate one has to be able to preserve the area behind it. Making the mouse cursor appear to move really involves repeatedly copying the bytes behind it to a safe place, drawing the cursor, and then putting the copied bytes back where they were before the cursor moves on to a new location.

The functions to copy the background and then restore it, called CURSORBACK and HIDECURSOR herein, are pretty simple. They behave a bit like getimage and putimage; but because they operate in very predictable circumstances, they can be written to avoid any bit shifting or other processor-intensive data manipulation. Wherever the mouse cursor is, the area behind it can be no more than three bytes across by sixteen lines deep. Calculating where in the 24-bit wide field the mouse cursor resides can be a bit tricky, as we've seen, but this doesn't really matter to CURSORBACK and HIDECURSOR. They simply work with the whole 24 by 16 pixel area the mouse cursor might inhabit.

Finally, we'll need a function for the Microsoft mouse driver to call every time the mouse moves. Here's what it looks like:

```
MOUSEHANDLER  PROC  FAR
              PUSHF

              CLI

              LDATASEG

              MOV     [MOUSEB],BX

              CMP     [MOUSEF],0000H
              JL      MH1

              PUSH    AX
              PUSH    BX
              PUSH    CX
              PUSH    DX
              CALL    ERASECURSOR
              POP     DX
              POP     CX
              POP     BX
              POP     AX

              MOV     [MOUSEX],CX
              MOV     [MOUSEY],DX

              SHR     WORD PTR CS:[MOUSEX],1
                      SHR     WORD PTR CS:[MOUSEX],1

              CALL    CURSORBACK
```

```
                 CALL      DRAWCURSOR
        MH1:      POPF
                  RETF
        MOUSEHANDLER ENDP
```

When the mouse driver calls this function, the BX register will contain the current
button status. The first bit will be set if the left button is down and the second bit
will be set if the right button is down. The CX register will contain the current
horizontal position of the mouse and the DX register the current vertical position.
It's important to note that when this function is called, the DS register will contain
the data segment of the Microsoft mouse driver, rather than that of your
application. The function called by the driver must be sure to establish its own data
segment. In this case, it's taken care of by the LDATASEG macro.

A bit more will be said about the mouse management code toward the end of this
chapter.

Creating & managing 3-D buttons

With the advent of Windows 3.0, three-dimensional buttons seem to have become
all the rage. They're not actually that hard to do, and will help make any application
that uses a Windows-like interface seem a lot more contemporary and slick.

There is a catch to this, however. Buttons are part of a graphical user interface. The
complex part in managing a complete user interface is not in drawing the graphical
objects *per se*, but rather in keeping track of lots of objects and dealing with them
in a sensible, efficient way. The code to be examined herein will illustrate how to
draw and work with a few buttons. Be warned, though—if you try to write a whole
user interface this way, you'll wind up with a very large, very sloppy program that
won't work very well.

If you'd like to create your own graphical user interface along lines that won't leave
you enmired in a pit of virtual boa constrictors, you might want to have a look at my
book *Graphical User Interface Programming*, published by Windcrest.

Figure 3-9 illustrates some three-dimensional buttons.

3-9
Three-dimensional buttons.

The three-dimensional appearance of the buttons in FIG. 3-9 is achieved by simulating the appearance of light falling on a raised solid object. The object itself is light grey. The upper and left edges are shaded white, to simulate the areas light would be reflected from. The lower and right edges are shaded dark grey, to simulate the areas in shadow.

You can create three-dimensional buttons with much greater depth by increasing the size of the shaded areas. Consider, however, that buttons that seem to be raised half an inch from the surface of your monitor will arguably look a bit unreal.

This is a function to make a rectangular area look three-dimensional:

```
Fill3DBox(left,top,right,bottom)
        int left,top,right,bottom;
{

        FillRect(left,top,right,bottom,LIGHTGREY);
        DrawLine(left,top,right-1,top,WHITE);
        DrawLine(left,top+1,left,bottom-1,WHITE);

        DrawLine(left+3,bottom,right,bottom,DARKGREY);
        DrawLine(right,top+2,right,bottom-1,DARKGREY);
}
```

The Fill3DBox function uses calls to some of the other graphic primitives examined in this chapter. It fills a rectangular area with FillRect and then draws in the shaded areas. The FillRect function is called by DrawButton.

```
DrawButton(button)
        BUTTON *button;
{

        FillRect(button->frame.left+1,button->frame.top+1,
                button->frame.right-1,button->frame.bottom-1,
                WHITE);
        DrawLine(button->frame.left+1,button->frame.top,
                button->frame.right-1,button->frame.top,
                BLACK);
        DrawLine(button->frame.left,button->frame.top+1,
                button->frame.left,button->frame.bottom-1,
                BLACK);
        DrawLine(button->frame.right,button->frame.top+1,
                button->frame.right,button->frame.bottom-1,
                BLACK);
        DrawLine(button->frame.left+1,button->frame.bottom,
                button->frame.right-1,button->frame.bottom,
                BLACK);

        Fill3DBox(button->frame.left+1,button->frame.top+1,
                button->frame.right-1,button->frame.bottom-1);
        DrawString(button->frame.left+8,button->frame.top+4,
                button->text,DARKGREY,LIGHTGREY);
}
```

The `DrawButton` function draws the frame of the button and uses `Fill3DBox` to create its interior. Note that it uses four calls to `DrawLine` rather than one call to `FrameRect`. The four lines don't quite meet at the corners, and the one-pixel gaps help to create the illusion that the button being created has rounded corners.

The `DrawString` call puts the text in the button.

The argument passed to `DrawButton` is an object of the type BUTTON. Here's what it looks like:

```
typedef struct {
        RECT frame;
        char *text;
        } BUTTON;
```

This, in turn, uses another defined object, a RECT.

```
typedef struct {
        unsigned int left,top,right,bottom;
        } RECT;
```

A RECT object defines any rectangular area on the screen. The RECT object that appears in a BUTTON defines where the frame of the button resides. The `MakeButton` function sets up the elements of a BUTTON object passed to it, including the RECT that defines its frame. The resulting button will be sized to fit the text that it contains.

```
MakeButton(left,top,string,button)
        unsigned int left,top;
        char *string;
        BUTTON *button;
{
        button->frame.left = left & 0xfff8;
        button->frame.right=button->frame.left+
            (strlen(string)<<3)+16;
        button->frame.top=top;
        button->frame.bottom=button->frame.top+FONTDEPTH+8;
        button->text=string;
}
```

Note that `MakeButton` rounds the left coordinate down to the nearest value that's evenly divisible by eight. This takes into account that even though the graphic drawing and filling functions can deal with values that aren't byte aligned, `DrawString` cannot.

Having created and drawn a button, the program that uses it must respond to clicking in it. This is called "tracking" a button. In this case, tracking involves drawing the button to make it look depressed, waiting for the mouse to be released and then redrawing it normally.

As will be dealt with shortly, when you click your mouse, your program can retrieve an object of the type POINT that will define its location at the time of the click. This is what a POINT looks like:

```
typedef struct {
        unsigned int x,y;
```

```
        } POINT;
```
You can decide whether a mouse click has taken place within the area defined by a
BUTTON object by using the function `PointInRect`. It looks like this.

```
PointInRect(p,r)
        POINT *p;
        RECT *r;
{
        if(p->x > r->left && p->x < r->right &&
           p->y > r->top  && p->y < r->bottom) return(1);
        else return (0) ;
}
```

The `PointInRect` function will return a true value if the POINT object passed to it
defines a point inside the RECT object.

Having noticed that the mouse has been clicked, a program managing one or more
buttons would test each one to see if the click has taken place within its frame. If a
click is found to be within a button, the program would call `TrackButton`, and
then whatever functions the button is intended to invoke. Here's the code for
`TrackButton`.

```
TrackButton(button)
        BUTTON *button;
{
        POINT p;

        FillRect(button->frame.left+1,button->frame.top+1,
                button->frame.right-1,
                button->frame.bottom-1,LIGHTGREY);
        DrawString(button->frame.left+8,button->frame.top+4,
                button->text,DARKGREY,LIGHTGREY);
        while(MouseDown(&p));
        DrawButton(button);
}
```

Some of this code will probably have to wait for a formal explanation of the mouse
functions in this chapter before it will make complete sense.

If you experiment with one of the paint packages on the companion disk for this
book, you'll probably notice a similarity between the buttons described in this
chapter and those in Desktop Paint. In fact, this code has been abstracted from
Desktop Paint. However, while the buttons are drawn and tracked by the same
code, the extensive library of functions to manage controls that drives Desktop
Paint is not discussed herein. As you might appreciate, a program that wanted to
manage an extensive list of controls by calling `PointInRect` to check each mouse
click for each control would get pretty unwieldy pretty quickly.

Capturing the screen to a PCX file

In a graphics mode, the screen of a VGA card is really just a somewhat oddly
structured bitmap. You can copy the bitmapped lines from the screen buffer and
write them to an image file if you like. The same code that created PCX files from
image fragments back in Chapter 2 can be used to create a PCX screen capture.

It's worth keeping in mind that commercial resident screen capture programs don't
usually support the super VGA graphics modes and as such won't capture the
screen of a super VGA card when it's in one of these modes. If you think the users

of your applications might require the ability to capture screens, you should probably build this feature in.

An integral screen capture function was required to capture the screen for FIG. 3-1 at the beginning of this chapter, for example.

Capturing a 16-color screen to a PCX file is fairly simple. A PCXHEAD object, as defined in Chapter 2, must be loaded with the appropriate dimension and color depth values and then written to the destination file. Each line can then be written to the file by bringing the four screen planes onto the bus for reading, one at a time, and calling the pcxwriteline function to compress them. Make sure the mouse cursor is hidden during the write.

The function to handle this in the test program to be described next is called DoSave. You'll find it to be functionally identical to the FRG2PCX code from chapter two, save for the calls to egareadplane in the main write loop.

The MOUSE16.ASM code module

When it's linked to a C language calling program, the MOUSE16 module will provide you with a complete mouse interface for use in an 800 by 600 pixel, 16-color super VGA graphics mode. It also contains selected graphic functions that benefit by being handled in assembly language.

Figure 3-10 illustrates the complete source code for MOUSE16.ASM.

3-10
The source code for MOUSE16.ASM.

```
;
;                       Mouse Functions for 16-colour
;                       Super VGA graphics
;

_AOFF           EQU     6  ;STACK OFFSET TO FIRST ARG

CURSORWIDE      EQU     16 ;CURSOR DIMENSIONS
CURSORDEEP      EQU     16
CURSORBYTES     EQU     (CURSORWIDE SHR 3)

SCREENWIDE      EQU     800;SCREEN DIMENSIONS
SCREENDEEP      EQU     600

FONTEIGHT       EQU     0  ;SET ONE OF THESE TRUE FOR THE
FONTSIXTEEN     EQU     1  ;SCREEN FONT SIZE

;SET ALL FOUR WRITE PLANES ON
FOURPLANES      MACRO
                PUSH    AX
                PUSH    DX
                MOV     DX,03C4H
                MOV     AL,02H
                OUT     DX,AL
                MOV     DX,03C5H
                MOV     AL,0FH
                OUT     DX,AL
                POP     DX
                POP     AX
                ENDM

;THIS MACRO FETCHES THE DATA SEGEMENT
```

```
LDATASEG        MACRO
                PUSH    AX
                MOV     AX,_DATA
                MOV     DS,AX
                POP     AX
                ENDM

; SET ONE OR MORE WRITE PLANES ON
EGAWRITEPLANE   MACRO   ARG
                PUSH    AX
                PUSH    DX
                MOV     DX,03C4H
                MOV     AL,02H
                OUT     DX,AL
                MOV     DX,03C5H
                MOV     AL,ARG
                OUT     DX,AL
                POP     DX
                POP     AX
                ENDM

; SET ONE READ PLANE ON
EGAREADPLANE    MACRO   ARG
                PUSH    AX
                PUSH    DX
                MOV     DX,03CEH
                MOV     AL,04H
                OUT     DX,AL
                MOV     DX,03CFH
                MOV     AL,ARG
                OUT     DX,AL
                POP     DX
                POP     AX
                ENDM

;SET THE CURRENT WRITE MODE
SETWRITEMODE    MACRO   ARG
                PUSH    AX
                PUSH    DX
                MOV     DX,03CEH
                MOV     AL,05H
                OUT     DX,AL
                MOV     DX,03CFH
                MOV     AL,ARG
                OUT     DX,AL
                POP     DX
                POP     AX
                ENDM

;SET THE WRITE MASK
SETBITMASK      MACRO   ARG
                PUSH    AX
                PUSH    DX
                PUSH    AX
                MOV     DX,03CEH
```

3-10
Continued.

```
                              MOV      AL,08H
                              OUT      DX,AL
                              POP      AX
                              MOV      DX,03CFH
                              MOV      AL,ARG
                              OUT      DX,AL
                              POP      DX
                              POP      AX
                              ENDM

              ;DO A LONG LOOP
              LNGLOOP         MACRO    ARG1
                              LOCAL    LAB1
                              DEC      CX
                              CMP      CX,0000H
                              JE       LAB1
                              JMP      ARG1
              LAB1:
                              ENDM

              MOUSE16_TEXT    SEGMENT BYTE PUBLIC ´CODE´
                              ASSUME  CS:MOUSE16_TEXT,DS:_DATA

              ;               ARG1 = X
              ;               ARG2 = Y
              ;               ARG3 = STRING
              ;               ARG4 = COLOUR
              ;               ARG6 = BACKGROUND
                              PUBLIC  _DrawString
              _DrawString     PROC     FAR
                              PUSH     BP
                              MOV      BP,SP
                              PUSH     DS
                              PUSH     ES

                              LDATASEG

                              CALL     HIDECURSOR
                              SETWRITEMODE      2

                              ;POINT TO THE SCREEN SEGMENT
                              MOV      AX,[_SCREENSEG]
                              MOV      ES,AX

                              ;POINT TO THE CORRECT BYTE
                              MOV      CL,3
                              SHR      WORD PTR [BP + _AOFF + 0],CL

                              ;LOOP THROUGH ALL THE LINES
                              MOV      CX,[_FONTDEPTH]
              DSO:            PUSH     CX
                              DEC      CX

                              ;GET THE BOTTOM LINE — WE COUNT BACKWARDS
                              MOV      BX,[BP + _AOFF + 2]
```

```
            ADD     BX,CX
            SHL     BX,1

            ;GET THE SCREEN POINTER
            LDATASEG
            MOV     DI,DS:[_SCREENTBL+BX]
            ADD     DI,[BP + _AOFF + 0]

            ;POINT TO THE START OF THE STRING
            MOV     SI,[BP + _AOFF + 4]
            MOV     DS,[BP + _AOFF + 6]

            ;STOP LOOPING WHEN A NULL BYTE IS REACHED
DS1:        MOV     AH,00H
            MOV     AL,DS:[SI]
            CMP     AL,00H
            JE      DS3

DS2:        PUSH    DS
            PUSH    SI

            ;FIND THE FONT CHARACTER
            MUL     [_FONTDEPTH]

            ;GET THE BYTE OFFSET
            MOV     BX,AX
            ADD     BX,CX

            PUSH    CX

            ;GET THE BYTE FROM THE FONT
            MOV     SI,[_FONTOFF]
            MOV     DS,[_FONTSEG]
            MOV     AH,DS:[SI+BX]

            ;GET THE FOREGROUND COLOUR
            MOV     CX,[BP + _AOFF + 8]

            ;SET THE BIT MASK
            SETBITMASK      AH

            ;DO THE DUMMY READ AND THE WRITE
            MOV     AL,ES:[DI]
            MOV     ES:[DI],CL

            ;GET THE BACKGROUND COLOR
            MOV     CX,[BP + _AOFF + 10]

            ;SET THE BIT MASK
            NOT     AH
            SETBITMASK      AH

            ;DO THE DUMMY READ AND WRITE
            MOV     AL,ES:[DI]
            MOV     ES:[DI],CL
```

The MOUSE16.ASM code module 137

```
                        POP      CX

                        INC      DI

                        POP      SI
                        POP      DS

                        INC      SI

                        JMP      DS1

        DS3:            POP      CX
                        LOOP     DS0

                        ;RESTORE THE BIT MASK TO ALL BITS ON
                        SETBITMASK OFFH

                        ;RESTORE WRITE MODE ZERO
                        SETWRITEMODE        0

                        LDATASEG
                        CALL     SHOWCURSOR

                        POP      ES
                        POP      DS
                        POP      BP
                        RET
        _DrawString     ENDP

                        PUBLIC   _InitMouse
        _InitMouse      PROC     FAR
                        PUSH     BP
                        MOV      BP,SP
                        PUSH     DS
                        PUSH     ES

                        LDATASEG

                        ;INITALIZE THE FONT POINTER
                        IF       FONTEIGHT
                        MOV      AX,1130H
                        MOV      BX,0300H
                        INT      10H
                        MOV      [_FONTSEG],ES
                        MOV      [_FONTOFF],BP
                        MOV      [_FONTDEPTH],0008H
                        ENDIF    ;FONTEIGHT

                        IF       FONTSIXTEEN
                        MOV      AX,1130H
                        MOV      BX,0600H
                        INT      10H
                        MOV      [_FONTSEG],ES
                        MOV      [_FONTOFF],BP
                        MOV      [_FONTDEPTH],0010H
                        ENDIF    ;FONTSIXTEEN
```

```
        ;SEE IF THERE'S A MOUSE HANDLER
        MOV     AX,3533H
        INT     21H
        MOV     AX,ES
        OR      AX,BX
        JZ      INITMOUSE1

        ;INITIALIZE THE MOUSE
        MOV     AX,0000H
        INT     33H

        ;CHECK TO SEE IT'S THERE
        CMP     AX,0000H
        JE      INITMOUSE1

        ;SET THE HORIZONTAL RANGE
        MOV     AX,0007H
        MOV     CX,0000H
        MOV     DX,[_SCREENWIDE]
        SUB     DX,CURSORWIDE
        SHL     DX,1
        SHL     DX,1
        INT     33H

        ;SET THE VERTICAL RANGE
        MOV     AX,0008H
        MOV     CX,0000H
        MOV     DX,[_SCREENDEEP]
        SUB     DX,CURSORDEEP
        INT     33H

        ;PUT THE CURSOR IN THE CENTRE OF THE SCREEN
        MOV     AX,0004H
        MOV     CX,[_SCREENWIDE]
        SHL     CX,1
        MOV     DX,[_SCREENDEEP]
        SHR     DX,1
        INT     33H

        ;SET THE MOUSE SENSITIVITY
        MOV     AX,000FH
        MOV     CX,0003H
        MOV     DX,0010H
        INT     33H

        ;SET THE INITIAL POSITION
        MOV     AX,[_SCREENWIDE]
        SHR     AX,1
        MOV     [MOUSEX],AX

        MOV     AX,[_SCREENDEEP]
        SHR     AX,1
        MOV     [MOUSEY],AX

;SHOW THE CURSOR
        CALL    SHOWCURSOR
```

```
                        ;SET THE MOUSE HANDLER HOOK
                        MOV     AX,CS
                        MOV     ES,AX
                        MOV     AX,000CH
                        MOV     CX,001FH
                        MOV     DX,OFFSET MOUSEHANDLER
                        INT     33H

                        ;SAY ALL IS WELL
                        MOV     AX,0FFFFH

INITMOUSE1:             POP     ES
                        POP     DS
                        POP     BP
                        RET
_InitMouse             ENDP

                        PUBLIC  _DeinitMouse
_DeinitMouse           PROC    FAR
                        PUSH    BP
                        MOV     BP,SP
                        PUSH    DS
                        PUSH    ES

                        MOV     AX,0000H
                        INT     33H

                        POP     ES
                        POP     DS
                        POP     BP
                        RET
_DeinitMouse           ENDP

;                       ARG1 = COLOUR TO CLEAR TO
                        PUBLIC  _ClearScreen
_ClearScreen           PROC    FAR
                        PUSH    BP
                        MOV     BP,SP
                        PUSH    DS
                        PUSH    ES

                        CALL    HIDECURSOR

                        MOV     CX,[_SCREENDEEP]
                        MOV     ES,[_SCREENSEG]

                        MOV     BX,0000H

                        SETWRITEMODE    2

                        MOV     AH,BYTE PTR [BP + _AOFF + 0]

CS1:                    PUSH    CX
                        PUSH    BX
```

```
                       SHL     BX,1
                       MOV     DI,[_SCREENTBL+BX]

                       MOV     CX,[_SCREENBYTES]

          CS2:         SETBITMASK OFFH

                       MOV     AL,ES:[DI]
                       MOV     ES:[DI],AH

                       INC     DI
                       LOOP    CS2

                       POP     BX
                       POP     CX

                       INC     BX

                       LOOP    CS1

                       SETBITMASK      OFFH
                       SETWRITEMODE    0

                       LDATASEG
                       CALL    SHOWCURSOR

                       FOURPLANES

                       POP     ES
                       POP     DS
                       POP     BP
                       RET
          _ClearScreen ENDP

                       PUBLIC  _MouseOn
          _MouseOn     PROC    FAR
                       PUSH    BP
                       MOV     BP,SP
                       PUSH    DS
                       PUSH    ES

                       LDATASEG
                       CALL    SHOWCURSOR

                       POP     ES
                       POP     DS
                       POP     BP
                       RET
          _MouseOn     ENDP

                       PUBLIC  _MouseOff
          _MouseOff    PROC    FAR
                       PUSH    BP
                       MOV     BP,SP
                       PUSH    DS
                       PUSH    ES
```

```
                        LDATASEG
                        CALL    HIDECURSOR

                        POP     ES
                        POP     DS
                        POP     BP
                        RET
_MouseOff               ENDP

                        PUBLIC  _MouseDown
_MouseDown              PROC    FAR
                        PUSH    BP
                        MOV     BP,SP
                        PUSH    DS
                        PUSH    ES

                        LDATASEG
                        MOV     DI,[BP + _AOFF + 0]
                        MOV     ES,[BP + _AOFF + 2]

                        MOV     AX,[MOUSEX]
                        ADD     AX,[SPOTX]
                        STOSW

                        MOV     AX,[MOUSEY]
                        ADD     AX,[SPOTY]
                        STOSW

                        MOV     AX,[MOUSEB]
                        AND     AX,0003H

                        POP     ES
                        POP     DS
                        POP     BP
                        RET
_MouseDown              ENDP

;                       ARG1 = CURSOR
;                       ARG2 = HOTSPOT X
;                       ARG3 = HOTSPOT Y
                        PUBLIC  _MouseCursor
_MouseCursor            PROC    FAR
                        PUSH    BP
                        MOV     BP,SP
                        PUSH    DS
                        PUSH    ES

                        LDATASEG
                        CALL    HIDECURSOR

                        MOV     SI,[BP+_AOFF+0]
                        MOV     DS,[BP+_AOFF+2]

                        MOV     AX,_DATA
                        MOV     ES,AX
                        MOV     DI,OFFSET DEFAULTCURSOR
```

```
                    MOV         CX,32
                    CLD
    MC1:            LODSW
                    XCHG        AL,AH
                    STOSW
                    LOOP        MC1

                    MOV         AX,[BP+_AOFF+4]
                    MOV         BX,[BP+_AOFF+6]

                    MOV         [SPOTX],AX
                    MOV         [SPOTY],BX

                    LDATASEG
                    CALL        SHOWCURSOR

                    POP         ES
                    POP         DS
                    POP         BP
                    RET
    _MouseCursor    ENDP

    ;
    ;                   INTERNAL FUNCTIONS
    ;

    ; HANDLE MOUSE MOVEMENT - THIS FUNCTION CALLED WHENEVER THE MOUSE
    ; CHANGES STATE. IT'S CALLED BY THE MOUSE DRIVER

    MOUSEHANDLER    PROC        FAR
                    PUSHF

                    CLI

                    LDATASEG

                    MOV         [MOUSEB],BX

                    CMP         [MOUSEF],0000H
                    JL          MH1

                    PUSH        AX
                    PUSH        BX
                    PUSH        CX
                    PUSH        DX
                    CALL        ERASECURSOR
                    POP         DX
                    POP         CX
                    POP         BX
                    POP         AX

                    MOV         [MOUSEX],CX
                    MOV         [MOUSEY],DX

                    SHR         WORD PTR [MOUSEX],1
                    SHR         WORD PTR [MOUSEX],1
```

```
                          CALL    CURSORBACK
                          CALL    DRAWCURSOR

        MH1:              POPF
                          RETF
        MOUSEHANDLER      ENDP

        DRAWCURSOR        PROC    NEAR

                          LDATASEG

                          FOURPLANES

                          MOV     CX,CURSORDEEP
                          MOV     BX,[MOUSEY]

                          MOV     SI,OFFSET DEFAULTCURSOR

                          MOV     DX,[MOUSEX]
                          AND     DX,0007H

                          MOV     DH,08H
                          SUB     DH,DL

                          SETWRITEMODE      2

        DC1:              PUSH    CX
                          PUSH    BX

                          ;GET THE LINE TO WRITE
                          SHL     BX,1
                          MOV     DI,[_SCREENTBL+BX]
                          MOV     ES,[_SCREENSEG]

                          ;POINT TO THE START OF THE CURSOR
                          MOV     AX,[MOUSEX]
                          MOV     CL,3
                          SHR     AX,CL
                          ADD     DI,AX

                          PUSH    DI

                          MOV     AL,DS:[SI]
                          NOT     AL
                          MOV     CL,DL
                          SHR     AL,CL

                          SETBITMASK AL
                          MOV     AL,ES:[DI]
                          MOV     BYTE PTR ES:[DI],00H

                          MOV     AH,DS:[SI]
                          NOT     AH
                          MOV     CL,DH
                          SHL     AH,CL
```

```
        INC     SI
        INC     DI

        MOV     AL,DS:[SI]
        NOT     AL
        MOV     CL,DL
        SHR     AL,CL
        OR      AL,AH

        SETBITMASK      AL
        MOV     AL,ES:[DI]
        MOV     BYTE PTR ES:[DI],00H

        MOV     AH,DS:[SI]
        NOT     AH
        MOV     CL,DH
        SHL     AH,CL
        MOV     AL,AH
        INC     SI
        INC     DI

        SETBITMASK      AL
        MOV     AL,ES:[DI]
        MOV     BYTE PTR ES:[DI],00H

        POP     DI
        PUSH    SI

        ADD     SI,30

        MOV     AL,DS:[SI]
        MOV     CL,DL
        SHR     AL,CL

        SETBITMASK      AL
        MOV     AL,ES:[DI]
        MOV     BYTE PTR ES:[DI],0FH

        MOV     AH,DS:[SI]
        MOV     CL,DH
        SHL     AH,CL
        INC     SI
        INC     DI

        MOV     AL,DS:[SI]
        MOV     CL,DL
        SHR     AL,CL
        OR      AL,AH

        SETBITMASK      AL
        MOV     AL,ES:[DI]
        MOV     BYTE PTR ES:[DI],0FH

        MOV     AH,DS:[SI]
        MOV     CL,DH
        SHL     AH,CL
```

```
                    MOV       AL,AH
                    INC       SI
                    INC       DI

                    SETBITMASK      AL
                    MOV       AL,ES:[DI]
                    MOV       BYTE PTR ES:[DI],0FH

                    POP       SI

                    POP       BX
                    POP       CX

                    INC       BX

                    LNGLOOP DC1

                    SETWRITEMODE    0
                    SETBITMASK      0FFH

                    RET
DRAWCURSOR          ENDP

;ERASE THE CURSOR
ERASECURSOR         PROC      NEAR

                    MOV       DX,0000H

                    MOV       CX,0004H
                    MOV       BX,0000H

EC1:                PUSH      CX
                    PUSH      BX

                    MOV       BH,01H
                    MOV       CL,BL
                    SHL       BH,CL

                    EGAWRITEPLANE   BH

                    MOV       BX,[MOUSEY]
                    MOV       CX,CURSORDEEP

EC2:                PUSH      CX
                    PUSH      BX

                    ;GET THE LINE TO WRITE
                    SHL       BX,1
                    MOV       DI,[_SCREENTBL+BX]
                    MOV       ES,[_SCREENSEG]

                    ;POINT TO THE FIRST BYTE
                    MOV       AX,[MOUSEX]
                    MOV       CL,3
                    SHR       AX,CL
                    ADD       DI,AX
```

```
                MOV       BX,DX

                MOV       AX,WORD PTR DS:[MOUSEBACK+BX]
                MOV       ES:[DI],AX
                MOV       AL,DS:[MOUSEBACK+BX+2]
                MOV       ES:[DI+2],AL

                ADD       DX,0003H

                POP       BX
                POP       CX

                INC       BX

                LOOP      EC2

                POP       BX
                POP       CX

                INC       BX

                LOOP      EC1

                FOURPLANES

                RET
ERASECURSOR     ENDP

;COPY THE CURSOR BACKGROUND TO MEMORY
CURSORBACK      PROC      NEAR

                LDATASEG

                MOV       DX,0000H

                MOV       CX,0004H
                MOV       BX,0000H

CC1:            PUSH      CX
                PUSH      BX

                EGAREADPLANE    BL

                MOV       BX,[MOUSEY]
                MOV       CX,CURSORDEEP

CC2:            PUSH      CX
                PUSH      BX

                ;GET THE LINE TO WRITE
                SHL       BX,1
                MOV       SI,[_SCREENTBL+BX]
                MOV       ES,[_SCREENSEG]

                ;POINT TO THE FIRST BYTE
```

```
                        MOV     AX,[MOUSEX]
                        MOV     CL,3
                        SHR     AX,CL
                        ADD     SI,AX

                        MOV     BX,DX

                        MOV     AX,ES:[SI]
                        MOV     WORD PTR DS:[MOUSEBACK+BX],AX
                        MOV     AL,ES:[SI+2]
                        MOV     DS:[MOUSEBACK+BX+2],AL

                        ADD     DX,0003H

                        POP     BX
                        POP     CX

                        INC     BX

                        LOOP    CC2

                        POP     BX
                        POP     CX

                        INC     BX

                        LOOP    CC1

                        FOURPLANES

                        RET
CURSORBACK              ENDP

                        PUBLIC HIDECURSOR
; MAKE THE CURSOR DISAPPEAR
HIDECURSOR              PROC    FAR
                        PUSHF
                        CLI
                        DEC     [MOUSEF]
                        CMP     [MOUSEF],-1
                        JL      HC1
                        CALL    ERASECURSOR

HC1:                    POPF
                        RET
HIDECURSOR              ENDP

                        PUBLIC SHOWCURSOR
; SHOW THE CURSOR
SHOWCURSOR              PROC    FAR
                        PUSHF
                        CLI
                        INC     [MOUSEF]
                        CMP     [MOUSEF],0000H
                        JG      SC1
```

```
                CALL    CURSORBACK
                CALL    DRAWCURSOR

SC1:            POPF
                RET
SHOWCURSOR      ENDP

MOUSE16_TEXT    ENDS

DGROUP          GROUP   _DATA,_BSS
_DATA           SEGMENT WORD PUBLIC 'DATA'

; THIS MACRO CREATES A TABLE
SCREENTABLE     MACRO   W,D
                X = 0
                REPT    D
                DW      X
                X = X + (W / 8)
                ENDM
                ENDM

                PUBLIC  _SCREENTBL,_SCREENSEG,_SCREENBYTES
                PUBLIC  _SCREENWIDE,_SCREENDEEP
                PUBLIC  _MASKTABLE,_BITTABLE
                PUBLIC  _FONTSEG,_FONTOFF,_FONTDEPTH

; SCREEN DIMENSIONS
_SCREENTBL      LABEL   WORD
                SCREENTABLE SCREENWIDE SCREENDEEP
_SCREENSEG      DW      0A000H
_SCREENBYTES    DW      SCREENWIDE / 8
_SCREENWIDE     DW      SCREENWIDE
_SCREENDEEP     DW      SCREENDEEP

; FONT DIMENSIONS AND POINTER
_FONTSEG        DW      ?
_FONTOFF        DW      ?
_FONTDEPTH      DW      ?

; MASK OBJECTS
_MASKTABLE      DB      80H,40H,20H,10H,08H,04H,02H,01H
_BITTABLE       DB      01H,02H,04H,08H,10H,20H,40H,80H

; WHERE THE CURSOR LIVES
DEFAULTCURSOR   DB      03FH,0FFH,01FH,0FFH
                DB      00FH,0FFH,007H,0FFH
                DB      003H,0FFH,001H,0FFH
                DB      000H,0FFH,000H,07FH
                DB      000H,03FH,000H,01FH
                DB      001H,0FFH,010H,0FFH
                DB      030H,0FFH,0F8H,07FH
                DB      0F8H,07FH,0FCH,07FH
                DB      000H,000H,040H,000H
                DB      060H,000H,070H,000H
                DB      078H,000H,07CH,000H
                DB      07EH,000H,07FH,000H
```

```
                          DB      07FH,080H,07CH,000H
                          DB      06CH,000H,046H,000H
                          DB      006H,000H,003H,000H
                          DB      003H,000H,000H,000H

SPOTX             DW      0000H
SPOTY             DW      0000H

; MOUSE POSITION AND BUTTONS
MOUSEX            DW      ?
MOUSEY            DW      ?
MOUSEB            DW      ?

; MOUSE CURSOR FLAG
MOUSEF            DW      -1              ;IF >= 0, MOUSE IS VISIBLE

; WHERE THE AREA BEHIND THE MOUSE CURSOR IS STORED
MOUSEBACK         DB      ((CURSORBYTES + 1) * CURSORDEEP * 4)
DUP (?)

_DATA             ENDS

_BSS              SEGMENT WORD PUBLIC 'BSS'

_BSS              ENDS

                  END
```

The following is a complete list of the functions provided by MOUSE16 in the order they appear in the source code. Note that some of these functions make use of the INT 33H mouse driver call. The parameters for INT 33H are documented in their entirety in the *Microsoft Mouse Programmer's Reference Guide*. While there's enough information to use the calls here for their functions in this module, you might want to get a copy of this book from Microsoft if you want to expand your understanding of the mouse driver.

DrawString(unsigned int x,unsigned int y,char *string,unsigned int forecolor,unsigned int backcolor)

The DrawString function draws text in the color defined by the forecolor argument against the color defined by the backcolor argument. The string is pointed to by the string argument, and should be terminated by a zero byte, just like a normal C language string. The rectangle which encloses the string will have its upper left corner at point (x,y). Note, however, that the x coordinate will be rounded down to the nearest byte boundary, as has been noted.

The DrawString function will draw in either eight or 16-point text, depending on the status of the FONTEIGHT and FONTSIXTEEN equates in MOUSE16.ASM. You'll find the eight point font to be pretty nearly unreadable at 800 by 600 pixels.

InitMouse(void)

The InitMouse function sets up the mouse manager. It also locates the font for DrawString and stores a pointer to it.

The code for `InitMouse` checks for the presence of a mouse driver and initializes it. It then sets the range of the mouse cursor's travel to be those of the screen's dimensions. Finally, it sets up the hook to the custom mouse handler code, MOUSEHANDLER, which has been discussed previously.

The `InitMouse` function will return a true value if all is well, and false one if the mouse driver couldn't be located.

Note that the screen dimensions and screen table are all set up at assembly time, so these do not have to be initialized. The screen table is created by the rather peculiar SCREENTABLE macro down toward the end of the MOUSE16.ASM listing. This is a repeating macro, and the apparently extraneous extra ENDM is in fact necessary. It generates D instances of a word of storage, with each instance incremented by W / 8.

The advantage in handling the screen table this way, rather than initializing it dynamically in `InitMouse`, is that it eliminates the albeit brief initial delay in calculating each of the 600 line offsets when `InitMouse` is called. There is a minor catch to this, however: both MASM and TASM are fairly slow at expanding this sort of macro, and MOUSE16 will take a while to assemble.

Deinit Mouse

The `Deinit Mouse` function disables the hook into the custom mouse handler previously installed by `InitMouse` and resets the mouse driver. It's extremely important to call this before returning control to DOS, as it will keep the mouse driver from leaping into the middle of whatever application you next run on your system—and thereby falling into a great cosmic nothingness in most cases—the first time the mouse moves.

ClearScreen(unsigned int color)

The `ClearScreen` function clears the screen to the color specified by its `color` argument. It was examined in detail earlier in this chapter.

MouseOn(void)

The `MouseOn` function makes the mouse cursor visible, and is usually called after a corresponding call to `MouseOff`.

MouseOff(void)

The `MouseOff` function hides the mouse cursor. You should make sure to call this function if you'll be drawing something on the screen that doesn't itself hide the mouse cursor, and then call `MouseOn` to reinstate it. If you hide the cursor for the time it takes to call a simple graphic function, the cursor won't actually seem to vanish, but you will avoid the cosmetic *faux pas* of drawing over the mouse cursor and having part of your drawing vanish when the mouse moves. Most of the graphic primitives, with the exception of `putpixel`, explicitly turn off the mouse cursor before they write to the screen and then turn it on again when they're done.

MouseDown(POINT *p)

The `MouseDown` function is exceedingly useful in writing code to interface with the mouse. When it's called, it will store the current location of the mouse cursor in the POINT object it's passed a pointer to and return an integer that defines the state of the mouse buttons at the time of the call. If n is the value returned by `MouseDown`, n & 1 will be true if the left mouse button is down and n & 2 will be true if the right mouse button is down.

The MOUSEHANDLER function that's called by the mouse driver sets the button status flag and the current mouse location every time the mouse moves or is clicked.

The location of the mouse cursor is the point where the upper left corner of the sixteen by sixteen pixel cursor resides on your screen plus the offset of the "hot spot." This will be dealt with in the explanation of MouseCursor.

MouseCursor(char *cursor,unsigned int x,unsigned int y)

The MouseCursor function will change the appearance of the mouse cursor. By default, it appears as an arrow pointing to the upper left. The current cursor is stored in the DEFAULTCURSOR buffer in MOUSE16.ASM.

A mouse cursor consists of the 32 bytes of the mask bitmap followed by the 32 bytes of the image bitmap, as was said earlier in this chapter.

The x and y arguments to MouseCursor represent the cursor "hot spot"—that is, where the location of the cursor is said to be in relation to the upper left corner of the cursor bitmap on your screen. For the standard arrow cursor, the hot spot would be at (0,0), which means that the location of the cursor would be at the upper left corner of the bitmap. For the hourglass cursor normally used to indicate a delay, the hot spot is typically set to (7,7), such that the location of the cursor is said to be at the center of the bitmap. This is of questionable relevance, as one rarely is given the opportunity to click on anything with a wait cursor.

The example C language calling function, to be presented in a moment, will illustrate two cursors for use with MouseCursor.

Calling MOUSE16 from C

Figure 3-11 is the complete C language source code for the program that generated FIG. 3-1, back at the beginning of this chapter. It's called TESTM16.C. It includes the various graphic functions covered in this chapter that aren't resident in MOUSE16, as well as a main function to exercise them. If you compile this program, you'll want to link it to MOUSE16.OBJ, as derived from MOUSE16.ASM. You'll also need MOUSE16.H, which will be presented in the next section of this chapter.

If you run into compilation or execution problems with TESTM16.C, check the setup of your compiler defaults, as explained in Chapter 1.

You'll probably recognize almost everything about TESTM16.C save for its main function, as all its secondary functions have been discussed at length in this chapter. If you write software that uses the techniques from this chapter, you'll no doubt want to abstract some of the functions used in TESTM16.C.

The palette table and the corresponding color defines at the top of TESTM16.C work together. This is a good default palette for 16-color graphics. Note that if you change the colors in the palette, you should change the names in the defines too.

The main function begins by looking for a command line argument to tell it what kind of super VGA card it should set itself up for. If it finds no argument, it will assume that it's to run in the standard 640 by 480 pixel VGA graphics mode. The card type, in thiscard, is passed to graphicmode, which will turn up presently.

```
/*
            Some 16 colour graphics

            Copyright (c) 1992 Alchemy Mindworks Inc.

            Links to MOUSE16.ASM
*/

#include "stdio.h"
#include "dos.h"
#include "alloc.h"
#include "mouse16.h"

/* colours in this sixteen-colour palette */
#define BLACK           0
#define BLUE            1
#define GREEN           2
#define CYAN            3
#define RED             4
#define MAGENTA         5
#define YELLOW          6
#define GREY            7
#define DARKGREY        8
#define LIGHTGREY       9
#define LIGHTBLUE       10
#define LIGHTGREEN      11
#define LIGHTRED        12
#define LIGHTYELLOW     13
#define LIGHTMAGENTA    14
#define WHITE           15

/* dimensions of the about box */
#define ABOUTLEFT       107
#define ABOUTTOP        50
#define ABOUTRIGHT      475
#define ABOUTBOTTOM     180

typedef struct          {
        char manufacturer;
        char version;
        char encoding;
        char bits_per_pixel;
        int xmin,ymin;
        int xmax,ymax;
        int hres;
        int vres;
        char palette[48];
        char reserved;
        char colour_planes;
        int bytes_per_line;
        int palette_type;
        char filler[58];
        } PCXHEAD;

char *farPtr(char *p,unsigned long l);
```

```
/* the sixteen-colour palette we'll use */
char palette[] = {
        0x00,0x00,0x00,
        0x00,0x00,0xaa,
        0x00,0xaa,0x00,
        0x00,0xaa,0xaa,
        0xaa,0x00,0x00,
        0xaa,0x00,0xaa,
        0xaa,0xaa,0x00,
        0xaa,0xaa,0xaa,
        0x55,0x55,0x55,
        0xcc,0xcc,0xcc,
        0x00,0x00,0xff,
        0x00,0xff,0x00,
        0xff,0x00,0x00,
        0xff,0xff,0x00,
        0xff,0x00,0xff,
        0xff,0xff,0xff
        };

unsigned int oldvesamode=0xffff;

main(argc,argv)
        int argc;
        char *argv[];
{
        BUTTON quit,pause,about,save;
        POINT p;
        int left,top,right,bottom;
        int i,alive=1,thiscard=VGA;

        /* see what kind of card is installed – sort of */
        if(argc > 1) {
                if(!stricmp(argv[1],"PARADISE")) thiscard=PARADISE;
                else if(!stricmp(argv[1],"ATI")) thiscard=ATI;
                else if(!stricmp(argv[1],"TSENG")) thiscard=TSENG;
                else if(!stricmp(argv[1],"TRIDENT")) thiscard=TRIDENT;
                else if(!stricmp(argv[1],"OAK")) thiscard=OAK;
                else if(!stricmp(argv[1],"VESA")) thiscard=VESA;
        }

        /* go for a graphics mode */
        if(!GraphicMode(thiscard)) {
                TextMode(thiscard);
                exit(1);
        }

        /* set the palette */
        SetVgaPalette(palette,16);

        /* clear the screen */
        ClearScreen(LIGHTGREY);

        /* draw a moire pattern */
        for(i=0;i<SCREENWIDE;i+=2)
            DrawLine(i,0,SCREENWIDE>>1,SCREENDEEP>>1,i);
```

```
for(i=0;i<SCREENDEEP;i+=2)
    DrawLine(SCREENWIDE>>1,SCREENDEEP>>1,SCREENWIDE-1,i,i);
for(i=SCREENWIDE-1;i>=0;i-=2)
    DrawLine(SCREENWIDE>>1,SCREENDEEP>>1,i,SCREENDEEP-1,i-1);
for(i=SCREENDEEP-1;i>=0;i-=2)
    DrawLine(0,i,SCREENWIDE>>1,SCREENDEEP>>1,i-1);

/* show the palette */
for(i=0;i<16;++i) {
        left=30+i*30;
        top=400;
        right=60+i*30;
        bottom=430;

        FillRect(left,top,right,bottom,i);
        FrameRect(left,top,right,bottom,BLACK);
}

/* show some example text */
i=100;
DrawString(128,i," This is blue on light green.        ",BLUE,LIGHTGREEN);
i+=FONTDEPTH;
DrawString(128,i," This is red on light yellow.        ",RED,LIGHTYELLOW);
i+=FONTDEPTH;
DrawString(128,i," This is light yellow on red.        ",LIGHTYELLOW,RED);
i+=FONTDEPTH;
DrawString(128,i," This is black on magenta (very ugly). ",BLACK,MAGENTA);
i+=FONTDEPTH;
DrawString(128,i," This is cyan on light grey.         ",CYAN,LIGHTGREY);
i+=FONTDEPTH;

/* create some buttons to click on */
MakeButton(SCREENWIDE-100,SCREENDEEP-60,"Quit",&quit);
DrawButton(&quit);

MakeButton(SCREENWIDE-200,SCREENDEEP-60,"Pause",&pause);
DrawButton(&pause);

MakeButton(SCREENWIDE-300,SCREENDEEP-60,"About",&about);
DrawButton(&about);

MakeButton(SCREENWIDE-400,SCREENDEEP-60,"Save",&save);
DrawButton(&save);

/* loop 'til we're done */
do {
        /* look for a mouse click */
        if(MouseDown(&p)) {
                if(PointInRect(&p,&quit)) {
                        TrackButton(&quit);
                        alive=0;
                }
                else if(PointInRect(&p,&pause)) {
                        TrackButton(&pause);
                        WaitCursor();
```

```
                                        delay(5000);
                                        ArrowCursor();
                        }
                        else if(PointInRect(&p,&about)) {
                                TrackButton(&about);
                                DoAbout();
                        }
                        else if(PointInRect(&p,&save)) {
                                TrackButton(&save);
                                DoSave("SCREEN00.PCX");
                        }
                }
        } while(alive);

        TextMode(thiscard);
}

/* save the screen to a PCX file */
DoSave(path)
        char *path;
{
        PCXHEAD pcx;
        FILE *fp;
        char *p;
        unsigned int i,j,n;

        /* create the destination file */
        if((fp=fopen(path,"wb"))==NULL) {
                beep();
                return;
        }

        memset((char *)&pcx,0,sizeof(PCXHEAD));
        memcpy(pcx.palette,palette,48);

        pcx.manufacturer=10;
        pcx.encoding=1;
        pcx.xmin=pcx.ymin=0;
        pcx.xmax=SCREENWIDE-1;
        pcx.ymax=SCREENDEEP-1;
        pcx.palette_type=1;
        pcx.bits_per_pixel=1;
        pcx.version=2;
        pcx.colour_planes=4;
        pcx.bytes_per_line=SCREENBYTES;

        WaitCursor();
        if(fwrite((char *)&pcx,1,sizeof(PCXHEAD),fp) != sizeof(PCXHEAD)) {
                fclose(fp);
                remove(path);
                ArrowCursor();
                beep();
                return;
        }
```

```
                for(i=0;i<SCREENDEEP;++i) {
                        p=MK_FP(SCREENSEG,SCREENTBL[i]);
                        MouseOff();
                        for(j=0;j<4;++j) {
                                egareadplane(j);
                                n=pcxwriteline(fp,p,pcx.bytes_per_line);

                                if(n != pcx.bytes_per_line) {
                                        fclose(fp);
                                        remove(path);
                                        MouseOn();
                                        ArrowCursor();
                                        beep();
                                        return;
                                }
                        }
                        MouseOn();
                }
        ArrowCursor();
        fclose(fp);
}

/* write one pcx line */
pcxwriteline(fp,p,n)
        FILE *fp;
        char *p;
        unsigned int n;
{
        unsigned int i=0,j=0,t=0;

        do {
                i=0;
                while((p[t+i]==p[t+i+1]) && ((t+i) < n) && (i < 63))++i;
                if(i>0) {
                        if(fputc(i | 0xc0,fp)==EOF) return(-1);
                        if(fputc(p[t],fp)==EOF) return(-1);
                        t+=i;
                        j+=2;
                }
                else {
                        if(((p[t]) & 0xc0)==0xc0) {
                                if(fputc(0xc1,fp)==EOF) return(-1);
                                ++j;
                        }
                        if(fputc(p[t++],fp)==EOF) return(-1);
                        ++j;
                }
        } while(t<n);
        return(n);
}

/* show the about box */
DoAbout()
{
        POINT pt;
```

```
BUTTON done;
char *p;
unsigned long size;
unsigned int i;

/* see how much memory the area behind it needs */
size=ImageSize16(ABOUTLEFT,ABOUTTOP,ABOUTRIGHT,ABOUTBOTTOM);

/* get a buffer */
if((p=farmalloc(size)) != NULL) {

        /* get the area behind the box */
        GetImage16(ABOUTLEFT,ABOUTTOP,ABOUTRIGHT,ABOUTBOTTOM,p);

        /* draw the box */
        FillRect(ABOUTLEFT,ABOUTTOP,ABOUTRIGHT,ABOUTBOTTOM,LIGHTBLUE);
        FrameRect(ABOUTLEFT,ABOUTTOP,ABOUTRIGHT,ABOUTBOTTOM,BLACK);

        /* add the Done button */
        MakeButton(ABOUTLEFT+16,ABOUTBOTTOM-32,"Done",&done);
        DrawButton(&done);

        /* show some text */
        i=ABOUTTOP+16;
        DrawString(ABOUTLEFT+16,i,"This is an example of sixteen
                                colour",BLACK,LIGHTBLUE);
        i+=FONTDEPTH;
        DrawString(ABOUTLEFT+16,i,"super VGA graphics. Copyright (c)
                                1902",BLACK,LIGHTBLUE);
        i+=FONTDEPTH;
        DrawString(ABOUTLEFT+16,i,"Mother Martha's Computer
                                Software",BLACK,LIGHTBLUE);
        i+=FONTDEPTH;
        DrawString(ABOUTLEFT+16,i,"Emporium Ltd. Use no
                                hooks.",BLACK,LIGHTBLUE);

        i=1;

        /* loop 'til we're done */
        do {
                if(MouseDown(&pt)) {
                        if(PointInRect(&pt,&done)) {
                                TrackButton(&done);
                                i=0;
                        } else beep();
                }
        } while(i);

        /* put the old screen back */
        PutImage16(ABOUTLEFT,ABOUTTOP,p);

        /* free the buffer */
        farfree(p);
} else beep();
}
```

```
GraphicMode(card)
      unsigned int card;
{
      union REGS r;
      struct SREGS sr;
      VESAINFO vi;
      VESABLOCK vb;
      unsigned int i;

      if(card==VGA) {
              r.x.ax=card;
              int86(0x10,&r,&r);
              SCREENWIDE=640;
              SCREENDEEP=480;
              SCREENBYTES=80;
              for(i=0;i<SCREENDEEP;++i) SCREENTBL[i]=i*SCREENBYTES;
      }
      else if(card==VESA) {
              /* check for a VESA BIOS */
              r.x.ax=0x4f00;
              r.x.di=FP_OFF((char *)&vb);
              sr.es=FP_SEG((char *)&vb);
              int86x(0x10,&r,&r,&sr);
              if(r.x.ax != 0x004f) return(0);

              /* see if this mode is supported */
              while(*vb.videomode != VESA && *vb.videomode != 0xffff)
                  (vb.videomode)++;

              if(*vb.videomode == 0xffff) return(0);

              /* get the VESA information */
              r.x.ax=0x4f01;
              r.x.cx=VESA;
              r.x.di=FP_OFF((char *)&vi);
              sr.es=FP_SEG((char *)&vi);
              int86x(0x10,&r,&r,&sr);

              /* set the screen segment */
              SCREENSEG=vi.windowsegment_a;

              /* get the current mode */
              r.x.ax=0x4f03;
              int86(0x10,&r,&r);
              oldvesamode=r.x.bx;

              /* set the new mode */
              r.x.ax=0x4f02;
              r.x.bx=VESA;
              int86(0x10,&r,&r);
      }
      else {
              r.x.ax=card;
              int86(0x10,&r,&r);
      }
```

```
              return(InitMouse());
          }

     TextMode(card)
          unsigned int card;
     {
          VESABLOCK vb;
          union REGS r;
          struct SREGS sr;

          r.x.ax=0x1200;
          r.x.bx=0x0031;
          int86(0x10,&r,&r);

          if(card==VESA && oldvesamode != 0xffff) {
               r.x.ax=0x4f00;
               r.x.di=FP_OFF((char *)&vb);
               sr.es=FP_SEG((char *)&vb);
               int86x(0x10,&r,&r,&sr);

               /* see if the old mode is supported */
               while(*vb.videomode != oldvesamode && *vb.videomode != 0xffff)
                    (vb.videomode)++;

               /* if not, select the standard text mode */
               if(*vb.videomode == 0xffff) {
                    r.x.ax=0x0003;
                    int86(0x10,&r,&r);
               }
               else {
                    r.x.ax=0x4f02;
                    r.x.bx=oldvesamode;
                    int86(0x10,&r,&r);
               }
          }
          else {
               r.x.ax=0x0003;
               int86(0x10,&r,&r);
          }
          DeinitMouse();
     }

     DrawLine(left,top,right,bottom,colour)
          int left,top,right,bottom,colour;
     {
          int temp,dx,dy,x,y,x_sign,y_sign,flag;

          MouseOff();
          dx = abs(right - left);
          dy = abs(bottom - top);
          if(((dx >= dy) && (left > right)) ||
             ((dy > dx) && (top > bottom))) {
                    temp = left;
                    left = right;
                    right = temp;
```

```
                        temp = top;
                        top = bottom;
                        bottom = temp;
                }
                if ((bottom - top) < 0) y_sign = -1;
                else y_sign = 1;
                if ((right - left) < 0) x_sign = -1;
                else x_sign = 1;
                if (dx >= dy) {
                        for (x=left,y=top,flag=0; x<=right; x++,flag+=dy) {
                                if (flag>=dx) {
                                        flag  -= dx;
                                        y+= y_sign;
                                }
                                setpixel(x,y,colour);
                        }
                }
                else {
                        for (x=left,y=top,flag=0; y<=bottom; y++,flag+=dx) {
                                if (flag>=dy) {
                                        flag  -= dy;
                                        x+=x_sign;
                                }
                                setpixel(x,y,colour);
                        }
                }
        MouseOn();
}

#pragma warn -aus
FillRect(left,top,right,bottom,colour)
        int left,top,right,bottom,colour;
{
        char *p,bf[100];
        int a,i,j,width,depth,bleft,bytes,xleft,xright,pleft,pright;

        MouseOff();
        xleft=left & 0xfff8;
        xright=right;
        if(xright & 0x0007) xright=(xright | 0x0007)+1;
        width=xright-xleft;
        depth=bottom-top;
        bleft=xleft>>3;
        pleft=left-xleft;
        pright=pleft+(right-left);
        bytes=pixels2bytes(width)+1;

        memset(bf,0,bytes);

        for(i=pleft;i<=pright;++i) bf[i>>3] |= masktable[i & 0x0007];

        setwritemode(2);
        for(i=0;i<=depth;++i) {
                p=MK_FP(SCREENSEG,SCREENTBL[top+i]+bleft);
                for(j=0;j<bytes;++j) {
```

```
                                        setbitmask(bf[j]);
                                        a=p[j];
                                        p[j]=colour;
                            }
                    }
            setbitmask(0xff);
            setwritemode(0);
            MouseOn();
    }
    #pragma warn +aus

    FrameRect(left,top,right,bottom,colour)
            unsigned int left,top,right,bottom,colour;
    {
            DrawLine(left,top,right,top,colour);
            DrawLine(left,bottom,right,bottom,colour);
            DrawLine(left,top,left,bottom,colour);
            DrawLine(right,top,right,bottom,colour);
    }

    SetVgaPalette(p,n)
            char *p;
            unsigned int n;
    {
            union REGS r;
            int i;

            for(i=0;i<n;++i) {
                    r.h.dh=*p++>>2;
                    r.h.ch=*p++>>2;
                    r.h.cl=*p++>>2;
                    r.x.bx=i;
                    r.x.ax=0x1010;
                    int86(0x10,&r,&r);
            }

            r.x.bx=0x0000;
            for(i=0;i<n;++i) {
                    r.x.ax=0x1000;
                    int86(0x10,&r,&r);
                    r.x.bx+=0x0101;
            }
    }

    MakeButton(left,top,string,button)
            unsigned int left,top;
            char *string;
            BUTTON *button;
    {
            button->frame.left = left & 0xfff8;
            button->frame.right=button->frame.left+(strlen(string)<<3)+16;
            button->frame.top=top;
            button->frame.bottom=button->frame.top+FONTDEPTH+8;
            button->text=string;
    }
```

```
DrawButton(button)
        BUTTON *button;
{
        FillRect(button->frame.left+1,button->frame.top+1,
                button->frame.right-1,button->frame.bottom-1,WHITE);
        DrawLine(button->frame.left+1,button->frame.top,
                button->frame.right-1,button->frame.top,BLACK);
        DrawLine(button->frame.left,button->frame.top+1,
                button->frame.left,button->frame.bottom-1,BLACK);
        DrawLine(button->frame.right,button->frame.top+1,
                button->frame.right,button->frame.bottom-1,BLACK);
        DrawLine(button->frame.left+1,button->frame.bottom,
                button->frame.right-1,button->frame.bottom,BLACK);
        Fill3DBox(button->frame.left+1,button->frame.top+1,
                button->frame.right-1,button->frame.bottom-1);

        DrawString(button->frame.left+8,button->frame.top+4,
                button->text,DARKGREY,LIGHTGREY);
}

TrackButton(button)
        BUTTON *button;
{
        POINT p;

        FillRect(button->frame.left+1,button->frame.top+1,
                button->frame.right-1,button->frame.bottom-1,LIGHTGREY);
        DrawString(button->frame.left+8,button->frame.top+4,
                button->text,DARKGREY,LIGHTGREY);
        while(MouseDown(&p));
        DrawButton(button);
}

Fill3DBox(left,top,right,bottom)
        int left,top,right,bottom;
{
        FillRect(left,top,right,bottom,LIGHTGREY);
        DrawLine(left,top,right-1,top,WHITE);
        DrawLine(left,top+1,left,bottom-1,WHITE);

        DrawLine(left+3,bottom,right,bottom,DARKGREY);
        DrawLine(right,top+2,right,bottom-1,DARKGREY);
}

PointInRect(p,r)/* return true if point is in rect */
        POINT *p;
        RECT *r;
{
        if(p->x > r->left && p->x < r->right &&
           p->y > r->top  && p->y < r->bottom) return(1);
        else return(0);
}

WaitCursor()
{
```

```
static char cursor[] = {
        0x00,0x00,0x00,0x00,
        0x00,0x00,0x01,0x80,
        0x03,0xC0,0x07,0xE0,
        0x0F,0xF0,0x07,0xE0,
        0x03,0xC0,0x01,0x80,
        0x00,0x00,0x00,0x00,
        0x00,0x00,0x00,0x00,
        0xFF,0xFF,0xFF,0xFF,

        0x00,0x00,0xFE,0x7F,
        0x06,0x60,0x0C,0x30,
        0x18,0x18,0x30,0x0C,
        0x60,0x06,0xC0,0x03,
        0x60,0x06,0x30,0x0C,
        0x98,0x19,0xCC,0x33,
        0xE6,0x67,0xFE,0x7F,
        0x00,0x00,0x00,0x00 };

MouseCursor(cursor,7,7);
}

ArrowCursor()
{
        static char cursor[] = {
        0xFF,0x3F,0xFF,0x1F,
        0xFF,0x0F,0xFF,0x07,
        0xFF,0x03,0xFF,0x01,
        0xFF,0x00,0x7F,0x00,
        0x3F,0x00,0x1F,0x00,
        0xFF,0x01,0xFF,0x10,
        0xFF,0x30,0x7F,0xF8,
        0x7F,0xF8,0x7F,0xFC,
        0x00,0x00,0x00,0x40,
        0x00,0x60,0x00,0x70,
        0x00,0x78,0x00,0x7C,
        0x00,0x7E,0x00,0x7F,
        0x80,0x7F,0x00,0x7C,
        0x00,0x6C,0x00,0x46,
        0x00,0x06,0x00,0x03,
        0x00,0x03,0x00,0x00 };

MouseCursor(cursor,0,0);
}

#pragma warn -aus
PutImage16(left,top,p)
        unsigned int left,top;
        char *p;
{
        char mask[100];
        char *scr;
        int start;
        unsigned int a,i,j,n,r,x,y,w,nn;
```

```
MouseOff();
x=ImageWidth(p);
y=ImageDepth(p);
p+=4;

w=pixels2bytes(x);
r=left & 0x0007;
n=8-r;
start=left>>3;

j=r+x;
memset(mask,0x00,SCREENBYTES);
for(i=r;i<j;++i) mask[i>>3] |= masktable[i & 0x0007];
for(i=0;i<y;++i) {
        scr=MK_FP(SCREENSEG,SCREENTBL[i+top]+start);
        egawriteplane(8);
        a=0;
        for(j=0;j<w;++j) {
                setbitmask(mask[j]);
                nn=scr[j];
                scr[j] = ((p[j] >> r) | a);
                a=(p[j] << n);
        }
        setbitmask(mask[j]);
                nn=scr[j];
        scr[j]=a;
        p+=w;

        egawriteplane(4);
        a=0;
        for(j=0;j<w;++j) {
                setbitmask(mask[j]);
                nn=scr[j];
                scr[j] = ((p[j] >> r) | a);
                a=(p[j] << n);
        }
        setbitmask(mask[j]);
        nn=scr[j];scr[j]=a;
        p+=w;

        egawriteplane(2);
        a=0;
        for(j=0;j<w;++j) {
                setbitmask(mask[j]);
                nn=scr[j];
                scr[j] = ((p[j] >> r) | a);
                a=(p[j] << n);
        }
        setbitmask(mask[j]);
                nn=scr[j];
        scr[j]=a;
        p+=w;

        egawriteplane(1);
        a=0;
```

```
                        for(j=0;j<w;++j) {
                                setbitmask(mask[j]);
                                nn=scr[j];
                                scr[j] = ((p[j] >> r) | a);
                                a=(p[j] << n);
                        }
                                setbitmask(mask[j]);
                        nn=scr[j];
                        scr[j]=a;
                        p=farPtr(p,(long)w);
                }
                fourplanes();
                setbitmask(0xff);
                MouseOn();
        }
        #pragma warn +aus

        GetImage16(left,top,right,bottom,p)
                unsigned int left,top,right,bottom;
                char *p;
        {
                char *scr;
                int start;
                unsigned int a,i,j,n,r,x,y,w;

                MouseOff();
                x=right-left+1;
                y=bottom-top+1;
                *p++=(x-1);
                *p++=(x-1)>>8;
                *p++=(y-1);
                *p++=(y-1)>>8;

                w=pixels2bytes(x);
                r=left & 0x0007;
                n=8-r;
                start=left>>3;

                for(i=0;i<y;++i) {
                        scr=MK_FP(SCREENSEG,SCREENTBL[i+top]+start);
                        a=0;
                        egareadplane(3);
                        for(j=0;j<w;++j) {
                                a=(scr[j+1] >> n);
                                p[j] = ((scr[j] << r) | a);
                        }
                        p+=w;
                        a=0;
                        egareadplane(2);
                        for(j=0;j<w;++j) {
                                a=(scr[j+1] >> n);
                                p[j] = ((scr[j] << r) | a);
                        }
                        p+=w;
                        a=0;
```

```
                egareadplane(1);
                for(j=0;j<w;++j) {
                        a=(scr[j+1] >> n);
                        p[j] = ((scr[j] << r) | a);
                }
                p+=w;
                a=0;
                egareadplane(0);
                for(j=0;j<w;++j) {
                        a=(scr[j+1] >> n);
                        p[j] = ((scr[j] << r) | a);
                }
                p=farPtr(p,(long)w);
        }
        MouseOn();
}

char *farPtr(p,l)
        char *p;
        unsigned long l;
{
        unsigned int seg,off;

        seg = FP_SEG(p);
        off = FP_OFF(p);
        seg += (off / 16);
        off &= 0x000f;
        off += (unsigned int)(l & 0x000fL);
        seg += (l / 16L);
        p = MK_FP(seg,off);
        return(p);
}
```

The first bit of actual graphics in the main function of TESTM16.C is the code that
draws the moire pattern, the radial lines that fill the screen. This exercises
DrawLine. The odd patterns it generates result from the rounding errors is the
Bresenham's line algorithm interfering with the lines of the screen.

Following the code that draws a moire, main draws sixteen boxes with the palette
colors in them using FillRect. It then draws some example text with
DrawString and sets up four buttons. Most of the rest of the function is occupied
by a loop to manage the buttons.

The Quit button terminates the loop by setting the alive variable false. The Pause
button exercises the MouseCursor function by changing the cursor to an hourglass
and pausing for five seconds. The About button will display an About box by
calling the DoAbout function. The Save button will create a file called
SCREEN00.PCX that will contain a captured image of the current screen.

The About box in TESTM16.C illustrates the use of a number of graphic function
calls. It saves the area behind the box with GetImage16, uses FillRect and
FrameRect to draw the box, DrawText to say what the box is about and then the

button-related functions to draw and manage the button that banishes the box. The PutImage16 function restores the area behind the box.

As an aside, this application of PutImage16 and GetImage16 doesn't make for particularly snappy dialog boxes; in a sense, it represents severe overkill. There's an alternate approach examined in *Graphical User Interface Programming*.

Here's a list of the functions in TESTM16.C that you might want to excise for use in your own software.

DoSave(char *path)

The DoSave function will create a PCX file of your current graphic screen at the moment it's called. The path argument should be a complete path and file name, or just a file name if you want the file to appear in the current directory. This includes the extension PCX.

GraphicMode(unsigned int card)

The GraphicMode function will initialize the graphic mode specified by the card argument. The constants it will recognize are defined in MOUSE16.H. Aside from several super VGA modes, it will also allow for standard VGA graphics. In this case, it will redefine the SCREENWIDE, SCREENDEEP, SCREENBYTES and SCREENTBL objects in MOUSE16. The GraphicMode function will call InitMouse once it has established a graphic mode, and return whatever InitMouse returns.

TextMode(unsigned int card)

The TextMode function will return the screen to text mode and deinitialize the mouse handler.

DrawLine(unsigned int left,unsigned int top,unsigned int right,unsigned int bottom,unsigned int color)

The DrawLine function will draw a line from (left,top) to (right,bottom) in the color defined by its color argument.

FillRect(unsigned int left,unsigned int top,unsigned int right,unsigned int bottom,unsigned int color)

The FillRect function will fill a rectangular area defined by its first four arguments with color.

FrameRect(unsigned int left,unsigned int top,unsigned int right,unsigned int bottom,unsigned int color)

The FrameRect function will draw a rectangle around the area defined by its first four arguments in color.

SetVgaPalette(char *palette,int colors)

The SetVgaPalette function will set the current 16-color VGA palette. The palette argument should be a pointer to a table of three-byte RGB color values. The colors argument is the number of colors to set—this will usually be sixteen.

MakeButton(unsigned int left,unsigned int top,char *string,BUTTON *button)

The MakeButton function sets up a BUTTON object to display a button with its upper left corner at (left,top) and its text set to string. It will set the frame element of the button so that its upper left corner corresponds to the left and top arguments to MakeButton; the left value will be rounded down to the nearest 8-bit boundary, as was discussed earlier in this chapter. The bottom of the frame will be set based on the current font size. The right edge of the frame will be set based on the length of the string to be used by the button.

Note that a BUTTON object doesn't store the text for the button it defines, but only a pointer to it. As such, the text passed to MakeButton must be static.

DrawButton(BUTTON *button)

The DrawButton function—perhaps predictably—draws a button on the screen. The BUTTON object passed to it should have been set up by a previous call to MakeButton.

TrackButton(BUTTON *button)

The TrackButton function will manage a button once it has been established that a mouse click has taken place within its boundaries.

Fill3DBox(unsigned int left,unsigned int top,unsigned int right,unsigned int bottom)

The Fill3DBOX function is called by DrawButton and probably won't be of much use to other aspects of your software directly.

PointInRect(POINT *p,RECT *r)

The PointInRect function will return a true value if POINT p is within RECT r, or a false value if it's not.

WaitCursor(void)

The WaitCursor function will cause the current cursor to change to an hourglass. It should be called prior to any operation that will take a while to perform.

ArrowCursor(void)

The ArrowCursor function will cause the current cursor to revert to a standard arrow cursor. It can be called after a call to WaitCursor or to any other function that redefines the mouse cursor's appearance.

PutImage16(unsigned int left,unsigned int top,char *p)

The PutImage16 function will paint a standard BGI-style 16-color image fragment pointed to by p on the screen, such that its upper left corner resides at (left,top). The fragment can be larger than 64K.

GetImage16(unsigned int left,unsigned int top,unsigned int right,unsigned int bottom,char *p)

The GetImage16 will capture a standard BGI-style image fragment from the screen area bounded by its first four arguments into the buffer at p. The size of the buffer passed to GetImage16 should be calculated by a call to ImageSize16. Note that while the buffers set up by GetImage16 are structured like those created by getimage, they are not constrained to fit in less than 64K of memory.

unsigned long ImageSize16(unsigned int left,unsigned int top,unsigned int right,unsigned int bottom)

The `ImageSize16` function returns a long integer that contains the number of bytes required to create a `GetImage16` buffer to hold the screen fragment defined by its four arguments.

char *farPtr(char *, unsigned long l)

The `farPtr` function returns a properly normalized pointer to the memory at p + 1.

The MOUSE16.H header

The MOUSE16.H file should be included in any source code that makes calls to MOUSE16. It also contains some structures used by the functions in TESTM16.C. It's illustrated in FIG. 3-12.

The list of mode numbers for the various VGA cards at the top of MOUSE16.H can be expanded a bit, should you discover that your card isn't on it. John Bridges maintains a public domain library of VGA card information called VGAKIT, which provides a list of the mode numbers for most super VGA cards, among other things. It can be found in the GO PICS forum of CompuServe, among other places. Here are a few additional mode numbers for 800 by 600 pixel, sixteen color super VGA graphics based on the information in VGAKIT.

```
#define AHEAD            0x6a
#define CHIPSANDTECH     0x70
#define EVEREX           0x02¹
#define GENOA            0x79²
#define NCR              0x58
#define VIDEOSEVEN       0x62³

¹AX = 0x0070, BL = 0x02
²0x6a also works
³AX = 0x6f05, BL = 0x62
```

John Bridges adds new information to VGAKIT periodically.

The `extern` declarations in MOUSE16.H allow a C language program to get at a number of useful objects in MOUSE16. The SCREENWIDE, SCREENDEEP, SCREENBYTES, SCREENSEG, and SCREENTBL objects have been discussed previously. The `masktable` and `bittable` objects have turned up informally in a few places; they'll be dealt with in detail in the next section. The `FONTDEPTH` value represents the vertical size of the system font in lines. The horizontal value will always be eight. The `FONTSEG` and `FONTOFF` values represent a pointer into the VGA BIOS where the system font being used resides.

Note that MOUSE16.H includes prototypes for all the functions discussed in this chapter. If you modify the functions such that their arguments or return values change, make sure you modify the prototypes too.

3-12
The MOUSE16.H header file.

```
/*
          Header for MOUSE16
*/

#define VGA       0x12
#define PARADISE  0x58
#define ATI       0x54
```

```
#define TSENG        0x29
#define TRIDENT      0x5b
#define OAK          0x52
#define VESA         0x0102

#define COLOURDEPTH 4

#define RGB_RED      0
#define RGB_GREEN    1
#define RGB_BLUE     2
#define RGB_SIZE     3

typedef struct {
        unsigned int x,y;
        } POINT;

typedef struct {
        unsigned int left,top,right,bottom;
        } RECT;

typedef struct {
        RECT frame;
        char *text;
        } BUTTON;

typedef struct{
        char vesasig[4];
        unsigned int version;
        char *oemstring;
        char capabilities[4];
        unsigned int *videomode;
        unsigned int memory;
        char reserved[242];
        } VESABLOCK;

typedef struct {
        unsigned int modeattributes;
        char windowattr_a;
        char windowattr_b;
        unsigned int granularity;
        unsigned int windowsize;
        unsigned int windowsegment_a;
        unsigned int windowsegment_b;
        int (*windowptr)();
        unsigned int bytesperline;
        /* new additions */
        unsigned int xres;
        unsigned int yres;
        char xcharsize;
        char ycharsize;
        char numberofplanes;
        char bitsperpixel;
        char banks;
        char memorymodel;
        char banksize;
```

```c
                char imagepages;
                char reserved1;
                char redmask;
                char redfield;
                char greenmask;
                char greenfield;
                char bluemask;
                char bluefield;
                char resmask;
                char resfield;
                char directcolour;
                char reserved2[216];
                } VESAINFO;

#define setpixel(x,y,c) { char *p; \
                p=MK_FP(0xa000,SCREENTBL[(y)]+((x)>>3)); \
                outp(0x3ce,8); outp(0x3cf,masktable[(x) & 0x0007]); \
                outp(0x3ce,5); outp(0x3cf,2); \
                *p=*p; *p=(c); \
                outp(0x3ce,5); outp(0x3cf,0); \
                outp(0x3ce,8); outp(0x3cf,255); }

#define fourplanes()        { outportb(0x3c4,0x02); outportb(0x3c5,0x0f);}
#define pixels2bytes(n)     ((n+7)/8)
#define ImageWidth(p)       (1+p[0]+(p[1] << 8))
#define ImageDepth(p)       (1+p[2]+(p[3] << 8))
#define ImageBytes(p)       (pixels2bytes((1+p[0]+(p[1] << 8))))

#define egawriteplane(n)    { outp(0x3c4,2); outp(0x3c5,(n)); }
#define egareadplane(n)       { outp(0x3ce,4); outp(0x3cf,(n)); }
#define setbitmask(n)       { outp(0x3ce,8); outp(0x3cf,(n)); }
#define setwritemode(n)       { outp(0x3ce,5); outp(0x3cf,(n)); }

#define greyvalue(r,g,b)        (((r*30)/100) + ((g*59)/100) + ((b*11)/100))

#define beep()                  putchar(7)

#ifndef max
#define max(a,b)            (((a)>(b))?(a):(b))
#endif
#ifndef min
#define min(a,b)            (((a)<(b))?(a):(b))
#endif

#define ImageSize16(l,t,r,b)        (4L+(long)(1+pixels2bytes(max(r,l)-\
                            min(r,l)))*4L*(long)(1+max(b,t)-min(b,t)))

unsigned int InitMouse(void);
void DeinitMouse(void);
void MouseOn(void);
void MouseOff(void);
unsigned int MouseDown(POINT *p);
void MouseCursor(char *cursor,unsigned int x,unsigned int y);
void DrawString(unsigned x,unsigned int y,char *p,unsigned int c,
                unsigned int b);
```

```
extern unsigned int SCREENTBL[];
extern unsigned int SCREENWIDE;
extern unsigned int SCREENDEEP;
extern unsigned int SCREENBYTES;
extern unsigned int SCREENSEG;
extern char masktable[];
extern char bittable[];
extern unsigned int FONTDEPTH;
extern unsigned int FONTSEG;
extern unsigned int FONTOFF;
```

Bit fields:
The last word
about
masktable

In examining both monochrome and 16-color images, we've expressed all the image data thus far as image planes. A *plane* is a string of bits stored in bytes. When really dedicated programmers get together for a hot night of swapping algorithms, they refer to strings of bytes used this way as a "bit field." Really dedicated programmers are those who've had extra fingers surgically attached to their hands so they can count on them in hexadecimal.

Bit fields aren't all that hard to understand—by now you should have them by the throat—but they're a bit tricky to work with effectively because a PC's processor thinks that the smallest object worth considering is a byte. It lacks any operators to work directly with bits.

The way around this is to use masks. Masks allow you to deal with specific bits stored in bytes. A PC's processor gets along well enough with bits if it can be allowed to disguise them in this form.

In this example, let's allow that p points to a bit field—this can be one line of a monochrome image or one plane of a 16-color image. We'd like to know if bit x is high or low.

To begin with, it would be handy to know which byte in p the bit in question is stored in. Because there are eight bits in a byte, bit x must reside at p[x / 8]. Division by eight is equivalent to shifting x right by three places, save that shifting bits is a lot quicker. As such, we can express the byte that contains bit x as being p[x >> 3].

To determine whether a particular pixel is on or off in a byte, you would AND the byte with a mask that represents the position of the pixel and test the result. The mask is a byte with only one bit set. You can calculate the mask to determine the position of the pixel at x as 0x80 >> (x & 7). As such, if (p[x >> 3] & (0x80 >> (x & 7))) is non-zero, bit x is set. If it's zero, bit x isn't set.

Calculating 0x80 >> (x & 7) is time consuming if you'll be doing it a lot. You can reduce the time it takes to work out each mask by observing that there are only eight possible results for this calculation. They can be stored in a table. The table, predictably, is masktable.

```
char masktable[8]= { 0x80,0x40,0x20,0x10,0x08,0x04,0x02,0x01 };
```

With this table available, the calculation of a bit mask can be reduced to masktable[x & 7].

Bitwise manipulation can be used to test and manipulate bits in a bit field. We've seen what's involved in testing bits. Much the same approach is used when you want to modify the individual bits in a string of bytes. Once again, in these examples the bit field in question will be pointed to by p and the position of the bit to be dealt with will be x.

The easiest bitwise manipulation is setting a bit on. It's done by ORing a mask with one byte of a bit field. This is how you'd do it:

```
p[x >> 3] |= masktable[x & 7];
```

To turn a bit off, you must AND the appropriate byte with the inverse of the mask that you would have used to set the bit on by ORing it. This has the effect of leaving all the existing bits unaffected save for the one which you wanted to turn off, which will be masked. It's done like this:

```
p[x >> 3] &= masktable[x & 7];
```

Finally, to flip a bit—that is, to invert its state—you can XOR a mask with the bit field, like this:

```
p[x >> 3] ^= masktable[x & 7];
```

You'll find that masktable has all sorts of applications in bitmapped graphics. Note that in the programs in this chapter, it's defined in the MOUSE16.ASM assembly language file, rather than in C. It's accessible in both languages, of course.

Understanding VESA

The VESA specification is another of the things that has turned up informally throughout this chapter without much of an explanation. In some applications, this is largely acceptable; we've been making fairly elementary use of VESA thus far.

This section will deal with VESA in detail. As was touched on in Chapter 1, a super VGA card with a VESA BIOS will allow you to switch graphic modes and perform several other fundamental graphic functions using a somewhat standardized interface. In fact, the VESA specification hasn't been interpreted all that consistently by some super VGA card manufacturers, so the fact that a card claims to have a VESA BIOS isn't all that much of a guarantee that you'll be able to drive it using VESA calls. This problem gets worse in dealing with 256-color and high-color graphics through VESA.

A VESA card will tell software that wants to drive it which super VGA modes are available, and a few other incidental things, such as who made the card. It will provide a way to enable graphics modes and to change display pages. The latter isn't something you'll need to know until we get into 256-color graphics.

Software can communicate with a VESA BIOS through INT 10H. Calls for VESA functions always have 4FH in the AH register. To begin with, this is the call to ask a VESA BIOS for information about itself.

```
VESABLOCK vb;
union REGS r;
struct SREGS sr;

r.x.ax=0x4f00;
r.x.di=FP_OFF((char *)&vb);
sr.es=FP_SEG((char *)&vb);
int86x(0x10,&r,&r,&sr);
```

```
if(r.x.ax != 0x004f) {
        /* there is no VESA BIOS present */
}
```

This bit of code will return with the value 004FH in the AX register if it's successful.
As this is unlikely to happen if no VESA BIOS is present, it's a good way to check
for VESA capability.

The ES:DI pointer passed to INT 10H for this call should point to a VESABLOCK
object. Here's what it looks like:

```
typedef struct{
        char vesasig[4];
        unsigned int version;
        char *oemstring;
        char capabilities[4];
        unsigned int *videomode;
        unsigned int memory;
        char reserved[242];
        } VESABLOCK;
```

The VESABLOCK will be filled in by the INT 10H VESA handler in this call. The
vesasig element will—perhaps predictably—hold the string "VESA". The version
element will be the version number of the VESA BIOS. The high order byte is the
major version and the low order byte is the minor version. The current version as of
this writing is 1.3—the version element for a current VESA BIOS would hold the
value 0103H.

The oemstring element is a far pointer to a string that defines who manufactured
the card in question. This is a normal C language null terminated string.

The capabilities element is a set of bit fields, most of which are unused in
the current implementation of VESA. These can be ignored for the applications
in this book.

The videomode element points to a table of integers in the VESA BIOS that define
which VESA mode numbers the BIOS can handle. The list will be terminated by the
value FFFFH. We'll deal with VESA mode numbers in a moment.

The memory element specifies the number of 64K memory blocks the card supports.

The VESA standard defines specific mode numbers for a variety of text and graphic
modes. It also allows for custom modes, that is, for mode numbers defined by
individual manufacturers for their own use. While very open ended, this has meant
that a few VESA cards have used the VESA interface in fairly peculiar ways.

Here's a list of the standard VESA mode numbers:

```
0100H    640 by 400, 256 colors
0101H    640 by 480, 256 colors
0102H    800 by 600, 16 colors
0103H    800 by 600, 256 colors
0104H    1024 by 768, 16 colors
0105H    1024 by 768, 256 colors
0106H    1280 by 1024, 16 colors
0107H    1280 by 1024, 256 colors
0108H    80 by 60 column text
```

```
0109H    132 by 25 column text
010AH    132 by 43 column text
010BH    132 by 50 column text
010CH    132 by 60 column text
010DH    320 by 200, 32768 colors
010EH    320 by 200, 65536 colors
010FH    320 by 200, 16,777,216 colors
0110H    640 by 480, 32768 colors
0111H    640 by 480, 65536 colors
0112H    640 by 480, 16,777,216 colors
0113H    800 by 600, 32768 colors
0114H    800 by 600, 65536 colors
0115H    800 by 600, 16,777,216 colors
0116H    1024 by 768, 32768 colors
0117H    1024 by 768, 65536 colors
0118H    1024 by 768, 16,777,216 colors
0119H    1280 by 1024, 32768 colors
011AH    1280 by 1024, 65536 colors
011BH    1280 by 1024, 16,777,216 colors
```

It's worth noting that not all cards support all these modes. In fact, many cards with VESA support turn out not even to support VESA modes for all their capabilities.

You can find out if a card supports a particular mode by scanning through the list of integers pointed to by the videomode element in a VESABLOCK. For example, if you wanted to find out if a particular card supported 800 by 600, 16-color graphics— VESA mode 102H—you would perform the foregoing VESA status call and then do this:

```
while(*vb.videomode != 0x0102 &&
        *vb.videomode != 0xffff) (vb.videomode)++;

if(*vb.videomode == 0xffff) {
        /* the mode isn't supported */
}
```

Once you've determined that the VESA mode you're interested in is supported by the card you're working with, you can have the BIOS fetch another block of information about it. Here's the call to do this:

```
VESAINFO vi;
union REGS r;
struct SREGS sr;

r.x.ax=0x4f01;
r.x.di=FP_OFF((char *)&vi);
sr.es=FP_SEG((char *)&vi);
int86x(0x10,&r,&r,&sr);
```

The VESAINFO structure is quite a lot more involved than the VESABLOCK was— and, in fairness, you won't need any of it to work with the graphic functions described in this chapter. Here's what it looks like:

```
typedef struct {
        unsigned int modeattributes;
        char windowattr_a;
        char windowattr_b;
```

```
        unsigned int granularity;
        unsigned int windowsize;
        unsigned int windowsegment_a;
        unsigned int windowsegment_b;
        int (*windowptr)();
        unsigned int bytesperline;
        /* new additions */
        unsigned int xres;
        unsigned int yres;
        char xcharsize;
        char ycharsize;
        char numberofplanes;
        char bitsperpixel;
        char banks;
        char memorymodel;
        char banksize;
        char imagepages;
        char reserved1;
        char redmask;
        char redfield;
        char greenmask;
        char greenfield;
        char bluemask;
        char bluefield;
        char resmask;
        char resfield;
        char directcolor;
        char reserved2[216];
        } VESAINFO;
```

Not all of the information in a VESAINFO struct is of immediate use to the code in this book. We'll have a look at some of the more important fields here.

The modeattributes field is a collection of flags. Here's what the bits mean:

Bit 0: This will be high if the mode is supported in hardware.

Bit 2: This will be high if the output functions are supported by the BIOS.

Bit 3: This will be high if the mode is color.

Bit 4: This will be high if the mode is a graphics mode.

You can usually ignore this field.

The windowsize element specifies the size of the screen window in kilobytes. The windowsegment_a and windowsegment_b elements specify the video buffer screen segments.

The windowptr element is a pointer to a function that can be called to switch video pages, something that will be of use in the next chapter.

The bytesperline element specifies the size of one screen line in bytes.

Having learned everything you can about a VESA BIOS and the mode you want to use, you can actually select the mode and get down to something useful like this:

```
    union REGS r;
```

```
r.x.ax=0x4f02;
r.x.bx=MODENUMBER;
int86(0x10,&r,&r);
```

Finally, you can have a VESA BIOS tell you what the current mode is. The absolutely correct way to change modes under VESA is to find the current mode number, change modes, and then restore the previous mode when you're done working with the new mode. This is how you can retrieve the current mode:

```
union REGS r;
```

```
r.x.ax=0x4f03;
int86(0x10,&r,&r);
```

The mode number will be in r.x.bx.

Because a VESA BIOS will tell you quite a lot about itself, it's possible to write a program to list all the available modes of a VESA card. Figure 3-13 illustrates one.

This section has dealt with those areas of VESA that pertain to the code in this book. If you'd like to read the entire VESA specification, contact the

Video Electronics Standards Association
1330 S. Bascom Av. Suite D
San Jose, California 95128-4502.

3-13
The source code for
VESACARD.

```
/*
                VESA card explorer

                Copyright(c) 1992 Alchemy Mindworks Inc.
*/

#include "stdio.h"
#include "dos.h"
#include "alloc.h"

typedef struct {
        char sig[4];
        unsigned int version;
        char far *oemstring;
        char capabilities[4];
        unsigned int *videomode;
        unsigned int memory;
        char reserved[242];
        } VESABLOCK;

typedef struct {
        unsigned int attrib;
        char wina_attrib;
        char winb_attrib;
        unsigned int wingran;
        unsigned int winsize;
        unsigned int win_aseg;
        unsigned int win_bseg;
        int (*winfunc)();
```

```
            unsigned int bytesperline;
            unsigned int xres;
            unsigned int yres;
            char xchar;
            char ychar;
            char planecount;
            char bitsperpixel;
            char bankcount;
            char memorymodel;
            char banksize;
            char imagepagecount;
            } VESAMODE;

unsigned int linecount=0;

main()
{
        say("VESA card explorer copyright (c) 1992 Alchemy Mindworks Inc.");
        say("");

        if(!vesa()) say("No VESA BIOS extension found");
}

vesa()
{
        VESAMODE *vm;
        VESABLOCK vb;
        union REGS r;
        struct SREGS sr;
        char b[64],p[256];

        r.x.ax=0x4f00;
        sr.es=FP_SEG(&vb);
        r.x.di=FP_OFF(&vb);
        int86x(0x10,&r,&r,&sr);
        if(r.x.ax != 0x004f) return(0);
        if(memcmp(vb.sig,"VESA",4)) return(0);

        say("Vesa BIOS extension found");
        sprintf(b,"Version %d.%d",vb.version >> 8,vb.version & 0x00ff);
        say(b);
        say(vb.oemstring);
        sprintf(b,"%lu kilobytes of memory on board",(long)vb.memory*64L);
        say(b);

        say("Graphics modes supported:");
        for(;;*vb.videomode++) {
                if(*vb.videomode==0xffff) break;
                sprintf(b,"\t\tMode %04.4X:",*vb.videomode);
                say(b);
                switch(*vb.videomode) {
                        case 0x0100: say("\t\t640 by 400, 256 colours"); break;
                        case 0x0101: say("\t\t640 by 480, 256 colours"); break;
                        case 0x0102: say("\t\t800 by 600, 16 colours"); break;
                        case 0x0103: say("\t\t800 by 600, 256 colours"); break;
```

```
                        case 0x0104: say("\t\t1024 by 768, 16 colours"); break;
                        case 0x0105: say("\t\t1024 by 768, 256 colours"); break;
                        case 0x0106: say("\t\t1280 by 1024, 16 colours"); break;
                        case 0x0107: say("\t\t1280 by 1024, 256 colours"); break;
                        case 0x0108: say("\t\t80 by 60 column text"); continue;
                        case 0x0109: say("\t\t132 by 25 column text"); continue;
                        case 0x010a: say("\t\t132 by 43 column text"); continue;
                        case 0x010b: say("\t\t132 by 50 column text"); continue;
                        case 0x010c: say("\t\t132 by 60 column text"); continue;
                        case 0x010d: say("\t\t320 by 200, 32768 colours"); break;
                        case 0x010e: say("\t\t320 by 200, 65536 colours"); break;
                        case 0x010f: say("\t\t320 by 200, 16,777,216 colours"); break;
                        case 0x0110: say("\t\t640 by 480, 32768 colours"); break;
                        case 0x0111: say("\t\t640 by 480, 65536 colours"); break;
                        case 0x0112: say("\t\t640 by 380, 16,777,216 colours"); break;
                        case 0x0113: say("\t\t800 by 600, 32768 colours"); break;
                        case 0x0114: say("\t\t800 by 600, 65536 colours"); break;
                        case 0x0115: say("\t\t800 by 600, 16,777,216 colours"); break;
                        case 0x0116: say("\t\t1024 by 768, 32768 colours"); break;
                        case 0x0117: say("\t\t1024 by 768, 65536 colours"); break;
                        case 0x0118: say("\t\t1024 by 768, 16,777,216 colours"); break;
                        case 0x0119: say("\t\t1280 by 1024, 32768 colours"); break;
                        case 0x011a: say("\t\t1280 by 1024, 65536 colours"); break;
                        case 0x011b: say("\t\t1280 by 1024, 16,777,216 colours"); break;
                        default:
                                sprintf(b,"\t\tMode %XH - unknown",*vb.videomode);
                                say(b);
                                break;
                }

        r.x.ax=0x4f01;
        r.x.cx=*vb.videomode;
        sr.es=FP_SEG(p);
        r.x.di=FP_OFF(p);
        int86x(0x10,&r,&r,&sr);

        vm=(VESAMODE *)p;

        sprintf(b,"\t\t\tMode attributes: %04.4XH",vm->attrib); say(b);
        sprintf(b,"\t\t\tWindow A attributes: %02.2XH",vm->wina_attrib); say(b);
        sprintf(b,"\t\t\tWindow B attributes: %02.2XH",vm->winb_attrib); say(b);
        sprintf(b,"\t\t\tWindow granularity: %04.4XH",vm->wingran); say(b);
        sprintf(b,"\t\t\tWindow size: %04.4XH",vm->winsize); say(b);
        sprintf(b,"\t\t\tWindow A segment: %04.4XH",vm->win_aseg); say(b);
        sprintf(b,"\t\t\tWindow B segment: %04.4XH",vm->win_bseg); say(b);
        sprintf(b,"\t\t\tWindow function pointer: %p",vm->winfunc); say(b);

        sprintf(b,"\t\t\tBytes per line: %d",vm->bytesperline); say(b);

        sprintf(b,"\t\t\tX resolution: %d",vm->xres); say(b);
        sprintf(b,"\t\t\tY resolution: %d",vm->yres); say(b);
        sprintf(b,"\t\t\tX character size: %d",vm->xchar); say(b);
        sprintf(b,"\t\t\tY character size: %d",vm->ychar); say(b);
        sprintf(b,"\t\t\tMemory planes: %d",vm->planecount); say(b);
        sprintf(b,"\t\t\tBits per pixel: %d",vm->bitsperpixel); say(b);
```

```
                    sprintf(b,"\t\t\tBanks: %d",vm->bankcount); say(b);
                    sprintf(b,"\t\t\tMemory model: %d",vm->memorymodel); say(b);
                    sprintf(b,"\t\t\tBank size: %d",vm->banksize); say(b);
                    sprintf(b,"\t\t\tImage pages: %d",vm->imagepagecount); say(b);
        }
        say("");

        return(1);
}

say(s)
        char *s;
{

        puts(s);
        if(++linecount >= 24) {
                printf("[ More ]");
                getch();
                printf("\r            \r");
                linecount=0;
        }
}
```

Being able to work in the 16-color super VGA graphics modes seems to be a prerequisite for writing many sorts of ostensibly serious software. While many programmers will look at 16-color graphics and scoff loudly at a display architecture with enough backward compatibility to bend itself into a mobius strip, the modest memory and display requirements of 16-color graphics pretty well ensure that anything you write to run these modes will be usable by almost everyone with a computer made after the battle of Hastings. The same can't be said for the more interesting—but unquestionably more hardware hungry—256-color and high-color modes.

Keep in mind that even VGA cards made prior to the battle of Hastings have a respectable resolution at sixteen colors, and most basic VGA cards still offer 800 by 600 pixels at sixteen colors to run Windows. Basic VGA cards cost well under a hundred dollars, probably replacing mice as the cheapest peripherals available for Christmas presents and bribes for the very easily suborned. If one tenth of everyone with a card having the capability of running sixteen colors at 640 by 480 pixels or better springs for a copy of your software, you'll be able to buy yourself a universe and retire.

I consider it enlightening in reflection that of the two paint packages on the companion disk for this book—Desktop Paint 16 and Desktop Paint 256—the 256-color one has won hands down in individual sales, but the 16-color package gets sold in site licenses to businesses in far greater quantities than its ostensibly more powerful cousin.

Applications for 16-color graphics

256-Color graphics

Bawdy tales & questionable pictures

"There's no future in time travel."
—Graffiti

The 16-color graphic modes described in Chapter 3 are a good choice for ostensibly serious software. The 256-color modes to be dealt with in this chapter are well suited for getting together with a room full of pixels and having a good time. While not quite up to the imaging standards of the high-color super VGA modes—we'll deal with them in the next chapter—256-color graphic modes allow you to display pictures of photographic quality on a super VGA monitor, and to work in a pretty impressive range of colors.

The standard IBM VGA 256-color mode, mode 13H, is arguably too coarse to do anything serious with. Save for the really low cost "basic" super VGA cards, pretty well all super VGA adapters will let you work with at least 640 by 400 pixels at 256 colors, a decided improvement. However, as you might well have anticipated if you've read the previous chapter, all the super VGA 256-color modes are implemented differently by different manufacturers. For reasons to be dealt with in a moment, the problem of working with 256-color super VGA graphics is quite a bit more complex than it was for the 16-color modes.

This chapter will illustrate code to perform the 256-color equivalents of the 16-color functions from Chapter 3. Specifically, when you reach the end of it you'll have functions to do the following:

❏ Initialize a super VGA graphics mode
❏ Clear the screen
❏ Set the VGA palette

- ❏ Set pixels
- ❏ Draw lines
- ❏ Draw rectangles
- ❏ Fill rectangles
- ❏ Draw text
- ❏ Get and put image fragments
- ❏ Animate a mouse cursor
- ❏ Create and manage three-dimensional buttons
- ❏ Save graphic screen to a PCX file

Figure 4-1 illustrates the screen of the example program that will be created with the code in this chapter. While similar in appearance to FIG. 3-1 from the previous chapter, you'll note that the screen dimensions are different—which has caused the four buttons to change position relative to the other objects on the screen—and that there are a lot more palette tiles.

If you compile and run the example program from this chapter, you'll find that the screen colors are a bit different too.

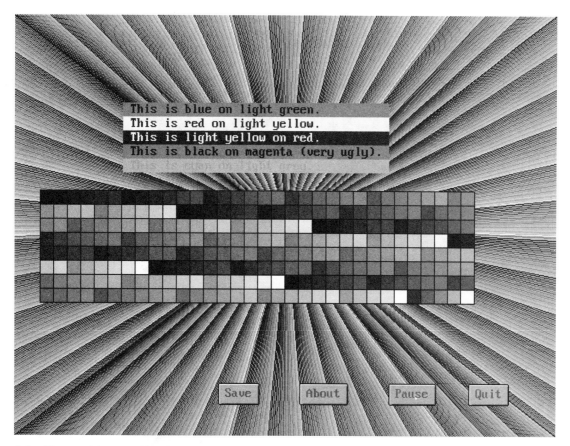

4-1 *The graphic created by the example program in this chapter.*

One of the things that makes 256-color graphics so interesting is the ability to integrate scanned photographs with machine-generated graphics. While this is something that won't be dealt with in detail in this chapter, you'll find that it's fairly easy to do, if you begin with the graphic file code from Chapter 2 and the buttons and drawing primitives to be presented here.

Figure 4-2 illustrates the screen of Desktop Paint 256, one of the programs from the companion disk of this book. It uses essentially the same code as the example in FIG. 4-1 did.

While there's a fairly elaborate graphical user interface library behind Desktop Paint 256—much the same one that was mentioned in Chapter 3—the graphic primitives it uses are not much more complicated than the ones in this chapter.

As with Chapter 3, the discussions of the graphic functions in this chapter are accompanied by code fragments to help you follow the whole circus as you go. In some cases these fragments have been simplified a bit to make them easier to follow. The complete—and wholly functional—code module will be presented toward the end of this chapter.

4-2 *Desktop Paint 256.*

As with the code in Chapter 3, the program in this chapter will consist of an assembly language program that does most of the work, a C language calling program and a C language header that sets up access to the assembly language functions. These are MOUSE256.ASM, TESTM256.C, and MOUSE256.H respectively.

As of this writing, super VGA cards with 256-color support are available with between 256K and 1 megabyte of video memory. The video memory has nothing to do with the memory in your system—it's the exclusive province of the super VGA card it's plugged into and is only used to store graphics.

You can work out the memory requirements in bytes of a 256-color graphic mode by multiplying its dimensions together, there being one byte per pixel in these modes. Divide the resulting value by 1024, the number of bytes in a kilobyte, to find the number of kilobytes of memory involved. Here's what the commonly used modes will call for:

640 by 400	250K
640 by 480	300K
800 by 600	470K
1024 by 768	768K
1280 by 768	960K

There are a number of things to keep in mind about these values. To begin with, the 640 by 400 pixel modes, on those cards that support them, are usually included for versions of the cards with only 256K of memory. This mode doesn't look very attractive. The aspect ratio of the 640 by 480 pixel mode is much more natural.

Super VGA cards usually come with 256K, 512K, or 1 megabyte of memory on board. In many cases, you can update the memory on a card with less than one megabyte by plugging in some additional chips and changing a few jumpers.

A card with 512K of memory on board will support 640 by 480 pixels at 256 colors. Most of them will also support 800 by 600, although this is by no means true of all cards. In addition to merely having enough memory to support the higher resolution modes, a super VGA card must also have the hardware on board to run at the higher sync rates of higher resolution modes.

Finally, before you attempt to display graphics in modes beyond 640 by 480 at 256 colors, make certain your monitor is designed to sync at these rates. You can toast a low end monitor quite substantially by running it in a graphic mode that it wasn't designed to support.

The code in this chapter will work with the 640 by 480 pixel, 256-color modes of the super VGA cards this book supports. We'll look at how you can modify it to work with other modes later on. You'll need at least 512K of memory on your display card to use the functions in this chapter as they stand.

For the most part, all super VGA cards manage their modes and memory in similar ways. There are two important distinctions between the super VGA chip sets of the various VGA card manufacturers. The first is how one actually enables a super VGA graphic mode, a problem similar to the one dealt with in Chapter 3. The solution is similar, too.

The second problem is one that didn't come up in Chapter 3. At 640 by 480 pixels in 256 colors, the video buffer is 300K long. However, a VGA card is only allowed to occupy one memory segment, or 64K, with its display memory. No matter how much memory a display card has, it can only appear in the memory space from A000:0000H through A000:FFFFH.

Super VGA cards get around this problem by using paged memory. The memory on a super VGA card can be made visible in the 64K "page frame" at A000:0000H one page at a time, where each page is 64K long.

Unlike the memory planes in the 16-color modes, the super VGA memory pages are pretty easy to work with—with one notable catch, to be explained in a moment. Let's begin by setting a pixel at location (10,14) on a 640 by 480 pixel, 256-color screen. Because each pixel is one byte and each line is 640 bytes long, this pixel is located at location 14 * 640 + 10, or 8970. This is well within the first 64K of screen memory; you could set this pixel by creating a pointer to this offset in segment A000H and writing to it.

Now, let's set a pixel at (10,150). This pixel resides at location 150 * 640 + 10, or 96,010. This is clearly not within the first 64K. On a super VGA card, you would get around this by changing pages. Specifically, you'd work out the page number by dividing this value by the number of bytes in one page; that's 96,010 / 65,535, or 1 in integer math. Next, you'd tell the super VGA card to make memory page one appear in the page frame at A000:0000H. Finally, you'd work out the offset into this page like this:

```
offset = location - (65535 * pagenumber);
```

In this case, this works out to 96,010 - (65,535 * 1), or 30,475. With page one visible in the page frame, you could create a far pointer to this location and set the pixel.

By switching pages as need be, all the video memory in a super VGA screen buffer can be accessed. This is more complicated than simply writing to the screen buffer directly, of course, but it's really the only way the fairly claustrophobic memory architecture of a PC lets a large screen buffer be managed.

The previously alluded-to second problem in working with the diverse super VGA cards, then, is how your software is to instruct them to change pages. There's no standard BIOS call or other operation for doing this; in all cases, it requires some pretty inscrutable register fiddling. Each of the cards in question has its own layout of registers, and hence it's own bit of code to fiddle them.

This chapter will deal with the hardware-specific code for the cards being examined in this book. If you'd like to expand it to deal with additional cards in their 256-color modes, you'll need not only the appropriate mode numbers but also the functions to change pages. This latter problem is usually a bit more awkward to solve in the absence of documentation from the manufacturer of the card in question.

John Bridges' VGAKIT, mentioned in the previous chapter, is a superb resource in this respect.

One way around this problem, of course, is to use VESA, rather than the native hardware mode of a display card. This assumes, of course, that the card in question either has a VESA BIOS or can be coerced into thinking it does with a suitable TSR. You should be warned, however, that not all VESA implementation work properly, and that graphic-intensive applications such as the ones in this chapter are among the more likely things to upset imperfect VESA cards. In developing the code for this chapter I encountered a disturbingly large number of VESA cards that wouldn't work with it—or anything else that used the same VESA graphic modes and facilities.

If the code to be presented here doesn't work on your VESA board, you might just have a funky VESA implementation.

As a final note, like the code in Chapter 3, there's an assembly language module involved in this program as well. Unlike the one in Chapter 3, this one's a bit enormous. It's called MOUSE256.ASM. The inherently simpler structure of 256-color graphic modes makes writing graphic primitives a lot simpler, but this is more than offset by the relatively large amounts of memory involved. To make the 256-color graphic functions run at a workable speed, a lot more of them have been handled in assembly language, rather than in C.

Assembly language lends itself to much tighter code and smaller applications, but it requires voluminous source listings. You'll find the complete listing of MOUSE256.ASM toward the end of this chapter.

As with the 16-color graphic modes, there are two considerations in selecting the mode you want to work with. The first is in simply knowing the magic number that will turn it on. The second is in setting up a table of pointers to address the screen lines quickly. The first problem is easily solved:

Initializing a super VGA graphic mode

```
#define PARADISE   0x5f
#define ATI        0x62
#define TSENG      0x2e
#define TRIDENT    0x5d
#define OAK        0x53
#define VESA       0x0101
```

In all cases save for VESA, these values are passed in the AX register to INT 10H to select the mode in question.

The second problem is one of such scope and enormity as to make lesser problems gaze up at it in awe and admiration, quaking in its shadow and building statues to pay homage to its awkwardness.

There are few cases in which you'll want to write just one pixel to the screen. In drawings lines, capturing and painting image fragments, painting text, and so on, strings of bytes must be moved to and from the screen memory address space. In most cases, this isn't a lot more difficult to do than setting a single pixel. However, there are four lines on a 640 by 480 pixel, 256-color screen in which the breaks between pages occur. These breaks don't even fall conveniently between screen lines. This means that for these four lines, the first part of the line is on one page and the second part is on the next higher page.

This does complicate writing to the screen buffer to no small extent.

In Chapter 3, we looked at how a program can set up a table of offsets into the screen buffer, such that the address of any line can be found by indexing into the table. Much the same thing can be done in the 256-color modes, save that each entry in the table must contain not only the offset into the screen memory, but also the number of the page where the memory in question resides. Finally, it must contain a flag to tell the code that will read and write to the screen memory whether a line is one of those with a break in the middle. These lines must be handled differently.

This is a bit of code to handle the creation of such a table. The table lives at _SCREENTBL. Each entry is two words long. The first word is the offset into the screen memory. Of the second word, the low order byte is the page number and the high order byte is a flag for broken lines. In this example, the numbers 640 and 480 refer to the screen dimensions.

```
          MOV   CX,480
          MOV   BX,0000H
          MOV   SI,OFFSET _SCREENTBL
MT1:  PUSH  CX
          MOV   AX,640
          MUL   BX
          AND   DX,00FFH
          MOV   CX,0FFFEH
          SUB   CX,640
          CMP   AX,CX
          JB    MT2
          MOV   DH,0FFH

MT2:  MOV   DS:[SI],AX
          MOV   DS:[SI+2],DX
          ADD   SI,4
          INC   BX
          POP   CX
          LOOP  MT1
```

The MOUSE256.ASM module calls this function MAKETABLE.

In addition to setting up the screen dimensions and the screen pointer table—as was done in Chapter 3—the initialization code in this chapter will also set up an indirect function pointer called SETBANK. This points to whichever procedure is appropriate for setting the screen memory page on the card being used. Handling the bank setting this way allows the banks to be changed quickly, something that's important for operations like animating a mouse cursor.

The graphic and mouse initialization have been combined into the InitMouse function in MOUSE256.ASM. The mouse initialization remains unchanged from that of MOUSE16.ASM. Note, however, that all the VESA functions have been ported to assembly language in this version of InitMouse.

The page switching functions in MOUSE256.ASM are down near the end of the listing. They're named as follows:

Paradise   SETBANK_PAR

ATI   SETBANK_ATI

Tseng Labs	SETBANK_TNG
Trident	SETBANK_TRI
Oak	SETBANK_OAK
VESA	SETBANK_VSA

Understanding what these functions are actually up to would require some pretty serious grappling with the low level hardware of the cards in question. There's pretty well no need to do so—just call the appropriate bit of code and get on with your application.

The SETBANK_VSA function is a bit different from the others. Rather than fiddling registers, a VESA board allows you to change banks through a standardized call to the VESA BIOS. There are two ways to perform this call—either through INT 10H with AX set to 4F05H and DX set to the bank number, or by doing a far indirect call to the address in the WINFUNPTR element of the VESAINFO struct returned by the BIOS, assuming this pointer isn't NULL. The latter is quite a bit faster.

The bank number for a VESA card isn't constrained to be the same as that of the other display cards being dealt with in this chapter, as a VESA card need not have 64K screen memory pages. Most do, of course, as a VESA BIOS usually just makes calls to the real display hardware of the card it supports. However, to support the possibility of different page sizes, the FINDVESASHIFT function in MOUSE26.ASM works out the real bank size based on the information returned in a VESAINFO struct and stores it such that SETBANK_VSA can work out the correct bank number to pass to the BIOS when it's asked to change pages.

The VESA initialization is handled by INITVESA in MOUSE256.ASM. It also handles creating the line start table, which could be a bit different from the one set up by MAKETABLE for the other card types.

While having SCREENTBL correctly set up will allow you to address all the pixels on the screen, writing code that does so effectively requires a few more tools. Because strings of bytes written to the screen might cross a page boundary, you can't use the normal STOSB and MOVSB string instructions. These machine instructions were not created to deal with the page boundaries of VGA cards correctly.

Addressing the screen

The MOUSE256 code module includes a number of functions and macros that replace simple string instructions and pointer manipulations. The first is the VGALINE function, which will return a pointer to the line specified in the BX register as ES:DI. In fact, it also handles changing the screen memory page appropriately and setting a flag to tell other code whether the line being addressed has a break in it.

Here's what it looks like:

```
VGALINE PROC  NEAR
        PUSH  AX
        PUSH  BX
        PUSH  CX
        PUSH  DX
```

```
            LDATASEG
            SHL       BX,1
            SHL       BX,1
            MOV       DI,[_SCREENTBL+BX]
            MOV       AX,[_SCREENTBL+2+BX]
            CALL      CS:[SETBANK]
            MOV       [PAGEBREAK],AH
            MOV       ES,[_SCREENSEG]
            POP       DX
            POP       CX
            POP       BX
            POP       AX
            RET
    VALINE  ENDP
```

Note that the bank setting functions—one of which will be addressed by
SETBANK—will ignore attempts to change banks when the bank number being
selected is the same as that of the current bank. The value in PAGEBREAK will be
true if the line pointed to by ES:DI has a break in it.

There are also a number of macros defined up near the top of MOUSE256.ASM.
These are "safe" versions of the usual string and byte move instructions. They're
aware of the possibility of a string in the screen memory straddling a page break,
and will change pages accordingly.

To begin with, the INCPAGE macro is called by several of the other macros to
increment the current page number, should a page break be encountered.

```
    INCPAGE MACRO
            PUSH   AX
            MOV    AX,[CODEPAGE]
            INC    AX
            CALL   VGABANK
            POP    AX
            ENDM
```

The CHECKPAGE macro decides whether to call INCPAGE. It's called after DI has
been incremented when it's used to write to the screen buffer. The only case in
which DI should contain zero is if it has wrapped around past the end of its
segment, indicating that the page should be incremented.

```
    CHECKPAGE MACRO
            LOCAL    LAB1
            CMP      DI,0000H
            JNE      LAB1
            INCPAGE
    LAB1:
            ENDM
```

The GRAFADD_DI macro adds an offset to DI. However, it's a lot more complicated
than the usual ADD DI,AX instruction because it checks to see if doing so would
mean that the new value of DI should point into a different page. If this would
happen, it calls INCPAGE.

```
    GRAFADD_DI MACRO   ARG1
            LOCAL    LAB1
            PUSH     AX
```

```
            MOV     AX,DI
            ADD     DI,ARG1
            CMP     AX,DI
            JBE     LAB1
            INCPAGE
    LAB1:
            POP     AX
            ENDM
```

The GRAF_STOSB macro performs a normal STOSB machine instruction and then checks to make sure the end of a page hasn't been reached, adjusting the page if need be.

```
GRAF_STOSB  MACRO
            CLD
            STOSB
            CHECKPAGE
            ENDM
```

The limitation in GRAF_STOSB is that it won't work with the REPNE prefix, as it's not a real machine instruction. As such, we'll need a macro to handle this, too:

```
GRAF_REPNESTOSB  MACRO
                 LOCAL    LAB1,LAB2
                 CLD
                 CMP      [PAGEBREAK],00H
                 JNE      LAB1
            REPNE STOSB
                 JMP      LAB2
    LAB1:        STOSB
                 CHECKPAGE
                 LOOP     LAB1
    LAB2:
                 ENDM
```

The GRAF_REPNESTOSB macro is the first one to make use of the PAGEBREAK flag. If PAGEBREAK is zero, indicating that the line being addressed has no break, it can use a normal REPNE STOSB instruction without concern that doing so might wrap past a page boundary. If the PAGEBREAK flag isn't zero, it handles the string move one byte at a time, calling CHECKPAGE after each byte to make sure it hasn't crossed the page boundary. This is a lot slower, of course, but as it only happens in four places on the screen it's not too crippling.

There's also an equivalent macro for REPNE MOVSB.

```
GRAF_REPNEMOVSB  MACRO
                 LOCAL    LAB1,LAB2
                 CLD
                 CMP      [PAGEBREAK],00H
                 JNE      LAB1
            REPNE MOVSB
                 JMP      LAB2
    LAB1:        MOVSB
                 CHECKPAGE
                 LOOP     LAB1
    LAB2:
                 ENDM
```

These macros will turn up throughout the code to be dealt with in this chapter. They're reasonably transparent, with one important catch. Some of them refer to objects in the common data segment of the program. The DS register must be set to _DATA prior to invoking those that do, or they'll behave unpredictably. With its fairly limited selection of segment registers, an 8086-series processor can make this a bit of a juggling act.

The LDATASEG macro will set DS to _DATA.

Clearing the screen

Clearing the screen in a 256-color mode is almost effortless. All that's involved in writing the same value to every byte in the screen memory as quickly as possible. The GRAF_REPNESTOSB macro makes this fairly painless.

```
_ClearScreen  PROC    FAR
              PUSH    BP
              MOV     BP,SP
              PUSH    DS
              PUSH    ES

              LDATASEG
              CALL    HIDECURSOR
              MOV     CX,[_SCREENDEEP]
              MOV     BX,0000H
CS1:          PUSH    CX
              PUSH    BX
              CALL    VGALINE
              MOV     AL,BYTE PTR [BP + _AOFF + 0]
              MOV     CX,[_SCREENWIDE]
              GRAF_REPNESTOSB
              POP     BX
              POP     CX
              INC     BX
              LOOP    CS1

              LDATASEG
              CALL    SHOWCURSOR
              POP     ES
              POP     DS
              POP     BP
              RET
_ClearScreen  ENDP
```

The ClearScreen function illustrates the use of VGALINE. It also makes calls to HIDECURSOR and SHOWCURSOR. While these functions haven't been formally discussed in conjunction with MOUSE256, they're identical to those in MOUSE16.

Setting the VGA palette

The code to set the VGA palette is one of the few parts of the 256-color graphic package that can be handled in C without any real penalty. Here's the complete SetVgaPalette function.

```
SetVgaPalette(p,n)
        char *p;
        unsigned int n;
{
        int i;
```

```
                 outp(0x3c6,0xff);
                 for(i=0;i<n;++i) {
                         outp(0x3c8,i);
                         outp(0x3c9,(*p++) >> 2);
                         outp(0x3c9,(*p++) >> 2);
                         outp(0x3c9,(*p++) >> 2);
                 }
         }
```

The 256-color SetVgaPalette function is called just like its 16-color counterpart from the previous chapter, although its internal workings are different. Rather than using BIOS calls to set the palette colors, it manipulates the display card registers directly. A 256-color palette takes a significant amount of time to set if you handle it through BIOS calls.

The TESTM256.C program that will call the functions in MOUSE256 includes an example 256-color palette. The color names from the previous chapter are also included, although their values have been modified to reflect comparable colors in this palette. As with the 16-color graphics program, if you change the palette colors, the color names won't mean much anymore.

Setting individual pixels in a 256-color graphic mode is fairly elementary. The vertical coordinate of the pixel to be set forms the argument to pass to VGALINE. The horizontal coordinate can be added to the resulting ES:DI pointer with GRAFADD_DI to derive an offset into the line, with page changes as necessary.

Setting pixels

Here's the function to get it together:

```
_SetPixel  PROC    FAR
           PUSH    BP
           MOV     BP,SP
           PUSH    DS
           PUSH    ES

           LDATASEG

           MOV     DX,[BP+_AOFF+0]
           MOV     BX,[BP+_AOFF+2]
           MOV     AX,[BP+_AOFF+4]
           GRAF_PUTPIXEL

           POP     ES
           POP     DS
           POP     BP
           RET
_SetPixel  ENDP
```

The GRAF_PUTPIXEL macro combines GRAFADD_DI and STOSB.

Drawing lines

The theoretical process for drawing lines was explained in the previous chapter. The DrawLine function for 256-color graphics will use Bresenham's algorithm too, although the implementation will be a bit different. In the 16-color DrawLine function, the code to set pixels could be handled as a C language macro, resulting in acceptably quick code. In this case, however, the DrawLine function would have to call SetPixel from the MOUSE256 module if it were to be written in C. The overhead of doing a call every time a pixel was to be set would slow DrawLine down to a fairly embarrassing degree. The solution is to implement Bresenham's algorithm in assembly language.

The assembly language DrawLine is shown in FIG. 4-3. It's nothing like as easy to understand as the C language version from Chapter 3, although it is remarkably quick. Note that the 8086-series processors don't really have enough machine registers to handle all the values required of the implement DrawLine, and some of the variables are stored on the stack.

If you'd like to improve on the performance of the 16-color DrawLine function from the last chapter, try porting this DrawLine to MOUSE16.ASM and deleting DrawLine from the TESTM16.C source file. You'll have to replace the GRAF_PUTPIXEL macro expansions with code to set 16-color pixels in write mode two.

4-3
The DrawLine function implemented in assembly language.

```
LINE_DELTAX     EQU     2
LINE_DELTAY     EQU     4
LINE_HALFX      EQU     6
LINE_HALFY      EQU     8
LINE_COUNT      EQU     10
LINE_ADJ        EQU     12

;THIS FUNCTION DRAWS A LINE
;        ARGS      -       LEFT
;                          TOP
;                          RIGHT
;                          BOTTOM
;                          COLOUR
;        RETURNS   -       VOID
                 PUBLIC   _DrawLine
_DrawLine        PROC     FAR
                 PUSH     BP
                 MOV      BP,SP
                 SUB      SP,LINE_ADJ
                 PUSH     DS
                 PUSH     ES

                 LDATASEG

                 FIXRECT

                 CALL     HIDECURSOR

                 MOV      AX,[BP+_AOFF+6]
                 SUB      AX,[BP+_AOFF+2];BOTTOM - TOP = DELTA Y

                 MOV      SI,1
                 JGE      LINE1
                 MOV      SI,-1
                 NEG      AX
LINE1:           MOV      [BP - LINE_DELTAY],AX

                 MOV      AX,[BP+_AOFF+4]
                 SUB      AX,[BP+_AOFF+0];RIGHT - LEFT = DELTA X
```

```
                    MOV       DI,1
                    JGE       LINE2
                    MOV       DI,-1
                    NEG       AX

LINE2:              MOV       [BP - LINE_DELTAX],AX

                    MOV       AX,[BP - LINE_DELTAX]
                    CMP       AX,[BP - LINE_DELTAY]
                    JL        LINE3

                    ;HANDLE SLOPE < 1

                    MOV       AX,[BP - LINE_DELTAX]
                    SHR       AX,1
                    MOV       [BP - LINE_HALFX],AX

                    MOV       CX,[BP+_AOFF+0]
                    MOV       DX,[BP+_AOFF+2]
                    MOV       BX,0000H
                    MOV       AX,[BP - LINE_DELTAX]
                    MOV       [BP - LINE_COUNT],AX

LINE5:              PUSH      BX                    ;PLOT THE PIXEL
                    PUSH      DI
                    PUSH      DX
                    MOV       BX,DX
                    MOV       DX,CX
                    MOV       AX,[BP+_AOFF+8]
                    GRAF_PUTPIXEL
                    POP       DX
                    POP       DI
                    POP       BX

                    ADD       CX,DI
                    ADD       BX,[BP - LINE_DELTAY]
                    CMP       BX,[BP - LINE_HALFX]
                    JLE       LINE6
                    SUB       BX,[BP - LINE_DELTAX]
                    ADD       DX,SI

LINE6:              DEC       WORD PTR [BP - LINE_COUNT]
                    JGE       LINE5

                    JMP       LINE4

                    ; HANDLE SLOPE > 1
LINE3:              MOV       AX,[BP - LINE_DELTAY]
                    SHR       AX,1
                    MOV       [BP - LINE_HALFY],AX

                    MOV       CX,[BP+_AOFF+0]
                    MOV       DX,[BP+_AOFF+2]
                    MOV       BX,0000H
                    MOV       AX,[BP - LINE_DELTAY]
```

```
                              MOV       [BP - LINE_COUNT],AX
              LINE7:          PUSH      BX                    ;PLOT THE PIXEL
                              PUSH      DI
                              PUSH      DX
                              MOV       BX,DX
                              MOV       DX,CX
                              MOV       AX,[BP+_AOFF+8]
                              GRAF_PUTPIXEL
                              POP       DX
                              POP       DI
                              POP       BX

                              ADD       DX,SI
                              ADD       BX,[BP - LINE_DELTAX]
                              CMP       BX,[BP - LINE_HALFY]
                              JLE       LINE8
                              SUB       BX,[BP - LINE_DELTAY]
                              ADD       CX,DI

              LINE8:          DEC       WORD PTR [BP - LINE_COUNT]
                              JGE       LINE7

              LINE4:          LDATASEG
                              CALL      SHOWCURSOR

                              POP       ES
                              POP       DS
                              ADD       SP,LINE_ADJ
                              POP       BP
                              RET
              _DrawLine       ENDP
```

Drawing & filling rectangles

Unlike the 16-color graphic function to draw rectangles, the FrameRect function in MOUSE256 doesn't make calls to DrawLine but rather does the drawing internally. This can run quite a bit faster than DrawLine, as the lines of a rectangle are constrained to be either perfectly horizontal or perfectly vertical. There are no slope calculations involved. The extra speed of handling this line drawing as a special case helps to compensate for the generally slower performance of 256-color graphics.

Figure 4-4 illustrates the 256-color FrameRect function.

```
              ;THIS FUNCTION DRAWS A RECTANGLE
              ;       ARGS       -        LEFT
              ;                           TOP
              ;                           RIGHT
              ;                           BOTTOM
              ;                           COLOUR
              ;       RETURNS    -        VOID
                              PUBLIC    _FrameRect
              _FrameRect      PROC      FAR
                              PUSH      BP
```

```
            MOV      BP,SP
            PUSH     DS
            PUSH     ES

            LDATASEG

            FIXRECTDIR
            FIXRECT

            CALL     HIDECURSOR

            MOV      BX,[BP+_AOFF+2] ;TOP LINE
            MOV      CX,[BP+_AOFF+6] ;BOTTOM LINE
            SUB      CX,BX

            MOV      DX,[BP+_AOFF+4]
            SUB      DX,[BP+_AOFF+0] ;GET WIDTH

;           DRAW TOP LINE
            PUSH     CX
            PUSH     BX
            CALL     VGALINE
            GRAFADD_DI [BP+_AOFF+0]

            MOV      CX,DX
            INC      CX
            MOV      AX,[BP+_AOFF+8] ;COLOUR

            GRAF_REPNESTOSB

            POP      BX
            POP      CX

;           DRAW SIDES
FR1:        PUSH     CX
            PUSH     DX
            INC      BX

            PUSH     DX
            MOV      DX,[BP+_AOFF+0] ;LEFT
            MOV      AX,[BP+_AOFF+8] ;COLOUR
            GRAF_PUTPIXEL

            POP      CX
            ADD      DX,CX
            GRAF_PUTPIXEL

            POP      DX
            POP      CX
            LOOP     FR1

;           DRAW BOTTOM LINE
            CALL     VGALINE
            GRAFADD_DI [BP+_AOFF+0]
```

```
                    MOV      CX,DX
                    INC      CX
                    MOV      AX,[BP+_AOFF+8] ;COLOUR

                    GRAF_REPNESTOSB

                    LDATASEG
                    CALL     SHOWCURSOR

                    POP      ES
                    POP      DS
                    POP      BP
                    RET
_FrameRect          ENDP
```

In drawing a rectangle, the two horizontal lines are pretty easy. After the line to be written to is found using a call to VGALINE, the offset to the left edge of the rectangle can be calculated with the GRAFADD_DI macro, which adds the LEFT argument to the ES:DI pointer returned by VGALINE. The width of the rectangle can be filled with the appropriate byte value using GRAF_REPNESTOSB.

Filling rectangles in 256-color graphics is a lot like drawing them. The FillRect function, as illustrated in FIG. 4-5, really just draws the top line of FrameRect over and over again, until the entire depth of the rectangle has been covered. Fortunately, there's nothing very elaborate happening in this code, and it all works very quickly.

The VGA gurus from the last chapter haven't turned up much in this one, but one thing they're likely to observe in this code is that FillRect could be speeded up measurably by writing words rather than bytes—with a single STOSB at the beginning and end of a line if its dimensions happened to be odd. This is based on the observation that it takes half as many STOSW instructions as it does STOSB instructions to fill a buffer with bytes. You might want to see if you can find a way to modify FillRect to implement this strategy if you're really concerned about performance. Having said this, you might want to see FillRect in action before you set about this task, as it's pretty snappy as it stands.

4-5
The FillRect function.

```
;THIS FUNCTION FILLS A RECTANGLE
;       ARGS       -       LEFT
;                          TOP
;                          RIGHT
;                          BOTTOM
;                          COLOUR
;       RETURNS    -       VOID
                    PUBLIC_FillRect
_FillRect           PROC FAR
                    PUSH BP
                    MOV  BP,SP
                    PUSH DS
                    PUSH ES

                    LDATASEG

                    FIXRECTDIR
```

```
                FIXRECT

                CALL       HIDECURSOR

                MOV        BX,[BP+_AOFF+2]   ;TOP LINE
                MOV        CX,[BP+_AOFF+6]   ;BOTTOM LINE
                SUB        CX,BX
                INC        CX

                MOV        DX,[BP+_AOFF+4]
                SUB        DX,[BP+_AOFF+0]   ;GET WIDTH

IR1:            PUSH       CX
                PUSH       BX
                CALL       VGALINE
                GRAFADD_DI [BP+_AOFF+0]

                MOV        CX,DX
                INC        CX
                MOV        AX,[BP+_AOFF+8]   ;COLOUR

                GRAF_REPNESTOSB

                POP        BX
                POP        CX
                INC        BX
                LOOP       IR1

                LDATASEG
                CALL       SHOWCURSOR

                POP        ES
                POP        DS
                POP        BP
                RET
_FillRect       ENDP
```

Drawing text

Text drawing was described in detail in Chapter 3, and the DrawString function for 256-color graphics needn't be all that different from its 16-color ancestor. It still uses the VGA BIOS as a source of font patterns and addresses them in essentially the same way. The difference is that each byte of the source font must be translated into eight bytes worth of pixels because each pixel is a bit, rather than a byte. This is one of the few instances wherein it's genuinely easier to write a function for 16-color graphics than it is for 256 colors.

Having said this, keep in mind that you don't have to keep track of any bit masks or different write modes in the 256-color version of DrawString, arguably something of a measure of compensation.

Figure 4-6 illustrates the source code for DrawString. If it looks familiar, it's because save for the bit that actually writes to the screen, it's identical to the DrawString function from the previous chapter.

```
                      ;THIS FUNCTION DRAWS A STRING OF TEXT
                      ;            ARG1 = X
                      ;            ARG2 = Y
                      ;            ARG3 = STRING
                      ;            ARG4 = COLOUR
                      ;            ARG6 = BACKGROUND
                      PUBLIC    _DrawString
      _DrawString     PROC      FAR
                      PUSH      BP
                      MOV       BP,SP
                      PUSH      DS
                      PUSH      ES

                      LDATASEG

                      CALL      HIDECURSOR

                      ;LOOP THROUGH ALL THE LINES
                      MOV       CX,[_FONTDEPTH]
      DS0:            PUSH      CX
                      DEC       CX

                      ;GET THE BOTTOM LINE — WE COUNT BACKWARDS
                      MOV       BX,[BP + _AOFF + 2]
                      ADD       BX,CX

                      ;GET THE SCREEN POINTER
                      LDATASEG
                      CALL      VGALINE
                      GRAFADD_DI          [BP+_AOFF+0]

                      ;POINT TO THE START OF THE STRING
                      MOV       SI,[BP + _AOFF + 4]
                      MOV       DS,[BP + _AOFF + 6]

                      ;STOP LOOPING WHEN A NULL BYTE IS REACHED
      DS1:            MOV       AH,00H
                      MOV       AL,DS:[SI]
                      CMP       AL,00H
                      JE        DS5

      DS2:            PUSH      DS
                      PUSH      SI

                      ;FIND THE FONT CHARACTER
                      MUL       [_FONTDEPTH]

                      ;GET THE BYTE OFFSET
                      MOV       BX,AX
                      ADD       BX,CX

                      PUSH      CX

                      ;GET THE BYTE FROM THE FONT
                      MOV       SI,[_FONTOFF]
```

```
        MOV        DS,[_FONTSEG]
        MOV        AH,DS:[SI+BX]

        MOV        CX,0008H
        MOV        BX,0000H

        LDATASEG

DS3:            MOV        AL,BYTE PTR [BP + _AOFF + 8]
                TEST       AH,[_MASKTABLE + BX]
                JNZ        DS4
                MOV        AL,BYTE PTR [BP + _AOFF + 10]

DS4:            INC        BX
                GRAF_STOSB
                LOOP       DS3

                POP        CX

                POP        SI
                POP        DS
                INC        SI
                JMP        DS1

DS5:            POP        CX
                LOOP       DS0

                LDATASEG
                CALL       SHOWCURSOR

                POP        ES
                POP        DS
                POP        BP
                RET
_DrawString     ENDP
```

The part of DrawString that handles writing to the screen makes use of the
masktable object discussed at the end of Chapter 3. This bit of code expects to
find one byte of font data in the AH register. It will write eight bytes to the screen at
ES:DI. Any bytes which correspond to set bits in AH will be written in the
foreground color. The remaining bytes will be written in the background color.

```
        MOV        CX,0008H
        MOV        BX,0000H

  DS3:  MOV        AL,BYTE PTR [BP + _AOFF + 8]
        TEST       AH,[_MASKTABLE + BX]
        JNZ        DS4
        NOV        AL,BYTE PTR [BP + _AOFF + 10]

  DS4:  INC        BX
        GRAF_STOSB
        LOOP       DS3
```

In this code fragment, BX addresses successively higher entries in `masktable`, which are tested against the font data in AH. As a result of the test, AL will contain either argument eight or argument ten of `DrawString`, the foreground and background colors respectively. The GRAF_STOSB macro writes AL to the screen.

As an aside, it's worth noting that because `DrawString` finds its font data in the VGA BIOS of the machine it's running on, the text it draws will look like the normal text mode characters on your monitor. If you use the 16-point text, you'll find that the usual high-order IBM screen characters are also available. The only catch to this—albeit a small one—is that the appearance of the text drawn by your applications may change slightly from machine to machine. Not all VGA BIOSs have identical internal fonts.

This will not affect either the meaning or the legibility of the text in your applications, of course. However, you might find that the text in your programs doesn't look exactly like that in FIG. 4-1.

Moving image fragments

The 256-color equivalents to the Turbo C `getimage` and `putimage` functions behave much like their 16-color counterparts from Chapter 3. They will handle image fragments larger than 64K and they work in whatever super VGA modes MOUSE256 will, something that the standard Borland BGI drivers do not allow for. Finally, they're impressively quick.

Inasmuch as the 256-color modes don't require any bit shifting, the code for `GetImage256` and `PutImage256` can be pretty elementary. However, for many of the same reasons as applied to the previous functions in this chapter, these two must be handled in assembly language as well. Figure 4-7 illustrates the code for `GetImage256` and `PutImage256`.

4-7
The GetImage256 *and* PutImage256 *functions.*

```
;THIS FUNCTION COPIES AN IMAGE FRAGMENT FROM THE SCREEN
;       ARGS        -       LEFT
;                           TOP
;                           RIGHT
;                           BOTTOM
;                           IMAGE
;       RETURNS     -       VOID
                PUBLIC      _GetImage256
_GetImage256    PROC        FAR
                PUSH        BP
                MOV         BP,SP
                PUSH        DS
                PUSH        ES

                LDATASEG

                FIXRECTDIR
                FIXRECT

                CALL        HIDECURSOR

                MOV         AX,[_SCREENWIDE]

                MOV         DX,[BP+_AOFF+4]         ;GET WIDTH
                SUB         DX,[BP+_AOFF+0]
```

```
              MOV      CX,[BP+_AOFF+6]        ;GET DEPTH
              SUB      CX,[BP+_AOFF+2]

              MOV      SI,[BP+_AOFF+8]        ;GET IMAGE
              MOV      DS,[BP+_AOFF+10]

              NORMALIZE                               ;NORMALIZE POINTER

              MOV      DS:[SI],DX              ;SAVE SIZE VALUES
              MOV      DS:[SI+2],CX
              ADD      SI,0004H

              INC      CX                     ;GET REAL SIZE VALUES
              INC      DX

GI1:          PUSH     CX
              PUSH     DX

              PUSH     DS
              LDATASEG
              MOV      BX,[BP+_AOFF+2]
              CALL     VGALINE
              GRAFADD_DI [BP+_AOFF+0]
              POP      DS
              INC      WORD PTR [BP+_AOFF+2]

              POP      CX
              PUSH     CX

GI2:          MOV      AL,ES:[DI]
              MOV      DS:[SI],AL
              INC      SI
              PUSH     DS
              LDATASEG
              GRAFADD_DI 0001H
              POP      DS
              LOOP     GI2

              PUSH     DS
              LDATASEG
              MOV      AX,[_SCREENWIDE]
              POP      DS
              NORMALIZE

              POP      DX
              POP      CX
              LOOP     GI1

              LDATASEG

              CALL     SHOWCURSOR

              POP      ES
              POP      DS
```

```
                                    POP      BP
                                    RET
_GetImage256                        ENDP

;THIS FUNCTION COPIES AN IMAGE FRAGMENT TO THE SCREEN
;          ARGS      -       X
;                            Y
;                            IMAGE
;          RETURNS -         VOID
                                    PUBLIC   _PutImage256
_PutImage256                        PROC     FAR
                                    PUSH     BP
                                    MOV      BP,SP
                                    PUSH     DS
                                    PUSH     ES

                                    CALL     HIDECURSOR

                                    MOV      SI,[BP+_AOFF+4]
                                    MOV      DS,[BP+_AOFF+6]

                                    MOV      DX,DS:[SI + 0]        ;GET WIDTH
                                    INC      DX
                                    MOV      CX,DS:[SI + 2]        ;GET DEPTH
                                    INC      CX
                                    ADD      SI,0004H

PI1:                                PUSH     CX
                                    PUSH     DX

                                    PUSH     DS
                                    LDATASEG
                                    MOV      BX,[BP+_AOFF+2]
                                    CALL     VGALINE
                                    GRAFADD_DI [BP+_AOFF+0]
                                    POP      DS

                                    INC      WORD PTR [BP+_AOFF+2]
                                    POP      CX
                                    PUSH     CX

                                    CLD
PI2:                                MOV      AL,DS:[SI]

                                    PUSH     DS
                                    LDATASEG
                                    GRAF_STOSB
                                    POP      DS

                                    INC      SI
                                    LOOP     PI2

                                    PUSH     DS
                                    LDATASEG
                                    MOV      AX,[_SCREENWIDE]
```

```
            POP      DS
            NORMALIZE

            POP      DX
            POP      CX
            LOOP     PI1

            LDATASEG
            CALL     SHOWCURSOR

            POP      ES
            POP      DS
            POP      BP
            RET
_PutImage256    ENDP
```

For the most part, these functions just copy strings of bytes from a source buffer to a destination buffer. Whichever buffer is in fact the screen must be addressed using VGALINE and the appropriate GRAF macros. The buffer in memory—the image fragment being gotten or saved—can be dealt with using normal pointer arithmetic with the addition of a new macro, called NORMALIZE.

The NORMALIZE macro deals with the problem of the offset of a simple pointer wrapping around—much the same thing that farPtr took care of in TESTM16 in the previous chapter. The NORMALIZE macro always adjusts DS:SI. Here's what it looks like:

```
     ;NORMALIZE THE POINTER IN DS:SI, SCREEN WIDTH IN AX
     NORMALIZE MACRO
            LOCAL   LAB1
            PUSH    AX
            PUSH    CX
            MOV     CX,0FFFFH
            SUB     CX,AX
            MOV     AX,CX
            CMP     SI,AX
            JB      LAB1
            MOV     AX,SI
            MOV     CL,4
            SHR     AX,CL

            MOV     CX,DS
            ADD     CX,AX
            MOV     DS,CX
            AND     SI,000FH

            LAB1:   POP      CX
            POP     AX
            ENDM
```

To begin with, NORMALIZE does nothing to DS:SI if SI is more than the width of the screen in bytes away from wrapping. In this case, a value can be safely added to it without fear of its wrapping around. If it does find that SI requires adjustment, it works out the number of 16-byte paragraphs represented by SI and adds them to

DS. It then reduces SI by a corresponding amount. When NORMALIZE gets done with it, SI will be no larger than fifteen.

It's worth noting that while the `GetImage256` and `PutImage256` perform analogous functions to the Turbo C `getimage` and `putimage` functions, the 256-color functions are inherently simpler. There is no operator argument for `PutImage256`—it can only do the equivalent of the COPY_PUT option—and neither function will deal correctly with an attempt to get or put image fragments that extend off the screen. In fact, attempting to use `PutImage256` with a fragment that extends past the bottom of the screen may have very nasty results, as this will cause data to be written to screen lines that aren't defined in SCREENTBL.

Animate a mouse cursor

If you hacked and bludgeoned your way through the underbrush and venomous creatures of the shadows that populated the 16-color mouse code from Chapter 3, you'll find the corresponding functions for MOUSE256 to be little more than a quick Maori firewalk by comparison. The principals are all pretty well the same, and in fact most of the code has been lifted in its entirety from MOUSE16. As was noted earlier, `InitMouse` includes the graphic initialization in MOUSE256 as well, but you'll find that the latter half of this function is identical to its 16-color counterpart.

The CURSORBACK and ERASECURSOR functions do exactly what they did in MOUSE16—they just do it with more bytes. The DRAWCURSOR code is a bit different. Like `DrawString`, it works with a source bitmap which is monochrome and a destination which is byte-oriented in 256 colors.

Unlike the 16-color mouse functions, this DRAWCURSOR just paints the appropriate bytes to the screen based on the bits set in the DEFAULTCURSOR bitmapped image. The cursor structure is the same as it was in MOUSE16. The DRAWCURSOR code uses two objects in the data segment—VGAWHITE and VGABLACK. It assumes that these will have been set by the application that calls `InitMouse` such that they represent suitable colors in the current palette. Note that DRAWCURSOR doesn't know anything about what these colors really represent. If you load light blue into VGAWHITE and neon green into VGABLACK you'll see a mouse cursor drawn in really ugly colors.

If you write a program that uses MOUSE256 and changes its palette in the course of its operation, make sure you have it update VGABLACK and VGAWHITE. There are macros defined in MOUSE256.H—to be examined later in this chapter—to handle this.

In fact, there are five of these defined colors in MOUSE256—VGABLACK, VGAWHITE, VGAGREY, VGALIGHTGREY, and VGADARKGREY. The grey colors are used in drawing buttons. While they don't all have to be in MOUSE256.ASM, it's arguably convenient to keep them all in one place.

All the other mouse-related functions—`MouseOn`, `MouseOff`, `MouseDown`, and `MouseCursor` behave just like they did in Chapter 3. In fact, they're identical.

Creating & managing 3-D buttons

The button functions in the 256-color graphic package are effectively identical to those in the 16-color package from Chapter 3. The only difference is the way the colors are set—rather than using the color constants directly, the functions to draw and tack buttons fetch the grey colors from MOUSE256.ASM through macros defined in MOUSE256.H.

Clearly, this has no real effect on the way the functions work. You will, however, find it serves as a more convenient way to keep track of these system colors in a large application if the current palette changes periodically.

Saving a graphic screen to a PCX file

The `DoSave` function for a 256-color screen is very much like the one for a 16-color screen from Chapter 3. The PCXHEAD object is set up a bit differently, as befits 256-color graphics, and a 256-color palette must be tacked onto the end of the compressed image data, as dealt with in Chapter 2. The only significant change in the way this implementation of `DoSave` works is the way it fetches lines from the screen buffer.

In the 16-color `DoSave` function, it was possible to fetch a line of screen data by simply creating a pointer into the appropriate part of segment A000H. This worked because all of the memory could be made to appear in this address space in a convenient form, with no possibility of page breaks occurring anywhere awkwardly. Clearly this is not the case with the 256-color graphic modes.

Making `DoSave` work requires the use of one last assembly language call. The `GetScreenLine` function will fill a buffer with the screen line it's asked for, dealing with any page breaks it may encounter in the process. Here's what it looks like:

```
_GetScreenLine  PROC      FAR
                PUSH      BP
                MOV       BP,SP
                PUSH      DS
                PUSH      ES

                LDATASEG
                BX,[BP+_AOFF+4]
                CALL      VGALINE

                MOV       CX,[_SCREENWIDE]

                MOV       SI,[BP+_AOFF+0]
                MOV       DS,[BP+_AOFF+2]
RL1:            PUSH      CX
                MOV       AL,ES:[DI]
                MOV       DS:[SI],AL
                INC       SI
                PUSH      DS
                LDATASEG
                GRAFADD_DI      0001H
                POP       DS
                POP       CX
                LOOP      RL1

                POP       ES
                POP       DS
                POP       BP
                RET
_GetScreenLine  ENDP
```

You might find that you have cause to write more elaborate functions along the lines of GetScreenLine to get and put sections of lines. For example, the Desktop Paint 256 package on the companion disk for this book uses a variation on this function to fetch the screen line sections that reside within its drawing window.

Figure 4-8 illustrates the modified DoSave function.

4-8
The DoSave
function to save a
256-color screen
to a PCX *file*

```
/* save the screen to a PCX file */
DoSave(path)
    char *path;
{
    PCXHEAD pcx;
    FILE *fp;
    char *p;
    unsigned int i,n;

    /* create the destination file */
    if((fp=fopen(path,"wb"))==NULL) {
        beep();
        return;
    }

    if((p=malloc(SCREENWIDE))==NULL) {
        beep();
        fclose(fp);
        return;
    }

    memset((char *)&pcx,0,sizeof(PCXHEAD));
    memcpy(pcx.palette,palette,48);

    pcx.manufacturer=10;
    pcx.encoding=1;
    pcx.xmin=pcx.ymin=0;
    pcx.xmax=SCREENWIDE-1;
    pcx.ymax=SCREENDEEP-1;
    pcx.palette_type=1;
    pcx.bits_per_pixel=8;
    pcx.version=5;
    pcx.colour_planes=1;
    pcx.bytes_per_line=SCREENWIDE;

    WaitCursor();
    if(fwrite((char *)&pcx,1,sizeof(PCXHEAD),fp) != sizeof(PCXHEAD)) {
        free(p);
        fclose(fp);
        remove(path);
        ArrowCursor();
        beep();
        return;
    }

    for(i=0;i<SCREENDEEP;++i) {
        MouseOff();
        GetScreenLine(p,i);
```

```
                MouseOn();
                n=pcxwriteline(fp,p,pcx.bytes_per_line);

                if(n != pcx.bytes_per_line) {
                        free(p);
                        fclose(fp);
                        remove(path);
                        ArrowCursor();
                        beep();
                        return;
                }
        }

        fputc(12,fp);
        if(fwrite(palette,1,768,fp) != 768) {
                free(p);
                fclose(fp);
                remove(path);
                ArrowCursor();
                beep();
                return;
        }

        ArrowCursor();
        free(p);
        fclose(fp);
}

/* write one pcx line */
pcxwriteline(fp,p,n)
        FILE *fp;
        char *p;
        unsigned int n;
{
        unsigned int i=0,j=0,t=0;

        do {
                i=0;
                while((p[t+i]==p[t+i+1]) && ((t+i) < n) && (i < 63))++i;
                if(i>0) {
                        if(fputc(i | 0xc0,fp)==EOF) return(-1);
                        if(fputc(p[t],fp)==EOF) return(-1);
                        t+=i;
                        j+=2;
                }
                else {
                        if(((p[t]) & 0xc0)==0xc0) {
                                if(fputc(0xc1,fp)==EOF) return(-1);
                                ++j;
                        }
                        if(fputc(p[t++],fp)==EOF) return(-1);
                        ++j;
                }
        } while(t<n);
        return(n);
}
```

When it's linked to a C language calling program, the MOUSE256 module will provide you with a complete mouse interface and numerous graphic functions for use in any 256-color super VGA graphics mode—with a few catches. As it's set up here, it expects to run in a 640 by 480 pixel mode, and it will only deal with those cards it knows how to support.

Figure 4-9 illustrates the complete source code for MOUSE256.ASM.

4-9

The source code for MOUSE256.ASM.

```
;
;                       Mouse Functions for 256-colour
;                       Super VGA graphics
;

_AOFF           EQU     6               ;STACK OFFSET TO FIRST ARG

PARADISE        EQU     005FH
ATI             EQU     0062H
TSENG           EQU     002EH
TRIDENT         EQU     005DH
OAK             EQU     0053H
VESA            EQU     0101H

CURSORWIDE      EQU     16              ;CURSOR DIMENSIONS
CURSORDEEP      EQU     16

FONTEIGHT       EQU     0               ;SET ONE OF THESE TRUE FOR THE
FONTSIXTEEN     EQU     1               ;SCREEN FONT SIZE

TABLEDEEP       EQU     480             ;NUMBER OF ITEMS IN THE
                                        ;SCREEN TABLE

; MAKE SURE THE RECTANGLE ON THE STACK IS WITHIN SCREEN
LIMITS
FIXRECT         MACRO
                LOCAL   LAB1,LAB2,LAB3,LAB4
                PUSH    AX
                CMP     WORD PTR [BP+_AOFF+0],0000H
                JGE     LAB1
                MOV     WORD PTR [BP+_AOFF+0],0000H
LAB1:           CMP     WORD PTR [BP+_AOFF+2],0000H
                JGE     LAB2
                MOV     WORD PTR [BP+_AOFF+2],0000H
LAB2:           MOV     AX,[_SCREENWIDE]
                DEC     AX
                CMP     WORD PTR [BP+_AOFF+4],AX
                JL      LAB3
                MOV     WORD PTR [BP+_AOFF+4],AX
LAB3:           MOV     AX,[_SCREENDEEP]
                DEC     AX
                CMP     WORD PTR [BP+_AOFF+6],AX
                JL      LAB4
                MOV     WORD PTR [BP+_AOFF+6],AX
LAB4:           POP     AX
                ENDM
```

```
; MAKE SURE THE RECTANGLE ON THE STACK PROPERLY ORIENTED
FIXRECTDIR      MACRO
                LOCAL   LAB1,LAB2
                MOV     AX,[BP+_AOFF+0]
                MOV     BX,[BP+_AOFF+4]
                CMP     AX,BX
                JL      LAB1
                MOV     [BP+_AOFF+0],BX
                MOV     [BP+_AOFF+4],AX

LAB1:           MOV     AX,[BP+_AOFF+2]
                MOV     BX,[BP+_AOFF+6]
                CMP     AX,BX
                JL      LAB2
                MOV     [BP+_AOFF+2],BX
                MOV     [BP+_AOFF+6],AX
LAB2:
                ENDM

;NORMALIZE THE POINTER IN DS:SI, SCREEN WIDTH IN AX
NORMALIZE       MACRO
                LOCAL   LAB1
                PUSH    AX
                PUSH    CX
                MOV     CX,0FFFFH
                SUB     CX,AX
                MOV     AX,CX
                CMP     SI,AX
                JB      LAB1
                MOV AX,SI                       ;SEE HOW MANY SEGMENTS ARE
                MOV CL,4                         ;...IN SI (SI DIV 16)
                SHR AX,CL

                MOV CX,DS                        ;ADD THEM TO THE DATA SEGMENT
                ADD CX,AX                        ;...(YOU CAN'T JUST ADD DS,AX)
                MOV     DS,CX
                AND     SI,000FH                 ;ADJUST SI (SI MOD 16)

LAB1:           POP     CX
                POP     AX
                ENDM

INCPAGE         MACRO   ;INCREMENT THE PAGE
                PUSH    AX
                MOV     AX,[CODEPAGE]
                INC     AX
                CALL    VGABANK
                POP     AX
                ENDM

CHECKPAGE       MACRO   ;HANDLE PAGE BOUNDARIES
                LOCAL   LAB1
                CMP     DI,0000H
                JNE     LAB1
                INCPAGE
```

4-9
Continued.

```
         LAB1:
                         ENDM

         GRAFADD_DI      MACRO   ARG1      ;ADD THE ARGUMENT TO DI WITH PAGE SWITCHING
                         LOCAL   LAB1
                         PUSH    AX
                         MOV     AX,DI
                         ADD     DI,ARG1
                         CMP     AX,DI
                         JBE     LAB1
                         INCPAGE
         LAB1:
                         POP     AX
                         ENDM

         GRAF_STOSB      MACRO   ;STORE A BIT AT DS:SI WITH PAGE SWITCH
                         CLD
                         STOSB
                         CHECKPAGE
                         ENDM

         GRAF_REPNESTOSB MACRO   ;DO STORE STRING TO ES:DI WITH PAGE SWITCH
                         LOCAL   LAB1,LAB2
                         CLD
                         CMP     [PAGEBREAK],00H
                         JNE     LAB1
                 REPNE   STOSB
                         JMP     LAB2
         LAB1:           STOSB
                         CHECKPAGE
                         LOOP    LAB1
         LAB2:
                         ENDM

         GRAF_REPNEMOVSB MACRO   ;DO MOVE STRING FROM DS:SI TO ES:DI WITH PAGE SWITCH
                         LOCAL   LAB1,LAB2
                         CLD
                         CMP     [PAGEBREAK],00H
                         JNE     LAB1
                 REPNE   MOVSB
                         JMP     LAB2
         LAB1:           MOVSB
                         CHECKPAGE
                         LOOP    LAB1
         LAB2:
                         ENDM

         GRAF_PUTPIXEL   MACRO   ;SET THE PIXEL AT (DX,BX) TO AL
                         PUSH    AX
                         CALL    VGALINE
                         GRAFADD_DI DX
                         POP     AX
                         STOSB
                         ENDM
```

```
GRAF_NOTPIXEL    MACRO    ;INVERT THE PIXEL AT (DX,BX)
                 CALL     VGALINE
                 GRAFADD_DI DX
                 NOT      BYTE PTR ES:[DI]
                 ENDM

;THIS MACRO FETCHES THE DATA SEGEMENT
LDATASEG         MACRO
                 PUSH     AX
                 MOV      AX,_DATA
                 MOV      DS,AX
                 POP      AX
                 ENDM

;DO A LONG LOOP
LNGLOOP          MACRO    ARG1
                 LOCAL    LAB1
                 DEC      CX
                 CMP      CX,0000H
                 JE       LAB1
                 JMP      ARG1
LAB1:
                 ENDM

MOUSE256_TEXT    SEGMENT BYTE PUBLIC ´CODE´
                 ASSUME   CS:MOUSE256_TEXT,DS:_DATA

;THIS FUNCTION COPIES ONE LINE OF VGA DATA FROM THE SCREEN
;        ARGS      -        POINTER TO THE DATA
;                           LINE NUMBER
;        RETURNS   -        VOID
                 PUBLIC   _GetScreenLine
_GetScreenLine   PROC     FAR
                 PUSH     BP
                 MOV      BP,SP
                 PUSH     DS
                 PUSH     ES

                 LDATASEG
                 MOV      BX,[BP+_AOFF+4]
                 CALL     VGALINE

                 MOV      CX,[_SCREENWIDE]

                 MOV      SI,[BP+_AOFF+0]
                 MOV      DS,[BP+_AOFF+2]

RL1:             PUSH     CX
                 MOV      AL,ES:[DI]
                 MOV      DS:[SI],AL
                 INC      SI
                 PUSH     DS
                 LDATASEG
                 GRAFADD_DI 0001H
                 POP      DS
```

```
                        POP     CX
                        LOOP    RL1

                        POP     ES
                        POP     DS
                        POP     BP
                        RET
        _GetScreenLine  ENDP

        ;THIS FUNCTION COPIES AN IMAGE FRAGMENT FROM THE SCREEN
        ;       ARGS    -       LEFT
        ;                       TOP
        ;                       RIGHT
        ;                       BOTTOM
        ;                       IMAGE
        ;       RETURNS -       VOID
                        PUBLIC  _GetImage256
        _GetImage256    PROC    FAR
                        PUSH    BP
                        MOV     BP,SP
                        PUSH    DS
                        PUSH    ES

                        LDATASEG

                        FIXRECTDIR
                        FIXRECT

                        CALL    HIDECURSOR

                        MOV     AX,[_SCREENWIDE]

                        MOV     DX,[BP+_AOFF+4]         ;GET WIDTH
                        SUB     DX,[BP+_AOFF+0]

                        MOV     CX,[BP+_AOFF+6]         ;GET DEPTH
                        SUB     CX,[BP+_AOFF+2]

                        MOV     SI,[BP+_AOFF+8]        ;GET IMAGE
                        MOV     DS,[BP+_AOFF+10]

                        NORMALIZE                              ;NORMALIZE POINTER

                        MOV     DS:[SI],DX                    ;SAVE SIZE VALUES
                        MOV     DS:[SI+2],CX
                        ADD     SI,0004H

                        INC     CX                           ;GET REAL SIZE VALUES
                        INC     DX

        GI1:            PUSH    CX
                        PUSH    DX

                        PUSH    DS
                        LDATASEG
```

```
                MOV     BX,[BP+_AOFF+2]
                CALL    VGALINE
                GRAFADD_DI [BP+_AOFF+0]
                POP     DS
                INC     WORD PTR [BP+_AOFF+2]

                POP     CX
                PUSH    CX

GI2:            MOV     AL,ES:[DI]
                MOV     DS:[SI],AL
                INC     SI
                PUSH    DS
                LDATASEG
                GRAFADD_DI 0001H
                POP     DS
                LOOP    GI2

                PUSH    DS
                LDATASEG
                MOV     AX,[_SCREENWIDE]
                POP     DS
                NORMALIZE

                POP     DX
                POP     CX
                LOOP    GI1

                LDATASEG

                CALL    SHOWCURSOR

                POP     ES
                POP     DS
                POP     BP
                RET
_GetImage256    ENDP

;THIS FUNCTION COPIES AN IMAGE FRAGMENT TO THE SCREEN
;       ARGS    -       X
;                       Y
;                       IMAGE
;       RETURNS -       VOID
                PUBLIC  _PutImage256
_PutImage256    PROC    FAR
                PUSH    BP
                MOV     BP,SP
                PUSH    DS
                PUSH    ES

                CALL    HIDECURSOR

                MOV     SI,[BP+_AOFF+4]
                MOV     DS,[BP+_AOFF+6]
```

```
                              MOV      DX,DS:[SI + 0]          ;GET WIDTH
                              INC      DX
                              MOV      CX,DS:[SI + 2]          ;GET DEPTH
                              INC      CX
                              ADD      SI,0004H

                  PI1:        PUSH     CX
                              PUSH     DX

                              PUSH     DS
                              LDATASEG
                              MOV      BX,[BP+_AOFF+2]
                              CALL     VGALINE
                              GRAFADD_DI [BP+_AOFF+0]
                              POP      DS

                              INC      WORD PTR [BP+_AOFF+2]
                              POP      CX
                              PUSH     CX

                              CLD
                  PI2:        MOV      AL,DS:[SI]

                              PUSH     DS
                              LDATASEG
                              GRAF_STOSB
                              POP      DS

                              INC      SI
                              LOOP     PI2

                              PUSH     DS
                              LDATASEG
                              MOV      AX,[_SCREENWIDE]
                              POP      DS
                              NORMALIZE

                              POP      DX
                              POP      CX
                              LOOP     PI1

                              LDATASEG
                              CALL     SHOWCURSOR

                              POP      ES
                              POP      DS
                              POP      BP
                              RET
      _PutImage256            ENDP

      ;THIS FUNCTION SETS THE PIXEL AT (X,Y) TO COLOUR
      ;        ARGS      -        X
      ;                           Y
      ;                           COLOUR
      ;        RETURNS   -        VOID
```

```
                    PUBLIC  _SetPixel
_SetPixel           PROC    FAR
                    PUSH    BP
                    MOV     BP,SP
                    PUSH    DS
                    PUSH    ES

                    LDATASEG

                    MOV     DX,[BP+_AOFF+0]
                    MOV     BX,[BP+_AOFF+2]
                    MOV     AX,[BP+_AOFF+4]
                    GRAF_PUTPIXEL

                    POP     ES
                    POP     DS
                    POP     BP
                    RET
_SetPixel           ENDP

;THIS FUNCTION DRAWS A RECTANGLE
;       ARGS      -         LEFT
;                           TOP
;                           RIGHT
;                           BOTTOM
;                           COLOUR
;       RETURNS   -         VOID
                    PUBLIC  _FrameRect
_FrameRect          PROC    FAR
                    PUSH    BP
                    MOV     BP,SP
                    PUSH    DS
                    PUSH    ES

                    LDATASEG

                    FIXRECTDIR
                    FIXRECT

                    CALL    HIDECURSOR

                    MOV     BX,[BP+_AOFF+2] ;TOP LINE
                    MOV     CX,[BP+_AOFF+6] ;BOTTOM LINE
                    SUB     CX,BX

                    MOV     DX,[BP+_AOFF+4]
                    SUB     DX,[BP+_AOFF+0] ;GET WIDTH

;                   DRAW TOP LINE
                    PUSH    CX
                    PUSH    BX
                    CALL    VGALINE
                    GRAFADD_DI [BP+_AOFF+0]

                    MOV     CX,DX
```

```
                          INC     CX
                          MOV     AX,[BP+_AOFF+8] ;COLOUR

                          GRAF_REPNESTOSB

                          POP     BX
                          POP     CX

;                         DRAW SIDES
FR1:                      PUSH    CX
                          PUSH    DX
                          INC     BX

                          PUSH    DX
                          MOV     DX,[BP+_AOFF+0] ;LEFT
                          MOV     AX,[BP+_AOFF+8] ;COLOUR
                          GRAF_PUTPIXEL

                          POP     CX
                          ADD     DX,CX
                          GRAF_PUTPIXEL

                          POP     DX
                          POP     CX
                          LOOP    FR1

;                         DRAW BOTTOM LINE
                          CALL    VGALINE
                          GRAFADD_DI [BP+_AOFF+0]

                          MOV     CX,DX
                          INC     CX
                          MOV     AX,[BP+_AOFF+8] ;COLOUR

                          GRAF_REPNESTOSB

                          LDATASEG
                          CALL    SHOWCURSOR

                          POP     ES
                          POP     DS
                          POP     BP
                          RET
_FrameRect                ENDP

;THIS FUNCTION FILLS A RECTANGLE
;         ARGS    -       LEFT
;                         TOP
;                         RIGHT
;                         BOTTOM
;                         COLOUR
;         RETURNS -       VOID
                          PUBLIC  _FillRect
_FillRect                 PROC    FAR
                          PUSH    BP
```

```
                MOV       BP,SP
                PUSH      DS
                PUSH      ES

                LDATASEG

                FIXRECTDIR
                FIXRECT

                CALL      HIDECURSOR

                MOV       BX,[BP+_AOFF+2] ;TOP LINE
                MOV       CX,[BP+_AOFF+6] ;BOTTOM LINE
                SUB       CX,BX
                INC       CX

                MOV       DX,[BP+_AOFF+4]
                SUB       DX,[BP+_AOFF+0] ;GET WIDTH

IR1:            PUSH      CX
                PUSH      BX
                CALL      VGALINE
                GRAFADD_DI [BP+_AOFF+0]

                MOV       CX,DX
                INC       CX
                MOV       AX,[BP+_AOFF+8] ;COLOUR

                GRAF_REPNESTOSB

                POP       BX
                POP       CX
                INC       BX
                LOOP      IR1

                LDATASEG
                CALL      SHOWCURSOR

                POP       ES
                POP       DS
                POP       BP
                RET
_FillRect       ENDP

LINE_DELTAX     EQU       2
LINE_DELTAY     EQU       4
LINE_HALFX      EQU       6
LINE_HALFY      EQU       8
LINE_COUNT      EQU       10
LINE_ADJ        EQU       12

;THIS FUNCTION DRAWS A LINE
;       ARGS      -       LEFT
;                         TOP
;                         RIGHT
```

```
;                       BOTTOM
;                       COLOUR
;        RETURNS -      VOID
              PUBLIC   _DrawLine
_DrawLine     PROC     FAR
              PUSH     BP
              MOV      BP,SP
              SUB      SP,LINE_ADJ
              PUSH     DS
              PUSH     ES

              LDATASEG

              FIXRECT

              CALL     HIDECURSOR

              MOV      AX,[BP+_AOFF+6]
              SUB      AX,[BP+_AOFF+2] ;BOTTOM - TOP = DELTA Y

              MOV      SI,1
              JGE      LINE1
              MOV      SI,-1
              NEG      AX
LINE1:        MOV      [BP - LINE_DELTAY],AX

              MOV      AX,[BP+_AOFF+4]
              SUB      AX,[BP+_AOFF+0] ;RIGHT - LEFT = DELTA X

              MOV      DI,1
              JGE      LINE2
              MOV      DI,-1
              NEG      AX

LINE2:        MOV      [BP - LINE_DELTAX],AX

              MOV      AX,[BP - LINE_DELTAX]
              CMP      AX,[BP - LINE_DELTAY]
              JL       LINE3

              ;HANDLE SLOPE < 1

              MOV      AX,[BP - LINE_DELTAX]
              SHR      AX,1
              MOV      [BP - LINE_HALFX],AX

              MOV      CX,[BP+_AOFF+0]
              MOV      DX,[BP+_AOFF+2]
              MOV      BX,0000H
              MOV      AX,[BP - LINE_DELTAX]
              MOV      [BP - LINE_COUNT],AX

LINE5:        PUSH     BX              ;PLOT THE PIXEL
              PUSH     DI
              PUSH     DX
```

```
                        MOV        BX,DX
                        MOV        DX,CX
                        MOV        AX,[BP+_AOFF+8]
                        GRAF_PUTPIXEL
                        POP        DX
                        POP        DI
                        POP        BX

                        ADD        CX,DI
                        ADD        BX,[BP - LINE_DELTAY]
                        CMP        BX,[BP - LINE_HALFX]
                        JLE        LINE6
                        SUB        BX,[BP - LINE_DELTAX]
                        ADD        DX,SI

LINE6:                  DEC        WORD PTR [BP - LINE_COUNT]
                        JGE        LINE5

                        JMP        LINE4

                        ; HANDLE SLOPE > 1
LINE3:                  MOV        AX,[BP - LINE_DELTAY]
                        SHR        AX,1
                        MOV        [BP - LINE_HALFY],AX

                        MOV        CX,[BP+_AOFF+0]
                        MOV        DX,[BP+_AOFF+2]
                        MOV        BX,0000H
                        MOV        AX,[BP - LINE_DELTAY]
                        MOV        [BP - LINE_COUNT],AX

LINE7:                  PUSH       BX                   ;PLOT THE PIXEL
                        PUSH       DI
                        PUSH       DX
                        MOV        BX,DX
                        MOV        DX,CX
                        MOV        AX,[BP+_AOFF+8]
                        GRAF_PUTPIXEL
                        POP        DX
                        POP        DI
                        POP        BX

                        ADD        DX,SI
                        ADD        BX,[BP - LINE_DELTAX]
                        CMP        BX,[BP - LINE_HALFY]
                        JLE        LINE8
                        SUB        BX,[BP - LINE_DELTAY]
                        ADD        CX,DI

LINE8:                  DEC        WORD PTR [BP - LINE_COUNT]
                        JGE        LINE7

LINE4:                  LDATASEG
                        CALL       SHOWCURSOR
```

```
                          POP     ES
                          POP     DS
                          ADD     SP,LINE_ADJ
                          POP     BP
                          RET
     _DrawLine            ENDP

     ;THIS FUNCTION DRAWS A STRING OF TEXT
     ;        ARG1 = X
     ;        ARG2 = Y
     ;        ARG3 = STRING
     ;        ARG4 = COLOUR
     ;        ARG6 = BACKGROUND
                          PUBLIC  _DrawString
     _DrawString          PROC    FAR
                          PUSH    BP
                          MOV     BP,SP
                          PUSH    DS
                          PUSH    ES

                          LDATASEG

                          CALL    HIDECURSOR

                          ;LOOP THROUGH ALL THE LINES
                          MOV     CX,[_FONTDEPTH]
     DS0:                 PUSH    CX
                          DEC     CX

                          ;GET THE BOTTOM LINE — WE COUNT BACKWARDS
                          MOV     BX,[BP + _AOFF + 2]
                          ADD     BX,CX

                          ;GET THE SCREEN POINTER
                          LDATASEG
                          CALL    VGALINE
                          GRAFADD_DI      [BP+_AOFF+0]

                          ;POINT TO THE START OF THE STRING
                          MOV     SI,[BP + _AOFF + 4]
                          MOV     DS,[BP + _AOFF + 6]

                          ;STOP LOOPING WHEN A NULL BYTE IS REACHED
     DS1:                 MOV     AH,00H
                          MOV     AL,DS:[SI]
                          CMP     AL,00H
                          JE      DS5

     DS2:                 PUSH    DS
                          PUSH    SI

                          ;FIND THE FONT CHARACTER
                          MUL     [_FONTDEPTH]

                          ;GET THE BYTE OFFSET
```

```
                    MOV     BX,AX
                    ADD     BX,CX

                    PUSH    CX

                    ;GET THE BYTE FROM THE FONT
                    MOV     SI,[_FONTOFF]
                    MOV     DS,[_FONTSEG]
                    MOV     AH,DS:[SI+BX]

                    MOV     CX,0008H
                    MOV     BX,0000H

                    LDATASEG

DS3:                MOV     AL,BYTE PTR [BP + _AOFF + 8]
                    TEST    AH,[_MASKTABLE + BX]
                    JNZ     DS4
                    MOV     AL,BYTE PTR [BP + _AOFF + 10]

DS4:                INC     BX
                    GRAF_STOSB
                    LOOP    DS3

                    POP     CX

                    POP     SI
                    POP     DS
                    INC     SI
                    JMP     DS1

DS5:                POP     CX
                    LOOP    DS0

                    LDATASEG
                    CALL    SHOWCURSOR

                    POP     ES
                    POP     DS
                    POP     BP
                    RET
_DrawString         ENDP

;THIS FUNCTION INITIALIZES THE MOUSE AND GRAPHIC MODE
;       ARGS      -         SCREENWIDE
;                           SCREENDEEP
;                           CARD
;       RETURNS   -         TRUE FOR INTIALIZED
                    PUBLIC  _InitMouse
_InitMouse          PROC    FAR
                    PUSH    BP
                    MOV     BP,SP
                    PUSH    DS
                    PUSH    ES
```

4-9
Continued.

```
        LDATASEG

        MOV     [CODEPAGE],OFFFFH

        MOV     AX,[BP + _AOFF + 0]
        MOV     [_SCREENWIDE],AX

        MOV     AX,[BP + _AOFF + 2]
        MOV     [_SCREENDEEP],AX

        MOV     AX,[BP + _AOFF + 4]
        MOV     [_CARD],AX

        MOV     AX,CS
        MOV     CS:[SETBANK_SEG],AX

        CMP     [_CARD],PARADISE
        JNE     INITMOUSE1

        MOV     AX,OFFSET SETBANK_PAR
        MOV     CS:[SETBANK_OFF],AX
        CALL    MAKETABLE

        MOV     AX,[_CARD]
        INT     10H

        JMP     INITMOUSE7
INITMOUSE1:     CMP     [_CARD],ATI
        JNE     INITMOUSE2

        MOV     AX,OFFSET SETBANK_ATI
        MOV     CS:[SETBANK_OFF],AX
        CALL    MAKETABLE

        MOV     AX,0C000H
        MOV     ES,AX
        MOV     AX,ES:[0010H]
        MOV     CS:[ATIREG],AX

        MOV     AX,[_CARD]
        INT     10H

        JMP     INITMOUSE7
INITMOUSE2:     CMP     [_CARD],TSENG
        JNE     INITMOUSE3

        MOV     AX,OFFSET SETBANK_TNG
        MOV     CS:[SETBANK_OFF],AX
        CALL    MAKETABLE

        MOV     DX,03C4H                        ;SET
                                                ;TSENG
                                                ;REGISTERS

        MOV     AL,0
        OUT     DX,AL
        MOV     DX,03C5H
```

```
                IN        AL,DX
                AND       AL,0FEH
                OUT       DX,AL
                MOV       DX,03CEH
                MOV       AL,06H
                OUT       DX,AL
                MOV       DX,03CFH
                IN        AL,DX
                XOR       AL,06H
                OR        AL,02H
                OUT       DX,AL

                MOV       AX,[_CARD]
                INT       10H

                JMP       INITMOUSE7
INITMOUSE3:     CMP       [_CARD],TRIDENT
                JNE       INITMOUSE4

                MOV       AX,OFFSET SETBANK_TRI
                MOV       CS:[SETBANK_OFF],AX
                CALL      MAKETABLE

                MOV       AX,[_CARD]
                INT       10H

                JMP       INITMOUSE7
INITMOUSE4:     CMP       [_CARD],OAK
                JNE       INITMOUSE5

                MOV       AX,OFFSET SETBANK_OAK
                MOV       CS:[SETBANK_OFF],AX
                CALL      MAKETABLE

                MOV       AX,[_CARD]
                INT       10H

                JMP       INITMOUSE7
INITMOUSE5:     CMP       [_CARD],VESA
                JNE       INITMOUSE6

                MOV       AX,OFFSET SETBANK_VSA
                MOV       CS:[SETBANK_OFF],AX
                CALL      INITVESA

                JMP       INITMOUSE7
INITMOUSE6:     MOV       AX,0000H
                JMP       INITMOUSE8

INITMOUSE7:     ;INTITALIZE THE FONT POINTER
                IF        FONTEIGHT
                MOV       AX,1130H
                MOV       BX,0300H
                INT       10H
                MOV       [_FONTSEG],ES
```

```
MOV     [_FONTOFF],BP
MOV     [_FONTDEPTH],0008H
ENDIF   ;FONTEIGHT

IF      FONTSIXTEEN
MOV     AX,1130H
MOV     BX,0600H
INT     10H
MOV     [_FONTSEG],ES
MOV     [_FONTOFF],BP
MOV     [_FONTDEPTH],0010H
ENDIF   ;FONTSIXTEEN

;SEE IF THERE'S A MOUSE HANDLER
MOV     AX,3533H
INT     21H
MOV     AX,ES
OR      AX,BX
JZ      INITMOUSE8

;INITIALIZE THE MOUSE
MOV     AX,0000H
INT     33H

;CHECK TO SEE IT'S THERE
CMP     AX,0000H
JE      INITMOUSE8

;SET THE HORIZONTAL RANGE
MOV     AX,0007H
MOV     CX,0000H
MOV     DX,[_SCREENWIDE]
SUB     DX,CURSORWIDE
SHL     DX,1
SHL     DX,1
INT     33H

;SET THE VERTICAL RANGE
MOV     AX,0008H
MOV     CX,0000H
MOV     DX,[_SCREENDEEP]
SUB     DX,CURSORDEEP
INT     33H

;PUT THE CURSOR IN THE CENTRE OF THE SCREEN
MOV     AX,0004H
MOV     CX,[_SCREENWIDE]
SHL     CX,1
MOV     DX,[_SCREENDEEP]
SHR     DX,1
INT     33H

;SET THE MOUSE SENSITIVITY
MOV     AX,000FH
MOV     CX,0003H
```

```
          MOV     DX,0010H
          INT     33H

          ;SET THE INITIAL POSITION
          MOV     AX,[_SCREENWIDE]
          SHR     AX,1
          MOV     [MOUSEX],AX

          MOV     AX,[_SCREENDEEP]
          SHR     AX,1
          MOV     [MOUSEY],AX

          ;SHOW THE CURSOR
          CALL    SHOWCURSOR

          ;SET THE MOUSE HANDLER HOOK
          MOV     AX,CS
          MOV     ES,AX
          MOV     AX,000CH
          MOV     CX,001FH
          MOV     DX,OFFSET MOUSEHANDLER
          INT     33H

          ;SAY ALL IS WELL
          MOV     AX,0FFFFH

INITMOUSE8:   POP     ES
              POP     DS
              POP     BP
              RET
_InitMouse    ENDP

              PUBLIC  _DeinitMouse
_DeinitMouse  PROC    FAR
              PUSH    BP
              MOV     BP,SP
              PUSH    DS
              PUSH    ES

              LDATASEG

              MOV     AX,0000H                    ;MOUSE OFF
              INT     33H

              CMP     [_CARD],VESA
              JNE     DM3
              CMP     [OLDVESAMODE],0FFFFH
              JE      DM3

              MOV     DI,WORD PTR [VIDEOMODE+0]    ;IF THE OLD MODE
              MOV     ES,WORD PTR [VIDEOMODE+2]    ;IS A LEGAL VESA
                                                  ;MODE, CHANGE TO
DM1:          MOV     AX,ES:[DI]                  ;IT... OTHERWISE
              ADD     DI,0002H                    ;RETURN TO THE
                                                  ;STANDARD TEXT
```

```
        4-9                         CMP     AX,0FFFFH               ;MODE
     Continued.                     JE      DM2
                                    CMP     AX,[OLDVESAMODE]
                                    JE      DM2
                                    JMP     DM1

                    DM2:            CMP     AX,0FFFFH               ;MODE NOT FOUND
                                    JE      DM3

                                    MOV     AX,4F02H
                                    MOV     BX,[OLDVESAMODE]
                                    INT     10H

                                    JMP     DM4

                    DM3:            MOV     AX,0003H
                                    INT     10H

                    DM4:            POP     ES
                                    POP     DS
                                    POP     BP
                                    RET
     _DeinitMouse   ENDP

                    ;               ARG1 = COLOUR TO CLEAR TO
                                    PUBLIC  _ClearScreen
     _ClearScreen   PROC    FAR
                                    PUSH    BP
                                    MOV     BP,SP
                                    PUSH    DS
                                    PUSH    ES

                                    LDATASEG

                                    CALL    HIDECURSOR

                                    MOV     CX,[_SCREENDEEP]
                                    MOV     BX,0000H

                    CS1:            PUSH    CX
                                    PUSH    BX

                                    CALL    VGALINE
                                    MOV     AL,BYTE PTR [BP + _AOFF + 0]
                                    MOV     CX,[_SCREENWIDE]
                                    GRAF_REPNESTOSB

                                    POP     BX
                                    POP     CX
                                    INC     BX
                                    LOOP    CS1

                                    LDATASEG
                                    CALL    SHOWCURSOR
```

```
                            POP     ES
                            POP     DS
                            POP     BP
                            RET
_ClearScreen                ENDP


                            PUBLIC  _MouseOn
_MouseOn                    PROC    FAR
                            PUSH    BP
                            MOV     BP,SP
                            PUSH    DS
                            PUSH    ES

                            LDATASEG
                            CALL    SHOWCURSOR

                            POP     ES
                            POP     DS
                            POP     BP
                            RET
_MouseOn                    ENDP


                            PUBLIC  _MouseOff
_MouseOff                   PROC    FAR
                            PUSH    BP
                            MOV     BP,SP
                            PUSH    DS
                            PUSH    ES

                            LDATASEG
                            CALL    HIDECURSOR

                            POP     ES
                            POP     DS
                            POP     BP
                            RET
_MouseOff                   ENDP


                            PUBLIC  _MouseDown
_MouseDown                  PROC    FAR
                            PUSH    BP
                            MOV     BP,SP
                            PUSH    DS
                            PUSH    ES

                            LDATASEG

                            MOV     DI,[BP + _AOFF + 0]
                            MOV     ES,[BP + _AOFF + 2]

                            MOV     AX,[MOUSEX]
                            ADD     AX,[SPOTX]
                            STOSW

                            MOV     AX,[MOUSEY]
```

```
                              ADD     AX,[SPOTY]
                              STOSW

                              MOV     AX,[MOUSEB]
                              AND     AX,0003H

                              POP     ES
                              POP     DS
                              POP     BP
                              RET
_MouseDown                    ENDP

;                             ARG1 = CURSOR
;                             ARG2 = HOTSPOT X
;                             ARG3 = HOTSPOT Y
                              PUBLIC  _MouseCursor
_MouseCursor                  PROC    FAR
                              PUSH    BP
                              MOV     BP,SP
                              PUSH    DS
                              PUSH    ES

                              LDATASEG
                              CALL    HIDECURSOR

                              MOV     SI,[BP+_AOFF+0]
                              MOV     DS,[BP+_AOFF+2]

                              MOV     AX,_DATA
                              MOV     ES,AX
                              MOV     DI,OFFSET DEFAULTCURSOR

                              MOV     CX,32
                              CLD
MC1:                          LODSW
                              XCHG    AL,AH
                              STOSW
                              LOOP    MC1

                              MOV     AX,[BP+_AOFF+4]
                              MOV     BX,[BP+_AOFF+6]

                              MOV     [SPOTX],AX
                              MOV     [SPOTY],BX

                              LDATASEG
                              CALL    SHOWCURSOR

                              POP     ES
                              POP     DS
                              POP     BP
                              RET
_MouseCursor                  ENDP

;
```

```
;               INTERNAL FUNCTIONS
;

;MAKE A LINE START TABLE WITH FLAGS FOR PAGE BREAKS
MAKETABLE       PROC    NEAR
                MOV     CX,[_SCREENDEEP]                ;DEPTH OF SCREEN
                MOV     BX,0000H                        ;ZERO LINE COUNTER
                MOV     SI,OFFSET _SCREENTBL            ;POINT TO TABLE

MT1:            PUSH    CX
                MOV     AX,[_SCREENWIDE]                ;WIDTH OF SCREEEN
                MUL     BX                              ;TIMES LINE NUMBER

                AND     DX,00FFH

                MOV     CX,0FFFEH
                SUB     CX,[_SCREENWIDE]

                CMP     AX,CX                           ;SEE IF WE WILL
                JB      MT2                             ;EXCEED A PAGE BOUNDARY

                MOV     DH,0FFH

MT2:            MOV     DS:[SI],AX                      ;SAVE THE VALUES
                MOV     DS:[SI+2],DX                    ;IN OUR LOOKUP TABLE
                ADD     SI,4                            ;AND POINT TO THE
                INC     BX                              ;NEXT LINE AND

                POP     CX                              ;ENTRY
                LOOP    MT1

                RET
MAKETABLE       ENDP

; HANDLE MOUSE MOVEMENT - THIS FUNCTION CALLED WHENEVER THE MOUSE
; CHANGES STATE. IT'S CALLED BY THE MOUSE DRIVER

MOUSEHANDLER    PROC    FAR
                PUSHF

                CLI

                LDATASEG

                MOV     [MOUSEB],BX

                CMP     [MOUSEF],0000H
                JL      MH1

                PUSH    AX
                PUSH    BX
                PUSH    CX
                PUSH    DX
                CALL    ERASECURSOR
                POP     DX
```

```
                            POP     CX
                            POP     BX
                            POP     AX

                            MOV     [MOUSEX].CX
                            MOV     [MOUSEY].DX

                            SHR     WORD PTR [MOUSEX].1
                            SHR     WORD PTR [MOUSEX].1

                            CALL    CURSORBACK
                            CALL    DRAWCURSOR

MH1:                        POPF
                            RETF
MOUSEHANDLER                ENDP

DRAWCURSOR                  PROC    NEAR

                            LDATASEG

                            MOV     CX.CURSORDEEP
                            MOV     BX.[MOUSEY]

                            MOV     SI.OFFSET DEFAULTCURSOR

DC1:                        PUSH    CX
                            PUSH    BX

                            CALL    VGALINE
                            GRAFADD_DI      [MOUSEX]

                            MOV     CX.CURSORWIDE
                            MOV     BX.0000H

DC2:                        PUSH    CX
                            MOV     CX.BX
                            MOV     DX.8000H
                            SHR     DX.CL
                            MOV     AX.DS:[SI]
                            XCHG    AH.AL
                            TEST    AX.DX
                            JNZ     DC3
                            MOV     AX.[_VGABLACK]
                            GRAF_STOSB
                            JMP     DC4

DC3:                        GRAFADD_DI      1

DC4:                        POP     CX
                            INC     BX

                            LOOP    DC2

                            POP     BX
```

```
                      PUSH      BX

                      CALL      VGALINE
                      GRAFADD_DI        [MOUSEX]

                      MOV       CX,CURSORWIDE
                      MOV       BX,0000H

DC5:                  PUSH      CX
                      MOV       CX,BX
                      MOV       DX,8000H
                      SHR       DX,CL
                      MOV       AX,DS:[SI+32]
                      XCHG      AH,AL
                      TEST      AX,DX
                      JZ        DC6
                      MOV       AX,[_VGAWHITE]
                      GRAF_STOSB
                      JMP       DC7

DC6:                  GRAFADD_DI        1

DC7:                  POP       CX
                      INC       BX

                      LOOP      DC5

                      POP       BX
                      POP       CX

                      INC       BX
                      ADD       SI,0002H

                      LNGLOOP DC1

                      RET
DRAWCURSOR            ENDP

;ERASE THE CURSOR
ERASECURSOR           PROC      NEAR

                      LDATASEG

                      MOV       CX,CURSORDEEP
                      MOV       BX,[MOUSEY]

                      MOV       SI,OFFSET MOUSEBACK

EC1:                  PUSH      CX

                      CALL      VGALINE
                      GRAFADD_DI        [MOUSEX]

                      MOV       CX,CURSORWIDE
                      GRAF_REPNEMOVSB
```

```
                                POP     CX
                                INC     BX
                                LOOP    EC1

                                RET
ERASECURSOR     ENDP

;COPY THE CURSOR BACKGROUND TO MEMORY
CURSORBACK      PROC    NEAR

                                LDATASEG

                                MOV     CX,CURSORDEEP
                                MOV     BX,[MOUSEY]

                                MOV     SI,OFFSET MOUSEBACK

CC1:                            PUSH    CX

                                CALL    VGALINE
                                GRAFADD_DI      [MOUSEX]

                                MOV     CX,CURSORWIDE
CC2:                            MOV     AL,ES:[DI]
                                MOV     DS:[SI],AL
                                INC     SI
                                GRAFADD_DI 0001H
                                LOOP    CC2

                                POP     CX
                                INC     BX
                                LOOP    CC1

                                RET
CURSORBACK      ENDP

; MAKE THE CURSOR DISAPPEAR
                                PUBLIC  HIDECURSOR
HIDECURSOR      PROC    FAR
                                PUSHF
                                CLI
                                DEC     [MOUSEF]
                                CMP     [MOUSEF],-1
                                JL      HC1
                                CALL    ERASECURSOR

HC1:                            POPF
                                RET
HIDECURSOR      ENDP

; SHOW THE CURSOR
                                PUBLIC  SHOWCURSOR
SHOWCURSOR      PROC    FAR
                                PUSHF
```

```
                      CLI
                      INC       [MOUSEF]
                      CMP       [MOUSEF],0000H
                      JG        SC1
                      CALL      CURSORBACK
                      CALL      DRAWCURSOR

SC1:                  POPF
                      RET
SHOWCURSOR            ENDP

;INITIALIZE A VESA BOARD
INITVESA`             PROC      NEAR
                      MOV       AX,_DATA
                      MOV       ES,AX
                      MOV       AX,4F00H
                      MOV       DI,OFFSET VESABLOCK
                      INT       10H
                      CMP       AX,004FH
                      JE        IV1
                      MOV       AX,0000H
                      RET

IV1:                  MOV       SI,WORD PTR [VIDEOMODE]
                      MOV       ES,WORD PTR [VIDEOMODE+2]

IV2:                  MOV       AX,ES:[SI]
                      ADD       SI,0002H
                      CMP       AX,0FFFFH
                      JE        IV3
                      CMP       AX,VESA
                      JE        IV4
                      JMP       IV2

IV3:                  MOV       AX,0000H
                      RET

IV4:                  MOV       AX,_DATA
                      MOV       ES,AX
                      MOV       AX,4F01H
                      MOV       CX,VESA
                      MOV       DI,OFFSET VESAINFO
                      INT       10H

                      MOV       AX,[WIN_ASEG]
                      MOV       [_SCREENSEG],AX

                      MOV       AX,4F03H
                      INT       10H
                      MOV       [OLDVESAMODE],BX

                      MOV       AX,4F02H
                      MOV       BX,VESA
                      INT       10H
```

```
                    CALL    FINDVESASHIFT
                    MOV     [BANKSHIFT],AX

                    MOV     AX,[WINSIZE]
                    MOV     BX,0400H
                    MUL     BX
                    SUB     AX,0002H
                    SUB     AX,[BYTESPERLINE]
                    MOV     [BANKSIZE],AX

                    MOV     CX,[YRES]               ;DEPTH OF SCREEN
                    SUB     BX,BX                   ;ZERO LINE COUNTER
                    MOV     SI,OFFSET _SCREENTBL    ;POINT TO TABLE

IV5:                PUSH    CX
                    MOV     AX,[BYTESPERLINE]       ;WIDTH OF SCREEEN
                    MUL     BX                      ;TIMES LINE NUMBER

                    AND     DX,7FFFH

                    CMP     AX,[BANKSIZE]           ;SEE IF WE WILL EXCEED THE
                                                    ;BLOCK

                    JB      IV6

                    OR      DX,1000H

IV6:                MOV     DS:[SI],AX              ;SAVE THE VALUES
                    MOV     DS:[SI+2],DX            ;IN OUR LOOKUP TABLE
                    ADD     SI,4                    ;AND POINT TO THE
                    INC     BX                      ;NEXT LINE AND
                    POP     CX                      ;ENTRY
                    LOOP    IV5

                    MOV     AX,0FFFFH

                    RET
INITVESA            ENDP

;FIND THE SHIFT VALUE FOR VESA BANK NUMBERS
FINDVESASHIFT       PROC    NEAR
                    MOV     DX,0000H
                    MOV     AX,CS:[WINSIZE]
                    DIV     CS:[WINGRAN]

                    CMP     AX,0040H
                    JNE     FVS1
                    MOV     AX,0006H
                    RET

FVS1:               CMP     AX,0020H
                    JNE     FVS2
                    MOV     AX,0005H
                    RET

FVS2:               CMP     AX,0010H
```

```
              JNE      FVS3
              MOV      AX,0004H
              RET

FVS3:         CMP      AX,0008H
              JNE      FVS4
              MOV      AX,0003H
              RET

FVS4:         CMP      AX,0004H
              JNE      FVS6
              MOV      AX,0002H
              RET

FVS6:         CMP      AX,0002H
              JNE      FVS7
              MOV      AX,0001H
              RET

FVS7:         MOV      AX,0000H
              RET
FINDVESASHIFT ENDP

;             RETURN A POINTER IN ES:DI TO THE SCREEN LINE IN BX
              PUBLIC   VGALINE
VGALINE       PROC     FAR
              PUSH     AX
              PUSH     BX
              PUSH     CX
              PUSH     DX

              LDATASEG

              SHL      BX,1
              SHL      BX,1

              MOV      DI,[_SCREENTBL + BX]
              MOV      AX,[_SCREENTBL + 2 + BX]

              CALL     CS:[SETBANK]
              MOV      [PAGEBREAK],AH
              MOV      ES,[_SCREENSEG]

              POP      DX
              POP      CX
              POP      BX
              POP      AX
              RET
VGALINE       ENDP

;SWITCH TO THE BANK IN AX
              PUBLIC   VGABANK
VGABANK       PROC     FAR
              CALL     CS:[SETBANK]
              RET
```

The MOUSE.256ASM code module 237

```
             VGABANK        ENDP

             DUMMY          PROC    FAR
                            RET
             DUMMY          ENDP

             SETBANK_ATI    PROC    FAR
                            CMP     AX,[CODEPAGE]
                            JE      SETB_ATI1

                            MOV     [CODEPAGE],AX

                            PUSH    AX
                            PUSH    CX
                            PUSH    DX

                            MOV     DX,[ATIREG]

                            MOV     CX,AX
                            PUSHF
                            CLI
                            MOV     AL,0B2H
                            OUT     DX,AL
                            INC     DL
                            IN      AL,DX
                            MOV     AH,AL
                            AND     AH,0E1H
                            SHL     CL,1
                            OR      AH,CL
                            MOV     AL,0B2H
                            DEC     DL
                            OUT     DX,AX
                            POPF
                            POP     DX
                            POP     CX
                            POP     AX

             SETB_ATI1:     RET
             SETBANK_ATI    ENDP

             SETBANK_TRI    PROC    FAR
                            CMP     AX,[CODEPAGE]
                            JE      SETB_TRI1

                            MOV     [CODEPAGE],AX

                            PUSH    AX
                            PUSH    BX
                            PUSH    DX

                            MOV     DX,3CEH   ;SET PAGE SIZE TO 64K
                            MOV     AL,6
                            OUT     DX,AL
                            INC     DL
                            IN      AL,DX
```

```
                    DEC     DL
                    OR      AL,4
                    MOV     AH,AL
                    MOV     AL,6
                    OUT     DX,AX

                    MOV     DL,0C4H   ;SWITCH TO BPS MODE
                    MOV     AL,0BH
                    OUT     DX,AL
                    INC     DL
                    IN      AL,DX
                    DEC     DL

                    MOV     BX,[CODEPAGE]
                    MOV     AH,BL
                    XOR     AH,2
                    MOV     DX,3C4H
                    MOV     AL,0EH
                    OUT     DX,AX

                    POP     DX
                    POP     BX
                    POP     AX

SETB_TRI1:          RET
SETBANK_TRI         ENDP

SETBANK_TNG         PROC    FAR
                    CMP     AX,[CODEPAGE]
                    JE      SETB_TNG1

                    MOV     [CODEPAGE],AX
                    PUSH    AX
                    PUSH    DX
                    MOV     AH,AL
                    MOV     DX,3BFH
                    MOV     AL,3
                    OUT     DX,AL
                    MOV     DL,0D8H
                    MOV     AL,0A0H
                    OUT     DX,AL
                    AND     AH,15
                    MOV     AL,AH
                    SHL     AL,1
                    SHL     AL,1
                    SHL     AL,1
                    SHL     AL,1
                    OR      AL,AH
                    MOV     DL,0CDH
                    OUT     DX,AL
                    POP     DX
                    POP     AX

SETB_TNG1:          RET
SETBANK_TNG         ENDP
```

```
         4-9   SETBANK_PAR     PROC    FAR
      Continued.               CMP     AX,[CODEPAGE]
                               JE      SETB_PAR1

                               PUSH    AX
                               PUSH    CX
                               PUSH    DX

                               AND     AX,00FFH
                               MOV     [CODEPAGE],AX

                               MOV     DX,03CEH
                               MOV     AX,050FH
                               OUT     DX,AX

                               MOV     AX,[CODEPAGE]
                               MOV     CL,12
                               SHL     AX,CL
                               OR      AX,0009H
                               OUT     DX,AX

                               POP     DX
                               POP     CX
                               POP     AX

               SETB_PAR1:      RET
               SETBANK_PAR     ENDP

               SETBANK_OAK     PROC    FAR
                               CMP     AX,[CODEPAGE]
                               JE      SETB_OAK1

                               MOV     [CODEPAGE],AX

                               PUSH    AX
                               PUSH    DX
                               AND     AL,15
                               MOV     AH,AL
                               SHL     AL,1
                               SHL     AL,1
                               SHL     AL,1
                               SHL     AL,1
                               OR      AH,AL
                               MOV     AL,11H
                               MOV     DX,3DEH
                               OUT     DX,AX
                               POP     DX
                               POP     AX

               SETB_OAK1:      RET
               SETBANK_OAK     ENDP

               SETBANK_VSA     PROC    FAR

                               PUSH    AX
```

```
                      CMP       AX,[CODEPAGE]
                      JE        SETB_VSA4

                      MOV       [CODEPAGE],AX

                      PUSH      BX
                      PUSH      CX
                      PUSH      DX

                      MOV       DX,AX
                      AND       DX,00FFH
                      MOV       CX,[BANKSHIFT]
                      SHL       DX,CL
                      MOV       BX,0000H
                      MOV       AX,4F05H
                      CMP       WORD PTR CS:[WINFUNPTR+2],0000H
                      JNE       SETB_VSA2

                      MOV       DX,[CODEPAGE]
                      AND       DX,00FFH
                      INT       10H

                      JMP       SETB_VSA3

SETB_VSA2:            CALL      CS:[WINFUNPTR]

SETB_VSA3:            POP       DX
                      POP       CX
                      POP       BX

SETB_VSA4:            POP       AX
                      RET
SETBANK_VSA           ENDP

SETBANK               LABEL     DWORD
SETBANK_OFF           DW        DUMMY
SETBANK_SEG           DW        MOUSE256_TEXT

MOUSE256_TEXT         ENDS

DGROUP                GROUP     _DATA,_BSS
_DATA                 SEGMENT WORD PUBLIC 'DATA'

                      PUBLIC    _SCREENTBL,_SCREENSEG,
                      PUBLIC    _SCREENWIDE,_SCREENDEEP
                      PUBLIC    _MASKTABLE,_BITTABLE
                      PUBLIC    _FONTSEG,_FONTOFF,_FONTDEPTH
                      PUBLIC    _VGAWHITE,_VGABLACK,_VGAGREY
                      PUBLIC    _VGALIGHTGREY,_VGADARKGREY
                      PUBLIC    _CARD
                      PUBLIC    CODEPAGE
; SCREEN DIMENSIONS
_SCREENTBL            DW        (TABLEDEEP * 2) DUP (?)
_SCREENSEG            DW        0A000H
```

```
4-9           _SCREENWIDE        DW      640
Continued.    _SCREENDEEP        DW      480

              ; FONT DIMENSIONS AND POINTER
              _FONTSEGDW         ?
              _FONTOFFDW         ?
              _FONTDEPTH         DW      ?

              ; MASK OBJECTS
              _MASKTABLE         DB      80H,40H,20H,10H,08H,04H,02H,01H
              _BITTABLE          DB      01H,02H,04H,08H,10H,20H,40H,80H

              ;COLOURS
              _VGABLACK          DW      0
              _VGAWHITE          DW      0
              _VGAGREY           DW      0
              _VGALIGHTGREY      DW      0
              _VGADARKGREY       DW      0

              ;VGA CARD TYPE
              _CARD              DW      0

              CODEPAGE           DW      0
              ATIREG             DW      0
              PAGEBREAK          DB      0

              ; WHERE THE CURSOR LIVES
              DEFAULTCURSOR      DB      03FH,0FFH,01FH,0FFH
                                 DB      00FH,0FFH,007H,0FFH
                                 DB      003H,0FFH,001H,0FFH
                                 DB      000H,0FFH,000H,07FH
                                 DB      000H,03FH,000H,01FH
                                 DB      001H,0FFH,010H,0FFH
                                 DB      030H,0FFH,0F8H,07FH
                                 DB      0F8H,07FH,0FCH,07FH
                                 DB      000H,000H,040H,000H
                                 DB      060H,000H,070H,000H
                                 DB      078H,000H,07CH,000H
                                 DB      07EH,000H,07FH,000H
                                 DB      07FH,080H,07CH,000H
                                 DB      06CH,000H,046H,000H
                                 DB      006H,000H,003H,000H
                                 DB      003H,000H,000H,000H

              SPOTX              DW      0000H
              SPOTY              DW      0000H

              ; MOUSE POSITION AND BUTTONS
              MOUSEX             DW      ?
              MOUSEY             DW      ?
              MOUSEB             DW      ?

              ; MOUSE CURSOR FLAG
              MOUSEF             DW      -1          ;IF >= 0, MOUSE IS VISIBLE
```

```
; WHERE THE AREA BEHIND THE MOUSE CURSOR IS STORED
MOUSEBACK        DB       (CURSORWIDE * CURSORDEEP) DUP (?)

VESABLOCK        LABEL    WORD
VESASIG          DB       4 DUP (0)
VESAVERSION      DW       0
OEMSTRING        DD       0
CAPABILITIES     DB       4 DUP (0)
VIDEOMODE        DD       0
TOTALMEMORY      DW       0
                 DB       242 DUP (0)

VESAINFO         LABEL    WORD
MODE_ATTR        DW       ?
WINA_ATTR        DB       ?
WINB_ATTR        DB       ?
WINGRAN          DW       ?
WINSIZE          DW       ?
WIN_ASEG         DW       ?
WIN_BSEG         DW       ?
WINFUNPTR        DD       ?
BYTESPERLINE     DW       ?
XRES             DW       ?
YRES             DW       ?
XCHARSIZE        DB       ?
YCHARSIZE        DB       ?
PLANECOUNT       DB       ?
BITXPERPIXEL     DB       ?
BANCKCOUNT       DB       ?
MEMORYMODEL      DB       ?
BANKVSIZE        DB       ?
PAGECOUNT        DB       ?
RESERVED1        DB       ?
MASKS            DB       8 DUP (0)
DIRECTCOLOUR     DB       ?
RESERVED2        DB       216 DUP (0)

OLDVESAMODE      DW       0FFFFH
BANKSHIFT        DW       0
BANKSIZEDW       0

_DATA            ENDS

_BSS             SEGMENT WORD PUBLIC 'BSS'

_BSS             ENDS

                 END
```

The following is a complete list of the functions provided by MOUSE256, in the order they appear in the source code. These functions are similar to those in MOUSE16 (from Chapter 3), although note that a few have different arguments and more of them are handled in assembly language in this version of the code.

GetScreenLine(char *line,unsigned int number)

The `GetScreenLine` function will copy the bytes from line `number` into the buffer at `line`. It's the responsibility of the calling function to make sure that the buffer at `line` is big enough to hold at least SCREENWIDE bytes and that `number` is in the range of 0 through SCREENDEEP-1.

GetImage256(unsigned int left,unsigned int top,unsigned int right,unsigned int bottom,char *p)

The `GetImage256` will capture a standard BGI-style image fragment from the screen area bounded by its first four arguments into the buffer at p. The size of the buffer passed to `GetImage256` should be calculated by the `ImageSize256` macro, which can be found in MOUSE256.H. Note that while the buffers set up by `GetImage256` are structured like those created by `getimage`, they are not constrained to fit in less than 64K of memory.

PutImage256(unsigned int left,unsigned int top,char *p)

The `PutImage256` function will paint a standard BGI-style 256-color image fragment pointed to by p on the screen, such that its upper left corner resides at (`left,top`). The fragment can be larger than 64K.

SetPixel(unsigned int x,unsigned int y,unsigned int color)

The `SetPixel` function will set the pixel at (`x,y`) to `color`. Note that the `SetPixel` function does not turn off the mouse cursor when it writes; be sure to do so before using `SetPixel`, and then turn it back on when you're done setting pixels.

FrameRect(unsigned int left,unsigned int top,unsigned int right,unsigned int bottom,unsigned int color)

The `FrameRect` function will draw a rectangle around the area defined by its first four arguments in `color`.

FillRect(unsigned int left,unsigned int top,unsigned int right,unsigned int bottom,unsigned int color)

The `FillRect` function will fill a rectangular area defined by its first four arguments with `color`.

DrawLine(unsigned int left,unsigned int top,unsigned int right,unsigned int bottom,unsigned int color)

The `DrawLine` function will draw a line from (`left,top`) to (`right,bottom`) in the color defined by its `color` argument.

DrawString(unsigned int x,unsigned int y,char *string,unsigned int forecolor,unsigned int backcolor)

The `DrawString` function draws text in the color defined by the `forecolor` argument against the color defined by the `backcolor` argument. The string is pointed to by the `string` argument and should be terminated by a zero byte, just like a normal C language string. The rectangle that encloses the string will have its upper left corner at point (x,y).

The `DrawString` function will draw in either 8-or 16-point text, depending on the status of the FONTEIGHT and FONTSIXTEEN equates in MOUSE256.ASM. Both fonts are readable at 640 by 480—the 8-point font can be drawn more rapidly and occupies less screen space. The 16-point font looks better.

InitMouse(unsigned int width,unsigned int depth,unsigned int card)

The `InitMouse` function sets up a suitable graphic mode for the card in question and the mouse manager. It also locates the font for `DrawString` and stores a pointer to it.

The code for `InitMouse` checks for the presence of a mouse driver and then initializes it. It then sets the range of the mouse cursor's travel to be those of the screen's dimensions. Finally, it sets up the hook to the custom mouse handler code, MOUSEHANDLER, which has been covered previously.

The `InitMouse` function will return a true value if all is well and a false one if the mouse driver couldn't be located.

The SCREENTBL line start table array is set up by `InitMouse` based on the card type. Unlike the 16-color version of `InitMouse`, this can't be handled at assembly time.

DeinitMouse(void)

The `DeinitMouse` function disables the hook into the custom mouse handler previously installed by `InitMouse` and resets the mouse driver. It also returns the screen to text mode. As with the 16-color version of `DeinitMouse`, it's extremely important to call this before returning control to DOS, as it will keep the mouse driver from leaping into the middle of whatever application you next run on your system—and thereby falling into roughly the same great cosmic nothingness in most cases—the first time the mouse moves.

ClearScreen(unsigned int color)

The `ClearScreen` function clears the screen to the color specified by its `color` argument. It was examined in detail earlier in this chapter.

MouseOn(void)

The `MouseOn` function makes the mouse cursor visible, and is usually called after a corresponding call to `MouseOff`.

MouseOff(void)

The `MouseOff` function hides the mouse cursor. You should make sure to call this function if you'll be drawing something on the screen that doesn't itself hide the mouse cursor, and then call `MouseOn` to reinstate it. The `SetPixel` function, for example, does not intrinsically hide the mouse cursor.

MouseDown(POINT *p)

The `MouseDown` function is exceedingly useful in writing code to interface with the mouse. When it's called, it will store the current location of the mouse cursor in the POINT object it's passed a pointer to, and return an integer that defines the state of the mouse buttons at the time of the call. If n is the value returned by `MouseDown`, n & 1 will be true if the left mouse button is down and n & 2 will be true if the right mouse button is down.

The MOUSEHANDLER function that's called by the mouse driver sets the button status flag and the current mouse location every time the mouse moves or is clicked.

The location of the mouse cursor is the point where the upper left corner of the sixteen by sixteen pixel cursor resides on your screen plus the offset of the "hot spot." This will be dealt with when we look at MouseCursor.

MouseCursor(char *cursor,unsigned int x,unsigned int y)

The MouseCursor function will change the appearance of the mouse cursor. By default, it appears as an arrow pointing to the upper left. The current cursor is stored in the DEFAULTCURSOR buffer in MOUSE256.ASM. Note that the cursor format for MOUSE256 is identical to that of MOUSE16.

A mouse cursor consists of the 32 bytes of the mask bitmap followed by the 32 bytes of the image bitmap, as was explained in Chapter 3. A more complete explanation of the "hot spot" values can also be found in Chapter 3.

Calling MOUSE256 from C

Figure 4-10 is the complete C language source code for TESTM256.C, the program that generated FIG. 4-1, back at the beginning of this chapter. It includes the few graphic functions covered in this chapter that aren't resident in MOUSE256, as well as a main function to exercise them. If you compile this program, you'll want to link it to MOUSE256.OBJ, as derived from MOUSE256.ASM. You'll also need MOUSE256.H, which will be presented in the next section of this chapter.

4-10
The source code for TESTM256.C.

```
/*
        Some 256 colour graphics

        Copyright (c) 1992 Alchemy Mindworks Inc.

        Links to MOUSE256.ASM
*/

#include "stdio.h"
#include "dos.h"
#include "alloc.h"
#include "mouse256.h"

/* colours in this 256-colour palette */
#define BLACK           0
#define BLUE            126
#define GREEN           31
#define CYAN            246
#define RED             3
#define MAGENTA         143
#define YELLOW          41
#define GREY            253
#define DARKGREY        252
#define LIGHTGREY       254
#define LIGHTBLUE       192
#define LIGHTGREEN      36
```

```
#define LIGHTRED          5
#define LIGHTYELLOW       125
#define LIGHTMAGENTA      227
#define WHITE             255

/* dimensions of the about box */
#define ABOUTLEFT         107
#define ABOUTTOP          50
#define ABOUTRIGHT        475
#define ABOUTBOTTOM       180

typedef struct {
        char manufacturer;
        char version;
        char encoding;
        char bits_per_pixel;
        int xmin,ymin;
        int xmax,ymax;
        int hres;
        int vres;
        char palette[48];
        char reserved;
        char colour_planes;
        int bytes_per_line;
        int palette_type;
        char filler[58];
        } PCXHEAD;

/* the 256-colour palette we'll use */
char palette[] = {
        0x00,0x00,0x00,0x57,0x00,0x00,0x83,0x00,
        0x00,0xab,0x00,0x00,0xd7,0x00,0x00,0xff,
        0x00,0x00,0x00,0x2b,0x00,0x57,0x2b,0x00,
        0x83,0x2b,0x00,0xab,0x2b,0x00,0xd7,0x2b,
        0x00,0xff,0x2b,0x00,0x00,0x57,0x00,0x57,
        0x57,0x00,0x83,0x57,0x00,0xab,0x57,0x00,
        0xd7,0x57,0x00,0xff,0x57,0x00,0x00,0x83,
        0x00,0x57,0x83,0x00,0x83,0x83,0x00,0xab,
        0x83,0x00,0xd7,0x83,0x00,0xff,0x83,0x00,
        0x00,0xab,0x00,0x57,0xab,0x00,0x83,0xab,
        0x00,0xab,0xab,0x00,0xd7,0xab,0x00,0xff,
        0xab,0x00,0x00,0xd7,0x00,0x57,0xd7,0x00,
        0x83,0xd7,0x00,0xab,0xd7,0x00,0xd7,0xd7,
        0x00,0xff,0xd7,0x00,0x00,0xff,0x00,0x57,
        0xff,0x00,0x83,0xff,0x00,0xab,0xff,0x00,
        0xd7,0xff,0x00,0xff,0xff,0x00,0x00,0x00,
        0x57,0x57,0x00,0x57,0x83,0x00,0x57,0xab,
        0x00,0x57,0xd7,0x00,0x57,0xff,0x00,0x57,
        0x00,0x2b,0x57,0x57,0x2b,0x57,0x83,0x2b,
        0x57,0xab,0x2b,0x57,0xd7,0x2b,0x57,0xff,
        0x2b,0x57,0x00,0x57,0x57,0x57,0x57,0x57,
        0x83,0x57,0x57,0xab,0x57,0x57,0xd7,0x57,
        0x57,0xff,0x57,0x57,0x00,0x83,0x57,0x57,
        0x83,0x57,0x83,0x83,0x57,0xab,0x83,0x57,
        0xd7,0x83,0x57,0xff,0x83,0x57,0x00,0xab,
```

```
0x57,0x57,0xab,0x57,0x83,0xab,0x57,0xab,
0xab,0x57,0xd7,0xab,0x57,0xff,0xab,0x57,
0x00,0xd7,0x57,0x57,0xd7,0x57,0x83,0xd7,
0x57,0xab,0xd7,0x57,0xd7,0xd7,0x57,0xff,
0xd7,0x57,0x00,0xff,0x57,0x57,0xff,0x57,
0x83,0xff,0x57,0xab,0xff,0x57,0xd7,0xff,
0x57,0xff,0xff,0x57,0x00,0x00,0x83,0x57,
0x00,0x83,0x83,0x00,0x83,0xab,0x00,0x83,
0xd7,0x00,0x83,0xff,0x00,0x83,0x00,0x2b,
0x83,0x57,0x2b,0x83,0x83,0x2b,0x83,0xab,
0x2b,0x83,0xd7,0x2b,0x83,0xff,0x2b,0x83,
0x00,0x57,0x83,0x57,0x57,0x83,0x83,0x57,
0x83,0xab,0x57,0x83,0xd7,0x57,0x83,0xff,
0x57,0x83,0x00,0x83,0x83,0x57,0x83,0x83,
0x83,0x83,0x83,0xab,0x83,0x83,0xd7,0x83,
0x83,0xff,0x83,0x83,0x00,0xab,0x83,0x57,
0xab,0x83,0x83,0xab,0x83,0xab,0xab,0x83,
0xd7,0xab,0x83,0xff,0xab,0x83,0x00,0xd7,
0x83,0x57,0xd7,0x83,0x83,0xd7,0x83,0xab,
0xd7,0x83,0xd7,0xd7,0x83,0xff,0xd7,0x83,
0x00,0xff,0x83,0x57,0xff,0x83,0x83,0xff,
0x83,0xab,0xff,0x83,0xd7,0xff,0x83,0xff,
0xff,0x83,0x00,0x00,0xab,0x57,0x00,0xab,
0x83,0x00,0xab,0xab,0x00,0xab,0xd7,0x00,
0xab,0xff,0x00,0xab,0x00,0x2b,0xab,0x57,
0x2b,0xab,0x83,0x2b,0xab,0xab,0x2b,0xab,
0xd7,0x2b,0xab,0xff,0x2b,0xab,0x00,0x57,
0xab,0x57,0x57,0xab,0x83,0x57,0xab,0xab,
0x57,0xab,0xd7,0x57,0xab,0xff,0x57,0xab,
0x00,0x83,0xab,0x57,0x83,0xab,0x83,0x83,
0xab,0xab,0x83,0xab,0xd7,0x83,0xab,0xff,
0x83,0xab,0x00,0xab,0xab,0x57,0xab,0xab,
0x83,0xab,0xab,0xab,0xab,0xab,0xd7,0xab,
0xab,0xff,0xab,0xab,0x00,0xd7,0xab,0x57,
0xd7,0xab,0x83,0xd7,0xab,0xab,0xd7,0xab,
0xd7,0xd7,0xab,0xff,0xd7,0xab,0x00,0xff,
0xab,0x57,0xff,0xab,0x83,0xff,0xab,0xab,
0xff,0xab,0xd7,0xff,0xab,0xff,0xff,0xab,
0x00,0x00,0xd7,0x57,0x00,0xd7,0x83,0x00,
0xd7,0xab,0x00,0xd7,0xd7,0x00,0xd7,0xff,
0x00,0xd7,0x00,0x2b,0xd7,0x57,0x2b,0xd7,
0x83,0x2b,0xd7,0xab,0x2b,0xd7,0xd7,0x2b,
0xd7,0xff,0x2b,0xd7,0x00,0x57,0xd7,0x57,
0x57,0xd7,0x83,0x57,0xd7,0xab,0x57,0xd7,
0xd7,0x57,0xd7,0xff,0x57,0xd7,0x00,0x83,
0xd7,0x57,0x83,0xd7,0x83,0x83,0xd7,0xab,
0x83,0xd7,0xd7,0x83,0xd7,0xff,0x83,0xd7,
0x00,0xab,0xd7,0x57,0xab,0xd7,0x83,0xab,
0xd7,0xab,0xab,0xd7,0xd7,0xab,0xd7,0xff,
0xab,0xd7,0x00,0xd7,0xd7,0x57,0xd7,0xd7,
0x83,0xd7,0xd7,0xab,0xd7,0xd7,0xd7,0xd7,
0xd7,0xff,0xd7,0xd7,0x00,0xff,0xd7,0x57,
0xff,0xd7,0x83,0xff,0xd7,0xab,0xff,0xd7,
0xd7,0xff,0xd7,0xff,0xff,0xd7,0x00,0x00,
0xff,0x57,0x00,0xff,0x83,0x00,0xff,0xab,
```

```
            0x00,0xff,0xd7,0x00,0xff,0xff,0x00,0xff,
            0x00,0x2b,0xff,0x57,0x2b,0xff,0x83,0x2b,
            0xff,0xab,0x2b,0xff,0xd7,0x2b,0xff,0xff,
            0x2b,0xff,0x00,0x57,0xff,0x57,0x57,0xff,
            0x83,0x57,0xff,0xab,0x57,0xff,0xd7,0x57,
            0xff,0xff,0x57,0xff,0x00,0x83,0xff,0x57,
            0x83,0xff,0x83,0x83,0xff,0xab,0x83,0xff,
            0xd7,0x83,0xff,0xff,0x83,0xff,0x00,0xab,
            0xff,0x57,0xab,0xff,0x83,0xab,0xff,0xab,
            0xab,0xff,0xd7,0xab,0xff,0xff,0xab,0xff,
            0x00,0xd7,0xff,0x57,0xd7,0xff,0x83,0xd7,
            0xff,0xab,0xd7,0xff,0xd7,0xd7,0xff,0xff,
            0xd7,0xff,0x00,0xff,0xff,0x57,0xff,0xff,
            0x83,0xff,0xff,0xab,0xff,0xff,0xd7,0xff,
            0xff,0x3f,0x3f,0x3f,0x6b,0x6b,0x6b,0x97,
            0x97,0x97,0xc3,0xc3,0xc3,0xff,0xff,0xff
            };

main(argc,argv)
        int argc;
        char *argv[];
{
        BUTTON quit,pause,about,save;
        POINT p;
        int left,top,right,bottom;
        int i,alive=1,thiscard=0xffff;

        /* see what kind of card is installed - sort of */
        if(argc > 1) {
            if(!stricmp(argv[1],"PARADISE")) thiscard=PARADISE;
            else if(!stricmp(argv[1],"ATI")) thiscard=ATI;
            else if(!stricmp(argv[1],"TSENG")) thiscard=TSENG;
            else if(!stricmp(argv[1],"TRIDENT")) thiscard=TRIDENT;
            else if(!stricmp(argv[1],"OAK")) thiscard=OAK;
            else if(!stricmp(argv[1],"VESA")) thiscard=VESA;
        }

        /* go for a graphics mode */
        if(!InitMouse(640,480,thiscard)) exit(1);

        /* set the palette */
        SetVgaPalette(palette,256);

        SetVgaWhite(WHITE);
        SetVgaBlack(BLACK);
        SetVgaGrey(GREY);
        SetVgaLightGrey(LIGHTGREY);
        SetVgaDarkGrey(DARKGREY);

        /* clear the screen */
        ClearScreen(GetVgaLightGrey());

        /* draw a moire pattern */
        for(i=0;i<SCREENWIDE;i+=2)
            DrawLine(i,0,SCREENWIDE>>1,SCREENDEEP>>1,i);
```

```
for(i=0;i<SCREENDEEP;i+=2)
    DrawLine(SCREENWIDE>>1,SCREENDEEP>>1,SCREENWIDE-1,i,i);
for(i=SCREENWIDE-1;i>=0;i-=2)
    DrawLine(SCREENWIDE>>1,SCREENDEEP>>1,i,SCREENDEEP-1,i-1);
for(i=SCREENDEEP-1;i>=0;i-=2)
    DrawLine(0,i,SCREENWIDE>>1,SCREENDEEP>>1,i-1);

/* show the palette */
for(i=0;i<256;++i) {
    left=30+(i % 32)*16;
    top=200+(i / 32)*16;
    right=left+16;
    bottom=top+16;
    FillRect(left,top,right,bottom,i);
    FrameRect(left,top,right,bottom,GetVgaBlack());
}

/* show some example text */
i=100;
DrawString(128,i," This is blue on light green.           ",BLUE,LIGHTGREEN);
i+=FONTDEPTH;
DrawString(128,i," This is red on light yellow.           ",RED,LIGHTYELLOW);
i+=FONTDEPTH;
DrawString(128,i," This is light yellow on red.           ",LIGHTYELLOW,RED);
i+=FONTDEPTH;
DrawString(128,i," This is black on magenta (very ugly). ",BLACK,MAGENTA);
i+=FONTDEPTH;
DrawString(128,i," This is cyan on light grey.           ",CYAN,LIGHTGREY);
i+=FONTDEPTH;

/* create some buttons to click on */
MakeButton(SCREENWIDE-100,SCREENDEEP-60,"Quit",&quit);
DrawButton(&quit);

MakeButton(SCREENWIDE-200,SCREENDEEP-60,"Pause",&pause);
DrawButton(&pause);

MakeButton(SCREENWIDE-300,SCREENDEEP-60,"About",&about);
DrawButton(&about);

MakeButton(SCREENWIDE-400,SCREENDEEP-60,"Save",&save);
DrawButton(&save);

/* loop 'til we're done */
do {
        /* look for a mouse click */
        if(MouseDown(&p)) {
                if(PointInRect(&p,&quit)) {
                        TrackButton(&quit);
                        alive=0;
                }
                else if(PointInRect(&p,&pause)) {
                        TrackButton(&pause);
                        WaitCursor();
                        delay(5000);
                        ArrowCursor();
```

```
                                }
                                else if(PointInRect(&p,&about)) {
                                        TrackButton(&about);
                                        DoAbout();
                                }
                                else if(PointInRect(&p,&save)) {
                                        TrackButton(&save);
                                        DoSave("SCREEN00.PCX");
                                }
                        }
                }
        } while(alive);

        DeinitMouse();
}

/* save the screen to a PCX file */
DoSave(path)
        char *path;
{
        PCXHEAD pcx;
        FILE *fp;
        char *p;
        unsigned int i,n;

        /* create the destination file */
        if((fp=fopen(path,"wb"))==NULL) {
                beep();
                return;
        }

        if((p=malloc(SCREENWIDE))==NULL) {
                beep();
                fclose(fp);
                return;
        }

        memset((char *)&pcx,0,sizeof(PCXHEAD));
        memcpy(pcx.palette,palette,48);

        pcx.manufacturer=10;
        pcx.encoding=1;
        pcx.xmin=pcx.ymin=0;
        pcx.xmax=SCREENWIDE-1;
        pcx.ymax=SCREENDEEP-1;
        pcx.palette_type=1;
        pcx.bits_per_pixel=8;
        pcx.version=5;
        pcx.colour_planes=1;
        pcx.bytes_per_line=SCREENWIDE;

        WaitCursor();
        if(fwrite((char *)&pcx,1,sizeof(PCXHEAD),fp) != sizeof(PCXHEAD)) {
                free(p);
                fclose(fp);
                remove(path);
```

```
                              ArrowCursor();
                              beep();
                              return;
              }

              for(i=0;i<SCREENDEEP;++i) {
                              MouseOff();
                              GetScreenLine(p,i);
                              MouseOn();
                              n=pcxwriteline(fp,p,pcx.bytes_per_line);

                              if(n != pcx.bytes_per_line) {
                              free(p);
                              fclose(fp);
                              remove(path);
                              ArrowCursor();
                              beep();
                              return;
                               }
              }

              fputc(12,fp);
              if(fwrite(palette,1,768,fp) != 768) {
                  free(p);
                  fclose(fp);
                  remove(path);
                  ArrowCursor();
                  beep();
                  return;
              }

              ArrowCursor();
              free(p);
              fclose(fp);
      }

      /* write one pcx line */
      pcxwriteline(fp,p,n)
              FILE *fp;
              char *p;
              unsigned int n;
      {
              unsigned int i=0,j=0,t=0;

              do {
                      i=0;
                      while((p[t+i]==p[t+i+1]) && ((t+i) < n) && (i < 63))++i;
                      if(i>0) {
                              if(fputc(i | 0xc0,fp)==EOF) return(-1);
                              if(fputc(p[t],fp)==EOF) return(-1);
                              t+=i;
                              j+=2;
                      }
              else {
                      if(((p[t]) & 0xc0)==0xc0) {
```

```
                                        if(fputc(0xc1,fp)==EOF) return(-1);
                                        ++j;
                                }
                                if(fputc(p[t++],fp)==EOF) return(-1);
                                ++j;
                        }
                } while(t<n);
                return(n);
}

/* show the about box */
DoAbout()
{
        POINT pt;
        BUTTON done;
        char *p;
        unsigned long size;
        unsigned int i;

        /* see how much memory the area behind it needs */
        size=ImageSize256(ABOUTLEFT,ABOUTTOP,ABOUTRIGHT,ABOUTBOTTOM);

        /* get a buffer */
        if((p=farmalloc(size)) != NULL) {

            /* get the area behind the box */
            GetImage256(ABOUTLEFT,ABOUTTOP,ABOUTRIGHT,ABOUTBOTTOM,p);

            /* draw the box */
            FillRect(ABOUTLEFT,ABOUTTOP,ABOUTRIGHT,ABOUTBOTTOM,LIGHTBLUE);
            FrameRect(ABOUTLEFT,ABOUTTOP,ABOUTRIGHT,ABOUTBOTTOM,BLACK);

            /* add the Done button */
            MakeButton(ABOUTLEFT+16,ABOUTBOTTOM-32,"Done",&done);
            DrawButton(&done);

            /* show some text */
            i=ABOUTTOP+16;
            DrawString(ABOUTLEFT+16,i,"This is an example of 256 colour",BLACK,LIGHTBLUE);
            i+=FONTDEPTH;
            DrawString(ABOUTLEFT+16,i,"super VGA graphics. Copyright (c) 1902",BLACK,LIGHTBLUE);
            i+=FONTDEPTH;
            DrawString(ABOUTLEFT+16,i,"Mother Martha's Computer Software",BLACK,LIGHTBLUE);
            i+=FONTDEPTH;
            DrawString(ABOUTLEFT+16,i,"Emporium Ltd. Use no hooks.",BLACK,LIGHTBLUE);

            i=1;

            /* loop 'til we're done */
            do {
                if(MouseDown(&pt)) {
                        if(PointInRect(&pt,&done)) {
                                TrackButton(&done);
                                        i=0;
                        } else beep();
```

```
                                    }
                        } while(i);

                        /* put the old screen back */
                        PutImage256(ABOUTLEFT,ABOUTTOP,p);

                        /* free the buffer */
                        farfree(p);
                } else beep();
}

SetVgaPalette(p,n)
        char *p;
        unsigned int n;
{
        int i;

        outp(0x3c6,0xff);
        for(i=0;i<n;++i) {
                outp(0x3c8,i);
                outp(0x3c9,(*p++) >> 2);
                outp(0x3c9,(*p++) >> 2);
                outp(0x3c9,(*p++) >> 2);
        }
}

MakeButton(left,top,string,button)
        unsigned int left,top;
        char *string;
        BUTTON *button;
{
        button->frame.left = left & 0xfff8;
        button->frame.right=button->frame.left+(strlen(string)<<3)+16;
        button->frame.top=top;
        button->frame.bottom=button->frame.top+FONTDEPTH+8;
        button->text=string;
}

DrawButton(button)
        BUTTON *button;
{
        FillRect(button->frame.left+1,button->frame.top+1,
                button->frame.right-1,button->frame.bottom-1,GetVgaWhite());
        DrawLine(button->frame.left+1,button->frame.top,
                button->frame.right-1,button->frame.top,GetVgaBlack());
        DrawLine(button->frame.left,button->frame.top+1,
                button->frame.left,button->frame.bottom-1,GetVgaBlack());
        DrawLine(button->frame.right,button->frame.top+1,
                button->frame.right,button->frame.bottom-1,GetVgaBlack());
        DrawLine(button->frame.left+1,button->frame.bottom,
                button->frame.right-1,button->frame.bottom,GetVgaBlack());
        Fill3DBox(button->frame.left+1,button->frame.top+1,
                        button->frame.right-1,button->frame.bottom-1);

        DrawString(button->frame.left+8,button->frame.top+4,
                button->text,GetVgaDarkGrey(),GetVgaLightGrey());
```

```
        }

TrackButton(button)
        BUTTON *button;
{
        POINT p;

        FillRect(button->frame.left+1,button->frame.top+1,
                        button->frame.right-1,button->frame.bottom-1,GetVgaLightGrey());

        DrawString(button->frame.left+8,button->frame.top+4,
                                button->text,GetVgaDarkGrey(),GetVgaLightGrey());
        while(MouseDown(&p));
        DrawButton(button);
}

Fill3DBox(left,top,right,bottom)
        int left,top,right,bottom;
{
        FillRect(left,top,right,bottom,GetVgaLightGrey());
        DrawLine(left,top,right-1,top,GetVgaWhite());
        DrawLine(left,top+1,left,bottom-1,GetVgaWhite());

        DrawLine(left+3,bottom,right,bottom,GetVgaDarkGrey());
        DrawLine(right,top+2,right,bottom-1,GetVgaDarkGrey());
}

PointInRect(p,r)/* return true if point is in rect */
        POINT *p;
        RECT *r;
{
        if(p->x > r->left && p->x < r->right &&
           p->y > r->top  && p->y < r->bottom) return(1);
        else return(0);
}

WaitCursor()
{
        static char cursor[] = {
            0x00,0x00,0x00,0x00,
            0x00,0x00,0x01,0x80,
            0x03,0xC0,0x07,0xE0,
            0x0F,0xF0,0x07,0xE0,
            0x03,0xC0,0x01,0x80,
            0x00,0x00,0x00,0x00,
            0x00,0x00,0x00,0x00,
            0xFF,0xFF,0xFF,0xFF,

            0x00,0x00,0xFE,0x7F,
            0x06,0x60,0x0C,0x30,
            0x18,0x18,0x30,0x0C,
            0x60,0x06,0xC0,0x03,
            0x60,0x06,0x30,0x0C,
            0x98,0x19,0xCC,0x33,
            0xE6,0x67,0xFE,0x7F,
            0x00,0x00,0x00,0x00 };
```

```
                    MouseCursor(cursor,7,7);
                }

ArrowCursor()
{
    static char cursor[] = {
        0xFF,0x3F,0xFF,0x1F,
        0xFF,0x0F,0xFF,0x07,
        0xFF,0x03,0xFF,0x01,
        0xFF,0x00,0x7F,0x00,
        0x3F,0x00,0x1F,0x00,
        0xFF,0x01,0xFF,0x10,
        0xFF,0x30,0x7F,0xF8,
        0x7F,0xF8,0x7F,0xFC,
        0x00,0x00,0x00,0x40,
        0x00,0x60,0x00,0x70,
        0x00,0x78,0x00,0x7C,
        0x00,0x7E,0x00,0x7F,
        0x80,0x7F,0x00,0x7C,
        0x00,0x6C,0x00,0x46,
        0x00,0x06,0x00,0x03,
        0x00,0x03,0x00,0x00  };

    MouseCursor(cursor,0,0);
}
```

If you run into compilation or execution problems with TESTM256.C, check the setup of your compiler defaults, as explained in Chapter 1.

Pretty well everything that's happening in TESTM256.C happened in TESTM16.C, in the previous chapter. The only real difference is the size of the palette, and the number of palette tiles that are drawn as a result of this.

The `main` function begins by looking for a command line argument to tell it what kind of super VGA card it should set itself up for. Unlike TESTM16, this program can't run on a standard VGA card. If it doesn't find an argument to tell it which card it's to run with, it will return to DOS.

The card type, in `thiscard`, is passed to `InitMouse`.

The first bit of actual graphics in the `main` function of TESTM256.C is the drawing of the moire pattern, the radial lines that fill the screen. This bit of code exercises `DrawLine`.

Following the code that draws a moire, `main` draws 256 boxes with the palette colors in them using `FillRect`. It then draws some example text with `DrawString` and sets up four buttons. Most of the rest of the function is occupied by a loop to manage the buttons.

The Quit button terminates the loop by setting the `alive` variable false. The `Pause` button exercises the `MouseCursor` function by changing the cursor to an hourglass and pausing for five seconds. The `About` button will display an About box by calling the `DoAbout` function. The Save button will create a file called

SCREEN00.PCX that will contain a captured image of the current screen. The `About` and `DoSave` functions work just like they did in TESTM16.

Here's a list of the functions in TESTM256.C that you might want to excise for use in your own software. It's quite a bit shorter than the one for TESTM16, as most of the 256-color graphic functions are in MOUSE256.

DoSave(char *path)

The `DoSave` function will create a PCX file of your current graphic screen at the moment it's called. The `path` argument should be a complete path and file name, or just a file name if you want the file to appear in the current directory. This includes the extension PCX.

SetVgaPalette(char *palette,int colors)

The `SetVgaPalette` function will set the current 16-color VGA palette. The `palette` argument should be a pointer to a table of three-byte RGB color values. The `colors` argument is the number of colors to set—this will usually be 256.

MakeButton(unsigned int left,unsigned int top,char *string, BUTTON *button)

The `MakeButton` function sets up a BUTTON object to display a button with its upper left corner at (`left,top`) and its text set to `string`. It will set the `frame` element of the button so that its upper left corner corresponds to the `left` and `top` arguments to `MakeButton`. The bottom of the frame will be set based on the current font size. The right edge of the frame will be set based on the length of the string to be used by the button.

Note that a BUTTON object doesn't store the text for the button it defines, but only a pointer to it. As such, the text passed to `MakeButton` must be static.

DrawButton(BUTTON *button)

The `DrawButton` function—perhaps predictably—draws a button on the screen. The BUTTON object passed to it should have been set up by a previous call to `MakeButton`.

TrackButton(BUTTON *button)

The `TrackButton` function will manage a button once it has been established that a mouse click has taken place within its boundaries.

Fill3DBox(unsigned int left,unsigned int top,unsigned int right,unsigned int bottom)

The `Fill3DBOX` function is called by `DrawButton`, and probably won't be of much use to other aspects of your software directly.

PointInRect(POINT *p,RECT *r)

The `PointInRect` function will return a true value if POINT p is within RECT r, or a false value if it's not.

WaitCursor(void)

The WaitCursor function will cause the current cursor to change to an hourglass. It should be called prior to any operation which will take a while to perform.

ArrowCursor(void)

The ArrowCursor function will cause the current cursor to revert to a standard arrow cursor. It can be called after a call to WaitCursor, or to any other function that redefines the mouse cursor's appearance.

The MOUSE256.H header

The MOUSE256.H file should be included in any C language source code that makes calls to MOUSE256. It also contains some structures used by the functions in TESTM256.C. It's illustrated in FIG. 4-11.

As with MOUSE16, the list of mode numbers for the various VGA cards at the top of MOUSE256.H can be expanded a bit. In this case, you might want to do so to use either a 640 by 400 pixel, 256-color graphic mode if you have a super VGA card with only 256K of memory on it. Alternately, you might want to try an 800 by 600 or 1024 by 768 pixel mode if you have a higher-end card.

4-11
The MOUSE256.H header file.

```
/*
        Header for MOUSE256
*/

#define PARADISE      0x5f
#define ATI           0x62
#define TSENG         0x2e
#define TRIDENT       0x5d
#define OAK           0x53
#define VESA          0x0101

#define COLOURDEPTH 8

#define RGB_RED       0
#define RGB_GREEN     1
#define RGB_BLUE      2
#define RGB_SIZE      3

typedef struct {
        unsigned int x,y;
        } POINT;

typedef struct {
        unsigned int left,top,right,bottom;
        } RECT;

typedef struct {
        RECT frame;
        char *text;
        } BUTTON;

#define pixels2bytes(n)     ((n+7)/8)
#define ImageWidth(p)       (1+p[0]+(p[1] << 8))
#define ImageDepth(p)       (1+p[2]+(p[3] << 8))
```

```
#define SetVgaWhite(n)              { VGAWHITE=(n); }
#define SetVgaBlack(n)              { VGABLACK=(n); }
#define SetVgaGrey(n)               { VGAGREY=(n); }
#define SetVgaLightGrey(n)          { VGALIGHTGREY=(n); }
#define SetVgaDarkGrey(n)   { VGADARKGREY=(n); }

#define GetVgaWhite()           VGAWHITE
#define GetVgaBlack()           VGABLACK
#define GetVgaGrey()            VGAGREY
#define GetVgaLightGrey()   VGALIGHTGREY
#define GetVgaDarkGrey()    VGADARKGREY

#define greyvalue(r,g,b)        (((r*30)/100) + ((g*59)/100) + ((b*11)/100))

#define beep()                  putchar(7)

#ifndef max
#define max(a,b)                (((a)>(b))?(a):(b))
#endif
#ifndef min
#define min(a,b)                (((a)<(b))?(a):(b))
#endif

#define ImageSize256(l,t,r,b)   (4L+(long)(1+max(r,l)-min(r,l))*\
                                (long)(1+max(b,t)-min(b,t)))

unsigned int InitMouse(unsigned int screenwide,unsigned int screendeep,
                    unsigned int card);
void DeinitMouse(void);
void MouseOn(void);
void MouseOff(void);
unsigned int MouseDown(POINT *p);
void MouseCursor(char *cursor,unsigned int x,unsigned int y);
void DrawString(unsigned x,unsigned int y,char *p,unsigned int c,
            unsigned int b);
void PutImage256(unsigned int left,unsigned int top,char *p);
void GetImage256(unsigned int left,unsigned int top,unsigned int right,
            unsigned int bottom,char *p);

extern unsigned int SCREENTBL[];
extern unsigned int SCREENWIDE;
extern unsigned int SCREENDEEP;
extern unsigned int SCREENSEG;
extern char masktable[];
extern char bittable[];
extern unsigned int FONTDEPTH;
extern unsigned int FONTSEG;
extern unsigned int FONTOFF;
extern unsigned int VGAWHITE;
extern unsigned int VGABLACK;
extern unsigned int VGALIGHTGREY;
extern unsigned int VGADARKGREY;
extern unsigned int VGAGREY;
```

In all cases, keep in mind that you must change the screen mode and the screen dimensions. Finally, make very certain you change the TABLEDEEP equate in MOUSE256.ASM to reflect the maximum possible screen depth, lest SCREENTBL exceed its bounds and overwrite something useful in your code.

To begin with, here are the mode numbers for the 640 by 400 pixel, 256-color modes:

```
#define PARADISE  0x5e
#define ATI       0x61
#define TSENG     0x2f
#define TRIDENT   0x5c
#define OAK       None
#define VESA      0x0100
```

You'll note that each of these values differ from their corresponding 640 by 480 modes by one. Unfortunately, they're not consistent in this: some of them are one higher and others one lower.

These are the mode numbers for the 800 by 600 pixel, 256-color modes:

```
#define PARADISE  0x5c
#define ATI       0x63
#define TSENG     0x30
#define TRIDENT   0x5e
#define OAK       0x54
#define VESA      0x0103
```

Finally, here are the mode numbers for the 1024 by 768 pixel, 256-color modes:

```
#define PARADISE  0x60
#define ATI       0x64
#define TSENG     0x38
#define TRIDENT   0x5f
#define OAK       0x59
#define VESA      0x0105
```

It's quite practical to support all these modes in your applications, although you'll need a more elaborate method of defining them than has been used in this chapter. Note, for example, that the mode number for the Trident 800 by 600 pixel mode is the same as that of the Paradise 640 by 400 pixel mode.

It's also important to keep in mind that not all cards support all these modes even if they do appear to have the memory to do so. There are a number of ATI cards that have 512K on board but won't do 800 by 600 pixels at 256 colors, presumably so they won't encroach on the sales of more expensive ATI cards that do.

The extern declarations in MOUSE256.H allow a C language program to get at a number of useful objects in MOUSE256. The SCREENWIDE, SCREENDEEP, SCREENSEG, and SCREENTBL objects have been described previously, as have masktable and bittable. The FONTDEPTH value represents the vertical size of the system font in lines. The horizontal value will always be eight. The FONTSEG and FONTOFF values represent a pointer into the VGA BIOS where the system font being used resides. These values behave in the same way as they did in MOUSE16.

The macro `ImageSize256` returns a value that defines the number of bytes required for a `GetImage256` buffer, just as the `imagesize` function does for a normal Turbo C `getimage` fragment. You can regard it as a function:

```
unsigned long ImageSize256(unsigned int left,unsigned int
top,unsigned int right,unsigned int bottom)
```

The `ImageSize256` function returns a long integer that contains the number of bytes required to create a `GetImage256` buffer to hold the screen fragment defined by its four arguments.

Applications for 256-color graphics

In the closing paragraphs of Chapter 3, I suggested that real-world business applications seemed to get along best with the 16-color graphic modes. While this is unquestionably true, a lot of high-end super VGA cards have been sold nonetheless. The ability to work with graphics that simulate real life on a monitor is somehow appealing of itself. It's also not without its practical applications; if it takes a bit more vision to appreciate them, you might consider this to be a filter that rejects the short-sighted.

Software that makes use of the 16-color business graphic modes of a super VGA card might help you see more. Software that uses the 256-color modes can help you see better. Relatively little of the passion and poetry of the human spirit has been inspired by a well-rounded integer.

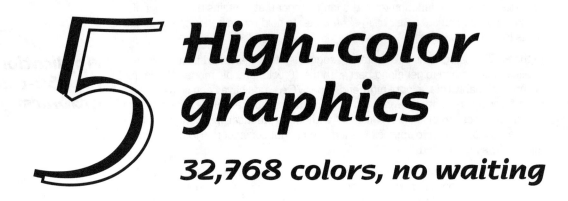

5 *High-color graphics*

32,768 colors, no waiting

"The days of the digital watch are numbered."
—Graffiti

A growing number of high-end super VGA cards offer high-color graphics. A bit mysterious in some respects—and almost universally unsupported by most applications—these modes offer the potential for an almost unlimited range of colors. They don't restrict the software that drives them to finite color palettes. Things that are impractically slow in a 256-color mode can often be handled in no time at all using high-color graphics.

There are a few drawbacks to the high-color display modes, most of them involving memory in one way or another. It requires a megabyte of display memory to support super VGA high-color graphics, and if you intend to work with bitmapped images in these modes, plan on having a lot of system memory to hold your pictures as well. A 640 by 480 pixel picture stored in the same pixel format as a high-color display will require 600K of memory.

This means that moving images to the screen can be a bit time consuming as well.

A secondary consideration is that relatively few users have display adapters capable of supporting high-color graphics. As of this writing, only three of the manufacturers of conventional super VGA hardware—Paradise, ATI and Tseng Labs—offer high-color support. Some of the more esoteric chip sets, such as the S3 graphic accelerator, have high-color modes as well. This latter group of cards can usually be dealt with as VESA devices.

In addition to the usual VGA hardware, a super VGA card with high-color support requires an external digital to analog converter chip to handle high color. This is referred to as a RAMDAC on Paradise hardware and as a Sierra DAC, indicating its manufacturer, on Tseng Labs boards. The Tseng Labs cards that offer high-color support use the 4000-series chip set with some extra hardware, and are as such referred to as 4000X.

The lack of color palettes arguably makes the somewhat gluttonous memory demands of high-color graphics worth accepting. These modes allow you to draw in any color you like, in as many colors at once as there are pixels on your screen. The actual maximum number of different colors a high-color mode can support is 2^{15}, or 32,768.

Despite the fairly exotic nature of high-color graphics, you can do pretty well the same things in a high-color mode as you can with the 256-color super VGA modes—and quite a lot more besides. Figure 5-1 illustrates a variation on the example graphic that has turned up in the previous two chapters. This one was created by a variation on the foregoing two graphic packages that runs in a 640 by 480 pixel high-color mode.

5-1 *The graphic created by the example program in this chapter.*

The almost unlimited number of colors available in a high-color mode has made it possible to do some different things in FIG. 5-1. To begin with, integrating the photographic fragment in the upper left corner was agreeably easy. In a 256-color mode, merging two graphics can be something of a juggling act with chainsaws, as doing so usually means combining two disparate color palettes into one—hopefully without introducing too noticeable a color shift in either image. In a high-color mode, inasmuch as there are no palettes involved, you can simply paint one image over another and get on with whatever comes next.

The image fragment was imported as a FRG file, created with PCX2FRG from Chapter 2. We'll look at this process in detail a bit later.

The other new element in FIG. 5-1 is the color display that replaces the palette tiles from the previous chapters. It would be impractical to display 32,768 color tiles. This color display suggests the range of colors available in a high-color graphic mode, but it by no means displays all the available colors. At 640 by 480, it will display 600 colors out of a possible 32,768.

The high-color graphic package to be examined in this chapter will have pretty well all the same facilities as the one in Chapter 4—save that it will only support those few super VGA cards which have high-color modes, and that it will deal with color a bit differently. In fact, the assembly language modules are remarkably similar—three quarters of the work in transforming MOUSE256.ASM from Chapter 4 into the MOUSE-HI.ASM module in this chapter was involved in changing STOSB instructions to STOSWs. Aside from the fact that each pixel is represented by a word rather than a byte in a high-color mode, high-color super VGA graphics can be managed very much as the 256-color modes were.

Here's a list of the functions the code in this chapter will provide you with:

❏ Initialize a high-color graphics mode
❏ Clear the screen
❏ Set pixels
❏ Draw lines
❏ Draw rectangles
❏ Fill rectangles
❏ Draw text
❏ Get and put image fragments
❏ Animate a mouse cursor
❏ Create and manage three-dimensional buttons
❏ Save a graphic screen to a PCX file
❏ Load an image fragment from the disk and display it

The only thing that really distinguishes this list from the one in the previous chapter is that there's no palette to set.

High color   As was dealt with in Chapter 1, high color is true RGB color modified somewhat to fit in confined quarters. The three bytes of an RGB color can be compressed into two bytes—one word—if the color depth of each is reduced from eight to five bits. This reduces the number of bits of color information to fifteen bits per pixel, which will fit in a 16-bit word with one bit left over. Reprised from Chapter 1, FIG. 5-2 illustrates the relationship of a high color 15-bit pixel to a true color 24-bit pixel.

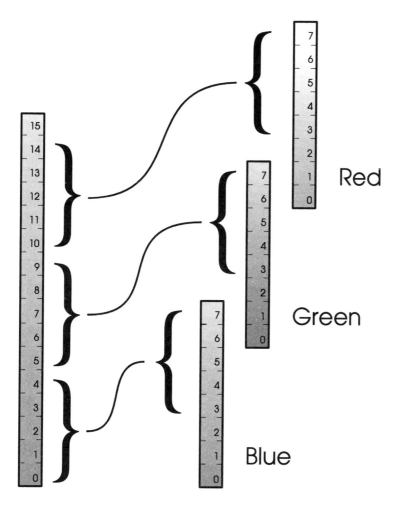

5-2
The relationship between a 24-bit pixel and a 15-bit pixel.

The process of getting a 24-bit color value into the structure of a high-color pixel would seem rather awkward at first, entailing quite a lot of bit shifting and manipulation. In a sense this is true, but it's not as much of a problem as it first appears. As long as you define colors using 15 bits, rather than 24, you can treat high-color pixels as simple integer values. They can be exceedingly fast to work with in this form.

To begin with, here's a macro to translate a normal RGB color definition into a high color pixel value:

```
#define HIGHCOLOUR(r,g,b) \
                ((((((unsigned int)r >> 3) & 0x1f) << 10) + \
                (((((unsigned int)g >> 3) & 0x1f) << 5) + \
                (((unsigned int)b >> 3) & 0x1f))
```

The HIGHCOLOUR macro performs the bit shifts necessary to compress the three color indices of its arguments into a single integer. For example, this is how you would define bright red:

```
unsigned int red;
red=HIGHCOLOUR(255,0,0);
```

While a bit involved to look at, the HIGHCOLOUR macro actually works fairly quickly, as it's not actually called upon to use any really complex processor instructions.

It's also useful to be able to extract the individual color components of a high-color pixel. Here are three macros to handle this. These turned up informally in Chapter 2.

```
#define HIGHRED(c)    (((((c) >> 10) & 0x1f) << 3)
#define HIGHGREEN(c)  (((((c) >> 5) & 0x1f) << 3)
#define HIGHBLUE(c)   (((c) & 0x1f) << 3)
```

The argument c to one of these macros should be a high-color pixel. The value returned by the macro will be one of the three 8-bit color values in a 24-bit color definition. The three low order bits will be set to zero.

The organization of a high-color graphic screen buffer is similar to that of the buffer of a 256-color mode, save that each pixel is a word rather than a byte. The same approach to addressing the screen—using a table of offsets and page numbers—can be applied to high-color graphics. There will, of course, be only half as many pixels per screen page.

If you're of a disposition to leaf through books before you get down to reading them, you'll probably have noticed that this chapter is a lot shorter than the previous one despite its covering much the same material, albeit for a different graphic mode. In fact, it manages its brevity by leaving out a lot of redundant explanation. Most of the code in this chapter is identical to that of the last one—only the macros that directly access the screen buffer have changed. They'll be examined in the next section.

You should find that if you've read Chapter 4, most of the functions in this chapter will be pretty easy to work through. Specifically, there will be no explicit discussion of the functions to clear the screen, set pixels, draw lines and rectangles, fill rectangles, draw text, get and put image fragments, animate a mouse cursor, or manage buttons.

Initializing a high-color graphic mode

The code for selecting a high-color graphic mode isn't much more complicated than was the equivalent function for handling the 256-color super VGA modes—made arguably simpler by there being fewer super VGA cards with high-color facilities. We'll be working with 640 by 480 pixel high-color modes in the following example program—the changes to work in 800 by 600 pixels will be dealt with toward the end of this chapter.

To begin with, here are the mode numbers for the high-color modes we'll be working with:

```
PARADISE  EQU  0062H
ATI       EQU  0072H
TSENG     EQU  002EH
VESA      EQU  0110H
```

There are no mode numbers for the Trident or Oak Technologies cards, as these cards don't currently support high color. You might have noticed that the Tseng

Labs mode number is identical to the one for the 256-color 640 by 480 pixel mode used in the previous chapter. We'll get to that in a moment.

Selecting the Paradise high-color mode is really easy:

```
MOV AX,0062H
INT 10H
```

The ATI mode is almost as easy:

```
MOV AX,0C000H
MOV ES,AX
MOV AX,ES:[0010H]
MOV CS:[ATIREG],AX

MOV AX,0072H
INT 10H
```

The four MOV instructions before the INT 10H call fetch the port address of the ATI VGA controller chip, for later use by the bank switching function.

The Tseng Labs mode change is somewhat more involved—for reasons not easily explained—as it involves doing a bit of register juggling as well as the BIOS call to change modes. Note also that the BIOS call requires two parameters.

```
MOV     DX,03C4H
        MOV AL,0
        OUT DX,AL
        MOV DX,03C5H
        IN  AL,DX
        AND AL,0FEH
        OUT DX,AL
        MOV DX,03CEH
        MOV AL,06H
        OUT DX,AL
        MOV DX,03CFH
        IN  AL,DX
        XOR AL,06H
        OR  AL,02H
        OUT DX,AL
MOV AX,10F0H
MOV BX,002EH
INT 10H
```

The VESA mode change behaves as it did in the foregoing two chapters.

Having set up the appropriate screen mode for you card, you'll need a line start table like the one used in the previous chapter. Here's the function to create it:

```
MAKETABLE PROC NEAR
          MOV  CX,480
          MOV  BX,0000H
          MOV  SI,OFFSET _SCREENTBL
MT1:      PUSH CX
          MOV  AX,640
```

```
                    SHL    AX,1
                    MUL    BX

                    AND    DX,00FFH

                    PUSH   AX
                    MOV    CX,0FFFEH
                    MOV    AX,640
                    SHL    AX,1
                    SUB    CX,AX
                    POP    AX

                    CMP    AX,CX
                    JB     MT2

                    MOV    DH,0FFH

        MT2:        MOV    DS:[SI],AX
                    MOV    DS:[SI+2],DX
                    ADD    SI,4
                    INC    BX

                    POP    CX
                    LOOP   MT1

                    RET
        MAKETABLE   ENDP
```

The instances of 640 and 480 in the foregoing code refer to the dimensions of the screen—they'll turn up as references to SCREENWIDE and SCREENDEEP in the working example of this code.

This version of MAKETABLE differs from the one in the previous chapter only in that all the screen width values are shifted left by one place, that is, that they're multiplied by two. This reflects the fact that each pixel on the screen is two bytes wide, rather than one, and that as such there will be only half as many lines per page as there would be in a corresponding 256-color mode.

The screen access macros introduced in Chapter 4 will also turn up in a very slightly modified form in this chapter, in that they must move words rather than bytes, and they must address pixels using word-width alignment. This latter point usually just means shifting the horizontal coordinate of a pixel left by one place.

The GRAFADD_DI macro is an example of this. It shifts the value to be added to DI left by one. In a sense this probably isn't the correct way to do this—the value passed to GRAFADD_DI should probably have been adjusted before GRAFADD_DI was called—but this arrangement works in all the instances in which GRAFADD_DI is used in the example code. We'll allow that GRAFADD_DI adds pixels, rather than bytes. In this case, pixels happen to be two bytes wide.

```
        GRAFADD_DI  MACRO   ARG1
                    LOCAL   LAB1
                    PUSH    AX
                    PUSH    BX
                    MOV     AX,DI
                    MOV     BX,ARG1
```

```
            SHL     BX,1
            ADD     DI,BX
            CMP     AX,DI
            JBE     LAB1
            INCPAGE
LAB1:
            POP     BX
            POP     AX
            ENDM
```

Note that you can't use AX as an argument to GRAFADD_DI—there's no case in the code in this chapter where this occurs.

The various replacements for the STOSB and MOVSB instructions from Chapter 4 have become replacements for STOSW and MOVSW in this one. They work the same way, keeping track of page changes on lines that have breaks in them. Here's the one to store one word at ES:DI:

```
GRAF_STOSW    MACRO
              CLD
              STOSW
              CHECKPAGE
              ENDM
```

This macro will store CX words at ES:DI

```
GRAF_REPNESTOSW    MACRO
                   LOCAL     LAB1,LAB2
                   CLD
                   CMP       [PAGEBREAK],00H
                   JNE       LAB1
REPNE              STOSW
                   JMP       LAB2
LAB1:              STOSW
                   CHECKPAGE
                   LOOP      LAB1
LAB2:
                   ENDM
```

Finally, this macro will move CX words from DS:SI to ES:DI. Note that DS:SI must point to a buffer in the common data segment; be careful that you don't try to use this macro to move data from, say, an allocated buffer to the screen.

```
GRAF_REPNEMOVSW    MACRO
                   LOCAL     LAB1,LAB2
                   CLD
                   CMP       [PAGEBREAK],00H
                   JNE       LAB1
            REPNE   MOVSW
                    JMP       LAB2
LAB1:               MOVSW
                    CHECKPAGE
                    LOOP      LAB1
LAB2:
                    ENDM
```

The GRAF_PUTPIXEL macro works just like it did in Chapter 4, save that it writes a word rather than a byte.

```
GRAF_PUTPIXEL  MACRO      ;SET THE PIXEL AT (DX,BX) TO AL
               PUSH    AX
               CALL    VGALINE
               GRAFADD_DI DX
               POP     AX
               STOSW
               ENDM
```

The VGALINE function, as called by these macros and by most of the functions to be dealt with in this chapter, is the same one as was used in the previous chapter.

Save a graphic screen to a PCX file

As with most of the other functions in this chapter, the DoSave function to save a graphic screen to a PCX file isn't all that different from its predecessors. The PCXHEAD object used to define the file header contains slightly altered values, of course, and the line data is structured differently. Actually, the line data requires moderately extensive swabbing, as the lines returned by GetScreenLine are stored as two-byte high-color pixels while a PCX file wants each line to be stored as three planes of 8-bit color indices.

Figure 5-3 illustrates the DoSave function for a high-color screen. This will create a 24-bit PCX file.

The only fairly sneaky part of DoSave is the three loops to extract the individual color components of the lines returned by GetScreenLine. These use the HIGHRED, HIGHGREEN, and HIGHBLUE macros to extract the color components of the high-color pixels in each line, such that the final PCX file will be correctly structured.

5-3

The DoSave *function to save a high-color screen to a PCX file.*

```
/* save the screen to a PCX file */
DoSave(path)
     char *path;
{

     PCXHEAD pcx;
     FILE *fp;
     char *ps,*pd;
     unsigned int i,j,n,*ip;

     /* create the destination file */
     if((fp=fopen(path,"wb"))==NULL) {
             beep();
             return;
     }

     if((ps=malloc(SCREENWIDE*sizeof(unsigned int)))==NULL) {
             beep();
             fclose(fp);
             return;
     }

     if((pd=malloc(SCREENWIDE))==NULL) {
             free(ps);
             beep();
```

```
          fclose(fp);
          return;
}

memset((char *)&pcx,0,sizeof(PCXHEAD));

pcx.manufacturer=10;
pcx.encoding=1;
pcx.xmin=pcx.ymin=0;
pcx.xmax=SCREENWIDE-1;
pcx.ymax=SCREENDEEP-1;
pcx.bits_per_pixel=8;
pcx.version=5;
pcx.colour_planes=3;
pcx.bytes_per_line=SCREENWIDE;

WaitCursor();
if(fwrite((char *)&pcx,1,sizeof(PCXHEAD),fp) != sizeof(PCXHEAD)) {
          free(pd);
          free(ps);
          fclose(fp);
          remove(path);
          ArrowCursor();
          beep();
          return;
}

for(i=0;i<SCREENDEEP;++i) {
          MouseOff();
          GetScreenLine(ps,i);
          MouseOn();

          /* extract the red components */
          ip=(unsigned int *)ps;
          for(j=0;j<SCREENWIDE;++j) pd[j]=HIGHRED(ip[j]);
          n=pcxwriteline(fp,pd,pcx.bytes_per_line);

          /* extract the green components */
          ip=(unsigned int *)ps;
          for(j=0;j<SCREENWIDE;++j) pd[j]=HIGHGREEN(ip[j]);
          n=pcxwriteline(fp,pd,pcx.bytes_per_line);

          /* extract the blue components */
          ip=(unsigned int *)ps;
          for(j=0;j<SCREENWIDE;++j) pd[j]=HIGHBLUE(ip[j]);
          n=pcxwriteline(fp,pd,pcx.bytes_per_line);

          if(n != pcx.bytes_per_line) {
                  free(pd);
                  free(ps);
                  fclose(fp);
                  remove(path);
                  ArrowCursor();
                  beep();
                  return;
```

```
                                      }
                            }

                ArrowCursor();
                free(pd);
                free(ps);
                fclose(fp);
        }

        /* write one pcx line */
        pcxwriteline(fp,p,n)
                FILE *fp;
                char *p;
                unsigned int n;
        {
                unsigned int i=0,j=0,t=0;

                do {
                        i=0;
                        while((p[t+i]==p[t+i+1]) && ((t+i) < n) && (i < 63))++i;
                        if(i>0) {
                                if(fputc(i | 0xc0,fp)==EOF) return(-1);
                                if(fputc(p[t],fp)==EOF) return(-1);
                                t+=i;
                                j+=2;
                        }
                        else {
                                if(((p[t]) & 0xc0)==0xc0) {
                                        if(fputc(0xc1,fp)==EOF) return(-1);
                                        ++j;
                                }
                                if(fputc(p[t++],fp)==EOF) return(-1);
                                ++j;
                        }
                } while(t<n);
                return(n);
        }
```

Displaying an image fragment

The photograph back in FIG. 5-1 was imported from a FRG file on disk. As was touched on earlier in this chapter, this is a relatively painless undertaking in a high color graphic mode because of the lack of a fixed screen palette. Here's the code to handle it:

```
if((frg=loadfrag(FRGFILE)) != NULL) {
        PutImageHi(10,10,frg);
        farfree(frg);
}
```

In fact, the code in the example program for this chapter is a bit more involved, as it frames the image and draws a drop shadow behind it. All the foregoing code fragment does is call loadfrag to fetch the image from disk, PutImageHi to display it on the screen and then `farfree` to deallocate the buffer it occupied. This call will place the image with its upper left coordinates at location (10,10). The fragment file name is defined by the constant FRGFILE.

The `loadfrag` function will open a FRG file, allocate a buffer to hold the image fragment portion of it and then load the image into the buffer. It will return either a pointer to the allocated buffer or NULL if something went wrong. Among the things that can go wrong are the lack of existence of the image fragment file, bad reads, a color depth of other than sixteen bits, or insufficient memory to hold the fragment.

Figure 5-4 illustrates `loadfrag`. Pretty well everything it's up to should be familiar from Chapter 2.

As an aside, if you'll be writing an application to work with high-color bitmaps of any size, you should probably give careful thought to its memory requirements. Consider that not only does a full 640 by 480 pixel high-color screen image exceed what will fit in one memory segment—it exceeds the available free conventional memory on most systems. If you'll be working with large image fragments and a large application, plan on writing versions of `GetImageHi` and `PutImageHi` that can use extended or expanded memory for image buffers. There's a complete discussion of extended and expanded memory in my books *Bitmapped Graphics* and *Supercharged Bitmapped Graphics*, both published by Windcrest.

5-4
The `loadfrag` *function to load the image of a FRG file into a buffer.*

```
/* load a fragment into a buffer and return a pointer to the image */
char *loadfrag(s)
        char *s;
{
        FILE *fp;
        IMAGEHEAD ih;
        char *p,*pr;
        unsigned int i;

        if((fp=fopen(s,"rb")) == NULL) return(NULL);

        if(fread((char *)&ih,1,sizeof(IMAGEHEAD),fp) != sizeof(IMAGEHEAD)) {
                fclose(fp);
                return(NULL);
        }

        if(ih.bits != 16) {
                fclose(fp);
                return(NULL);
        }

        if((p=farmalloc(4L+(long)ih.bytes*(long)ih.depth)) == NULL) {
                fclose(fp);
                return(NULL);
        }

        fseek(fp,ih.image,SEEK_SET);

        pr=p;
```

```
                    pr+=fread(pr,1,4,fp);

                    for(i=0;i<ih.depth;++i) {
                            if(fread(pr,1,ih.bytes,fp) != ih.bytes) {
                                    farfree(p);
                                    fclose(fp);
                                    return(NULL);
                            }
                            pr=farPtr(pr,(long)ih.bytes);
                    }
                    fclose(fp);
                    return(p);
            }
```

The MOUSE-HI.ASM code module

When it's linked to a C language calling program, the MOUSE-HI module will provide you with a complete mouse interface and several ancillary graphic functions for use with one of the aforementioned high-color graphic modes.

Figure 5-5 illustrates the complete source code for MOUSE-HI.ASM.

```
;
;                       Mouse Functions for high colour
;                       Super VGA graphics
;

_AOFF           EQU     6       ;STACK OFFSET TO FIRST ARG

PARADISE        EQU     0062H
ATI             EQU     0072H
TSENG           EQU     002EH
VESA            EQU     0110H

CURSORWIDE      EQU     16      ;CURSOR DIMENSIONS
CURSORDEEP      EQU     16

FONTEIGHT       EQU     0       ;SET ONE OF THESE TRUE FOR THE
FONTSIXTEEN     EQU     1       ;SCREEN FONT SIZE

TABLEDEEP       EQU     480     ;NUMBER OF ITEMS IN THE SCREEN
                                ;TABLE

; MAKE SURE THE RECTANGLE ON THE STACK IS WITHIN SCREEN LIMITS
FIXRECT         MACRO
                LOCAL   LAB1,LAB2,LAB3,LAB4
                PUSH    AX
                CMP     WORD PTR [BP+_AOFF+0],0000H
                JGE     LAB1
                MOV     WORD PTR [BP+_AOFF+0],0000H
LAB1:           CMP     WORD PTR [BP+_AOFF+2],0000H
                JGE     LAB2
                MOV     WORD PTR [BP+_AOFF+2],0000H
LAB2:           MOV     AX,[_SCREENWIDE]
```

```
                    DEC     AX
                    CMP     WORD PTR [BP+_AOFF+4],AX
                    JL      LAB3
                    MOV     WORD PTR [BP+_AOFF+4],AX
LAB3:               MOV     AX,[_SCREENDEEP]
                    DEC     AX
                    CMP     WORD PTR [BP+_AOFF+6],AX
                    JL      LAB4
                    MOV     WORD PTR [BP+_AOFF+6],AX
LAB4:               POP     AX
                    ENDM

; MAKE SURE THE RECTANGLE ON THE STACK PROPERLY ORIENTED
FIXRECTDIR          MACRO
                    LOCAL   LAB1,LAB2
                    MOV     AX,[BP+_AOFF+0]
                    MOV     BX,[BP+_AOFF+4]
                    CMP     AX,BX
                    JL      LAB1
                    MOV     [BP+_AOFF+0],BX
                    MOV     [BP+_AOFF+4],AX

LAB1:               MOV     AX,[BP+_AOFF+2]
                    MOV     BX,[BP+_AOFF+6]
                    CMP     AX,BX
                    JL      LAB2
                    MOV     [BP+_AOFF+2],BX
                    MOV     [BP+_AOFF+6],AX
LAB2:
                    ENDM

;NORMALIZE THE POINTER IN DS:SI, SCREEN WIDTH IN AX
NORMALIZE           MACRO
                    LOCAL   LAB1
                    PUSH    AX
                    PUSH    CX
                    MOV     CX,0FFFFH
                    SUB     CX,AX
                    MOV     AX,CX
                    CMP     SI,AX
                    JB      LAB1
                    MOV     AX,SI                   ;SEE HOW MANY SEGMENTS ARE
                    MOV     CL,4                    ;...IN SI (SI DIV 16)
                    SHR     AX,CL

                    MOV     CX,DS                   ;ADD THEM TO THE DATA SEGMENT
                    ADD     CX,AX                   ;...(YOU CAN'T JUST ADD DS,AX)
                    MOV     DS,CX
                    AND     SI,000FH                ;ADJUST SI (SI MOD 16)
LAB1:               POP     CX
                    POP     AX
                    ENDM

INCPAGE             MACRO   ;INCREMENT THE PAGE
```

```
                              PUSH    AX
                              MOV     AX,[CODEPAGE]
                              INC     AX
                              CALL    VGABANK
                              POP     AX
                              ENDM

            CHECKPAGE         MACRO    ;HANDLE PAGE BOUNDARIES
                              LOCAL   LAB1
                              CMP     DI,0000H
                              JNE     LAB1
                              INCPAGE
            LAB1:
                              ENDM


            GRAFADD_DI        MACRO   ARG1        ;ADD THE ARGUMENT TO DI WITH PAGE
                                                  ;SWITCHING
                              LOCAL   LAB1
                              PUSH    AX
                              PUSH    BX
                              MOV     AX,DI
                              MOV     BX,ARG1
                              SHL     BX,1
                              ADD     DI,BX
                              CMP     AX,DI
                              JBE     LAB1
                              INCPAGE
            LAB1:
                              POP     BX
                              POP     AX
                              ENDM

            GRAF_STOSW        MACRO    ;STORE A BIT AT DS:SI WITH PAGE SWITCH
                              CLD
                              STOSW
                              CHECKPAGE
                              ENDM

            GRAF_REPNESTOSW   MACRO               ;DO STORE STRING TO ES:DI WITH PAGE
                                                  ;SWITCH
                              LOCAL   LAB1,LAB2
                              CLD
                              CMP     [PAGEBREAK],00H
                              JNE     LAB1
                        REPNE STOSW
                              JMP     LAB2
            LAB1:             STOSW
                              CHECKPAGE
                              LOOP    LAB1
            LAB2:
                              ENDM

            GRAF_REPNEMOVSW MACRO  ;DO MOVE STRING FROM DS:SI TO ES:DI WITH PAGE
                                   ;SWITCH
```

```
               LOCAL   LAB1,LAB2
               CLD
               CMP     [PAGEBREAK],00H
               JNE     LAB1
         REPNE MOVSW
               JMP     LAB2
LAB1:          MOVSW
               CHECKPAGE
               LOOP    LAB1
LAB2:
               ENDM

GRAF_PUTPIXEL  MACRO   ;SET THE PIXEL AT (DX,BX) TO AL
               PUSH    AX
               CALL    VGALINE
               GRAFADD_DI DX
               POP     AX
               STOSW
               ENDM

;THIS MACRO FETCHES THE DATA SEGEMENT
LDATASEG       MACRO
               PUSH    AX
               MOV     AX,_DATA
               MOV     DS,AX
               POP     AX
               ENDM

;DO A LONG LOOP
LNGLOOP        MACRO   ARG1
               LOCAL   LAB1
               DEC     CX
               CMP     CX,0000H
               JE      LAB1
               JMP     ARG1
LAB1:
               ENDM

MOUSE_HI_TEXT  SEGMENT BYTE PUBLIC 'CODE'
               ASSUME CS:MOUSE_HI_TEXT,DS:_DATA

;THIS FUNCTION COPIES ONE LINE OF VGA DATA FROM THE SCREEN
;      ARGS    -         POINTER TO THE DATA
;                        LINE NUMBER
;              RETURNS-VOID
               PUBLIC  _GetScreenLine
_GetScreenLine PROC     FAR
               PUSH    BP
               MOV     BP,SP
               PUSH    DS
               PUSH    ES

               LDATASEG
               MOV     BX,[BP+_AOFF+4]
               CALL    VGALINE
```

```
                      MOV       CX,[_SCREENWIDE]

                      MOV       SI,[BP+_AOFF+0]
                      MOV       DS,[BP+_AOFF+2]

          RL1:        PUSH      CX
                      MOV       AX,ES:[DI]
                      MOV       DS:[SI],AX
                      ADD       SI,0002H
                      PUSH      DS
                      LDATASEG
                      GRAFADD_DI 0001H
                      POP       DS
                      POP       CX
                      LOOP      RL1

                      POP       ES
                      POP       DS
                      POP       BP
                      RET
_GetScreenLine ENDP

;THIS FUNCTION COPIES AN IMAGE FRAGMENT FROM THE SCREEN
;       ARGS    -LEFT
;                       TOP
;                       RIGHT
;                       BOTTOM
;                       IMAGE
;       RETURNS-        VOID
                      PUBLIC  _GetImageHi
_GetImageHi     PROC    FAR
                      PUSH      BP
                      MOV       BP,SP
                      PUSH      DS
                      PUSH      ES

                      LDATASEG

                      FIXRECTDIR
                      FIXRECT

                      CALL      HIDECURSOR

                      MOV       AX,[_SCREENWIDE]

                      MOV       DX,[BP+_AOFF+4]          ;GET WIDTH
                      SUB       DX,[BP+_AOFF+0]

                      MOV       CX,[BP+_AOFF+6]          ;GET DEPTH
                      SUB       CX,[BP+_AOFF+2]

                      MOV       SI,[BP+_AOFF+8]          ;GET IMAGE
                      MOV       DS,[BP+_AOFF+10]

                      NORMALIZE                         ;NORMALIZE POINTER
```

```
                MOV     DS:[SI],DX          ;SAVE SIZE VALUES
                MOV     DS:[SI+2],CX
                ADD     SI,0004H

                INC     CX                  ;GET REAL SIZE VALUES
                INC     DX

GI1:            PUSH    CX
                PUSH    DX

                PUSH    DS
                LDATASEG
                MOV     BX,[BP+_AOFF+2]
                CALL    VGALINE
                GRAFADD_DI[BP+_AOFF+0]
                POP     DS
                INC     WORD PTR [BP+_AOFF+2]

                POP     CX
                PUSH    CX

GI2:            MOV     AX,ES:[DI]
                MOV     DS:[SI],AX
                ADD     SI,0002H
                PUSH    DS
                LDATASEG
                GRAFADD_DI 0001H
                POP     DS
                LOOP    GI2

                PUSH    DS
                LDATASEG
                MOV     AX,[_SCREENWIDE]
                POP     DS
                NORMALIZE

                POP     DX
                POP     CX
                LNGLOOP GI1

                LDATASEG

                CALL    SHOWCURSOR

                POP     ES
                POP     DS
                POP     BP
                RET
_GetImageHi     ENDP

;THIS FUNCTION COPIES AN IMAGE FRAGMENT TO THE SCREEN
;       ARGS            -X
;                       Y
;                       IMAGE
;               RETURNS-VOID
```

```
                        PUBLIC  _PutImageHi
        _PutImageHi     PROC    FAR
                        PUSH    BP
                        MOV     BP,SP
                        PUSH    DS
                        PUSH    ES

                        CALL    HIDECURSOR

                        MOV     SI,[BP+_AOFF+4]
                        MOV     DS,[BP+_AOFF+6]

                        MOV     DX,DS:[SI + 0]              ;GET WIDTH
                        INC     DX
                        MOV     CX,DS:[SI + 2]              ;GET DEPTH
                        INC     CX
                        ADD     SI,0004H

PI1:                    PUSH    CX
                        PUSH    DX

                        PUSH    DS
                        LDATASEG
                        MOV     BX,[BP+_AOFF+2]
                        CALL    VGALINE
                        GRAFADD_DI[BP+_AOFF+0]
                        POP     DS

                        INC     WORD PTR [BP+_AOFF+2]
                        POP     CX
                        PUSH    CX

                        CLD
PI2:                    MOV     AX,DS:[SI]

                        PUSH    DS
                        LDATASEG
                        GRAF_STOSW
                        POP     DS

                        ADD     SI,0002H
                        LOOP    PI2

                        PUSH    DS
                        LDATASEG
                        MOV     AX,[_SCREENWIDE]
                        POP     DS
                        NORMALIZE

                        POP     DX
                        POP     CX
                        LNGLOOP PI1

                        LDATASEG
                        CALL    SHOWCURSOR
```

```
                    POP     ES
                    POP     DS
                    POP     BP
                    RET
_PutImageHi         ENDP

;THIS FUNCTION SETS THE PIXEL AT (X,Y) TO COLOUR
;       ARGS    -       X
;                       Y
;                       COLOUR
;               RETURNS-VOID
                    PUBLIC  _SetPixel
_SetPixel           PROC    FAR
                    PUSH    BP
                    MOV     BP,SP
                    PUSH    DS
                    PUSH    ES

                    LDATASEG

                    MOV     DX,[BP+_AOFF+0]
                    MOV     BX,[BP+_AOFF+2]
                    MOV     AX,[BP+_AOFF+4]
                    GRAF_PUTPIXEL

                    POP     ES
                    POP     DS
                    POP     BP
                    RET
_SetPixel           ENDP

;THIS FUNCTION DRAWS A RECTANGLE
;       ARGS    -       LEFT
;                       TOP
;                       RIGHT
;                       BOTTOM
;                       COLOUR
;               RETURNS-VOID
                    PUBLIC  _FrameRect
_FrameRect          PROC    FAR
                    PUSH    BP
                    MOV     BP,SP
                    PUSH    DS
                    PUSH    ES

                    LDATASEG

                    FIXRECTDIR
                    FIXRECT

                    CALL    HIDECURSOR

                    MOV     BX,[BP+_AOFF+2]     ;TOP LINE
                    MOV     CX,[BP+_AOFF+6]     ;BOTTOM LINE
                    SUB     CX,BX
```

```
                              MOV    DX,[BP+_AOFF+4]
                              SUB    DX,[BP+_AOFF+0]      ;GET WIDTH

        ;                     DRAW TOP LINE
                              PUSH   CX
                              PUSH   BX
                              CALL   VGALINE
                              GRAFADD_DI [BP+_AOFF+0]

                              MOV    CX,DX
                              INC    CX
                              MOV    AX,[BP+_AOFF+8]      ;COLOUR

                              GRAF_REPNESTOSW

                              POP    BX
                              POP    CX

        ;                     DRAW SIDES
        FR1:                  PUSH   CX
                              PUSH   DX
                              INC    BX

                              PUSH   DX
                              MOV    DX,[BP+_AOFF+0]    ;LEFT
                              MOV    AX,[BP+_AOFF+8]    ;COLOUR
                              GRAF_PUTPIXEL

                              POP    CX
                              ADD    DX,CX
                              GRAF_PUTPIXEL

                              POP    DX
                              POP    CX
                              LOOP   FR1

        ;                     DRAW BOTTOM LINE
                              CALL   VGALINE
                              GRAFADD_DI [BP+_AOFF+0]

                              MOV    CX,DX
                              INC    CX
                              MOV    AX,[BP+_AOFF+8]     ;COLOUR

                              GRAF_REPNESTOSW

                              LDATASEG
                              CALL   SHOWCURSOR

                              POP    ES
                              POP    DS
                              POP    BP
                              RET
        _FrameRect            ENDP
```

```
;THIS FUNCTION FILLS A RECTANGLE
;       ARGS    -       LEFT
;                       TOP
;                       RIGHT
;                       BOTTOM
;                       COLOUR
;               RETURNS-VOID
                PUBLIC  _FillRect
_FillRect       PROC    FAR
                PUSH    BP
                MOV     BP,SP
                PUSH    DS
                PUSH    ES

                LDATASEG

                FIXRECTDIR
                FIXRECT

                CALL    HIDECURSOR

                MOV     BX,[BP+_AOFF+2]   ;TOP LINE
                MOV     CX,[BP+_AOFF+6]   ;BOTTOM LINE
                SUB     CX,BX
                INC     CX

                MOV     DX,[BP+_AOFF+4]
                SUB     DX,[BP+_AOFF+0]   ;GET WIDTH

IR1:            PUSH    CX
                PUSH    BX
                CALL    VGALINE
                GRAFADD_DI [BP+_AOFF+0]

                MOV     CX,DX
                INC     CX
                MOV     AX,[BP+_AOFF+8]   ;COLOUR

                GRAF_REPNESTOSW

                POP     BX
                POP     CX
                INC     BX
                LOOP    IR1

                LDATASEG
                CALL    SHOWCURSOR

                POP     ES
                POP     DS
                POP     BP
                RET
_FillRect       ENDP

LINE_DELTAX     EQU     2
```

```
            LINE_DELTAY    EQU     4
            LINE_HALFX     EQU     6
            LINE_HALFY     EQU     8
            LINE_COUNT     EQU     10
            LINE_ADJ       EQU     12

            ;THIS FUNCTION DRAWS A LINE
            ;       ARGS    -       LEFT
            ;                       TOP
            ;                       RIGHT
            ;                       BOTTOM
            ;                       COLOUR
            ;               RETURNS-VOID
                        PUBLIC  _DrawLine
_DrawLine   PROC    FAR
            PUSH    BP
            MOV     BP,SP
            SUB     SP,LINE_ADJ
            PUSH    DS
            PUSH    ES

            LDATASEG

            FIXRECT

            CALL    HIDECURSOR

            MOV     AX,[BP+_AOFF+6]
            SUB     AX,[BP+_AOFF+2]     ;BOTTOM - TOP = DELTA Y

            MOV     SI,1
            JGE     LINE1
            MOV     SI,-1
            NEG     AX
LINE1:      MOV     [BP - LINE_DELTAY],AX

            MOV     AX,[BP+_AOFF+4]
            SUB     AX,[BP+_AOFF+0]     ;RIGHT - LEFT = DELTA X

            MOV     DI,1
            JGE     LINE2
            MOV     DI,-1
            NEG     AX

LINE2:      MOV     [BP - LINE_DELTAX],AX

            MOV     AX,[BP - LINE_DELTAX]
            CMP     AX,[BP - LINE_DELTAY]
            JL      LINE3

            ;HANDLE SLOPE < 1

            MOV     AX,[BP - LINE_DELTAX]
            SHR     AX,1
            MOV     [BP - LINE_HALFX],AX
```

```
            MOV     CX,[BP+_AOFF+0]
            MOV     DX,[BP+_AOFF+2]
            MOV     BX,0000H
            MOV     AX,[BP - LINE_DELTAX]
            MOV     [BP - LINE_COUNT],AX

LINE5:      PUSH    BX                      ;PLOT THE PIXEL
            PUSH    DI
            PUSH    DX
            MOV     BX,DX
            MOV     DX,CX
            MOV     AX,[BP+_AOFF+8]
            GRAF_PUTPIXEL
            POP     DX
            POP     DI
            POP     BX

            ADD     CX,DI
            ADD     BX,[BP - LINE_DELTAY]
            CMP     BX,[BP - LINE_HALFX]
            JLE     LINE6
            SUB     BX,[BP - LINE_DELTAX]
            ADD     DX,SI

LINE6:      DEC     WORD PTR [BP - LINE_COUNT]
            JGE     LINE5

            JMP     LINE4

            ; HANDLE SLOPE > 1
LINE3:      MOV     AX,[BP - LINE_DELTAY]
            SHR     AX,1
            MOV     [BP - LINE_HALFY],AX

            MOV     CX,[BP+_AOFF+0]
            MOV     DX,[BP+_AOFF+2]
            MOV     BX,0000H
            MOV     AX,[BP - LINE_DELTAY]
            MOV     [BP - LINE_COUNT],AX

LINE7:      PUSH    BX                      ;PLOT THE PIXEL
            PUSH    DI
            PUSH    DX
            MOV     BX,DX
            MOV     DX,CX
            MOV     AX,[BP+_AOFF+8]
            GRAF_PUTPIXEL
            POP     DX
            POP     DI
            POP     BX

            ADD     DX,SI
            ADD     BX,[BP - LINE_DELTAX]
            CMP     BX,[BP - LINE_HALFY]
```

```
                              JLE     LINE8
                              SUB     BX,[BP - LINE_DELTAY]
                              ADD     CX,DI

          LINE8:              DEC     WORD PTR [BP - LINE_COUNT]
                              JGE     LINE7

          LINE4:              LDATASEG
                              CALL    SHOWCURSOR

                              POP     ES
                              POP     DS
                              ADD     SP,LINE_ADJ
                              POP     BP
                              RET
          _DrawLine           ENDP

          ;THIS FUNCTION DRAWS A STRING OF TEXT
          ;                   ARG1 = X
          ;                   ARG2 = Y
          ;                   ARG3 = STRING
          ;                   ARG4 = COLOUR
          ;                   ARG6 = BACKGROUND
                              PUBLIC  _DrawString
          _DrawString         PROC    FAR
                              PUSH    BP
                              MOV     BP,SP
                              PUSH    DS
                              PUSH    ES

                              LDATASEG

                              CALL    HIDECURSOR

                              ;LOOP THROUGH ALL THE LINES
                              MOV     CX,[_FONTDEPTH]
          DS0:                PUSH    CX
                              DEC     CX

                              ;GET THE BOTTOM LINE — WE COUNT BACKWARDS
                              MOV     BX,[BP + _AOFF + 2]
                              ADD     BX,CX

                              ;GET THE SCREEN POINTER
                              LDATASEG
                              CALL    VGALINE
                              GRAFADD_DI      [BP+_AOFF+0]

                              ;POINT TO THE START OF THE STRING
                              MOV     SI,[BP + _AOFF + 4]
                              MOV     DS,[BP + _AOFF + 6]

                              ;STOP LOOPING WHEN A NULL BYTE IS REACHED
          DS1:                MOV     AH,00H
                              MOV     AL,DS:[SI]
```

```
                    CMP     AL,00H
                    JE      DS5

DS2:                PUSH    DS
                    PUSH    SI

                    ;FIND THE FONT CHARACTER
                    MUL     [_FONTDEPTH]

                    ;GET THE BYTE OFFSET
                    MOV     BX,AX
                    ADD     BX,CX

                    PUSH    CX

                    ;GET THE BYTE FROM THE FONT
                    MOV     SI,[_FONTOFF]
                    MOV     DS,[_FONTSEG]
                    MOV     DH,DS:[SI+BX]

                    MOV     CX,0008H
                    MOV     BX,0000H

                    LDATASEG

DS3:                MOV     AX,[BP + _AOFF + 8]
                    TEST    DH,[_MASKTABLE + BX]
                    JNZ     DS4
                    MOV     AX,[BP + _AOFF + 10]

DS4:                INC     BX
                    GRAF_STOSW
                    LOOP    DS3

                    POP     CX

                    POP     SI
                    POP     DS
                    INC     SI
                    JMP     DS1

DS5:                POP     CX
                    LNGLOOP DS0

                    LDATASEG
                    CALL    SHOWCURSOR

                    POP     ES
                    POP     DS
                    POP     BP
                    RET
_DrawString         ENDP

;THIS FUNCTION INITIALIZES THE MOUSE AND GRAPHIC MODE
;       ARGS    -       SCREENWIDE
```

```
;                    SCREENDEEP
;                    CARD
;       RETURNS-TRUE FOR INTIALIZED
                PUBLIC_InitMouse
_InitMouse      PROC    FAR
                PUSH    BP
                MOV     BP,SP
                PUSH    DS
                PUSH    ES

                LDATASEG

                MOV     [CODEPAGE],0FFFFH

                MOV     AX,[BP + _AOFF + 0]
                MOV     [_SCREENWIDE],AX

                MOV     AX,[BP + _AOFF + 2]
                MOV     [_SCREENDEEP],AX

                MOV     AX,[BP + _AOFF + 4]
                MOV     [_CARD],AX

                MOV     AX,CS
                MOV     CS:[SETBANK_SEG],AX

                CMP     [_CARD],PARADISE
                JNE     INITMOUSE1

                MOV     AX,OFFSET SETBANK_PAR
                MOV     CS:[SETBANK_OFF],AX
                CALL    MAKETABLE

                MOV     AX,[_CARD]
                INT     10H

                JMP     INITMOUSE5
INITMOUSE1:     CMP     [_CARD],ATI
                JNE     INITMOUSE2

                MOV     AX,OFFSET SETBANK_ATI
                MOV     CS:[SETBANK_OFF],AX
                CALL    MAKETABLE

                MOV     AX,0C000H
                MOV     ES,AX
                MOV     AX,ES:[0010H]
                MOV     CS:[ATIREG],AX

                MOV     AX,[_CARD]
                INT     10H

                JMP     INITMOUSE4
INITMOUSE2:     CMP     [_CARD],TSENG
                JNE     INITMOUSE3
```

```
                MOV     AX,OFFSET SETBANK_ATI
                MOV     CS:[SETBANK_OFF],AX
                CALL    MAKETABLE

                MOV     DX,03C4H                    ;SET
                MOV     AL,0                        ;TSENG
                OUT     DX,AL                       ;REGISTERS
                MOV     DX,03C5H
                IN      AL,DX
                AND     AL,0FEH
                OUT     DX,AL
                MOV     DX,03CEH
                MOV     AL,06H
                OUT     DX,AL
                MOV     DX,03CFH
                IN      AL,DX
                XOR     AL,06H
                OR      AL,02H
                OUT     DX,AL

                MOV     AX,10F0H
                MOV     BX,[_CARD]
                INT     10H

                JMP     INITMOUSE5

INITMOUSE3:     CMP     [_CARD],VESA
                JNE     INITMOUSE4

                MOV     AX,OFFSET SETBANK_VSA
                MOV     CS:[SETBANK_OFF],AX
                CALL    INITVESA

                JMP     INITMOUSE5

INITMOUSE4:     MOV     AX,0000H
                JMP     INITMOUSE6

INITMOUSE5:     ;INTITALIZE THE FONT POINTER
                IF      FONTEIGHT
                MOV     AX,1130H
                MOV     BX,0300H
                INT     10H
                MOV     [_FONTSEG],ES
                MOV     [_FONTOFF],BP
                MOV     [_FONTDEPTH],0008H
                ENDIF   ;FONTEIGHT

                IF      FONTSIXTEEN
                MOV     AX,1130H
                MOV     BX,0600H
                INT     10H
                MOV     [_FONTSEG],ES
                MOV     [_FONTOFF],BP
```

```
        MOV    [_FONTDEPTH],0010H
        ENDIF  ;FONTSIXTEEN

        ;SEE IF THERE'S A MOUSE HANDLER
        MOV    AX,3533H
        INT    21H
        MOV    AX,ES
        OR     AX,BX
        JZ     INITMOUSE5

        ;INITIALIZE THE MOUSE
        MOV    AX,0000H
        INT    33H

        ;CHECK TO SEE IT'S THERE
        CMP    AX,0000H
        JE     INITMOUSE5

        ;SET THE HORIZONTAL RANGE
        MOV    AX,0007H
        MOV    CX,0000H
        MOV    DX,[_SCREENWIDE]
        SUB    DX,CURSORWIDE
        SHL    DX,1
        SHL    DX,1
        INT    33H

        ;SET THE VERTICAL RANGE
        MOV    AX,0008H
        MOV    CX,0000H
        MOV    DX,[_SCREENDEEP]
        SUB    DX,CURSORDEEP
        INT    33H

        ;PUT THE CURSOR IN THE CENTRE OF THE SCREEN
        MOV    AX,0004H
        MOV    CX,[_SCREENWIDE]
        SHL    CX,1
        MOV    DX,[_SCREENDEEP]
        SHR    DX,1
        INT    33H

        ;SET THE MOUSE SENSITIVITY
        MOV    AX,000FH
        MOV    CX,0003H
        MOV    DX,0010H
        INT    33H

        ;SET THE INITIAL POSITION
        MOV    AX,[_SCREENWIDE]
        SHR    AX,1
        MOV    [MOUSEX],AX

        MOV    AX,[_SCREENDEEP]
        SHR    AX,1
        MOV    [MOUSEY],AX
```

```
                ;SHOW THE CURSOR
                CALL    SHOWCURSOR

                ;SET THE MOUSE HANDLER HOOK
                MOV     AX,CS
                MOV     ES,AX
                MOV     AX,000CH
                MOV     CX,001FH
                MOV     DX,OFFSET MOUSEHANDLER
                INT     33H

                ;SAY ALL IS WELL
                MOV     AX,0FFFFH

INITMOUSE6:     POP     ES
                POP     DS
                POP     BP
                RET
_InitMouse      ENDP

                PUBLIC  _DeinitMouse
_DeinitMouse    PROC    FAR
                PUSH    BP
                MOV     BP,SP
                PUSH    DS
                PUSH    ES

                LDATASEG

                MOV     AX,0000H                ;MOUSE OFF
                INT     33H

                CMP     [_CARD],VESA
                JNE     DM3
                CMP     [OLDVESAMODE],0FFFFH
                JE      DM3

                MOV     DI,WORD PTR [VIDEOMODE+0]        ;IF THE OLD MODE
                MOV     ES,WORD PTR [VIDEOMODE+2]        ;IS A LEGAL VESA
                                                        ;MODE, CHANGE TO
DM1:            MOV     AX,ES:[DI]                      ;IT... OTHERWISE
                ADD     DI,0002H                        ;RETURN TO THE
                                                        ;STANDARD TEXT
                CMP     AX,0FFFFH                       ;MODE
                JE      DM2
                CMP     AX,[OLDVESAMODE]
                JE      DM2
                JMP     DM1

DM2:            CMP     AX,0FFFFH                       ;MODE NOT FOUND
                JE      DM3

                MOV     AX,4F02H
                MOV     BX,[OLDVESAMODE]
```

```
                           INT      10H

                           JMP      DM4

DM3:                       MOV      AX,0003H
                           INT      10H

DM4:                       POP      ES
                           POP      DS
                           POP      BP
                           RET
_DeinitMouse               ENDP

;                          ARG1 = COLOUR TO CLEAR TO
                           PUBLIC  _ClearScreen
_ClearScreen               PROC     FAR
                           PUSH     BP
                           MOV      BP,SP
                           PUSH     DS
                           PUSH     ES

                           LDATASEG

                           CALL     HIDECURSOR

                           MOV      CX,[_SCREENDEEP]
                           MOV      BX,0000H

CS1:                       PUSH     CX
                           PUSH     BX

                           CALL     VGALINE
                           MOV      AL,BYTE PTR [BP + _AOFF + 0]
                           MOV      CX,[_SCREENWIDE]
                           GRAF_REPNESTOSW

                           POP      BX
                           POP      CX
                           INC      BX
                           LOOP     CS1

                           LDATASEG
                           CALL     SHOWCURSOR

                           POP      ES
                           POP      DS
                           POP      BP
                           RET
_ClearScreen               ENDP

                           PUBLIC  _MouseOn
_MouseOn                   PROC     FAR
                           PUSH     BP
                           MOV      BP,SP
                           PUSH     DS
```

```
                    PUSH    ES

                    LDATASEG
                    CALL    SHOWCURSOR

                    POP     ES
                    POP     DS
                    POP     BP
                    RET
_MouseOn            ENDP

                    PUBLIC  _MouseOff
_MouseOff           PROC    FAR
                    PUSH    BP
                    MOV     BP,SP
                    PUSH    DS
                    PUSH    ES

                    LDATASEG
                    CALL    HIDECURSOR

                    POP     ES
                    POP     DS
                    POP     BP
                    RET
_MouseOff           ENDP

                    PUBLIC  _MouseDown
_MouseDown          PROC    FAR
                    PUSH    BP
                    MOV     BP,SP
                    PUSH    DS
                    PUSH    ES

                    LDATASEG

                    MOV     DI,[BP + _AOFF + 0]
                    MOV     ES,[BP + _AOFF + 2]

                    MOV     AX,[MOUSEX]
                    ADD     AX,[SPOTX]
                    STOSW

                    MOV     AX,[MOUSEY]
                    ADD     AX,[SPOTY]
                    STOSW

                    MOV     AX,[MOUSEB]
                    AND     AX,0003H

                    POP     ES
                    POP     DS
                    POP     BP
                    RET
_MouseDown          ENDP
```

```
              ;              ARG1 = CURSOR
              ;              ARG2 = HOTSPOT X
              ;              ARG3 = HOTSPOT Y
                             PUBLIC  _MouseCursor
    _MouseCursor   PROC      FAR
                   PUSH      BP
                   MOV       BP,SP
                   PUSH      DS
                   PUSH      ES

                   LDATASEG
                   CALL      HIDECURSOR

                   MOV       SI,[BP+_AOFF+0]
                   MOV       DS,[BP+_AOFF+2]

                   MOV       AX,_DATA
                   MOV       ES,AX
                   MOV       DI,OFFSET DEFAULTCURSOR

                   MOV       CX,32
                   CLD
    MC1:           LODSW
                   XCHG      AL,AH
                   STOSW
                   LOOP      MC1

                   MOV       AX,[BP+_AOFF+4]
                   MOV       BX,[BP+_AOFF+6]

                   MOV       [SPOTX],AX
                   MOV       [SPOTY],BX

                   LDATASEG
                   CALL      SHOWCURSOR

                   POP       ES
                   POP       DS
                   POP       BP
                   RET
    _MouseCursor   ENDP


              ;
              ;              INTERNAL FUNCTIONS
              ;


    ;MAKE A LINE START TABLE WITH FLAGS FOR PAGE BREAKS
    MAKETABLE      PROC      NEAR
                   MOV       CX,[_SCREENDEEP]        ;DEPTH OF SCREEN
                   MOV       BX,0000H                ;ZERO LINE COUNTER
                   MOV       SI,OFFSET _SCREENTBL    ;POINT TO TABLE

    MT1:           PUSH      CX
                   MOV       AX,[_SCREENWIDE]        ;WIDTH OF SCREEEN
                   SHL       AX,1
```

```
                MUL     BX                          ;TIMES LINE NUMBER

                AND     DX,00FFH

                PUSH    AX
                MOV     CX,0FFFEH
                MOV     AX,[_SCREENWIDE]
                SHL     AX,1
                SUB     CX,AX
                POP     AX

                CMP     AX,CX                       ;SEE IF WE WILL
                JB      MT2                         ;EXCEED A PAGE BOUNDARY

                MOV     DH,0FFH

MT2:            MOV     DS:[SI],AX                  ;SAVE THE VALUES
                MOV     DS:[SI+2],DX                ;IN OUR LOOKUP TABLE
                ADD     SI,4                        ;AND POINT TO THE
                INC     BX                          ;NEXT LINE AND

                POP     CX                          ;ENTRY
                LOOP    MT1

                RET
MAKETABLE       ENDP

; HANDLE MOUSE MOVEMENT - THIS FUNCTION CALLED WHENEVER THE MOUSE
; CHANGES STATE. IT'S CALLED BY THE MOUSE DRIVER

MOUSEHANDLER    PROC    FAR
                PUSHF

                CLI

                LDATASEG

                MOV     [MOUSEB],BX

                CMP     [MOUSEF],0000H
                JL      MH1

                PUSH    AX
                PUSH    BX
                PUSH    CX
                PUSH    DX
                CALL    ERASECURSOR
                POP     DX
                POP     CX
                POP     BX
                POP     AX

                MOV     [MOUSEX],CX
                MOV     [MOUSEY],DX
```

```
                              SHR     WORD PTR [MOUSEX],1
                              SHR     WORD PTR [MOUSEX],1

                              CALL    CURSORBACK
                              CALL    DRAWCURSOR

MH1:                          POPF
                              RETF
MOUSEHANDLER                  ENDP

DRAWCURSOR                    PROC    NEAR

                              LDATASEG

                              MOV     CX,CURSORDEEP
                              MOV     BX,[MOUSEY]

                              MOV     SI,OFFSET DEFAULTCURSOR

DC1:                          PUSH    CX
                              PUSH    BX

                              CALL    VGALINE
                              GRAFADD_DI          [MOUSEX]

                              MOV     CX,CURSORWIDE
                              MOV     BX,0000H

DC2:                          PUSH    CX
                              MOV     CX,BX
                              MOV     DX,8000H
                              SHR     DX,CL
                              MOV     AX,DS:[SI]
                              XCHG    AH,AL
                              TEST    AX,DX
                              JNZ     DC3
                              MOV     AX,[_VGABLACK]
                              GRAF_STOSW
                              JMP     DC4

DC3:                          GRAFADD_DI          1

DC4:                          POP     CX
                              INC     BX

                              LOOP    DC2

                              POP     BX
                              PUSH    BX

                              CALL    VGALINE
                              GRAFADD_DI          [MOUSEX]

                              MOV     CX,CURSORWIDE
                              MOV     BX,0000H
```

```
          DC5:              PUSH    CX
                            MOV     CX,BX
                            MOV     DX,8000H
                            SHR     DX,CL
                            MOV     AX,DS:[SI+32]
                            XCHG    AH,AL
                            TEST    AX,DX
                            JZ      DC6
                            MOV     AX,[_VGAWHITE]
                            GRAF_STOSW
                            JMP     DC7

          DC6:              GRAFADD_DI           1

          DC7:              POP     CX
                            INC     BX

                            LOOP    DC5

                            POP     BX
                            POP     CX

                            INC     BX
                            ADD     SI,0002H

                            LNGLOOP DC1

                            RET
DRAWCURSOR                  ENDP

;ERASE THE CURSOR
ERASECURSOR       PROC      NEAR

                            LDATASEG

                            MOV     CX,CURSORDEEP
                            MOV     BX,[MOUSEY]

                            MOV     SI,OFFSET MOUSEBACK

          EC1:              PUSH    CX

                            CALL    VGALINE
                            GRAFADD_DI           [MOUSEX]

                            MOV     CX,CURSORWIDE
                            GRAF_REPNEMOVSW

                            POP     CX
                            INC     BX
                            LOOP    EC1

                            RET
ERASECURSOR                 ENDP
```

```
                     ;COPY THE CURSOR BACKGROUND TO MEMORY
                     CURSORBACK      PROC    NEAR

                                     LDATASEG

                                     MOV     CX,CURSORDEEP
                                     MOV     BX,[MOUSEY]

                                     MOV     SI,OFFSET MOUSEBACK

            CC1:                     PUSH    CX

                                     CALL    VGALINE
                                     GRAFADD_DI          [MOUSEX]

                                     MOV     CX,CURSORWIDE
            CC2:                     MOV     AX,ES:[DI]
                                     MOV     DS:[SI],AX
                                     ADD     SI,0002H
                                     GRAFADD_DI 0001H
                                     LOOP    CC2

                                     POP     CX
                                     INC     BX
                                     LOOP    CC1

                                     RET
            CURSORBACK      ENDP

            ; MAKE THE CURSOR DISAPPEAR
                            PUBLIC HIDECURSOR
            HIDECURSOR      PROC    FAR
                            PUSHF
                            CLI
                            DEC     [MOUSEF]
                            CMP     [MOUSEF],-1
                            JL      HC1
                            CALL    ERASECURSOR

            HC1:            POPF
                            RET
            HIDECURSOR      ENDP

            ; SHOW THE CURSOR
                            PUBLIC SHOWCURSOR
            SHOWCURSOR      PROC    FAR
                            PUSHF
                            CLI
                            INC     [MOUSEF]
                            CMP     [MOUSEF],0000H
                            JG      SC1
                            CALL    CURSORBACK
                            CALL    DRAWCURSOR

            SC1:            POPF
```

```
                        RET
SHOWCURSOR      ENDP

;INITIALIZE A VESA BOARD
INITVESAPROC    NEAR
                        MOV     AX,_DATA
                        MOV     ES,AX
                        MOV     AX,4F00H
                        MOV     DI,OFFSET VESABLOCK
                        INT     10H
                        CMP     AX,004FH
                        JE      IV1
                        MOV     AX,0000H
                        RET

IV1:            MOV     SI,WORD PTR [VIDEOMODE]
                        MOV     ES,WORD PTR [VIDEOMODE+2]

IV2:            MOV     AX,ES:[SI]
                        ADD     SI,0002H
                        CMP     AX,0FFFFH
                        JE      IV3
                        CMP     AX,VESA
                        JE      IV4
                        JMP     IV2

IV3:            MOV     AX,0000H
                        RET

IV4:            MOV     AX,_DATA
                        MOV     ES,AX
                        MOV     AX,4F01H
                        MOV     CX,VESA
                        MOV     DI,OFFSET VESAINFO
                        INT     10H

                        MOV     AX,[WIN_ASEG]
                        MOV     [_SCREENSEG],AX

                        MOV     AX,4F03H
                        INT     10H
                        MOV     [OLDVESAMODE],BX

                        MOV     AX,4F02H
                        MOV     BX,VESA
                        INT     10H

                        CALL    FINDVESASHIFT
                        MOV     [BANKSHIFT],AX

                        MOV     AX,[WINSIZE]
                        MOV     BX,0400H
                        MUL     BX
                        SUB     AX,0002H
                        SUB     AX,[BYTESPERLINE]
```

```
                        MOV     [BANKSIZE],AX

                        MOV     CX,[YRES]               ;DEPTH OF SCREEN
                        SUB     BX,BX                   ;ZERO LINE COUNTER
                        MOV     SI,OFFSET _SCREENTBL    ;POINT TO TABLE

        IV5:            PUSH    CX
                        MOV     AX,[BYTESPERLINE]       ;WIDTH OF SCREEEN
                        MUL     BX                      ;TIMES LINE NUMBER

                        AND     DX,7FFFH

                        CMP     AX,[BANKSIZE]           ;SEE IF WE WILL EXCEED
        THE BLOCK
                        JB      IV6

                        OR      DX,1000H

        IV6:            MOV     DS:[SI],AX              ;SAVE THE VALUES
                        MOV     DS:[SI+2],DX            ;IN OUR LOOKUP TABLE
                        ADD     SI,4                    ;AND POINT TO THE
                        INC     BX                      ;NEXT LINE AND
                        POP     CX                      ;ENTRY
                        LOOP    IV5

                        MOV     AX,0FFFFH

                        RET
        INITVESA        ENDP

        ;FIND THE SHIFT VALUE FOR VESA BANK NUMBERS
        FINDVESASHIFT   PROC    NEAR
                        MOV     DX,0000H
                        MOV     AX,CS:[WINSIZE]
                        DIV     CS:[WINGRAN]

                        CMP     AX,0040H
                        JNE     FVS1
                        MOV     AX,0006H
                        RET

        FVS1:           CMP     AX,0020H
                        JNE     FVS2
                        MOV     AX,0005H
                        RET

        FVS2:           CMP     AX,0010H
                        JNE     FVS3
                        MOV     AX,0004H
                        RET

        FVS3:           CMP     AX,0008H
                        JNE     FVS4
                        MOV     AX,0003H
```

```
                    RET

FVS4:               CMP     AX,0004H
                    JNE     FVS6
                    MOV     AX,0002H
                    RET

FVS6:               CMP     AX,0002H
                    JNE     FVS7
                    MOV     AX,0001H
                    RET

FVS7:               MOV     AX,0000H
                    RET
FINDVESASHIFT       ENDP

;                   RETURN A POINTER IN ES:DI TO THE SCREEN LINE IN BX
                    PUBLIC  VGALINE
VGALINE             PROC    FAR
                    PUSH    AX
                    PUSH    BX
                    PUSH    CX
                    PUSH    DX

                    LDATASEG

                    SHL     BX,1
                    SHL     BX,1

                    MOV     DI,[_SCREENTBL + BX]
                    MOV     AX,[_SCREENTBL + 2 + BX]

                    CALL    CS:[SETBANK]
                    MOV     [PAGEBREAK],AH
                    MOV     ES,[_SCREENSEG]

                    POP     DX
                    POP     CX
                    POP     BX
                    POP     AX
                    RET
VGALINE             ENDP

;SWITCH TO THE BANK IN AX
                    PUBLIC  VGABANK
VGABANK             PROC    FAR
                    CALL    CS:[SETBANK]
                    RET
VGABANK             ENDP

DUMMY               PROC    FAR
                    RET
DUMMY               ENDP
```

```
              SETBANK_ATI    PROC    FAR
                             CMP     AX,[CODEPAGE]
                             JE      SETB_ATI1

                             MOV     [CODEPAGE],AX

                             PUSH    AX
                             PUSH    CX
                             PUSH    DX

                             MOV     DX,[ATIREG]

                             MOV     CX,AX
                             PUSHF
                             CLI
                             MOV     AL,0B2H
                             OUT     DX,AL
                             INC     DL
                             IN      AL,DX
                             MOV     AH,AL
                             AND     AH,0E1H
                             SHL     CL,1
                             OR      AH,CL
                             MOV     AL,0B2H
                             DEC     DL
                             OUT     DX,AX
                             POPF
                             POP     DX
                             POP     CX
                             POP     AX

              SETB_ATI1:     RET
              SETBANK_ATI    ENDP

              SETBANK_TNG    PROC    FAR
                             CMP     AX,[CODEPAGE]
                             JE      SETB_TNG1

                             MOV     [CODEPAGE],AX
                             PUSH    AX
                             PUSH    DX
                             MOV     AH,AL
                             MOV     DX,3BFH
                             MOV     AL,3
                             OUT     DX,AL
                             MOV     DL,0D8H
                             MOV     AL,0A0H
                             OUT     DX,AL
                             AND     AH,15
                             MOV     AL,AH
                             SHL     AL,1
                             SHL     AL,1
                             SHL     AL,1
                             SHL     AL,1
                             OR      AL,AH
```

```
                         MOV       DL,0CDH
                         OUT       DX,AL
                         POP       DX
                         POP       AX

SETB_TNG1:               RET
SETBANK_TNG              ENDP

SETBANK_PAR              PROC      FAR
                         CMP       AX,[CODEPAGE]
                         JE        SETB_PAR1

                         PUSH      AX
                         PUSH      CX
                         PUSH      DX

                         AND       AX,00FFH
                         MOV       [CODEPAGE],AX

                         MOV       DX,03CEH
                         MOV       AX,050FH
                         OUT       DX,AX

                         MOV       AX,[CODEPAGE]
                         MOV       CL,12
                         SHL       AX,CL
                         OR        AX,0009H
                         OUT       DX,AX

                         POP       DX
                         POP       CX
                         POP       AX

SETB_PAR1:               RET
SETBANK_PAR              ENDP

SETBANK_VSA              PROC      FAR

                         PUSH      AX

                         CMP       AX,[CODEPAGE]
                         JE        SETB_VSA4

                         MOV       [CODEPAGE],AX

                         PUSH      BX
                         PUSH      CX
                         PUSH      DX

                         MOV       DX,AX
                         AND       DX,00FFH
                         MOV       CX,[BANKSHIFT]
                         SHL       DX,CL
                         MOV       BX,0000H
                         MOV       AX,4F05H
```

```
                            CMP     WORD PTR CS:[WINFUNPTR+2],0000H
                            JNE     SETB_VSA2

                            MOV     DX,[CODEPAGE]
                            AND     DX,00FFH
                            INT     10H

                            JMP     SETB_VSA3

SETB_VSA2:      CALL    CS:[WINFUNPTR]

SETB_VSA3:      POP     DX
                            POP     CX
                            POP     BX

SETB_VSA4:      POP     AX
                            RET
SETBANK_VSA     ENDP

SETBANK         LABEL   DWORD
SETBANK_OFF     DW      DUMMY
SETBANK_SEG     DW      MOUSE_HI_TEXT

MOUSE_HI_TEXT   ENDS

DGROUP                  GROUP   _DATA,_BSS
_DATA                   SEGMENT WORD PUBLIC 'DATA'

                            PUBLIC  _SCREENTBL,_SCREENSEG,
                            PUBLIC  _SCREENWIDE,_SCREENDEEP
                            PUBLIC  _MASKTABLE,_BITTABLE
                            PUBLIC  _FONTSEG,_FONTOFF,_FONTDEPTH
                            PUBLIC  _VGAWHITE,_VGABLACK,_VGAGREY
                            PUBLIC  _VGALIGHTGREY,_VGADARKGREY
                            PUBLIC  _CARD
                            PUBLIC  CODEPAGE

; SCREEN DIMENSIONS
_SCREENTBL      DW      (TABLEDEEP * 2) DUP (?)
_SCREENSEG      DW      0A000H
_SCREENWIDE     DW      640
_SCREENDEEP     DW      480

; FONT DIMENSIONS AND POINTER
_FONTSEG        DW      ?
_FONTOFF        DW      ?
_FONTDEPTH      DW      ?

; MASK OBJECTS
_MASKTABLE      DB      80H,40H,20H,10H,08H,04H,02H,01H
_BITTABLE       DB      01H,02H,04H,08H,10H,20H,40H,80H

;COLOURS
_VGABLACK       DW      0000H
_VGAWHITE       DW      8FFFH
```

```
_VGAGREY         DW      0
_VGALIGHTGREY    DW      0
_VGADARKGREY     DW      0

;VGA CARD TYPE
_CARD            DW      0

CODEPAGE         DW      0
ATIREG           DW      0
PAGEBREAK        DB      0

; WHERE THE CURSOR LIVES
DEFAULTCURSOR    DB      03FH,0FFH,01FH,0FFH
                 DB      00FH,0FFH,007H,0FFH
                 DB      003H,0FFH,001H,0FFH
                 DB      000H,0FFH,000H,07FH
                 DB      000H,03FH,000H,01FH
                 DB      001H,0FFH,010H,0FFH
                 DB      030H,0FFH,0F8H,07FH
                 DB      0F8H,07FH,0FCH,07FH
                 DB      000H,000H,040H,000H
                 DB      060H,000H,070H,000H
                 DB      078H,000H,07CH,000H
                 DB      07EH,000H,07FH,000H
                 DB      07FH,080H,07CH,000H
                 DB      06CH,000H,046H,000H
                 DB      006H,000H,003H,000H
                 DB      003H,000H,000H,000H

SPOTX            DW      0000H
SPOTY            DW      0000H

; MOUSE POSITION AND BUTTONS
MOUSEX           DW      ?
MOUSEY           DW      ?
MOUSEB           DW      ?

; MOUSE CURSOR FLAG
MOUSEF           DW      -1              ;IF >= 0, MOUSE IS VISIBLE

; WHERE THE AREA BEHIND THE MOUSE CURSOR IS STORED
MOUSEBACK        DB      (CURSORWIDE * CURSORDEEP * 2) DUP (?)

VESABLOCK        LABEL   WORD
VESASIG          DB      4 DUP (0)
VESAVERSION      DW      0
OEMSTRING        DD      0
CAPABILITIES     DB      4 DUP (0)
VIDEOMODE        DD      0
TOTALMEMORY      DW      0
                 DB      242 DUP (0)

VESAINFO         LABEL   WORD
MODE_ATTR        DW      ?
WINA_ATTR        DB      ?
```

```
WINB_ATTR        DB      ?
WINGRAN          DW      ?
WINSIZE          DW      ?
WIN_ASEG         DW      ?
WIN_BSEG         DW      ?
WINFUNPTR        DD      ?
BYTESPERLINE     DW      ?
XRES             DW      ?
YRES             DW      ?
XCHARSIZE        DB      ?
YCHARSIZE        DB      ?
PLANECOUNT       DB      ?
BITXPERPIXEL     DB      ?
BANCKCOUNT       DB      ?
MEMORYMODEL      DB      ?
BANKVSIZE        DB      ?
PAGECOUNT        DB      ?
RESERVED1        DB      ?
MASKS            DB      8 DUP (0)
DIRECTCOLOUR     DB      ?
RESERVED2        DB      216 DUP (0)

OLDVESAMODE      DW      OFFFFH
BANKSHIFT        DW      0
BANKSIZE         DW      0

_DATA            ENDS

_BSS             SEGMENT WORD PUBLIC 'BSS'

_BSS             ENDS

                 END
```

The following is a list of the functions provided by MOUSE-HI, in the order they appear in the source code. These functions can be called exactly as they were in Chapter 4, except as noted.

GetScreenLine(char *line,unsigned int number)

The GetScreenLine function will copy the words from line number into the buffer at line. It's the responsibility of the calling function to make sure that the buffer at line is big enough to hold at least SCREENWIDE words—SCREENWIDE * 2 bytes—and that number is in the range of 0 through SCREENDEEP-1. Note that the buffer for the high-color GetScreenLine must be twice the size of the one for the 256-color version of this function.

GetImageHi(unsigned int left,unsigned int top,unsigned int right,unsigned int bottom,char *p)

The GetImageHi will capture an image fragment from the screen area bounded by its first four arguments into the buffer at p. The size of the buffer passed to GetImageHi should be calculated by the ImageSizeHi macro, which can be

found in MOUSE-HI.H. In theory, this function behaves in the same way the
Borland `getimage` function would if `getimage` supported high-color graphic
modes.

PutImageHi(unsigned int left,unsigned int top,char *p)

The `PutImageHi` function will paint an image fragment pointed to by p on the
screen, such that its upper left corner resides at (`left`,`top`).

SetPixel(unsigned int x,unsigned int y,unsigned int color)

The `SetPixel` function will set the pixel at (`x`,`y`) to `color`. Note that the
`SetPixel` function does not turn off the mouse cursor when it writes—be sure to
do so before using `SetPixel`, and then turn it back on when you're done setting
pixels. The value passed as `color` should be a high-color pixel.

FrameRect(unsigned int left,unsigned int top,unsigned int right,unsigned int bottom,unsigned int color)

The `FrameRect` function will draw a rectangle around the area defined by its first
four arguments in `color`. The value passed as `color` should be a high-color pixel.

FillRect(unsigned int left,unsigned int top,unsigned int right,unsigned int bottom,unsigned int color)

The `FillRect` function will fill a rectangular area defined by its first four
arguments with `color`. The value passed as `color` should be a high-color pixel.

DrawLine(unsigned int left,unsigned int top,unsigned int right,unsigned int bottom,unsigned int color)

The `DrawLine` function will draw a line from (`left`,`top`) to (`right`,`bottom`)
in the color defined by its `color` argument. The value passed as `color` should be a
high-color pixel.

DrawString(unsigned int x,unsigned int y,char *string,unsigned int forecolor,unsigned int backcolor)

The `DrawString` function draws text in the color defined by the `forecolor`
argument against the color defined by the `backcolor` argument. The string is
pointed to by the `string` argument, and should be terminated by a zero byte, just
like a normal C language string. The rectangle that encloses the string will have its
upper left corner at point (x,y).

The `DrawString` function will draw in either 8-or 16-point text, depending on the
status of the FONTEIGHT and FONTSIXTEEN equates in MOUSE256.ASM. Both
fonts are readable at 640 by 480. The 8-point font can be drawn more rapidly and
occupies less screen space, while the 16-point font looks better.

The values passed as `forecolor` and `backcolor` should be high-color pixels.

InitMouse(unsigned int width,unsigned int depth,unsigned int card)

The `InitMouse` function sets up a suitable graphic mode for the card in question
and the mouse manager. It also locates the font for `DrawString` and stores a
pointer to it.

The code for InitMouse checks for the presence of a mouse driver and then initializes it. It then sets the range of the mouse cursor's travel to be those of the screen's dimensions. Finally, it sets up a hook to the custom mouse handler code, MOUSEHANDLER, which has been explained previously.

The InitMouse function will return a true value if all is well, and false one if the mouse driver couldn't be located.

The SCREENTBL line start table array is set up by InitMouse based on the card type.

DeinitMouse(void)

The DeinitMouse function disables the hook into the custom mouse handler previously installed by InitMouse and resets the mouse driver. It also returns the screen to text mode. It's extremely important to call this before returning control to DOS.

ClearScreen(unsigned int color)

The ClearScreen function clears the screen to the color specified by its color argument. The value passed as color should be a high-color pixel.

MouseOn(void)

The MouseOn function makes the mouse cursor visible and is usually called after a corresponding call to MouseOff.

MouseOff(void)

The MouseOff function hides the mouse cursor. You should make sure to call this function if you'll be drawing something on the screen which doesn't itself hide the mouse cursor, and then call MouseOn to reinstate it. The SetPixel function, for example, does not intrinsically hide the mouse cursor.

MouseDown(POINT *p)

The MouseDown function is exceedingly useful in writing code to interface with the mouse. When it's called, it will store the current location of the mouse cursor in the POINT object it's passed a pointer to, and return an integer that defines the state of the mouse buttons at the time of the call. If n is the value returned by MouseDown, n & 1 will be true if the left mouse button is down and n & 2 will be true if the right mouse button is down.

The MOUSEHANDLER function that's called by the mouse driver sets the button status flag and the current mouse location every time the mouse moves or is clicked.

The location of the mouse cursor is the point where the upper left corner of the 16 by 16 pixel cursor resides on your screen plus the offset of the "hot spot." This will be dealt with in the discussion of MouseCursor.

MouseCursor(char *cursor,unsigned int x,unsigned int y)

The MouseCursor function will change the appearance of the mouse cursor. By default, it appears as an arrow pointing to the upper left. The current cursor is stored in the DEFAULTCURSOR buffer in MOUSE-HI.ASM. Note that the cursor format for MOUSE-HI is identical to that of MOUSE16.

A mouse cursor consists of the 32 bytes of the mask bitmap followed by the 32 bytes of the image bitmap, as was discussed in Chapter 3. The x and y "hot spot" values were also explained in Chapter 3.

Figure 5-6 is the complete C language source code for TESTM-HI.C, the program that generated FIG. 5-1. As with TESTM256, it includes the graphic functions covered in this chapter that aren't resident in MOUSE-HI, as well as a `main` function to exercise them. If you compile this program, you'll want to link it to MOUSE-HI.OBJ, as derived from MOUSE-HI.ASM. You'll also need MOUSE-HI.H, which will be presented in the next section of this chapter.

Calling
MOUSE-HI
from C

5-6
The source code for TESTM-HI.C.

```
/*
        Some high-colour graphics

        Copyright (c) 1992 Alchemy Mindworks Inc.

        Links to MOUSE-HI.ASM
*/

#include "stdio.h"
#include "dos.h"
#include "alloc.h"
#include "mouse-hi.h"

/* some useful colours */
#define BLACK           HIGHCOLOUR(0x00,0x00,0x00)
#define BLUE            HIGHCOLOUR(0x00,0x00,0xaa)
#define GREEN           HIGHCOLOUR(0x00,0xaa,0x00)
#define CYAN            HIGHCOLOUR(0x00,0xaa,0xaa)
#define RED             HIGHCOLOUR(0xaa,0x00,0x00)
#define MAGENTA         HIGHCOLOUR(0xaa,0x00,0xaa)
#define YELLOW          HIGHCOLOUR(0xaa,0xaa,0x00)
#define GREY            HIGHCOLOUR(0xaa,0xaa,0xaa)
#define DARKGREY        HIGHCOLOUR(0x55,0x55,0x55)
#define LIGHTGREY       HIGHCOLOUR(0xcc,0xcc,0xcc)
#define LIGHTBLUE       HIGHCOLOUR(0x00,0x00,0xff)
#define LIGHTGREEN      HIGHCOLOUR(0x00,0xff,0x00)
#define LIGHTRED        HIGHCOLOUR(0xff,0x00,0x00)
#define LIGHTYELLOW     HIGHCOLOUR(0xff,0xff,0x00)
#define LIGHTMAGENTA    HIGHCOLOUR(0xff,0x00,0xff)
#define WHITE           HIGHCOLOUR(0xff,0xff,0xff)

/* dimensions of the about box */
#define ABOUTLEFT       107
#define ABOUTTOP        50
#define ABOUTRIGHT      475
#define ABOUTBOTTOM     180

#define FRGFILE         "TESTM-HI.FRG"

typedef struct {
```

```
            char manufacturer;
            char version;
            char encoding;
            char bits_per_pixel;
            int xmin,ymin;
            int xmax,ymax;
            int hres;
            int vres;
            char palette[48];
            char reserved;
            char colour_planes;
            int bytes_per_line;
            int palette_type;
            char filler[58];
            } PCXHEAD;

    typedef struct {
            char sig[4];
            unsigned int width,depth,bits,bytes,planebytes;
            unsigned long palette;
            unsigned long image;
            } IMAGEHEAD;

    char *farPtr(char *p,unsigned long l);
    char *loadfrag(char *s);

    main(argc,argv)
            int argc;
            char *argv[];
    {
            static int colourtable[16] = {
                    BLACK,BLUE,GREEN,CYAN,
                    RED,MAGENTA,YELLOW,GREY,
                    DARKGREY,LIGHTGREY,LIGHTBLUE,LIGHTGREEN,
                    LIGHTRED,LIGHTYELLOW,LIGHTMAGENTA,WHITE
            };

            BUTTON quit,pause,about,save;
            POINT p;
            char *frg;
            double red,green,blue,ri,gi,bi;
            int i,alive=1,thiscard=0xffff;

            /* see what kind of card is installed — sort of */
            if(argc > 1) {
                    if(!stricmp(argv[1],"PARADISE")) thiscard=PARADISE;
                    else if(!stricmp(argv[1],"ATI")) thiscard=ATI;
                    else if(!stricmp(argv[1],"TSENG")) thiscard=TSENG;
                    else if(!stricmp(argv[1],"VESA")) thiscard=VESA;
            }

            /* go for a graphics mode */
            if(!InitMouse(640,480,thiscard)) exit(1);

            SetVgaWhite(WHITE);
```

```
SetVgaBlack(BLACK);
SetVgaGrey(GREY);
SetVgaLightGrey(LIGHTGREY);
SetVgaDarkGrey(DARKGREY);

/* clear the screen */
ClearScreen(GetVgaLightGrey());

/* draw a moire pattern */
for(i=0;i<SCREENWIDE;i+=2)
    DrawLine(i,0,SCREENWIDE>>1,SCREENDEEP>>1,colourtable[i & 15]);
for(i=0;i<SCREENDEEP;i+=2)
    DrawLine(SCREENWIDE>>1,SCREENDEEP>>1,SCREENWIDE-1,i,colourtable[i & 15]);
for(i=SCREENWIDE-1;i>=0;i-=2)
    DrawLine(SCREENWIDE>>1,SCREENDEEP>>1,i,SCREENDEEP-1,colourtable[(i-1) & 15]);
for(i=SCREENDEEP-1;i>=0;i-=2)
    DrawLine(0,i,SCREENWIDE>>1,SCREENDEEP>>1,colourtable[(i-1) & 15]);

red=green=blue=0;
ri=(double)256/(double)(SCREENWIDE-40)*1;
gi=(double)256/(double)(SCREENWIDE-40)*5;
bi=(double)256/(double)(SCREENWIDE-40)*3;

for(i=0;i<(SCREENWIDE-40);++i) {
        DrawLine(20+i,300,20+i,400,HIGHCOLOUR((int)red,(int)green,(int)blue));

        if((red+ri) > 255 || (red+ri) < 0) ri=ri*-1;
        if((green+gi) > 255 || (green+gi) < 0) gi=gi*-1;
        if((blue+bi) > 255 || (blue+bi) < 0) bi=bi*-1;

        red+=ri;
        green+=gi;
        blue+=bi;
}

/* display an image fragment */

WaitCursor();
if((frg=loadfrag(FRGFILE)) != NULL) {
        FillRect(15,15,15+ImageWidth(frg),15+ImageDepth(frg),DARKGREY);
        PutImageHi(10,10,frg);
        FrameRect(10,10,10+ImageWidth(frg),10+ImageDepth(frg),BLACK);
        farfree(frg);
}
ArrowCursor();

/* show some example text */
i=100;
DrawString(200,i," This is blue on light green.          ",BLUE,LIGHTGREEN);
i+=FONTDEPTH;
DrawString(200,i," This is red on light yellow.          ",RED,LIGHTYELLOW);
i+=FONTDEPTH;
DrawString(200,i," This is light yellow on red.          ",LIGHTYELLOW,RED);
i+=FONTDEPTH;
DrawString(200,i," This is black on magenta (very ugly). ",BLACK,MAGENTA);
i+=FONTDEPTH;
```

```
DrawString(200,i," This is cyan on light grey.                ",CYAN,LIGHTGREY);
i+=FONTDEPTH;

/* create some buttons to click on */
MakeButton(SCREENWIDE-100,SCREENDEEP-60,"Quit",&quit);
DrawButton(&quit);

MakeButton(SCREENWIDE-200,SCREENDEEP-60,"Pause",&pause);
DrawButton(&pause);

MakeButton(SCREENWIDE-300,SCREENDEEP-60,"About",&about);
DrawButton(&about);

MakeButton(SCREENWIDE-400,SCREENDEEP-60,"Save",&save);
DrawButton(&save);

/* loop 'til we're done */
do {
        /* look for a mouse click */
        if(MouseDown(&p)) {
                if(PointInRect(&p,&quit)) {
                        TrackButton(&quit);
                        alive=0;
                }
                else if(PointInRect(&p,&pause)) {
                        TrackButton(&pause);
                        WaitCursor();
                        delay(5000);
                        ArrowCursor();
                }
                else if(PointInRect(&p,&about)) {
                        TrackButton(&about);
                        DoAbout();
                }
                else if(PointInRect(&p,&save)) {
                        TrackButton(&save);
                        DoSave("SCREEN00.PCX");
                }
        }
} while(alive);

DeinitMouse();
}

/* save the screen to a PCX file */
DoSave(path)
        char *path;
{
        PCXHEAD pcx;
        FILE *fp;
        char *ps,*pd;
        unsigned int i,j,n,*ip;

        /* create the destination file */
        if((fp=fopen(path,"wb"))==NULL) {
```

```
                beep();
                return;
        }

        if((ps=malloc(SCREENWIDE*sizeof(unsigned int)))==NULL) {
                beep();
                fclose(fp);
                return;
        }

        if((pd=malloc(SCREENWIDE))==NULL) {
                free(ps);
                beep();
                fclose(fp);
                return;
        }

        memset((char *)&pcx,0,sizeof(PCXHEAD));

        pcx.manufacturer=10;
        pcx.encoding=1;
        pcx.xmin=pcx.ymin=0;
        pcx.xmax=SCREENWIDE-1;
        pcx.ymax=SCREENDEEP-1;
        pcx.bits_per_pixel=8;
        pcx.version=5;
        pcx.colour_planes=3;
        pcx.bytes_per_line=SCREENWIDE;

        WaitCursor();
        if(fwrite((char *)&pcx,1,sizeof(PCXHEAD),fp) != sizeof(PCXHEAD)) {
                free(pd);
                free(ps);
                fclose(fp);
                remove(path);
                ArrowCursor();
                beep();
                return;
        }

        for(i=0;i<SCREENDEEP;++i) {
                MouseOff();
                GetScreenLine(ps,i);
                MouseOn();

                /* extract the red components */
                ip=(unsigned int *)ps;
                for(j=0;j<SCREENWIDE;++j) pd[j]=HIGHRED(ip[j]);
                n=pcxwriteline(fp,pd,pcx.bytes_per_line);

                /* extract the green components */
                ip=(unsigned int *)ps;
                for(j=0;j<SCREENWIDE;++j) pd[j]=HIGHGREEN(ip[j]);
                n=pcxwriteline(fp,pd,pcx.bytes_per_line);
```

```
                    /* extract the blue components */
                    ip=(unsigned int *)ps;
                    for(j=0;j<SCREENWIDE;++j) pd[j]=HIGHBLUE(ip[j]);
                    n=pcxwriteline(fp,pd,pcx.bytes_per_line);

                    if(n != pcx.bytes_per_line) {
                            free(pd);
                            free(ps);
                            fclose(fp);
                            remove(path);
                            ArrowCursor();
                            beep();
                            return;

                    }
            }

        ArrowCursor();
        free(pd);
        free(ps);
        fclose(fp);
}

/* write one pcx line */
pcxwriteline(fp,p,n)
        FILE *fp;
        char *p;
        unsigned int n;
{
        unsigned int i=0,j=0,t=0;

        do {
                i=0;
                while((p[t+i]==p[t+i+1]) && ((t+i) < n) && (i < 63))++i;
                if(i>0) {
                        if(fputc(i | 0xc0,fp)==EOF) return(-1);
                        if(fputc(p[t],fp)==EOF) return(-1);
                        t+=i;
                        j+=2;
                }
                else {
                        if(((p[t]) & 0xc0)==0xc0) {
                                if(fputc(0xc1,fp)==EOF) return(-1);
                                ++j;
                        }
                        if(fputc(p[t++],fp)==EOF) return(-1);
                        ++j;

                }
        } while(t<n);
        return(n);
}

/* show the about box */
DoAbout()
{
        POINT pt;
```

```
            BUTTON done;
            char *p;
            unsigned long size;
            unsigned int i;

            /* see how much memory the area behind it needs */
            size=ImageSizeHi(ABOUTLEFT,ABOUTTOP,ABOUTRIGHT,ABOUTBOTTOM);

            /* get a buffer */
            if((p=farmalloc(size)) != NULL) {

                    /* get the area behind the box */
                    GetImageHi(ABOUTLEFT,ABOUTTOP,ABOUTRIGHT,ABOUTBOTTOM,p);

                    /* draw the box */
                    FillRect(ABOUTLEFT,ABOUTTOP,ABOUTRIGHT,ABOUTBOTTOM,LIGHTBLUE);
                    FrameRect(ABOUTLEFT,ABOUTTOP,ABOUTRIGHT,ABOUTBOTTOM,BLACK);

                    /* add the Done button */
                    MakeButton(ABOUTLEFT+16,ABOUTBOTTOM-32,"Done",&done);
                    DrawButton(&done);

                    /* show some text */
                    i=ABOUTTOP+16;
                    DrawString(ABOUTLEFT+16,i,"This is an example of 256 colour",BLACK,LIGHTBLUE);
                    i+=FONTDEPTH;
                    DrawString(ABOUTLEFT+16,i,"super VGA graphics. Copyright (c) 1902",BLACK,LIGHTBLUE);
                    i+=FONTDEPTH;
                    DrawString(ABOUTLEFT+16,i,"Mother Martha's Computer Software",BLACK,LIGHTBLUE);
                    i+=FONTDEPTH;
                    DrawString(ABOUTLEFT+16,i,"Emporium Ltd. Use no hooks.",BLACK,LIGHTBLUE);

                    i=1;

                    /* loop 'til we're done */
                    do {
                            if(MouseDown(&pt)) {
                                    if(PointInRect(&pt,&done)) {
                                      TrackButton(&done);
                                      i=0;
                                      } else beep();
                                    }
                    } while(i);

                    /* put the old screen back */
                    PutImageHi(ABOUTLEFT,ABOUTTOP,p);

                    /* free the buffer */
                    farfree(p);
            } else beep();
    }

MakeButton(left,top,string,button)
        unsigned int left,top;
        char *string;
```

```
                BUTTON *button;

                button->frame.left = left & 0xfff8;
                button->frame.right=button->frame.left+(strlen(string)<<3)+16;
                button->frame.top=top;
                button->frame.bottom=button->frame.top+FONTDEPTH+8;
                button->text=string;
        }

    DrawButton(button)
                BUTTON *button;
        {
                FillRect(button->frame.left+1,button->frame.top+1,
                        button->frame.right-1,button->frame.bottom-1,GetVgaWhite());
                DrawLine(button->frame.left+1,button->frame.top,
                        button->frame.right-1,button->frame.top,GetVgaBlack());
                DrawLine(button->frame.left,button->frame.top+1,
                        button->frame.left,button->frame.bottom-1,GetVgaBlack());
                DrawLine(button->frame.right,button->frame.top+1,
                        button->frame.right,button->frame.bottom-1,GetVgaBlack());
                DrawLine(button->frame.left+1,button->frame.bottom,
                        button->frame.right-1,button->frame.bottom,GetVgaBlack());
                Fill3DBox(button->frame.left+1,button->frame.top+1,
                        button->frame.right-1,button->frame.bottom-1);

                DrawString(button->frame.left+8,button->frame.top+4,
                        button->text,GetVgaDarkGrey(),GetVgaLightGrey());
        }

    TrackButton(button)
                BUTTON *button;
        {
                POINT p;

                FillRect(button->frame.left+1,button->frame.top+1,
                        button->frame.right-1,button->frame.bottom-
                        1,GetVgaLightGrey());

                DrawString(button->frame.left+8,button->frame.top+4,
                        button->text,GetVgaDarkGrey(),GetVgaLightGrey());
                while(MouseDown(&p));
                DrawButton(button);
        }

    Fill3DBox(left,top,right,bottom)
                int left,top,right,bottom;
        {
                FillRect(left,top,right,bottom,GetVgaLightGrey());
                DrawLine(left,top,right-1,top,GetVgaWhite());
                DrawLine(left,top+1,left,bottom-1,GetVgaWhite());

                DrawLine(left+3,bottom,right,bottom,GetVgaDarkGrey());
                DrawLine(right,top+2,right,bottom-1,GetVgaDarkGrey());
        }

    PointInRect(p,r)/* return true if point is in rect */
```

```
        POINT *p;
        RECT *r;
{
        if(p->x > r->left && p->x < r->right &&
           p->y > r->top  && p->y < r->bottom) return(1);
        else return(0);
}

WaitCursor()
{
        static char cursor[] = {
                0x00,0x00,0x00,0x00,
                0x00,0x00,0x01,0x80,
                0x03,0xC0,0x07,0xE0,
                0x0F,0xF0,0x07,0xE0,
                0x03,0xC0,0x01,0x80,
                0x00,0x00,0x00,0x00,
                0x00,0x00,0x00,0x00,
                0xFF,0xFF,0xFF,0xFF,

                0x00,0x00,0xFE,0x7F,
                0x06,0x60,0x0C,0x30,
                0x18,0x18,0x30,0x0C,
                0x60,0x06,0xC0,0x03,
                0x60,0x06,0x30,0x0C,
                0x98,0x19,0xCC,0x33,
                0xE6,0x67,0xFE,0x7F,
                0x00,0x00,0x00,0x00 };

        MouseCursor(cursor,7,7);
}

ArrowCursor()
{
        static char cursor[] = {
                0xFF,0x3F,0xFF,0x1F,
                0xFF,0x0F,0xFF,0x07,
                0xFF,0x03,0xFF,0x01,
                0xFF,0x00,0x7F,0x00,
                0x3F,0x00,0x1F,0x00,
                0xFF,0x01,0xFF,0x10,
                0xFF,0x30,0x7F,0xF8,
                0x7F,0xF8,0x7F,0xFC,
                0x00,0x00,0x00,0x40,
                0x00,0x60,0x00,0x70,
                0x00,0x78,0x00,0x7C,
                0x00,0x7E,0x00,0x7F,
                0x80,0x7F,0x00,0x7C,
                0x00,0x6C,0x00,0x46,
                0x00,0x06,0x00,0x03,
                0x00,0x03,0x00,0x00 };

        MouseCursor(cursor,0,0);
}
```

```
/* load a fragment into a buffer and return a pointer to the image */
char *loadfrag(s)
        char *s;
{
        FILE *fp;
        IMAGEHEAD ih;
        char *p,*pr;
        unsigned int i;

        if((fp=fopen(s,"rb")) == NULL) return(NULL);

        if(fread((char *)&ih,1,sizeof(IMAGEHEAD),fp) != sizeof(IMAGEHEAD))
        {
                fclose(fp);
                return(NULL);
        }

        if(ih.bits != 16) {
                fclose(fp);
                return(NULL);
        }

        if((p=farmalloc(4L+(long)ih.bytes*(long)ih.depth)) == NULL) {
                fclose(fp);
                return(NULL);
        }

        fseek(fp,ih.image,SEEK_SET);

        pr=p;

        pr+=fread(pr,1,4,fp);

        for(i=0;i<ih.depth;++i) {
                if(fread(pr,1,ih.bytes,fp) != ih.bytes) {
                        farfree(p);
                        fclose(fp);
                        return(NULL);
                }
                pr=farPtr(pr,(long)ih.bytes);
        }
        fclose(fp);
        return(p);
}

char *farPtr(p,l)
        char *p;
        unsigned long l;
{
        unsigned int seg,off;

        seg = FP_SEG(p);
        off = FP_OFF(p);
        seg += (off / 16);
        off &= 0x000f;
```

```
        off += (unsigned int)(1 & 0x000fL);
        seg += (1 / 16L);
        p = MK_FP(seg,off);                    \
        return(p);
}
```

The main function of TESTM-HI behaves pretty much like that of TESTM256 from Chapter 4, with a few notable differences. There are fewer display card options, and there's an extra bit of code included to load and display a FRG image fragment file. The file should be named MOUSE-HI.FRG; there's a suitable FRG file on the companion disk for this book, should you lack a way to create one easily.

Note that if no file is available in the current subdirectory of your hard drive, TESTM-HI will simply ignore it and move on to the next part of the display.

The other aspect of the main function of TESTM-HI that differs from its predecessors is the way the palette display works. It creates a color fountain that runs from pure black to pure white, with as many colors in between as it can manage with 600 pixels. All the floating point math really just creates three transitions for the three color indices of subtractive color.

Here's a list of the functions in TESTM-HI.C that you might want to use in your own software.

DoSave(char *path)

The DoSave function will create a PCX file of your current graphic screen at the moment it's called. The path argument should be a complete path and file name, or just a file name if you want the file to appear in the current directory. This includes the extension PCX.

MakeButton(unsigned int left,unsigned int top,char *string, BUTTON *button)

The MakeButton function sets up a BUTTON object to display a button with its upper left corner at (left,top) and its text set to string. It will set the frame element of the button so that its upper left corner corresponds to the left and top arguments to MakeButton. The bottom of the frame will be set based on the current font size. The right edge of the frame will be set based on the length of the string to be used by the button.

DrawButton(BUTTON *button)

The DrawButton function draws a button on the screen. The BUTTON object passed to it should have been set up by a previous call to MakeButton.

TrackButton(BUTTON *button)

The TrackButton function will manage a button once it has been established that a mouse click has taken place within its boundaries.

Fill3DBox(unsigned int left,unsigned int top,unsigned int right,unsigned int bottom)

The Fill3DBOX function is called by DrawButton and probably won't be of much use to other aspects of your software directly.

PointInRect(POINT *p,RECT *r)

The `PointInRect` function will return a true value if POINT p is within RECT r or a false value if it's not.

WaitCursor(void)

The `WaitCursor` function will cause the current cursor to change to an hourglass. It should be called prior to any operation that will take a while to perform.

ArrowCursor(void)

The `ArrowCursor` function will cause the current cursor to revert to a standard arrow cursor. It can be called after a call to `WaitCursor` or to any other function that redefines the mouse cursor's appearance.

The MOUSE-HI.H header

The MOUSE-HI.H file should be included in any C language source code that makes calls to MOUSE-HI. It also contains some structures used by the functions in TESTM-HI.C. It's illustrated in FIG. 5-7.

5-7
The MOUSE-HI.H header file.

```
/*
            Header for MOUSE-HI
*/

#define PARADISE            0x62
#define ATI                 0x72
#define TSENG               0x2e
#define VESA                0x0110

#define COLOURDEPTH         16

#define RGB_RED             0
#define RGB_GREEN           1
#define RGB_BLUE            2
#define RGB_SIZE            3

typedef struct {
        unsigned int x,y;
        } POINT;

typedef struct {
        unsigned int left,top,right,bottom;
        } RECT;

typedef struct {
        RECT frame;
        char *text;
        } BUTTON;

#define pixels2bytes(n) ((n+7)/8)
#define ImageWidth(p)   (1+p[0]+(p[1] << 8))
#define ImageDepth(p)   (1+p[2]+(p[3] << 8))

#define SetVgaWhite(n)              { VGAWHITE=(n); }
#define SetVgaBlack(n)              { VGABLACK=(n); }
```

```c
#define SetVgaGrey(n)              { VGAGREY=(n); }
#define SetVgaLightGrey(n)         { VGALIGHTGREY=(n); }
#define SetVgaDarkGrey(n)          { VGADARKGREY=(n); }

#define GetVgaWhite()              (VGAWHITE & 0x7fff)
#define GetVgaBlack()              (VGABLACK & 0x7fff)
#define GetVgaGrey()               (VGAGREY & 0x7fff)
#define GetVgaLightGrey()          (VGALIGHTGREY & 0x7fff)
#define GetVgaDarkGrey()           (VGADARKGREY & 0x7fff)

#define greyvalue(r,g,b)           (((r*30)/100) + ((g*59)/100) + ((b*11)/100))

#define beep()                     putchar(7)

#ifndef max
#define max(a,b)                   (((a)>(b))?(a):(b))
#endif
#ifndef min
#define min(a,b)                   (((a)<(b))?(a):(b))
#endif

#define ImageSizeHi(l,t,r,b)       (4L+2L*(long)(1+max(r,l)-min(r,l))*\
                                   (long)(1+max(b,t)-min(b,t)))

#define HIGHRED(c)      (((((c) >> 10) & 0x1f) << 3)
#define HIGHGREEN(c)    (((((c) >> 5) & 0x1f) << 3)
#define HIGHBLUE(c)     ((((c) & 0x1f) < 3)

#define HIGHCOLOUR(r,g,b) (((((unsigned int)r > 3) & 0x1f) < 10) + \
                          ((((unsigned int)g > 3) & 0x1f) < 5) + \
                          (((unsigned int)b > 3) & 0x1f))

unsigned int InitMouse(unsigned int screenwide,unsigned int screendeep,
                       unsigned int card);
void DeinitMouse(void);
void MouseOn(void);
void MouseOff(void);
unsigned int MouseDown(POINT *p);
void MouseCursor(char *cursor,unsigned int x,unsigned int y);
void DrawString(unsigned x,unsigned int y,char *p,unsigned int c,
                unsigned int b);
void PutImageHi(unsigned int left,unsigned int top,char *p);
void GetImageHi(unsigned int left,unsigned int top,unsigned int right,
                unsigned int bottom,char *p);

extern unsigned int SCREENTBL[];
extern unsigned int SCREENWIDE;
extern unsigned int SCREENDEEP;
extern unsigned int SCREENSEG;
extern char masktable[];
extern char bittable[];
extern unsigned int FONTDEPTH;
extern unsigned int FONTSEG;
extern unsigned int FONTOFF;
extern unsigned int VGAWHITE;
```

```
extern unsigned int VGABLACK;
extern unsigned int VGALIGHTGREY;
extern unsigned int VGADARKGREY;
extern unsigned int VGAGREY;
```

You can add a few more modes to the list of mode numbers at the top of MOUSE-HI.H, although the pickings aren't as thick as they were in the 256-color version of the graphic package. Specifically, both the Tseng Labs and Paradise cards have 800 by 600 pixel highcolor modes available as well. To select the 800 by 600 pixel high-color mode on a a Paradise card, you would do this:

```
MOV AX,0063H
INT 10H
```

To select the same mode on a Tseng Labs 4000X card, you'd need the following bit of code. Note that this is identical to that used to select the 640 by 480 pixel high-color mode, save for the arguments to INT 10H.

```
MOV     DX,03C4H
    MOV     AL,0
    OUT     DX,AL
    MOV     DX,03C5H
    IN      AL,DX
    AND     AL,0FEH
    OUT     DX,AL
    MOV     DX,03CEH
    MOV     AL,06H
    OUT     DX,AL
    MOV     DX,03CFH
    IN      AL,DX
    XOR     AL,06H
    OR      AL,02H
    OUT     DX,AL

MOV         AX,10F0H
MOV         BX,0030H
INT         10H
```

If you decide to include these modes in MOUSE-HI.ASM, make sure you modify the screen dimensions and the TABLEDEEP equate to reflect the new values.

As has been noted earlier in this chapter, the HIGHRED, HIGHGREEN, and HIGHBLUE macros will extract individual color indices from a high-color pixel. The HIGHCOLOUR macro will combine the red, green, and blue components of an RGB color into a high-color pixel.

The macro ImageSizeHi returns a value that defines the number of bytes required for a GetImageHi buffer, just as the imagesize function does for a normal Turbo C getimage fragment. You can regard it as a function:

```
unsigned long ImageSizeHi(unsigned int left,unsigned int
    top,unsigned int right,unsigned int bottom)
```

By the time this book gets to press, Desktop Paint 16 and Desktop Paint 256 will have been joined by Desktop Paint HI—predictably, a 16-bit paint package. I confess that this is one of the few applications for high-color graphics that I've thought of to date. A high-color arcade game is an engaging thought, although there probably aren't that many people with $500 super VGA cards who are interested in tying them up to zap aliens from the ninth dimension.

The great thing about high-color graphics is that with the right hardware, there's nothing your mind can imagine that your software can't do. The only real drawback to this at the moment is that so few people have the right hardware.

High-end graphic applications seem to be one of the really hot areas of growth in PC applications at the moment; if your imagination naturally works in technicolor, you'll probably find that what it comes up with can be most readily achieved using the technology covered in this chapter.

Applications for high-color graphics

Display fonts

Living in interesting times

"Sects, sects, sects... is that all monks think about?"
—Graffiti

One of the things that makes desktop publishing a lot more fun than it seems it should be is the ability of most desktop publishing software to use extra fonts. Typography is a wonderfully expressive medium, and you can do a lot to make any display text—printed pages or graphic screen displays—much more interesting through the use of well chosen type faces.

Part of your perception of this book, for example, has probably been determined by its typography. If it had been designed using monospaced typewriter type, for example, you probably wouldn't have taken it seriously and it would still be languishing on a shelf somewhere.

In fact, type can be incredibly evocative. People who design books, magazine articles, and such are usually very much aware of the subtleties of choosing type. To be sure, you can be a lot more subtle when your display medium is a 2540 dot per inch phototypesetter, rather than a 75 dot per inch monitor. Some of the refinements of type are lost—or, at least, not really worth perusing—on a graphic display.

You can still do a lot with display type in super VGA graphic programs, and being able to use text other than that of the system font that's turned up in the foregoing chapters can do a lot to make your applications look professional.

Figure 6-1 illustrates some display type in a super VGA graphic program. The programs to be presented in this chapter will generate this screen in the 16, 256, and high-color super VGA modes.

This is 8 point Swiss
This is 9 point Swiss
This is 10 point Swiss
This is 12 point Swiss

This is 16 point Swiss

This is 18 point Swiss

This is 20 point Swiss

This is 24 point Swiss

This is 28 point Swiss

This is 36 point Swiss

This is 8 point Dutch
This is 9 point Dutch
This is 10 point Dutch
This is 12 point Dutch

This is 16 point Dutch

This is 18 point Dutch

This is 20 point Dutch

This is 28 point Dutch

This is 12 point Courier

This is 24 point Courier

6-1
*Some display type in a
super VGA graphic
program.*

Save   Quit

It's worth noting that the fonts in FIG. 6-1 are by no means the only ones you can use with the font functions to be covered in this chapter. There are a lot of available screen display fonts—we'll be looking at tools to use quite a few of them. Figure 6-2 illustrates a somewhat larger library of fonts that could be used with the functions in this chapter.

Most of the fonts in Fig. 6-2 have come from Macintosh applications. They include the Macintosh system fonts, a number of commercial third-party Macintosh fonts, and some fonts that came from the Mac conference of a local bulletin board. We'll deal with this Macintosh lore later in this chapter.

There are two problems in using these attractive fonts. The first is that they're a bit trickier to work with than the screen fonts were. The second is that there is no source of readily available bitmapped screen fonts for PC applications. The first problem can be solved with some assembly language. The second one requires some legislation.

6-2
Quite a few more display fonts.

We'll leave the legal questions until later in this chapter too.

This is 24 point Gazelle

THIS IS 24 POINT GLOSS

𝕿his is 24 point Gregorian

This is 24 point Los Angeles

THIS IS 24 POINT PIERCE

This is 14 point Venice

𝕿his is 18 point Wartburg

This is 24 point Future

THIS IS 18 POINT ATHENS

The fonts and font code in this chapter are derived from my book *Graphical User Interface Programming*, also published by Windcrest. It includes a more detailed treatment of screen fonts, as well as the source code for the conversion programs and other utilities to be discussed in this chapter. While you won't need the information in *Graphical User Interface Programming* just to work with fonts—the functions in this chapter will more than suffice for that—you might want to consult this book if you'd like to manipulate fonts, especially fonts from other sources.

The *Graphical User Interface Programming* book also includes a more complete set of functions to manipulate resources, another topic that will turn up in this chapter.

The thing that makes working with display fonts a lot more involved than using the system font has to do with the way type is set. The text in display fonts, like the text you're reading now, is proportionally spaced. This means that each character on a line occupies only as much horizontal space as it requires. The real estate allocated to the letter "i", for example, will be considerably smaller than that of the letter "M". This allows a lot more text to be fit on a line—assuming all the letters aren't M's—and it makes for much more readable type as well.

Fonts & font resources

By comparison, the text created by a typewriter or a simple dot matrix printer is monospaced. The type used to set the program listings in this book is also monospaced. All the characters occupy the same width on a line. While it's arguably not as attractive as proportionally spaced type, text set in a monospaced font is pretty well essential for anything in which the characters must line up vertically. Program listings—especially C language listings with a lot of indentation—can be made pretty well unreadable by setting them in a proportionally spaced font.

In a sense, the system font used in the earlier chapters of this book stored each character as a bitmapped image fragment. In theory you might devise a way to handle proportionally spaced text this way as well, with each character stored in a putimage fragment suited to its width. This would not make for a particularly accessible font format, however, and it would be awkward to manage. Perhaps more to the point, however, this is not the way existing font formats work.

While the font format to be dealt with in the first part of this chapter is synthetic—it was created for use with the Desktop Paint packages that come bundled with this book—it's derived from several extant commercial font formats. As such, its method for storing character bitmaps leans a bit on the formats to which its owes its ancestry.

The code in this book will expect proportionally spaced fonts to be stored as a font header followed by a character bitmap. It's easier to understand the header if you begin by looking at the bitmap. Figure 6-3 illustrates part of a font bitmap.

In a proportionally spaced font, there is a single very long bitmap with each character in the font set sequentially. The individual bits of each character will be extracted from the font bitmap when the font is being used. While this is a tad complex to manage, it involves only the simplest of processor instructions, and as such can be made to run pretty quickly.

ABCDEFGHIJKLMNOPQRSTUVWXYZ

6-3 *Part of a font bitmap.*

The bitmap is preceded by a header that looks like this:

```
typedef struct {
        char name[FONTNAMESIZE+1];
        char number;
        char pointsize;
        char charwide[(MAXFONTCHAR-MINFONTCHAR)+1];
        unsigned int charoff[(MAXFONTCHAR-MINFONTCHAR)+1];
        unsigned int bitmapwidth;
        unsigned int bitmapdepth;
        unsigned int bitmapbytes;
        unsigned int widestchar;
        unsigned int padwidth;
        unsigned int spacewidth;
        } FONT;
```

The following constants will also prove useful:

```
#define MINFONTCHAR   0
#define MAXFONTCHAR   255
#define FONTNAMESIZE 32
```

The `name` field of a FONT object holds the font name—this is a somewhat peculiar issue, and one that we'll cover in greater detail shortly. The `number` field contains the font number, which will also become more relevant later in this chapter. The `pointsize` field contains the point size of the font.

Points are the unit of measurement of type. A point is about $1/72$ of an inch, although strictly speaking there is no absolute definition of the size of one point. Because one pixel on an average size monitor will be about $1/75$ of an inch, it's convenient to regard a point and a pixel as being more or less the same size. Type designers and professional graphic artists typically become incensed about this sort of wanton informality.

In fact, the `pointsize` field doesn't actually have anything to do with the way proportionally spaced type is used—it's only used to define the way it's named. The real application of the `pointsize` field will be dealt with in conjunction with the `number` field.

The `charwide` field of a FONT object is an array of values that represents the width in pixels of each character in the font. There are 256 ASCII characters and, as such, 256 possible font characters. In fact, few fonts define characters for all the possible characters in a font. Some of the entries in the `charwide` array will be 0.

The `charwide` array assumes that no font will have characters that are more than 255 pixels wide, a fairly safe assumption for screen fonts.

The charoff element of a FONT object is an array of unsigned integers that specifies the number of pixels between the left edge of the bitmap of the font in question and the left edge of each character in the array. This allows a function that wants to work with the font to find each character in the bitmap quickly. It also means that multiple ASCII character codes can display the same character on screen by having the same charoff elements. Macintosh fonts use this facility to manage a dummy character that's used for characters having no explicit character pattern.

The bitmapwidth and bitmapdepth elements of a FONT object define the dimensions of the character bitmap. The bitmapbytes value defines the number of bytes in a line—this would usually be equal to pixels2bytes(font.bitmapwidth). The widestchar element defines the number of pixels in the widest character. The spacewidth defines the number of pixels in a space character—that is, ASCII character 32. A space character is not defined in the font bitmap in many cases. The padwidth element defines the number of extra pixels to be added between characters when they're displayed.

Some applications will want to adjust the size of a space character dynamically, such as to feather lines.

The character bitmap of a font appears immediately after the FONT object, that is, at sizeof(FONT) bytes beyond the start of the font.

Figure 6-4 illustrates how text is displayed using the information in a FONT object and its accompanying font bitmap.

6-4
How bits are copied from a font bitmap to the screen.

It's possible to write a function in C to display text using a FONT object. In fact, this is how Desktop Paint 16 handles painting text with its text tool. While agreeably fast in sixteen colors—as it can use the setpixel macro—it runs into difficulties in the 256 and high-color super VGA modes, where each pixel would require a call to the SetPixel function. This is what the C language function looks like.

```
DrawFontString(s,font,x,y,color)
        char *s;
        FONT *font;
        int x,y,color;
```

```
{
            char *bmp;
            int n,i,j,k,kl,cp,cb;

            n=strlen(s);
            bmp=((char *)font)+sizeof(FONT);

            MouseOff();
            for(i=0;i<font->bitmapdepth;++i) {
                if((y+i) >=SCREENDEEP) break;
                cb=x;
                for(j=0;j<n;++j) {
                        if(s[j]!=32) {
                                kl=font->charwide[s[j]];
                                cp=font->charoff[s[j]];
                                for(k=0;k<kl;++k) {
                                        if(bmp[cp>>3] &
                                            masktable[cp & 0x0007])
                                            setpixel(cb, y+i, color) ;
                                        ++cb;
                                        ++cp;
                                }
                                cb+=font->padwidth;
                        } else cb+=(font->spacewidth+font->padwidth);
                }
                bmp+=font->bitmapbytes;
            }
            MouseOn();
}
```

It's pretty easy to follow what's happening in DrawFontString. The string passed as s is painted on the screen one line at a time. Screen pointers are derived from SCREENTBL to address the screen buffer. Each character in the string is used as an index into the charwide array of the FONT object passed to DrawFontString to find the width of the character to be drawn, and then into the charoff array to find its offset in the character bitmap, bmp. Having located the bitmap section for a character, its bits are copied to the screen.

Actually, only the set bits are copied. The DrawFontString function doesn't paint anything in the background of the text it draws. The bits are read and written using the masktable array.

Because the C language DrawFontString function would be a bit slow in super VGA modes with more color depth, the code in this chapter will use an assembly language version of the function. As you'll have observed in the foregoing three chapters, modifying assembly language functions to handle different color depths is fairly uninvolved. As such, the 16-color font code will use an assembly language DrawFontString function too, even though it could be handled in C.

We'll have a look at the real DrawFontString in a moment.

Organizing fonts as resources The simplest way to use a font of the sort just described would be to store it in a binary file and load it from the disk when it was required. While this is arguably a workable way to handle one font, it would be a messy way to deal with lots of fonts. Applications which use lots of little files tie up an untoward amount of hard drive space in file granulation, and run the risk of having some of their dependant files accidentally deleted.

The Desktop Paint packages that use the fonts we've been looking at here handle storing them in a somewhat different way. They manage fonts as "resources." The concept of resources is something else borrowed from the Macintosh—it also turns up in applications written for Microsoft Windows. A *resource* is a block of data stored in a file with a lot of other blocks of data. Each resource has a type and a number—in this context, a type will be a 4-byte string.

The resource format use by Desktop Paint—and by the code in this chapter— structures its resource files as "linked lists." This means that each resource contains a pointer to the next resource, such that an application reading the file can step from one resource to the next until it finds the one it's after. This isn't actually the fastest way to organize a resource file, but it is the most flexible. It allows a resource file to be manipulated without requiring large amounts of memory.

In the resource format to be used herein, resources are constrained to be no larger than 64K long. This is adequate for even fairly large fonts. The extension for resource files is RES.

A resource file always starts with a resource file header. This is what one looks like:

```
typedef struct {
        char id[8];
        char description[65];
        unsigned int count;
        } RESHEAD;
```

The id field of a RESHEAD object will always hold the signature string for a resource file. This is how it's defined:

```
#define RESID "ALCHRSRC"
```

While you can use whatever signature string you want, note that the utilities provided on the companion disk for this book expect to work with resource files structured this way.

The description field can contain an optional text description of the nature of a resource file. It can usually be ignored. The count field defines the number of resources in the file. The first byte after the RESHEAD object will be the beginning of the first resource in the file.

Each resource is preceded by a RESOURCE object, essentially a local header for the resource data. While the resource data can be anything your application requires, the local resource header is fixed, such that it can be read and interpreted in a standard manner. This is the definition of a RESOURCE object:

```
typedef struct {
        char type[4];
        unsigned long number;
        unsigned int size;
        } RESOURCE;
```

The `type` element of a RESOURCE object will be the 4-byte string that identifies the type of the resource in question. The type for a font is—perhaps predictably—"FONT". As you'll discover if you have looked at the resource file for Desktop Paint 16, there are lots of other sorts of data that can be stored as resources. This chapter will only deal with resources of the type FONT. One of the handy things about the structure of a resource file is that it's easy to ignore resources you're not interested in.

Note that resource types are case-sensitive. The resource types "FONT" and "font" would designate different resources.

Every resource has a unique number for its type, as found in the `number` field of a RESOURCE object. You can have resources with different types and the same number. The resource numbers allow software that manages a resource file to keep track of individual resources. Resource numbers are long integers—they can be very large. There is also an illegal resource number, which is defined like this:

```
#define BADRECNUM 0xffffffffL
```

The BADRECNUM constant is used in much the same way the NULL pointer constant is under C—it's handy for indicating an illegal return value or the end of a list of resource numbers.

The `size` field of a RESOURCE object specifies the number of bytes in its attendant resource. If `fp` is a file pointer to a resource file and a RESOURCE object has just been read, seeking forward by `size` bytes will locate the next RESOURCE object.

Figure 6-5 illustrates `loadfont`, a function to find a specific FONT resource in a resource file and load it into memory. It assumes that the resource type will be "FONT", and as such it only needs to know the number of the FONT resource to be loaded.

6-5

The `loadfont` function.

```
FONT *loadfont(s,n)
        char *s;
        unsigned long n;
{
        RESHEAD rh;
        RESOURCE rc;
        FONT *font;
        FILE *fp;
        unsigned int i;

        /* open the resource file */
        if((fp=fopen(s,"rb")) == NULL) return(NULL);

        /* read the header */
        if(fread((char *)&rh,1,sizeof(RESHEAD),fp) != sizeof(RESHEAD)) {
                fclose(fp);
                return(NULL);
        }

        /* make sure it's a resource file */
        if(memcmp(rh.id,RESID,8)) {
                fclose(fp);
                return(NULL);
```

```
        }

        /* look at all the resources */
        for(i=0;i<rh.count;++i) {

                /* fetch the resource */
                if(fread((char *)&rc,1,sizeof(RESOURCE),fp) != sizeof(RESOURCE)) {
                        fclose(fp);
                        return(NULL);
                }

                /* if it's a font and it's the one we want, load it */
                if(!memcmp(rc.type,FONTID,4) && rc.number == n) {

                        /* allocate a buffer for the data */
                        if((font=(FONT *)malloc(rc.size)) == NULL) {
                                fclose(fp);
                                return(NULL);
                        }

                        /* read the data */
                        if(fread((char *)font,1,rc.size,fp) != rc.size) {
                                free((char *)font);
                                fclose(fp);
                                return(NULL);
                        }

                        /* we're done -- go away */
                        fclose(fp);
                        return(font);
                }

                /* otherwise, seek to the next resource */
                fseek(fp,(unsigned long)rc.size,SEEK_CUR);
        }

        /* resource not found */
        fclose(fp);
        return(NULL);
}
```

The loadfont function begins by opening the resource file it's passed as an argument and reading its RESHEAD header object. It then steps through all the resources in the file looking for one with the type "FONT"—defined here as the constant FONTID—and the number n. If it finds such a resource, it will allocate a buffer of size bytes and load the data into it. If it doesn't, it will return a NULL pointer.

If you write applications to use display fonts, you'll have the choice of either loading all the fonts in a resource file into memory when your application boots up or of loading each one as it's required and then discarding it when you're done with it. The first approach allows whatever functions that require fonts to get at them pretty well instantly. The second minimizes the amount of memory that will be tied up by fonts; by their nature, fonts can get a bit memory hungry.

Font resource organization

As we'll see in a moment, you can manipulate the fonts in a resource file pretty easily. Ideally, applications that use lots of display fonts should be structured to allow their compliment of fonts to be adjusted by their users. Desktop Paint, for example, does this—it allows its users to delete fonts they don't require and to add fonts that they've converted from other sources, something else to be covered presently. Desktop Paint is designed to read its resource file and determine the list of available fonts from it.

Fonts usually appear in families. For example, FIG. 6-6 illustrates the family for the font Times Roman—or, more correctly, for the font Dutch.

If you look back at the definition of a FONT object, you'll note that each font has a number. This is not the same as a RESOURCE object's number. Every font family in a resource file should have a unique number. By convention, the number for the Dutch font is 14. Font numbers can range from 0 through 255.

An application that works with lots of fonts should read through its resource file and group the fonts it finds by family—or, more correctly, by the font numbers that differentiate the font families. In a resource file that contained the fonts illustrated in FIG. 6-6, there would be numerous fonts having the font number fourteen. Each would have a different point size.

Within reason, an application that works with fonts this way will allow its users to add any fonts they choose to it.

This is 9 point Times Roman

This is 10 point Times Roman

This is 12 point Times Roman

This is 14 point Times Roman

This is 18 point Times Roman

This is 20 point Times Roman

This is 24 point Times Roman

OR PERHAPS IT'S ALL DUTCH

6-6
The font family for Times Roman.

Manipulating resources

The example programs in this chapter will use the resource file from the Desktop Paint 16 application as a source of font resources. You might want to extract it from the DTPE10.ZIP file on the companion disk for this book. You'll also want the resource tools from the companion disk, as stored in RESTOOLS.ZIP.

The principal utility for working with resources is RMOVER.EXE. It's a bit inelegant, but it allows you to manipulate resource files pretty effectively. Specifically, RMOVER will allow you to create a resource file and add resources to it, to extract resources from a resource file and write them to a new resource file, to delete resources from a resource file and to list all the resources in a resource file. We'll use the DTPE.RES file from Desktop Paint 16 in the following examples.

To begin with, you might want to see what resources are in DTPE.RES. Here's the command to do so:

```
RMOVER DTPE /L
```

The first argument to RMOVER is always the name of the principal resource file you want to work with. The file extension is optional. The /L argument tells RMOVER to list the contents of DTPE.RES. In this case, the list will go on for quite a while— Desktop Paint 16 stores its fonts, its help screens, parts of its code, and numerous other resources in DTPE.RES, for a total 134 resources in the distribution version of the package. Most of this won't be of much interest to you.

Here's the listing for the fonts:

Rsrc 0013 - type:FONT - nmbr:000000002 - 02063 bytes Swiss 9pt #242

Rsrc 0014 - type:FONT - nmbr:000000003 - 02111 bytes Swiss 10pt #242

Rsrc 0015 - type:FONT - nmbr:000000004 - 02645 bytes Swiss 12pt #242

Rsrc 0016 - type:FONT - nmbr:000000005 - 03479 bytes Swiss 14pt #242

Rsrc 0017 - type:FONT - nmbr:000000006 - 04775 bytes Swiss 18pt #242

Rsrc 0018 - type:FONT - nmbr:000000007 - 05759 bytes Swiss 20pt #242

Rsrc 0019 - type:FONT - nmbr:000000008 - 07479 bytes Swiss 24pt #242

Rsrc 0020 - type:FONT - nmbr:000000009 - 03215 bytes OldEngish 18pt #243

Rsrc 0021 - type:FONT - nmbr:000000010 - 01937 bytes Monospace 9pt #244

Rsrc 0022 - type:FONT - nmbr:000000011 - 02375 bytes Monospace 12pt #244

Rsrc 0023 - type:FONT - nmbr:000000012 - 01943 bytes Dutch 9pt #245

Rsrc 0024 - type:FONT - nmbr:000000013 - 02111 bytes Dutch 10pt #245

Rsrc 0025 - type:FONT - nmbr:000000014 - 02645 bytes Dutch 12pt #245

Rsrc 0026 - type:FONT - nmbr:000000015 - 03263 bytes Dutch 14pt #245

Rsrc 0027 - type:FONT - nmbr:000000016 - 04427 bytes Dutch 18pt #245

Rsrc 0028 - type:FONT - nmbr:000000017 - 05171 bytes Dutch 20pt #245

Rsrc 0029 - type:FONT - nmbr:000000018 - 06743 bytes Dutch 24pt #245

The font names, numbers, and point sizes are listed in the right column. In most cases, RMOVER doesn't know what's in a resource. However, there are a few common resource types—such as FONT resources—that it will investigate in greater detail.

Here's how you would extract a resource from DTPE.RES to a new resource file. In this example we'll extract the 18-point Old English font to a file called OLDENG18.RES.

```
RMOVER DTPE /E /FOLDENG18 /TFONT /N9
```

The first argument passed to RMOVER is the name of the source resource file. The /E argument is the command to extract a resource. The /F argument specifies the name of the file the resource will be written to. The /T argument specifies the resource type—note that this must be in uppercase, as resource types are case-sensitive. The /N argument specifies the resource number. The resource number is the one from the center column in the RMOVER listing, the one with "nmbr:" preceding it.

When it's extracting a resource, RMOVER will create the destination file. Note that the order of the arguments preceded by slashes doesn't matter.

Here's how you'd add a new font resource to DTPE.RES. In this example, we'll add the resource file NEWFNT36.RES to DTPE.RES—assuming that such a file existed.

```
RMOVER DTPE /A /FNEWFNT36
```

The /A argument tells RMOVER to add one or more resources to DTPE.RES. The /F argument specifies the name of the resource file to have its contents added to DTPE. If NEWFNT36.RES contains more than one resource, they'll all be added to DTPE.RES. In cases where the resource types and numbers in the resources to be added would conflict with existing resources, RMOVER will change the numbers of the incoming resources.

Finally, here's how you would delete a resource. In this example, we'll delete the 18-point Old English font from DTPE.RES.

```
RMOVER DTPE /D /TFONT /N9
```

The /D argument is the command to delete. The /T and /N arguments behave as they did for the /E function.

Looking at fonts   While the RMOVER utility will tell you the names and point sizes of font resources, it's quite a lot more interesting to see fonts as they're supposed to be seen—in graphics mode. The SEEFONT.EXE utility from the companion disk for this book will allow you to do so. It's in the RESTOOLS.ZIP archive along with RMOVER. The SEEFONT program will open any resource file and let you browse all the fonts therein.

You will need a Microsoft-compatible mouse and mouse driver loaded to use SEEFONT. To run it, type

```
SEEFONT
```

Select the Open item from the SEEFONT File menu. In this example, we'll look at the fonts in DTPE.RES. Select DTPE.RES from the Open File dialog box and then click on Ok. A window like the one in FIG. 6-7 will appear. This is a list of all the fonts in DTPE.RES. Select one and click on Ok.

Once you select a font from the SEEFONT selector dialog, the program will load it into memory and display it. Figure 6-8 illustrates the display for the 18-point Old English font from DTPE.RES. The SEEFONT program will display some information

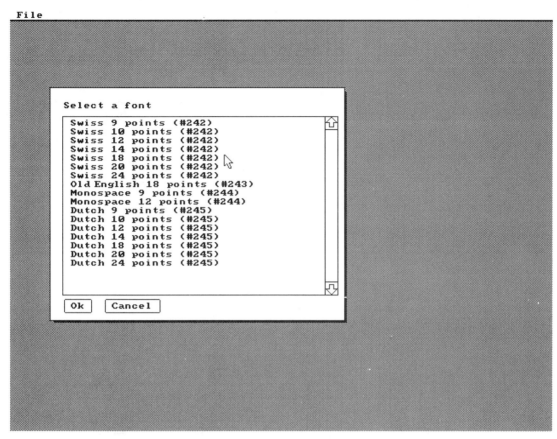

6-7 *The Selector in SEEFONT.*

about the font in question at the top of the screen and then the font characters in the larger of its two work spaces. If there's room, it will also display the string "The quick brown fox obfuscated the lazy dog."

Few things are more pathetic than an obfuscated dog.

The fonts included with Desktop Paint 16 have been modified somewhat, in that they only contain character definitions for the characters from 32 through 127. All the other characters in these fonts are blank. This was done to make DTPE.RES compress into a smaller archive, something that's important for shareware applications. Most fonts will have a full set of high-order special characters too. Figure 6-9 (on page 339) illustrates the SEEFONT display for the Meath font. This is a commercial font from Cassady and Greene.

The high-order characters—the ones ranging from 128 through 255—will vary depending on where a font has originated from. The Meath font in FIG. 6-8 was derived from a Ventura Publisher screen font. Your applications are free to use these extra characters, of course—as long as you keep in mind that they might not be the same in all fonts.

```
        FONT NAME: Venice          BITMAP WIDTH: 1152
      FONT NUMBER: 246             BITMAP BYTES: 144
       POINT SIZE: 14
       FONT DEPTH: 19
 WIDEST CHARACTER: 21
```

□□□□□□□□□□□□□□□□□□□□□□□□ !"#$%&'()*+,-./0123456789:;<=>?□ABCDEFGH1

JKLMNOPQRSTUVWXYZ[\]^_`abcdefghijklmnopqrstuvwxyz{|}~□ÅÅÇÉÑÖ

Üáàâäãåçéèêëíìîïñóòôöõúùûü□□□□□□□ß□□□´□□ÆØ□□□□□□□□□□□□□□

□œø¿i□□□□□«»□ÀÃÕŒœ--""""□□ÿ

The quick brown fox obfuscated the lazy dog...

6-8 *The SEEFONT application.*

Of font names & lawyers

The next section of this chapter will deal with getting screen fonts for your applications by abstracting them from other applications. This might seem a bit questionable—bordering on the recklessly illegal—but in fact, it's neither. The legal situation surrounding fonts is unusually peculiar.

Note that the following information is not legal council—you might want to check it out with a lawyer if you're uncertain about it.

The United States Copyright Office decided in September, 1988, that typeface designs cannot be registered—and hence protected—under the copyright act. The complete text of this decision is in the Federal Register volume 53, number 189, docket 86-4. The reason for this decision is unusual: the Copyright Office decided that if typefaces could be copyrighted, the copyright holders might be in a position to regulate their use—that is, to define what could and could not be typeset using the copyrighted faces. Because virtually all printed words are typeset in one face or another, this might have given the holders of typeface copyrights the ability to regulate what was printed.

```
            FONT NAME: Meath          BITMAP WIDTH: 2321
          FONT NUMBER: 202            BITMAP BYTES: 292
           POINT SIZE: 24
           FONT DEPTH: 24
      WIDEST CHARACTER: 31
```

!"#$%&'()*+,-./0123456789:;<=>?@ABCDEFGHIJKLM
NOPQRSTUVWXYZ[\]^_`abcdefghijklmnopqrstuvwxy
z{|}~ÇüéâäàåçêëèïÅÅÉæÆôöòûùÿÖÜ¢£■áíóúñÑªº¿⌐¬ı«
»ãõØøœŒλÂÃÕ§ᵗᵗ⑨©®™…⊗--˙ÁÂÈÊÈÏÌÍÎÏÓÒÔ ÙÚ
ÛŸß / ↵→⊔▬□

The quick brown fox obfuscated the lazy dog...

6-9 *The high-order characters in a commercial font.*

In theory, this means that you can use any fonts you acquire from any source in your applications without having to be concerned as to who created them. In practice, there are two catches to this. The first is that while the design of a font cannot be copyrighted, its name most certainly can be. The commercial trade names of fonts such as Helvetica and Times Roman cannot be used without the authorization of their owners. In this case, their owner is the International Typeface Corporation, which as of this writing is owned by Letraset.

Applications that want to use these fonts without having them licensed can do so, provided they name the fonts differently. By convention, the Helvetica font is usually known by the pseudonym Swiss and the Times Roman font by the pseudonym Dutch. The origins of these names are a bit obscure. The Helvetti were an ancient Celtic tribe who inhabited what is now Switzerland. The Times Roman font is referred to as a "serif" font—the little picks at the ends of the characters in Times Roman are called serifs. The word serif is derived from the Dutch word *shreef*, which means "stroke."

As an aside, while it's wholly illegal to sell an application that uses copyrighted font names without the permission of the owners of the copyright, you can name the fonts you use "in house" anything you like. As such, you can rename fonts like Swiss and Dutch to Helvetica and Times Roman, so long as you don't distribute them this way. You can also provide the users of your applications with a way to do this.

The second catch in using commercial fonts is a bit less well-defined. Not all law suits are undertaken because the instigator of the suit thinks they're right. Sometimes they just think they have enough money to make sure they'll win. The Apple Corporation, for example, has a history of suing much smaller companies for alleged copyright and patent violations knowing that the defendants in such cases won't have anywhere near the financial resources to weather such a suit.

Consider that Apple attempted to sue Microsoft and Hewlett Packard over their Windows and New Wave user interfaces respectively, on the grounds that they looked and felt too much like the Macintosh Finder. Apple had, in fact, abstracted the look and feel of the Finder from Xerox some years before.

This is an area where common sense can keep you out of trouble far more readily than a lawyer can. It's both unwise and arguably unethical to use someone else's fonts to write applications that compete with them. It would not be a particularly good idea to use the fonts that come with Ventura Publisher to write your own desktop publishing package, for example.

As a final note on this issue, you'll probably observe that some PC-based applications use real copyrighted font names, such as Times Roman and Helvetica, and some use pseudonyms, such as Swiss and Dutch. In most cases, this has to do with the sorts of printers they'll be driving. When Adobe, the creators of the PostScript printer language, set out to write PostScript, they licensed the font designs and names for a number of typefaces from the International Typeface Corporation. This included Helvetica and Times Roman. Since that time, Adobe has gone on to license hundreds of other traditional faces for release as PostScript fonts. You can buy a CD-ROM of these faces as the Adobe Typeface Library.

Because PostScript devices are the primary laser printers for Macintosh systems, Mac applications tend to use the PostScript typeface names.

When Hewlett Packard created its LaserJet laser printers—the other sort of laser printers commonly used by PC systems—it did not license its fonts from anyone. It created similar fonts of its own. As such, applications that print to a LaserJet typically do not come with fonts having "real" names.

Where font resources come from

The quickest way to obtain a modest selection of screen fonts for your own applications is to abstract them from the Desktop Paint resources files. Use RMOVER to extract each of the FONT resources to individual resources, and then add them all back into a single common resource file. While a bit time-consuming— taking as much as several minutes if you don't type particularly quickly—it's a great deal easier than all the other approaches to obtaining fonts.

The only limitation in this is that there's a fairly restricted range of fonts included with the Desktop Paint packages. If you'd like to expand on the font selection, you'll have to quest further afield.

As was noted at the beginning of this chapter, there are no commercial sources of bitmapped screen fonts for PC applications *per se*, as there are for the Macintosh. There are, however, several applications that use screen fonts in proprietary formats. As such, you can obtain screen fonts by converting them from the forms they're used in commercially to the resource format examined in this chapter.

There are three utilities provided with the companion disk for this book that will handle this conversion. They're part of the RESTOOLS.ZIP archive. Specifically, the MAC2FONT.EXE program will convert Macintosh fonts into FONT resource files. The GEM2FONT.EXE program will convert the screen fonts used by the GEM version of Ventura Publisher, as well as the fonts of several other GEM-based applications. The WIN2FONT.EXE program will convert Windows FNT files. All three probably deserve a bit more explanation.

While the inner workings of these programs will not be covered in detail in this chapter, note that their source code is presented in *Graphical User Interface Programming*, should you want to see what they're up to.

Converting GEM screen fonts

Ventura Publisher has evolved into a fairly enormous application for Windows and OS/2, but it began life running under a modified version of the Digital Research GEM environment, its authors having begun work on the project when they were employees of Digital Research. Its authors have now gone on to do other things, and Ventura Publisher is owned by Xerox as of this writing.

While the Windows version of Ventura Publisher is considerably more capable than its GEM-based forbearer, it's also quite a bit slower, as Windows applications are wont to be. In addition, it requires an order of magnitude more hardware resources. As such, the GEM version of Ventura persists.

Unlike Windows applications, which are able to call upon the TrueType font manager to whistle up some screen fonts when they're called for, GEM requires that all fonts be provided as individual font files. In order to be able to display fonts on screen, the GEM version of Ventura Publisher is accompanied by several dozen screen font files, all having the extension EGA or VGA, depending upon the type of display card you installed the software for.

Note that Ventura uses the EGA and VGA extensions for screen drivers as well.

Figure 6-10 illustrates the compliment of screen fonts available under Ventura Publisher if you've installed the package for a PostScript printer.

You can convert any GEM Ventura screen font into a font resource file using the GEM2FONT.EXE utility, as found in the RESTOOLS.ZIP archive on the companion disk for this book. In this example, we'll look at converting the DUTCV36N.VGA Ventura screen font into DUTCH36.RES.

To begin with, note that you can work out quite a lot about the Ventura screen fonts from their file names. The first four characters are a truncation of the name of the font in the file—DUTC for Dutch, SWIS for Swiss, COUR for Courier, and so on. The digits are the point size. The last character in the name is the effect—N stands for Normal. In theory, there could be other effects, such as I for Italic or B for bold, but these usually don't turn up. Ventura creates italic and bold fonts internally from the corresponding normal fonts.

The file DUTCV36N.VGA contains the 36-point Dutch screen font. To convert it to a usable FONT resource, you would do this:

```
GEM2FONT DUTCV36N.VGA DUTCH36.RES /F14 /P36 /NDutch
```

8 point Helvetica

8 point Helvetica

9 point Helvetica

10 point Helvetica

11 point Helvetica

12 point Helvetica

14 point Helvetica

16 point Helvetica

18 point Helvetica

20 point Helvetica

22 point Helvetica

24 point Helvetica

28 point Helvetica

36 point Helvetica

36 point Times Roman

28 point Times Roman

24 point Times Roman

22 point Times Roman

20 point Times Roman

18 point Times Roman

16 point Times Roman

14 point Times Roman

12 point Times Roman

11 point Times Roman

10 point Times Roman

9 point Times Roman

8 point Times Roman

```
12 point Courier
```

20 point Courier

24 point Courier

6-10   *The GEM Ventura Publisher screen fonts.*

The first argument to GEM2FONT is the name of the source GEM screen font file. The second argument is the name of the resource file to be written. The /F14 argument defines the font number for the resource. By convention, this will be 14 for Times Roman, or Dutch, and 2 for Helvetica, or Swiss. Of course, you can use any number you like—the range is 0 through 255. You should make certain you use the same number for all the point sizes in a font family, however.

The /P option defines the point size and the /N option defines the name of the font. You could make this /NTimesRoman if you wanted to, assuming the font will be exclusively for your own use.

If you look at the resulting DUTCH36.RES file with SEEFONT, you should see a screen like the one in FIG. 6-11.

Aside from the fonts that come with Ventura Publisher—a fairly pedestrian appointment of typefaces—there are all sorts of other screen fonts available as GEM font files. Most of the manufacturers of third-party printer fonts for Ventura accompanied them with corresponding screen fonts. You'll also find Ventura fonts, complete with their corresponding screen fonts, on bulletin boards.

```
         FONT NAME: Dutch          BITMAP WIDTH: 4339
       FONT NUMBER: 245            BITMAP BYTES: 544
        POINT SIZE: 36
        FONT DEPTH: 55
   WIDEST CHARACTER: 61
```

!"#$%&'()*+,-./01234
56789:;<=>?@ABCDE
FGHIJKLMNOPQRST
UVWXYZ[\]^_'abcdefg
hijklmnopqrstuvwxyz{|}

6-11 *The 36-point Dutch font from Ventura.*

Microsoft Windows has a long and oftentimes conflicting history of font formats. The present Windows 3.1 package includes the TrueType font manager, which maintains its fonts as vector outline files which are scaled internally when they're required as screen or printer fonts. Creating the equivalent of the TrueType manager is well beyond the scope of this book.

Prior to the appearance of TrueType, Windows applications found their fonts where they could. Some, such as Corel Draw, used proprietary font formats. The Adobe Type Manager package allowed type one PostScript fonts to be used as screen fonts. In the absence of any other alternative, Windows came with a selection of bitmapped screen fonts. These were created as FNT files, which were in turn compiled into FON resource files.

The WIN2FONT.EXE utility will convert Windows FNT files to FONT resources. Its syntax is identical to that of GEM2FONT.

While FNT files do exist, they're nowhere near as common as they once were. With the introduction of TrueType, there has been a decreasing interest in dedicated bitmapped screen fonts for Windows.

Converting windows FNT files

Converting Macintosh FONT resources

The most fertile source of bitmapped screen fonts is arguably a Macintosh. Because the Macintosh embodies font support in its operating system, creating a common pool of fonts for applications to draw on, it has been practical to offer third-party screen fonts for use with the Mac. There are a lot of commercial font packages for the Macintosh, and buckets of fonts floating about in the public domain.

In many cases, you needn't actually have anything to do with a Macintosh to use Mac fonts.

The file structure of a Macintosh is fundamentally different than that of a PC. Every file is said to have two *forks*, or sections: the *data* fork and the *resource* fork. The data fork contains unstructured data, such as a bitmapped image or the text of a word processing document. The resource fork contains resources, similar in concept to the font resources that have been examined in this chapter. Note, however, that the internal structure of Macintosh resources is completely different.

Macintosh applications themselves are structured as lots of blocks of code stored as resources.

When a Macintosh application is ported to another system, a way must be found to preserve the two-fork structure of a Mac file in a universe that gets along quite well with one fork. There are several ways to manage this, depending on the medium used to export files from a Macintosh. Exporting a Mac file over a local area network, such as TOPS, will typically leave you with two files—one for the data fork and one for the resource fork. Exporting a Mac file over a serial cable or a modem will usually combine the two files into one, with a header preceding them to assist in their subsequent restoration should the file be returned to a Macintosh. This header is known informally as a "Macbinary" header.

Macintosh users can store files in archives similar in concept to ZIP files. The most popular application for doing this on a Macintosh is a shareware package called StuffIt, written by Raymond Lau. It produces files with the extension SIT. StuffIt archives are often found on bulletin boards.

There are several PC utilities that will unpack a StuffIt file into something that's useful on a PC. One of these is UnStuffit, written by R. Scott McGinnis of

Caber Software
P.O. Box 3607 Mdse Mart
Chicago, IL 60654-0607

The UnStuffIt utility offers a number of options that will make working with Macintosh fonts a great deal easier. UnStuffIt can be found on most large bulletin boards.

If you have UnStuffIt and a modem, you should be able to find a considerable wealth of public domain fonts in the Macintosh conferences of most large bulletin boards. Note that Macintosh applications frequently include fonts built into themselves.

Figure 6-12 illustrates some Macintosh fonts I found over about an hour of browsing.

24 POINT EIRE

36 point Atlantis

24 point Italy

24 point Bell Medium

24 POINT ZIRKLE

24 POINT CRYPT

36 point CDeath

12 point Calcutta

12 point Cape

6-12
*Some Macintosh fonts from
a bulletin board.*

Once you've found a SIT file that contains Macintosh fonts—or, more properly, Macintosh FONT resources—you can convert them to FONT resources for use with the functions in this chapter as follows. Begin by extracting the font files from a SIT—when UnStuffIt prompts you to include a Macbinary header, answer "yes." Next, use the MAC2FONT utility from the RESTOOLS.ZIP archive on the companion disk of this book to convert the Macintosh font resource to individual font resource files with the extension RES.

Because a Macintosh font resource file will usually contain multiple fonts, MAC2FONT only requires one command line argument—that of the extracted Macintosh font resource file to be unpacked, as generated by UnStuffIt. It will then prompt you for the other information it requires for each font to be extracted—specifically, the name, point size, font number, and RES file name for each entry in the original file. Make sure you use the same font number for the various members of the same font family.

If you have access to a Macintosh and a way to port Mac files to a PC, you can also work with some of the commercial Macintosh fonts and with the Mac system fonts if you like. Macintosh fonts are stored in files with the icons illustrated in FIG. 6-13.

Use the Macintosh Font DA Mover application to copy the fonts you want to use in a Mac font file to a new file. It's a good idea to keep the size of the font files you create to no more than about 200K each; you can, of course, create lots of font files. Create a StuffIt archive with your new font files using the Macintosh StuffIt

Old font file icon

6-13

The icons used to indicate font files on a Macintosh.

New font file icon

application and port the archives to a PC. You can treat the ported files as you would SIT files downloaded from a bulletin board.

My favorite Macintosh font collection—all of it suitable for porting to a PC—is Cassady and Greene's *Fluent Fonts* package. The commercial font examples in this chapter were drawn from it.

You'll probably find that it takes a bit of experience to work with Macintosh font files. The tools involved and the procedures for creating workable FONT resources might seem a bit funky at first. You'll likely find this to be especially true if making off with fonts leads you to work with a Macintosh for the first time. Some of the newer models come with self-adhesive mice, such that having touched one you'll require the assistance of a good surgeon to extricate yourself from the system.

Font display functions

The code in this chapter will provide your programs with a single principal function, DrawFontString. Passed a string to draw, the coordinates to draw it at, the color the text is to appear in and a pointer to a FONT object, it will draw the text on the screen. This chapter will look at three variations on this function, one each for the 16, 256, and high-color modes.

As an aside, these functions have been written by transliterating the C language DrawFontString code dealt with earlier in this chapter. If you're interested in digging through the assembly language version of DrawFontString in detail, you should be able to recognize the original structure of the C code. Of course, the assembly language implementation does run a fair bit faster.

Figure 6-14 illustrates the 16-color version of DrawFontString. This block of code is intended to be used as a complete assembly language module called FONT-16.ASM. It makes calls to some of the functions in MOUSE16.ASM. If you want to, you can simply move the DrawFontString code to MOUSE16.ASM.

If you understood how the C language DrawFontString function worked, you should have no difficulty with its assembly language counterpart. Alternately, of course, you can just use the code and not bother understanding what it's up to.

Figure 6-15 illustrates a C language calling program to make DrawFontString do something interesting. This program is called TESTF16.C. It expects to find the DTPE.RES file from Desktop Paint 16 in the current directory; make sure you extract this from the DTPE10.ZIP file on the companion disk for this book before you run the TESTF16 program. It will search through DTPE.RES, find all the FONT resources, and display some text in each on the screen.

```
;                   Font Functions for 16-colour
;                   Super VGA graphics
;

_AOFF            EQU      6          ;STACK OFFSET TO FIRST ARG

MINFONTCHAR      EQU      0          ;LOWEST NUMBER FOR A FONT
                                     ;CHARACTER
MAXFONTCHAR      EQU      255        ;HIGHEST NUMBER FOR A FOTN
                                     ;CHARACTER
FONTNAMESIZE     EQU      32         ;MAXIMUM SIZE OF A FONT NAME

FONT             STRUC
                 FN_NAME        DB      (FONTNAMESIZE+1) DUP (?)
                 FN_NUMBER      DB      ?
                 FN_POINTSIZE   DB      ?
                 FN_CHARWIDE    DB      (MAXFONTCHAR-MINFONTCHAR+1) DUP (?)
                 FN_CHAROFF     DW      (MAXFONTCHAR-MINFONTCHAR+1) DUP (?)
                 FN_BITMAPWIDTH DW      ?
                 FN_BITMAPDEPTH DW      ?
                 FN_BITMAPBYTES DW      ?
                 FN_WIDESTCHAR  DW      ?
                 FN_PADWIDTH    DW      ?
                 FN_SPACEWIDTH  DW      ?
FONT             ENDS

;THIS MACRO FETCHES THE DATA SEGEMENT
LDATASEG         MACRO
                 PUSH     AX
                 MOV      AX,_DATA
                 MOV      DS,AX
                 POP      AX
                 ENDM

;SET THE CURRENT WRITE MODE
SETWRITEMODE     MACRO    ARG
                 PUSH     AX
                 PUSH     DX
                 MOV      DX,03CEH
                 MOV      AL,05H
                 OUT      DX,AL
                 MOV      DX,03CFH
                 MOV      AL,ARG
                 OUT      DX,AL
                 POP      DX
                 POP      AX
                 ENDM

;SET THE WRITE MASK
SETBITMASK       MACRO    ARG
                 PUSH     AX
                 PUSH     DX
                 PUSH     AX
                 MOV      DX,03CEH
```

6-14
The source code for
FONT-16.ASM.

```
6-14          MOV     AL,08H
Continued.    OUT     DX,AL
              POP     AX
              MOV     DX,03CFH
              MOV     AL,ARG
              OUT     DX,AL
              POP     DX
              POP     AX
              ENDM

;DO A LONG LOOP
LNGLOOP       MACRO   ARG1
              LOCAL   LAB1
              DEC     CX
              CMP     CX,0000H
              JE      LAB1
              JMP     ARG1
LAB1:
              ENDM

DRAWFN_CB       EQU     2
DRAWFN_CP       EQU     4
DRAWFN_KL       EQU     6
DRAWFN_J        EQU     8
DRAWFN_I        EQU     10
DRAWFN_N        EQU     12
DRAWFN_BMPOFF   EQU     14
DRAWFN_BMPSEG   EQU     16
DRAWFN_PR       EQU     18
DRAWFN_ADJUST   EQU     20

              EXTRN HIDECURSOR:FAR
              EXTRN SHOWCURSOR:FAR

FONT16_TEXT     SEGMENT BYTE PUBLIC ´CODE´
              ASSUME  CS:FONT16_TEXT,DS:_DATA

;             ARG1 = X
;             ARG2 = Y
;             ARG3 = STRING
;             ARG4 = COLOUR
;             ARG6 = FONT
              PUBLIC  _DrawFontString
_DrawFontString PROC    FAR
              PUSH    BP
              MOV     BP,SP
              SUB     SP,DRAWFN_ADJUST
              PUSH    DS
              PUSH    ES

              LDATASEG

              CALL    HIDECURSOR
              SETWRITEMODE    2
```

```
                ;POINT TO THE SCREEN SEGMENT
                MOV     AX,[_SCREENSEG]
                MOV     ES,AX

                ;FETCH THE STRING
                MOV     SI,[BP + _AOFF + 4]
                MOV     DS,[BP + _AOFF + 6]

                ;SEE HOW LONG IT IS
                MOV     WORD PTR [BP - DRAWFN_N],0000H
DF1:            LODSB
                CMP     AL,00H
                JE      DF2

                INC     WORD PTR [BP - DRAWFN_N]
                JMP     DF1

                ;FETCH THE FONT POINTER
DF2:            MOV     SI,[BP + _AOFF + 10]
                MOV     DS,[BP + _AOFF + 12]

                ;SAVE A POINTER TO THE FONT BITMAP
                MOV     [BP - DRAWFN_BMPOFF],SI
                MOV     [BP - DRAWFN_BMPSEG],DS
                ADD     WORD PTR [BP - DRAWFN_BMPOFF],SIZE FONT

                ;GET THE FONT DEPTH
                MOV     CX,DS:[SI + FN_BITMAPDEPTH]
                MOV     WORD PTR [BP - DRAWFN_I],0000H

DF3:            PUSH    CX

                ;FETCH A POINTER TO THE CURRENT SCREEN LINE
                LDATASEG
                MOV     BX,[BP + _AOFF + 2]
                MOV     AX,[BP - DRAWFN_I]
                ADD     BX,AX
                SHL     BX,1
                MOV     AX,[_SCREENTBL + BX]
                MOV     [BP - DRAWFN_PR],AX

                ;FETCH THE LEFT COORDINATE
                MOV     AX,[BP + _AOFF + 0]
                MOV     [BP - DRAWFN_CB],AX

                MOV     CX,[BP - DRAWFN_N]
                MOV     WORD PTR [BP - DRAWFN_J],0000H
DF4:            PUSH    CX

                ;FETCH A CHARACTER FROM THE STRING
                MOV     SI,[BP + _AOFF + 4]
                MOV     DS,[BP + _AOFF + 6]
                MOV     BX,[BP - DRAWFN_J]
                MOV     AL,DS:[SI + BX]
```

```
                        ;FETCH A POINTER TO THE FONT
                        MOV    SI,[BP + _AOFF + 10]
                        MOV    DS,[BP + _AOFF + 12]

                        ;CHECK FOR SPACE CHARACTER
                        CMP    AL,20H
                        JNE    DF5

                        ;IF IT'S A SPACE, JUST PAD RIGHT AND CONTINUE
                        MOV    AX,[BP - DRAWFN_CB]
                        ADD    AX,DS:[SI + FN_SPACEWIDTH]
                        ADD    AX,DS:[SI + FN_PADWIDTH]
                        MOV    [BP - DRAWFN_CB],AX
                        JMP    DF8

                        ;IF IT'S NOT A SPACE, DRAW THE CHARACTER
DF5:                    MOV    BL,AL
                        AND    BX,00FFH

                        MOV    AL,DS:[SI + FN_CHARWIDE + BX]
                        AND    AX,00FFH
                        MOV    [BP - DRAWFN_KL],AX

                        SHL    BX,1
                        MOV    AX,DS:[SI + FN_CHAROFF + BX]
                        MOV    [BP - DRAWFN_CP],AX

                        ;LOOP FOR THE CHARACTER WIDTH
                        MOV    CX,[BP - DRAWFN_KL]
DF6:                    PUSH   CX

                        ;SEE IF THIS BIT IS SET IN THE CHARACTER BITMAP
                        LDATASEG
                        MOV    BX,[BP - DRAWFN_CP]
                        AND    BX,0007H
                        MOV    AL,[_MASKTABLE + BX]

                        MOV    SI,[BP - DRAWFN_BMPOFF]
                        MOV    DS,[BP - DRAWFN_BMPSEG]
                        MOV    BX,[BP - DRAWFN_CP]
                        MOV    CL,3
                        SHR    BX,CL
                        TEST   DS:[SI + BX],AL
                        JZ     DF7

                        ;IT'S SET - DRAW THE PIXEL
                        LDATASEG
                        MOV    BX,[BP - DRAWFN_CB]
                        AND    BX,0007H
                        MOV    AH,[_MASKTABLE + BX]
                        SETBITMASK    AH

                        ;GET A POINTER TO THE LINE
                        MOV    BX,[BP - DRAWFN_CB]
```

```
               MOV     CL,3
               SHR     BX,CL
               MOV     DI,[BP - DRAWFN_PR]

               MOV     AX,[BP + _AOFF + 8]
               MOV     AH,ES:[DI + BX]
               MOV     ES:[DI + BX],AL

DF7:           INC     WORD PTR [BP - DRAWFN_CB]
               INC     WORD PTR [BP - DRAWFN_CP]

               POP     CX
               LOOP    DF6

               ;PAD OVER BY THE PAD WIDTH
               MOV     SI,[BP + _AOFF + 10]
               MOV     DS,[BP + _AOFF + 12]
               MOV     AX,DS:[SI + FN_PADWIDTH]
               ADD     [BP - DRAWFN_CB],AX

DF8:           POP     CX
               INC     WORD PTR [BP - DRAWFN_J]
               LNGLOOP DF4

               ;POINT TO THE NEXT LINE OF THE FONT BITMAP
               MOV     SI,[BP + _AOFF + 10]
               MOV     DS,[BP + _AOFF + 12]
               MOV     AX,DS:[SI + FN_BITMAPBYTES]
               ADD     [BP - DRAWFN_BMPOFF],AX

               POP     CX
               INC     WORD PTR [BP - DRAWFN_I]

               ;MAKE SURE WE WON'T BE WRITING PAST THE END OF THE SCREEN
               LDATASEG
               MOV     AX,[BP + _AOFF + 2]
               ADD     AX,[BP - DRAWFN_I]
               CMP     AX,[_SCREENDEEP]
               JGE     DF9

               LNGLOOP DF3

               ;RESTORE THE BIT MASK TO ALL BITS ON
DF9:           SETBITMASK      0FFH

               ;RESTORE WRITE MODE ZERO
               SETWRITEMODE    0

               LDATASEG
               CALL    SHOWCURSOR

               POP     ES
               POP     DS
               ADD     SP,DRAWFN_ADJUST
               POP     BP
```

```
                           RET
_DrawFontString ENDP

FONT16_TEXT        ENDS

DGROUP             GROUP   _DATA,_BSS
_DATA              SEGMENT WORD PUBLIC 'DATA'

                   EXTRN _SCREENTBL:WORD
                   EXTRN _SCREENSEG:WORD
                   EXTRN _SCREENBYTES:WORD
                   EXTRN _SCREENWIDE:WORD
                   EXTRN _SCREENDEEP:WORD
                   EXTRN _MASKTABLE:BYTE
                   EXTRN _BITTABLE:BYTE

_DATA              ENDS

_BSS               SEGMENT WORD PUBLIC 'BSS'

_BSS               ENDS

                   END
```

```
/*
            Using fonts in sixteen colors

            Copyright (c) 1992 Alchemy Mindworks Inc.

            Links to MOUSE16.ASM
            Links to FONT-16.ASM
*/

#include "stdio.h"
#include "dos.h"
#include "alloc.h"
#include "mouse16.h"

#define MINFONTCHAR     0          /* lowest number font character */
#define MAXFONTCHAR     255        /* highest number font character */
#define FONTNAMESIZE    32         /* maximum size of a font name */

#define BADRECNUM       0xffffffffL    /* illegal record number */

typedef struct {
        char name[FONTNAMESIZE+1];
        char number;
        char pointsize;
        char charwide[(MAXFONTCHAR-MINFONTCHAR)+1];
        unsigned int charoff[(MAXFONTCHAR-MINFONTCHAR)+1];
        unsigned int bitmapwidth;
        unsigned int bitmapdepth;
```

```
              unsigned int bitmapbytes;
              unsigned int widestchar;
              unsigned int padwidth;
              unsigned int spacewidth;
              } FONT;

typedef struct {
              char id[8];
              char description[65];
              unsigned int count;
              } RESHEAD;

typedef struct {
              char type[4];
              unsigned long number;
              unsigned int size;
              } RESOURCE;

typedef struct  {
              char manufacturer;
              char version;
              char encoding;
              char bits_per_pixel;
              int xmin,ymin;
              int xmax,ymax;
              int hres;
              int vres;
              char palette[48];
              char reserved;
              char colour_planes;
              int bytes_per_line;
              int palette_type;
              char filler[58];
              } PCXHEAD;

/* colours in this sixteen-colour palette */
#define BLACK            0
#define BLU              1
#define GREEN            2
#define CYAN             3
#define RED              4
#define MAGENTA          5
#define YELLOW           6
#define GREY             7
#define DARKGREY         8
#define LIGHTGREY        9
#define LIGHTBLUE        10
#define LIGHTGREEN       11
#define LIGHTRED         12
#define LIGHTYELLOW      13
#define LIGHTMAGENTA     14
#define WHITE            15

#define RESID            "ALCHRSRC"
#define FONTFILE         "DTPE.RES"
```

```
#define FONTID          "FONT"

void DrawFontString(unsigned int x,unsigned int y,char *string,\
                    unsigned int colour,FONT *font);
FONT *loadfont(char *s,unsigned long n);
unsigned long *countfonts(char *s);

/* the sixteen-colour palette we'll use */
char palette[] = {
        0x00,0x00,0x00,
        0x00,0x00,0xaa,
        0x00,0xaa,0x00,
        0x00,0xaa,0xaa,
        0xaa,0x00,0x00,
        0xaa,0x00,0xaa,
        0xaa,0xaa,0x00,
        0xaa,0xaa,0xaa,
        0x55,0x55,0x55,
        0xcc,0xcc,0xcc,
        0x00,0x00,0xff,
        0x00,0xff,0x00,
        0xff,0x00,0x00,
        0xff,0xff,0x00,
        0xff,0x00,0xff,
        0xff,0xff,0xff
        };

unsigned int oldvesamode=0xffff;

main(argc,argv)
        int argc;
        char *argv[];
{
        static char colourtable[8]= {
                BLACK,RED,LIGHTRED,LIGHTYELLOW,
                LIGHTBLUE,YELLOW,GREEN,DARKGREY
        };

        FONT *thefont;
        BUTTON save,quit;
        POINT p;
        char b[128];
        unsigned long *lp;
        int i=10,j=0,k,n=0,alive=1,thiscard=VGA;

        if((lp=countfonts(FONTFILE))== NULL || lp[0]==BADRECNUM) {
                puts("Can't find fonts");
                exit(1);
        }

        /* see what kind of card is installed -- sort of */
        if(argc > 1) {
                if(!stricmp(argv[1],"PARADISE")) thiscard=PARADISE;
                else if(!stricmp(argv[1],"ATI")) thiscard=ATI;
                else if(!stricmp(argv[1],"TSENG")) thiscard=TSENG;
```

```
              else if(!stricmp(argv[1],"TRIDENT")) thiscard=TRIDENT;
              else if(!stricmp(argv[1],"OAK")) thiscard=OAK;
              else if(!stricmp(argv[1],"VESA")) thiscard=VESA;
      }

      /* go for a graphics mode */
      if(!GraphicMode(thiscard)) {
              TextMode(thiscard);
              exit(1);
      }

      /* set the palette */
      SetVgaPalette(palette,16);

      /* clear the screen */
      ClearScreen(LIGHTGREY);

      /* show the fonts */
      do {
              if((thefont=loadfont(FONTFILE,lp[n++])) != NULL) {
                      sprintf(b,"This is %u point %s",
                          thefont->pointsize,thefont->name);
                      k=(SCREENWIDE-FontStringLength(b,thefont))/2;
                      DrawFontString(k,i,b,colourtable[j % 8],thefont);
                      i+=thefont->bitmapdepth;
                      free((char *)thefont);
                      ++j;
              }
      } while(lp[n] != BADRECNUM && thefont != NULL && i < SCREENDEEP);

      free((char *)lp);

      /* create a button to click on */
      MakeButton(SCREENWIDE-100,SCREENDEEP-60,"Quit",&quit);
      DrawButton(&quit);

      MakeButton(SCREENWIDE-200,SCREENDEEP-60,"Save",&save);
      DrawButton(&save);

      /* loop 'til we're done */
      do {
              /* look for a mouse click */
              if(MouseDown(&p)) {
                      if(PointInRect(&p,&quit)) {
                              TrackButton(&quit);
                              alive=0;
                      }
                      else if(PointInRect(&p,&save)) {
                              TrackButton(&save);
                              DoSave("SCREEN00.PCX");
                      }
              }
      } while(alive);

      TextMode(thiscard);
```

```
/* save the screen to a PCX file */
DoSave(path)
        char *path;
{

        PCXHEAD pcx;
        FILE *fp;
        char *p;
        unsigned int i,j,n;

        /* create the destination file */
        if((fp=fopen(path,"wb"))==NULL) {
                beep();
                return;
        }

        memset((char *)&pcx,0,sizeof(PCXHEAD));
        memcpy(pcx.palette,palette,48);

        pcx.manufacturer=10;
        pcx.encoding=1;
        pcx.xmin=pcx.ymin=0;
        pcx.xmax=SCREENWIDE-1;
        pcx.ymax=SCREENDEEP-1;
        pcx.palette_type=1;
        pcx.bits_per_pixel=1;
        pcx.version=2;
        pcx.colour_planes=4;
        pcx.bytes_per_line=SCREENBYTES;

        WaitCursor();
        if(fwrite((char *)&pcx,1,sizeof(PCXHEAD),fp) != sizeof(PCXHEAD)) {
                fclose(fp);
                remove(path);
                ArrowCursor();
                beep();
                return;
        }

        for(i=0;i<SCREENDEEP;++i) {
                p=MK_FP(SCREENSEG,SCREENTBL[i]);
                MouseOff();
                for(j=0;j<4;++j) {
                        egareadplane(j);
                        n=pcxwriteline(fp,p,pcx.bytes_per_line);

                        if(n != pcx.bytes_per_line) {
                                fclose(fp);
                                remove(path);
                                MouseOn();
                                ArrowCursor();
                                beep();
                                return;
                        }
```

```
                }
                MouseOn();
        }
        ArrowCursor();
        fclose(fp);
}

/* write one pcx line */
pcxwriteline(fp,p,n)
        FILE *fp;
        char *p;
        unsigned int n;
{
        unsigned int i=0,j=0,t=0;

        do {
                i=0;
                while((p[t+i]==p[t+i+1]) && ((t+i) < n) && (i < 63))++i;
                if(i>0) {
                        if(fputc(i | 0xc0,fp)==EOF) return(-1);
                        if(fputc(p[t],fp)==EOF) return(-1);
                        t+=i;
                        j+=2;
                }
                else {
                        if(((p[t]) & 0xc0)==0xc0) {
                                if(fputc(0xc1,fp)==EOF) return(-1);
                                ++j;
                        }
                        if(fputc(p[t++],fp)==EOF) return(-1);
                        ++j;
                }
        } while(t<n);
        return(n);
}


FontStringLength(s,font)
        char *s;
        FONT *font;
{
        unsigned int a=0;

        /* add up the character widths of all the characters in the string */
        while(*s) a+=font->charwide[*s++];
        return(a);
}

unsigned long *countfonts(s)
        char *s;
{
        RESHEAD rh;
        RESOURCE rc;
        unsigned long *lp;
        FILE *fp;
```

```
            unsigned int i,j;

            /* open the resource file */
            if((fp=fopen(s,"rb")) == NULL) return(NULL);

            /* read the header */
            if(fread((char *)&rh,1,sizeof(RESHEAD),fp) != sizeof(RESHEAD)) {
                    fclose(fp);
                    return(NULL);
            }

            /* make sure it's a resource file */
            if(memcmp(rh.id,RESID,8)) {
                    fclose(fp);
                    return(NULL);
            }

            /* allocate a buffer for the numbers */
            if((lp=(unsigned long *)malloc((1+rh.count)*sizeof(unsigned long))) == NULL) {
                fclose(fp);
                return(NULL);
            }

            /* set the end of the buffer */
            lp[0]=BADRECNUM;

            /* step through each resource */
            for(i=j=0;i<rh.count;++i) {

                    /* fetch the resource */
                    if(fread((char *)&rc,1,sizeof(RESOURCE),fp) != sizeof(RESOURCE)) {
                            fclose(fp);
                            return(lp);
                    }

                    /* if it's a font, add it to the list */
                    if(!memcmp(rc.type,FONTID,4)) {
                            lp[j++]=rc.number;
                            lp[j]=BADRECNUM;
                    }

                    /* seek to the next resource */
                    fseek(fp,(unsigned long)rc.size,SEEK_CUR);
            }

            fclose(fp);
            return(lp);
    }

FONT *loadfont(s,n)
        char *s;
        unsigned long n;
    {
        RESHEAD rh;
        RESOURCE rc;
```

```
FONT *font;
FILE *fp;
unsigned int i;

/* open the resource file */
if((fp=fopen(s,"rb")) == NULL) return(NULL);

/* read the header */
if(fread((char *)&rh,1,sizeof(RESHEAD),fp) != sizeof(RESHEAD)) {
        fclose(fp);
        return(NULL);
}

/* make sure it's a resource file */
if(memcmp(rh.id,RESID,8)) {
        fclose(fp);
        return(NULL);
}

/* look at all the resources */
for(i=0;i<rh.count;++i) {

        /* fetch the resource */
        if(fread((char *)&rc,1,sizeof(RESOURCE),fp) != sizeof(RESOURCE)) {
                fclose(fp);
                return(NULL);
        }

        /* if it's a font and it's the one we want, load it */
        if(!memcmp(rc.type,FONTID,4) && rc.number == n) {

                /* allocate a buffer for the data */
                if((font=(FONT *)malloc(rc.size)) == NULL) {
                        fclose(fp);
                        return(NULL);
                }

                /* read the data */
                if(fread((char *)font,1,rc.size,fp) != rc.size) {
                        free((char *)font);
                        fclose(fp);
                        return(NULL);
                }

                /* we're done -- go away */
                fclose(fp);
                return(font);
        }

        /* otherwise, seek to the next resource */
        fseek(fp,(unsigned long)rc.size,SEEK_CUR);
}

/* resource not found */
fclose(fp);
```

```
                    return(NULL);
            }

    GraphicMode(card)
            unsigned int card;
    {
            union REGS r;
            struct SREGS sr;
            VESAINFO vi;
            VESABLOCK vb;
            unsigned int i;

            if(card==VGA) {
                    r.x.ax=card;
                    int86(0x10,&r,&r);
                    SCREENWIDE=640;
                    SCREENDEEP=480;
                    SCREENBYTES=80;
                    for(i=0;i<SCREENDEEP;++i) SCREENTBL[i]=i*SCREENBYTES;
            }
            else if(card==VESA) {
                    /* check for a VESA BIOS */
                    r.x.ax=0x4f00;
                    r.x.di=FP_OFF((char *)&vb);
                    sr.es=FP_SEG((char *)&vb);
                    int86x(0x10,&r,&r,&sr);
                    if(r.x.ax != 0x004f) return(0);

                    /* see if this mode is supported */
                    while(*vb.videomode != VESA && *vb.videomode != 0xffff)
                        (vb.videomode)++;

                    if(*vb.videomode == 0xffff) return(0);

                    /* get the VESA information */
                    r.x.ax=0x4f01;
                    r.x.cx=VESA;
                    r.x.di=FP_OFF((char *)&vi);
                    sr.es=FP_SEG((char *)&vi);
                    int86x(0x10,&r,&r,&sr);

                    /* set the screen segment */
                    SCREENSEG=vi.windowsegment_a;

                    /* get the current mode */
                    r.x.ax=0x4f03;
                    int86(0x10,&r,&r);
                    oldvesamode=r.x.bx;

                    /* set the new mode */
                    r.x.ax=0x4f02;
                    r.x.bx=VESA;
                    int86(0x10,&r,&r);
            }
            else {
```

```
                        r.x.ax=card;
                        int86(0x10,&r,&r);
            }
            return(InitMouse());
}

TextMode(card)
        unsigned int card;
{
        union REGS r;

        r.x.ax=0x1200;
        r.x.bx=0x0031;
        int86(0x10,&r,&r);

        if(card==VESA && oldvesamode != 0xffff) {
                r.x.ax=0x4f02;
                r.x.bx=oldvesamode;
                int86(0x10,&r,&r);
        }
        else {
                r.x.ax=0x0003;
                int86(0x10,&r,&r);
        }
        DeinitMouse();
}

DrawLine(left,top,right,bottom,colour)
        int left,top,right,bottom,colour;
{
        int temp,dx,dy,x,y,x_sign,y_sign,flag;

        MouseOff();
        dx = abs(right - left);
        dy = abs(bottom - top);
        if(((dx >= dy) && (left > right)) ||
           ((dy > dx) && (top > bottom))) {
                temp = left;
                left = right;
                right = temp;
                temp = top;
                top = bottom;
                bottom = temp;
        }
        if ((bottom - top) < 0) y_sign = -1;
        else y_sign = 1;
        if ((right - left) < 0) x_sign = -1;
        else x_sign = 1;
        if (dx >= dy) {
                for (x=left,y=top,flag=0; x<=right; x++,flag+=dy) {
                        if (flag>=dx) {
                                flag -= dx;
                                y+= y_sign;
                        }
                        setpixel(x,y,colour);
```

```
                                    }
                            }
                    else {
                            for (x=left,y=top,flag=0; y<=bottom; y++,flag+=dx) {
                                    if (flag>=dy) {
                                            flag -= dy;
                                            x+=x_sign;
                                    }
                                    setpixel(x,y,colour);
                            }
                    }
                    MouseOn();
            }

            #pragma warn -aus
            FillRect(left,top,right,bottom,colour)
                    int left,top,right,bottom,colour;
            {
                    char *p,bf[100];
                    int a,i,j,width,depth,bleft,bytes,xleft,xright,pleft,pright;

                    MouseOff();
                    xleft=left & 0xfff8;
                    xright=right;
                    if(xright & 0x0007) xright=(xright | 0x0007)+1;
                    width=xright-xleft;
                    depth=bottom-top;
                    bleft=xleft>3;
                    pleft=left-xleft;
                    pright=pleft+(right-left);
                    bytes=pixels2bytes(width)+1;

                    memset(bf,0,bytes);

                    for(i=pleft;i<=pright;++i) bf[i>>3] |= masktable[i & 0x0007];

                    setwritemode(2);
                    for(i=0;i<=depth;++i) {
                            p=MK_FP(SCREENSEG,SCREENTBL[top+i]+bleft);
                            for(j=0;j<bytes;++j) {
                                    setbitmask(bf[j]);
                                    a=p[j];
                                    p[j]=colour;
                            }
                    }
                    setbitmask(0xff);
                    setwritemode(0);
                    MouseOn();
            }
            #pragma warn +aus

            FrameRect(left,top,right,bottom,colour)
                    unsigned int left,top,right,bottom,colour;
            {
                    DrawLine(left,top,right,top,colour);
```

```
        DrawLine(left,bottom,right,bottom,colour);
        DrawLine(left,top,left,bottom,colour);
        DrawLine(right,top,right,bottom,colour);
}

SetVgaPalette(p,n)
        char *p;
        unsigned int n;
{
        union REGS r;
        int i;

        for(i=0;i<n;++i) {
                r.h.dh=*p++>>2;
                r.h.ch=*p++>>2;
                r.h.cl=*p++>>2;
                r.x.bx=i;
                r.x.ax=0x1010;
                int86(0x10,&r,&r);
        }

        r.x.bx=0x0000;
        for(i=0;i<n;++i) {
                r.x.ax=0x1000;
                int86(0x10,&r,&r);
                r.x.bx+=0x0101;
        }
}

MakeButton(left,top,string,button)
        unsigned int left,top;
        char *string;
        BUTTON *button;
{
        button->frame.left = left & 0xfff8;
        button->frame.right=button->frame.left+(strlen(string)<3)+16;
        button->frame.top=top;
        button->frame.bottom=button->frame.top+FONTDEPTH+8;
        button->text=string;
}

DrawButton(button)
        BUTTON *button;
{
        FillRect(button->frame.left+1,button->frame.top+1,
                button->frame.right-1,button->frame.bottom-1,WHITE);
        DrawLine(button->frame.left+1,button->frame.top,
                button->frame.right-1,button->frame.top,BLACK);
        DrawLine(button->frame.left,button->frame.top+1,
                button->frame.left,button->frame.bottom-1,BLACK);
        DrawLine(button->frame.right,button->frame.top+1,
                button->frame.right,button->frame.bottom-1,BLACK);
        DrawLine(button->frame.left+1,button->frame.bottom,
                button->frame.right-1,button->frame.bottom,BLACK);
        Fill3DBox(button->frame.left+1,button->frame.top+1,
```

```
                                    button->frame.right-1,button->frame.bottom-1);

                    DrawString(button->frame.left+8,button->frame.top+4,
                            button->text,DARKGREY,LIGHTGREY);
        }

TrackButton(button)
        BUTTON *button;
{
        POINT p;

        FillRect(button->frame.left+1,button->frame.top+1,
                button->frame.right-1,button->frame.bottom-1,LIGHTGREY);
        DrawString(button->frame.left+8,button->frame.top+4,
                button->text,DARKGREY,LIGHTGREY);
        while(MouseDown(&p));
        DrawButton(button);
}

Fill3DBox(left,top,right,bottom)
        int left,top,right,bottom;
{
        FillRect(left,top,right,bottom,LIGHTGREY);
        DrawLine(left,top,right-1,top,WHITE);
        DrawLine(left,top+1,left,bottom-1,WHITE);

        DrawLine(left+3,bottom,right,bottom,DARKGREY);
        DrawLine(right,top+2,right,bottom-1,DARKGREY);
}

PointInRect(p,r)/* return true if point is in rect */
        POINT *p;
        RECT *r;
{
        if(p->x > r->left && p->x < r->right &&
           p->y > r->top  && p->y < r->bottom) return(1);
        else return(0);
}

WaitCursor()
{
        static char cursor[] = {
                0x00,0x00,0x00,0x00,
                0x00,0x00,0x01,0x80,
                0x03,0xC0,0x07,0xE0,
                0x0F,0xF0,0x07,0xE0,
                0x03,0xC0,0x01,0x80,
                0x00,0x00,0x00,0x00,
                0x00,0x00,0x00,0x00,
                0xFF,0xFF,0xFF,0xFF,

                0x00,0x00,0xFE,0x7F,
                0x06,0x60,0x0C,0x30,
                0x18,0x18,0x30,0x0C,
                0x60,0x06,0xC0,0x03,
```

```
                    0x60,0x06,0x30,0x0C,
                    0x98,0x19,0xCC,0x33,
                    0xE6,0x67,0xFE,0x7F,
                    0x00,0x00,0x00,0x00 };

            MouseCursor(cursor,7,7);
}

ArrowCursor()
{
            static char cursor[] = {
                    0xFF,0x3F,0xFF,0x1F,
                    0xFF,0x0F,0xFF,0x07,
                    0xFF,0x03,0xFF,0x01,
                    0xFF,0x00,0x7F,0x00,
                    0x3F,0x00,0x1F,0x00,
                    0xFF,0x01,0xFF,0x10,
                    0xFF,0x30,0x7F,0xF8,
                    0x7F,0xF8,0x7F,0xFC,
                    0x00,0x00,0x00,0x40,
                    0x00,0x60,0x00,0x70,
                    0x00,0x78,0x00,0x7C,
                    0x00,0x7E,0x00,0x7F,
                    0x80,0x7F,0x00,0x7C,
                    0x00,0x6C,0x00,0x46,
                    0x00,0x06,0x00,0x03,
                    0x00,0x03,0x00,0x00 };

            MouseCursor(cursor,0,0);
}
```

The result should look something like FIG. 6-1, back at the beginning of this chapter. The fonts themselves might vary.

There are a few ancillary functions in TESTF16.C that you might find useful in your own applications. The countfonts function will look through all the fonts in a resource file and return an array of long integers with the number of each FONT resource in the file. The last entry in the list will be the value BADRECNUM, indicating the end of the list.

The loadfont function will fetch a specified FONT resource from the disk and return a pointer to it. Note that the number passed to it is the font resource number, not the position of the resource in the resource file. Passing 12 as this argument, for example, will cause loadfont to fetch the FONT resource which has its number field set to 12, not the twelfth FONT resource in the resource file.

Finally, the FontStringLength function will return the length of a text string in pixels, based on the font passed to it. Keep in mind that, because display fonts are proportionally spaced, there is no obvious relationship between the number of characters in a string and the amount of screen real estate the string will occupy in a particular font. The FontStringLength function works out the length of a string in pixels by adding up the charwide array elements for each character in the string.

Note that TESTF16 includes a button to save the screen to a PCX file, as the example mouse programs did. This isn't necessary in experimenting with the DrawFontString function—it was included solely to allow FIG. 6-1 to be created.

To compile and link TESTF16.C into TESTF16.EXE, you should begin by assembling FONT-16.ASM, to produce FONT-16.OBJ. The MOUSE16.OBJ file, left over from Chapter 3, will also be required. Create a Turbo C project file to link the following modules, or a MAKE file if you're not working in the integrated development environment:

    TESTF16.C
    MOUSE16.OBJ
    FONT-16.OBJ

The TESTF16 program isn't all that interesting to look at—you'll probably be able to think of much more practical applications for the font functions in this chapter.

As you'll no doubt appreciate by now, modifying the font functions to work in a 256-color graphics mode is fairly elementary. The write mode two code in DrawFontString must be replaced with calls to the appropriate GRAF macros and the display palette will get somewhat bigger but pretty well all the functionality of the code will be about the same.

6-16
The source code for FONT-256.ASM

```
;
;               Font Functions for 256-colour
;               Super VGA graphics
;

_AOFF           EQU     6               ;STACK OFFSET TO FIRST ARG

MINFONTCHAR     EQU     0               ;LOWEST NUMBER FOR A FONT CHARACTER
MAXFONTCHAR     EQU     255             ;HIGHEST NUMBER FOR A FONT CHARACTER
FONTNAMESIZE    EQU     32              ;MAXIMUM SIZE OF A FONT NAME

FONT            STRUC
                FN_NAME         DB      (FONTNAMESIZE+1) DUP (?)
                FN_NUMBER       DB      ?
                FN_POINTSIZE    DB      ?
                FN_CHARWIDE     DB      (MAXFONTCHAR-MINFONTCHAR+1) DUP (?)
                FN_CHAROFF      DW      (MAXFONTCHAR-MINFONTCHAR+1) DUP (?)
                FN_BITMAPWIDTH  DW      ?
                FN_BITMAPDEPTH  DW      ?
                FN_BITMAPBYTES  DW      ?
                FN_WIDESTCHAR   DW      ?
                FN_PADWIDTH     DW      ?
                FN_SPACEWIDTH   DW      ?
FONT            ENDS

INCPAGE         MACRO   ;INCREMENT THE PAGE
                PUSH    AX
                MOV     AX,[CODEPAGE]
```

```
                        INC      AX
                        CALL     VGABANK
                        POP      AX
                        ENDM

CHECKPAGE               MACRO    ;HANDLE PAGE BOUNDARIES
                        LOCAL    LAB1
                        CMP      DI,0000H
                        JNE      LAB1
                        INCPAGE
LAB1:
                        ENDM

GRAFADD_DI              MACRO    ARG1    ;ADD THE ARGUMENT TO DI WITH PAGE SWITCHING
                        LOCAL    LAB1
                        PUSH     AX
                        MOV      AX,DI
                        ADD      DI,ARG1
                        CMP      AX,DI
                        JBE      LAB1
                        INCPAGE
LAB1:
                        POP      AX
                        ENDM

GRAF_STOSB              MACRO    ;STORE A BIT AT DS:SI WITH PAGE SWITCH
                        CLD
                        STOSB
                        CHECKPAGE
                        ENDM

;THIS MACRO FETCHES THE DATA SEGEMENT
LDATASEG                MACRO
                        PUSH     AX
                        MOV      AX,_DATA
                        MOV      DS,AX
                        POP      AX
                        ENDM

;DO A LONG LOOP
LNGLOOP                 MACRO    ARG1
                        LOCAL    LAB1
                        DEC      CX
                        CMP      CX,0000H
                        JE       LAB1
                        JMP      ARG1
LAB1:
                        ENDM

DRAWFN_CB               EQU      2
DRAWFN_CP               EQU      4
DRAWFN_KL               EQU      6
DRAWFN_J                EQU      8
DRAWFN_I                EQU      10
DRAWFN_N                EQU      12
```

```
6-16        DRAWFN_BMPOFF    EQU       14
Continued.  DRAWFN_BMPSEG    EQU       16
            DRAWFN_ADJUST    EQU       18

                             EXTRN HIDECURSOR:FAR
                             EXTRN SHOWCURSOR:FAR
                             EXTRN VGABANK:FAR
                             EXTRN VGALINE:FAR

FONT256_TEXT                 SEGMENT BYTE PUBLIC 'CODE'
                             ASSUME  CS:FONT256_TEXT,DS:_DATA

;                            ARG1 = X
;                            ARG2 = Y
;                            ARG3 = STRING
;                            ARG4 = COLOUR
;                            ARG6 = FONT
                             PUBLIC  _DrawFontString
_DrawFontString PROC         FAR
                PUSH         BP
                MOV          BP,SP
                SUB          SP,DRAWFN_ADJUST
                PUSH         DS
                PUSH         ES

                             LDATASEG

                             CALL    HIDECURSOR

                             ;FETCH THE STRING
                             MOV     SI,[BP + _AOFF + 4]
                             MOV     DS,[BP + _AOFF + 6]

                             ;SEE HOW LONG IT IS
                             MOV     WORD PTR [BP - DRAWFN_N],0000H
DF1:                         LODSB
                             CMP     AL,00H
                             JE      DF2

                             INC     WORD PTR [BP - DRAWFN_N]
                             JMP     DF1

                             ;FETCH THE FONT POINTER
DF2:                         MOV     SI,[BP + _AOFF + 10]
                             MOV     DS,[BP + _AOFF + 12]

                             ;SAVE A POINTER TO THE FONT BITMAP
                             MOV     [BP - DRAWFN_BMPOFF],SI
                             MOV     [BP - DRAWFN_BMPSEG],DS
                             ADD     WORD PTR [BP - DRAWFN_BMPOFF],SIZE FONT

                             ;GET THE FONT DEPTH
                             MOV     CX,DS:[SI + FN_BITMAPDEPTH]
                             MOV     WORD PTR [BP - DRAWFN_I],0000H
```

```
DF3:            PUSH    CX

                ;FETCH THE LEFT COORDINATE
                MOV     AX,[BP + _AOFF + 0]
                MOV     [BP - DRAWFN_CB],AX

                MOV     CX,[BP - DRAWFN_N]
                MOV     WORD PTR [BP - DRAWFN_J],0000H
DF4:            PUSH    CX

                ;FETCH A CHARACTER FROM THE STRING
                MOV     SI,[BP + _AOFF + 4]
                MOV     DS,[BP + _AOFF + 6]
                MOV     BX,[BP - DRAWFN_J]
                MOV     AL,DS:[SI + BX]

                ;FETCH A POINTER TO THE FONT
                MOV     SI,[BP + _AOFF + 10]
                MOV     DS,[BP + _AOFF + 12]

                ;CHECK FOR SPACE CHARACTER
                CMP     AL,20H
                JNE     DF5

                ;IF IT'S A SPACE, JUST PAD RIGHT AND CONTINUE
                MOV     AX,[BP - DRAWFN_CB]
                ADD     AX,DS:[SI + FN_SPACEWIDTH]
                ADD     AX,DS:[SI + FN_PADWIDTH]
                MOV     [BP - DRAWFN_CB],AX
                JMP     DF8

                ;IF IT'S NOT A SPACE, DRAW THE CHARACTER
DF5:            MOV     BL,AL
                AND     BX,00FFH

                MOV     AL,DS:[SI + FN_CHARWIDE + BX]
                AND     AX,00FFH
                MOV     [BP - DRAWFN_KL],AX

                SHL     BX,1
                MOV     AX,DS:[SI + FN_CHAROFF + BX]
                MOV     [BP - DRAWFN_CP],AX

                ;LOOP FOR THE CHARACTER WIDTH
                MOV     CX,[BP - DRAWFN_KL]
DF6:            PUSH    CX

                ;SEE IF THIS BIT IS SET IN THE CHARACTER BITMAP
                LDATASEG
                MOV     BX,[BP - DRAWFN_CP]
                AND     BX,0007H
                MOV     AL,[_MASKTABLE + BX]

                MOV     SI,[BP - DRAWFN_BMPOFF]
```

```
                MOV     DS,[BP - DRAWFN_BMPSEG]
                MOV     BX,[BP - DRAWFN_CP]
                MOV     CL,3
                SHR     BX,CL
                TEST    DS:[SI + BX],AL
                JZ      DF7

                ;GET A POINTER TO THE LINE
                MOV     BX,[BP + _AOFF + 2]
                MOV     AX,[BP - DRAWFN_I]
                ADD     BX,AX
                CALL    VGALINE
                GRAFADD_DI [BP-DRAWFN_CB]

                ;WRITE THE PIXEL
                MOV     AX,[BP + _AOFF + 8]
                GRAF_STOSB

DF7:            INC     WORD PTR [BP - DRAWFN_CB]
                INC     WORD PTR [BP - DRAWFN_CP]

                POP     CX
                LOOP    DF6

                ;PAD OVER BY THE PAD WIDTH
                MOV     SI,[BP + _AOFF + 10]
                MOV     DS,[BP + _AOFF + 12]
                MOV     AX,DS:[SI + FN_PADWIDTH]
                ADD     [BP - DRAWFN_CB],AX

DF8:            POP     CX
                INC     WORD PTR [BP - DRAWFN_J]
                LNGLOOP DF4

                ;POINT TO THE NEXT LINE OF THE FONT BITMAP
                MOV     SI,[BP + _AOFF + 10]
                MOV     DS,[BP + _AOFF + 12]
                MOV     AX,DS:[SI + FN_BITMAPBYTES]
                ADD     [BP - DRAWFN_BMPOFF],AX

                POP     CX
                INC     WORD PTR [BP - DRAWFN_I]

                ;MAKE SURE WE WON'T BE WRITING PAST THE END OF THE SCREEN
                LDATASEG
                MOV     AX,[BP + _AOFF + 2]
                ADD     AX,[BP - DRAWFN_I]
                CMP     AX,[_SCREENDEEP]
                JGE     DF9

                LNGLOOP DF3

                ;RESTORE THE BIT MASK TO ALL BITS ON
DF9:            LDATASEG
                CALL    SHOWCURSOR
```

```
                POP     ES
                POP     DS
                ADD     SP,DRAWFN_ADJUST
                POP     BP
                RET
_DrawFontString ENDP

FONT256_TEXT    ENDS

DGROUP          GROUP   _DATA,_BSS
_DATA           SEGMENT WORD PUBLIC 'DATA'

                EXTRN   _SCREENTBL:WORD
                EXTRN   _SCREENSEG:WORD
                EXTRN   _SCREENBYTES:WORD
                EXTRN   _SCREENWIDE:WORD
                EXTRN   _SCREENDEEP:WORD
                EXTRN   _MASKTABLE:BYTE
                EXTRN   _BITTABLE:BYTE
                EXTRN   CODEPAGE:WORD

_DATA           ENDS

_BSS            SEGMENT WORD PUBLIC 'BSS'

_BSS            ENDS

                END
```

As with the 16-color DrawFontString function, you can see how the code in FIG. 6-15 works by linking it to a C language calling program. The TESTF256.C program is in FIG. 6-17—it works pretty well like the TESTF16 program.

```
/*
        Using fonts in 256 colors

        Copyright (c) 1992 Alchemy Mindworks Inc.

        Links to MOUSE256.ASM
        Links to FONT-256.ASM
*/

#include "stdio.h"
#include "dos.h"
#include "alloc.h"
#include "mouse256.h"

#define MINFONTCHAR     0          /* lowest number font character */
#define MAXFONTCHAR     255        /* highest number font character */
#define FONTNAMESIZE    32         /* maximum size of a font name */

#define BADRECNUM       0xffffffffL    /* illegal record number */
```

6-17
The source code for
TESTF256.C.

```
6-17      typedef struct {
Continued.        char name[FONTNAMESIZE+1];
                  char number;
                  char pointsize;
                  char charwide[(MAXFONTCHAR-MINFONTCHAR)+1];
                  unsigned int charoff[(MAXFONTCHAR-MINFONTCHAR)+1];
                  unsigned int bitmapwidth;
                  unsigned int bitmapdepth;
                  unsigned int bitmapbytes;
                  unsigned int widestchar;
                  unsigned int padwidth;
                  unsigned int spacewidth;
                  } FONT;

          typedef struct {
                  char id[8];
                  char description[65];
                  unsigned int count;
                  } RESHEAD;

          typedef struct {
                  char type[4];
                  unsigned long number;
                  unsigned int size;
                  } RESOURCE;

          typedef struct  {
                  char manufacturer;
                  char version;
                  char encoding;
                  char bits_per_pixel;
                  int xmin,ymin;
                  int xmax,ymax;
                  int hres;
                  int vres;
                  char palette[48];
                  char reserved;
                  char colour_planes;
                  int bytes_per_line;
                  int palette_type;
                  char filler[58];
                  } PCXHEAD;

          /* colours in this 256-colour palette */
          #define BLACK          0
          #define BLUE           126
          #define GREEN          31
          #define CYAN           246
          #define RED            3
          #define MAGENTA        143
          #define YELLOW         41
          #define GREY           253
          #define DARKGREY       252
          #define LIGHTGREY      254
          #define LIGHTBLUE      192
```

```
#define LIGHTGREEN        36
#define LIGHTRED          5
#define LIGHTYELLOW       125
#define LIGHTMAGENTA      227
#define WHITE             255

#define RESID             "ALCHRSRC"
#define FONTFILE          "DTPE.RES"
#define FONTID            "FONT"

void DrawFontString(unsigned int x,unsigned int y,char *string,\
                    unsigned int colour,FONT *font);
FONT *loadfont(char *s,unsigned long n);
unsigned long *countfonts(char *s);

/* the 256-colour palette we'll use */
char palette[] = {
        0x00,0x00,0x00,0x57,0x00,0x00,0x83,0x00,
        0x00,0xab,0x00,0x00,0xd7,0x00,0x00,0xff,
        0x00,0x00,0x00,0x2b,0x00,0x57,0x2b,0x00,
        0x83,0x2b,0x00,0xab,0x2b,0x00,0xd7,0x2b,
        0x00,0xff,0x2b,0x00,0x00,0x57,0x00,0x57,
        0x57,0x00,0x83,0x57,0x00,0xab,0x57,0x00,
        0xd7,0x57,0x00,0xff,0x57,0x00,0x00,0x83,
        0x00,0x57,0x83,0x00,0x83,0x83,0x00,0xab,
        0x83,0x00,0xd7,0x83,0x00,0xff,0x83,0x00,
        0x00,0xab,0x00,0x57,0xab,0x00,0x83,0xab,
        0x00,0xab,0xab,0x00,0xd7,0xab,0x00,0xff,
        0xab,0x00,0x00,0xd7,0x00,0x57,0xd7,0x00,
        0x83,0xd7,0x00,0xab,0xd7,0x00,0xd7,0xd7,
        0x00,0xff,0xd7,0x00,0x00,0xff,0x00,0x57,
        0xff,0x00,0x83,0xff,0x00,0xab,0xff,0x00,
        0xd7,0xff,0x00,0xff,0xff,0x00,0x00,0x00,
        0x57,0x57,0x00,0x57,0x83,0x00,0x57,0xab,
        0x00,0x57,0xd7,0x00,0x57,0xff,0x00,0x57,
        0x00,0x2b,0x57,0x57,0x2b,0x57,0x83,0x2b,
        0x57,0xab,0x2b,0x57,0xd7,0x2b,0x57,0xff,
        0x2b,0x57,0x00,0x57,0x57,0x57,0x57,0x57,
        0x83,0x57,0x57,0xab,0x57,0x57,0xd7,0x57,
        0x57,0xff,0x57,0x57,0x00,0x83,0x57,0x57,
        0x83,0x57,0x83,0x83,0x57,0xab,0x83,0x57,
        0xd7,0x83,0x57,0xff,0x83,0x57,0x00,0xab,
        0x57,0x57,0xab,0x57,0x83,0xab,0x57,0xab,
        0xab,0x57,0xd7,0xab,0x57,0xff,0xab,0x57,
        0x00,0xd7,0x57,0x57,0xd7,0x57,0x83,0xd7,
        0x57,0xab,0xd7,0x57,0xd7,0xd7,0x57,0xff,
        0xd7,0x57,0x00,0xff,0x57,0x57,0xff,0x57,
        0x83,0xff,0x57,0xab,0xff,0x57,0xd7,0xff,
        0x57,0xff,0xff,0x57,0x00,0x00,0x83,0x57,
        0x00,0x83,0x83,0x00,0x83,0xab,0x00,0x83,
        0xd7,0x00,0x83,0xff,0x00,0x83,0x00,0x2b,
        0x83,0x57,0x2b,0x83,0x83,0x2b,0x83,0xab,
        0x2b,0x83,0xd7,0x2b,0x83,0xff,0x2b,0x83,
        0x00,0x57,0x83,0x57,0x57,0x83,0x83,0x57,
        0x83,0xab,0x57,0x83,0xd7,0x57,0x83,0xff,
```

```
0x57,0x83,0x00,0x83,0x83,0x57,0x83,0x83,
0x83,0x83,0x83,0xab,0x83,0x83,0xd7,0x83,
0x83,0xff,0x83,0x83,0x00,0xab,0x83,0x57,
0xab,0x83,0x83,0xab,0x83,0xab,0xab,0x83,
0xd7,0xab,0x83,0xff,0xab,0x83,0x00,0xd7,
0x83,0x57,0xd7,0x83,0x83,0xd7,0x83,0xab,
0xd7,0x83,0xd7,0xd7,0x83,0xff,0xd7,0x83,
0x00,0xff,0x83,0x57,0xff,0x83,0x83,0xff,
0x83,0xab,0xff,0x83,0xd7,0xff,0x83,0xff,
0xff,0x83,0x00,0x00,0xab,0x57,0x00,0xab,
0x83,0x00,0xab,0xab,0x00,0xab,0xd7,0x00,
0xab,0xff,0x00,0xab,0x00,0x2b,0xab,0x57,
0x2b,0xab,0x83,0x2b,0xab,0xab,0x2b,0xab,
0xd7,0x2b,0xab,0xff,0x2b,0xab,0x00,0x57,
0xab,0x57,0x57,0xab,0x83,0x57,0xab,0xab,
0x57,0xab,0xd7,0x57,0xab,0xff,0x57,0xab,
0x00,0x83,0xab,0x57,0x83,0xab,0x83,0x83,
0xab,0xab,0x83,0xab,0xd7,0x83,0xab,0xff,
0x83,0xab,0x00,0xab,0xab,0x57,0xab,0xab,
0x83,0xab,0xab,0xab,0xab,0xab,0xd7,0xab,
0xab,0xff,0xab,0xab,0x00,0xd7,0xab,0x57,
0xd7,0xab,0x83,0xd7,0xab,0xab,0xd7,0xab,
0xd7,0xd7,0xab,0xff,0xd7,0xab,0x00,0xff,
0xab,0x57,0xff,0xab,0x83,0xff,0xab,0xab,
0xff,0xab,0xd7,0xff,0xab,0xff,0xff,0xab,
0x00,0x00,0xd7,0x57,0x00,0xd7,0x83,0x00,
0xd7,0xab,0x00,0xd7,0xd7,0x00,0xd7,0xff,
0x00,0xd7,0x00,0x2b,0xd7,0x57,0x2b,0xd7,
0x83,0x2b,0xd7,0xab,0x2b,0xd7,0xd7,0x2b,
0xd7,0xff,0x2b,0xd7,0x00,0x57,0xd7,0x57,
0x57,0xd7,0x83,0x57,0xd7,0xab,0x57,0xd7,
0xd7,0x57,0xd7,0xff,0x57,0xd7,0x00,0x83,
0xd7,0x57,0x83,0xd7,0x83,0x83,0xd7,0xab,
0x83,0xd7,0xd7,0x83,0xd7,0xff,0x83,0xd7,
0x00,0xab,0xd7,0x57,0xab,0xd7,0x83,0xab,
0xd7,0xab,0xab,0xd7,0xd7,0xab,0xd7,0xff,
0xab,0xd7,0x00,0xd7,0xd7,0x57,0xd7,0xd7,
0x83,0xd7,0xd7,0xab,0xd7,0xd7,0xd7,0xd7,
0xd7,0xff,0xd7,0xd7,0x00,0xff,0xd7,0x57,
0xff,0xd7,0x83,0xff,0xd7,0xab,0xff,0xd7,
0xd7,0xff,0xd7,0xff,0xff,0xd7,0x00,0x00,
0xff,0x57,0x00,0xff,0x83,0x00,0xff,0xab,
0x00,0xff,0xd7,0x00,0xff,0xff,0x00,0xff,
0x00,0x2b,0xff,0x57,0x2b,0xff,0x83,0x2b,
0xff,0xab,0x2b,0xff,0xd7,0x2b,0xff,0xff,
0x2b,0xff,0x00,0x57,0xff,0x57,0x57,0xff,
0x83,0x57,0xff,0xab,0x57,0xff,0xd7,0x57,
0xff,0xff,0x57,0xff,0x00,0x83,0xff,0x57,
0x83,0xff,0x83,0x83,0xff,0xab,0x83,0xff,
0xd7,0x83,0xff,0xff,0x83,0xff,0x00,0xab,
0xff,0x57,0xab,0xff,0x83,0xab,0xff,0xab,
0xab,0xff,0xd7,0xab,0xff,0xff,0xab,0xff,
0x00,0xd7,0xff,0x57,0xd7,0xff,0x83,0xd7,
0xff,0xab,0xd7,0xff,0xd7,0xd7,0xff,0xff,
0xd7,0xff,0x00,0xff,0xff,0x57,0xff,0xff,
```

```
        0x83,0xff,0xff,0xab,0xff,0xff,0xd7,0xff,
        0xff,0x3f,0x3f,0x3f,0x6b,0x6b,0x6b,0x97,
        0x97,0x97,0xc3,0xc3,0xc3,0xff,0xff,0xff
        };

main(argc,argv)
        int argc;
        char *argv[];
{
        static char colourtable[8]= {
                BLACK,RED,LIGHTRED,LIGHTYELLOW,
                LIGHTBLUE,YELLOW,GREEN,DARKGREY
        };

        FONT *thefont;
        BUTTON save,quit;
        POINT p;
        char b[128];
        unsigned long *lp;
        int i=10,j=0,k,n=0,alive=1,thiscard=0xffff;

        if((lp=countfonts(FONTFILE))== NULL || lp[0]==BADRECNUM) {
                puts("Can't find fonts");
                exit(1);
        }

        /* see what kind of card is installed -- sort of */
        if(argc > 1) {
                if(!stricmp(argv[1],"PARADISE")) thiscard=PARADISE;
                else if(!stricmp(argv[1],"ATI")) thiscard=ATI;
                else if(!stricmp(argv[1],"TSENG")) thiscard=TSENG;
                else if(!stricmp(argv[1],"TRIDENT")) thiscard=TRIDENT;
                else if(!stricmp(argv[1],"OAK")) thiscard=OAK;
                else if(!stricmp(argv[1],"VESA")) thiscard=VESA;
        }

        /* go for a graphics mode */
        if(!InitMouse(640,480,thiscard)) exit(1);

        /* set the palette */
        SetVgaPalette(palette,256);

        SetVgaWhite(WHITE);
        SetVgaBlack(BLACK);
        SetVgaGrey(GREY);
        SetVgaLightGrey(LIGHTGREY);
        SetVgaDarkGrey(DARKGREY);

        /* clear the screen */
        ClearScreen(GetVgaLightGrey());

        /* show the fonts */
        do {
                if((thefont=loadfont(FONTFILE,lp[n++])) != NULL) {
                        sprintf(b,"This is %u point %s",
                            thefont->pointsize,thefont->name);
```

```
                                        k=(SCREENWIDE-FontStringLength(b,thefont))/2;
                                        DrawFontString(k,i,b,colourtable[j % 8],thefont);
                                        i+=thefont->bitmapdepth;
                                        free((char *)thefont);
                                        ++j;
                        }
                } while(lp[n] != BADRECNUM && thefont != NULL && i < SCREENDEEP);

                free((char *)lp);

                /* create a button to click on */
                MakeButton(SCREENWIDE-100,SCREENDEEP-60,"Quit",&quit);
                DrawButton(&quit);

                MakeButton(SCREENWIDE-200,SCREENDEEP-60,"Save",&save);
                DrawButton(&save);

                /* loop 'til we're done */
                do {
                        /* look for a mouse click */
                        if(MouseDown(&p)) {
                                if(PointInRect(&p,&quit)) {
                                        TrackButton(&quit);
                                        alive=0;
                                }
                                else if(PointInRect(&p,&save)) {
                                        TrackButton(&save);
                                        DoSave("SCREEN00.PCX");
                                }
                        }
                } while(alive);

                DeinitMouse();
        }

/* save the screen to a PCX file */
DoSave(path)
        char *path;
{
        PCXHEAD pcx;
        FILE *fp;
        char *p;
        unsigned int i,n;

        /* create the destination file */
        if((fp=fopen(path,"wb"))==NULL) {
                beep();
                return;
        }

        if((p=malloc(SCREENWIDE))==NULL) {
                beep();
                fclose(fp);
                return;
        }
```

```
memset((char *)&pcx,0,sizeof(PCXHEAD));
memcpy(pcx.palette,palette,48);

pcx.manufacturer=10;
pcx.encoding=1;
pcx.xmin=pcx.ymin=0;
pcx.xmax=SCREENWIDE-1;
pcx.ymax=SCREENDEEP-1;
pcx.palette_type=1;
pcx.bits_per_pixel=8;
pcx.version=5;
pcx.colour_planes=1;
pcx.bytes_per_line=SCREENWIDE;

WaitCursor();
if(fwrite((char *)&pcx,1,sizeof(PCXHEAD),fp) != sizeof(PCXHEAD)) {
        free(p);
        fclose(fp);
        remove(path);
        ArrowCursor();
        beep();
        return;
}

for(i=0;i<SCREENDEEP;++i) {
        MouseOff();
        GetScreenLine(p,i);
        MouseOn();
        n=pcxwriteline(fp,p,pcx.bytes_per_line);

        if(n != pcx.bytes_per_line) {
                free(p);
                fclose(fp);
                remove(path);
                ArrowCursor();
                beep();
                return;
        }
}

fputc(12,fp);
if(fwrite(palette,1,768,fp) != 768) {
        free(p);
        fclose(fp);
        remove(path);
        ArrowCursor();
        beep();
        return;
}

ArrowCursor();
free(p);
fclose(fp);
}
```

```
/* write one pcx line */
pcxwriteline(fp,p,n)
        FILE *fp;
        char *p;
        unsigned int n;
{
        unsigned int i=0,j=0,t=0;

        do {
                i=0;
                while((p[t+i]==p[t+i+1]) && ((t+i) < n) && (i < 63))++i;
                if(i>0) {
                        if(fputc(i | 0xc0,fp)==EOF) return(-1);
                        if(fputc(p[t],fp)==EOF) return(-1);
                        t+=i;
                        j+=2;
                }
                else {
                        if(((p[t]) & 0xc0)==0xc0) {
                                if(fputc(0xc1,fp)==EOF) return(-1);
                                ++j;
                        }
                        if(fputc(p[t++],fp)==EOF) return(-1);
                        ++j;

                }
        } while(t<n);
        return(n);
}


FontStringLength(s,font)
        char *s;
        FONT *font;
{
        unsigned int a=0;

        /* add up the character widths of all the characters in the string */
        while(*s) a+=font->charwide[*s++];
        return(a);
}

unsigned long *countfonts(s)
        char *s;
{
        RESHEAD rh;
        RESOURCE rc;
        unsigned long *lp;
        FILE *fp;
        unsigned int i,j;

        /* open the resource file */
        if((fp=fopen(s,"rb")) == NULL) return(NULL);

        /* read the header */
        if(fread((char *)&rh,1,sizeof(RESHEAD),fp) != sizeof(RESHEAD)) {
```

```
                        fclose(fp);
                        return(NULL);
        }

        /* make sure it's a resource file */
        if(memcmp(rh.id,RESID,8)) {
                        fclose(fp);
                        return(NULL);
        }

        /* allocate a buffer for the numbers */
        if((lp=(unsigned long *)malloc((1+rh.count)*sizeof(unsigned long))) == NULL) {
                        fclose(fp);
                        return(NULL);
        }

        /* set the end of the buffer */
        lp[0]=BADRECNUM;

        /* step through each resource */
        for(i=j=0;i<rh.count;++i) {

                        /* fetch the resource */
                        if(fread((char *)&rc,1,sizeof(RESOURCE),fp) != sizeof(RESOURCE)) {
                                fclose(fp);
                                return(lp);
                        }

                        /* if it's a font, add it to the list */
                        if(!memcmp(rc.type,FONTID,4)) {
                                lp[j++]=rc.number;
                                lp[j]=BADRECNUM;
                        }

                        /* seek to the next resource */
                        fseek(fp,(unsigned long)rc.size,SEEK_CUR);
        }

        fclose(fp);
        return(lp);
}

FONT *loadfont(s,n)
        char *s;
        unsigned long n;
{
        RESHEAD rh;
        RESOURCE rc;
        FONT *font;
        FILE *fp;
        unsigned int i;

        /* open the resource file */
        if((fp=fopen(s,"rb")) == NULL) return(NULL);
```

```
                /* read the header */
                if(fread((char *)&rh,1,sizeof(RESHEAD),fp) != sizeof(RESHEAD)) {
                        fclose(fp);
                        return(NULL);
                }

                /* make sure it's a resource file */
                if(memcmp(rh.id,RESID,8)) {
                        fclose(fp);
                        return(NULL);
                }

                /* look at all the resources */
                for(i=0;i<rh.count;++i) {

                        /* fetch the resource */
                        if(fread((char *)&rc,1,sizeof(RESOURCE),fp) != sizeof(RESOURCE)) {
                                fclose(fp);
                                return(NULL);
                        }

                        /* if it's a font and it's the one we want, load it */
                        if(!memcmp(rc.type,FONTID,4) && rc.number == n) {

                                /* allocate a buffer for the data */
                                if((font=(FONT *)malloc(rc.size)) == NULL) {
                                        fclose(fp);
                                        return(NULL);
                                }

                                /* read the data */
                                if(fread((char *)font,1,rc.size,fp) != rc.size) {
                                        free((char *)font);
                                        fclose(fp);
                                        return(NULL);
                                }

                                /* we're done -- go away */
                                fclose(fp);
                                return(font);
                        }

                        /* otherwise, seek to the next resource */
                        fseek(fp,(unsigned long)rc.size,SEEK_CUR);
                }

                /* resource not found */
                fclose(fp);
                return(NULL);
        }

        SetVgaPalette(p,n)
                char *p;
                unsigned int n;
        {
```

```
        int i;

        outp(0x3c6,0xff);
        for(i=0;i<n;++i) {
                outp(0x3c8,i);
                outp(0x3c9,(*p++) >> 2);
                outp(0x3c9,(*p++) >> 2);
                outp(0x3c9,(*p++) >> 2);
        }
}

MakeButton(left,top,string,button)
        unsigned int left,top;
        char *string;
        BUTTON *button;
{
        button->frame.left = left & 0xfff8;
        button->frame.right=button->frame.left+(strlen(string)<<3)+16;
        button->frame.top=top;
        button->frame.bottom=button->frame.top+FONTDEPTH+8;
        button->text=string;
}

DrawButton(button)
        BUTTON *button;
{
        FillRect(button->frame.left+1,button->frame.top+1,
                button->frame.right-1,button->frame.bottom-1,GetVgaWhite());
        DrawLine(button->frame.left+1,button->frame.top,
                button->frame.right-1,button->frame.top,GetVgaBlack());
        DrawLine(button->frame.left,button->frame.top+1,
                button->frame.left,button->frame.bottom-1,GetVgaBlack());
        DrawLine(button->frame.right,button->frame.top+1,
                button->frame.right,button->frame.bottom-1,GetVgaBlack());
        DrawLine(button->frame.left+1,button->frame.bottom,
                button->frame.right-1,button->frame.bottom,GetVgaBlack());
        Fill3DBox(button->frame.left+1,button->frame.top+1,
                button->frame.right-1,button->frame.bottom-1);

        DrawString(button->frame.left+8,button->frame.top+4,
                button->text,GetVgaDarkGrey(),GetVgaLightGrey());
}

TrackButton(button)
        BUTTON *button;
{
        POINT p;

        FillRect(button->frame.left+1,button->frame.top+1,
                button->frame.right-1,button->frame.bottom-1,GetVgaLightGrey());

        DrawString(button->frame.left+8,button->frame.top+4,
                button->text,GetVgaDarkGrey(),GetVgaLightGrey());
        while(MouseDown(&p));
        DrawButton(button);
```

```
}

Fill3DBox(left,top,right,bottom)
        int left,top,right,bottom;
{
        FillRect(left,top,right,bottom,GetVgaLightGrey());
        DrawLine(left,top,right-1,top,GetVgaWhite());
        DrawLine(left,top+1,left,bottom-1,GetVgaWhite());

        DrawLine(left+3,bottom,right,bottom,GetVgaDarkGrey());
        DrawLine(right,top+2,right,bottom-1,GetVgaDarkGrey());
}

PointInRect(p,r)/* return true if point is in rect */
        POINT *p;
        RECT *r;
{
        if(p->x > r->left && p->x < r->right &&
           p->y > r->top  && p->y < r->bottom) return(1);
        else return(0);
}

WaitCursor()
{
        static char cursor[] = {
                0x00,0x00,0x00,0x00,
                0x00,0x00,0x01,0x80,
                0x03,0xC0,0x07,0xE0,
                0x0F,0xF0,0x07,0xE0,
                0x03,0xC0,0x01,0x80,
                0x00,0x00,0x00,0x00,
                0x00,0x00,0x00,0x00,
                0xFF,0xFF,0xFF,0xFF,

                0x00,0x00,0xFE,0x7F,
                0x06,0x60,0x0C,0x30,
                0x18,0x18,0x30,0x0C,
                0x60,0x06,0xC0,0x03,
                0x60,0x06,0x30,0x0C,
                0x98,0x19,0xCC,0x33,
                0xE6,0x67,0xFE,0x7F,
                0x00,0x00,0x00,0x00 };

        MouseCursor(cursor,7,7);
}

ArrowCursor()
{
        static char cursor[] = {
                0xFF,0x3F,0xFF,0x1F,
                0xFF,0x0F,0xFF,0x07,
                0xFF,0x03,0xFF,0x01,
                0xFF,0x00,0x7F,0x00,
                0x3F,0x00,0x1F,0x00,
                0xFF,0x01,0xFF,0x10,
```

```
                    0xFF,0x30,0x7F,0xF8,
                    0x7F,0xF8,0x7F,0xFC,
                    0x00,0x00,0x00,0x40,
                    0x00,0x60,0x00,0x70,
                    0x00,0x78,0x00,0x7C,
                    0x00,0x7E,0x00,0x7F,
                    0x80,0x7F,0x00,0x7C,
                    0x00,0x6C,0x00,0x46,
                    0x00,0x06,0x00,0x03,
                    0x00,0x03,0x00,0x00  };

        MouseCursor(cursor,0,0);
}
```

In order to create TESTF256, you should link the following files:

TESTF256.C
MOUSE256.OBJ
FONT-256.OBJ

Using display fonts in a high-color graphics mode is, if anything, still simpler than using them in a 256-color mode. The DrawFontString function is almost identical, save that it must write a word for each pixel, rather than a byte. The FONT-HI.ASM code is shown in FIG. 6-18.

6-18
The source code for
FONT-HI.ASM.

```
;
;               Font Functions for high colour
;               Super VGA graphics
;

_AOFF           EQU     6           ;STACK OFFSET TO FIRST ARG

MINFONTCHAR     EQU     0           ;LOWEST NUMBER FOR A FONT CHARACTER
MAXFONTCHAR     EQU     255         ;HIGHEST NUMBER FOR A FONT CHARACTER
FONTNAMESIZE    EQU     32          ;MAXIMUM SIZE OF A FONT NAME

FONT            STRUC
                FN_NAME         DB      (FONTNAMESIZE+1) DUP (?)
                FN_NUMBER       DB      ?
                FN_POINTSIZE    DB      ?
                FN_CHARWIDE     DB      (MAXFONTCHAR-MINFONTCHAR+1) DUP (?)
                FN_CHAROFF      DW      (MAXFONTCHAR-MINFONTCHAR+1) DUP (?)
                FN_BITMAPWIDTH  DW      ?
                FN_BITMAPDEPTH  DW      ?
                FN_BITMAPBYTES  DW      ?
                FN_WIDESTCHAR   DW      ?
                FN_PADWIDTH     DW      ?
                FN_SPACEWIDTH   DW      ?
FONT            ENDS

INCPAGE         MACRO   ;INCREMENT THE PAGE
```

```
                        PUSH    AX
                        MOV     AX,[CODEPAGE]
                        INC     AX
                        CALL    VGABANK
                        POP     AX
                        ENDM

        CHECKPAGE       MACRO   ;HANDLE PAGE BOUNDARIES
                        LOCAL   LAB1
                        CMP     DI,0000H
                        JNE     LAB1
                        INCPAGE
        LAB1:
                        ENDM

        GRAFADD_DI      MACRO   ARG1        ;ADD THE ARGUMENT TO DI WITH PAGE SWITCHING
                        LOCAL   LAB1
                        PUSH    AX
                        PUSH    BX
                        MOV     AX,DI
                        MOV     BX,ARG1
                        SHL     BX,1
                        ADD     DI,BX
                        CMP     AX,DI
                        JBE     LAB1
                        INCPAGE
        LAB1:
                        POP     BX
                        POP     AX
                        ENDM

        GRAF_STOSW      MACRO   ;STORE A BIT AT DS:SI WITH PAGE SWITCH
                        CLD
                        STOSW
                        CHECKPAGE
                        ENDM

        ;THIS MACRO FETCHES THE DATA SEGEMENT
        LDATASEG        MACRO
                        PUSH    AX
                        MOV     AX,_DATA
                        MOV     DS,AX
                        POP     AX
                        ENDM

        ;DO A LONG LOOP
        LNGLOOP         MACRO   ARG1
                        LOCAL   LAB1
                        DEC     CX
                        CMP     CX,0000H
                        JE      LAB1
                        JMP     ARG1
        LAB1:
                        ENDM
```

```
DRAWFN_CB         EQU      2
DRAWFN_CP         EQU      4
DRAWFN_KL         EQU      6
DRAWFN_J          EQU      8
DRAWFN_I          EQU      10
DRAWFN_N          EQU      12
DRAWFN_BMPOFF     EQU      14
DRAWFN_BMPSEG     EQU      16
DRAWFN_ADJUST     EQU      18

                  EXTRN HIDECURSOR:FAR
                  EXTRN SHOWCURSOR:FAR
                  EXTRN VGABANK:FAR
                  EXTRN VGALINE:FAR

FONT_HI_TEXT      SEGMENT BYTE PUBLIC 'CODE'
                  ASSUME  CS:FONT_HI_TEXT,DS:_DATA

;                 ARG1 = X
;                 ARG2 = Y
;                 ARG3 = STRING
;                 ARG4 = COLOUR
;                 ARG6 = FONT
                  PUBLIC  _DrawFontString
_DrawFontString PROC     FAR
                  PUSH     BP
                  MOV      BP,SP
                  SUB      SP,DRAWFN_ADJUST
                  PUSH     DS
                  PUSH     ES

                  LDATASEG

                  CALL     HIDECURSOR

                  ;FETCH THE STRING
                  MOV      SI,[BP + _AOFF + 4]
                  MOV      DS,[BP + _AOFF + 6]

                  ;SEE HOW LONG IT IS
                  MOV      WORD PTR [BP - DRAWFN_N],0000H
DF1:              LODSB
                  CMP      AL,00H
                  JE       DF2

                  INC      WORD PTR [BP - DRAWFN_N]
                  JMP      DF1

                  ;FETCH THE FONT POINTER
DF2:              MOV      SI,[BP + _AOFF + 10]
                  MOV      DS,[BP + _AOFF + 12]

                  ;SAVE A POINTER TO THE FONT BITMAP
                  MOV      [BP - DRAWFN_BMPOFF],SI
                  MOV      [BP - DRAWFN_BMPSEG],DS
```

```
                          ADD      WORD PTR [BP - DRAWFN_BMPOFF],SIZE FONT

                          ;GET THE FONT DEPTH
                          MOV      CX,DS:[SI + FN_BITMAPDEPTH]
                          MOV      WORD PTR [BP - DRAWFN_I],0000H

              DF3:        PUSH     CX

                          ;FETCH THE LEFT COORDINATE
                          MOV      AX,[BP + _AOFF + 0]
                          MOV      [BP - DRAWFN_CB],AX

                          MOV      CX,[BP - DRAWFN_N]
                          MOV      WORD PTR [BP - DRAWFN_J],0000H

              DF4:        PUSH     CX

                          ;FETCH A CHARACTER FROM THE STRING
                          MOV      SI,[BP + _AOFF + 4]
                          MOV      DS,[BP + _AOFF + 6]
                          MOV      BX,[BP - DRAWFN_J]
                          MOV      AL,DS:[SI + BX]

                          ;FETCH A POINTER TO THE FONT
                          MOV      SI,[BP + _AOFF + 10]
                          MOV      DS,[BP + _AOFF + 12]

                          ;CHECK FOR SPACE CHARACTER
                          CMP      AL,20H
                          JNE      DF5

                          ;IF IT'S A SPACE, JUST PAD RIGHT AND CONTINUE
                          MOV      AX,[BP - DRAWFN_CB]
                          ADD      AX,DS:[SI + FN_SPACEWIDTH]
                          ADD      AX,DS:[SI + FN_PADWIDTH]
                          MOV      [BP - DRAWFN_CB],AX
                          JMP      DF8

                          ;IF IT'S NOT A SPACE, DRAW THE CHARACTER
              DF5:        MOV      BL,AL
                          AND      BX,00FFH

                          MOV      AL,DS:[SI + FN_CHARWIDE + BX]
                          AND      AX,00FFH
                          MOV      [BP - DRAWFN_KL],AX

                          SHL      BX,1
                          MOV      AX,DS:[SI + FN_CHAROFF + BX]
                          MOV      [BP - DRAWFN_CP],AX

                          ;LOOP FOR THE CHARACTER WIDTH
                          MOV      CX,[BP - DRAWFN_KL]
              DF6:        PUSH     CX

                          ;SEE IF THIS BIT IS SET IN THE CHARACTER BITMAP
```

```
            LDATASEG
            MOV      BX,[BP - DRAWFN_CP]
            AND      BX,0007H
            MOV      AL,[_MASKTABLE + BX]

            MOV      SI,[BP - DRAWFN_BMPOFF]
            MOV      DS,[BP - DRAWFN_BMPSEG]
            MOV      BX,[BP - DRAWFN_CP]
            MOV      CL,3
            SHR      BX,CL
            TEST     DS:[SI + BX],AL
            JZ       DF7

            ;GET A POINTER TO THE LINE
            MOV      BX,[BP + _AOFF + 2]
            MOV      AX,[BP - DRAWFN_I]
            ADD      BX,AX
            CALL     VGALINE
            GRAFADD_DI [BP-DRAWFN_CB]

            ;WRITE THE PIXEL
            MOV      AX,[BP + _AOFF + 8]
            GRAF_STOSW

DF7:        INC      WORD PTR [BP - DRAWFN_CB]
            INC      WORD PTR [BP - DRAWFN_CP]

            POP      CX
            LOOP     DF6

            ;PAD OVER BY THE PAD WIDTH
            MOV      SI,[BP + _AOFF + 10]
            MOV      DS,[BP + _AOFF + 12]
            MOV      AX,DS:[SI + FN_PADWIDTH]
            ADD      [BP - DRAWFN_CB],AX

DF8:        POP      CX
            INC      WORD PTR [BP - DRAWFN_J]
            LNGLOOP  DF4

            ;POINT TO THE NEXT LINE OF THE FONT BITMAP
            MOV      SI,[BP + _AOFF + 10]
            MOV      DS,[BP + _AOFF + 12]
            MOV      AX,DS:[SI + FN_BITMAPBYTES]
            ADD      [BP - DRAWFN_BMPOFF],AX

            POP      CX
            INC      WORD PTR [BP - DRAWFN_I]

            ;MAKE SURE WE WON'T BE WRITING PAST THE END OF THE SCREEN
            LDATASEG
            MOV      AX,[BP + _AOFF + 2]
            ADD      AX,[BP - DRAWFN_I]
            CMP      AX,[_SCREENDEEP]
            JGE      DF9
```

```
                                          LNGLOOP DF3

                                          ;RESTORE THE BIT MASK TO ALL BITS ON
                        DF9:              LDATASEG
                                          CALL     SHOWCURSOR

                                          POP      ES
                                          POP      DS
                                          ADD      SP,DRAWFN_ADJUST
                                          POP      BP
                                          RET
                        _DrawFontString ENDP

                        FONT_HI_TEXT     ENDS

                        DGROUP           GROUP    _DATA,_BSS
                        _DATA            SEGMENT WORD PUBLIC 'DATA'

                                          EXTRN _SCREENTBL:WORD
                                          EXTRN _SCREENSEG:WORD
                                          EXTRN _SCREENBYTES:WORD
                                          EXTRN _SCREENWIDE:WORD
                                          EXTRN _SCREENDEEP:WORD
                                          EXTRN _MASKTABLE:BYTE
                                          EXTRN _BITTABLE:BYTE
                                          EXTRN CODEPAGE:WORD

                        _DATA            ENDS

                        _BSS             SEGMENT WORD PUBLIC 'BSS'

                        _BSS             ENDS

                                          END
```

Finally, the C language calling program for the high-color `DrawFontString` can be found in FIG. 6-19. It does pretty much what the foregoing two test programs have done, save that it uses the high-color image structure examined in Chapter 5.

```
/*
            Using fonts in high colour

            Copyright (c) 1992 Alchemy Mindworks Inc.

            Links to MOUSE-HI.ASM
            Links to FONT-HI.ASM
*/

#include "stdio.h"
#include "dos.h"
#include "alloc.h"
#include "mouse-hi.h"
```

```
#define MINFONTCHAR        0           /* lowest number font character */
#define MAXFONTCHAR        255         /* highest number font character */
#define FONTNAMESIZE       32          /* maximum size of a font name */

#define BADRECNUM          0xffffffffL     /* illegal record number */

typedef struct {
        char name[FONTNAMESIZE+1];
        char number;
        char pointsize;
        char charwide[(MAXFONTCHAR-MINFONTCHAR)+1];
        unsigned int charoff[(MAXFONTCHAR-MINFONTCHAR)+1];
        unsigned int bitmapwidth;
        unsigned int bitmapdepth;
        unsigned int bitmapbytes;
        unsigned int widestchar;
        unsigned int padwidth;
        unsigned int spacewidth;
        } FONT;

typedef struct {
        char id[8];
        char description[65];
        unsigned int count;
        } RESHEAD;

typedef struct {
        char type[4];
        unsigned long number;
        unsigned int size;
        } RESOURCE;

typedef struct  {
        char manufacturer;
        char version;
        char encoding;
        char bits_per_pixel;
        int xmin,ymin;
        int xmax,ymax;
        int hres;
        int vres;
        char palette[48];
        char reserved;
        char colour_planes;
        int bytes_per_line;
        int palette_type;
        char filler[58];
        } PCXHEAD;

/* some useful colours */
#define BLACK              HIGHCOLOUR(0x00,0x00,0x00)
#define BLUE               HIGHCOLOUR(0x00,0x00,0xaa)
#define GREEN              HIGHCOLOUR(0x00,0xaa,0x00)
#define CYAN               HIGHCOLOUR(0x00,0xaa,0xaa)
#define RED                HIGHCOLOUR(0xaa,0x00,0x00)
```

6-19
Continued.

```
#define MAGENTA          HIGHCOLOUR(0xaa,0x00,0xaa)
#define YELLOW           HIGHCOLOUR(0xaa,0xaa,0x00)
#define GREY             HIGHCOLOUR(0xaa,0xaa,0xaa)
#define DARKGREY         HIGHCOLOUR(0x55,0x55,0x55)
#define LIGHTGREY        HIGHCOLOUR(0xcc,0xcc,0xcc)
#define LIGHTBLUE        HIGHCOLOUR(0x00,0x00,0xff)
#define LIGHTGREEN       HIGHCOLOUR(0x00,0xff,0x00)
#define LIGHTRED         HIGHCOLOUR(0xff,0x00,0x00)
#define LIGHTYELLOW      HIGHCOLOUR(0xff,0xff,0x00)
#define LIGHTMAGENTA     HIGHCOLOUR(0xff,0x00,0xff)
#define WHITE            HIGHCOLOUR(0xff,0xff,0xff)

#define RESID            "ALCHRSRC"
#define FONTFILE         "DTPE.RES"
#define FONTID           "FONT"

void DrawFontString(unsigned int x,unsigned int y,char *string,\
                    unsigned int colour,FONT *font);
FONT *loadfont(char *s,unsigned long n);
unsigned long *countfonts(char *s);

main(argc,argv)
        int argc;
        char *argv[];
{
        static unsigned int colourtable[8]= {
                BLACK,RED,LIGHTRED,LIGHTYELLOW,
                LIGHTBLUE,YELLOW,GREEN,DARKGREY
        };

        FONT *thefont;
        BUTTON save,quit;
        POINT p;
        char b[128];
        unsigned long *lp;
        int i=10,j=0,k,n=0,alive=1,thiscard=0xffff;

        if((lp=countfonts(FONTFILE))== NULL || lp[0]==BADRECNUM) {
                puts("Can't find fonts");
                exit(1);
        }

        /* see what kind of card is installed - sort of */
        if(argc > 1) {
                if(!stricmp(argv[1],"PARADISE")) thiscard=PARADISE;
                else if(!stricmp(argv[1],"ATI")) thiscard=ATI;
                else if(!stricmp(argv[1],"TSENG")) thiscard=TSENG;
        }

        /* go for a graphics mode */
        if(!InitMouse(640,480,thiscard)) exit(1);

        SetVgaWhite(WHITE);
        SetVgaBlack(BLACK);
        SetVgaGrey(GREY);
```

```
                SetVgaLightGrey(LIGHTGREY);
                SetVgaDarkGrey(DARKGREY);

                /* clear the screen */
                ClearScreen(GetVgaLightGrey());

                /* show the fonts */
                do {
                        if((thefont=loadfont(FONTFILE,lp[n++])) != NULL) {
                                sprintf(b,"This is %u point %s",
                                    thefont->pointsize,thefont->name);
                                k=(SCREENWIDE-FontStringLength(b,thefont))/2;
                                DrawFontString(k,i,b,colourtable[j % 8],thefont);
                                i+=thefont->bitmapdepth;
                                free((char *)thefont);
                                ++j;
                        }
                } while(lp[n] != BADRECNUM && thefont != NULL && i < SCREENDEEP);

                free((char *)lp);

                /* create a button to click on */
                MakeButton(SCREENWIDE-100,SCREENDEEP-60,"Quit",&quit);
                DrawButton(&quit);

                MakeButton(SCREENWIDE-200,SCREENDEEP-60,"Save",&save);
                DrawButton(&save);

                /* loop 'til we're done */
                do {
                        /* look for a mouse click */
                        if(MouseDown(&p)) {
                                if(PointInRect(&p,&quit)) {
                                        TrackButton(&quit);
                                        alive=0;
                                }
                                else if(PointInRect(&p,&save)) {
                                        TrackButton(&save);
                                        DoSave("SCREEN00.PCX");
                                }
                        }
                } while(alive);

                DeinitMouse();
}

/* save the screen to a PCX file */
DoSave(path)
        char *path;
{
        PCXHEAD pcx;
        FILE *fp;
        char *ps,*pd;
        unsigned int i,j,n,*ip;
```

```
/* create the destination file */
if((fp=fopen(path,"wb"))==NULL) {
        beep();
        return;
}

if((ps=malloc(SCREENWIDE*sizeof(unsigned int)))==NULL) {
        beep();
        fclose(fp);
        return;
}

if((pd=malloc(SCREENWIDE))==NULL) {
        free(ps);
        beep();
        fclose(fp);
        return;
}

memset((char *)&pcx,0,sizeof(PCXHEAD));

pcx.manufacturer=10;
pcx.encoding=1;
pcx.xmin=pcx.ymin=0;
pcx.xmax=SCREENWIDE-1;
pcx.ymax=SCREENDEEP-1;
pcx.bits_per_pixel=8;
pcx.version=5;
pcx.colour_planes=3;
pcx.bytes_per_line=SCREENWIDE;

WaitCursor();
if(fwrite((char *)&pcx,1,sizeof(PCXHEAD),fp) != sizeof(PCXHEAD))
{
        free(pd);
        free(ps);
        fclose(fp);
        remove(path);
        ArrowCursor();
        beep();
        return;
}

for(i=0;i<SCREENDEEP;++i) {
        MouseOff();
        GetScreenLine(ps,i);
        MouseOn();

        /* extract the red components */
        ip=(unsigned int *)ps;
        for(j=0;j<SCREENWIDE;++j) pd[j]=HIGHRED(ip[j]);
        n=pcxwriteline(fp,pd,pcx.bytes_per_line);

        /* extract the green components */
        ip=(unsigned int *)ps;
```

```
                        for(j=0;j<SCREENWIDE;++j) pd[j]=HIGHGREEN(ip[j]);
                        n=pcxwriteline(fp,pd,pcx.bytes_per_line);

                        /* extract the blue components */
                        ip=(unsigned int *)ps;
                        for(j=0;j<SCREENWIDE;++j) pd[j]=HIGHBLUE(ip[j]);
                        n=pcxwriteline(fp,pd,pcx.bytes_per_line);

                        if(n != pcx.bytes_per_line) {
                                free(pd);
                                free(ps);
                                fclose(fp);
                                remove(path);
                                ArrowCursor();
                                beep();
                                return;
                        }
                }

        ArrowCursor();
        free(pd);
        free(ps);
        fclose(fp);
}

/* write one pcx line */
pcxwriteline(fp,p,n)
        FILE *fp;
        char *p;
        unsigned int n;
{
        unsigned int i=0,j=0,t=0;

        do {
                i=0;
                while((p[t+i]==p[t+i+1]) && ((t+i) < n) && (i < 63))++i;
                if(i>0) {
                        if(fputc(i | 0xc0,fp)==EOF) return(-1);
                        if(fputc(p[t],fp)==EOF) return(-1);
                        t+=i;
                        j+=2;
                }
                else {
                        if(((p[t]) & 0xc0)==0xc0) {
                                if(fputc(0xc1,fp)==EOF) return(-1);
                                ++j;
                        }
                        if(fputc(p[t++],fp)==EOF) return(-1);
                        ++j;
                }
        } while(t<n);
        return(n);
}
```

```
       FontStringLength(s,font)
                char *s;
                FONT *font;
      {
                unsigned int a=0;

                /* add up the character widths of all the characters in the string
                    */
                while(*s) a+=font->charwide[*s++];
                return(a);
      }

      unsigned long *countfonts(s)
                char *s;
      {
                RESHEAD rh;
                RESOURCE rc;
                unsigned long *lp;
                FILE *fp;
                unsigned int i,j;

                /* open the resource file */
                if((fp=fopen(s,"rb")) == NULL) return(NULL);

                /* read the header */
                if(fread((char *)&rh,1,sizeof(RESHEAD),fp) != sizeof(RESHEAD)) {
                        fclose(fp);
                        return(NULL);
                }

                /* make sure it's a resource file */
                if(memcmp(rh.id,RESID,8)) {
                        fclose(fp);
                        return(NULL);
                }

                /* allocate a buffer for the numbers */
                if((lp=(unsigned long *)malloc((1+rh.count)*sizeof(unsigned long))) == NULL) {
                        fclose(fp);
                        return(NULL);
                }

                /* set the end of the buffer */
                lp[0]=BADRECNUM;

                /* step through each resource */
                for(i=j=0;i<rh.count;++i) {

                        /* fetch the resource */
                        if(fread((char *)&rc,1,sizeof(RESOURCE),fp) !=
                        sizeof(RESOURCE)) {
                                fclose(fp);
                                return(lp);
                        }
```

```
                    /* if it's a font, add it to the list */
                    if(!memcmp(rc.type,FONTID,4)) {
                            lp[j++]=rc.number;
                            lp[j]=BADRECNUM;
                    }

                    /* seek to the next resource */
                    fseek(fp,(unsigned long)rc.size,SEEK_CUR);
            }

        fclose(fp);
        return(lp);
}

FONT *loadfont(s,n)
        char *s;
        unsigned long n;
{
        RESHEAD rh;
        RESOURCE rc;
        FONT *font;
        FILE *fp;
        unsigned int i;

        /* open the resource file */
        if((fp=fopen(s,"rb")) == NULL) return(NULL);

        /* read the header */
        if(fread((char *)&rh,1,sizeof(RESHEAD),fp) != sizeof(RESHEAD)) {
                fclose(fp);
                return(NULL);
        }

        /* make sure it's a resource file */
        if(memcmp(rh.id,RESID,8)) {
                fclose(fp);
                return(NULL);
        }

        /* look at all the resources */
        for(i=0;i<rh.count;++i) {

                /* fetch the resource */
                if(fread((char *)&rc,1,sizeof(RESOURCE),fp) != sizeof(RESOURCE)) {
                        fclose(fp);
                        return(NULL);
                }

                /* if it's a font and it's the one we want, load it */
                if(!memcmp(rc.type,FONTID,4) && rc.number == n) {

                        /* allocate a buffer for the data */
                        if((font=(FONT *)malloc(rc.size)) == NULL) {
                                fclose(fp);
                                return(NULL);
```

```
                                 }

                                 /* read the data */
                                 if(fread((char *)font,1,rc.size,fp) != rc.size) {
                                         free((char *)font);
                                         fclose(fp);
                                         return(NULL);
                                 }

                                 /* we're done -- go away */
                                 fclose(fp);
                                 return(font);
                        }

                        /* otherwise, seek to the next resource */
                        fseek(fp,(unsigned long)rc.size,SEEK_CUR);
                }

        /* resource not found */
        fclose(fp);
        return(NULL);
}

MakeButton(left,top,string,button)
        unsigned int left,top;
        char *string;
        BUTTON *button;
{
        button->frame.left = left & 0xfff8;
        button->frame.right=button->frame.left+(strlen(string)<3)+16;
        button->frame.top=top;
        button->frame.bottom=button->frame.top+FONTDEPTH+8;
        button->text=string;
}

DrawButton(button)
        BUTTON *button;
{
        FillRect(button->frame.left+1,button->frame.top+1,
                button->frame.right-1,button->frame.bottom-
                1,GetVgaWhite());
        DrawLine(button->frame.left+1,button->frame.top,
                button->frame.right-1,button->frame.top,GetVgaBlack());
        DrawLine(button->frame.left,button->frame.top+1,
                button->frame.left,button->frame.bottom-1,GetVgaBlack());
        DrawLine(button->frame.right,button->frame.top+1,
                button->frame.right,button->frame.bottom-
                1,GetVgaBlack());
        DrawLine(button->frame.left+1,button->frame.bottom,
                button->frame.right-1,button-
                >frame.bottom,GetVgaBlack());
        Fill3DBox(button->frame.left+1,button->frame.top+1,
                button->frame.right-1,button->frame.bottom-1);

        DrawString(button->frame.left+8,button->frame.top+4,
                button->text,GetVgaDarkGrey(),GetVgaLightGrey());
```

```
}

TrackButton(button)
        BUTTON *button;
{
        POINT p;

        FillRect(button->frame.left+1,button->frame.top+1,
                button->frame.right-1,button->frame.bottom-1,GetVgaLightGrey());

        DrawString(button->frame.left+8,button->frame.top+4,
                button->text,GetVgaDarkGrey(),GetVgaLightGrey());
        while(MouseDown(&p));
        DrawButton(button);
}

Fill3DBox(left,top,right,bottom)
        int left,top,right,bottom;
{
        FillRect(left,top,right,bottom,GetVgaLightGrey());
        DrawLine(left,top,right-1,top,GetVgaWhite());
        DrawLine(left,top+1,left,bottom-1,GetVgaWhite());

        DrawLine(left+3,bottom,right,bottom,GetVgaDarkGrey());
        DrawLine(right,top+2,right,bottom-1,GetVgaDarkGrey());
}

PointInRect(p,r)/* return true if point is in rect */
        POINT *p;
        RECT *r;
{
        if(p->x > r->left && p->x < r->right &&
           p->y > r->top  && p->y < r->bottom) return(1);
        else return(0);
}

WaitCursor()
{
        static char cursor[] = {
                0x00,0x00,0x00,0x00,
                0x00,0x00,0x01,0x80,
                0x03,0xC0,0x07,0xE0,
                0x0F,0xF0,0x07,0xE0,
                0x03,0xC0,0x01,0x80,
                0x00,0x00,0x00,0x00,
                0x00,0x00,0x00,0x00,
                0xFF,0xFF,0xFF,0xFF,

                0x00,0x00,0xFE,0x7F,
                0x06,0x60,0x0C,0x30,
                0x18,0x18,0x30,0x0C,
                0x60,0x06,0xC0,0x03,
                0x60,0x06,0x30,0x0C,
                0x98,0x19,0xCC,0x33,
                0xE6,0x67,0xFE,0x7F,
```

```
                            0x00,0x00,0x00,0x00 };

                MouseCursor(cursor,7,7);
        }

ArrowCursor()
{
        static char cursor[] = {
                0xFF,0x3F,0xFF,0x1F,
                0xFF,0x0F,0xFF,0x07,
                0xFF,0x03,0xFF,0x01,
                0xFF,0x00,0x7F,0x00,
                0x3F,0x00,0x1F,0x00,
                0xFF,0x01,0xFF,0x10,
                0xFF,0x30,0x7F,0xF8,
                0x7F,0xF8,0x7F,0xFC,
                0x00,0x00,0x00,0x40,
                0x00,0x60,0x00,0x70,
                0x00,0x78,0x00,0x7C,
                0x00,0x7E,0x00,0x7F,
                0x80,0x7F,0x00,0x7C,
                0x00,0x6C,0x00,0x46,
                0x00,0x06,0x00,0x03,
                0x00,0x03,0x00,0x00 };

        MouseCursor(cursor,0,0);
}
```

You should create a project or a MAKE file to link the following files, creating TESTF-HI.EXE

TESTF-HI.C
MOUSE-HI.OBJ
FONT-HI.OBJ

Note that each of the EXE programs generated in this chapter expects to see a command line argument to tell it which sort of display card it will be working with. These arguments are the same as the ones used in Chapters 3 through 5 for the mouse and graphics test programs. The TESTF16 program will default to the standard 640 by 480 pixel VGA mode in the absence of one. The TESTF256 and TESTF-HI will return to DOS immediately, as the standard VGA modes don't really provide them with workable defaults.

Furthering fonts

The code in this chapter will provide you with fast, tight functions to draw text using font resources. In most applications that use more than a few fonts, however, a large part of making your software work effectively will involve managing font resources. Of necessity, the font management code dealt with in this chapter— essentially countfonts and loadfonts—is a bit primitive.

If you understand how the resource structure of fonts work, you should have little difficulty in writing a more effective resource manager. Alternately, you can work with effectively the same resource manager that Desktop Paint does. It's included in the *Graphical User Interface Programming* book mentioned earlier in this chapter.

7 Printing super VGA graphics

Guttenberg's revenge

"That was zen, this is tao."
—Graffiti

Hard copy rarely looks as good as what you can display on a monitor, but it's tangible and a lot easier to ship. Its warranty isn't voided if you drop it, and when you don't want it anymore, it's easily disposed of. We use errant hard copy to light fires—wood heat changes one's perspective of technology to some extent.

Printing super VGA graphics to the current generation of hard copy devices is a bit of a challenge, mostly because the current generation is pretty varied. There are a few mutants in with the good seeds as well. Printers, unlike super VGA display cards, are not constrained to behave themselves in a way that's calculated to make the universe a warmer and friendlier place for software authors.

As a rule, printing graphics is a relatively unpleasant undertaking for software. Printers are slow, hard to communicate with, and make the mindless chaos of super VGA display standards look like a well-thought-out, disciplined organization by comparison. Most of the popular printer standards were in fact designed by trans-dimensional alien life forms who have plans to take over western civilization while everyone's busy trying to figure out why their printers keep misfeeding.

This isn't an assertion you're likely to find documented in the manual for your printer, of course.

This chapter would be lying pretty substantially if it suggested that it will tell you everything there is to know about graphic printing. It will, however, provide you with functions to print super VGA screens to any of four broad classes of printers in any of the three basic super VGA graphic modes we've covered throughout this book. For practical purposes, these functions will allow you to support most of the worthwhile printers currently in use with PC systems—albeit with a few compromises in some cases.

Specifically, the `DoPrintScreen` functions in this chapter will drive the following printers:

❏ Any LaserJet Plus-compatible printer
❏ Any PostScript printer
❏ Any Epson FX80-compatible printer
❏ Any Hewlett-Packard PaintJet or Deskjet 500C

7-1
The hard copy generated by the programs in this chapter, printed from 16-color, 256-color, and high-color screens respectively.

These will unquestionably require a bit of explaining. Figure 7-1 illustrates the three screens these programs will create. These images were actually printed by a PostScript printer.

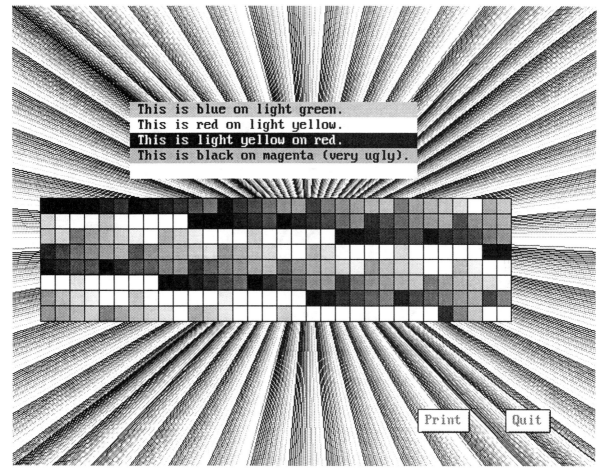

7-1 *Continued.*

The three programs to be presented later in this chapter will generate text screens and print them to the printer of your choice. There is one program each for 16, 256, and high-color graphics.

While the example `DoPrintScreen` functions to be dealt with here print the graphics they find on their screens, keep in mind that a super VGA screen is really just a bitmap—if a rather peculiarly structured one in some modes. As such, you should encounter little difficulty in modifying these functions to print bitmaps stored in memory, for example, or in an FRG file.

Printer basics

The simplest way to regard a graphics printer is as a bitmap—this is, in effect, how one will treat the paper running through it. A printer can print the dots of its virtual bitmap as dots of ink or toner on paper. If you manipulate the bitmap such that some of the dots are on and some of them off, you can print images.

For practical purposes, you can't just send a simple bitmap of the type that's turned up in this book to a printer. Image data destined for a printer must be encoded in a

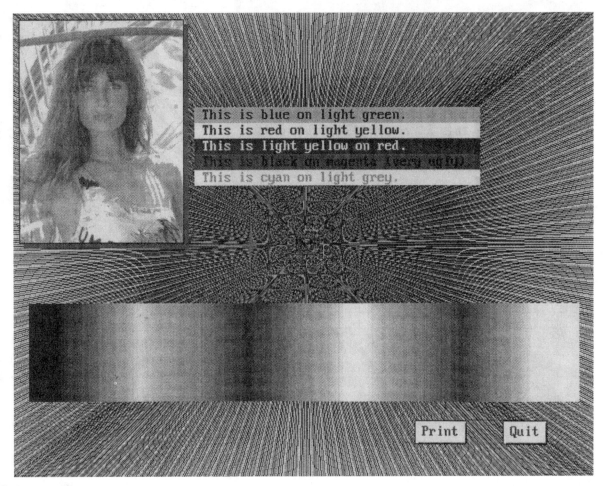

7-1 *Continued.*

way that will make sense to the printer in question. Just as super VGA cards from
different sources require different driver code to make them work, so do different
types of printers. In fact, the differences among printers are somewhat more radical.

In printing a super VGA bitmap—that is, in translating between a screen bitmap
and a printer bitmap—a printer driver must deal with several limitations of printers.
To begin with, printers don't have palettes. A monochrome laser printer, for
example, can't print grey—its engine can only handle black dots on white paper. In
order to make such a printer represent colors or grey levels, some way must be
found to simulate grey with black and white.

A similar problem occurs in discussing color inkjet printers. A DeskJet 500C, one of
the printers to be dealt with in this chapter, can really only print in one of three colors:
cyan, magenta, and yellow. None of these are terribly attractive colors, and in order to
coerce a more useful range of colors from a Deskjet, some stealth will be required.

Secondly, printers are mechanical devices, and in some cases the data sent to them must be structured in a way to make it compatible with the mechanics of a printer's hardware. There are few cases wherein this will prove to be particularly convenient.

The final problem in driving a printer is that a parallel printer port, as found on a PC, is a rather inelegant bit of hardware that hasn't changed since printers first replaced cave painting as a primary hard copy device. Applications running under DOS that want to drive a PC's printer port usually have to juggle a few bits and interrupts to make it happen reliably.

The foregoing list of printer types was presented in the order of increasing driver complexity. While by no means the least expensive type of printer on the list, Hewlett-Packard LaserJet Plus printers—and printers compatible with them—are about the simplest sorts of printers to drive if you'll be printing graphics. We'll begin by looking at them.

It was noted earlier that a graphics printer is really a sort of bitmap. Laser printers are very large bitmaps, as the dots of a laser printer's engine are exceedingly small. At 300 dots per inch, a laser printer represents a bitmap of 2400 by 3150 pixels, or 7,560,000 pixels in total. This is the actual printable area of an 8.5" by 11" page on a laser printer; most lasers have an unprintable margin about a quarter of an inch around their printing areas.

LaserJet printing

Driving a printer like this by sending it a huge bitmap for each page would be exceedingly time consuming, and it would entail having about a megabyte of spare memory in your computer to generate each bitmap that the printer is to print. This would be a very involved undertaking just to print a letter, for example.

To make laser printers somewhat more useful, the interface between a laser printer's engine and your computer includes a "printer control language." The printer control language for a Hewlett-Packard LaserJet printer is called *PCL*—which stands, rather unimaginatively, for printer control language.

In its simplest sense, PCL allows you to deal with a LaserJet in one of several ways, depending on what you want to print. You can treat a LaserJet as a "dumb teletype," which means that it will print whatever text you send it in the way a simple dot matrix printer would. It will print such text in very well formed twelve-point Courier type, however, in the way a simple dot matrix printer certainly would not.

The PCL language also allows you to define other fonts to print text in. This will allow suitable software to print complex pages with multiple typefaces and such.

Finally, you can send bitmaps to a PCL printer. As with text, you can position a bitmap anywhere on the page being created. The basic PCL language only allows for monochrome bitmaps, however.

A LaserJet printer will print whatever it's sent, save for escape characters (ASCII character 27). If it receives an escape character followed by one of a predefined sequence of codes, it will interpret the data as a command. These "escape sequences" allow you to change fonts, position the printer's cursor, and code up bitmapped line data, for example. The list of PCL escape sequences is pretty extensive, and most of it is beyond the scope of this chapter to deal with.

The DoPrintScreen function in this chapter will only concern itself with dumping a simple bitmap to a LaserJet.

Thus far we've examined LaserJets as a single class of printers. In fact, there are numerous variations on the original Hewlett-Packard LaserJet. An authentic first-generation LaserJet won't work with the code in this chapter—a LaserJet requires at least a megabyte of memory to print graphics. The original LaserJet only came with 512K.

The LaserJet Plus printer, a slightly less antediluvian device, supported basic PCL and had enough memory to handle graphics. It was widely emulated, and most low cost "personal" laser printers are in effect LaserJet Plus machines. The DoPrintScreen functions in this chapter will drive any of these printers.

In recent years, Hewlett Packard has released newer LaserJets—the LaserJet II, III, and 4 printers. These printers support a superset of the facilities of original PCL—they use what's called PCL 5. The DoPrintScreen functions in this chapter will drive these newer LaserJets, although if you're interested in digging into the workings of PCL 5, you'll find that you can improve on their performance considerably.

The arguable drawback to PCL 5 printers is that most of the LaserJet-compatible printers currently in use don't support the advanced features of PCL 5. If you want to support all LaserJet-compatible printers, you should limit your software to using only the basic PCL features. As such, the LaserJet drivers in this chapter will work with the original LaserJet Plus implementation of the language.

Simple dithering

In printing a color graphic—such as the screens generated by the test programs earlier in this book—a printer driver is confronted by two basic problems. The first one involves converting colors to grey levels. The second one is representing grey levels as black and white dots, assuming that the printer in question has no facilities for doing internal halftoning.

The first problem is easily solved using the greyvalue macro from Chapter 2. This will replace any RGB color with a corresponding grey level ranging from 0 through 255—that is, from pure black through pure white. In theory, the grey levels generated by greyvalue represent the luminosity, or relative brightness, of the colors they're derived from.

Representing a grey-scale image as black and white dots is a much more nettlesome problem, and one for which there is no perfect solution. Printers that provide internal halftoning facilities—such as the PostScript printer that generated FIG. 7-1— can generate variable size spots based on the density of the source image being printed, much as photographic halftones in newspapers and magazines do. Unfortunately, they lose considerable image resolution in doing so. Perhaps more to the point, this is not a facility that's available under the basic PCL language.

Representing more grey levels or colors than really exist on a computer is typically handled through a process called *dithering*. As a simple example, you can create a very convincing 50 percent grey area by alternating black and white pixels. You can apply dithering techniques to complex bitmapped images as well.

There are a number of approaches to dithering images. The simplest is called *Bayer dithering*. Figure 7-2 illustrates a graphic that has been halftoned and Bayer dithered.

The results of Bayer dithering are far from exemplary, but Bayer dithering has a number of fairly worthwhile characteristics. Specifically, it's very fast, easy to implement and requires virtually no memory overhead to operate. More sophisticated dithering algorithms—usually referred to as "error diffused" dithering—can take hundreds of times longer to run than a Bayer dither.

There's a much more complete description of image dithering in my book *Bitmapped Graphics*, published by Windcrest.

Bayer dithering represents a good compromise in writing a function to dump a graphic screen to a printer. Figure 7-3 (on page 407) illustrates one of the Bayer dither screen captures from the programs in this chapter.

7-2   *Halftoning and Bayer dithering a color graphic. Downloaded from Rose Media, (416) 733-2285.*

7-2 *Continued.*

Just as it's easy to implement, Bayer dithering is easy to understand. It's based on an eight by eight matrix of values, as illustrated here:

```
char bayerPattern[8][8] = {
         0,32, 8,40, 2,34,10,42,
        48,16,56,24,50,18,58,26,
        12,44, 4,36,14,46, 6,38,
        60,28,52,20,62,30,54,22,
         3,35,11,43, 1,33, 9,41,
        51,19,59,27,49,17,57,25,
        15,47, 7,39,13,45, 5,37,
        63,31,55,23,61,29,53,21 };
```

There are 64 different values in the bayerPattern array, ranging from 0 through 63. As such, an image to be Bayer dithered should have no more than 64 distinct grey levels. The values returned by the greyvalue macro can range from 0 through 256. They can be converted to the required range by shifting them right by two places.

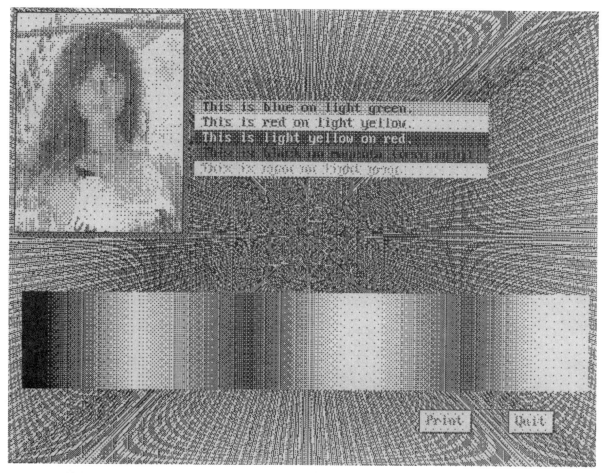

7-3 *A Bayer dither of one of the images from Fig. 7-1.*

Each pixel to be Bayer dithered is compared against the bayerPattern matrix based on its location. Allowing that p points to a line of grey pixels set up by greyvalue and that y is the number of the line, here's how you would Bayer-dither the line:

```
int i;
for(i=0;i<LINEWIDE;++i) {
        if((p[i] >> 2) > bayerPattern[y & 7][i & 7]) {
                /* this is a white pixel */
        }
        else {
                /* this is a black pixel */
        }
}
```

The result of dithering an image using the Bayer dithering pattern is to impose a fixed pattern of alternating black and white areas on it, based on the original density of the pixels. This isn't all that convincing as halftone procedures go, as witnessed by FIG. 7-2, but it can be surprisingly good.

It's probably worth observing that the test screens generated by the programs in this chapter are pathologically bad cases for dithering. Dithering imposes a repeating pattern on an image. The test screens create moires, or interference patterns, between the matrix of pixels on your screen and the radial lines in the screen pattern. Overlayed by the pattern of the Bayer matrix, the screen images can be seen to take on some additional interference characteristics—which don't look all that interesting.

LaserJet escape sequences

Printing a bitmap to a LaserJet-compatible printer only requires a fraction of the voluminous library of escape sequences the PCL language offers. Specifically, a LaserJet driver should be able to do the following:

❏ Reset the printer
❏ Set the printer resolution
❏ Position the upper left corner of the bitmap to be printed.
❏ Send the bitmap data
❏ Eject the page

As was noted earlier, all the escape sequences used to drive a LaserJet consist of character 27 followed by some data. Ejecting a completed page is an exception to this—it's handled by sending a formfeed character, ASCII character 12.

This is the escape sequence to reinitialize a LaserJet to its power-up condition:

```
\033E
```

This is a C language string. The \033 character is the octal representation of 27—for historical reasons, C is somewhat enamored of octal. Most compilers will allow you to write this as \x1b as well (that is, in hexadecimal).

As an aside, one of the most useful bits of hardware you can invest in to make software easier to write is a Texas Instruments TI-36 calculator. Among other things, it will convert among decimal, binary, hexadecimal, and octal values.

A LaserJet's engine prints at 300 dots per inch, but you can tell it to run in any of four resolution modes, these being 75, 100, 150, and 300 dots per inch. The lower resolution modes print with larger pixels and thus will generate bigger graphics, all other things being equal. A super VGA screen printed at 300 dots per inch will come out looking like a bad design for a postage stamp—the 100 dot per inch resolution will print an 800 by 600 pixel screen such that it just fits across a normal 8.5" by 11" page.

Here's the escape sequence to select 100 dot per inch graphics on a LaserJet:

```
\033*T100R
```

The 100 in the above string is the resolution—you can replace this with one of the other three legal resolution values to select a different resolution. Most PCL implementations will default to 75 dots per inch printing if you attempt to feed them illegal values in this escape sequence.

The default unit of measurement on a LaserJet is the "decipoint," which is a more elaborate word for dot. Because a LaserJet prints at 300 dots per inch, one decipoint is ⅟₃₀₀ of an inch. Here are the escape sequences to position the printer's cursor twenty dots from the left and twenty dots from the top of the page respectively:

```
\033*p20x
\033*p20Y
```

Finally, prior to sending a LaserJet some graphics, you must tell it to expect them by sending it this escape sequence:

```
\033*r1A
```

The 1 in the foregoing escape sequence tells the printer that the upper left corner of the graphic should appear at the current cursor location.

Having initialized the printer, you can send it graphics one line at a time. Each line should be preceded by an escape sequence. This is how you'd send a line of 80 bytes of graphic information:

```
\033*b80W
```

Having sent this escape sequence, the printer would interpret the subsequent 80 bytes as bitmap data. It would then return its cursor to the left edge of the graphic and move down a line, ready for the next line of graphics. In the case of the DoPrintScreen function to be dealt with in this chapter, the bitmap data will actually be dithered from the graphics on your screen.

When all the bitmap lines have been sent, you should tell the printer not to expect anymore graphics for a while by sending it this escape sequence:

```
\033*rB
```

Finally, this is what you'd send a LaserJet to tell it to eject its page:

```
\014
```

A LaserJet accepts monochrome bitmaps in almost the same format as they're stored for display, which makes setting them up to print relatively easy. This won't prove to be the case for any of the other printers to be covered in this chapter, all of which will require a certain amount of data manipulation.

PostScript printing

The PostScript language does pretty much what PCL does—and hundreds of other things as well. PostScript being a rich and fairly complete interpreted programming language rather than a set of escape sequences, there's little you can conceive of that PostScript can't render on paper.

In driving a PostScript printer, an application actually writes a program that defines the graphics to be printed and then downloads it to the printer, where a resident PostScript interpreter executes it. This is analogous to writing a BASIC program to print text to the screen and then having the Microsoft BASIC interpreter run it. PostScript is somewhat more obtuse than BASIC.

Actually, PostScript is somewhat more obtuse than C, which should give you some idea of its magnitude of user-unfriendliness. Among other things, PostScript is a postfix language, like FORTH. This means that its arguments precede its operators. For example, in C, one might move the cursor with a statement like:

```
gotoxy(100,320);
```

Under PostScript, an analogous instruction would be:

```
100 320 moveto
```

Learning to write PostScript programs is a pretty monstrous undertaking. This chapter won't even begin to explore the dark and seething catacombs of PostScript. Printing a few bitmaps doesn't really require a great deal of PostScript expertise. You'll probably find that you can use the functions from the code to be presented herein without really getting into how it works.

The following is a bit of PostScript code. It's used to print bitmaps.

```
/screensize 0 def
/width 640 def
/height 480 def
/pixwidth 460 def
/pixheight 345 def
/picstr width string def
screensize 0 ne {
        screensize 45 {
                abs exch abs 2 copy add 1 gt
                {1 sub dup mul exch 1 sub dup mul add 1 sub }
                { dup mul exch dup mul add 1 exch sub }
                ifelse
        } setscreen
} if
/dopic {
        gsave width height 8
        [width 0 0 height neg 0 height]
        {currentfile picstr readhexstring pop}
        image grestore
} def
/showname {
        /Courier findfont 12 scalefont setfont
        20 20 moveto (This is a picture) show
} def
showname
40 50 translate pixwidth pixheight scale
dopic
```

This program—with two additional elements of code, to be dealt with in a moment—will display a graphic on a PostScript printer. The graphic must have the dimensions 640 by 480 pixels and have eight bits of color. The DoPrintScreen function in this chapter will handle this code slightly differently, replacing these fixed values by whatever dimensions are called for.

Note the screensize definition at the top of the PostScript program. If this is set to 0, as it is here, the graphic will be printed using the printer's internal halftoning algorithm. You can change this to some other value to specify the number of spots per inch for halftoning. You might want to try fairly small numbers to produce very coarse screens—20 to 30 is a good place to start.

Note also the showname definition. This function will print some text at the bottom of the page when a graphic is printed. This isn't used *per se* in the DoPrintScreen functions in this chapter, but you might want to implement it if you'd like to add a few words to your hard copy.

When this program executes, it will attempt to read 307,200 hexadecimal numbers from the standard input file for the printer—that is, one for every pixel in the image. The standard input file is, in fact, the printer port. This code should be followed immediately by a lot of hex data. Each hexadecimal number should consist of two characters—numbers less than 10H must be padded with zeros. In theory, a PostScript printer doesn't care how long a line of input data is; in practice, it's a good idea to introduce a carriage return into the data after every few dozen numbers.

Each number represents the grey level of the pixel it corresponds to.

When all the numbers have been read, the PostScript interpreter will expect to find some legal PostScript code. In this case, we'd like the printer to eject its page. The PostScript instruction for this is:

```
showpage\r\n
```

The only way any of this can go badly wrong is if you provide too few or too many hexadecimal numbers for the dopic PostScript function to interpret. If you send too few, the program will lunch out on whatever comes next. In this case, it will be the showpage instruction, leaving nothing to tell the printer to eject its page. If you send down too much image data, the printer will think that the leftover numbers are to be interpreted as PostScript instructions.

One of the drawbacks to PostScript programming is that PostScript printers aren't terribly vociferous about communicating their problems. Most of the time they hang when they're confronted with bad programs, or they fail to print anything and just go idle after a few minutes.

As an aside, note that PostScript is a large and relatively slow language. In addition, printing an 8-bit graphic as a halftone to a PostScript printer involves sending sixteen times as much data to the printer as handling the same image as a dithered monochrome bitmap on a LaserJet—there will be eight bits per pixel, rather than one, and each 8-bit value will be represented by two characters for a hexadecimal number. Printing a screen to a PostScript printer can take several minutes. It's not hung—it's just thinking hard.

Printing graphics to a dot matrix printer offers new scope and dimension to the word "funky." A bit like a hand-cranked printing press with a maintenance agreement, a dot matrix printer is awkward to deal with at the best of times. You'll find that getting one to generate pictures will be quite the journey into bit juggling.

Dot matrix printing

Of all the poorly defined standards encountered in this book, none will even begin to explore the fantastic confusion of dot matrix printers. Virtually every manufacturer of high-end dot matrix printers has adopted a unique command structure. Writing drivers to print to state-of-the-art 24-pin printers requires that you buy a lot of printers.

If there is a common standard, it's the one defined by a very old printer: the Epson FX-80. While long since discontinued by its manufacturer, the ghost of the FX-80 lives on in most dot matrix printers in that most of them will emulate its escape sequences. The catch in this is that the FX-80 was an 8-pin printer—it produced relatively coarse type and graphics. Printers that emulate it might be capable of much better output in their higher resolution modes, but if you drive one using the Epson FX-80 commands, it will produce work no better than an FX-80 would.

This situation is workable for printing screens, which are relatively coarse. As such, the dot matrix drivers to be covered in this chapter will work with most dot matrix printers. However, if you find you want to print more sophisticated graphics at higher resolutions, you'll have to get into writing dedicated drivers for every printer you want to support.

As an aside, I should note that this code was developed using an authentic antique Epson FX-80 rather than another printer emulating one. This printer turned up at a garage sale for ten dollars, knocked down to eight when its owner couldn't find the plastic cover for the print mechanism. This is probably about average for an FX-80 at the moment.

Should you have thus far avoided investigating the workings of a dot matrix printer, it's probably worth having a quick look at how these things work. As its name might imply, a dot matrix printer's print head consists of a matrix of pins. When called upon to print, selected pins will launch themselves forward through a typewriter ribbon, leaving smudges of ink or carbon on the paper behind the ribbon. Early dot matrix printers used a matrix of eight by eight pins. More sophisticated "near letter quality" printers have pin matrices with 24 pins on a side.

The author of the phrase "near letter quality" clearly had a more liberal interpretation of the word "near" than you or I might.

In printing graphics with a dot matrix printer, only one vertical row of pins is used. In an eight-pin printer, the printer prints a horizontal band of pixels eight dots deep with each pass of its print head. Each position of the print head as it moves across the paper is controlled by one byte of graphic data sent to the printer, but the orientation of the bytes is fundamentally different from that used to store bitmaps in memory.

Figure 7-4 illustrates the relationship of bitmap data to a dot matrix printer's idea of graphics.

In order to print a bitmap, a dot matrix printer driver must separate it into bands and send down each band. In the case of an FX-80, each band is eight lines deep. Each band must be preceded by an escape sequence to tell the printer how long it will be. This is the one we'll use in this chapter:

```
\033*\006LH
```

The bytes L and H aren't really sent as such. They represent the two bytes of an unsigned integer that defines the length of the band in pixels. To print a 640 pixel line, then the L byte would be 80H, or 128, and the H byte would be 02H.

This is a function to print an eight-line bitmap fragment to an Epson FX-80 printer:

```
PrintEpsonBuffer()
{
        char *p;
        int c,i,j,m;

        p_string("\033*\006");
        p_char(SCREENWIDE);
        p_char(SCREENWIDE >> 8);
```

```
for(i=0;i<SCREENWIDE;++i) {
        c=0;
        p=lpbuf+(i>>3);
        m=masktable[i & 0x0007];
        for(j=0;j<EPSON_LINEDEEP;++j) {
                if(*p & m) c |= masktable[j];
                p+=SCREENBYTES;
        }
        p_char(~c);
}
p_string("\015\033J\030");
}
```

The functions p_char and p_string will be explained in greater detail later in this chapter.

Having printed one band of a bitmap, you must send an escape sequence to move the print head back to the left edge of the page and down to be in position for the next band. Unfortunately, an FX-80 doesn't have a standard way of doing this. You can move the print head to the left of the page by sending a carriage return and then move it down by using this escape sequence:

\033JN

In this case, the byte N is the number of $\frac{1}{216}$ of an inch to move the print head down. The value 030 octal, or $\frac{24}{216}$ of an inch, was determined experimentally. Unfortunately, this value isn't consistent among different FX-80 emulations. You might find that on some printers it results in a slight overlap between bands, or a slight gap, and must be adjusted a bit.

7-4

The relationship between bitmap data and dot matrix printer data.

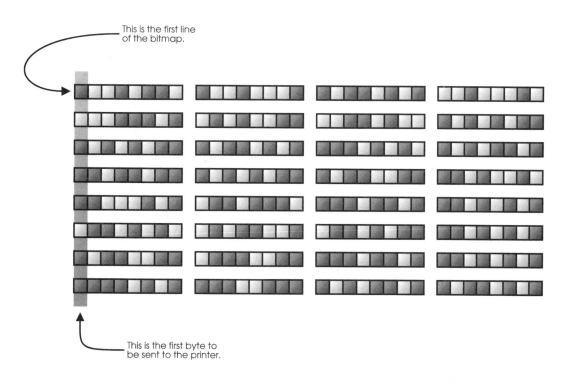

This is the first line of the bitmap.

This is the first byte to be sent to the printer.

As you'll observe in the example programs later in this chapter, the DoPrintScreen functions work with one line of the source image at a time. The PrintEpsonBuffer function wants to be handed eight lines at a time. As such, the screen printing code buffers the lines until it has collected eight of them and then sends the whole works to PrintEpsonBuffer.

As with printing to a LaserJet, a dot matrix printer can only handle black and white. The same dithering strategy that was used to simulate halftones on a LaserJet will be used for the dot matrix driver.

DeskJet 500C printing

The Hewlett-Packard DeskJet 500C is a pretty amazing printer—or, at least, it is if it's driven correctly. It can print in color at 300 dots per inch. It's dead quiet, uses regular bond paper, and doesn't require a three-year engineering course to maintain. It does, however, have pretty peculiar requirements of its drivers, and it's relatively expensive to operate.

This latter observation probably deserves some qualification. The DeskJet 500C's pages cost more than, say, monochrome laser printer output. They're marginally more expensive than color dot matrix output too, although they look worlds better. They're a lot cheaper than color output from a wax transfer color PostScript printer—even ignoring the relative costs of the two printers involved. A DeskJet 500C costs about a tenth as much as QMS ColorScript color PostScript printer.

The salient aspect of driving a DeskJet 500C is that its print engine is fairly unsophisticated. If it's to do anything clever, you'll have to write the software to do it. The DeskJet 500C driver to be covered herein uses the engine to its best advantage, and you'll be surprised at what it can accomplish.

Under the right circumstances, the output of a DeskJet 500C can look almost photographic.

In Chapter 1 of this book, we looked at additive color synthesis—that is, the way color works on a monitor. Color printing uses the opposite approach, perhaps not surprisingly referred to as subtractive color. This is based on the observation that monitors are by nature black and paper is by nature white. Unless you buy a very cheap monitor from Sears with a screen that glares badly, a monitor in its quiescent state reflects no light. A sheet of white paper reflects all colors of visible light more or less equally.

In order to make a sheet of white paper appear colored, its ability to reflect all colors of light must be modified such that only the desired color is reflected. Painting some colored ink on it will handle this. If you put green ink on a page, for example, the green areas will reflect green light well and other colors of light poorly. As white light is a fusion of all colors, the green ink will serve as a sort of filter.

There are three primary colors in subtractive color synthesis, these being cyan, magenta and yellow. These are, in fact, the opposite colors to the primary colors of additive synthesis, as follows:

```
GREEN + BLUE = CYAN
RED + BLUE   = MAGENTA
RED + GREEN  = YELLOW
```

You can see this for yourself if you play with the palette adjustment controls of the Desktop Paint 16 package on the companion disk for this book.

As an aside, it's worth noting that commercial color printing uses four primary colors rather than three. The fourth one is black. Unlike as with a monitor, on which all the colors are theoretically pure, it's impractical to manufacture absolutely pure inks. While it's impossible for your eye to tell whether an area of cyan ink is really cyan, it's relatively easy to spot black that isn't really black. Creating black by mixing the three primary subtractive colors—called "process" black— will usually leave you with a muddy brown color in commercial printing. On a DeskJet 500C, process black usually tends toward green, the color shift becoming more pronounced for ink cartridges that are nearing the ends of their lives.

Commercial printing gets around this problem by replacing areas of process grey or black with solid black ink. This isn't something a DeskJet 500C can manage.

A DeskJet 500C's print engine can print colored dots $\frac{1}{300}$ of an inch across in the three primary subtractive colors. Unfortunately, this is the only thing it can do. If it's to print a complete spectrum of colors, they'll have to be formed from this initially fairly limited range of colors.

The problem of printing grey levels on a LaserJet is very similar in concept to the one of printing lots of colors on an engine that really only knows how to do a few of them. The solution in the same, too. The extra colors can be had by dithering.

Unlike as with monochrome graphics, color Bayer dithering can look remarkably good. The improvement is due primarily to the way it will be used in this chapter. Rather than printing each pixel with one dot of the print engine, as was done for the monochrome LaserJet driver, we'll use a three by three pixel matrix to represent each source image pixel. While a bit more complex to implement, the results of driving a DeskJet 500C this way can be pretty remarkable.

Color Bayer dithering works very much like monochrome dithering, save that each of the three color indices of an RGB color is compared individually to the Bayer matrix.

The Deskjet 500C driver in this chapter will run the printer at 300 dots per inch, but it will have an effective resolution of 100 dots per inch. At a distance of about a foot or more, it's impossible to see the individual pixels on a page printed this way, and the colors look pretty natural.

In fact, the individual pixels of a DeskJet 500C page don't have terribly good definition because they're formed by drops of liquid ink that tend to distort a bit when they hit the page and begin to soak in. While this degrades the quality of graphics with hard lines to some extent, it tends to improve the appearance of printed bitmaps, especially of scanned photographs.

If you work with a DeskJet 500C a bit, you'll find that the type of paper you use can have a considerable bearing on the quality of the images that finally lurch into the output hopper of your printer. While the DeskJet will print on regular bond paper, you can get noticeably better results from better grades of paper. The DeskJet 500C comes with a package of example paper that's well suited to the rigors of inkjet printing.

There's another bit of arcania associated with color printing—that of device "gamma." While a frequently used term, it's often misapplied. In its simplest sense, gamma is the difference between the color characteristics of an output device—a monitor or a color printer, for example—and the color perception of a human eye. In most cases, the gamma of an output device will prove to be unpleasantly non-linear. For example, if you print 100 percent red on a DeskJet next to 50 percent red, the 50 percent red area probably won't look to be half the brightness of the 100 percent red area. The DeskJet 500C tends to make colors look unnaturally dark.

Colors to be printed to a DeskJet 500C should be precompensated for the gamma of the printer. This is handled by using them as indices into a lookup table called a "gamma curve." The correct gamma value for a DeskJet 500C is about 0.3. This is the code to generate the curve, as derived from the Hewlett-Packard DeskJet 500C software developer's guide.

```
CreateGammaCurve(curve,gamma)
        char *curve;
        double gamma;
    {
            int i;

            for(i=0;i<256;++i)
                curve[i]=(int)(255 * pow((double)i/255,
                    (double)gamma) + (double)0.5);
    }
```

The `CreateGammaCurve` function will generate a 256-entry lookup table at `curve` based on the gamma value passed to it as `gamma`. Figure 7-5 illustrates the gamma curve for a gamma of 0.3.

Finally, it's worth noting that while the DeskJet 500C and the earlier Hewlett-Packard PaintJet printers used different print engines, they're driven in much the same way. If you have a PaintJet, you should be able to use the DeskJet driver in this chapter with no modification, save that the maximum resolution of a PaintJet's engine is 180 dots per inch, rather than 300 for a DeskJet.

Driving a DeskJet 500C

The DeskJet 500C is driven using a superset of the basic PCL language described earlier in this chapter. In fact, if you load the black ink cartridge into a DeskJet, it will behave like a normal PCL monochrome LaserJet, save that you can't use cursor positioning controls that would require the print head to move back up the page it's printing on.

With its color ink cartridge installed, attempting to print text or monochrome graphics to a DeskJet 500C will stop the printer and put it into an error state. Its "Change Cartridge" light will flash, indicating that it's not in a good mood. With its color cartridge in place, a DeskJet 500C only wants to print color graphics.

You can initialize a DeskJet 500C for printing bitmaps using much the same set of escape sequences, as was required to drive a LaserJet earlier in this chapter. Note that we'll be using 300 dot per inch printing resolution rather than 100 dots per inch. There are, in addition, four more escape sequences required.

To begin with, because color is represented using additive RGB color values in dealing with bitmapped graphics, it would be convenient to use these numbers to drive the DeskJet as well. It turns out that the printer can do the conversion

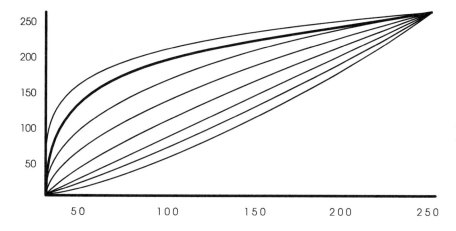

internally. This first escape sequence tells it to expect RGB colors, rather than colors expressed as percentages of cyan, magenta, and yellow.

```
\033*r3U
```

One of the things that really slows down complex printing is the time it takes to get the printed data from your computer to your printer. The DeskJet offers a way to cheat on this for some types of graphics by allowing the data that's sent to it to be run-length compressed, much as the lines of a PCX file are. It will then uncompress the data it receives internally before it's printed.

As was touched on in Chapter 2, run-length compression works notoriously badly for dithered images—these being the sorts of images we'll be printing using the code in this chapter. As such, we'll tell the DeskJet not to use any of its compressed modes with this escape sequence:

```
\033*b0M
```

Having sent this escape sequence, the printer will expect to receive uncompressed bitmap lines, just like the LaserJet did earlier in this chapter.

The next two escape sequences affect the way a DeskJet 500C handles color. The first one sets the ink depletion level. Ink depletion is an algorithmic process for removing ostensibly unnecessary dots from the image. It both reduces the ink consumption for large bitmaps and improves the color definition.

```
\033*o2D
```

This has specified a 25 percent depletion level.

Printer shingling modifies the order in which colored dots are printed. By default, the sixteen ink nozzles of a DeskJet's print head will lay down a band of lines in one pass. If this is changed such that each band requires four passes, laying down an interlaced checkerboard of dots, the tendency for the dots to bleed will be reduced considerably. The dots laid down by the first pass will have an opportunity to dry before the second pass comes by. This escape sequence sets up the shingling:

```
\033*o1Q
```

Note that the gamma value of 0.3 mentioned earlier is based on the assumption that these depletion and shingling values will be used.

The line data sent to a DeskJet 500C to print color images consists of three planes per printed line. Having selected the RGB color option several escape sequences back, the first plane defines whether red dots will appear for each bit in the line. The next plane determines whether green dots will appear. The third plane determines whether blue dots will appear. Each bit in one plane corresponds to one pixel on the page being printed.

In fact, the printer will be using multiple colors to create red, green, and blue dots.

If you regard the planes as being weighted values, there are eight possible combinations of bits across three planes, and as such eight possible colors:

Color	Red	Green	Blue	Value
Black	0	0	0	0
Red	1	0	1	1
Green	0	1	0	2
Yellow	1	1	0	3
Blue	0	0	1	4
Magenta	1	0	1	5
Cyan	0	1	1	6
White	1	1	1	7

In fact, the internal software of the printer, knowing that it really has a print engine that prints with subtractive colors, will invert this palette. However, as it happens transparently to the software that will be driving the printer—and as it has no effect on the final printed pages the printer will produce—we can ignore this and use the more convenient color model.

In printing a line of bitmapped data to a DeskJet 500C, then, we'll begin with the line represented as an array of RGB values. First off, we must create a red plane from this line by stepping through each of the red components of the pixels and comparing them against a Bayer matrix, as was done in the monochrome LaserJet driver. This will result in a single image plane, with one bit per pixel. Anywhere a bit is set, the printer will print a red dot. Having downloaded this line to the printer, we can do the same thing for the green and blue planes.

The escape sequence for downloading the red and green planes is:

    \033*b80V

This tells the printer to expect 80 bytes of data, the number of bytes for one plane of a 640 by 480 pixel screen. The sequence for the blue plane is a bit different:

    \033*b80W

This tells the printer that at the conclusion of this plane, all three planes will have been sent and the next line can be expected.

When an entire bitmap has been printed to a DeskJet, the printer should be deinitialized and its page ejected just as was done for a monochrome LaserJet page.

In the `DoPrintScreen` function to be dealt with next, the source lines will be expanded by a factor of three prior to dithering, and each line will be dithered and downloaded three times. This allows each pixel in the source image to be represented by more pixels in the printed image, resulting in much better color definition—albeit at a considerable penalty in download time. In practice, the DeskJet 500C is not a particularly fast printer, and whatever extra download time this driver entails is dwarfed by the time it takes the print engine itself to work.

If you decide to experiment with the DeskJet 500C printing functions in this chapter, you might want to keep something in mind about this approach to improving the color definition of a DeskJet. It's very effective, but its effectiveness varies at different expansion factors. So do the colors it represents. If you print the same image using different amounts of expansion, you'll probably notice a slight color shift.

This far we've look at what to send to various types of printers but not at how to actually send them. In fact, communicating with a printer is something of a problem on a PC. The proper and accepted way of doing so has something of a drawback in that it doesn't actually work; at least, it doesn't work if you'll be printing graphics.

Communicating with a printer

The proper and accepted way to talk to a printer is to use the C language streamed file functions with the file handle `stdprn`. For example, you can send a string to the printer connected to LPT1 very simply like this:

```
fprintf(stdprn,"It must have been the roses.");
```

Unfortunately, this approach actually sends the string through DOS, which turns out not to check the printer status as diligently as it might—for the most part DOS only wants to check for errors after the fact. As few printers can buffer a whole screen worth of image data all at once, this is almost certain to lose a few bytes here and there. As a rule, all the bytes in a graphic are equally important.

You can get around this problem by getting around DOS and mediating directly with the BIOS interrupt that deals with printing. The `p_char` function will print one character to a printer port. However, unlike DOS, it will wait until the port is free before it sends anything down the wire. This means that if your printer has put things on hold while it thinks about the last batch of data it was sent, `p_char` will wait until it's in a communicative mood again.

```
p_char(c)
        int c;
{
        union REGS r;
        do {
                r.h.ah = 2;
                r.x.dx = PRINTERPORT;
                int86(0x17,&r,&r);
        } while(!(r.h.ah & 0x80));
```

```
                      r.h.ah = 0;
                      r.h.al = c;
                      r.x.dx = PRINTERPORT;
                      int86(0x17,&r,&r);
            }
```

The value of PRINTERPORT defines which of the available hardware printer ports will be used. It will be 0 for LPT1, 1 for LPT2 and so on.

The p_char function uses two calls to INT 17H, the BIOS function that handles the printer port. The first one checks the status of the port, looping until it becomes free. The second one actually sends the character passed to p_char to the printer.

Now this code might look a little nasty, in that if the printer port in question never becomes free, this function will loop forever. In practice, this won't happen—it's worth noting that if you turn a printer off, it will look like a perpetually free port. You can build in a time-out if you want, but this can enormously complicate the software that uses this function, as it must then include some way to handle time-out errors.

The p_string function will print a C language string using multiple calls to p_char:

```
      p_string(s)
              char *s;
      {
              while(*s) p_char(*s++);
      }
```

These functions will turn up throughout the example programs to be covered next.

Printing a 16-color screen

Figure 7-6 illustrates the source code for the first of three programs to exercise a version of DoPrintScreen. This one will generate a 16-color test image similar to the program in Chapter 3. If you click on the Print button, it will send the screen to your printer. This program is called TESTP16.C.

7-6
The source code for
TESTP16.C.

```
/*
              Printing a super VGA screen

              Copyright (c) 1992 Alchemy Mindworks Inc.

              Links to MOUSE16.ASM
*/

#include "stdio.h"
#include "dos.h"
#include "alloc.h"
#include "math.h"
#include "mouse16.h"

/* colours in this sixteen-colour palette */
#define BLACK           0
#define BLUE            1
```

```
#define GREEN           2
#define CYAN            3
#define RED             4
#define MAGENTA         5
#define YELLOW          6
#define GREY            7
#define DARKGREY        8
#define LIGHTGREY       9
#define LIGHTBLUE       10
#define LIGHTGREEN      11
#define LIGHTRED        12
#define LIGHTYELLOW     13
#define LIGHTMAGENTA    14
#define WHITE           15

/* dimensions of the about box */
#define ABOUTLEFT       107
#define ABOUTTOP        50
#define ABOUTRIGHT      475
#define ABOUTBOTTOM     180

#define LASERJET        1
#define POSTSCRIPT      2
#define DESKJET         3
#define EPSONFX80       4

#define LPT1            0
#define LPT2            1
#define LPT3            2

#define PRINTERPORT     LPT1

#define DESKJET_GAMMA   0.3

#define EPSON_LINEDEEP  8

#define COLOUREXPANSION 3

/* the sixteen-colour palette we'll use */
char palette[] = {
        0x00,0x00,0x00,
        0x00,0x00,0xaa,
        0x00,0xaa,0x00,
        0x00,0xaa,0xaa,
        0xaa,0x00,0x00,
        0xaa,0x00,0xaa,
        0xaa,0xaa,0x00,
        0xaa,0xaa,0xaa,
        0x55,0x55,0x55,
        0xcc,0xcc,0xcc,
        0x00,0x00,0xff,
        0x00,0xff,0x00,
        0xff,0x00,0x00,
        0xff,0xff,0x00,
        0xff,0x00,0xff,
```

```
        0xff,0xff,0xff
        };

char bayerPattern[8][8] = {
     0,32, 8,40, 2,34,10,42,
    48,16,56,24,50,18,58,26,
    12,44, 4,36,14,46, 6,38,
    60,28,52,20,62,30,54,22,
     3,35,11,43, 1,33, 9,41,
    51,19,59,27,49,17,57,25,
    15,47, 7,39,13,45, 5,37,
    63,31,55,23,61,29,53,21 };

char greymap[]= {
        0x00,0x00,0x00,0x00,0x00,0x00,0x00,0x00,
        0x00,0x00,0x00,0x00,0x00,0x00,0x00,0x00,
        0x00,0x00,0x00,0x00,0x00,0x00,0x00,0x00,
        0x00,0x00,0x00,0x00,0x00,0x00,0x00,0x00,
        0x00,0x01,0x02,0x06,0x08,0x0B,0x0D,0x10,
        0x12,0x16,0x17,0x1B,0x1C,0x20,0x22,0x23,
        0x27,0x29,0x2C,0x2E,0x2F,0x33,0x35,0x36,
        0x3A,0x3C,0x3D,0x3F,0x43,0x44,0x46,0x49,
        0x4B,0x4D,0x4F,0x50,0x54,0x56,0x57,0x59,
        0x5B,0x5E,0x60,0x62,0x63,0x65,0x67,0x69,
        0x6C,0x6E,0x70,0x71,0x73,0x75,0x76,0x77,
        0x79,0x7B,0x7C,0x7E,0x80,0x82,0x83,0x87,
        0x89,0x8A,0x8C,0x8E,0x8F,0x91,0x93,0x95,
        0x95,0x96,0x98,0x9A,0x9C,0x9D,0x9F,0xA1,
        0xA3,0xA4,0xA6,0xA8,0xA9,0xAB,0xAD,0xAF,
        0xAF,0xB0,0xB2,0xB4,0xB6,0xB7,0xB9,0xBB,
        0xBB,0xBD,0xBE,0xC0,0xC2,0xC3,0xC5,0xC5,
        0xC7,0xC9,0xCA,0xCC,0xCE,0xCE,0xD0,0xD1,
        0xD3,0xD5,0xD5,0xD6,0xD8,0xDA,0xDC,0xDC,
        0xDD,0xDF,0xE1,0xE1,0xE3,0xE4,0xE6,0xE6,
        0xE8,0xEA,0xEB,0xEB,0xED,0xEF,0xF0,0xF0,
        0xF2,0xF4,0xF6,0xF6,0xF7,0xF9,0xF9,0xFB,
        0xFD,0xFE,0xFE,0xFF,0xFF,0xFF,0xFF,0xFF,
        0xFF,0xFF,0xFF,0xFF,0xFF,0xFF,0xFF,0xFF,
        0xFF,0xFF,0xFF,0xFF,0xFF,0xFF,0xFF,0xFF,
        0xFF,0xFF,0xFF,0xFF,0xFF,0xFF,0xFF,0xFF,
        0xFF,0xFF,0xFF,0xFF,0xFF,0xFF,0xFF,0xFF,
        0xFF,0xFF,0xFF,0xFF,0xFF,0xFF,0xFF,0xFF,
        0xFF,0xFF,0xFF,0xFF,0xFF,0xFF,0xFF,0xFF,
        0xFF,0xFF,0xFF,0xFF,0xFF,0xFF,0xFF,0xFF,
        0xFF,0xFF,0xFF,0xFF,0xFF,0xFF,0xFF,0xFF,
        0xFF,0xFF,0xFF,0xFF,0xFF,0xFF,0xFF,0xFF
        };

char gamma[256];

char *lpbuf=NULL;
int lplines=0;

unsigned int oldvesamode=0xffff;
```

```
main(argc,argv)
        int argc;
        char *argv[];
{

        BUTTON quit,print;
        POINT p;
        int left,top,right,bottom;
        int i,alive=1,thiscard=VGA,thisprinter=LASERJET;

        /* see what kind of card is installed — sort of */
        if(argc > 1) {
                if(!stricmp(argv[1],"PARADISE")) thiscard=PARADISE;
                else if(!stricmp(argv[1],"ATI")) thiscard=ATI;
                else if(!stricmp(argv[1],"TSENG")) thiscard=TSENG;
                else if(!stricmp(argv[1],"TRIDENT")) thiscard=TRIDENT;
                else if(!stricmp(argv[1],"OAK")) thiscard=OAK;
                else if(!stricmp(argv[1],"VESA")) thiscard=VESA;
        }

        if(argc > 2) {
                if(!stricmp(argv[2],"LASERJET")) thisprinter=LASERJET;
                else if(!stricmp(argv[2],"POSTSCRIPT")) thisprinter=POSTSCRIPT;
                else if(!stricmp(argv[2],"DESKJET")) thisprinter=DESKJET;
                else if(!stricmp(argv[2],"EPSONFX80")) thisprinter=EPSONFX80;
        }

        /* go for a graphics mode */
        if(!GraphicMode(thiscard)) {
                TextMode(thiscard);
                exit(1);
        }

        /* set the palette */
        SetVgaPalette(palette,16);

        /* clear the screen */
        ClearScreen(LIGHTGREY);

        /* draw a moire pattern */
        for(i=0;i<SCREENWIDE;i+=2)
            DrawLine(i,0,SCREENWIDE>>1,SCREENDEEP>1,i);
        for(i=0;i<SCREENDEEP;i+=2)
            DrawLine(SCREENWIDE>>1,SCREENDEEP>>1,SCREENWIDE-1,i,i);
        for(i=SCREENWIDE-1;i>=0;i-=2)
            DrawLine(SCREENWIDE>>1,SCREENDEEP>>1,i,SCREENDEEP-1,i-1);
        for(i=SCREENDEEP-1;i>=0;i-=2)
            DrawLine(0,i,SCREENWIDE>>1,SCREENDEEP>>1,i-1);

        /* show the palette */
        for(i=0;i<16;++i) {
                left=30+i*30;
                top=400;
                right=60+i*30;
                bottom=430;
```

```
                        FillRect(left,top,right,bottom,i);
                        FrameRect(left,top,right,bottom,BLACK);
        }

        /* show some example text */
        i=100;
        DrawString(128,i," This is blue on light green.           ",BLUE,LIGHTGREEN);
        i+=FONTDEPTH;
        DrawString(128,i," This is red on light yellow.           ",RED,LIGHTYELLOW);
        i+=FONTDEPTH;
        DrawString(128,i," This is light yellow on red.           ",LIGHTYELLOW,RED);
        i+=FONTDEPTH;
        DrawString(128,i," This is black on magenta (very ugly). ",BLACK,MAGENTA);
        i+=FONTDEPTH;
        DrawString(128,i," This is cyan on light grey.            ",CYAN,LIGHTGREY);
        i+=FONTDEPTH;

        /* create some buttons to click on */
        MakeButton(SCREENWIDE-100,SCREENDEEP-60,"Quit",&quit);
        DrawButton(&quit);

        MakeButton(SCREENWIDE-200,SCREENDEEP-60,"Print",&print);
        DrawButton(&print);

        /* loop 'til we're done */
        do {
                /* look for a mouse click */
                if(MouseDown(&p)) {
                        if(PointInRect(&p,&quit)) {
                                TrackButton(&quit);
                                alive=0;
                        }
                        else if(PointInRect(&p,&print)) {
                                TrackButton(&print);
                                DoPrintScreen(thisprinter);
                        }
                }
        } while(alive);

        TextMode(thiscard);
}

/* print the screen */
DoPrintScreen(printer)
        unsigned int printer;
{
        char *p,*ps,*pd,*pl;
        unsigned int i,j;

        if((p=malloc(SCREENBYTES * COLOURDEPTH)) == NULL) {
                beep();
                return;
        }

        if((pl=malloc(SCREENWIDE)) == NULL) {
```

```
                free(p);
                beep();
                return;
        }

        WaitCursor();
        if(!InitPrinter(printer)) {
                free(pl);
                free(p);
                ArrowCursor();
                beep();
                return;
        }

        for(i=0;i<SCREENDEEP;++i) {
                MouseOff();
                ps=MK_FP(SCREENSEG,SCREENTBL[i]);
                pd=p;
                for(j=0;j<COLOURDEPTH;++j) {
                        egareadplane(j);
                        memcpy(pd,ps,SCREENBYTES);
                        pd+=SCREENBYTES;
                }
                MouseOn();

                for(j=0;j<SCREENWIDE;++j)
                    pl[j]=GetBitPixel(p,COLOURDEPTH,SCREENBYTES,j);

                PrintLine(pl,i,printer);

        }
        DeinitPrinter(printer);
        ArrowCursor();

        free(pl);
        free(p);
}

/* set up the printer to print an image */
InitPrinter(printer)
        unsigned int printer;
{
        static char posthead[]=
                "/screensize %d def\r\n"
                "/width %d def\r\n"
                "/height %d def\r\n"
                "/pixwidth %f def\r\n"
                "/pixheight %f def\r\n"
                "/picstr width string def\r\n"
                "screensize 0 ne {\r\n"
                "screensize 45 { abs exch abs 2 copy add 1 gt\r\n"
                "{ 1 sub dup mul exch 1 sub dup mul add 1 sub }\r\n"
                "{ dup mul exch dup mul add 1 exch sub }\r\n"
                "ifelse } setscreen\r\n"
                "} if\r\n"
```

```
                      "/dopic {\r\n"
                      "gsave width height 8\r\n"
                      "[width 0 0 height neg 0 height]\r\n"
                      "{currentfile picstr readhexstring pop}\r\n"
          "image grestore } def\r\n"
          "/showname {\r\n"
          "/Courier findfont 12 scalefont setfont\r\n"
          "20 20 moveto (%s) show\r\n"
          "} def\r\n"
          "showname\r\n"
          "40 50 translate pixwidth pixheight scale\r\n"
          "dopic\r\n";

   char *lb,s[64];

   switch(printer) {
          case LASERJET:
                 p_string("\033E");
                 p_string("\033*t100R");
                 p_string("\033*p20X");
                 p_string("\033*p20Y");
                 p_string("\033*r1A");
                 break;
          case POSTSCRIPT:
                 if((lb=malloc(4096)) == NULL) return(0);
                 sprintf(lb,posthead,0,SCREENWIDE,SCREENDEEP,
                     (double)SCREENWIDE/1.39,(double)SCREENDEEP/1.39,"");
                 p_string(lb);
                 free(lb);
                 break;
          case DESKJET:
                 CreateGammaCurve(gamma,(double)DESKJET_GAMMA);
                 p_string("\033E");
                 p_string("\033*OoOL");

                 sprintf(s,"\033*r%uS",SCREENWIDE*COLOUREXPANSION);
                 p_string(s);
                 p_string("\033*r3U");
                 p_string("\033*bOM");

                 p_string("\033*o2D");
                 p_string("\033*o1Q");

                 p_string("\033*t300R");
                 p_string("\033*p20X");
                 p_string("\033*p20Y");
                 p_string("\033*r1A");
                 break;
          case EPSONFX80:
                 p_string("\033@");
                 if((lpbuf=malloc(EPSON_LINEDEEP*SCREENBYTES))==NULL)
                        return(0);
                 lplines=0;
                 break;
   }
```

```
                return(1);
}

/* close down the printer after printing an image */
DeinitPrinter(printer)
        unsigned int printer;
{
        switch(printer) {
                case LASERJET:
                        p_string("\033*rB");
                        p_string("\014");
                        break;
                case POSTSCRIPT:
                        p_string("showpage\r\n");
                        break;
                case DESKJET:
                        p_string("\033*rB");
                        p_string("\014");
                        break;
                case EPSONFX80:
                        if(lplines) PrintEpsonBuffer();
                        free(lpbuf);
                        p_string("\033@");
                        break;
        }
}

/* print one line of an image */
PrintLine(line,number,printer)
        char *line;
        unsigned int number,printer;
{
        char *pd,*pl,*pr,*ps,s[64];
        int c,i,j,k,n;

        switch(printer) {
                case LASERJET:
                        if((ps=malloc(SCREENBYTES)) != NULL) {
                                memset(ps,0,SCREENBYTES);
                                for(i=0;i<SCREENWIDE;++i) {
                                        pr=palette+line[i]*RGB_SIZE;
                                        c=greymap[greyvalue(pr[RGB_RED],
                                          pr[RGB_GREEN],pr[RGB_BLUE])];
                                        if((c >> 2) > bayerPattern[i & 0x0007][number & 0x0007])
                                            ps[i>>3] |= masktable[i & 0x0007];
                                }
                                sprintf(s,"\033*b%dW",SCREENBYTES);
                                p_string(s);
                                for(i=0;i<SCREENBYTES;++i) p_char(~ps[i]);
                                free(ps);
                        }
                        break;
                case POSTSCRIPT:
                        for(i=0;i<SCREENWIDE;++i) {
                                pr=palette+line[i]*RGB_SIZE;
```

```
                                c=greymap[greyvalue(pr[RGB_RED],
                                    pr[RGB_GREEN],pr[RGB_BLUE])];
                                    sprintf(s,"%02.2X",c & 0xff);
                                    p_string(s);
                                    if(!((i+1) % 32)) p_string("\r\n");
                }
            p_string("\r\n");
            break;
        case DESKJET:
            /* allocate a buffer to expand the line into */
            if((ps=malloc(SCREENWIDE*COLOUREXPANSION*RGB_SIZE)) == NULL) return;

            /* allocate a buffer to put the planes in */
            if((pl=malloc(SCREENBYTES*COLOUREXPANSION)) == NULL) {
                    free(ps);
                    return;
            }

            pd=ps;

            for(i=0;i<SCREENWIDE;++i) {
                    pr=palette+line[i]*RGB_SIZE;
                    for(j=0;j<COLOUREXPANSION;++j) {
                     pd[RGB_RED]=gamma[pr[RGB_RED]];
                     pd[RGB_GREEN]=gamma[pr[RGB_GREEN]];
                     pd[RGB_BLUE]=gamma[pr[RGB_BLUE]];
                     pd+=RGB_SIZE;
                     }
            }

            n=number*COLOUREXPANSION;

            for(i=0;i<COLOUREXPANSION;++i) {

                    /* dither the red line */
                    pd=ps;
                    memset(pl,0,SCREENBYTES*COLOUREXPANSION);
                    k=SCREENWIDE*COLOUREXPANSION;
                    for(j=0;j<k;++j) {
                            c=(pd[RGB_RED] >> 2);
                            if(c >= bayerPattern[j & 0x0007][n & 0x0007])
                                pl[j >> 3] |= masktable[j & 0x0007];
                            else
                                pl[j >> 3] &= ~masktable[j & 0x0007];
                            pd+=RGB_SIZE;
                    }
                    sprintf(s,"\033*b%dV",SCREENBYTES*COLOUREXPANSION);
                    p_string(s);
                    k=SCREENBYTES*COLOUREXPANSION;
                    for(j=0;j<k;++j) p_char(pl[j]);

                    /* dither the green line */
                    pd=ps;
                    memset(pl,0,SCREENBYTES*COLOUREXPANSION);
                    k=SCREENWIDE*COLOUREXPANSION;
```

```
                                   for(j=0;j<k;++j) {
                                           c=(pd[RGB_GREEN] >> 2);
                                           if(c >= bayerPattern[j & 0x0007][n & 0x0007])
                                                   pl[j >> 3] |= masktable[j & 0x0007];
                                           else
                                                   pl[j >> 3] &= ~masktable[j & 0x0007];
                                           pd+=RGB_SIZE;
                                   }
                                   sprintf(s,"\033*b%dV",SCREENBYTES*COLOUREXPANSION);
                                   p_string(s);
                                   k=SCREENBYTES*COLOUREXPANSION;
                                   for(j=0;j<k;++j) p_char(pl[j]);

                                   /* dither the blue line */
                                   pd=ps;
                                   memset(pl,0,SCREENBYTES*COLOUREXPANSION);
                                   k=SCREENWIDE*COLOUREXPANSION;
                                   for(j=0;j<k;++j) {
                                           c=(pd[RGB_BLUE] >> 2);
                                           if(c >= bayerPattern[j & 0x0007][n & 0x0007])
                                                   pl[j >> 3] |= masktable[j & 0x0007];
                                           else
                                                   pl[j >> 3] &= ~masktable[j & 0x0007];
                                           pd+=RGB_SIZE;
                                   }
                                   sprintf(s,"\033*b%dW",SCREENBYTES*COLOUREXPANSION);
                                   p_string(s);
                                   k=SCREENBYTES*COLOUREXPANSION;
                                   for(j=0;j<k;++j) p_char(pl[j]);

                                   ++n;
                           }
                           free(pl);
                           free(ps);
                           break;
                   case EPSONFX80:
                           if(lplines >= EPSON_LINEDEEP) PrintEpsonBuffer();
                           ps=lpbuf+lplines*SCREENBYTES;
                           memset(ps,0,SCREENBYTES);
                           for(i=0;i<SCREENWIDE;++i) {
                                   pr=palette+line[i]*RGB_SIZE;
                                   c=greymap[greyvalue(pr[RGB_RED],
                                     pr[RGB_GREEN],pr[RGB_BLUE])];
                                   if((c >> 2) > bayerPattern[i & 0x0007][number & 0x0007])
                                           ps[i>>3] |= masktable[i & 0x0007];
                           }
                           ++lplines;
                           break;
               }
       }

PrintEpsonBuffer()
{
       char *p;
       int c,i,j,m;
```

```
                        p_string("\033*\006");
                        p_char(SCREENWIDE);
                        p_char(SCREENWIDE >> 8);

                        for(i=0;i<SCREENWIDE;++i) {
                                c=0;
                                p=lpbuf+(i>>3);
                                m=masktable[i & 0x0007];
                                for(j=0;j<EPSON_LINEDEEP;++j) {
                                        if(*p & m) c |= masktable[j];
                                        p+=SCREENBYTES;
                                }
                                p_char(~c);
                        }
                        p_string("\015\033J\030");
                        lplines=0;
                        memset(lpbuf,0,EPSON_LINEDEEP*SCREENBYTES);
        }

CreateGammaCurve(curve,gamma)
        char *curve;
        double gamma;
{
        int i;

        for(i=0;i<256;++i)
            curve[i]=(int)(255 * pow((double)i/255,(double)
            gamma) + (double)0.5);
}

/* get one pixel from a planar image line */
GetBitPixel(p,bits,width,pos)
        char *p;
        int bits,width,pos;
{
        int c=0,i,byte,mask;

        byte=pos>>3;
        mask=masktable[pos & 0x0007];

        for(i=0;i<bits;++i) {
                if(p[byte] & mask) c |= bittable[i];
                p+=width;
        }

        return(c);
}

p_string(s)
        char *s;
{
        while(*s) p_char(*s++);
}
```

```
p_char(c)
        int c;
{
        union REGS r;

        do {
                r.h.ah = 2;
                r.x.dx = PRINTERPORT;
                int86(0x17,&r,&r);
        } while(!(r.h.ah & 0x80));

        r.h.ah = 0;
        r.h.al = c;
        r.x.dx = PRINTERPORT;
        int86(0x17,&r,&r);
}

GraphicMode(card)
        unsigned int card;
{
        union REGS r;
        struct SREGS sr;
        VESAINFO vi;
        VESABLOCK vb;
        unsigned int i;

        if(card==VGA) {
                r.x.ax=card;
                int86(0x10,&r,&r);
                SCREENWIDE=640;
                SCREENDEEP=480;
                SCREENBYTES=80;
                for(i=0;i<SCREENDEEP;++i) SCREENTBL[i]=i*SCREENBYTES;
        }
        else if(card==VESA) {
                /* check for a VESA BIOS */
                r.x.ax=0x4f00;
                r.x.di=FP_OFF((char *)&vb);
                sr.es=FP_SEG((char *)&vb);
                int86x(0x10,&r,&r,&sr);
                if(r.x.ax != 0x004f) return(0);

                /* see if this mode is supported */
                while(*vb.videomode != VESA && *vb.videomode != 0xffff)
                    (vb.videomode)++;

                if(*vb.videomode == 0xffff) return(0);

                /* get the VESA information */
                r.x.ax=0x4f01;
                r.x.cx=VESA;
                r.x.di=FP_OFF((char *)&vi);
                sr.es=FP_SEG((char *)&vi);
                int86x(0x10,&r,&r,&sr);
```

```
                        /* set the screen segment */
                        SCREENSEG=vi.windowsegment_a;

                        /* get the current mode */
                        r.x.ax=0x4f03;
                        int86(0x10,&r,&r);
                        oldvesamode=r.x.bx;

                        /* set the new mode */
                        r.x.ax=0x4f02;
                        r.x.bx=VESA;
                        int86(0x10,&r,&r);
                }
                else {
                        r.x.ax=card;
                        int86(0x10,&r,&r);
                }
                return(InitMouse());
        }

TextMode(card)
        unsigned int card;
{
        union REGS r;

        r.x.ax=0x1200;
        r.x.bx=0x0031;
        int86(0x10,&r,&r);

        if(card==VESA && oldvesamode != 0xffff) {
                r.x.ax=0x4f02;
                r.x.bx=oldvesamode;
                int86(0x10,&r,&r);
        }
        else {
                r.x.ax=0x0003;
                int86(0x10,&r,&r);
        }
        DeinitMouse();
}

DrawLine(left,top,right,bottom,colour)
        int left,top,right,bottom,colour;
{
        int temp,dx,dy,x,y,x_sign,y_sign,flag;

        MouseOff();
        dx = abs(right - left);
        dy = abs(bottom - top);
        if(((dx >= dy) && (left > right)) ||
           ((dy > dx) && (top > bottom))) {
                temp = left;
                left = right;
                right = temp;
                temp = top;
```

```
                  top = bottom;
                  bottom = temp;
          }
          if ((bottom - top) < 0) y_sign = -1;
          else y_sign = 1;
          if ((right - left) < 0) x_sign = -1;
          else x_sign = 1;
          if (dx >= dy) {
                  for (x=left,y=top,flag=0; x<=right; x++,flag+=dy) {
                          if (flag>=dx) {
                                  flag -= dx;
                                  y+= y_sign;
                          }
                          setpixel(x,y,colour);
                  }
          }
          else {
                  for (x=left,y=top,flag=0; y<=bottom; y++,flag+=dx) {
                          if (flag>=dy) {
                                  flag -= dy;
                                  x+=x_sign;
                          }
                          setpixel(x,y,colour);
                  }
          }
          MouseOn();
}

#pragma warn -aus
FillRect(left,top,right,bottom,colour)
          int left,top,right,bottom,colour;
{
          char *p,bf[100];
          int a,i,j,width,depth,bleft,bytes,xleft,xright,pleft,pright;

          MouseOff();
          xleft=left & 0xfff8;
          xright=right;
          if(xright & 0x0007) xright=(xright | 0x0007)+1;
          width=xright-xleft;
          depth=bottom-top;
          bleft=xleft>>3;
          pleft=left-xleft;
          pright=pleft+(right-left);
          bytes=pixels2bytes(width)+1;

          memset(bf,0,bytes);

          for(i=pleft;i<=pright;++i) bf[i>>3] |= masktable[i & 0x0007];

          setwritemode(2);
          for(i=0;i<=depth;++i) {
                  p=MK_FP(SCREENSEG,SCREENTBL[top+i]+bleft);
                  for(j=0;j<bytes;++j) {
                          setbitmask(bf[j]);
```

```
                                                a=p[j];
                                                p[j]=colour;
                                     }
                              }
                        setbitmask(0xff);
                        setwritemode(0);
                        MouseOn();
              }
              #pragma warn +aus

              FrameRect(left,top,right,bottom,colour)
                        unsigned int left,top,right,bottom,colour;
              {
                        DrawLine(left,top,right,top,colour);
                        DrawLine(left,bottom,right,bottom,colour);
                        DrawLine(left,top,left,bottom,colour);
                        DrawLine(right,top,right,bottom,colour);
              }

              SetVgaPalette(p,n)
                        char *p;
                        unsigned int n;
              {
                        union REGS r;
                        int i;

                        for(i=0;i<n;++i) {
                                r.h.dh=*p++>>2;
                                r.h.ch=*p++>>2;
                                r.h.cl=*p++>>2;
                                r.x.bx=i;
                                r.x.ax=0x1010;
                                int86(0x10,&r,&r);
                        }

                        r.x.bx=0x0000;
                        for(i=0;i<n;++i) {
                                r.x.ax=0x1000;
                                int86(0x10,&r,&r);
                                r.x.bx+=0x0101;
                        }
              }

              MakeButton(left,top,string,button)
                        unsigned int left,top;
                        char *string;
                        BUTTON *button;
              {
                        button->frame.left = left & 0xfff8;
                        button->frame.right=button->frame.left+(strlen
                        (string)<<3)+16;
                        button->frame.top=top;
                        button->frame.bottom=button->frame.top+FONTDEPTH+8;
                        button->text=string;
              }
```

```
DrawButton(button)
        BUTTON *button;
{
        FillRect(button->frame.left+1,button->frame.top+1,
                button->frame.right-1,button->frame.bottom-1,WHITE);
        DrawLine(button->frame.left+1,button->frame.top,
                button->frame.right-1,button->frame.top,BLACK);
        DrawLine(button->frame.left,button->frame.top+1,
                button->frame.left,button->frame.bottom-1,BLACK);
        DrawLine(button->frame.right,button->frame.top+1,
                button->frame.right,button->frame.bottom-1,BLACK);
        DrawLine(button->frame.left+1,button->frame.bottom,
                button->frame.right-1,button->frame.bottom,BLACK);
        Fill3DBox(button->frame.left+1,button->frame.top+1,
                button->frame.right-1,button->frame.bottom-1);

        DrawString(button->frame.left+8,button->frame.top+4,
                button->text,DARKGREY,LIGHTGREY);
}

TrackButton(button)
        BUTTON *button;
{
        POINT p;

        FillRect(button->frame.left+1,button->frame.top+1,
                button->frame.right-1,button->frame.bottom-1,LIGHTGREY);
        DrawString(button->frame.left+8,button->frame.top+4,
                button->text,DARKGREY,LIGHTGREY);
        while(MouseDown(&p));
        DrawButton(button);
}

Fill3DBox(left,top,right,bottom)
        int left,top,right,bottom;
{
        FillRect(left,top,right,bottom,LIGHTGREY);
        DrawLine(left,top,right-1,top,WHITE);
        DrawLine(left,top+1,left,bottom-1,WHITE);

        DrawLine(left+3,bottom,right,bottom,DARKGREY);
        DrawLine(right,top+2,right,bottom-1,DARKGREY);
}

PointInRect(p,r)/* return true if point is in rect */
        POINT *p;
        RECT *r;
{
        if(p->x > r->left && p->x < r->right &&
           p->y > r->top  && p->y < r->bottom) return(1);
        else return(0);
}

WaitCursor()
{
```

```
        static char cursor[] = {
                0x00,0x00,0x00,0x00,
                0x00,0x00,0x01,0x80,
                0x03,0xC0,0x07,0xE0,
                0x0F,0xF0,0x07,0xE0,
                0x03,0xC0,0x01,0x80,
                0x00,0x00,0x00,0x00,
                0x00,0x00,0x00,0x00,
                0xFF,0xFF,0xFF,0xFF,

                0x00,0x00,0xFE,0x7F,
                0x06,0x60,0x0C,0x30,
                0x18,0x18,0x30,0x0C,
                0x60,0x06,0xC0,0x03,
                0x60,0x06,0x30,0x0C,
                0x98,0x19,0xCC,0x33,
                0xE6,0x67,0xFE,0x7F,
                0x00,0x00,0x00,0x00 };

        MouseCursor(cursor,7,7);
}

ArrowCursor()
{
        static char cursor[] = {
                0xFF,0x3F,0xFF,0x1F,
                0xFF,0x0F,0xFF,0x07,
                0xFF,0x03,0xFF,0x01,
                0xFF,0x00,0x7F,0x00,
                0x3F,0x00,0x1F,0x00,
                0xFF,0x01,0xFF,0x10,
                0xFF,0x30,0x7F,0xF8,
                0x7F,0xF8,0x7F,0xFC,
                0x00,0x00,0x00,0x40,
                0x00,0x60,0x00,0x70,
                0x00,0x78,0x00,0x7C,
                0x00,0x7E,0x00,0x7F,
                0x80,0x7F,0x00,0x7C,
                0x00,0x6C,0x00,0x46,
                0x00,0x06,0x00,0x03,
                0x00,0x03,0x00,0x00 };

        MouseCursor(cursor,0,0);
}
```

The TESTP16.C program must link to MOUSE16. It expects to be run with two command line arguments—the type of display card you'll be using and the type of printer it should assume is connected to your computer. The display card types are as they were in Chapter 3. The printer names can be:

POSTSCRIPT
LASERJET
EPSONFX80
DESKJET

For example, to use a Paradise card and a Deskjet printer, you would run the program as:

```
TESTP16 PARADISE DESKJET
```

In a sense, TESTP16 is the most complicated of the three example programs as it must convert from planar image lines to byte-oriented pixels. This is handled by the GetBitPixel function, which extracts individual pixel values from a set of interleaved planes.

There's yet another peculiar object in this program—to wit, greymap. One more imponderable lookup table, the purpose of greymap might not be immediately obvious. It compensates for the non-linear characteristics of monochrome laser printers, similar to the way a gamma curve does for color output devices. Left to its own devices, a laser printer will produce somewhat flat, low contrast printouts. The absolute grey levels produced by the greyvalue macro aren't represented very accurately at the extremes of the grey scale by a printer. The greymap table is a contrast expansion curve that remaps the grey levels of greymap so the resulting hard copy will look natural.

The TESTP256.C program is illustrated in FIG. 7-7. As you might expect, it wants to link to MOUSE256, from Chapter 4. There's very little happening in TESTP256 that hasn't been dealt with previously.

If anything, the TESTP256.C program is a bit simpler than its 16-color counterpart. The image lines fetched from the screen buffer by GetScreenLine are byte-oriented and, as such, require no massaging. This also serves to make TESTP256 a bit faster. To keep the amount of juggling down to a minimum, the line buffers passed to PrintLine are set up as arrays of RGB pixels. Depending on the type of printer you've told TESTP256 to print to, these pixels might have to be further manipulated. A LaserJet, for example, will require that they be converted to grey and then dithered. A DeskJet can use them more or less as they are, dithering them down to three color planes.

Printing a 256-color screen

7-7
The source code for TESTP256.C.

```
/*

        Printing a super VGA screen

        Copyright (c) 1992 Alchemy Mindworks Inc.

        Links to MOUSE256.ASM
*/

#include "stdio.h"
#include "dos.h"
#include "alloc.h"
#include "math.h"
#include "mouse256.h"

/* colours in this 256-colour palette */
#define BLACK           0
#define BLUE            126
#define GREEN           31
#define CYAN            246
```

```
#define RED               3
#define MAGENTA           143
#define YELLOW            41
#define GREY              253
#define DARKGREY          252
#define LIGHTGREY         254
#define LIGHTBLUE         192
#define LIGHTGREEN        36
#define LIGHTRED          5
#define LIGHTYELLOW       125
#define LIGHTMAGENTA      227
#define WHITE             255

/* dimensions of the about box */
#define ABOUTLEFT         107
#define ABOUTTOP          50
#define ABOUTRIGHT        475
#define ABOUTBOTTOM       180

#define LASERJET          1
#define POSTSCRIPT        2
#define DESKJET           3
#define EPSONFX80         4

#define LPT1              0
#define LPT2              1
#define LPT3              2

#define PRINTERPORT       LPT1

#define DESKJET_GAMMA     0.3

#define EPSON_LINEDEEP    8

#define COLOUREXPANSION 3

/* the 256-colour palette we'll use */
char palette[] = {
        0x00,0x00,0x00,0x57,0x00,0x00,0x83,0x00,
        0x00,0xab,0x00,0xd7,0x00,0x00,0x00,0xff,
        0x00,0x00,0x00,0x2b,0x00,0x57,0x2b,0x00,
        0x83,0x2b,0x00,0xab,0x2b,0x00,0xd7,0x2b,
        0x00,0xff,0x2b,0x00,0x00,0x57,0x00,0x57,
        0x57,0x00,0x83,0x57,0x00,0xab,0x57,0x00,
        0xd7,0x57,0x00,0xff,0x57,0x00,0x00,0x83,
        0x00,0x57,0x83,0x00,0x83,0x83,0x00,0xab,
        0x83,0x00,0xd7,0x83,0x00,0xff,0x83,0x00,
        0x00,0xab,0x00,0x57,0xab,0x00,0x83,0xab,
        0x00,0xab,0xab,0x00,0xd7,0xab,0x00,0xff,
        0xab,0x00,0x00,0xd7,0x00,0x57,0xd7,0x00,
        0x83,0xd7,0x00,0xab,0xd7,0x00,0xd7,0xd7,
        0x00,0xff,0xd7,0x00,0x00,0xff,0x00,0x57,
        0xff,0x00,0x83,0xff,0x00,0xab,0xff,0x00,
        0xd7,0xff,0x00,0xff,0xff,0x00,0x00,0x00,
        0x57,0x57,0x00,0x57,0x83,0x00,0x57,0xab,
```

```
0x00,0x57,0xd7,0x00,0x57,0xff,0x00,0x57,
0x00,0x2b,0x57,0x57,0x2b,0x57,0x83,0x2b,
0x57,0xab,0x2b,0x57,0xd7,0x2b,0x57,0xff,
0x2b,0x57,0x00,0x57,0x57,0x57,0x57,0x57,
0x83,0x57,0x57,0xab,0x57,0x57,0xd7,0x57,
0x57,0xff,0x57,0x57,0x00,0x83,0x57,0x57,
0x83,0x57,0x83,0x83,0x57,0xab,0x83,0x57,
0xd7,0x83,0x57,0xff,0x83,0x57,0x00,0xab,
0x57,0x57,0xab,0x57,0x83,0xab,0x57,0xab,
0xab,0x57,0xd7,0xab,0x57,0xff,0xab,0x57,
0x00,0xd7,0x57,0x57,0xd7,0x57,0x83,0xd7,
0x57,0xab,0xd7,0x57,0xd7,0xd7,0x57,0xff,
0xd7,0x57,0x00,0xff,0x57,0x57,0xff,0x57,
0x83,0xff,0x57,0xab,0xff,0x57,0xd7,0xff,
0x57,0xff,0xff,0x57,0x00,0x00,0x83,0x57,
0x00,0x83,0x83,0x00,0x83,0xab,0x00,0x83,
0xd7,0x00,0x83,0xff,0x00,0x83,0x00,0x2b,
0x83,0x57,0x2b,0x83,0x83,0x2b,0x83,0xab,
0x2b,0x83,0xd7,0x2b,0x83,0xff,0x2b,0x83,
0x00,0x57,0x83,0x57,0x57,0x83,0x83,0x57,
0x83,0xab,0x57,0x83,0xd7,0x57,0x83,0xff,
0x57,0x83,0x00,0x83,0x83,0x57,0x83,0x83,
0x83,0x83,0x83,0xab,0x83,0x83,0xd7,0x83,
0x83,0xff,0x83,0x83,0x00,0xab,0x83,0x57,
0xab,0x83,0x83,0xab,0x83,0xab,0xab,0x83,
0xd7,0xab,0x83,0xff,0xab,0x83,0x00,0xd7,
0x83,0x57,0xd7,0x83,0x83,0xd7,0x83,0xab,
0xd7,0x83,0xd7,0xd7,0x83,0xff,0xd7,0x83,
0x00,0xff,0x83,0x57,0xff,0x83,0x83,0xff,
0x83,0xab,0xff,0x83,0xd7,0xff,0x83,0xff,
0xff,0x83,0x00,0x00,0xab,0x57,0x00,0xab,
0x83,0x00,0xab,0xab,0x00,0xab,0xd7,0x00,
0xab,0xff,0x00,0xab,0x00,0x2b,0xab,0x57,
0x2b,0xab,0x83,0x2b,0xab,0xab,0x2b,0xab,
0xd7,0x2b,0xab,0xff,0x2b,0xab,0x00,0x57,
0xab,0x57,0x57,0xab,0x83,0x57,0xab,0xab,
0x57,0xab,0xd7,0x57,0xab,0xff,0x57,0xab,
0x00,0x83,0xab,0x57,0x83,0xab,0x83,0x83,
0xab,0xab,0x83,0xab,0xd7,0x83,0xab,0xff,
0x83,0xab,0x00,0xab,0xab,0x57,0xab,0xab,
0x83,0xab,0xab,0xab,0xab,0xd7,0xab,
0xab,0xff,0xab,0xab,0x00,0xd7,0xab,0x57,
0xd7,0xab,0x83,0xd7,0xab,0xab,0xd7,0xab,
0xd7,0xd7,0xab,0xff,0xd7,0xab,0x00,0xff,
0xab,0x57,0xff,0xab,0x83,0xff,0xab,0xab,
0xff,0xab,0xd7,0xff,0xab,0xff,0xff,0xab,
0x00,0x00,0xd7,0x57,0x00,0xd7,0x83,0x00,
0xd7,0xab,0x00,0xd7,0xd7,0x00,0xd7,0xff,
0x00,0xd7,0x00,0x2b,0xd7,0x57,0x2b,0xd7,
0x83,0x2b,0xd7,0xab,0x2b,0xd7,0xd7,0x2b,
0xd7,0xff,0x2b,0xd7,0x00,0x57,0xd7,0x57,
0x57,0xd7,0x83,0x57,0xd7,0xab,0x57,0xd7,
0xd7,0x57,0xd7,0xff,0x57,0xd7,0x00,0x83,
0xd7,0x57,0x83,0xd7,0x83,0x83,0xd7,0xab,
0x83,0xd7,0xd7,0x83,0xd7,0xff,0x83,0xd7,
```

```
        0x00,0xab,0xd7,0x57,0xab,0xd7,0x83,0xab,
        0xd7,0xab,0xab,0xd7,0xd7,0xab,0xd7,0xff,
        0xab,0xd7,0x00,0xd7,0xd7,0x57,0xd7,0xd7,
        0x83,0xd7,0xd7,0xab,0xd7,0xd7,0xd7,0xd7,
        0xd7,0xff,0xd7,0xd7,0x00,0xff,0xd7,0x57,
        0xff,0xd7,0x83,0xff,0xd7,0xab,0xff,0xd7,
        0xd7,0xff,0xd7,0xff,0xff,0xd7,0x00,0x00,
        0xff,0x57,0x00,0xff,0x83,0x00,0xff,0xab,
        0x00,0xff,0xd7,0x00,0xff,0xff,0x00,0xff,
        0x00,0x2b,0xff,0x57,0x2b,0xff,0x83,0x2b,
        0xff,0xab,0x2b,0xff,0xd7,0x2b,0xff,0xff,
        0x2b,0xff,0x00,0x57,0xff,0x57,0x57,0xff,
        0x83,0x57,0xff,0xab,0x57,0xff,0xd7,0x57,
        0xff,0xff,0x57,0xff,0x00,0x83,0xff,0x57,
        0x83,0xff,0x83,0x83,0xff,0xab,0x83,0xff,
        0xd7,0x83,0xff,0xff,0x83,0xff,0x00,0xab,
        0xff,0x57,0xab,0xff,0x83,0xab,0xff,0xab,
        0xab,0xff,0xd7,0xab,0xff,0xff,0xab,0xff,
        0x00,0xd7,0xff,0x57,0xd7,0xff,0x83,0xd7,
        0xff,0xab,0xd7,0xff,0xd7,0xd7,0xff,0xff,
        0xd7,0xff,0x00,0xff,0xff,0x57,0xff,0xff,
        0x83,0xff,0xff,0xab,0xff,0xff,0xd7,0xff,
        0xff,0x3f,0x3f,0x3f,0x6b,0x6b,0x6b,0x97,
        0x97,0x97,0xc3,0xc3,0xc3,0xff,0xff,0xff
        };

char bayerPattern[8][8] = {
         0,32, 8,40, 2,34,10,42,
        48,16,56,24,50,18,58,26,
        12,44, 4,36,14,46, 6,38,
        60,28,52,20,62,30,54,22,
         3,35,11,43, 1,33, 9,41,
        51,19,59,27,49,17,57,25,
        15,47, 7,39,13,45, 5,37,
        63,31,55,23,61,29,53,21 };

char greymap[]= {
        0x00,0x00,0x00,0x00,0x00,0x00,0x00,0x00,
        0x00,0x00,0x00,0x00,0x00,0x00,0x00,0x00,
        0x00,0x00,0x00,0x00,0x00,0x00,0x00,0x00,
        0x00,0x00,0x00,0x00,0x00,0x00,0x00,0x00,
        0x00,0x01,0x02,0x06,0x08,0x0B,0x0D,0x10,
        0x12,0x16,0x17,0x1B,0x1C,0x20,0x22,0x23,
        0x27,0x29,0x2C,0x2E,0x2F,0x33,0x35,0x36,
        0x3A,0x3C,0x3D,0x3F,0x43,0x44,0x46,0x49,
        0x4B,0x4D,0x4F,0x50,0x54,0x56,0x57,0x59,
        0x5B,0x5E,0x60,0x62,0x63,0x65,0x67,0x69,
        0x6C,0x6E,0x70,0x71,0x73,0x75,0x76,0x77,
        0x79,0x7B,0x7C,0x7E,0x80,0x82,0x83,0x87,
        0x89,0x8A,0x8C,0x8E,0x8F,0x91,0x93,0x95,
        0x95,0x96,0x98,0x9A,0x9C,0x9D,0x9F,0xA1,
        0xA3,0xA4,0xA6,0xA8,0xA9,0xAB,0xAD,0xAF,
        0xAF,0xB0,0xB2,0xB4,0xB6,0xB7,0xB9,0xBB,
        0xBB,0xBD,0xBE,0xC0,0xC2,0xC3,0xC5,0xC5,
        0xC7,0xC9,0xCA,0xCC,0xCE,0xCE,0xD0,0xD1,
```

```
            0xD3,0xD5,0xD5,0xD6,0xD8,0xDA,0xDC,0xDC,
            0xDD,0xDF,0xE1,0xE1,0xE3,0xE4,0xE6,0xE6,
            0xE8,0xEA,0xEB,0xEB,0xED,0xEF,0xF0,0xF0,
            0xF2,0xF4,0xF6,0xF6,0xF7,0xF9,0xF9,0xFB,
            0xFD,0xFE,0xFE,0xFF,0xFF,0xFF,0xFF,0xFF,
            0xFF,0xFF,0xFF,0xFF,0xFF,0xFF,0xFF,0xFF,
            0xFF,0xFF,0xFF,0xFF,0xFF,0xFF,0xFF,0xFF,
            0xFF,0xFF,0xFF,0xFF,0xFF,0xFF,0xFF,0xFF,
            0xFF,0xFF,0xFF,0xFF,0xFF,0xFF,0xFF,0xFF,
            0xFF,0xFF,0xFF,0xFF,0xFF,0xFF,0xFF,0xFF,
            0xFF,0xFF,0xFF,0xFF,0xFF,0xFF,0xFF,0xFF,
            0xFF,0xFF,0xFF,0xFF,0xFF,0xFF,0xFF,0xFF,
            0xFF,0xFF,0xFF,0xFF,0xFF,0xFF,0xFF,0xFF,
            0xFF,0xFF,0xFF,0xFF,0xFF,0xFF,0xFF,0xFF
            };

char gamma[256];

char *lpbuf=NULL;
int lplines=0;

unsigned int oldvesamode=0xffff;

main(argc,argv)
        int argc;
        char *argv[];
{
        BUTTON quit,print;
        POINT p;
        int left,top,right,bottom;
        int i,alive=1,thiscard=0xffff,thisprinter=LASERJET;

        /* see what kind of card is installed - sort of */
        if(argc > 1) {
                if(!stricmp(argv[1],"PARADISE")) thiscard=PARADISE;
                else if(!stricmp(argv[1],"ATI")) thiscard=ATI;
                else if(!stricmp(argv[1],"TSENG")) thiscard=TSENG;
                else if(!stricmp(argv[1],"TRIDENT")) thiscard=TRIDENT;
                else if(!stricmp(argv[1],"OAK")) thiscard=OAK;
                else if(!stricmp(argv[1],"VESA")) thiscard=VESA;
        }

        if(argc > 2) {
                if(!stricmp(argv[2],"LASERJET")) thisprinter=LASERJET;
                else if(!stricmp(argv[2],"POSTSCRIPT")) thisprinter=POSTSCRIPT;
                else if(!stricmp(argv[2],"DESKJET")) thisprinter=DESKJET;
                else if(!stricmp(argv[2],"EPSONFX80")) thisprinter=EPSONFX80;
        }

        /* go for a graphics mode */
        if(!InitMouse(640,480,thiscard)) exit(1);

        /* set the palette */
        SetVgaPalette(palette,256);
```

```
SetVgaWhite(WHITE);
SetVgaBlack(BLACK);
SetVgaGrey(GREY);
SetVgaLightGrey(LIGHTGREY);
SetVgaDarkGrey(DARKGREY);

/* clear the screen */
ClearScreen(GetVgaLightGrey());

/* draw a moire pattern */
for(i=0;i<SCREENWIDE;i+=2)
    DrawLine(i,0,SCREENWIDE>>1,SCREENDEEP>>1,i);
for(i=0;i<SCREENDEEP;i+=2)
    DrawLine(SCREENWIDE>>1,SCREENDEEP>>1,SCREENWIDE-1,i,i);
for(i=SCREENWIDE-1;i>=0;i-=2)
    DrawLine(SCREENWIDE>>1,SCREENDEEP>>1,i,SCREENDEEP-1,i-1);
for(i=SCREENDEEP-1;i>=0;i-=2)
    DrawLine(0,i,SCREENWIDE>>1,SCREENDEEP>>1,i-1);

/* show the palette */
for(i=0;i<256;++i) {
        left=30+(i % 32)*16;
        top=200+(i / 32)*16;
        right=left+16;
        bottom=top+16;
        FillRect(left,top,right,bottom,i);
        FrameRect(left,top,right,bottom,GetVgaBlack());
}

/* show some example text */
i=100;
DrawString(128,i," This is blue on light green.          ",BLUE,LIGHTGREEN);
i+=FONTDEPTH;
DrawString(128,i," This is red on light yellow.          ",RED,LIGHTYELLOW);
i+=FONTDEPTH;
DrawString(128,i," This is light yellow on red.          ",LIGHTYELLOW,RED);
i+=FONTDEPTH;
DrawString(128,i," This is black on magenta (very ugly). ",BLACK,MAGENTA);
i+=FONTDEPTH;
DrawString(128,i," This is cyan on light grey.           ",CYAN,LIGHTGREY);
i+=FONTDEPTH;

/* create some buttons to click on */
MakeButton(SCREENWIDE-100,SCREENDEEP-60,"Quit",&quit);
DrawButton(&quit);

MakeButton(SCREENWIDE-200,SCREENDEEP-60,"Print",&print);
DrawButton(&print);

/* loop 'til we're done */
do {
        /* look for a mouse click */
```

```
                if(MouseDown(&p)) {
                        if(PointInRect(&p,&quit)) {
                                TrackButton(&quit);
                                alive=0;
                        }
                        else if(PointInRect(&p,&print)) {
                                TrackButton(&print);
                                DoPrintScreen(thisprinter);
                        }
                }
        } while(alive);

        DeinitMouse();
}

/* print the screen */
DoPrintScreen(printer)
        unsigned int printer;
{
        char *p,*ps,*pr,*pt;
        unsigned int i,j;

        if((p=malloc(SCREENWIDE)) == NULL) {
                beep();
                return;
        }

        if((ps=malloc(SCREENWIDE * RGB_SIZE)) == NULL) {
                beep();
                return;
        }

        WaitCursor();
        if(!InitPrinter(printer)) {
                free(ps);
                free(p);
                ArrowCursor();
                beep();
                return;
        }

        for(i=0;i<SCREENDEEP;++i) {
                MouseOff();
                GetScreenLine(p,i);
                MouseOn();

                pr=ps;
                pt=p;
                for(j=0;j<SCREENWIDE;++j) {
                        *pr++=palette[*pt*RGB_SIZE+RGB_RED];
                        *pr++=palette[*pt*RGB_SIZE+RGB_GREEN];
                        *pr++=palette[*pt*RGB_SIZE+RGB_BLUE];
                        ++pt;
```

```
                    }
                    PrintLine(ps,i,printer);
            }
        DeinitPrinter(printer);
        ArrowCursor();

        free(ps);
        free(p);
}

/* set up the printer to print an image */
InitPrinter(printer)
        unsigned int printer;
{
        static char posthead[]=
                "/screensize %d def\r\n"
                "/width %d def\r\n"
                "/height %d def\r\n"
                "/pixwidth %f def\r\n"
                "/pixheight %f def\r\n"
                "/picstr width string def\r\n"
                "screensize 0 ne {\r\n"
                "screensize 45 { abs exch abs 2 copy add 1 gt\r\n"
                "{ 1 sub dup mul exch 1 sub dup mul add 1 sub }\r\n"
                "{ dup mul exch dup mul add 1 exch sub }\r\n"
                "ifelse } setscreen\r\n"
                "} if\r\n"
                "/dopic {\r\n"
                "gsave width height 8\r\n"
                "[width 0 0 height neg 0 height]\r\n"
                "{currentfile picstr readhexstring pop}\r\n"
                "image grestore } def\r\n"
                "/showname {\r\n"
                "/Courier findfont 12 scalefont setfont\r\n"
                "20 20 moveto (%s) show\r\n"
                "} def\r\n"
                "showname\r\n"
                "40 50 translate pixwidth pixheight scale\r\n"
                "dopic\r\n";

        char *lb,s[64];

        switch(printer) {
                case LASERJET:
                        p_string("\033E");
                        p_string("\033*t100R");
                        p_string("\033*p20X");
                        p_string("\033*p20Y");
                        p_string("\033*r1A");
                        break;
                case POSTSCRIPT:
                        if((lb=malloc(4096)) == NULL) return(0);
                        sprintf(lb,posthead,0,SCREENWIDE,SCREENDEEP,
                            (double)SCREENWIDE/1.39,(double)SCREENDEEP/1.39,"");
```

```
                        p_string(lb);
                        free(lb);
                        break;
            case DESKJET:
                        CreateGammaCurve(gamma,(double)DESKJET_GAMMA);
                        p_string("\033E");
                        p_string("\033*OoOL");

                        sprintf(s,"\033*r%uS",SCREENWIDE*COLOUREXPANSION);
                        p_string(s);
                        p_string("\033*r3U");
                        p_string("\033*b0M");

                        p_string("\033*o2D");
                        p_string("\033*o1Q");

                        p_string("\033*t300R");
                        p_string("\033*p20X");
                        p_string("\033*p20Y");
                        p_string("\033*r1A");
                        break;
            case EPSONFX80:
            p_string("\033@");

if((lpbuf=malloc(EPSON_LINEDEEP*pixels2bytes(SCREENWIDE)))==NULL)
                        return(0);
                        lplines=0;
                        break;
        }
        return(1);
}

/* close down the printer after printing an image */
DeinitPrinter(printer)
        unsigned int printer;
{
        switch(printer) {
                case LASERJET:
                        p_string("\033*rB");
                        p_string("\014");
                        break;
                case POSTSCRIPT:
                        p_string("showpage\r\n");
                        break;
                case DESKJET:
                        p_string("\033*rB");
                        p_string("\014");
                        break;
                case EPSONFX80:
                        if(lplines) PrintEpsonBuffer();
                        free(lpbuf);
                        p_string("\033@");
                        break;
        }
}
```

```
/* print one line of an image */
PrintLine(line,number,printer)
    char *line;
    unsigned int number,printer;
{
    char *pd,*pl,*pr,*ps,s[64];
    int c,i,j,k,n;

    switch(printer) {
        case LASERJET:
            if((ps=malloc(pixels2bytes(SCREENWIDE))) != NULL) {
                memset(ps,0,pixels2bytes(SCREENWIDE));
                for(i=0;i<SCREENWIDE;++i) {
                    c=greymap[greyvalue(line[RGB_RED],
                        line[RGB_GREEN],line[RGB_BLUE])];
                    if((c >> 2) > bayerPattern[i & 0x0007][number & 0x0007])
                        ps[i>>3] |= masktable[i & 0x0007];
                    line+=RGB_SIZE;
                }
                sprintf(s,"\033*b%dW",pixels2bytes(SCREENWIDE));
                p_string(s);
                for(i=0;i<pixels2bytes(SCREENWIDE);++i) p_char(~ps[i]);
                free(ps);
            }
            break;
        case POSTSCRIPT:
            for(i=0;i<SCREENWIDE;++i) {
                c=greymap[greyvalue(line[RGB_RED],
                    line[RGB_GREEN],line[RGB_BLUE])];
                sprintf(s,"%02.2X",c & 0xff);
                p_string(s);
                if(!((i+1) % 32)) p_string("\r\n");
                line+=RGB_SIZE;
            }
            p_string("\r\n");
            break;
        case DESKJET:
            /* allocate a buffer to expand the line into */
            if((ps=malloc(SCREENWIDE*COLOUREXPANSION*RGB_SIZE)) == NULL) return;

            /* allocate a buffer to put the planes in */
            if((pl=malloc(pixels2bytes(SCREENWIDE)*COLOUREXPANSION)) == NULL) {
                free(ps);
                return;
            }

            pd=ps;
            pr=line;
            for(i=0;i<SCREENWIDE;++i) {
                for(j=0;j<COLOUREXPANSION;++j) {
                    pd[RGB_RED]=gamma[pr[RGB_RED]];
                    pd[RGB_GREEN]=gamma[pr[RGB_GREEN]];
                    pd[RGB_BLUE]=gamma[pr[RGB_BLUE]];
                    pd+=RGB_SIZE;
                }
```

```
            pr+=RGB_SIZE;
    }

    n=number*COLOUREXPANSION;

    for(i=0;i<COLOUREXPANSION;++i) {

        /* dither the red line */
        pd=ps;
        k=SCREENWIDE*COLOUREXPANSION;
        for(j=0;j<k;++j) {
            c=(pd[RGB_RED] >> 2);
            if(c >= bayerPattern[j & 0x0007][n & 0x0007])
                pl[j >> 3] |= masktable[j & 0x0007];
            else
                pl[j >> 3] &= ~masktable[j & 0x0007];
            pd+=RGB_SIZE;
        }
        sprintf(s,"\033*b%dV",pixels2bytes(SCREENWIDE)*COLOUREXPANSION);
        p_string(s);
        k=pixels2bytes(SCREENWIDE)*COLOUREXPANSION;
        for(j=0;j<k;++j) p_char(pl[j]);

        /* dither the green line */
        pd=ps;
        k=SCREENWIDE*COLOUREXPANSION;
        for(j=0;j<k;++j) {
            c=(pd[RGB_GREEN] >> 2);
            if(c >= bayerPattern[j & 0x0007][n & 0x0007])
                pl[j >> 3] |= masktable[j & 0x0007];
            else
                pl[j >> 3] &= ~masktable[j & 0x0007];
            pd+=RGB_SIZE;
        }
        sprintf(s,"\033*b%dV",pixels2bytes(SCREENWIDE)*COLOUREXPANSION);
        p_string(s);
        k=pixels2bytes(SCREENWIDE)*COLOUREXPANSION;
        for(j=0;j<k;++j) p_char(pl[j]);

        /* dither the blue line */
        pd=ps;
        k=SCREENWIDE*COLOUREXPANSION;
        for(j=0;j<k;++j) {
            c=(pd[RGB_BLUE] >> 2);
            if(c >= bayerPattern[j & 0x0007][n & 0x0007])
                pl[j >> 3] |= masktable[j & 0x0007];
            else
                pl[j >> 3] &= ~masktable[j & 0x0007];
            pd+=RGB_SIZE;
        }
        sprintf(s,"\033*b%dW",pixels2bytes(SCREENWIDE)*COLOUREXPANSION);
        p_string(s);
        k=pixels2bytes(SCREENWIDE)*COLOUREXPANSION;
        for(j=0;j<k;++j) p_char(pl[j]);
```

```
                                      ++n;
                          }
                          free(pl);
                          free(ps);
                          break;
                  case EPSONFX80:
                          if(lplines >= EPSON_LINEDEEP) PrintEpsonBuffer();
                          ps=lpbuf+lplines*pixels2bytes(SCREENWIDE);
                          memset(ps,0,pixels2bytes(SCREENWIDE));
                          for(i=0;i<SCREENWIDE;++i) {
                                  c=greymap[greyvalue(line[RGB_RED],
                                    line[RGB_GREEN],line[RGB_BLUE])];
                                  if((c >> 2) > bayerPattern[i & 0x0007]
                                    [number & 0x0007])
                                      ps[i>>3] |= masktable[i & 0x0007];
                                  line+=RGB_SIZE;
                          }
                          ++lplines;
                          break;
          }
  }


  PrintEpsonBuffer()
  {
          char *p;
          int c,i,j,m;

          p_string("\033*\006");
          p_char(SCREENWIDE);
          p_char(SCREENWIDE >> 8);

          for(i=0;i<SCREENWIDE;++i) {
                  c=0;
                  p=lpbuf+(i>>3);
                  m=masktable[i & 0x0007];
                  for(j=0;j<EPSON_LINEDEEP;++j) {
                          if(*p & m) c |= masktable[j];
                          p+=pixels2bytes(SCREENWIDE);
                  }
                  p_char(~c);
          }
          p_string("\015\033J\030");
          lplines=0;
          memset(lpbuf,0,EPSON_LINEDEEP*pixels2bytes(SCREENWIDE));
  }

  CreateGammaCurve(curve,gamma)
          char *curve;
          double gamma;
  {
          int i;

          for(i=0;i<256;++i)
                  curve[i]=(int)(255 * pow((double)i/255,(double)gamma) +
  (double)0.5);
```

```
        }

/* get one pixel from a planar image line */
GetBitPixel(p,bits,width,pos)
        char *p;
        int bits,width,pos;
{
        int c=0,i,byte,mask;

        byte=pos>>3;
        mask=masktable[pos & 0x0007];

        for(i=0;i<bits;++i) {
                if(p[byte] & mask) c |= bittable[i];
                p+=width;
        }

        return(c);
}

p_string(s)
        char *s;
{
        while(*s) p_char(*s++);
}

p_char(c)
        int c;
{
        union REGS r;

        do {
                r.h.ah = 2;
                r.x.dx = PRINTERPORT;
                int86(0x17,&r,&r);
        } while(!(r.h.ah & 0x80));

        r.h.ah = 0;
        r.h.al = c;
        r.x.dx = PRINTERPORT;
        int86(0x17,&r,&r);
}

SetVgaPalette(p,n)
        char *p;
        unsigned int n;
{
        int i;

        outp(0x3c6,0xff);
        for(i=0;i<n;++i) {
                outp(0x3c8,i);
                outp(0x3c9,(*p++) >> 2);
                outp(0x3c9,(*p++) >> 2);
                outp(0x3c9,(*p++) >> 2);
```

```
                              }

                      }

        MakeButton(left,top,string,button)
                unsigned int left,top;
                char *string;
                BUTTON *button;
        {
                button->frame.left = left & 0xfff8;
                button->frame.right=button->frame.left+(strlen(string)<<3)+16;
                button->frame.top=top;
                button->frame.bottom=button->frame.top+FONTDEPTH+8;
                button->text=string;
        }

        DrawButton(button)
                BUTTON *button;
        {
                FillRect(button->frame.left+1,button->frame.top+1,
                        button->frame.right-1,button->frame.bottom-1,WHITE);
                DrawLine(button->frame.left+1,button->frame.top,
                        button->frame.right-1,button->frame.top,BLACK);
                DrawLine(button->frame.left,button->frame.top+1,
                        button->frame.left,button->frame.bottom-1,BLACK);
                DrawLine(button->frame.right,button->frame.top+1,
                        button->frame.right,button->frame.bottom-1,BLACK);
                DrawLine(button->frame.left+1,button->frame.bottom,
                        button->frame.right-1,button->frame.bottom,BLACK);
                Fill3DBox(button->frame.left+1,button->frame.top+1,
                        button->frame.right-1,button->frame.bottom-1);

                DrawString(button->frame.left+8,button->frame.top+4,
                        button->text,DARKGREY,LIGHTGREY);
        }

        TrackButton(button)
                BUTTON *button;
        {
                POINT p;

                FillRect(button->frame.left+1,button->frame.top+1,
                        button->frame.right-1,button->frame.bottom-1,LIGHTGREY);
                DrawString(button->frame.left+8,button->frame.top+4,
                        button->text,DARKGREY,LIGHTGREY);
                while(MouseDown(&p));
                DrawButton(button);
        }

        Fill3DBox(left,top,right,bottom)
                int left,top,right,bottom;
        {
                FillRect(left,top,right,bottom,LIGHTGREY);
                DrawLine(left,top,right-1,top,WHITE);
```

```
            DrawLine(left,top+1,left,bottom-1,WHITE);

            DrawLine(left+3,bottom,right,bottom,DARKGREY);
            DrawLine(right,top+2,right,bottom-1,DARKGREY);
}

PointInRect(p,r)/* return true if point is in rect */
        POINT *p;
        RECT *r;
{
        if(p->x > r->left && p->x < r->right &&
           p->y > r->top  && p->y < r->bottom) return(1);
        else return(0);
}

WaitCursor()
{
        static char cursor[] = {
                0x00,0x00,0x00,0x00,
                0x00,0x00,0x01,0x80,
                0x03,0xC0,0x07,0xE0,
                0x0F,0xF0,0x07,0xE0,
                0x03,0xC0,0x01,0x80,
                0x00,0x00,0x00,0x00,
                0x00,0x00,0x00,0x00,
                0xFF,0xFF,0xFF,0xFF,

                0x00,0x00,0xFE,0x7F,
                0x06,0x60,0x0C,0x30,
                0x18,0x18,0x30,0x0C,
                0x60,0x06,0xC0,0x03,
                0x60,0x06,0x30,0x0C,
                0x98,0x19,0xCC,0x33,
                0xE6,0x67,0xFE,0x7F,
                0x00,0x00,0x00,0x00 };

        MouseCursor(cursor,7,7);
}

ArrowCursor()
{
        static char cursor[] = {
                0xFF,0x3F,0xFF,0x1F,
                0xFF,0x0F,0xFF,0x07,
                0xFF,0x03,0xFF,0x01,
                0xFF,0x00,0x7F,0x00,
                0x3F,0x00,0x1F,0x00,
                0xFF,0x01,0xFF,0x10,
                0xFF,0x30,0x7F,0xF8,
                0x7F,0xF8,0x7F,0xFC,
                0x00,0x00,0x00,0x40,
                0x00,0x60,0x00,0x70,
                0x00,0x78,0x00,0x7C,
                0x00,0x7E,0x00,0x7F,
                0x80,0x7F,0x00,0x7C,
```

7-7
Continued.

```
                        0x00,0x6C,0x00,0x46,
                        0x00,0x06,0x00,0x03,
                        0x00,0x03,0x00,0x00 };

        MouseCursor(cursor,0,0);
}
```

Printing a high- color screen

The TESTP-HI.C program in FIG. 7-8 links to MOUSE-HI from Chapter 5. It illustrates how the `DoPrintScreen` function can be modified to work with a high-color display. While high-color cards are arguably the most exotic super VGA hardware, they represent the easiest displays to print from. The only data swabbing involved is in translating the 2-byte high-color pixels fetched by `GetScreenLine` into 3-byte RGB pixels for the `PrintLine` function, something that's all done with mirrors and macros. The `PrintLine` function itself is unchanged from TESTP256.

7-8
*The source code for
TESTP-HI.C.*

```
/*
        Printing a super VGA screen

        Copyright (c) 1992 Alchemy Mindworks Inc.

        Links to MOUSE-HI.ASM
/

#include "stdio.h"
#include "dos.h"
#include "alloc.h"
#include "math.h"
#include "mouse-hi.h"

/* some useful colours */
#define BLACK           HIGHCOLOUR(0x00,0x00,0x00)
#define BLUE            HIGHCOLOUR(0x00,0x00,0xaa)
#define GREEN           HIGHCOLOUR(0x00,0xaa,0x00)
#define CYAN            HIGHCOLOUR(0x00,0xaa,0xaa)
#define RED             HIGHCOLOUR(0xaa,0x00,0x00)
#define MAGENTA         HIGHCOLOUR(0xaa,0x00,0xaa)
#define YELLOW          HIGHCOLOUR(0xaa,0xaa,0x00)
#define GREY            HIGHCOLOUR(0xaa,0xaa,0xaa)
#define DARKGREY        HIGHCOLOUR(0x55,0x55,0x55)
#define LIGHTGREY       HIGHCOLOUR(0xcc,0xcc,0xcc)
#define LIGHTBLUE       HIGHCOLOUR(0x00,0x00,0xff)
#define LIGHTGREEN      HIGHCOLOUR(0x00,0xff,0x00)
#define LIGHTRED        HIGHCOLOUR(0xff,0x00,0x00)
#define LIGHTYELLOW     HIGHCOLOUR(0xff,0xff,0x00)
#define LIGHTMAGENTA    HIGHCOLOUR(0xff,0x00,0xff)
#define WHITE           HIGHCOLOUR(0xff,0xff,0xff)

/* dimensions of the about box */
#define ABOUTLEFT       107
#define ABOUTTOP        50
#define ABOUTRIGHT      475
#define ABOUTBOTTOM     180
```

```
#define FRGFILE          "TESTM-HI.FRG"

#define LASERJET         1
#define POSTSCRIPT       2
#define DESKJET          3
#define EPSONFX80        4

#define LPT1             0
#define LPT2             1
#define LPT3             2

#define PRINTERPORT      LPT1

#define DESKJET_GAMMA    0.3

#define EPSON_LINEDEEP   8

#define COLOUREXPANSION 3

typedef struct  {
        char manufacturer;
        char version;
        char encoding;
        char bits_per_pixel;
        int xmin,ymin;
        int xmax,ymax;
        int hres;
        int vres;
        char palette[48];
        char reserved;
        char colour_planes;
        int bytes_per_line;
        int palette_type;
        char filler[58];
        } PCXHEAD;

typedef struct {
        char sig[4];
        unsigned int width,depth,bits,bytes,planebytes;
        unsigned long palette;
        unsigned long image;
        } IMAGEHEAD;

char *farPtr(char *p,unsigned long l);
char *loadfrag(char *s);

char bayerPattern[8][8] = {
         0,32, 8,40, 2,34,10,42,
        48,16,56,24,50,18,58,26,
        12,44, 4,36,14,46, 6,38,
        60,28,52,20,62,30,54,22,
         3,35,11,43, 1,33, 9,41,
        51,19,59,27,49,17,57,25,
        15,47, 7,39,13,45, 5,37,
        63,31,55,23,61,29,53,21 };
```

```
char greymap[]= {
        0x00,0x00,0x00,0x00,0x00,0x00,0x00,0x00,
        0x00,0x00,0x00,0x00,0x00,0x00,0x00,0x00,
        0x00,0x00,0x00,0x00,0x00,0x00,0x00,0x00,
        0x00,0x00,0x00,0x00,0x00,0x00,0x00,0x00,
        0x00,0x01,0x02,0x06,0x08,0x0B,0x0D,0x10,
        0x12,0x16,0x17,0x1B,0x1C,0x20,0x22,0x23,
        0x27,0x29,0x2C,0x2E,0x2F,0x33,0x35,0x36,
        0x3A,0x3C,0x3D,0x3F,0x43,0x44,0x46,0x49,
        0x4B,0x4D,0x4F,0x50,0x54,0x56,0x57,0x59,
        0x5B,0x5E,0x60,0x62,0x63,0x65,0x67,0x69,
        0x6C,0x6E,0x70,0x71,0x73,0x75,0x76,0x77,
        0x79,0x7B,0x7C,0x7E,0x80,0x82,0x83,0x87,
        0x89,0x8A,0x8C,0x8E,0x8F,0x91,0x93,0x95,
        0x95,0x96,0x98,0x9A,0x9C,0x9D,0x9F,0xA1,
        0xA3,0xA4,0xA6,0xA8,0xA9,0xAB,0xAD,0xAF,
        0xAF,0xB0,0xB2,0xB4,0xB6,0xB7,0xB9,0xBB,
        0xBB,0xBD,0xBE,0xC0,0xC2,0xC3,0xC5,0xC5,
        0xC7,0xC9,0xCA,0xCC,0xCC,0xCE,0xCE,0xD0,0xD1,
        0xD3,0xD5,0xD5,0xD6,0xD8,0xDA,0xDC,0xDC,
        0xDD,0xDF,0xE1,0xE1,0xE3,0xE4,0xE6,0xE6,
        0xE8,0xEA,0xEB,0xEB,0xED,0xEF,0xF0,0xF0,
        0xF2,0xF4,0xF6,0xF6,0xF7,0xF9,0xF9,0xFB,
        0xFD,0xFE,0xFE,0xFF,0xFF,0xFF,0xFF,0xFF,
        0xFF,0xFF,0xFF,0xFF,0xFF,0xFF,0xFF,0xFF,
        0xFF,0xFF,0xFF,0xFF,0xFF,0xFF,0xFF,0xFF,
        0xFF,0xFF,0xFF,0xFF,0xFF,0xFF,0xFF,0xFF,
        0xFF,0xFF,0xFF,0xFF,0xFF,0xFF,0xFF,0xFF,
        0xFF,0xFF,0xFF,0xFF,0xFF,0xFF,0xFF,0xFF,
        0xFF,0xFF,0xFF,0xFF,0xFF,0xFF,0xFF,0xFF,
        0xFF,0xFF,0xFF,0xFF,0xFF,0xFF,0xFF,0xFF,
        0xFF,0xFF,0xFF,0xFF,0xFF,0xFF,0xFF,0xFF,
        0xFF,0xFF,0xFF,0xFF,0xFF,0xFF,0xFF,0xFF
        };

char gamma[256];

char *lpbuf=NULL;
int lplines=0;

main(argc,argv)
        int argc;
        char *argv[];
{
        static int colourtable[16] = {
                BLACK,BLUE,GREEN,CYAN,
                RED,MAGENTA,YELLOW,GREY,
                DARKGREY,LIGHTGREY,LIGHTBLUE,LIGHTGREEN,
                LIGHTRED,LIGHTYELLOW,LIGHTMAGENTA,WHITE
                };

        BUTTON quit,print;
        POINT p;
        char *frg;
        double red,green,blue,ri,gi,bi;
```

```
        int i,alive=1,thiscard=0xffff,thisprinter=LASERJET;

        /* see what kind of card is installed - sort of */
        if(argc > 1) {
                if(!stricmp(argv[1],"PARADISE")) thiscard=PARADISE;
                else if(!stricmp(argv[1],"ATI")) thiscard=ATI;
                else if(!stricmp(argv[1],"TSENG")) thiscard=TSENG;
        }

        if(argc > 2) {
                if(!stricmp(argv[2],"LASERJET")) thisprinter=LASERJET;
                else if(!stricmp(argv[2],"POSTSCRIPT")) thisprinter=POSTSCRIPT;
                else if(!stricmp(argv[2],"DESKJET")) thisprinter=DESKJET;
                else if(!stricmp(argv[2],"EPSONFX80")) thisprinter=EPSONFX80;
        }

        /* go for a graphics mode */
        if(!InitMouse(640,480,thiscard)) exit(1);

        SetVgaWhite(WHITE);
        SetVgaBlack(BLACK);
        SetVgaGrey(GREY);
        SetVgaLightGrey(LIGHTGREY);
        SetVgaDarkGrey(DARKGREY);

        /* clear the screen */
        ClearScreen(GetVgaLightGrey());

        /* draw a moire pattern */
        for(i=0;i<SCREENWIDE;i+=2)
            DrawLine(i,0,SCREENWIDE>>1,SCREENDEEP>>1,colourtable[i & 15]);
        for(i=0;i<SCREENDEEP;i+=2)
            DrawLine(SCREENWIDE>>1,SCREENDEEP>>1,SCREENWIDE-1,i,colourtable[i & 15]);
        for(i=SCREENWIDE-1;i>=0;i-=2)
            DrawLine(SCREENWIDE>>1,SCREENDEEP>>1,i,SCREENDEEP-1,colourtable[(i-1) & 15]);
        for(i=SCREENDEEP-1;i>=0;i-=2)
            DrawLine(0,i,SCREENWIDE>>1,SCREENDEEP>>1,colourtable[(i-1) & 15]);

        red=green=blue=0;
        ri=(double)256/(double)(SCREENWIDE-40)*1;
        gi=(double)256/(double)(SCREENWIDE-40)*5;
        bi=(double)256/(double)(SCREENWIDE-40)*3;

        for(i=0;i<(SCREENWIDE-40);++i) {
                DrawLine(20+i,300,20+i,400,HIGHCOLOUR((int)red,(int)green,(int)blue));

                if((red+ri) > 255 || (red+ri) < 0) ri=ri*-1;
                if((green+gi) > 255 || (green+gi) < 0) gi=gi*-1;
                if((blue+bi) > 255 || (blue+bi) < 0) bi=bi*-1;

                red+=ri;
                green+=gi;
                blue+=bi;
        }
```

```
/* display an image fragment */

WaitCursor();
if((frg=loadfrag(FRGFILE)) != NULL) {
        FillRect(15,15,15+ImageWidth(frg),15+ImageDepth(frg),DARKGREY);
        PutImageHi(10,10,frg);
        FrameRect(10,10,10+ImageWidth(frg),10+ImageDepth(frg),BLACK);
        farfree(frg);
}
ArrowCursor();

/* show some example text */
i=100;
DrawString(200,i," This is blue on light green.           ",BLUE,LIGHTGREEN);
i+=FONTDEPTH;
DrawString(200,i," This is red on light yellow.           ",RED,LIGHTYELLOW);
i+=FONTDEPTH;
DrawString(200,i," This is light yellow on red.           ",LIGHTYELLOW,RED);
i+=FONTDEPTH;
DrawString(200,i," This is black on magenta (very ugly). ",BLACK,MAGENTA);
i+=FONTDEPTH;
DrawString(200,i," This is cyan on light grey.           ",CYAN,LIGHTGREY);
i+=FONTDEPTH;

/* create some buttons to click on */
MakeButton(SCREENWIDE-100,SCREENDEEP-60,"Quit",&quit);
DrawButton(&quit);

MakeButton(SCREENWIDE-200,SCREENDEEP-60,"Print",&print);
DrawButton(&print);

/* loop 'til we're done */
do {
        /* look for a mouse click */
        if(MouseDown(&p)) {
                if(PointInRect(&p,&quit)) {
                        TrackButton(&quit);
                        alive=0;
                }
                else if(PointInRect(&p,&print)) {
                        TrackButton(&print);
                        DoPrintScreen(thisprinter);
                }
        }
} while(alive);

DeinitMouse();
}

/* print the screen */
DoPrintScreen(printer)
        unsigned int printer;
{
        char *p,*ps,*pr;
```

```
        unsigned int i,j,*ip;

        if((p=malloc(SCREENWIDE * sizeof(unsigned int))) == NULL) {
                beep();
                return;
        }

        if((ps=malloc(SCREENWIDE * RGB_SIZE)) == NULL) {
                beep();
                return;
        }

        WaitCursor();
        if(!InitPrinter(printer)) {
                free(ps);
                free(p);
                ArrowCursor();
                beep();
                return;
        }

        for(i=0;i<SCREENDEEP;++i) {
                MouseOff();
                GetScreenLine(p,i);
                MouseOn();

                ip=(unsigned int *)p;
                pr=ps;
                for(j=0;j<SCREENWIDE;++j) {
                        *pr++=HIGHRED(*ip);
                        *pr++=HIGHGREEN(*ip);
                        *pr++=HIGHBLUE(*ip);
                        ++ip;
                }

                PrintLine(ps,i,printer);

        }
        DeinitPrinter(printer);
        ArrowCursor();

        free(ps);
        free(p);
}

/* set up the printer to print an image */
InitPrinter(printer)
        unsigned int printer;
{
        static char posthead[]=
                "/screensize %d def\r\n"
                "/width %d def\r\n"
                "/height %d def\r\n"
                "/pixwidth %f def\r\n"
                "/pixheight %f def\r\n"
```

```
"/picstr width string def\r\n"
"screensize 0 ne {\r\n"
"screensize 45 { abs exch abs 2 copy add 1 gt\r\n"
"{ 1 sub dup mul exch 1 sub dup mul add 1 sub }\r\n"
"{ dup mul exch dup mul add 1 exch sub }\r\n"
"ifelse } setscreen\r\n"
"} if\r\n"
"/dopic {\r\n"
"gsave width height 8\r\n"
"[width 0 0 height neg 0 height]\r\n"
"{currentfile picstr readhexstring pop}\r\n"
"image grestore } def\r\n"
"/showname {\r\n"
"/Courier findfont 12 scalefont setfont\r\n"
"20 20 moveto (%s) show\r\n"
"} def\r\n"
"showname\r\n"
"40 50 translate pixwidth pixheight scale\r\n"
"dopic\r\n";

    char *lb,s[64];

    switch(printer) {
        case LASERJET:
            p_string("\033E");
            p_string("\033*t100R");
            p_string("\033*p20X");
            p_string("\033*p20Y");
            p_string("\033*r1A");
            break;
        case POSTSCRIPT:
            if((lb=malloc(4096)) == NULL) return(0);
            sprintf(lb,posthead,0,SCREENWIDE,SCREENDEEP,
(double)SCREENWIDE/1.39,(double)SCREENDEEP/1.39,"");
            p_string(lb);
            free(lb);
            break;
        case DESKJET:
            CreateGammaCurve(gamma,(double)DESKJET_GAMMA);
            p_string("\033E");
            p_string("\033*o0L");

sprintf(s,"\033*r%uS",SCREENWIDE*COLOUREXPANSION);
            p_string(s);
            p_string("\033*r3U");
            p_string("\033*b0M");

            p_string("\033*o2D");
            p_string("\033*o1Q");

            p_string("\033*t300R");
            p_string("\033*p20X");
            p_string("\033*p20Y");
```

```
                                p_string("\033*r1A");
                                break;
                        case EPSONFX80:
                                p_string("\033@");
                                if((lpbuf=malloc(EPSON_LINEDEEP*pixels2bytes(SCREENWIDE)))==NULL)
                                        return(0);
                                lplines=0;
                                break;
                }
        return(1);
}

/* close down the printer after printing an image */
DeinitPrinter(printer)
        unsigned int printer;
{
        switch(printer) {
                case LASERJET:
                        p_string("\033*rB");
                        p_string("\014");
                        break;
                case POSTSCRIPT:
                        p_string("showpage\r\n");
                        break;
                case DESKJET:
                        p_string("\033*rB");
                        p_string("\014");
                        break;
                case EPSONFX80:
                        if(lplines) PrintEpsonBuffer();
                        free(lpbuf);
                        p_string("\033@");
                        break;
        }
}

/* print one line of an image */
PrintLine(line,number,printer)
        char *line;
        unsigned int number,printer;
{
        char *pd,*pl,*pr,*ps,s[64];
        int c,i,j,k,n;

        switch(printer) {
                case LASERJET:
                        if((ps=malloc(pixels2bytes(SCREENWIDE))) != NULL) {
                                memset(ps,0,pixels2bytes(SCREENWIDE));
                                for(i=0;i<SCREENWIDE;++i) {
                                        c=greymap[greyvalue(line[RGB_RED],
                                          line[RGB_GREEN],line[RGB_BLUE])];
                                        if((c >> 2) > bayerPattern[i & 0x0007][number & 0x0007])
                                          ps[i>>3] |= masktable[i & 0x0007];
                                        line+=RGB_SIZE;
```

```
                                      sprintf(s,"\033*b%dW",pixels2bytes(SCREENWIDE));
                                      p_string(s);
                                      for(i=0;i<pixels2bytes(SCREENWIDE);++i) p_char(~ps[i]);
                                      free(ps);
                              }
                      break;
              case POSTSCRIPT:
                      for(i=0;i<SCREENWIDE;++i) {
                              c=greymap[greyvalue(line[RGB_RED],
                                 line[RGB_GREEN],line[RGB_BLUE])];
                              sprintf(s,"%02.2X",c & 0xff);
                              p_string(s);
                              if(!((i+1) % 32)) p_string("\r\n");
                              line+=RGB_SIZE;
                      }
                      p_string("\r\n");
                      break;
              case DESKJET:
                      /* allocate a buffer to expand the line into */
                      if((ps=malloc(SCREENWIDE*COLOUREXPANSION*RGB_SIZE)) == NULL) return;

                      /* allocate a buffer to put the planes in */
                      if((pl=malloc(pixels2bytes(SCREENWIDE)*COLOUREXPANSION)) == NULL) {
                              free(ps);
                              return;
                      }

                      pd=ps;
                      pr=line;
                      for(i=0;i<SCREENWIDE;++i) {
                              for(j=0;j<COLOUREXPANSION;++j) {
                                      pd[RGB_RED]=gamma[pr[RGB_RED]];
                                      pd[RGB_GREEN]=gamma[pr[RGB_GREEN]];
                                      pd[RGB_BLUE]=gamma[pr[RGB_BLUE]];
                                      pd+=RGB_SIZE;
                              }
                              pr+=RGB_SIZE;
                      }

                      n=number*COLOUREXPANSION;

                      for(i=0;i<COLOUREXPANSION;++i) {

                              /* dither the red line */
                              pd=ps;
                              k=SCREENWIDE*COLOUREXPANSION;
                              for(j=0;j<k;++j) {
                                      c=(pd[RGB_RED] >> 2);
                                      if(c >= bayerPattern[j & 0x0007][n & 0x0007])
                                          pl[j >> 3] |= masktable[j & 0x0007];
                                      else
                                          pl[j >> 3] &= ~masktable[j & 0x0007];
                                      pd+=RGB_SIZE;
```

```
                }
                sprintf(s,"\033*b%dV",pixels2bytes(SCREENWIDE)*COLOUREXPANSION);
                p_string(s);
                k=pixels2bytes(SCREENWIDE)*COLOUREXPANSION;
                for(j=0;j<k;++j) p_char(pl[j]);

                /* dither the green line */
                pd=ps;
                k=SCREENWIDE*COLOUREXPANSION;
                for(j=0;j<k;++j) {
                        c=(pd[RGB_GREEN] >> 2);
                        if(c >= bayerPattern[j & 0x0007][n & 0x0007])
                            pl[j >> 3] |= masktable[j & 0x0007];
                        else
                            pl[j >> 3] &= ~masktable[j & 0x0007];
                        pd+=RGB_SIZE;
                }
                sprintf(s,"\033*b%dV",pixels2bytes(SCREENWIDE)*COLOUREXPANSION);
                p_string(s);
                k=pixels2bytes(SCREENWIDE)*COLOUREXPANSION;
                for(j=0;j<k;++j) p_char(pl[j]);

                /* dither the blue line */
                pd=ps;
                k=SCREENWIDE*COLOUREXPANSION;
                for(j=0;j<k;++j) {
                        c=(pd[RGB_BLUE] >> 2);
                        if(c >= bayerPattern[j & 0x0007][n & 0x0007])
                            pl[j >> 3] |= masktable[j & 0x0007];
                        else
                            pl[j >> 3] &= ~masktable[j & 0x0007];
                        pd+=RGB_SIZE;
                }
                sprintf(s,"\033*b%dW",pixels2bytes(SCREENWIDE)*COLOUREXPANSION);
                p_string(s);
                k=pixels2bytes(SCREENWIDE)*COLOUREXPANSION;
                for(j=0;j<k;++j) p_char(pl[j]);

                ++n;

            }
            free(pl);
            free(ps);
            break;
    case EPSONFX80:
            if(lplines >= EPSON_LINEDEEP) PrintEpsonBuffer();
            ps=lpbuf+lplines*pixels2bytes(SCREENWIDE);
            memset(ps,0,pixels2bytes(SCREENWIDE));
            for(i=0;i<SCREENWIDE;++i) {
                    c=greymap[greyvalue(line[RGB_RED],line[RGB_GREEN],line[RGB_BLUE])];
                    if((c >> 2) > bayerPattern[i & 0x0007]
                       [number & 0x0007])
                        ps[i>>3] |= masktable[i & 0x0007];
                    line+=RGB_SIZE;
            }
```

```
                                        ++lplines;
                                        break;
                }
        }

        PrintEpsonBuffer()
        {
                char *p;
                int c,i,j,m;

                p_string("\033*\006");
                p_char(SCREENWIDE);
                p_char(SCREENWIDE >> 8);

                for(i=0;i<SCREENWIDE;++i) {
                        c=0;
                        p=lpbuf+(i>>3);
                        m=masktable[i & 0x0007];
                        for(j=0;j<EPSON_LINEDEEP;++j) {
                                if(*p & m) c |= masktable[j];
                                p+=pixels2bytes(SCREENWIDE);
                        }
                        p_char(~c);
                }
                p_string("\015\033J\030");
                lplines=0;

        memset(lpbuf,0,EPSON_LINEDEEP*pixels2bytes(SCREENWIDE));
        }

        CreateGammaCurve(curve,gamma)
                char *curve;
                double gamma;
        {
                int i;

                for(i=0;i<256;++i)
                        curve[i]=(int)(255 * pow((double)i/255,(double)
                        gamma) + (double)0.5);
        }

        /* get one pixel from a planar image line */
        GetBitPixel(p,bits,width,pos)
                char *p;
                int bits,width,pos;
        {
                int c=0,i,byte,mask;

                byte=pos>>3;
                mask=masktable[pos & 0x0007];

                for(i=0;i<bits;++i) {
                        if(p[byte] & mask) c |= bittable[i];
                        p+=width;
                }
```

```
                return(c);
}

p_string(s)
        char *s;
{
        while(*s) p_char(*s++);
}

p_char(c)
        int c;
{
        union REGS r;

        do {
                r.h.ah = 2;
                r.x.dx = PRINTERPORT;
                int86(0x17,&r,&r);
        } while(!(r.h.ah & 0x80));

        r.h.ah = 0;
        r.h.al = c;
        r.x.dx = PRINTERPORT;
        int86(0x17,&r,&r);
}

MakeButton(left,top,string,button)
        unsigned int left,top;
        char *string;
        BUTTON *button;
{
        button->frame.left = left & 0xfff8;
        button->frame.right=button->frame.left+(strlen(string)<<3)+16;
        button->frame.top=top;
        button->frame.bottom=button->frame.top+FONTDEPTH+8;
        button->text=string;
}

DrawButton(button)
        BUTTON *button;
{
        FillRect(button->frame.left+1,button->frame.top+1,
                button->frame.right-1,button->frame.bottom-1,GetVgaWhite());
        DrawLine(button->frame.left+1,button->frame.top,
                button->frame.right-1,button->frame.top,GetVgaBlack());
        DrawLine(button->frame.left,button->frame.top+1,
                button->frame.left,button->frame.bottom-1,GetVgaBlack());
        DrawLine(button->frame.right,button->frame.top+1,
                button->frame.right,button->frame.bottom-1,GetVgaBlack());
        DrawLine(button->frame.left+1,button->frame.bottom,
                button->frame.right-1,button->frame.bottom,GetVgaBlack());
        Fill3DBox(button->frame.left+1,button->frame.top+1,
                button->frame.right-1,button->frame.bottom-1);
```

```
                    DrawString(button->frame.left+8,button->frame.top+4,
                            button->text,GetVgaDarkGrey(),GetVgaLightGrey());
        }

TrackButton(button)
        BUTTON *button;
        {

        POINT p;

        FillRect(button->frame.left+1,button->frame.top+1,
                button->frame.right-1,button->frame.bottom-
                1,GetVgaLightGrey());

        DrawString(button->frame.left+8,button->frame.top+4,
                    button->text,GetVgaDarkGrey(),GetVgaLightGrey());
        while(MouseDown(&p));
        DrawButton(button);
        }

Fill3DBox(left,top,right,bottom)
        int left,top,right,bottom;
        {
        FillRect(left,top,right,bottom,GetVgaLightGrey());
        DrawLine(left,top,right-1,top,GetVgaWhite());
        DrawLine(left,top+1,left,bottom-1,GetVgaWhite());

        DrawLine(left+3,bottom,right,bottom,GetVgaDarkGrey());
        DrawLine(right,top+2,right,bottom-1,GetVgaDarkGrey());
        }

PointInRect(p,r)/* return true if point is in rect */
        POINT *p;
        RECT *r;
        {
        if(p->x > r->left && p->x < r->right &&
           p->y > r->top  && p->>y < r->bottom) return(1);
        else return(0);
        }

WaitCursor()
        {
        static char cursor[] = {
                0x00,0x00,0x00,0x00,
                0x00,0x00,0x01,0x80,
                0x03,0xC0,0x07,0xE0,
                0x0F,0xF0,0x07,0xE0,
                0x03,0xC0,0x01,0x80,
                0x00,0x00,0x00,0x00,
                0x00,0x00,0x00,0x00,
                0xFF,0xFF,0xFF,0xFF,

                0x00,0x00,0xFE,0x7F,
                0x06,0x60,0x0C,0x30,
                0x18,0x18,0x30,0x0C,
                0x60,0x06,0xC0,0x03,
```

```
                         0x60,0x06,0x30,0x0C,
                         0x98,0x19,0xCC,0x33,
                         0xE6,0x67,0xFE,0x7F,
                         0x00,0x00,0x00,0x00 };

        MouseCursor(cursor,7,7);
}

ArrowCursor()
{
        static char cursor[] = {
                 0xFF,0x3F,0xFF,0x1F,
                 0xFF,0x0F,0xFF,0x07,
                 0xFF,0x03,0xFF,0x01,
                 0xFF,0x00,0x7F,0x00,
                 0x3F,0x00,0x1F,0x00,
                 0xFF,0x01,0xFF,0x10,
                 0xFF,0x30,0x7F,0xF8,
                 0x7F,0xF8,0x7F,0xFC,
                 0x00,0x00,0x00,0x40,
                 0x00,0x60,0x00,0x70,
                 0x00,0x78,0x00,0x7C,
                 0x00,0x7E,0x00,0x7F,
                 0x80,0x7F,0x00,0x7C,
                 0x00,0x6C,0x00,0x46,
                 0x00,0x06,0x00,0x03,
                 0x00,0x03,0x00,0x00 };

        MouseCursor(cursor,0,0);
}

/* load a fragment into a buffer and return a pointer to the image */
char *loadfrag(s)
        char *s;
{

        FILE *fp;
        IMAGEHEAD ih;
        char *p,*pr;
        unsigned int i;

        if((fp=fopen(s,"rb")) == NULL) return(NULL);

        if(fread((char *)&ih,1,sizeof(IMAGEHEAD),fp) != sizeof(IMAGEHEAD)) {
                fclose(fp);
                return(NULL);
        }

        if(ih.bits != 16) {
                fclose(fp);
                return(NULL);
        }

        if((p=farmalloc(4L+(long)ih.bytes*(long)ih.depth)) == NULL) {
                fclose(fp);
                return(NULL);
```

```
                            }

            fseek(fp,ih.image,SEEK_SET);

            pr=p;

            pr+=fread(pr,1,4,fp);

            for(i=0;i<ih.depth;++i) {
                    if(fread(pr,1,ih.bytes,fp) != ih.bytes) {
                            farfree(p);
                            fclose(fp);
                            return(NULL);
                    }
                    pr=farPtr(pr,(long)ih.bytes);
            }
            fclose(fp);
            return(p);
    }

    char *farPtr(p,l)
            char *p;
            unsigned long l;
    {

            unsigned int seg,off;

            seg = FP_SEG(p);
            off = FP_OFF(p);
            seg += (off / 16);
            off &= 0x000f;
            off += (unsigned int)(l & 0x000fL);
            seg += (l / 16L);
            p = MK_FP(seg,off);
            return(p);

    }
```

If you want to provide your applications with the facility to dump their screens to a printer, you should have little difficulty in excising the appropriate bits of code from the example programs in this chapter and using them in your own works. There is an additional consideration in doing so, however.

In most cases, it takes a significant amount of time to print these screens. Especially in the case of a laser printer, there's no obvious indication that anything's happening when the screen is being printed. On a slow PostScript printer, for example, the long wait involved in printing a screen can look an awful lot like a hung system.

In printing a screen, it's not really practical to draw a bar graph to indicate the status of the print, as the bar graph would become part of the output. The ideal way to handle this would be to capture the screen to a buffer and then print from the buffer, such that you could maintain a status display on your screen. Unfortunately, this can require rather a lot of memory—at least 600K worth for high-color graphics.

At the very least a real-world graphic print screen function probably warrants a dialog box before it starts, advising the users of your software to go for a Coke. Alternately, you might think about having the `DoPrintScreen` function beep or click every twenty or thirty lines, or otherwise provide some indication of its activity.

Writing animated games

"Alice Goes to TechnologyLand"

"Madness takes its toll—Please have exact change."
—Graffiti

At three in the morning, the distinction between the inch-high creatures on your screen and the ones that might be running around in the shadows of your house can begin to blur somewhat. In a sense, it's well and proper that this is so. Both are to some extent figments of someone's imagination. In the former case they can be said to have impinged themselves on your imagination through a couple of dual density floppy disks.

Graphic adventure games are a true art form and, unlike stationary graphics, one that doesn't really have an antecedent in conventional media. Genuinely a creation of personal computers, the facility for blasting mutant radishes, nuking demented robots, questing after lost treasure, and otherwise proving a hero to the phosphor people is something that only comes with too much time in front of a keyboard.

If games are fun to play, they're immensely satisfying to write. You can create a complete universe in a game, populate it with creatures of your imagination, and wind its clockspring with physical laws to suit your whims. A well-crafted game can fuse both action and complex puzzle solving.

Figure 8-1 illustrates screens from several popular shareware games—Duke Nukem, Clyde's Adventures and Dark Castle, the latter a very old game of this genre on the Macintosh. I've probably wasted as much time playing these games and others like them as I required to write this book.

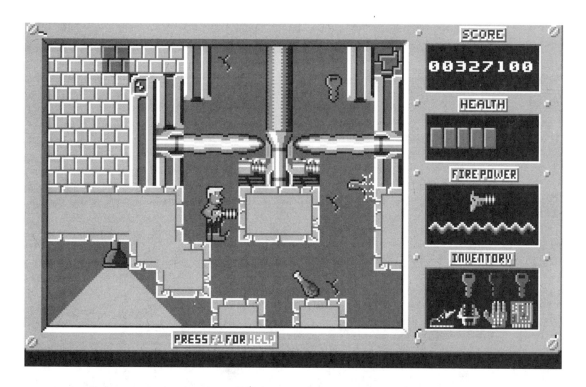

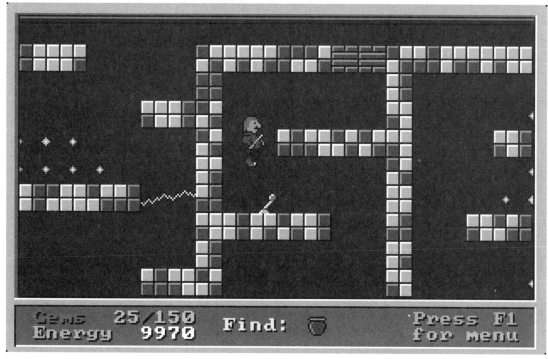

8-1 *Several alternate universes—Duke Nukem, Clyde's Adventures, and Dark Castle.*

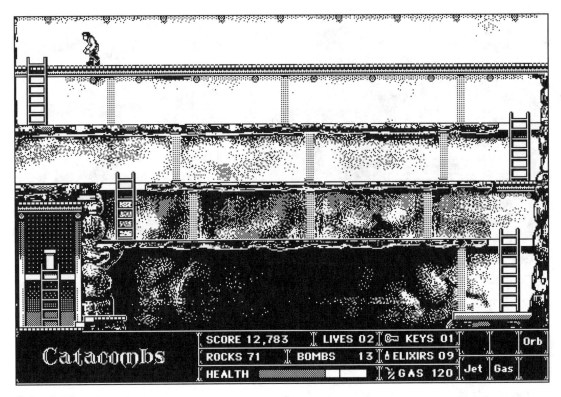

8-1 *Continued.*

The premise of graphic adventure games is usually pretty consistent, if the worlds and characters they present are not. You get to be a little animated adventurer who jumps and runs and teleports about the screen dispatching all sorts of nasties, searching for something salient to the plot of the game, and trying to find a way out of whatever trouble you've gotten into.

It's usually also the case that you should try to avoid becoming toast in the process.

The situations vary. Duke Nukem simply requires that the protagonist blast everything in his path to neutrinos. Dark Castle involves sophisticated puzzle solving. The various adventures of Commander Keen have taken the art of creating elaborate puzzles and menacing creatures to great lengths. Clyde's Adventures involve no weapons at all—Clyde himself is the only living thing in the game.

Writing one of these games is a worthy challenge and not something to be mastered easily. Aside from requiring some highly sophisticated graphic code, it also entails a pretty respectable degree of organization. While it's not always apparent when you play a graphic adventure game, there's a lot of clever data manipulation going on behind the hidden doors, secret chambers, and alternate universes.

This chapter will most certainly not tell you everything you need to write a graphic adventure game of your own; it will, however, get you started. Inasmuch as every game requires quite a lot of original code to make it go, this might be all a book really should hand you. You'll want to devise most of the working parts of a game yourself to suit your own perception of the warped reality of these synthetic worlds.

This chapter will look at a very simplified version of a game called *Alice* (alternately, *Alice in TechnologyLand*, *Alice through an Expired Warrantee*, *Lost Catacombs of a White Rabbit*, and so on—games require extreme titles to attract attention to themselves). At the time of Alice's creation, the idea of having a female protagonist in one of these things seemed pretty novel—in the interval between then and now Tim Sweeney's *Jill of the Jungle* turned up with much the same observation. It also embodied a wonderful aphorism—"This is a jungle, not Disneyland."

Figure 8-2 illustrates a screen from *Alice in TechnologyLand* as it will appear in this chapter. This includes some of the simple objects that will be used herein, as well as Alice herself. It seems fair to observe that as of this writing the real *Alice* is far from complete; every time it appears to be nearing completion someone seems to come up with a new twist for it, and it returns to the stellar fires of creation once more.

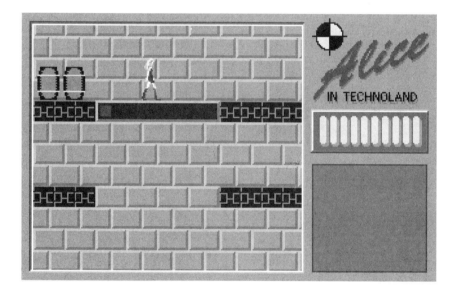

8-2
Alice in TechnologyLand.

The *Alice* in this chapter bears only a passing resemblance to the real game in progress. Reducing the fundamental code of the game down to something that didn't occupy most of this book was a challenge.

As this is a book about VGA graphics, this version of *Alice* has been created to run in a VGA graphics mode. The "real" version runs in a 320 by 200 pixel, 16-color EGA mode, with entirely different graphics. The 256-color mode has some interesting advantages, in that it allows for intricate, detailed graphics with lots of textures and clever uses of color. However, it also means that the bitmapped graphics that form the worlds of the game require a lot of memory. A game that runs in sixteen colors has about a quarter of the memory requirements, or, to look at it another way, can support worlds four times as big.

The action in this simplified version of *Alice* is pretty much in keeping with the basic tenets of these sorts of games. Alice can walk left and right and leap through holes in the floor. The room that she'll reside in is considerably larger than that which is visible in the screen window in FIG. 8-2. The complete room is shown in FIG. 8-3.

The object of this room is to get Alice from the upper left corner where the room begins around to that door in the lower left corner. In fact, this will be a pretty effortless journey, as the nasties that would normally appear in this room won't turn up in this example. The code in this chapter will concern itself with manifesting the objects in the room and animating Alice herself.

The problems involved in making this room work are actually fairly complex. The most obvious one is unquestionably that of making Alice appear to walk. This is accomplished using relatively simple cell animation. In fairness, because the screen display is quite coarse, the quality of the drawings would make Roger Rabbit want to rip his own ears out. There are certain practical considerations inherent in this—small screens call for small characters.

As an aside, drawing animation cells so they appear to walk naturally is also a bit tricky—very much more so in 256 colors, as it turns out, because of the way the cells are shaded. Originally the Alice in this game was created from the cells for the `16-color game, but the result was a very flat, uninteresting character. These cells were based on scanned photographs to some extent, with extensive retouching in Desktop Paint.

Making Alice walk is only a small part of the problem. Because the room in FIG. 8-3 is a good deal larger than the screen window in FIG. 8-2, the window must pan over the room as Alice progresses. In addition, some of the things in the room are solid—if Alice encounters one, she must jump over it to proceed. Knowing where the solid bits are and keeping track of them will require some stealth.

The floors are also solid bits. When Alice walks over a hole in the floor, she must drop down to the next level of the room.

While it won't be apparent in any of the preceding figures, the dark rectangular panels on the walls are animated as well. The lighter squares in them move in the direction Alice should probably walk. In fact, in the real version of the game, they turn out to be deliberately misleading from time to time. The code that makes the game go must manage these things too.

These panels are examples of an important class of game phenomena—things that move without human intervention.

Figure 8-3 probably looks like a huge drawn bitmap. In fact, it's nothing of the kind. The room as a whole was all created in data.

Managing objects

The room in FIG. 8-3 was created as a list of objects. An *object*—at least for the sake of this chapter—is a data structure that defines how the thing in question is to behave and a bitmap fragment that defines how it's to look. The bitmap fragments will, in fact, be FRG files of the sort that were dealt with in Chapter 2.

A complete room—a level, castle, catacombs, or whatever your game chooses to call it—really consists of a list of data objects. Each visible element in a room—such as one barrel, one of those direction signs, one floor tile, and so on—is an element in the list. If you draw every element in the list, you'll draw the entire room.

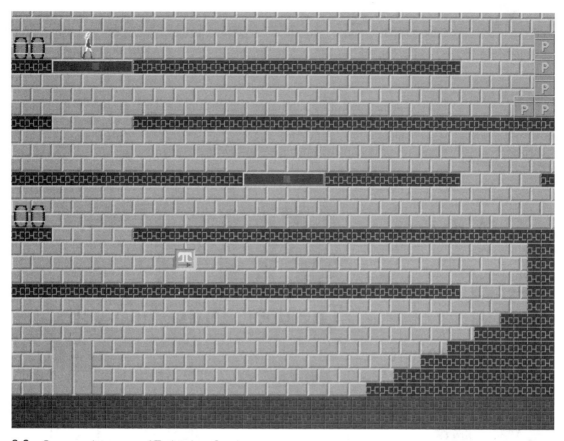

8-3 *One complete room of TechnologyLand.*

In fact, because the room is too big to draw in its entirety on a mode 13H screen, the code in this chapter will "draw" it in a virtual bitmap and then paint sections of it in the screen window as you pan around the room.

As an aside, the memory required for this virtual bitmap is the limiting factor to the size of the rooms you can create this way. At 256 colors, rooms much larger than 640 by 480 pixels will prove to be a problem.

To begin with, the definition of a room defines a tile object. This is actually just a grey rectangle with its sides shaded to make it look three-dimensional. It's used to fill the entire background of the room, creating the illusion of textured bricks. You can, of course, use other sorts of panels to create rooms with different appearances.

The floor tiles have the characteristic of being solid. Once again, they're fairly small objects—a length of floor consists of a lot of individual tile objects. The barrels are the same sorts of objects—that is, they're solid.

The signs set into the wall are "static" objects. Alice can pass before them, as they're considered to be part of the background.

Finally, the door in the lower left corner of the room is considered to be a special object. If Alice stands before it and someone hits the up arrow key to activate it, the door will open, Alice will vanish through it and the level will come to an end. In the example game in this chapter, the game will end as well.

Figure 8-4 illustrates the component parts of this room.

The program that manages the game will take the small graphic objects illustrated in FIG. 8-4 and assemble them into a complete room. In fact, it will do so based on the definition of this room shown in FIG. 8-5. The listing in FIG. 8-5 illustrates a very simple room definition language.

8-4

The component parts of a room in TechnologyLand.

 A barrel

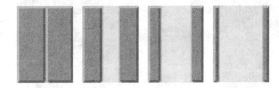

The door animation cells

The basement floor

The direction indicator

 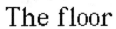 The floor

 A box
 A sign

 A wall

```
; Level three of Alice in Technology Land
DEFINE RoomWide 640
DEFINE RoomDeep 480
DEFINE RockBottom 440
DEFINE FloorTop1 312
DEFINE FloorTop2 248
DEFINE FloorTop3 184
DEFINE FloorTop4 120
DEFINE FloorTop5 56

;DEFINE A ROOM
ROOM RoomWide RoomDeep TILE.FRG

;THE FLOOR
SOLID 0 RockBottom BOTTOM.FRG
SOLID 64 RockBottom BOTTOM.FRG
SOLID 96 RockBottom BOTTOM.FRG
SOLID 160 RockBottom BOTTOM.FRG
SOLID 224 RockBottom BOTTOM.FRG
SOLID 288 RockBottom BOTTOM.FRG
SOLID 352 RockBottom BOTTOM.FRG
SOLID 416 RockBottom BOTTOM.FRG
SOLID 480 RockBottom BOTTOM.FRG
SOLID 496 RockBottom BOTTOM.FRG
SOLID 560 RockBottom BOTTOM.FRG
SOLID 624 RockBottom BOTTOM.FRG

;FIRST LEVEL
SOLID 0 FloorTop5 FLOOR.FRG
SOLID 48 FloorTop5 FLOOR.FRG
SOLID 96 FloorTop5 FLOOR.FRG
SOLID 144 FloorTop5 FLOOR.FRG
SOLID 144 FloorTop5 FLOOR.FRG
SOLID 192 FloorTop5 FLOOR.FRG
SOLID 240 FloorTop5 FLOOR.FRG
SOLID 288 FloorTop5 FLOOR.FRG
SOLID 336 FloorTop5 FLOOR.FRG
SOLID 384 FloorTop5 FLOOR.FRG
SOLID 432 FloorTop5 FLOOR.FRG
SOLID 480 FloorTop5 FLOOR.FRG

;BLINKING LIGHTS
INDICATOR 47 FloorTop5 3 DIRECT0.FRG DIRECT1.FRG DIRECT2.FRG
DIRECT3.FRG DIRECT4.FRG DIRECT5.FRG DIRECT6.FRG DIRECT7.FRG

SOLID 0 30 BARREL.FRG
SOLID 20 30 BARREL.FRG

;SECOND LEVEL
SOLID 0 FloorTop4 FLOOR.FRG
SOLID 144 FloorTop4 FLOOR.FRG
SOLID 144 FloorTop4 FLOOR.FRG
SOLID 192 FloorTop4 FLOOR.FRG
SOLID 240 FloorTop4 FLOOR.FRG
SOLID 288 FloorTop4 FLOOR.FRG
```

```
SOLID 336 FloorTop4 FLOOR.FRG
SOLID 384 FloorTop4 FLOOR.FRG
SOLID 432 FloorTop4 FLOOR.FRG
SOLID 480 FloorTop4 FLOOR.FRG
SOLID 528 FloorTop4 FLOOR.FRG
SOLID 576 FloorTop4 FLOOR.FRG
SOLID 624 FloorTop4 FLOOR.FRG

SOLID 616 96 PBOX.FRG
SOLID 592 96 PBOX.FRG
SOLID 616 72 PBOX.FRG
SOLID 616 48 PBOX.FRG
SOLID 616 24 PBOX.FRG

;THIRD LEVEL
SOLID 0 FloorTop3 FLOOR.FRG
SOLID 48 FloorTop3 FLOOR.FRG
SOLID 96 FloorTop3 FLOOR.FRG
SOLID 144 FloorTop3 FLOOR.FRG
SOLID 144 FloorTop3 FLOOR.FRG
SOLID 192 FloorTop3 FLOOR.FRG
SOLID 240 FloorTop3 FLOOR.FRG
SOLID 288 FloorTop3 FLOOR.FRG
SOLID 336 FloorTop3 FLOOR.FRG
SOLID 384 FloorTop3 FLOOR.FRG
SOLID 432 FloorTop3 FLOOR.FRG
SOLID 480 FloorTop3 FLOOR.FRG
SOLID 624 FloorTop3 FLOOR.FRG

SOLID 0 222 BARREL.FRG
SOLID 20 222 BARREL.FRG

;LET'S HAVE ONE OF THOSE ODD SIGNS
STATIC 192 272 SIGN.FRG

;MORE BLINKING LIGHTS
INDICATOR 271 FloorTop3 3 DIRECT0.FRG DIRECT1.FRG DIRECT2.FRG
DIRECT3.FRG DIRECT4.FRG DIRECT5.FRG DIRECT6.FRG DIRECT7.FRG

;FOURTH LEVEL
SOLID 0 FloorTop2 FLOOR.FRG
SOLID 144 FloorTop2 FLOOR.FRG
SOLID 144 FloorTop2 FLOOR.FRG
SOLID 192 FloorTop2 FLOOR.FRG
SOLID 240 FloorTop2 FLOOR.FRG
SOLID 288 FloorTop2 FLOOR.FRG
SOLID 336 FloorTop2 FLOOR.FRG
SOLID 384 FloorTop2 FLOOR.FRG
SOLID 480 FloorTop2 FLOOR.FRG
SOLID 528 FloorTop2 FLOOR.FRG
SOLID 576 FloorTop2 FLOOR.FRG
SOLID 624 FloorTop2 FLOOR.FRG

;FIFTH LEVEL
```

```
SOLID 0 FloorTop1 FLOOR.FRG
SOLID 48 FloorTop1 FLOOR.FRG
SOLID 96 FloorTop1 FLOOR.FRG
SOLID 144 FloorTop1 FLOOR.FRG
SOLID 144 FloorTop1 FLOOR.FRG
SOLID 192 FloorTop1 FLOOR.FRG
SOLID 240 FloorTop1 FLOOR.FRG
SOLID 288 FloorTop1 FLOOR.FRG
SOLID 336 FloorTop1 FLOOR.FRG
SOLID 384 FloorTop1 FLOOR.FRG
SOLID 432 FloorTop1 FLOOR.FRG
SOLID 480 FloorTop1 FLOOR.FRG
SOLID 624 FloorTop1 FLOOR.FRG

;SOME STAIRS
SOLID 608 264 WALLTILE.FRG
SOLID 624 264 WALLTILE.FRG
SOLID 592 344 FLOOR.FRG
SOLID 608 360 WALLTILE.FRG
SOLID 624 360 WALLTILE.FRG
SOLID 576 344 FLOOR.FRG
SOLID 544 360 FLOOR.FRG
SOLID 592 360 FLRTILE.FRG
SOLID 512 376 FLOOR.FRG
SOLID 560 376 FLOOR.FRG
SOLID 480 392 FLOOR.FRG
SOLID 528 392 FLOOR.FRG
SOLID 576 392 FLRTILE.FRG
SOLID 592 392 FLRTILE.FRG
SOLID 448 408 FLOOR.FRG
SOLID 496 408 FLOOR.FRG
SOLID 544 408 FLOOR.FRG
SOLID 592 408 FLRTILE.FRG
SOLID 416 424 FLOOR.FRG
SOLID 464 424 FLOOR.FRG
SOLID 512 424 FLOOR.FRG
SOLID 560 424 FLOOR.FRG

;AND FINALLY, THE DOOR
DOOR 48 376 DOOR0.FRG DOOR1.FRG DOOR2.FRG DOOR3.FRG DOOR3.FRG
DOOR2.FRG DOOR1.FRG DOOR0.FRG DOOR0.FRG DOOR0.FRG
```

As an aside, it's probably worth noting that in the real-world version of *Alice*—as
much as reality gets involved in this sort of thing—the rooms are defined in a
somewhat different format. Each room is a large binary object created by a room
editor program, in which each cell of the room is an object. Many games are
handled this way—as rooms defined in data and an "engine" to run the rooms.
Duke Nukem, for example, was created this way, allowing several third parties to
write room editors for it and at least one author, Tony Kamin, to create additional
Duke Nukem games by generating new level files.

The room definition language, as it's used in this chapter, has a fairly limited range of instructions. They are as follows:

```
ROOM Width Depth Path
SOLID X Y Path
STATIC X Y Path
INDICATOR X Y Timeslice Path0...PathX
DOOR X Y Path0...PathX
DEFINE String Value
```

The ROOM instruction should only appear once in a room definition. The Width and Depth arguments define the dimensions of the room bitmap in pixels—as was noted earlier, dimensions much above 640 by 480 pixels at 256 colors can start crowding your game software for memory. The Path argument is the path to a FRG file that defines a tile to fill the background with. This is a fairly simplistic way to create a textured background; more elaborate games can usually improve on this considerably.

The SOLID instruction defines the location of a solid object in the room. The X and Y arguments specify the upper left corner of the object. The Path argument is a path to a FRG file that defines the object.

The STATIC instruction defines objects that are part of the wall of the room, that is, which Alice can pass in front of. Its arguments are the same as those of SOLID.

The INDICATOR instruction defines an object that is animated and changes with time. The X and Y arguments define the upper left corner of the object. The Timeslice argument defines the number of time slice intervals between updates of the object on screen. Reducing this value will make the object appear to move or change more rapidly. The subsequent arguments, to a maximum of sixteen, define paths to FRG files that will form the cells of the object. When the object is animated, these will be displayed in the order they appear on the instruction line, repeating the sequence over and over again.

The DOOR instruction defines a door in the wall of the room. Alice can walk in front of it; if the door opens when she's before it, the level will terminate and, presumably, a new level will begin. The X and Y arguments define the upper left corner of the door. The subsequent arguments define the cells that will make up the door. If you look at the door definition in FIG. 8-5, you'll note that there are only four actual cells but that they're used twice—once to open the door and then in the reverse order to close it again.

Finally, the DEFINE instruction is a convenience of sorts. It allows you to define values as text strings. As such, in FIG. 8-5, the first floor level is defined as FloorTop1. This can make changing a room's contents a bit easier, as well as helping to make sense of the arguments to a long list of instructions.

Room definition files have the extension LVL—at least, they do in this game. Blank lines and lines beginning with semicolons are ignored by the room interpreter.

In creating a room, it's convenient to see the whole room before you actually attempt to play a game based on it. For one thing, in creating a real-world game, you'll probably have to battle your way through various nasties and perils to check all the real estate in a room; in a well-designed game, this should be at least modestly challenging, even for the game's author.

A room viewer will let you pan around a completed room as if it were a large bitmapped graphic. Figure 8-6 illustrates the source code for SHOWROOM.C, a program to let you tour the room defined back in FIG. 8-5.

8-6
The source code for SHOWROOM.C.

```
/*
        Room viewer

        Copyright (c) 1992 Alchemy Mindworks Inc.
*/

#include "stdio.h"
#include "dos.h"
#include "alloc.h"
#include "string.h"
#include "stdlib.h"
#include "ctype.h"

#define RGB_RED         0
#define RGB_GREEN       1
#define RGB_BLUE        2
#define RGB_SIZE        3

#define SCREENWIDE      320
#define SCREENDEEP      200

#define WINDOWLEFT      9
#define WINDOWTOP       9
#define WINDOWWIDE      207
#define WINDOWDEEP      183
#define TRANSPARENT     255

#define IMAGESIG        "IFRG"

#define MAXCELL         16
#define MAXARG          16
#define MAXDEFINE       32
#define DEFINESIZE      16

#define MAXWIDTH        800
#define MAXDEPTH        600

#define XSTEP           8
#define YSTEP           8

#define HOME            71 * 256
#define CURSOR_UP       72 * 256
#define CURSOR_LEFT     75 * 256
#define CURSOR_RIGHT    77 * 256
#define CURSOR_DOWN     80 * 256
#define END             79 * 256
```

```
#define  STATIC          0x0001
#define  SOLID           0x0002
#define  INDICATOR       0x0004
#define  DOOR            0x0008

#define  DOORTIME        0

#define  COPY_PUT        1
#define  TRANS_PUT       2

#define  ALT_D           0x2000
#define  ALT_R           0x1300
#define  ALT_S           0x1F00

#define  pixels2bytes(n) ((n+7)/8)
#define  ImageWidth(p)   (1+p[0]+(p[1] << 8))
#define  ImageDepth(p)   (1+p[2]+(p[3] << 8))
#define  beep()          putchar(7)

typedef struct {
        char sig[4];
        unsigned int width,depth,bits,bytes,planebytes;
        unsigned long palette;
        unsigned long image;
        } IMAGEHEAD;

typedef struct {
        unsigned int left,top,right,bottom;
        } RECT;

typedef struct OBJECT {
        struct OBJECT *next;
        RECT frame;
        char *cell[MAXCELL];
        unsigned int cellcount;
        unsigned int attributes;
        unsigned int timeslice;
        unsigned int thiscell;
        unsigned int timeleft;
        int (*proc)();
        char name[MAXCELL][9];
        } OBJECT;

typedef struct {
        char *tile;
        char *bitmap;
        OBJECT *objectlist;
        int width,depth;
        char name[9];
        } LEVEL;

typedef struct {
        int value;
        char name[MAXDEFINE+1];
        } DEFINE;
```

```
typedef struct   {
        char manufacturer;
        char version;
        char encoding;
        char bits_per_pixel;
        int xmin,ymin;
        int xmax,ymax;
        int hres;
        int vres;
        char palette[48];
        char reserved;
        char colour_planes;
        int bytes_per_line;
        int palette_type;
        char filler[58];
        } PCXHEAD;

char *farPtr(char *p,unsigned long l);
char *loadfrag(char *s,LEVEL *level);

char palette[] = {
        0x00,0x00,0x00,0x57,0x00,0x00,0x83,0x00,
        0x00,0xab,0x00,0x00,0xd7,0x00,0x00,0xff,
        0x00,0x00,0x00,0x2b,0x00,0x57,0x2b,0x00,
        0x83,0x2b,0x00,0xab,0x2b,0x00,0xd7,0x2b,
        0x00,0xff,0x2b,0x00,0x00,0x57,0x00,0x57,
        0x57,0x00,0x83,0x57,0x00,0xab,0x57,0x00,
        0xd7,0x57,0x00,0xff,0x57,0x00,0x00,0x83,
        0x00,0x57,0x83,0x00,0x83,0x83,0x00,0xab,
        0x83,0x00,0xd7,0x83,0x00,0xff,0x83,0x00,
        0x00,0xab,0x00,0x57,0xab,0x00,0x83,0xab,
        0x00,0xab,0xab,0x00,0xd7,0xab,0x00,0xff,
        0xab,0x00,0x00,0xd7,0x00,0x57,0xd7,0x00,
        0x83,0xd7,0x00,0xab,0xd7,0x00,0xd7,0xd7,
        0x00,0xff,0xd7,0x00,0x00,0xff,0x00,0x57,
        0xff,0x00,0x83,0xff,0x00,0xab,0xff,0x00,
        0xd7,0xff,0x00,0xff,0xff,0x00,0x00,0x00,
        0x57,0x57,0x00,0x57,0x83,0x00,0x57,0xab,
        0x00,0x57,0xd7,0x00,0x57,0xff,0x00,0x57,
        0x00,0x2b,0x57,0x57,0x2b,0x57,0x83,0x2b,
        0x57,0xab,0x2b,0x57,0xd7,0x2b,0x57,0xff,
        0x2b,0x57,0x00,0x57,0x57,0x57,0x57,0x57,
        0x83,0x57,0x57,0xab,0x57,0x57,0xd7,0x57,
        0x57,0xff,0x57,0x57,0x00,0x83,0x57,0x57,
        0x83,0x57,0x83,0x83,0x57,0xab,0x83,0x57,
        0xd7,0x83,0x57,0xff,0x83,0x57,0x00,0xab,
        0x57,0x57,0xab,0x57,0x83,0xab,0x57,0xab,
        0xab,0x57,0xd7,0xab,0x57,0xff,0xab,0x57,
        0x00,0xd7,0x57,0x57,0xd7,0x57,0x83,0xd7,
        0x57,0xab,0xd7,0x57,0xd7,0xd7,0x57,0xff,
        0xd7,0x57,0x00,0xff,0x57,0x57,0xff,0x57,
        0x83,0xff,0x57,0xab,0xff,0x57,0xd7,0xff,
        0x57,0xff,0xff,0x57,0x00,0x00,0x83,0x57,
        0x00,0x83,0x83,0x00,0x83,0xab,0x00,0x83,
        0xd7,0x00,0x83,0xff,0x00,0x83,0x00,0x2b,
```

```
0x83,0x57,0x2b,0x83,0x83,0x2b,0x83,0xab,
0x2b,0x83,0xd7,0x2b,0x83,0xff,0x2b,0x83,
0x00,0x57,0x83,0x57,0x57,0x83,0x83,0x57,
0x83,0xab,0x57,0x83,0xd7,0x57,0x83,0xff,
0x57,0x83,0x00,0x83,0x83,0x57,0x83,0x83,
0x83,0x83,0x83,0xab,0x83,0x83,0xd7,0x83,
0x83,0xff,0x83,0x83,0x00,0xab,0x83,0x57,
0xab,0x83,0x83,0xab,0x83,0xab,0xab,0x83,
0xd7,0xab,0x83,0xff,0xab,0x83,0x00,0xd7,
0x83,0x57,0xd7,0x83,0x83,0xd7,0x83,0xab,
0xd7,0x83,0xd7,0xd7,0x83,0xff,0xd7,0x83,
0x00,0xff,0x83,0x57,0xff,0x83,0x83,0xff,
0x83,0xab,0xff,0x83,0xd7,0xff,0x83,0xff,
0xff,0x83,0x00,0x00,0xab,0x57,0x00,0xab,
0x83,0x00,0xab,0xab,0x00,0xab,0xd7,0x00,
0xab,0xff,0x00,0xab,0x00,0x2b,0xab,0x57,
0x2b,0xab,0x83,0x2b,0xab,0xab,0x2b,0xab,
0xd7,0x2b,0xab,0xff,0x2b,0xab,0x00,0x57,
0xab,0x57,0x57,0xab,0x83,0x57,0xab,0xab,
0x57,0xab,0xd7,0x57,0xab,0xff,0x57,0xab,
0x00,0x83,0xab,0x57,0x83,0xab,0x83,0x83,
0xab,0xab,0x83,0xab,0xd7,0x83,0xab,0xff,
0x83,0xab,0x00,0xab,0xab,0x57,0xab,0xab,
0x83,0xab,0xab,0xab,0xab,0xab,0xd7,0xab,
0xab,0xff,0xab,0xab,0x00,0xd7,0xab,0x57,
0xd7,0xab,0x83,0xd7,0xab,0xab,0xd7,0xab,
0xd7,0xd7,0xab,0xff,0xd7,0xab,0x00,0xff,
0xab,0x57,0xff,0xab,0x83,0xff,0xab,0xab,
0xff,0xab,0xd7,0xff,0xab,0xff,0xff,0xab,
0x00,0x00,0xd7,0x57,0x00,0xd7,0x83,0x00,
0xd7,0xab,0x00,0xd7,0xd7,0x00,0xd7,0xff,
0x00,0xd7,0x00,0x2b,0xd7,0x57,0x2b,0xd7,
0x83,0x2b,0xd7,0xab,0x2b,0xd7,0xd7,0x2b,
0xd7,0xff,0x2b,0xd7,0x00,0x57,0xd7,0x57,
0x57,0xd7,0x83,0x57,0xd7,0xab,0x57,0xd7,
0xd7,0x57,0xd7,0xff,0x57,0xd7,0x00,0x83,
0xd7,0x57,0x83,0xd7,0x83,0x83,0xd7,0xab,
0x83,0xd7,0xd7,0x83,0xd7,0xff,0x83,0xd7,
0x00,0xab,0xd7,0x57,0xab,0xd7,0x83,0xab,
0xd7,0xab,0xab,0xd7,0xd7,0xab,0xd7,0xff,
0xab,0xd7,0x00,0xd7,0xd7,0x57,0xd7,0xd7,
0x83,0xd7,0xd7,0xab,0xd7,0xd7,0xd7,0xd7,
0xd7,0xff,0xd7,0xd7,0x00,0xff,0xd7,0x57,
0xff,0xd7,0x83,0xff,0xd7,0xab,0xff,0xd7,
0xd7,0xff,0xd7,0xff,0xff,0xd7,0x00,0x00,
0xff,0x57,0x00,0xff,0x83,0x00,0xff,0xab,
0x00,0xff,0xd7,0x00,0xff,0xff,0x00,0xff,
0x00,0x2b,0xff,0x57,0x2b,0xff,0x83,0x2b,
0xff,0xab,0x2b,0xff,0xd7,0x2b,0xff,0xff,
0x2b,0xff,0x00,0x57,0xff,0x57,0x57,0xff,
0x83,0x57,0xff,0xab,0x57,0xff,0xd7,0x57,
0xff,0xff,0x57,0xff,0x00,0x83,0xff,0x57,
0x83,0xff,0x83,0x83,0xff,0xab,0x83,0xff,
0xd7,0x83,0xff,0xff,0x83,0xff,0x00,0xab,
0xff,0x57,0xab,0xff,0x83,0xab,0xff,0xab,
```

```
        0xab,0xff,0xd7,0xab,0xff,0xff,0xab,0xff,
        0x00,0xd7,0xff,0x57,0xd7,0xff,0x83,0xd7,
        0xff,0xab,0xd7,0xff,0xd7,0xd7,0xff,0xff,
        0xd7,0xff,0x00,0xff,0xff,0x57,0xff,0xff,
        0x83,0xff,0xff,0xab,0xff,0xff,0xff,0xff,
        0xff,0x3f,0x3f,0x3f,0x6b,0x6b,0x6b,0x97,
        0x97,0x97,0xc3,0xc3,0xc3,0xff,0xff,0xff
        };

char masktable[8]={0x80,0x40,0x20,0x10,0x08,0x04,0x02,0x01};
char bittable[8]= {0x01,0x02,0x04,0x08,0x10,0x20,0x40,0x80};

char errormessage[7][48] = {
        "Ok",
        "File not found",
        "Invalid argument count",
        "Insufficient memory",
        "Image not found",
        "Level not defined",
        "Too many defines"
        };

int idle();

main(argc,argv)
        int argc;
        char *argv[];
{
        LEVEL level;
        unsigned long l;
        unsigned int n;

        puts("SHOWROOM version 1.0\r\n");

        if(argc <= 1)
            error("I need a path to a LVL file");

        if((n=LoadLevel(&level,argv[1])) == 0) {
                l=coreleft();
                graphics();
                setvgapalette(palette,256);
                ShowLevel(&level);
                text();
                printf("\n%lu bytes free\n",l);
        } else puts(errormessage[n]);
}

ShowLevel(level)
        LEVEL *level;
{
        OBJECT *op;
        char *screen;
        int c,wleft=0,wtop=0;

        if((screen=loadfrag("SCREEN.FRG",level)) != NULL) {
```

```
                        PutImage(0,0,screen,COPY_PUT);
                        free(screen);
            } else putchar(7);

      SetWindowFrame(WINDOWLEFT,WINDOWTOP,WINDOWLEFT+WINDOWWIDE,WINDOWTOP+WINDOWDEEP);
      SetWindowOff(0,0);

      StartTime(level);

      do {
      SetWindowOff(wleft,wtop);
            UpdateWindow();
            UpdateAll();

            c=GetKey();

            disable();
            switch(c) {
                  case ALT_D:
                        for(op=level->objectlist;op != NULL;op=op->next) {
                              if(op->attributes & DOOR) {
                                    OpenDoor(op);
                                    break;
                              }
                        }
                        break;
                  case ALT_S:
                        StopTime();
                        doSaveScreen("SCREEN00.PCX");
                        StartTime(level);
                        break;
                  case ALT_R:
                        StopTime();
                        doSaveBitmap("BITMAP00.PCX",level->bitmap,
                              level->width,level->depth,palette);
                        StartTime(level);
                        break;
                  case CURSOR_UP:
                        if((wtop-YSTEP) >= 0) wtop -= YSTEP;
                        else wtop=0;
                        break;
                  case CURSOR_DOWN:
                        if((wtop+YSTEP) < (level->depth-WINDOWDEEP)) wtop+=YSTEP;
                        else wtop=level->depth-WINDOWDEEP-1;
                        break;
                  case CURSOR_LEFT:
                        if((wleft-XSTEP) >= 0) {
                              wleft -= XSTEP;
                        }
                        break;
                  case CURSOR_RIGHT:
                        if((wleft+XSTEP) < (level->width-WINDOWWIDE)) {
                              wleft+=XSTEP;
                        }
                        break;
```

```
                              case HOME:
                                      wleft=wtop=0;
                                      break;
                              case END:
                                      wleft=level->width-WINDOWWIDE-1;
                                      wtop=level->depth-WINDOWDEEP-1;
                                      break;
                      }
                      enable();
              } while(c != 27);

              StopTime();
}


LoadLevel(level,path)
        LEVEL *level;
        char *path;
{
        DEFINE *define;
        FILE *fp;
        OBJECT *object,*op;
        char *p,*image,b[193],*arg[MAXARG];
        unsigned long size;
        unsigned int argindex,defineindex=0;
        int i,x,y,t;

        if((define=(DEFINE *)malloc(MAXDEFINE*sizeof(DEFINE))) == NULL)
            return(3);

        if((fp=fopen(path,"ra")) == NULL) {
                free((char *)define);
                return(1);
        }

        memset((char *)level,0,sizeof(LEVEL));

        do {
                if((p=fgets(b,192,fp)) != NULL) {
                        for(argindex=0;argindex<MAXARG && *p != 0;++argindex) {
                                while(*p <= 32 && *p != 0) *p++=0;
                                arg[argindex]=p;
                                while(*p > 32) ++p;
                        }

                        if(arg[0][0]==';') continue;

                        if(!stricmp(arg[0],"DEFINE")) {
                                if(defineindex < MAXDEFINE) {
                                        strcpy(define[defineindex].name,arg[1]);
                                        define[defineindex].value=atoi(arg[2]);
                                        ++defineindex;
                                }
                                else {
                                        free((char *)define);
                                        FreeLevel(level);
```

```
                                        fclose(fp);
                                        return(6);
                                }
                        }
                        else if(!stricmp(arg[0],"ROOM")) {
                        if(argindex < 3) return(2);
                        level->width=min(value(arg[1],define,defineindex),MAXWIDTH);
                        level->depth=min(value(arg[2],define,defineindex),MAXDEPTH);

                        size=(long)level->width*(long)level->depth;
                        if((level->bitmap=farmalloc(size))== NULL) {
                                free((char *)define);
                                fclose(fp);
                                return(3);
                        }

                        if((image=loadfrag(arg[3],level)) == NULL) {
                                free((char *)define);
                                FreeLevel(level);
                                fclose(fp);
                                return(4);
                        }
                        fnsplit(arg[3],NULL,NULL,level->name,NULL);

                        tileimage(level,image);
                        free(image);
                }
                else if(!stricmp(arg[0],"STATIC")) {
                        if((object=(OBJECT *)malloc(sizeof(OBJECT))) == NULL) {
                                free((char *)define);
                                FreeLevel(level);
                                fclose(fp);
                                return(3);
                        }

                        memset((char *)object,0,sizeof(OBJECT));

                        if(level->bitmap==NULL) {
                                free((char *)define);
                                FreeLevel(level);
                                fclose(fp);
                                return(5);
                        }
                        if(argindex < 3) return(2);

                        x=min(value(arg[1],define,defineindex),level->width);
                        y=min(value(arg[2],define,defineindex),level->depth);

                        if((image=loadfrag(arg[3],level)) == NULL) {
                                free((char *)define);
                                farfree(level->bitmap);
                                fclose(fp);
                                return(4);
                        }
                        placetile(level,image,x,y);
```

```
                    object->cellcount=1;
                    object->next=NULL;
                    object->frame.left=x;
                    object->frame.top=y;
                    object->frame.right=x+ImageWidth(image);
                    object->frame.bottom=y+ImageDepth(image);
                    object->cell[0]=image;
                    object->attributes=STATIC;
                    fnsplit(arg[3],NULL,NULL,object->name[0],NULL);

                    if(level->objectlist==NULL) level->objectlist=object;
                    else {
                            for(op=level->objectlist;op->next != NULL;op=op->next);
                            op->next=object;
                    }
            }
        else if(!stricmp(arg[0],"SOLID")) {
                if((object=(OBJECT *)malloc(sizeof(OBJECT))) == NULL) {
                        free((char *)define);
                        FreeLevel(level);
                        fclose(fp);
                        return(3);
                }

                memset((char *)object,0,sizeof(OBJECT));

                if(level->bitmap==NULL) {
                        free((char *)define);
                        FreeLevel(level);
                        fclose(fp);
                        return(5);
                }
                if(argindex < 3) return(2);

                x=min(value(arg[1],define,defineindex),level->width);
                y=min(value(arg[2],define,defineindex),level->depth);

                if((image=loadfrag(arg[3],level)) == NULL) {
                        free((char *)define);
                        FreeLevel(level);
                        fclose(fp);
                        return(4);
                }
                placetile(level,image,x,y);

                object->cellcount=1;
                object->next=NULL;
                object->frame.left=x;
                object->frame.top=y;
                object->frame.right=x+ImageWidth(image);
                object->frame.bottom=y+ImageDepth(image);
                object->cell[0]=image;
                object->attributes=SOLID;
                fnsplit(arg[3],NULL,NULL,object->name[0],NULL);
```

```
                              if(level->objectlist==NULL) level->objectlist=object;
                              else {
                                      for(op=level->objectlist;op->next != NULL;op=op->next);
                                      op->next=object;
                              }
                      }
                  else if(!stricmp(arg[0],"INDICATOR")) {
                          if((object=(OBJECT *)malloc(sizeof(OBJECT))) == NULL) {
                                  free((char *)define);
                                  FreeLevel(level);
                                  fclose(fp);
                                  return(3);
                          }

                          memset((char *)object,0,sizeof(OBJECT));

                          if(level->bitmap==NULL) {
                                  free((char *)define);
                                  FreeLevel(level);
                                  fclose(fp);
                                  return(5);
                          }
                          if(argindex < 3) return(2);

                          x=min(value(arg[1],define,defineindex),level->width);
                          y=min(value(arg[2],define,defineindex),level->depth);
                          t=value(arg[3],define,defineindex);

                          for(i=4;i<argindex-1 && object->cellcount < MAXCELL;++i) {
                                  if((object->cell[object->cellcount]=
                                      loadfrag(arg[i],level)) == NULL) {
                                      free((char *)define);
                                      FreeLevel(level);
                                      fclose(fp);
                                      return(4);
                                  }
                                  fnsplit(arg[i],NULL,NULL,
                                      object->name[object->cellcount],NULL);++object->cellcount;
                          }

                          if(object->cellcount==0) {
                                  free((char *)define);
                                  FreeLevel(level);
                                  fclose(fp);
                                  return(2);
                          }

                          object->next=NULL;
                          object->frame.left=x;
                          object->frame.top=y;
                          object->frame.right=x+ImageWidth(image);
                          object->frame.bottom=y+ImageDepth(image);
                          object->attributes=INDICATOR;
                          object->timeslice=t;
```

```
                        if(level->objectlist==NULL) level->objectlist=object;
                        else {
                                for(op=level->objectlist;op->next != NULL;op=op->next);
                                op->next=object;
                        }
                }
                else if(!stricmp(arg[0],"DOOR")) {
                        if((object=(OBJECT *)malloc(sizeof(OBJECT))) == NULL) {
                                free((char *)define);
                                FreeLevel(level);
                                fclose(fp);
                                return(3);
                        }

                        memset((char *)object,0,sizeof(OBJECT));

                        if(level->bitmap==NULL) {
                                free((char *)define);
                                FreeLevel(level);
                                fclose(fp);
                                return(5);
                        }
                        if(argindex < 3) return(2);

                        x=min(value(arg[1],define,defineindex),level->width);
                        y=min(value(arg[2],define,defineindex),level->depth);

                        for(i=3;i<argindex-1 && object->cellcount < MAXCELL;++i) {
                                if((object->cell[object->cellcount]=
                                    loadfrag(arg[i],level)) == NULL) {
                                        free((char *)define);
                                        FreeLevel(level);
                                        fclose(fp);
                                        return(4);
                                }
                                fnsplit(arg[i],NULL,NULL,
                                    object->name[object->cellcount],NULL);++object->cellcount;
                        }

                        if(object->cellcount==0) {
                                free((char *)define);
                                FreeLevel(level);
                                fclose(fp);
                                return(2);
                        }

                        placetile(level,object->cell[0],x,y);

                        object->next=NULL;
                        object->frame.left=x;
                        object->frame.top=y;
                        object->frame.right=x+ImageWidth(object->cell[0]);
                        object->frame.bottom=y+ImageDepth(object->cell[0]);
                        object->attributes=DOOR;
                        object->timeslice=DOORTIME;
```

```
                                             object->proc=idle;

                                             if(level->objectlist==NULL) level->objectlist=object;
                                             else {
                                                     for(op=level->objectlist;op->next != NULL;op=op->next);
                                                     op->next=object;
                                             }

                               }
                     }
          } while(p != NULL);

          fclose(fp);
          free((char *)define);
          return(0);
}

FreeLevel(level)
          LEVEL *level;
{
          OBJECT *op;
          char *p;
          int i;

          for(op=level->objectlist;
              level->objectlist != NULL && op != NULL;op=op->next) {
                  for(i=0;i<op->cellcount;++i) {
                          if(op->cell[i] != NULL) free(op->cell[i]);
                  }
                  p=(char *)op;
                  free(p);
          }

          free(level->bitmap);
          free(level->tile);
}

tileimage(level,image)
          LEVEL *level;
          char *image;
{
          int x,y,iw,id;

          iw=ImageWidth(image);
          id=ImageDepth(image);

          for(y=-(id/2);y<level->depth;) {
                  for(x=0;x<level->width;x+=iw) placetile(level,image,x,y);
                  y+=id;
                  for(x=-(iw/2);x<level->width;x+=iw) placetile(level,image,x,y);
                  y+=id;
          }
}

placetile(level,image,x,y)
          LEVEL *level;
```

```
            char *image;
            int x,y;
{
            char *pd,*ps;
            int i,j,iw,id;

            iw=ImageWidth(image);
            id=ImageDepth(image);
            image+=4;

            ps=image;

            for(i=0;i<id;++i) {
                    pd=farPtr(level->bitmap,(long)(y+i)*(long)level->width+(long)x);
                    for(j=0;j<iw;++j) {
                            if((x+j) >= 0 && (x+j) < level->width &&
                               (y+i) >= 0 && (y+i) < level->depth &&
                               *ps != TRANSPARENT) *pd=*ps;
                            ++ps;
                            ++pd;
                    }
            }
}

text()
{
            union REGS r;

            r.x.ax=0x0003;
            int86(0x10,&r,&r);
}

graphics()
{
            union REGS r;

            r.x.ax=0x0013;
            int86(0x10,&r,&r);
}

error(s)
            char *s;
{
            puts(s);
            exit(1);
}

setvgapalette(p,n)
            char *p;
            int n;
{
            int i;

            outp(0x3c6,0xff);
            for(i=0;i<n;++i) {
```

```
                        outp(0x3c8,i);
                        outp(0x3c9,(*p++) >> 2);
                        outp(0x3c9,(*p++) >> 2);
                        outp(0x3c9,(*p++) >> 2);
                }
        }

        char *loadfrag(s,level)
                char *s;
                LEVEL *level;
        {
                OBJECT *op;
                FILE *fp;
                IMAGEHEAD ih;
                char *p,*pr,name[16];
                unsigned int i;

                fnsplit(s,NULL,NULL,name,NULL);

                /* see if it's the background tile */
                if(!stricmp(level->name,name)) return(level->tile);

                /* see if it's a previously loaded object */
                if(level->objectlist != NULL) {
                        for(op=level->objectlist;op->next != NULL;op=op->next) {
                                for(i=0;i<op->cellcount;++i) {
                                        if(!stricmp(op->name[i],name))
                                                return(op->cell[i]);
                                }
                        }
                }

                /* load a new object */
                if((fp=fopen(s,"rb")) == NULL) return(NULL);

                if(fread((char *)&ih,1,sizeof(IMAGEHEAD),fp) != sizeof(IMAGEHEAD)) {
                        fclose(fp);
                        return(NULL);
                }

                if(ih.bits != 8) {
                        fclose(fp);
                        return(NULL);
                }

                if((p=farmalloc(4L+(long)ih.bytes*(long)ih.depth)) == NULL) {
                        fclose(fp);
                        return(NULL);
                }

                fseek(fp,ih.image,SEEK_SET);

                pr=p;

                pr+=fread(pr,1,4,fp);
```

```
                for(i=0;i<ih.depth;++i) {
                        if(fread(pr,1,ih.bytes,fp) != ih.bytes) {
                                farfree(p);
                                fclose(fp);
                                return(NULL);
                        }
                        pr=farPtr(pr,(long)ih.bytes);
                }
        fclose(fp);
        return(p);
}

char *farPtr(p,l)
        char *p;
        unsigned long l;
{
        unsigned int seg,off;

        seg = FP_SEG(p);
        off = FP_OFF(p);
        seg += (off / 16);
        off &= 0x000f;
        off += (unsigned int)(l & 0x000fL);
        seg += (l / 16L);
        p = MK_FP(seg,off);
        return(p);
}

GetKey()
{
        int c;

        c = getch();
        if(!(c & 0x00ff)) c = getch() << 8;
        return(c);
}

value(string,define,defineindex)
        char *string;
        DEFINE *define;
        unsigned int defineindex;
{
        int i;

        if(isdigit(string[0])) return(atoi(string));
        else {
                for(i=0;i<defineindex;++i) {
                        if(!stricmp(define[i].name,string))
                                return(define[i].value);
                }
        }
        return(-1);
}
```

```
/* save the screen to a PCX file */
DoSaveScreen(path)
        char *path;
{
        PCXHEAD pcx;
        FILE *fp;
        char *p;
        unsigned int i,n;

        /* create the destination file */
        if((fp=fopen(path,"wb"))==NULL) {
                beep();
                return;
        }

        memset((char *)&pcx,0,sizeof(PCXHEAD));
        memcpy(pcx.palette,palette,48);

        pcx.manufacturer=10;
        pcx.encoding=1;
        pcx.xmin=pcx.ymin=0;
        pcx.xmax=SCREENWIDE-1;
        pcx.ymax=SCREENDEEP-1;
        pcx.palette_type=1;
        pcx.bits_per_pixel=8;
        pcx.version=5;
        pcx.colour_planes=1;
        pcx.bytes_per_line=SCREENWIDE;

        if(fwrite((char *)&pcx,1,sizeof(PCXHEAD),fp) != sizeof(PCXHEAD)) {
                fclose(fp);
                remove(path);
                beep();
                return;
        }

        for(i=0;i<SCREENDEEP;++i) {
                p=MK_FP(0xa000,SCREENWIDE*i);
                n=pcxwriteline(fp,p,pcx.bytes_per_line);

                if(n != pcx.bytes_per_line) {
                        fclose(fp);
                        remove(path);
                        beep();
                        return;
                }
        }

        fputc(12,fp);
        if(fwrite(palette,1,768,fp) != 768) {
                free(p);
                fclose(fp);
                remove(path);
                beep();
                return;
```

```
                }

        fclose(fp);
}

/* save a bitmap to a PCX file */
DoSaveBitmap(path,bitmap,width,depth,palette)
        char *path,*bitmap;
        unsigned int width,depth;
        char *palette;
{
        PCXHEAD pcx;
        FILE *fp;
        char *p;
        unsigned int i,n;

        /* create the destination file */
        if((fp=fopen(path,"wb"))==NULL) {
                beep();
                return;
        }

        memset((char *)&pcx,0,sizeof(PCXHEAD));
        memcpy(pcx.palette,palette,48);

        pcx.manufacturer=10;
        pcx.encoding=1;
        pcx.xmin=pcx.ymin=0;
        pcx.xmax=width-1;
        pcx.ymax=depth-1;
        pcx.palette_type=1;
        pcx.bits_per_pixel=8;
        pcx.version=5;
        pcx.colour_planes=1;
        pcx.bytes_per_line=width;

        if(fwrite((char *)&pcx,1,sizeof(PCXHEAD),fp) != sizeof(PCXHEAD)) {
                fclose(fp);
                remove(path);
                beep();
                return;
        }

        for(i=0;i<depth;++i) {
                p=farPtr(bitmap,(long)width*(long)i);
                n=pcxwriteline(fp,p,pcx.bytes_per_line);

                if(n != pcx.bytes_per_line) {
                        fclose(fp);
                        remove(path);
                        beep();
                        return;
                }
        }
```

```
        fputc(12,fp);
        if(fwrite(palette,1,768,fp) != 768) {
                free(p);
                fclose(fp);
                remove(path);
                beep();
                return;
        }

        fclose(fp);
}

/* write one pcx line */
pcxwriteline(fp,p,n)
        FILE *fp;
        char *p;
        unsigned int n;
{
        unsigned int i=0,j=0,t=0;

        do {
                i=0;
                while((p[t+i]==p[t+i+1]) && ((t+i) < n) && (i < 63))++i;
                if(i>0) {
                        if(fputc(i | 0xc0,fp)==EOF) return(-1);
                        if(fputc(p[t],fp)==EOF) return(-1);
                        t+=i;
                        j+=2;
                }
                else {
                        if(((p[t]) & 0xc0)==0xc0) {
                                if(fputc(0xc1,fp)==EOF) return(-1);
                                ++j;
                        }
                        if(fputc(p[t++],fp)==EOF) return(-1);
                        ++j;
                }
        } while(t<n);
        return(n);
}

idle()
{

}
```

It's worth noting that SHOWROOM is not quite complete; if you attempt to compile it just now, you'll find that there are a few undefined functions—all of them in the ShowLevel code. They are provided by the assembly language module TIMESLIC.ASM, which will be dealt with toward the end of this chapter. If you'd like to create SHOWROOM.EXE now, you should get TIMESLIC.ASM from the companion disk for this book, assemble it to create TIMESLIC.OBJ, and create a project file that includes SHOWROOM.C and TIMESLIC.OBJ.

Perhaps predictably, TIMESLIC.ASM handles the time slicing functions for the programs in this chapter.

Most of the SHOWROOM program is actually involved in managing the graphic objects for the room and creating a rather large bitmap. There are two primary types of objects involved—one LEVEL and quite a number of OBJECT structures. You'll find them defined at the top of FIG. 8-6. They all get together in the LoadLevel function.

A room in the game consists of a LEVEL object, which includes a pointer to a linked list of OBJECT structures. Each OBJECT includes a pointer to the next object in the list, or to NULL if the OBJECT in question is the last one in the list. Every tile, barrel, blinking sign and door in a room is represented by an OBJECT structure. The data handling is actually quite complex, especially because the nature of objects varies a bit with their types.

The LoadRoom function opens an LVL file, such as the one in FIG. 8-5 and parses each line for the instructions mentioned earlier. It makes several common-sense assumptions about the LVL files it's passed—that you won't attempt to define any objects in a room until you define the room they'll reside in, for example—and in fairness its error checking isn't wholly bulletproof. It does produce very attractive rooms, however, as alternate universes go.

If you look through the LoadLevel function, you'll note that with the exception of the ROOM and DEFINE sections, each of the instruction handlers allocates memory for an OBJECT structure and tacks it into the next pointer chain of the current LEVEL structure for the room being created.

When an object is created for the current room, its bitmap—a FRG file—is loaded from disk by loadfrag. This function is actually a bit sneakier than it might appear. In creating a room, you'll usually use multiple instances of the same limited range of objects. For example, the floors in this level of Alice are made up of lots of tile objects. It would be a dead waste of time and memory to load each one from the disk once for each time it's used. As such, if you pass loadfrag the name of a FRG file, it will always return a pointer to the image you've asked for. However, it won't necessarily do so by allocating a new buffer and loading the image from disk. If it finds that the image has previously been loaded, and is pointed to by one of the OBJECT structures dangling from the current LEVEL, it will just return a pointer to the previously loaded iteration of the image.

Note that some of the instruction handlers will actually load multiple FRG files to handle animated objects.

Each OBJECT structure includes a pointer to its bitmap and values that define how the object is to be treated when it appears in a room. These include a definition of the rectangular space it will occupy, a constant that defines what sort of object it is and some information to handle time slicing—these latter elements will be manipulated by TIMESLIC.ASM.

When LoadLevel is complete, the LEVEL object passed to it will point to a pretty huge bitmap and a list of OBJECT structures defining the objects in the room. If you were to view the bitmap, it would look more or less like FIG. 8-3. In fact, the animated indicator elements would be missing—they won't actually be added until the room is brought to life.

The ShowLevel function is an exercise in unusual code—as well as a good example of how to best marry C and assembly language without having them go straight from the church to divorce court. It makes several calls into TIMESLIC.ASM; you might want to just pretend to understand what they're up to for the moment.

The ShowLevel function only knows how to work with mode 13H. It assumes the screen dimensions will be 320 by 200 pixels, and that the standard palette at the top of SHOWROOM.C will have been set. Note that this is a standard palette for these game examples; it's similar to the 256-color palette that has turned up elsewhere in this book, but it has nothing to do with the default VGA 256-color palette.

The ShowLevel function begins by attempting to load the FRG file SCREEN.FRG, which will provide it with the playing window from FIG. 8-2. I created this file by opening a new 256-color graphic in Desktop Paint 256 with the dimensions 320 by 200 pixels and drawing the elements of the playing window in it. Conveniently, the default color palette of Desktop Paint 256 that's used when you invoke the New function is more or less the same as the palette used by SHOWROOM. See the Desktop Paint 256 documentation for more information about using the default palette.

You can find SCREEN.FRG on the companion disk for this book. It's worth noting that the PutImage function called here to paint it on the screen is part of TIMESLIC.ASM—no Borland BGI calls are involved.

The SetWindowFrame and SetWindowOff functions are part of TIMESLIC.ASM. The former tells the assembly language module where the visible part of the game window is. The latter indicates where the window is relative to the large bitmap pointed to by the LEVEL structure. The StartTime function is also part of TIMESLIC.ASM; for the most part, it manages the animated indicators and doors in SHOWROOM.

The UpdateWindow function displays the appropriate portion of the bitmap in the screen window. Panning around the room involves nothing more clever than repainting the window with different fragments of the bitmap. The actual painting is handled by TIMESLIC.ASM; each time UpdateWindow is called, the playing window is refreshed from the large bitmap based on the values set by a previous call to SetWindowOff.

In fact, the whole ShowLevel function would be very simple indeed save for the existence of those animated indicator objects that have turned up throughout this chapter. As you pan across one, it has to keep moving, something that presents a bit of a problem. It would be fairly easy to simply paint the visible part of the indicator on the screen, but this would result in a moment wherein part of brick work behind it would be visible as the walls moved when you panned across one. Instead, the workings of TIMESLIC.ASM actually update the contents of the large bitmap as well as that of the screen window when an indicator is visible. This allows the little red dots to appear to move as well as keeping the big bitmap up to date should it be asked to pan.

Even with this in mind, ShowLevel is relatively easy to work though. In using calls into TIMESLIC.ASM to maintain its graphics, it sneaks past most of the complicated elements. Be warned—the assembly language involved is a pig.

In addition to allowing you to pan around an assembled room, SHOWROOM will let you save either the current screen or the whole bitmap to a PCX file. If you hit Alt-D, the screen will be saved to SCREEN00.PCX in the current directory. Hitting Alt-R will save the whole room to BITMAP00.PCX. While to some extent these facilities were included in SHOWROOM to create the figures for this chapter, you'll find the latter one especially handy in creating complex rooms. Using a super VGA file viewer, such as Graphic Workshop, you can view an entire room this way, rather than just the visible part as seen through the game window.

One of the somewhat unusual aspects of the graphic objects used in SHOWROOM is that they support transparency. This means, for example, that even though the barrels occupy a rectangular space but are not themselves rectangular, the area behind them will be visible. Transparency is handled by simply not writing any pixels in a graphic that are set to color 255. This appears as white in the SHOWROOM palette.

Animating the character in *Alice* is actually a bit easier than it might seem—mostly because of the way the room graphics are handled. The techniques for making something appear to move on a screen are fairly common. In animating Alice, the cells in FIG. 8-7 are repeatedly drawn one after another, displaced by a constant amount to make Alice appear to be moving.

See Alice run

As an aside, the cells in FIG. 8-7 look pretty chunky on paper; they're considerably more respectable looking in mode 13H. The characteristics of phosphor on glass tend to blend the individual pixels to produce lifelike shading.

8-7
The cells that make Alice appear to walk.

In fact, to make computer animation work, you should draw each cell by saving the area behind it, and then erase it by replacing the divot it created when it comes time to draw the next cell. This process can be fairly time consuming, even for small objects like Alice. In this case, it's not entirely necessary. The area behind Alice need not be preserved, as it's just a fragment of the large level bitmap. When it comes time to erase one cell prior to drawing the next one, the appropriate rectangular area of the bitmap can be copied to the screen.

In creating an animated game, it's worth noting that small objects can be animated a lot more readily than large ones. By keeping Alice to fairly modest dimensions, most of the pointer manipulation involved in handling the large bitmap can be performed with simple 16-bit calculations. The speed at which the animation cell code in TIMESLIC.ASM can manipulate the screen allows Alice to move without any flickering.

The four cells in FIG. 8-7 handle Alice walking right. They can be flipped horizontally to create four more cells, walking left. There is also one cell required for each of the two directions in which Alice can face as she falls when she jumps from one floor to the next.

Figure 8-8 illustrates the file ALICE.CHR, which defines Alice's actions. In this example the jumping cells are taken from the walking cells; in a more complex game, you'd probably want to design dedicated cells for Alice when she's airborne. In fact, there's nowhere for Alice to fall in this program—the jumping cells will turn up again in the next section of this chapter.

8-8

The definition for Alice's perambulations.

```
;Definition for Alice's animation

WALKRIGHT _RIGHT0.FRG _RIGHT1.FRG _RIGHT2.FRG _RIGHT3.FRG
WALKLEFT _LEFT0.FRG _LEFT1.FRG _LEFT2.FRG _LEFT3.FRG
JUMPRIGHT _RIGHT1.FRG
JUMPLEFT _LEFT1.FRG
START 104 14 4
```

The TESTWALK program in FIG. 8-9 will integrate ALICE.CHR and the FRG files it specifies to create a tiled room the size of your screen in which Alice can walk back and forth and jump around. The background of the room will be created by tiling yet another FRG file, as was done in the SHOWROOM program earlier in this chapter. Note that, once again, all the hard work—in this case the task of making Alice move—is handled by as yet mysterious code in TIMESLIC.ASM

As with SHOWROOM, you'll require a project file to link this program to TIMESLIC.OBJ in order to successfully run it. Alice will move back and forth in response to the left and right arrow keys. Hitting Esc will shut things down.

8-9

The source code for TESTWALK.C.

```
/*
        Show Alice Walking

        Copyright (c) 1992 Alchemy Mindworks Inc.
*/

#include "stdio.h"
#include "dos.h"
#include "alloc.h"
#include "string.h"
#include "stdlib.h"
#include "ctype.h"

#define RGB_RED         0
#define RGB_GREEN       1
#define RGB_BLUE        2
```

```
#define RGB_SIZE        3

#define WALKSTEP        8
#define WALKDELAY       80

#define SCREENWIDE      320
#define SCREENDEEP      200

#define TRANSPARENT     255
#define MAXARG          16
#define MAXCELL         16

#define IMAGESIG        "IFRG"

#define MAXWIDTH        800
#define MAXDEPTH        600

#define XSTEP           8
#define YSTEP           8

#define HOME            71 * 256
#define CURSOR_UP       72 * 256
#define CURSOR_LEFT     75 * 256
#define CURSOR_RIGHT    77 * 256
#define CURSOR_DOWN     80 * 256
#define END             79 * 256

#define ALTKEY          0x0008
#define CTRLKEY         0x0004
#define LEFTSHIFT       0x0002
#define RIGHTSHIFT      0x0001

#define WALKLEFT        1
#define WALKRIGHT       2
#define JUMPLEFT        3
#define JUMPRIGHT       4

#define pixels2bytes(n) ((n+7)/8)
#define ImageWidth(p)   (1+p[0]+(p[1] << 8))
#define ImageDepth(p)   (1+p[2]+(p[3] << 8))
#define beep()          putchar(7)

#define isctrlkey()     (bioskey(2) & CTRLKEY)

typedef struct {
        char sig[4];
        unsigned int
width,depth,bits,bytes,planebytes;
        unsigned long palette;
        unsigned long image;
        } IMAGEHEAD;

typedef struct {
        int left,top,right,bottom;
        } RECT;
```

```
typedef struct OBJECT {
        struct OBJECT *next;
        RECT frame;
        char *cell[MAXCELL];
        unsigned int cellcount;
        unsigned int attributes;
        unsigned int timeslice;
        unsigned int thiscell;
        unsigned int timeleft;
        int (*proc)();
        char name[MAXCELL][9];
        } OBJECT;

typedef struct {
        char *tile;
        char *bitmap;
        OBJECT *objectlist;
        int width,depth;
        char name[9];
        } LEVEL;

typedef struct {
        char *walkleft[MAXCELL];
        char *walkright[MAXCELL];
        char *jumpleft;
        char *jumpright;
        RECT leftframe;
        RECT rightframe;
        RECT leftjumpframe;
        RECT rightjumpframe;
        unsigned int action;
        unsigned int thiscell;
        unsigned int maxleft;
        unsigned int maxright;
        unsigned int xloc,yloc;
        } CHARACTER;

char *farPtr(char *p,unsigned long l);
char *loadfrag(char *s);

char palette[] = {
        0x00,0x00,0x00,0x57,0x00,0x00,0x83,0x00,
        0x00,0xab,0x00,0x00,0xd7,0x00,0x00,0xff,
        0x00,0x00,0x00,0x2b,0x00,0x57,0x2b,0x00,
        0x83,0x2b,0x00,0xab,0x2b,0x00,0xd7,0x2b,
        0x00,0xff,0x2b,0x00,0x00,0x57,0x00,0x57,
        0x57,0x00,0x83,0x57,0x00,0xab,0x57,0x00,
        0xd7,0x57,0x00,0xff,0x57,0x00,0x00,0x83,
        0x00,0x57,0x83,0x00,0x83,0x83,0x00,0xab,
        0x83,0x00,0xd7,0x83,0x00,0xff,0x83,0x00,
        0x00,0xab,0x00,0x57,0xab,0x00,0x83,0xab,
        0x00,0xab,0xab,0x00,0xd7,0xab,0x00,0xff,
        0xab,0x00,0x00,0xd7,0x00,0x57,0xd7,0x00,
        0x83,0xd7,0x00,0xab,0xd7,0x00,0xd7,0xd7,
        0x00,0xff,0xd7,0x00,0x00,0xff,0x00,0x57,
```

```
0xff,0x00,0x83,0xff,0x00,0xab,0xff,0x00,
0xd7,0xff,0x00,0xff,0xff,0x00,0x00,0x00,
0x57,0x57,0x00,0x57,0x83,0x00,0x57,0xab,
0x00,0x57,0xd7,0x00,0x57,0xff,0x00,0x57,
0x00,0x2b,0x57,0x57,0x2b,0x57,0x83,0x2b,
0x57,0xab,0x2b,0x57,0xd7,0x2b,0x57,0xff,
0x2b,0x57,0x00,0x57,0x57,0x57,0x57,0x57,
0x83,0x57,0x57,0xab,0x57,0x57,0xd7,0x57,
0x57,0xff,0x57,0x57,0x00,0x83,0x57,0x57,
0x83,0x57,0x83,0x83,0x57,0xab,0x83,0x57,
0xd7,0x83,0x57,0xff,0x83,0x57,0x00,0xab,
0x57,0x57,0xab,0x57,0x83,0xab,0x57,0xab,
0xab,0x57,0xd7,0xab,0x57,0xff,0xab,0x57,
0x00,0xd7,0x57,0x57,0xd7,0x57,0x83,0xd7,
0x57,0xab,0xd7,0x57,0xd7,0xd7,0x57,0xff,
0xd7,0x57,0x00,0xff,0x57,0x57,0xff,0x57,
0x83,0xff,0x57,0xab,0xff,0x57,0xd7,0xff,
0x57,0xff,0xff,0x57,0x00,0x00,0x83,0x57,
0x00,0x83,0x83,0x00,0x83,0xab,0x00,0x83,
0xd7,0x00,0x83,0xff,0x00,0x83,0x00,0x2b,
0x83,0x57,0x2b,0x83,0x83,0x2b,0x83,0xab,
0x2b,0x83,0xd7,0x2b,0x83,0xff,0x2b,0x83,
0x00,0x57,0x83,0x57,0x57,0x83,0x83,0x57,
0x83,0xab,0x57,0x83,0xd7,0x57,0x83,0xff,
0x57,0x83,0x00,0x83,0x83,0x57,0x83,0x83,
0x83,0x83,0x83,0xab,0x83,0x83,0xd7,0x83,
0x83,0xff,0x83,0x83,0x00,0xab,0x83,0x57,
0xab,0x83,0x83,0xab,0x83,0xab,0xab,0x83,
0xd7,0xab,0x83,0xff,0xab,0x83,0x00,0xd7,
0x83,0x57,0xd7,0x83,0x83,0xd7,0x83,0xab,
0xd7,0x83,0xd7,0xd7,0x83,0xff,0xd7,0x83,
0x00,0xff,0x83,0x57,0xff,0x83,0x83,0xff,
0x83,0xab,0xff,0x83,0xd7,0xff,0x83,0xff,
0xff,0x83,0x00,0x00,0xab,0x57,0x00,0xab,
0x83,0x00,0xab,0xab,0x00,0xab,0xd7,0x00,
0xab,0xff,0x00,0xab,0x00,0x2b,0xab,0x57,
0x2b,0xab,0x83,0x2b,0xab,0xab,0x2b,0xab,
0xd7,0x2b,0xab,0xff,0x2b,0xab,0x00,0x57,
0xab,0x57,0x57,0xab,0x83,0x57,0xab,0xab,
0x57,0xab,0xd7,0x57,0xab,0xff,0x57,0xab,
0x00,0x83,0xab,0x57,0x83,0xab,0x83,0x83,
0xab,0xab,0x83,0xab,0xd7,0x83,0xab,0xff,
0x83,0xab,0x00,0xab,0xab,0x57,0xab,0xab,
0x83,0xab,0xab,0xab,0xab,0xab,0xd7,0xab,
0xab,0xff,0xab,0xab,0x00,0xd7,0xab,0x57,
0xd7,0xab,0x83,0xd7,0xab,0xab,0xd7,0xab,
0xd7,0xd7,0xab,0xff,0xd7,0xab,0x00,0xff,
0xab,0x57,0xff,0xab,0x83,0xff,0xab,0xab,
0xff,0xab,0xd7,0xff,0xab,0xff,0xff,0xab,
0x00,0x00,0xd7,0x57,0x00,0xd7,0x83,0x00,
0xd7,0xab,0x00,0xd7,0xd7,0x00,0xd7,0xff,
0x00,0xd7,0x00,0x2b,0xd7,0x57,0x2b,0xd7,
0x83,0x2b,0xd7,0xab,0x2b,0xd7,0xd7,0x2b,
0xd7,0xff,0x2b,0xd7,0x00,0x57,0xd7,0x57,
0x57,0xd7,0x83,0x57,0xd7,0xab,0x57,0xd7,
```

```
                     0xd7,0x57,0xd7,0xff,0x57,0xd7,0x00,0x83,
                     0xd7,0x57,0x83,0xd7,0x83,0x83,0xd7,0xab,
                     0x83,0xd7,0xd7,0x83,0xd7,0xff,0x83,0xd7,
                     0x00,0xab,0xd7,0x57,0xab,0xd7,0x83,0xab,
                     0xd7,0xab,0xab,0xd7,0xd7,0xab,0xd7,0xff,
                     0xab,0xd7,0x00,0xd7,0xd7,0x57,0xd7,0xd7,
                     0x83,0xd7,0xd7,0xab,0xd7,0xd7,0xd7,0xd7,
                     0xd7,0xff,0xd7,0xd7,0x00,0xff,0xd7,0x57,
                     0xff,0xd7,0x83,0xff,0xd7,0xab,0xff,0xd7,
                     0xd7,0xff,0xd7,0xff,0xee,0xb8,0x00,0x00,
                     0xff,0x57,0x00,0xff,0x83,0x00,0xff,0xab,
                     0x00,0xff,0xd7,0x00,0xff,0xff,0x00,0xff,
                     0x00,0x2b,0xff,0x57,0x2b,0xff,0x83,0x2b,
                     0xff,0xab,0x2b,0xff,0xd7,0x2b,0xff,0xff,
                     0x2b,0xff,0x00,0x57,0xff,0x57,0x57,0xff,
                     0x83,0x57,0xff,0xab,0x57,0xff,0xd7,0x57,
                     0xff,0xff,0x57,0xff,0x00,0x83,0xff,0x57,
                     0x83,0xff,0x83,0x83,0xff,0xab,0x83,0xff,
                     0xd7,0x83,0xff,0xff,0x83,0xff,0x00,0xab,
                     0xff,0x57,0xab,0xff,0x83,0xab,0xff,0xab,
                     0xab,0xff,0xd7,0xab,0xff,0xff,0xab,0xff,
                     0x00,0xd7,0xff,0x57,0xd7,0xff,0x83,0xd7,
                     0xff,0xab,0xd7,0xff,0xd7,0xd7,0xff,0xff,
                     0xd7,0xff,0x00,0xff,0xff,0x57,0xff,0xff,
                     0x83,0xff,0xff,0xab,0xff,0xff,0xff,0xff,
                     0xff,0x3f,0x3f,0x3f,0x6b,0x6b,0x6b,0x97,
                     0x97,0x97,0xc3,0xc3,0xc3,0xff,0xff,0xff
                     };

     char masktable[8]={0x80,0x40,0x20,0x10,0x08,0x04,0x02,0x01};
     char bittable[8]= {0x01,0x02,0x04,0x08,0x10,0x20,0x40,0x80};

     char errormessage[7][48] = {
             "Ok",
             "File not found",
             "Invalid argument count",
             "Insufficient memory",
             "Image not found",
             "Level not defined",
             "Too many defines"
             };

main(argc,argv)
        int argc;
        char *argv[];
{
        CHARACTER character;
        unsigned long l;
        unsigned int n;

        puts("TESTWALK version 1.0\r\n");

        if(argc <= 1)
            error("I need a path to a CHR file");
```

```
        if((n=LoadCharacter(&character,argv[1])) == 0) {
                l=coreleft();
                graphics();
                setvgapalette(palette,256);
                TestWalk(&character);
                text();
                printf("\n%lu bytes free\n",l);
        } else puts(errormessage[n]);
}

TestWalk(character)
        CHARACTER *character;
{

        LEVEL level;
        int x,y,c,i,j,oldx=-1,oldy=-1;

        memset((char *)&level,0,sizeof(LEVEL));

        level.width=SCREENWIDE;
        level.depth=SCREENDEEP;

        x=(unsigned int)level.width*(unsigned int)level.depth;

        if((level.bitmap=malloc(x))==NULL) {
                beep();
                return;
        }

        memset(level.bitmap,253,x);

        if((level.tile=loadfrag("TILE.FRG")) != NULL)
            tileimage(&level,level.tile);

        memcpy(MK_FP(0xa000,0),level.bitmap,x);

        SetWindowFrame(0,0,SCREENWIDE,SCREENDEEP);
        SetWindowOff(0,0);

        StartTime(&level);

        character->action=WALKRIGHT;
        character->thiscell=0;

        SetCharacter(character);

        x=SCREENWIDE/2;
        y=SCREENDEEP/2;

        OffsetRect(&character->leftframe,x,y);
        OffsetRect(&character->rightframe,x,y);
        OffsetRect(&character->leftjumpframe,x,y);
        OffsetRect(&character->rightjumpframe,x,y);

        do {
                while(kbhit()) getch();
```

```
8-9          if(oldx != x || oldy != y) {
Continued.          oldx=x;
                    oldy=y;
                    PlaceCharacter(x,y);
              }
              delay(WALKDELAY);

              c=GetKey();

              switch(c) {
                    case CURSOR_LEFT:
                          i=character->leftframe.bottom-character->leftframe.top;
                          j=character->leftframe.right-character->leftframe.left;
                          SetRect(&character->leftframe,x,y,x+j,y+i);
                          if((character->leftframe.left-WALKSTEP) >= 0)
                              x-=WALKSTEP;
                          character->action=WALKLEFT;
                          break;
                    case CURSOR_RIGHT:
                          i=character->rightframe.bottom-character->rightframe.top;
                          j=character->rightframe.right-character->rightframe.left;
                          SetRect(&character->rightframe,x,y,x+j,y+i);
                          if((character->rightframe.right+WALKSTEP) < SCREENWIDE)
                              x+=WALKSTEP;
                          character->action=WALKRIGHT;
                          break;
              }
        } while(c != 27);

        StopTime();
}

LoadCharacter(character,path)
        CHARACTER *character;
        char *path;
{

        FILE *fp;
        char *p,b[193],*arg[MAXARG];
        unsigned int argindex;
        int i;

        if((fp=fopen(path,"ra")) == NULL) return(1);

        memset((char *)character,0,sizeof(CHARACTER));

        do {
              if((p=fgets(b,192,fp)) != NULL) {
                    for(argindex=0;argindex<MAXARG && *p != 0;++argindex) {
                          while(*p <= 32 && *p != 0) *p++=0;
                          arg[argindex]=p;
                          while(*p > 32) ++p;
                    }

                    if(arg[0][0]==';') continue;
```

```
if(!stricmp(arg[0],"WALKLEFT")) {

        if(argindex < 3) return(2);

        for(i=1;i<argindex-1 && character->maxleft < MAXCELL;++i) {
                if((character->walkleft[character->maxleft++]=
                    loadfrag(arg[i])) == NULL) {
                        FreeCharacter(character);
                        fclose(fp);
                        return(4);
                }
        }

        character->leftframe.left=0;
        character->leftframe.top=0;
        character->leftframe.right=ImageWidth(character->walkleft[0]);
        character->leftframe.bottom=ImageDepth(character->walkleft[0]);

        if(character->maxleft==0) {
                FreeCharacter(character);
                fclose(fp);
                return(2);
        }
}
else if(!stricmp(arg[0],"WALKRIGHT")) {

        if(argindex < 3) return(2);

        for(i=1;i<argindex-1 && character->maxright < MAXCELL;++i) {
                if((character->walkright[character->maxright++]=
                    loadfrag(arg[i])) == NULL) {
                        FreeCharacter(character);
                        fclose(fp);
                        return(4);
                }
        }

        character->rightframe.left=0;
        character->rightframe.top=0;
        character->rightframe.right=ImageWidth(character->walkright[0]);
        character->rightframe.bottom=ImageDepth(character->walkright[0]);

        if(character->maxright==0) {
                FreeCharacter(character);
                fclose(fp);
                return(2);
        }
}
else if(!stricmp(arg[0],"JUMPLEFT")) {

        if(argindex < 2) return(2);

        if((character->jumpleft=loadfrag(arg[1])) == NULL) {
                FreeCharacter(character);
                fclose(fp);
```

```
                                                        return(4);
                                        }

                                character->leftjumpframe.left=0;
                                character->leftjumpframe.top=0;
                                character->leftjumpframe.right=ImageWidth(character->jumpleft);
                                character->leftjumpframe.bottom=ImageDepth(character->jumpleft);
                        }
                        else if(!stricmp(arg[0],"JUMPRIGHT")) {

                                if(argindex < 2) return(2);

                                if((character->jumpright=
                                    loadfrag(arg[1])) == NULL) {
                                        FreeCharacter(character);
                                        fclose(fp);
                                        return(4);
                                }

                                character->rightjumpframe.left=0;
                                character->rightjumpframe.top=0;
                                character->rightjumpframe.right=ImageWidth(character->jumpright);
                                character->rightjumpframe.bottom=ImageDepth(character->jumpright);
                        }
                }
        } while(p != NULL);

        fclose(fp);
        return(0);
}

FreeCharacter(character)
        CHARACTER *character;
{
        int i;

        for(i=0;i<character->maxleft;++i) {
                if(character->walkleft[i] != NULL) free(character->walkleft[i]);
        }

        for(i=0;i<character->maxright;++i) {
                if(character->walkright[i] != NULL) free(character->walkright[i]);
        }

        if(character->jumpleft != NULL) free(character->jumpleft);
        if(character->jumpright != NULL) free(character->jumpright);
}

text()
{
        union REGS r;

        r.x.ax=0x0003;
        int86(0x10,&r,&r);
}
```

```
graphics()
{
        union REGS r;

        r.x.ax=0x0013;
        int86(0x10,&r,&r);
}

error(s)
        char *s;
{
        puts(s);
        exit(1);
}

setvgapalette(p,n)
        char *p;
        int n;
{
        int i;

        outp(0x3c6,0xff);
        for(i=0;i<n;++i) {
                outp(0x3c8,i);
                outp(0x3c9,(*p++) >> 2);
                outp(0x3c9,(*p++) >> 2);
                outp(0x3c9,(*p++) >> 2);
        }
}

char *loadfrag(s)
        char *s;
{
        FILE *fp;
        IMAGEHEAD ih;
        char *p,*pr;
        unsigned int i;

        if((fp=fopen(s,"rb")) == NULL) return(NULL);

        if(fread((char *)&ih,1,sizeof(IMAGEHEAD),fp) != sizeof(IMAGEHEAD)) {
                fclose(fp);
                return(NULL);
        }

        if(ih.bits != 8) {
                fclose(fp);
                return(NULL);
        }

        if((p=farmalloc(4L+(long)ih.bytes*(long)ih.depth)) == NULL) {
                fclose(fp);
                return(NULL);
        }
```

```
                fseek(fp,ih.image,SEEK_SET);

                pr=p;

                pr+=fread(pr,1,4,fp);

                for(i=0;i<ih.depth;++i) {
                        if(fread(pr,1,ih.bytes,fp) != ih.bytes) {
                                farfree(p);
                                fclose(fp);
                                return(NULL);
                        }
                        pr=farPtr(pr,(long)ih.bytes);
                }
                fclose(fp);
                return(p);
        }

char *farPtr(p,l)
        char *p;
        unsigned long l;
        {

        unsigned int seg,off;

        seg = FP_SEG(p);
        off = FP_OFF(p);
        seg += (off / 16);
        off &= 0x000f;
        off += (unsigned int)(l & 0x000fL);
        seg += (l / 16L);
        p = MK_FP(seg,off);
        return(p);
        }

IsRectOverlap(r1,r2)
        RECT *r1,*r2;
        {

        if(r1->right < r2->left) return(0);
        else if(r1->left > r2->right) return(0);
        else if(r1->bottom < r2->top) return(0);
        else if(r1->top > r2->bottom) return(0);
        else return(1);
        }

OffsetRect(r,x,y)
        RECT *r;
        int x,y;
        {

        r->left+=x;
        r->top+=y;
        r->right+=x;
        r->bottom+=y;
        }
```

```
SetRect(r,left,top,right,bottom)
        RECT *r;
        int left,top,right,bottom;
{
        r->left=left;
        r->top=top;
        r->right=right;
        r->bottom=bottom;
}

tileimage(level,image)
        LEVEL *level;
        char *image;
{
        int x,y,iw,id;

        iw=ImageWidth(image);
        id=ImageDepth(image);

        for(y=-(id/2);y<level->depth;) {
                for(x=0;x<level->width;x+=iw) placetile(level,image,x,y);
                y+=id;
                for(x=-(iw/2);x<level->width;x+=iw) placetile(level,image,x,y);
                y+=id;
        }
}

placetile(level,image,x,y)
        LEVEL *level;
        char *image;
        int x,y;
{
        char *pd,*ps;
        int i,j,iw,id;

        iw=ImageWidth(image);
        id=ImageDepth(image);
        image+=4;

        ps=image;

        for(i=0;i<id;++i) {
                pd=farPtr(level->bitmap,(long)(y+i)*(long)level->width+(long)x);
                for(j=0;j<iw;++j) {
                        if((x+j) >= 0 && (x+j) < level->width &&
                           (y+i) >= 0 && (y+i) < level->depth &&
                           *ps != TRANSPARENT) *pd=*ps;
                        ++ps;
                        ++pd;
                }
        }
}

GetKey()
{
```

8-9
Continued.

```
int c;

c = getch();
if(!(c & 0x00ff)) c = getch() << 8;
return(c);
}
```

A few minutes in TechnologyLand

The program to actually play the game is really just an integration of the SHOWROOM and TESTWALK programs, with one important addition. The PLAYGAME program in FIG. 8-10 replaces the arrow keys that pan over the room area with the movement of Alice herself. The only tricky bit is in knowing where Alice can move, such that she doesn't walk clear through a solid object, for example.

8-10
The source code for
PLAYGAME.C.

```
/*
        The game's a'foot

        Copyright (c) 1992 Alchemy Mindworks Inc.
*/

#include "stdio.h"
#include "dos.h"
#include "alloc.h"
#include "string.h"
#include "stdlib.h"
#include "ctype.h"

#define RGB_RED         0
#define RGB_GREEN       1
#define RGB_BLUE        2
#define RGB_SIZE        3

#define SCREENWIDE      320
#define SCREENDEEP      200

#define WINDOWLEFT      8
#define WINDOWTOP       8
#define WINDOWWIDE      208
#define WINDOWDEEP      184
#define TRANSPARENT     255

#define IMAGESIG        "IFRG"

#define MAXCELL         16
#define MAXARG          16
#define MAXDEFINE       32
#define DEFINESIZE      16

#define MAXWIDTH        800
#define MAXDEPTH        600

#define CURSOR_UP       72 * 256
```

```
#define CURSOR_LEFT       75 * 256
#define CURSOR_RIGHT      77 * 256

#define STATIC            0x0001
#define SOLID             0x0002
#define INDICATOR         0x0004
#define DOOR              0x0008

#define DOORTIME          0

#define COPY_PUT          1
#define TRANS_PUT         2

#define ALT_D             0x2000
#define ALT_R             0x1300
#define ALT_S             0x1F00

#define ALTKEY            0x0008
#define CTRLKEY           0x0004
#define LEFTSHIFT         0x0002
#define RIGHTSHIFT        0x0001

#define WALKLEFT          1
#define WALKRIGHT         2
#define JUMPLEFT          3
#define JUMPRIGHT         4

#define WALKSTEP          8
#define WALKDELAY         80

#define FALLDELAY         1

#define pixels2bytes(n)   ((n+7)/8)
#define ImageWidth(p)     (1+p[0]+(p[1] << 8))
#define ImageDepth(p)     (1+p[2]+(p[3] << 8))
#define beep()            putchar(7)

typedef struct {
        char sig[4];
        unsigned int width,depth,bits,bytes,planebytes;
        unsigned long palette;
        unsigned long image;
        } IMAGEHEAD;

typedef struct {
        int left,top,right,bottom;
        } RECT;

typedef struct OBJECT {
        struct OBJECT *next;
        RECT frame;
        char *cell[MAXCELL];
        unsigned int cellcount;
        unsigned int attributes;
        unsigned int timeslice;
```

```
unsigned int thiscell;
unsigned int timeleft;
int (*proc)();
char name[MAXCELL][9];
} OBJECT;

typedef struct {
    char *tile;
    char *bitmap;
    OBJECT *objectlist;
    int width,depth;
    char name[9];
} LEVEL;

typedef struct {
    int value;
    char name[MAXDEFINE+1];
} DEFINE;

typedef struct {
    char *walkleft[MAXCELL];
    char *walkright[MAXCELL];
    char *jumpleft;
    char *jumpright;
    RECT leftframe;
    RECT rightframe;
    RECT leftjumpframe;
    RECT rightjumpframe;
    unsigned int action;
    unsigned int thiscell;
    unsigned int maxleft;
    unsigned int maxright;
    unsigned int xloc,yloc;
} CHARACTER;

typedef struct   {
    char manufacturer;
    char version;
    char encoding;
    char bits_per_pixel;
    int xmin,ymin;
    int xmax,ymax;
    int hres;
    int vres;
    char palette[48];
    char reserved;
    char colour_planes;
    int bytes_per_line;
    int palette_type;
    char filler[58];
} PCXHEAD;

char *farPtr(char *p,unsigned long l);
char *loadfrag(char *s,LEVEL *level);
int EndLevel();
```

```
char palette[] = {
        0x00,0x00,0x00,0x57,0x00,0x00,0x83,0x00,
        0x00,0xab,0x00,0x00,0xd7,0x00,0x00,0xff,
        0x00,0x00,0x00,0x2b,0x00,0x57,0x2b,0x00,
        0x83,0x2b,0x00,0xab,0x2b,0x00,0xd7,0x2b,
        0x00,0xff,0x2b,0x00,0x00,0x57,0x00,0x57,
        0x57,0x00,0x83,0x57,0x00,0xab,0x57,0x00,
        0xd7,0x57,0x00,0xff,0x57,0x00,0x00,0x83,
        0x00,0x57,0x83,0x00,0x83,0x83,0x00,0xab,
        0x83,0x00,0xd7,0x83,0x00,0xff,0x83,0x00,
        0x00,0xab,0x00,0x57,0xab,0x00,0x83,0xab,
        0x00,0xab,0xab,0x00,0xd7,0xab,0x00,0xff,
        0xab,0x00,0x00,0xd7,0x00,0x57,0xd7,0x00,
        0x83,0xd7,0x00,0xab,0xd7,0x00,0xd7,0xd7,
        0x00,0xff,0xd7,0x00,0x00,0xff,0x00,0x57,
        0xff,0x00,0x83,0xff,0x00,0xab,0xff,0x00,
        0xd7,0xff,0x00,0xff,0xff,0x00,0x00,0x00,
        0x57,0x57,0x00,0x57,0x83,0x00,0x57,0xab,
        0x00,0x57,0xd7,0x00,0x57,0xff,0x00,0x57,
        0x00,0x2b,0x57,0x57,0x2b,0x57,0x83,0x2b,
        0x57,0xab,0x2b,0x57,0xd7,0x2b,0x57,0xff,
        0x2b,0x57,0x00,0x57,0x57,0x57,0x57,0x57,
        0x83,0x57,0x57,0xab,0x57,0x57,0xd7,0x57,
        0x57,0xff,0x57,0x57,0x00,0x83,0x57,0x57,
        0x83,0x57,0x83,0x83,0x57,0xab,0x83,0x57,
        0xd7,0x83,0x57,0xff,0x83,0x57,0x00,0xab,
        0x57,0x57,0xab,0x57,0x83,0xab,0x57,0xab,
        0xab,0x57,0xd7,0xab,0x57,0xff,0xab,0x57,
        0x00,0xd7,0x57,0x57,0xd7,0x57,0x83,0xd7,
        0x57,0xab,0xd7,0x57,0xd7,0xd7,0x57,0xff,
        0xd7,0x57,0x00,0xff,0x57,0x57,0xff,0x57,
        0x83,0xff,0x57,0xab,0xff,0x57,0xd7,0xff,
        0x57,0xff,0xff,0x57,0x00,0x00,0x83,0x57,
        0x00,0x83,0x83,0x00,0x83,0xab,0x00,0x83,
        0xd7,0x00,0x83,0xff,0x00,0x83,0x00,0x2b,
        0x83,0x57,0x2b,0x83,0x83,0x2b,0x83,0xab,
        0x2b,0x83,0xd7,0x2b,0x83,0xff,0x2b,0x83,
        0x00,0x57,0x83,0x57,0x57,0x83,0x83,0x57,
        0x83,0xab,0x57,0x83,0xd7,0x57,0x83,0xff,
        0x57,0x83,0x00,0x83,0x83,0x57,0x83,0x83,
        0x83,0x83,0x83,0xab,0x83,0x83,0xd7,0x83,
        0x83,0xff,0x83,0x83,0x00,0xab,0x83,0x57,
        0xab,0x83,0x83,0xab,0x83,0xab,0xab,0x83,
        0xd7,0xab,0x83,0xff,0xab,0x83,0x00,0xd7,
        0x83,0x57,0xd7,0x83,0x83,0xd7,0x83,0xab,
        0xd7,0x83,0xd7,0xd7,0x83,0xff,0xd7,0x83,
        0x00,0xff,0x83,0x57,0xff,0x83,0x83,0xff,
        0x83,0xab,0xff,0x83,0xd7,0xff,0x83,0xff,
        0xff,0x83,0x00,0x00,0xab,0x57,0x00,0xab,
        0x83,0x00,0xab,0xab,0x00,0xab,0xd7,0x00,
        0xab,0xff,0x00,0xab,0x00,0x2b,0xab,0x57,
        0x2b,0xab,0x83,0x2b,0xab,0xab,0x2b,0xab,
        0xd7,0x2b,0xab,0xff,0x2b,0xab,0x00,0x57,
        0xab,0x57,0x57,0xab,0x83,0x57,0xab,0xab,
        0x57,0xab,0xd7,0x57,0xab,0xff,0x57,0xab,
```

```
0x00,0x83,0xab,0x57,0x83,0xab,0x83,0x83,
0xab,0xab,0x83,0xab,0xd7,0x83,0xab,0xff,
0x83,0xab,0x00,0xab,0xab,0x57,0xab,0xab,
0x83,0xab,0xab,0xab,0xab,0xab,0xd7,0xab,
0xab,0xff,0xab,0xab,0x00,0xd7,0xab,0x57,
0xd7,0xab,0x83,0xd7,0xab,0xab,0xd7,0xab,
0xd7,0xd7,0xab,0xff,0xd7,0xab,0x00,0xff,
0xab,0x57,0xff,0xab,0x83,0xff,0xab,0xab,
0xff,0xab,0xd7,0xff,0xab,0xff,0xff,0xab,
0x00,0x00,0xd7,0x57,0x00,0xd7,0x83,0x00,
0xd7,0xab,0x00,0xd7,0xd7,0x00,0xd7,0xff,
0x00,0xd7,0x00,0x2b,0xd7,0x57,0x2b,0xd7,
0x83,0x2b,0xd7,0xab,0x2b,0xd7,0xd7,0x2b,
0xd7,0xff,0x2b,0xd7,0x00,0x57,0xd7,0x57,
0x57,0xd7,0x83,0x57,0xd7,0xab,0x57,0xd7,
0xd7,0x57,0xd7,0xff,0x57,0xd7,0x00,0x83,
0xd7,0x57,0x83,0xd7,0x83,0x83,0xd7,0xab,
0x83,0xd7,0xd7,0x83,0xd7,0xff,0x83,0xd7,
0x00,0xab,0xd7,0x57,0xab,0xd7,0x83,0xab,
0xd7,0xab,0xab,0xd7,0xd7,0xab,0xd7,0xff,
0xab,0xd7,0x00,0xd7,0xd7,0x57,0xd7,0xd7,
0x83,0xd7,0xd7,0xab,0xd7,0xd7,0xd7,0xd7,
0xd7,0xff,0xd7,0xd7,0x00,0xff,0xd7,0x57,
0xff,0xd7,0x83,0xff,0xd7,0xab,0xff,0xd7,
0xd7,0xff,0xd7,0xff,0xee,0xb8,0x00,0x00,
0xff,0x57,0x00,0xff,0x83,0x00,0xff,0xab,
0x00,0xff,0xd7,0x00,0xff,0xff,0x00,0xff,
0x00,0x2b,0xff,0x57,0x2b,0xff,0x83,0x2b,
0xff,0xab,0x2b,0xff,0xd7,0x2b,0xff,0xff,
0x2b,0xff,0x00,0x57,0xff,0x57,0x57,0xff,
0x83,0x57,0xff,0xab,0x57,0xff,0xd7,0x57,
0xff,0xff,0x57,0xff,0x00,0x83,0xff,0x57,
0x83,0xff,0x83,0x83,0xff,0xab,0x83,0xff,
0xd7,0x83,0xff,0xff,0x83,0xff,0x00,0xab,
0xff,0x57,0xab,0xff,0x83,0xab,0xff,0xab,
0xab,0xff,0xd7,0xab,0xff,0xff,0xab,0xff,
0x00,0xd7,0xff,0x57,0xd7,0xff,0x83,0xd7,
0xff,0xab,0xd7,0xff,0xd7,0xd7,0xff,0xff,
0xd7,0xff,0x00,0xff,0xff,0x57,0xff,0xff,
0x83,0xff,0xff,0xab,0xff,0xff,0xff,0xff,
0xff,0x3f,0x3f,0x3f,0x6b,0x6b,0x6b,0x97,
0x97,0x97,0xc3,0xc3,0xc3,0xff,0xff,0xff
};

char errormessage[7][48] = {
        "Ok",
        "File not found",
        "Invalid argument count",
        "Insufficient memory",
        "Image not found",
        "Level not defined",
        "Too many defines"
        };

int alive=1;
```

```
main(argc,argv)
        int argc;
        char *argv[];
{
        CHARACTER character;
        LEVEL level;
        unsigned long l;
        unsigned int n;

        puts("PLAYGAME version 1.0\r\n");

        if(argc <= 2)
            error("I need a path to a LVL file and a path to a CHR file");

        if((n=LoadLevel(&level,argv[1])) == 0) {
                if((n=LoadCharacter(&character,argv[2])) == 0) {
                        l=coreleft();
                        graphics();
                        setvgapalette(palette,256);
                        PlayLevel(&level,&character);
                        text();
                        printf("\n%lu bytes free\n",l);
                } else puts(errormessage[n]);
        } else puts(errormessage[n]);
}

PlayLevel(level,character)
        LEVEL *level;
        CHARACTER *character;
{
        OBJECT *op;
        RECT r,ro,window;
        char *screen;
        int x,y,c,i,j,oldx=-1,oldy=-1;
        int wleft=0,wtop=0,oldwleft=-1,oldwtop=-1;

        if((screen=loadfrag("SCREEN.FRG",NULL)) != NULL) {
                PutImage(0,0,screen,COPY_PUT);
                free(screen);
        } else putchar(7);


SetRect(&window,WINDOWLEFT,WINDOWTOP,WINDOWLEFT+WINDOWWIDE,WINDOWTOP+WINDOWDEEP);
        SetWindowFrame(window.left,window.top,window.right,window.bottom);
        SetWindowOff(0,0);
        StartTime(level);

        character->thiscell=0;
        SetCharacter(character);

        x=character->xloc;
        y=character->yloc;
        OffsetRect(&character->leftframe,x,y);
        OffsetRect(&character->rightframe,x,y);
        OffsetRect(&character->leftjumpframe,x,y);
```

```
OffsetRect(&character->rightjumpframe,x,y);

x=character->rightframe.right-character->rightframe.left;
y=character->rightframe.bottom-character->rightframe.top;

oldx=character->xloc;
oldy=character->yloc;

SetWindowOff(wleft,wtop);
UpdCharacter(character->xloc+window.left,character->yloc+window.top);
UpdateWindow();
UpdateAll();

do {
        SetWindowOff(wleft,wtop);

        while(kbhit()) getch();

        do {
                if(character->action==WALKLEFT || character->action==JUMPLEFT) {
                        i=character->leftframe.bottom-character->leftframe.top;
                        j=character->leftframe.right-character->leftframe.left;
                        SetRect(&character->leftframe,character->loc,character->yloc,
                                character->xloc+j,character->yloc+i);
                        mememcpy((char *)&r,(char *)&character->leftframe,sizeof(RECT));
                }

                else if(character->action==WALKRIGHT || character->action==JUMPRIGHT) {
                        i=character->rightframe.bottom-character->rightframe.top;
                        j=character->rightframe.right-character->rightframe.left;
                        SetRect(&character->rightframe,character->xloc,character->>yloc,
                                character->xloc+j,character->yloc+i);
                        memcpy((char *)&r,(char *)&character->rightframe,sizeof(RECT));
                }

                memcpy((char *)&ro,(char *)&r,sizeof(RECT));

                OffsetRect(&r,0,1);
                OffsetRect(&r,wleft,wtop);

                OffsetRect(&ro,0,WALKSTEP);
                OffsetRect(&ro,wleft,wtop);

                if((wtop+WINDOWDEEP+WALKSTEP) < level->depth) {
                        if((x=IsObstructed(&ro,level)) == 0) {

                                wtop+=WALKSTEP;
                                SetWindowOff(wleft,wtop);
                                UpdateWindow();
                                UpdateAll();

                                delay(FALLDELAY);
                                continue;
                        }
                }
```

```
                        if((x=IsObstructed(&r,level))==0) {
                                ++character->yloc;
                                PlaceCharacter(character->xloc+window.left,character->yloc+window.top);
                        }

                delay(FALLDELAY);
        } while(!x);

        if(oldx != character->xloc ||
           oldy != character->yloc ) {
                oldx=character->xloc;
                oldy=character->yloc;
                oldwleft=wleft;
                oldwtop=wtop;
                UpdateWindow();
                UpdateAll();
                PlaceCharacter(character->xloc+window.left,
                        character->yloc+window.top);
        }

        if(oldwleft != wleft ||
           oldwtop != wtop) {
                oldwleft=wleft;
                oldwtop=wtop;
                UpdateWindow();
                UpdateAll();
                UpdCharacter(character->xloc+window.left,
                        character->yloc+window.top);
        }

        delay(WALKDELAY);

        while(!kbhit() && alive);
        if(alive) c=GetKey();
        else c=0;

        switch(c) {
                case CURSOR_UP:
                        if(character->action==WALKLEFT || character->action==JUMPLEFT) {
                                i=character->leftframe.bottom-character->leftframe.top;
                                j=character->leftframe.right-character->leftframe.left;
                                SetRect(&character->leftframe,character->xloc,character->yloc,
                                        character->xloc+j,character->yloc+i);
                                memcpy((char *)&r,(char *)&character->leftframe,sizeof(RECT));
                        }
                        else if(character->action==WALKRIGHT || character->action==JUMPRIGHT)

                                i=character->rightframe.bottom-character->rightframe.top;
                                j=character->rightframe.right-character->rightframe.left;
                                SetRect(&character->rightframe,character->xloc,character->yloc,
                                        character->xloc+j,character->yloc+i);
                                memcpy((char *)&r,(char *)&character->rightframe,sizeof(RECT));
                        }

                        OffsetRect(&r,wleft,wtop);
```
{

```
                        for(op=level->objectlist;op != NULL;op=op->next) {
                                if((op->attributes & DOOR) &&
                                        IsRectOverlap(&r,&op->frame)) {
                                                OpenDoor(op);
                                                break;
                                }
                        }
                        break;
                case CURSOR_LEFT:
                        i=character->leftframe.bottom-character->leftframe.top;
                        j=character->leftframe.right-character->leftframe.left;
                        SetRect(&character->leftframe,character->xloc,character->yloc,
                            character->xloc+j,character->yloc+i);
                        memcpy((char *)&r,(char *)&character->leftframe,sizeof(RECT));
                        OffsetRect(&r,-WALKSTEP,0);
                        memcpy((char *)&ro,(char *)&r,sizeof(RECT));
                        OffsetRect(&ro,wleft,wtop);

                        if((wleft-WALKSTEP) >= 0) {
                                if(!IsObstructed(&ro,level))
                                        wleft-=WALKSTEP;
                        }
                        else if(!IsAtWall(&r,&window) &&
                          !IsObstructed(&ro,level))
                            character->xloc-=WALKSTEP;
                        character->action=WALKLEFT;
                        break;
                case CURSOR_RIGHT:
                        i=character->rightframe.bottom-character->rightframe.top;
                        j=character->rightframe.right-character->rightframe.left;
                        SetRect(&character->rightframe,character->xloc,character->yloc,
                            character->xloc+j,character->yloc+i);
                        memcpy((char *)&r,(char *)&character->rightframe,sizeof(RECT));
                        OffsetRect(&r,WALKSTEP,0);
                        memcpy((char *)&ro,(char *)&r,sizeof(RECT));
                        OffsetRect(&ro,wleft,wtop);

                        if((wleft+WINDOWWIDE+WALKSTEP) < level->width) {
                                if(!IsObstructed(&ro,level))
                                        wleft+=WALKSTEP;
                        }
                        else if(!IsAtWall(&r,&window) && !IsObstructed(&ro,level))
                            character->xloc+=WALKSTEP;
                        character->action=WALKRIGHT;
                        break;
                }
        } while(c != 27 && alive);

        StopTime();
}

LoadCharacter(character,path)
        CHARACTER *character;
        char *path;
{
```

```
FILE *fp;
char *p,b[193],*arg[MAXARG];
unsigned int argindex;
int i;

if((fp=fopen(path,"ra")) == NULL) return(1);

memset((char *)character,0,sizeof(CHARACTER));

do {
        if((p=fgets(b,192,fp)) != NULL) {
                for(argindex=0;argindex<MAXARG && *p != 0;++argindex) {
                        while(*p <= 32 && *p != 0) *p++=0;
                        arg[argindex]=p;
                        while(*p > 32) ++p;
                }

                if(arg[0][0]==';') continue;

                if(!stricmp(arg[0],"WALKLEFT")) {

                        if(argindex < 3) return(2);

                        for(i=1;i<argindex-1 && character->maxleft < MAXCELL;++i) {
                                if((character->walkleft[character->maxleft++]=
                                    loadfrag(arg[i],NULL)) == NULL) {
                                        FreeCharacter(character);
                                        fclose(fp);
                                        return(4);
                                }
                        }

                        character->leftframe.left=0;
                        character->leftframe.top=0;
                        character->leftframe.right=ImageWidth(character->walkleft[0]);
                        character->leftframe.bottom=ImageDepth(character->walkleft[0]);

                        if(character->maxleft==0) {
                                FreeCharacter(character);
                                fclose(fp);
                                return(2);
                        }
                }
                else if(!stricmp(arg[0],"WALKRIGHT")) {

                        if(argindex < 3) return(2);

                        for(i=1;i<argindex-1 && character->maxright < MAXCELL;++i) {
                                if((character->walkright[character->maxright++]=
                                    loadfrag(arg[i],NULL)) == NULL) {
                                        FreeCharacter(character);
                                        fclose(fp);
                                        return(4);
                                }
                        }
                }
```

```
                              character->rightframe.left=0;
                              character->rightframe.top=0;
                              character->rightframe.right=
                                ImageWidth(character->walkright[0]);
                              character->rightframe.bottom=
                                ImageDepth(character->walkright[0]);

                              if(character->maxright==0) {
                                      FreeCharacter(character);
                                      fclose(fp);
                                      return(2);
                              }
                      }
                      else if(!stricmp(arg[0],"JUMPLEFT")) {

                              if(argindex < 2) return(2);

                              if((character->jumpleft=
                                  loadfrag(arg[1],NULL)) == NULL) {
                                      FreeCharacter(character);
                                      fclose(fp);
                                      return(4);
                              }

                              character->leftjumpframe.left=0;
                              character->leftjumpframe.top=0;
                              character->leftjumpframe.right=
                                ImageWidth(character->jumpleft);
                              character->leftjumpframe.bottom=
                                ImageDepth(character->jumpleft);
                      }
                      else if(!stricmp(arg[0],"JUMPRIGHT")) {

                              if(argindex < 2) return(2);

                              if((character->jumpright=
                                  loadfrag(arg[1],NULL)) == NULL) {
                                      FreeCharacter(character);
                                      fclose(fp);
                                      return(4);
                              }

                              character->rightjumpframe.left=0;
                              character->rightjumpframe.top=0;
                              character->rightjumpframe.right=
                                ImageWidth(character->jumpright);
                              character->rightjumpframe.bottom=
                                ImageDepth(character->jumpright);
                      }
                      if(!stricmp(arg[0],"START")) {

                              if(argindex < 4) return(2);

                              character->xloc=atoi(arg[1]);
                              character->yloc=atoi(arg[2]);
                              character->action=atoi(arg[3]);
```

```
                            }

                    }
            } while(p != NULL);

            fclose(fp);
            return(0);
    }

FreeCharacter(character)
            CHARACTER *character;
    {
            int i;

            for(i=0;i<character->maxleft;++i) {
                    if(character->walkleft[i] != NULL)
                        free(character->walkleft[i]);
            }

            for(i=0;i<character->maxright;++i) {
                    if(character->walkright[i] != NULL)
                        free(character->walkright[i]);
            }

            if(character->jumpleft != NULL) free(character->jumpleft);
            if(character->jumpright != NULL) free(character->jumpright);
    }

LoadLevel(level,path)
            LEVEL *level;
            char *path;
    {
            DEFINE *define;
            FILE *fp;
            OBJECT *object,*op;
            char *p,*image,b[193],*arg[MAXARG];
            unsigned long size;
            unsigned int argindex,defineindex=0;
            int i,x,y,t;

            if((define=(DEFINE *)malloc(MAXDEFINE*sizeof(DEFINE))) == NULL)
                return(3);

            if((fp=fopen(path,"ra")) == NULL) {
                    free((char *)define);
                    return(1);
            }

            memset((char *)level,0,sizeof(LEVEL));

            do {
                    if((p=fgets(b,192,fp)) != NULL) {
                            for(argindex=0;argindex<MAXARG && *p != 0;++argindex) {
                                    while(*p <= 32 && *p != 0) *p++=0;
                                    arg[argindex]=p;
                                    while(*p > 32) ++p;
```

```
                       }

                       if(arg[0][0]==';') continue;

                       if(!stricmp(arg[0],"DEFINE")) {
                              if(defineindex < MAXDEFINE) {
                                     strcpy(define[defineindex].name,arg[1]);
                                     define[defineindex].value=atoi(arg[2]);
                                     ++defineindex;
                              }
                              else {
                                     free((char *)define);
                                     FreeLevel(level);
                                     fclose(fp);
                                     return(6);
                              }
                       }
                       else if(!stricmp(arg[0],"ROOM")) {
                              if(argindex < 3) return(2);
                              level->width=min(value(arg[1],define,defineindex),MAXWIDTH);
                              level->depth=min(value(arg[2],define,defineindex),MAXDEPTH);

                              size=(long)level->width*(long)level->depth;
                              if((level->bitmap=farmalloc(size))== NULL) {
                                     free((char *)define);
                                     fclose(fp);
                                     return(3);
                              }

                              if((image=loadfrag(arg[3],level)) == NULL) {
                                     free((char *)define);
                                     FreeLevel(level);
                                     fclose(fp);
                                     return(4);
                              }
                              fnsplit(arg[3],NULL,NULL,level->name,NULL);

                              tileimage(level,image);
                              free(image);
                       }
                       else if(!stricmp(arg[0],"STATIC")) {
                              if((object=(OBJECT *)malloc(sizeof(OBJECT))) == NULL) {
                                     free((char *)define);
                                     FreeLevel(level);
                                     fclose(fp);
                                     return(3);
                              }

                              memset((char *)object,0,sizeof(OBJECT));

                              if(level->bitmap==NULL) {
                                     free((char *)define);
                                     FreeLevel(level);
                                     fclose(fp);
                                     return(5);
                              }
```

```
                    if(argindex < 3) return(2);

                    x=min(value(arg[1],define,defineindex),level->width);
  y=min(value(arg[2],define,defineindex),level->depth);

                    if((image=loadfrag(arg[3],level)) == NULL) {
                            free((char *)define);
                            farfree(level->bitmap);
                            fclose(fp);
                            return(4);
                    }
                    placetile(level,image,x,y);

                    object->cellcount=1;
                    object->next=NULL;
                    object->frame.left=x;
                    object->frame.top=y;
                    object->frame.right=x+ImageWidth(image);
                    object->frame.bottom=y+ImageDepth(image);
                    object->cell[0]=image;
                    object->attributes=STATIC;
                    fnsplit(arg[3],NULL,NULL,object->name[0],NULL);

                    if(level->objectlist==NULL) level->objectlist=object;
                    else {
                            for(op=level->objectlist;op->next != NULL;op=op->next);
                            op->next=object;
                    }
            }
        else if(!stricmp(arg[0],"SOLID")) {
                    if((object=(OBJECT *)malloc(sizeof(OBJECT))) == NULL) {
                            free((char *)define);
                            FreeLevel(level);
                            fclose(fp);
                            return(3);
                    }

                    memset((char *)object,0,sizeof(OBJECT));

                    if(level->bitmap==NULL) {
                            free((char *)define);
                            FreeLevel(level);
                            fclose(fp);
                            return(5);
                    }
                    if(argindex < 3) return(2);

                    x=min(value(arg[1],define,defineindex),level->width);
                    y=min(value(arg[2],define,defineindex),level->depth);

                    if((image=loadfrag(arg[3],level)) == NULL) {
                            free((char *)define);
                            FreeLevel(level);
                            fclose(fp);
                            return(4);
                    }
```

```
                                    placetile(level,image,x,y);

                                    object->cellcount=1;
                                    object->next=NULL;
                                    object->frame.left=x;
                                    object->frame.top=y;
                                    object->frame.right=x+ImageWidth(image);
                                    object->frame.bottom=y+ImageDepth(image);
                                    object->cell[0]=image;
                                    object->attributes=SOLID;
                                    fnsplit(arg[3],NULL,NULL,object->name[0],NULL);

                                    if(level->objectlist==NULL) level->objectlist=object;
                                    else {
                                            for(op=level->objectlist;op->next != NULL;op=op->next);
                                            op->next=object;
                                    }
                    }
            else if(!stricmp(arg[0],"INDICATOR")) {
                    if((object=(OBJECT *)malloc(sizeof(OBJECT))) == NULL) {
                            free((char *)define);
                            FreeLevel(level);
                            fclose(fp);
                            return(3);
                    }

                    memset((char *)object,0,sizeof(OBJECT));

                    if(level->bitmap==NULL) {
                            free((char *)define);
                            FreeLevel(level);
                            fclose(fp);
                            return(5);
                    }
                    if(argindex < 3) return(2);

                    x=min(value(arg[1],define,defineindex),level->width);
                    y=min(value(arg[2],define,defineindex),level->depth);
                    t=value(arg[3],define,defineindex);

                    for(i=4;i<argindex-1 && object->cellcount < MAXCELL;++i) {
                            if((object->cell[object->cellcount]=
                                loadfrag(arg[i],level)) == NULL) {
                                    free((char *)define);
                                    FreeLevel(level);
                                    fclose(fp);
                                    return(4);
                            }
                            fnsplit(arg[i],NULL,NULL,
                                    object->name[object->cellcount],NULL);
                            ++object->cellcount;
                    }

                    if(object->cellcount==0) {
                            free((char *)define);
                            FreeLevel(level);
```

```
                                fclose(fp);
                                return(2);
                        }

                object->next=NULL;
                object->frame.left=x;
                object->frame.top=y;
                object->frame.right=x+ImageWidth(image);
                object->frame.bottom=y+ImageDepth(image);
                object->attributes=INDICATOR;
                object->timeslice=t;

                if(level->objectlist==NULL) level->objectlist=object;
                else {
                        for(op=level->objectlist;op->next != NULL;op=op->next);
                        op->next=object;
                }
        }
        else if(!stricmp(arg[0],"DOOR")) {
                if((object=(OBJECT *)malloc(sizeof(OBJECT))) == NULL) {
                        free((char *)define);
                        FreeLevel(level);
                        fclose(fp);
                        return(3);
                }

                memset((char *)object,0,sizeof(OBJECT));

                if(level->bitmap==NULL) {
                        free((char *)define);
                        FreeLevel(level);
                        fclose(fp);
                        return(5);
                }
                if(argindex < 3) return(2);

                x=min(value(arg[1],define,defineindex),level->width);
                y=min(value(arg[2],define,defineindex),level->depth);

                for(i=3;i<argindex-1 && object->cellcount < MAXCELL;++i) {
                        if((object->cell[object->cellcount]=
                            loadfrag(arg[i],level)) == NULL) {
                                free((char *)define);
                                FreeLevel(level);
                                fclose(fp);
                                return(4);
                        }
                        fnsplit(arg[i],NULL,NULL,
                            object->name[object->cellcount],NULL);
                        ++object->cellcount;
                }

                if(object->cellcount==0) {
                        free((char *)define);
                        FreeLevel(level);
                        fclose(fp);
```

```
                                                    return(2);
                                          }

                                          placetile(level,object->cell[0],x,y);

                                object->next=NULL;
                                object->frame.left=x;
                                object->frame.top=y;
                                object->frame.right=x+ImageWidth(object->cell[0]);
                                object->frame.bottom=y+ImageDepth(object->cell[0]);
                                object->attributes=DOOR;
                                object->timeslice=DOORTIME;
                                object->proc=EndLevel;

                                if(level->objectlist==NULL) level->objectlist=object;
                                else {
                                        for(op=level->objectlist;op->next != NULL;op=op->next);
                                        op->next=object;
                                }
                        }
                }
        } while(p != NULL);

        fclose(fp);
        free((char *)define);
        return(0);
}

FreeLevel(level)
        LEVEL *level;
{

        OBJECT *op;
        char *p;
        int i;

        for(op=level->objectlist;
            level->objectlist != NULL && op != NULL;op=op->next) {
                for(i=0;i<op->cellcount;++i) {
                        if(op->cell[i] != NULL) free(op->cell[i]);
                }
                p=(char *)op;
                free(p);
        }

        free(level->bitmap);
        free(level->tile);
}

tileimage(level,image)
        LEVEL *level;
        char *image;
{

        int x,y,iw,id;

        iw=ImageWidth(image);
        id=ImageDepth(image);
```

```
        for(y=-(id/2);y<level->depth;) {
                for(x=0;x<level->width;x+=iw) placetile(level,image,x,y);
                y+=id;
                for(x=-(iw/2);x<level->width;x+=iw)
                        placetile(level,image,x,y);
                y+=id;
        }
}

placetile(level,image,x,y)
        LEVEL *level;
        char *image;
        int x,y;
{
        char *pd,*ps;
        int i,j,iw,id;

        iw=ImageWidth(image);
        id=ImageDepth(image);
        image+=4;

        ps=image;

        for(i=0;i<id;++i) {
                pd=farPtr(level->bitmap,(long)(y+i)*(long)level->width+(long)x);
                for(j=0;j<iw;++j) {
                        if((x+j) >= 0 && (x+j) < level->width &&
                           (y+i) >= 0 && (y+i) < level->depth &&
                           *ps != TRANSPARENT) *pd=*ps;
                        ++ps;
                        ++pd;
                }
        }
}

text()
{
        union REGS r;

        r.x.ax=0x0003;
        int86(0x10,&r,&r);
}

graphics()
{
        union REGS r;

        r.x.ax=0x0013;
        int86(0x10,&r,&r);
}

error(s)
        char *s;
{
        puts(s);
```

```
            exit(1);
    }

setvgapalette(p,n)
        char *p;
        int n;
{
        int i;

        outp(0x3c6,0xff);
        for(i=0;i<n;++i) {
                outp(0x3c8,i);
                outp(0x3c9,(*p++) >> 2);
                outp(0x3c9,(*p++) >> 2);
                outp(0x3c9,(*p++) >> 2);
        }
}

char *loadfrag(s,level)
        char *s;
        LEVEL *level;
{
        OBJECT *op;
        FILE *fp;
        IMAGEHEAD ih;
        char *p,*pr,name[16];
        unsigned int i;

        fnsplit(s,NULL,NULL,name,NULL);

        if(level != NULL) {
                /* see if it's the background tile */
                if(!stricmp(level->name,name)) return(level->tile);

                /* see if it's a previously loaded object */
                if(level->objectlist != NULL) {
                        for(op=level->objectlist;op->next != NULL;op=op->next) {
                                for(i=0;i<op->cellcount;++i) {
                                        if(!stricmp(op->name[i],name))
                                                return(op->cell[i]);
                                }
                        }
                }
        }

        /* load a new object */
        if((fp=fopen(s,"rb")) == NULL) return(NULL);

        if(fread((char *)&ih,1,sizeof(IMAGEHEAD),fp) != sizeof(IMAGEHEAD))
        {
                fclose(fp);
                return(NULL);
        }

        if(ih.bits != 8) {
```

```
                fclose(fp);
                return(NULL);
        }

        if((p=farmalloc(4L+(long)ih.bytes*(long)ih.depth)) == NULL) {
                fclose(fp);
                return(NULL);
        }

        fseek(fp,ih.image,SEEK_SET);

        pr=p;

        pr+=fread(pr,1,4,fp);

        for(i=0;i<ih.depth;++i) {
                if(fread(pr,1,ih.bytes,fp) != ih.bytes) {
                        farfree(p);
                        fclose(fp);
                        return(NULL);
                }
                pr=farPtr(pr,(long)ih.bytes);
        }
        fclose(fp);
        return(p);
}

char *farPtr(p,l)
        char *p;
        unsigned long l;
{

        unsigned int seg,off;

        seg = FP_SEG(p);
        off = FP_OFF(p);
        seg += (off / 16);
        off &= 0x000f;
        off += (unsigned int)(l & 0x000fL);
        seg += (l / 16L);
        p = MK_FP(seg,off);
        return(p);
}

value(string,define,defineindex)
        char *string;
        DEFINE *define;
        unsigned int defineindex;
{

        int i;

        if(isdigit(string[0])) return(atoi(string));
        else {
                for(i=0;i<defineindex;++i) {
                        if(!stricmp(define[i].name,string))
                                return(define[i].value);
```

```
                              }
              }
              return(-1);
}

IsRectOverlap(r1,r2)
       RECT *r1,*r2;
{
       if(r1->right <= r2->left) return(0);
       else if(r1->left >= r2->right) return(0);
       else if(r1->bottom <= r2->top) return(0);
       else if(r1->top >= r2->bottom) return(0);
       else return(1);
}

OffsetRect(r,x,y)
       RECT *r;
       int x,y;
{
       r->left+=x;
       r->top+=y;
       r->right+=x;
       r->bottom+=y;
}

SetRect(r,left,top,right,bottom)
       RECT *r;
       int left,top,right,bottom;
{
       r->left=left;
       r->top=top;
       r->right=right;
       r->bottom=bottom;
}

IsAtWall(r,window)
       RECT *r,*window;
{
       if(r->right >= window->right) return(1);
       if(r->left < window->left) return(1);
       if(r->top < window->top) return(1);
       if(r->bottom >= window->bottom) return(1);
       return(0);
}

IsObstructed(r,level)
       RECT *r;
       LEVEL *level;
{
       OBJECT *op;

       for(op=level->objectlist;op != NULL;op=op->next) {
              if(op->attributes & SOLID) {
                     if(IsRectOverlap(r,&op->frame))
                     return(1);
```

```
                }
        }
        return(0);
}

GetKey()
{
        int c;

        c = getch();
        if(!(c & 0x00ff)) c = getch() << 8;
        return(c);
}

EndLevel()
{
        alive=0;
}
```

The locations of all the solid objects in a room are known—they're stored as
rectangular coordinates in entries of the OBJECT list for the room's LEVEL object.
When Alice wants to move, the game must determine whether she can do so by
working out the rectangular area she will occupy when she gets there and
comparing it to each frame element in the OBJECT list for the room that has a
SOLID attribute. If the proposed frame for Alice doesn't overlap any of the frames
for the solid objects, Alice can take a step. This requires a lot less time to perform
than it does to describe.

Comparing two rectangular area requires a function to see if rectangles overlap.
Here's what it looks like:

```
    IsRectOverlap(r1,r2)
            RECT *r1,*r2;
    {
            if(r1->right <= r2->left) return(0);
            else if(r1->left >= r2->right) return(0);
            else if(r1->bottom <= r2->top) return(0);
            else if(r1-top >= r2->bottom) return(0);
            else return(1);
    }
```

If IsRectOverlap returns a true value, the two RECT objects passed to it define
areas that at least partially overlap, and Alice should not be allowed to proceed.

Here's a function to invoke IsRectOverlap. It's called each time Alice wants to
move.

```
    IsObstructed(r,level)
            RECT *r;
            LEVEL *level;
    {
            OBJECT *op;

            for(op=level->objectlist;op != NULL;op=op->next) {
```

```
                            if(op->attributes & SOLID) {
                                if(IsRectOverlap(r,&op->frame))
                            return(1);
                    }
            }
        return(0);
    }
```

The IsObstructed function checks to make sure Alice isn't about to walk into a
barrel or other solid object. It does so by browsing the OBJECT list of the room.

The really involved aspect of Alice is actually the TIMESLIC.ASM assembly
language module, discussed hitherto only in oblique references. It's illustrated in
FIG. 8-11.

8-11
The source code for
TIMESLIC.ASM.

```
        ;
        ;                       Time Slice Functions
        ;                       Super VGA graphics
        ;                       Copyright (c) 1992 Alchemy Mindworks Inc.
        ;

        _AOFF           EQU     6               ;STACK OFFSET TO FIRST ARG

        SCREENWIDE      EQU     320             ;SCREEN DIMENSIONS
        SCREENDEEP      EQU     200

        DOWALKLEFT      EQU     0001H
        DOWALKRIGHT     EQU     0002H
        DOJUMPLEFT      EQU     0003H
        DOJUMPRIGHT     EQU     0004H

        INDICATOR       EQU     0004H
        DOOR            EQU     0008H

        MAXCELL         EQU     16

        TRANSPARENT     EQU     255

        COPY_PUT        EQU     1
        TRANS_PUT       EQU     2

        OBJECT          STRUC
                        NEXTOBJECT      DD      ?
                        FRAME           DW      4 DUP (?)
                        CELLPOINTER     DD      MAXCELL DUP (?)
                        CELLCOUNT       DW      ?
                        ATTRIBUTES      DW      ?
                        TIMESLICE       DW      ?
                        THISCELL        DW      ?
                        TIMELEFT        DW      ?
                        OBJECTPROC      DD      ?
                        OBJECTNAME      DB      (9 * MAXCELL) DUP (?)
        OBJECT          ENDS
```

```
LEVEL            STRUC
                 TILE           DD        ?
                 BITMAP         DD        ?
                 OBJECTLIST     DD        ?
                 LEVELWIDTH     DW        ?
                 LEVELDEPTH     DW        ?
                 LEVELNAME      DB        9 DUP (?)
LEVEL            ENDS

CHARACTEROBJ     STRUC
                 WALKLEFT       DD        MAXCELL DUP (?)
                 WALKRIGHT      DD        MAXCELL DUP (?)
                 JUMPLEFT       DD        ?
                 JUMPRIGHT      DD        ?
                 LEFTFRAME      DW        4 DUP (?)
                 RIGHTFRAME     DW        4 DUP (?)
                 LEFTJUMPFRAME  DW        4 DUP (?)
                 RIGHTJUMPFRAME DW        4 DUP (?)
                 ACTION         DW        ?
                 THISCHARCELL   DW        ?
                 MAXLEFT        DW        ?
                 MAXRIGHT       DW        ?
                 XLOC           DW        ?
                 YLOC           DW        ?
CHARACTEROBJ     ENDS

SCREENTABLE      MACRO     W,D
                 X = 0
                 REPT      D
                 DW        X
                 X = X + W
                 ENDM
                 ENDM

LDATASEG         MACRO
                 PUSH      AX
                 MOV       AX,_DATA
                 MOV       DS,AX
                 POP       AX
                 ENDM

;DO A LONG LOOP
LNGLOOP          MACRO     ARG1
                 LOCAL     LAB1
                 DEC       CX
                 CMP       CX,0000H
                 JE        LAB1
                 JMP       ARG1
LAB1:
                 ENDM

BEEP             MACRO
                 PUSH      AX
                 PUSH      BX
                 MOV       AX,0E07H
```

```
8-11                      MOV       BX,0000H
Continued.                INT       10H
                          POP       BX
                          POP       AX
                          ENDM

        TIMESLICE_TEXT  SEGMENT BYTE PUBLIC 'CODE'
                          ASSUME  CS:TIMESLICE_TEXT,DS:_DATA

        ;PLACE A CHARACTER ON THE SCREEN
        ;               ARGUMENTS         X
        ;                                 Y

                          PUBLIC  _PlaceCharacter
        _PlaceCharacter PROC    FAR
                          PUSH    BP
                          MOV     BP,SP
                          PUSH    DS
                          PUSH    ES
                          PUSHF

                          CLI

                          CALL    UPDATECOUNTERS

                          ;UNLESS THIS IS THE VERY FIRST PASS, REPLACE THE AREA
                          ;BEHIND THE CHARACTER WITH THE APPROPRIATE PART OF THE
                          ;LEVEL BITMAP

                          CMP     CS:[CHARACTER_X],-1
                          JE      PC2

                          CMP     CS:[CHARACTER_Y],-1
                          JE      PC2

                          PUSH    BP

                          MOV     DI,WORD PTR CS:[LEVELPOINTER+0]
                          MOV     ES,WORD PTR CS:[LEVELPOINTER+2]

                          MOV     AX,ES:[DI+LEVELWIDTH]
                          MOV     DX,0000H

                          MOV     BX,CS:[CHARACTER_Y]
                          SUB     BX,CS:[WINDOWTOP]
                          ADD     BX,CS:[TOPOFFSET]
                          MUL     BX

                          MOV     SI,WORD PTR ES:[DI+BITMAP+0]
                          MOV     DS,WORD PTR ES:[DI+BITMAP+2]

                          MOV     BP,ES:[DI+LEVELWIDTH]

                          CALL    FARPTR_SI
```

```
        ADD     SI,CS:[CHARACTER_X]
        ADD     SI,CS:[LEFTOFFSET]
        SUB     SI,CS:[WINDOWLEFT]

        MOV     BP,ES:[DI+LEVELWIDTH]

        PUSH    SI
        PUSH    DS
        CALL    GETCHARACTER

        POP     DS
        POP     SI

        MOV     AX,0A000H
        MOV     ES,AX

        MOV     AX,SCREENWIDE
        MUL     WORD PTR CS:[CHARACTER_Y]
        ADD     AX,CS:[CHARACTER_X]
        MOV     DI,AX

PC1:        PUSH    CX

        PUSH    SI
        PUSH    DI

        MOV     CX,BX
        CLD
REPNE   MOVSB

        POP     DI
        POP     SI

        ADD     SI,BP
        ADD     DI,SCREENWIDE

        POP     CX
        LOOP    PC1

        POP     BP

        ;NOW DRAW THE CHARACTER

PC2:        MOV     AX,[BP + _AOFF + 0]
        MOV     CS:[CHARACTER_X],AX
        MOV     AX,[BP + _AOFF + 2]
        MOV     CS:[CHARACTER_Y],AX

        CALL    GETCHARACTER

        MOV     AX,0A000H
        MOV     ES,AX

        MOV     AX,SCREENWIDE
        MUL     WORD PTR [BP + _AOFF + 2]
```

```
                              ADD       AX,[BP + _AOFF + 0]
                              MOV       DI,AX

                              LODSW
                              INC       AX
                              MOV       BX,AX

                              LODSW
                              INC       AX
                              MOV       CX,AX

              PC3:            PUSH      CX

                              PUSH      DI
                              MOV       CX,BX

              PC4:            LODSB
                              CMP       AL,TRANSPARENT
                              JE        PC5
                              MOV       ES:[DI],AL
              PC5:            INC       DI
                              LOOP      PC4

                              POP       DI

                              ADD       DI,SCREENWIDE

                              POP       CX
                              LOOP      PC3

                              POPF
                              POP       ES
                              POP       DS
                              POP       BP
                              RET
_PlaceCharacter ENDP

;UPDATE A CHARACTER POSITION WITHOUT DRAWING IT
;               ARGUMENTS          X
;                                  Y
;
                              PUBLIC    _UpdCharacter
_UpdCharacter   PROC      FAR
                              PUSH      BP
                              MOV       BP,SP
                              PUSH      DS
                              PUSH      ES
                              PUSHF

                              CLI

                              CALL      UPDATECOUNTERS

                              MOV       AX,[BP + _AOFF + 0]
                              MOV       CS:[CHARACTER_X],AX
```

```
              MOV       AX,[BP + _AOFF + 2]
              MOV       CS:[CHARACTER_Y],AX

              POPF
              POP       ES
              POP       DS
              POP       BP
              RET
_UpdCharacter ENDP

              PUBLIC    _SetCharacter
_SetCharacter PROC      FAR
              PUSH      BP
              MOV       BP,SP
              PUSH      DS
              PUSH      ES

              MOV       AX,[BP + _AOFF + 0]
              MOV       WORD PTR CS:[CHARACTER+0],AX

              MOV       AX,[BP + _AOFF + 2]
              MOV       WORD PTR CS:[CHARACTER+2],AX

              POP       ES
              POP       DS
              POP       BP
              RET
_SetCharacter ENDP

;PAINT AN IMAGE FRAGMENT ON THE SCREEN
;
;             ARGUMENTS       X
;                             Y
;                             POINTER TO IMAGE
;                             OP
              PUBLIC    _PutImage
_PutImage     PROC      FAR
              PUSH      BP
              MOV       BP,SP
              PUSH      DS
              PUSH      ES
              PUSHF

              CLI

              MOV       SI,[BP + _AOFF + 4]
              MOV       DS,[BP + _AOFF + 6]

              LODSW
              INC       AX
              MOV       DX,AX

              LODSW
              INC       AX
              MOV       CX,AX
```

```
                          MOV       BX,[BP + _AOFF + 2]

                          MOV       AX,0A000H
                          MOV       ES,AX

        PI1:              PUSH      BX
                          PUSH      CX

                          SHL       BX,1
                          MOV       DI,CS:[SCREENTBL+BX]

                          MOV       CX,DX
                          CLD
                          CMP       WORD PTR [BP + _AOFF + 8],COPY_PUT
                          JNE       PI2

             REPNE        MOVSB
                          JMP       PI5

        PI2:              CMP       WORD PTR [BP + _AOFF + 8],TRANS_PUT
                          JNE       PI5

        PI3:              LODSB
                          CMP       AL,TRANSPARENT
                          JE        PI4

                          MOV       ES:[DI],AL

        PI4:              INC       DI
                          LOOP      PI3

        PI5:              POP       CX
                          POP       BX
                          INC       BX
                          LOOP      PI1

                          POPF
                          POP       ES
                          POP       DS
                          POP       BP
                          RET
        _PutImage         ENDP

        ;UPDATE THE AREA WITHIN THE WINDOW
                          PUBLIC    _UpdateWindow
        _UpdateWindow     PROC      FAR
                          PUSH      BP
                          MOV       BP,SP
                          PUSH      DS
                          PUSH      ES
                          PUSHF

                          CLI
```

```
          CALL     GETCHARACTER

          LODSW
          INC      AX
          MOV      CS:[THISCHARWIDE],AX

          LODSW
          INC      AX
          MOV      CS:[THISCHARDEEP],AX

          MOV      WORD PTR CS:[THISCELLPTR+0],SI
          MOV      WORD PTR CS:[THISCELLPTR+2],DS

          MOV      DI,WORD PTR CS:[LEVELPOINTER+0]
          MOV      ES,WORD PTR CS:[LEVELPOINTER+2]

          MOV      SI,WORD PTR ES:[DI+BITMAP+0]
          MOV      DS,WORD PTR ES:[DI+BITMAP+2]

          MOV      AX,CS:[TOPOFFSET]
          MOV      DX,0000H
          MUL      WORD PTR ES:[DI+LEVELWIDTH]
          CALL     FARPTR_SI
          ADD      SI,CS:[LEFTOFFSET]

          MOV      DX,ES:[DI+LEVELWIDTH]

          MOV      AX,0A000H
          MOV      ES,AX

          MOV      BX,CS:[WINDOWTOP]
UW1:      PUSH     BX
          PUSH     DX
          SHL      BX,1
          MOV      DI,CS:[SCREENTBL+BX]
          ADD      DI,CS:[WINDOWLEFT]

          PUSH     SI
          PUSH     DI

          MOV      CX,CS:[WINDOWRIGHT]
          SUB      CX,CS:[WINDOWLEFT]
          CLD
REPNE     MOVSB

          POP      DI
          POP      SI

          ADD      DI,CS:[CHARACTER_X]
          SUB      DI,CS:[WINDOWLEFT]

          MOV      AX,DX
          MOV      DX,0000H
          CALL     FARPTR_SI
```

```
                            POP     DX
                            POP     BX

                            CMP     WORD PTR CS:[CHARACTER+2],0000H
                            JE      UW4

                            MOV     AX,CS:[CHARACTER_Y]
                            CMP     BX,AX
                            JL      UW4
                            ADD     AX,CS:[THISCHARDEEP]
                            CMP     BX,AX
                            JGE     UW4

                            PUSH    SI
                            PUSH    DS

                            MOV     SI,WORD PTR CS:[THISCELLPTR+0]
                            MOV     DS,WORD PTR CS:[THISCELLPTR+2]

                            MOV     CX,CS:[THISCHARWIDE]

UW2:                        LODSB
                            CMP     AL,TRANSPARENT
                            JE      UW3

                            MOV     ES:[DI],AL

UW3:                        INC     DI
                            LOOP    UW2

                            ADD     WORD PTR CS:[THISCELLPTR],16

                            POP     DS
                            POP     SI

UW4:                        INC     BX
                            CMP     BX,CS:[WINDOWBOTTOM]
                            JL      UW1

                            POPF
                            POP     ES
                            POP     DS
                            POP     BP
                            RET
_UpdateWindow               ENDP

;BEGIN SLICING TIME
;
;                           ARGUMENTS        POINTER TO LEVEL
;
                            PUBLIC  _StartTime
_StartTime                  PROC    FAR
                            PUSH    BP
                            MOV     BP,SP
                            PUSH    DS
```

```
                PUSH     ES

                MOV      CS:[LEFTOFFSET],0000H
                MOV      CS:[TOPOFFSET],0000H

                MOV      AX,[BP + _AOFF + 0]
                MOV      BX,[BP + _AOFF + 2]

                MOV      WORD PTR CS:[LEVELPOINTER+0],AX
                MOV      WORD PTR CS:[LEVELPOINTER+2],BX

                MOV      AX,351CH
                INT      21H
                MOV      WORD PTR CS:[OLDTIMER+0],BX
                MOV      WORD PTR CS:[OLDTIMER+2],ES

                MOV      AX,251CH
                MOV      DX,OFFSET HANDLER
                PUSH     CS
                POP      DS
                INT      21H

                POP      ES
                POP      DS
                POP      BP
                RET
_StartTime      ENDP

                PUBLIC   _StopTime
_StopTime       PROC     FAR
                PUSH     BP
                MOV      BP,SP
                PUSH     DS
                PUSH     ES

                MOV      AX,251CH
                MOV      DX,WORD PTR CS:[OLDTIMER+0]
                MOV      DS,WORD PTR CS:[OLDTIMER+2]
                INT      21H

                POP      ES
                POP      DS
                POP      BP
                RET
_StopTime       ENDP

;SET UP THE WINDOW DIMENSIONS
;
;               ARGUMENTS        LEFT
;                                TOP
;                                RIGHT
;                                BOTTOM

                PUBLIC   _SetWindowFrame
_SetWindowFrame PROC     FAR
```

```
                              PUSH    BP
                              MOV     BP,SP
                              PUSH    DS
                              PUSH    ES

                              MOV     AX,[BP + _AOFF + 0]
                              MOV     CS:[WINDOWLEFT],AX
                              MOV     AX,[BP + _AOFF + 2]
                              MOV     CS:[WINDOWTOP],AX
                              MOV     AX,[BP + _AOFF + 4]
                              MOV     CS:[WINDOWRIGHT],AX
                              MOV     AX,[BP + _AOFF + 6]
                              MOV     CS:[WINDOWBOTTOM],AX

                              POP     ES
                              POP     DS
                              POP     BP
                              RET
        _SetWindowFrame       ENDP

        ;SET UP THE WINDOW OFFSET
        ;
        ;             ARGUMENTS         LEFT
        ;                               TOP

                              PUBLIC  _SetWindowOff
        _SetWindowOff         PROC    FAR
                              PUSH    BP
                              MOV     BP,SP
                              PUSH    DS
                              PUSH    ES

                              MOV     AX,[BP + _AOFF + 0]
                              MOV     CS:[LEFTOFFSET],AX
                              MOV     AX,[BP + _AOFF + 2]
                              MOV     CS:[TOPOFFSET],AX

                              POP     ES
                              POP     DS
                              POP     BP
                              RET
        _SetWindowOff         ENDP

        ;UPDATE ALL THE OBJECTS
        ;
                              PUBLIC  _UpdateAll
        _UpdateAll            PROC    FAR
                              PUSH    BP
                              MOV     BP,SP
                              PUSH    DS
                              PUSH    ES
                              PUSHF

                              CLI
```

```
                CALL    UPDATE

                POPF
                POP     ES
                POP     DS
                POP     BP
                RET
_UpdateAll      ENDP

;OPEN A DOOR
;
;               ARGUMENTS       POINTER TO A DOOR OBJECT
                PUBLIC  _OpenDoor
_OpenDoor       PROC    FAR
                PUSH    BP
                MOV     BP,SP
                PUSH    DS
                PUSH    ES
                PUSHF

                CLI

                MOV     AX,[BP + _AOFF + 0]
                MOV     WORD PTR CS:[DOORPOINTER+0],AX

                MOV     AX,[BP + _AOFF + 2]
                MOV     WORD PTR CS:[DOORPOINTER+2],AX

                POPF
                POP     ES
                POP     DS
                POP     BP
                RET
_OpenDoor       ENDP

DRAWCELL        PROC    NEAR

                CMP     CS:[CHARACTER_X],-1
                JNE     DC0
                RET

DC0:            CMP     WORD PTR CS:[CHARACTER+2],0000H
                JNE     DC1
                RET

DC1:            PUSH    DI
                PUSH    ES

                CALL    GETCHARACTER

                MOV     AX,0A000H
                MOV     ES,AX

                MOV     AX,SCREENWIDE
                MUL     CS:[CHARACTER_Y]
```

```
                            ADD     AX,CS:[CHARACTER_X]
                            MOV     DI,AX

                            LODSW
                            INC     AX
                            MOV     BX,AX

                            LODSW
                            INC     AX
                            MOV     CX,AX
            DC2:            PUSH    CX

                            PUSH    DI
                            MOV     CX,BX

            DC3:            LODSB
                            CMP     AL,TRANSPARENT
                            JE      DC4
                            MOV     ES:[DI],AL
            DC4:            INC     DI
                            LOOP    DC3

                            POP     DI

                            ADD     DI,SCREENWIDE

                            POP     CX
                            LOOP    DC2

                            POP     ES
                            POP     DI
                            RET
            DRAWCELL        ENDP

            ;UPDATE ALL THE OBJECTS IN THE WINDOW
            UPDATE          PROC    NEAR

                            MOV     SI,WORD PTR CS:[LEVELPOINTER+0]
                            MOV     DS,WORD PTR CS:[LEVELPOINTER+2]

                            MOV     DI,WORD PTR DS:[SI+OBJECTLIST+0]
                            MOV     ES,WORD PTR DS:[SI+OBJECTLIST+2]

                            MOV     AX,ES
                            CMP     AX,0000H
                            JNE     UD1

                            RET

            UD1:            TEST    WORD PTR ES:[DI+ATTRIBUTES],INDICATOR
                            JZ      UD2

                            CMP     ES:[DI+TIMELEFT],0000H
                            JNE     UD1A
```

```
                CALL    SHOWTILE

                CALL    PLACETILE
                CALL    NEXTCELL

                MOV     AX,ES:[DI+TIMESLICE]
                MOV     ES:[DI+TIMELEFT],AX

                JMP     UD2

UD1A:           DEC     WORD PTR ES:[DI+TIMELEFT]

UD2:            TEST    WORD PTR ES:[DI+ATTRIBUTES],DOOR
                JZ      UD3

                CMP     DI,WORD PTR CS:[DOORPOINTER+0]
                JNZ     UD3

                MOV     AX,ES
                CMP     AX,WORD PTR CS:[DOORPOINTER+2]
                JNZ     UD3

                CMP     ES:[DI+TIMELEFT],0000H
                JNE     UD2C

                CALL    SHOWTILE

                CMP     WORD PTR ES:[DI+THISCELL],0003H
                JG      UD2A

                CALL    DRAWCELL

UD2A:           CALL    PLACETILE
                CALL    NEXTCELL

                CMP     WORD PTR ES:[DI+THISCELL],0000H
                JG      UD2B

                MOV     WORD PTR CS:[DOORPOINTER+0],0000H
                MOV     WORD PTR CS:[DOORPOINTER+2],0000H

                PUSH    DI
                PUSH    ES

                PUSH    DS
                MOV     AX,_DATA
                MOV     DS,AX

                MOV     AX,WORD PTR ES:[DI+OBJECTPROC]
                MOV     WORD PTR CS:[PROCPOINTER],AX
                MOV     AX,WORD PTR ES:[DI+OBJECTPROC+2]
                MOV     WORD PTR CS:[PROCPOINTER+2],AX

                CALL    CS:[PROCPOINTER]
```

```
                          POP      DS

                          POP      ES
                          POP      DI

          UD2B:           MOV      AX,ES:[DI+TIMESLICE]
                          MOV      ES:[DI+TIMELEFT],AX

                          JMP      UD3

          UD2C:           DEC      WORD PTR ES:[DI+TIMELEFT]

          UD3:            MOV      AX,WORD PTR ES:[DI+NEXTOBJECT+0]
                          MOV      BX,WORD PTR ES:[DI+NEXTOBJECT+2]

                          MOV      DI,AX
                          MOV      ES,BX

                          CMP      BX,0000H
                          JE       UDX
                          JMP      UD1

          UDX:            RET
          UPDATE          ENDP

          ;SHOW A TILE - THE OBJECT POINTER IS IN ES:DI
          SHOWTILE        PROC     NEAR

                          PUSH     SI
                          PUSH     DI

                          PUSH     DS
                          PUSH     ES

                          PUSH     BP

                          MOV      BX,ES:[DI+THISCELL]
                          SHL      BX,1
                          SHL      BX,1

          ST1:            MOV      SI,WORD PTR ES:[DI+CELLPOINTER+BX+0]
                          MOV      DS,WORD PTR ES:[DI+CELLPOINTER+BX+2]

                          LODSW
                          INC      AX
                          MOV      DX,AX

                          LODSW
                          INC      AX
                          MOV      CX,AX

                          MOV      BX,ES:[DI+FRAME+2]
                          SUB      BX,CS:[TOPOFFSET]
                          ADD      BX,CS:[WINDOWTOP]
                          MOV      BP,ES:[DI+FRAME+0]
```

```
                    SUB     BP,CS:[LEFTOFFSET]
                    ADD     BP,CS:[WINDOWLEFT]

                    MOV     AX,0A000H
                    MOV     ES,AX
     ST2:           PUSH    CX
                    PUSH    BX

                    CMP     BX,CS:[WINDOWTOP]
                    JL      ST5
                    CMP     BX,CS:[WINDOWBOTTOM]
                    JGE     ST5

                    SHL     BX,1
                    MOV     DI,CS:[SCREENTBL+BX]

                    MOV     AX,BP
                    ADD     DI,AX

                    MOV     CX,DX
                    CLD

                    PUSH    DX

                    MOV     DX,BP

     ST3:           LODSB
                    CMP     AL,TRANSPARENT
                    JE      ST4
                    CMP     DX,CS:[WINDOWLEFT]
                    JL      ST4
                    CMP     DX,CS:[WINDOWRIGHT]
                    JGE     ST4
                    MOV     ES:[DI],AL
     ST4:           INC     DI
                    INC     DX
                    LOOP    ST3

                    POP     DX

                    JMP     ST6

     ST5:           ADD     SI,DX

     ST6:           POP     BX
                    POP     CX
                    INC     BX
                    LOOP    ST2

                    POP     BP

                    POP     ES
                    POP     DS
                    POP     DI
```

```
                            POP      SI

                            RET
          SHOWTILE          ENDP

          ;PLACE A TILE - THE OBJECT POINTER IS IN ES:DI
          PLACETILE         PROC     NEAR

                            PUSH     SI
                            PUSH     DI

                            PUSH     DS
                            PUSH     ES

                            PUSH     BP

                            MOV      BX,ES:[DI+THISCELL]
                            SHL      BX,1
                            SHL      BX,1

                            MOV      SI,WORD PTR ES:[DI+CELLPOINTER+BX+0]
                            MOV      DS,WORD PTR ES:[DI+CELLPOINTER+BX+2]

                            LODSW
                            INC      AX
                            MOV      DX,AX              ;GET CELL WIDTH

                            LODSW
                            INC      AX
                            MOV      CX,AX              ;GET CELL DEPTH

                            MOV      BX,ES:[DI+FRAME+2]
                            SUB      BX,CS:[WINDOWTOP]
                            ADD      BX,CS:[WINDOWTOP]
                            MOV      BP,ES:[DI+FRAME+0]
                            SUB      BP,CS:[WINDOWLEFT]
                            ADD      BP,CS:[WINDOWLEFT]

          PT1:              PUSH     BX
                            PUSH     CX
                            MOV      DI,WORD PTR CS:[LEVELPOINTER+0]
                            MOV      ES,WORD PTR CS:[LEVELPOINTER+2]

                            MOV      AX,WORD PTR ES:[DI+LEVELDEPTH]
                            CMP      BX,AX
                            JGE      PT4

                            PUSH     DX
                            MOV      AX,ES:[DI+LEVELWIDTH]
                            MOV      CX,AX
                            MOV      DX,0000H
                            MUL      BX

                            MOV      BX,WORD PTR ES:[DI+BITMAP+0]
                            MOV      ES,WORD PTR ES:[DI+BITMAP+2]
```

```
                MOV       DI,BX

                CALL      FARPTR_DI
                POP       DX
                ADD       DI,BP

                MOV       BX,CX
                MOV       CX,DX

                PUSH      DX

                MOV       DX,BP

PT2:            LODSB
                CMP       AL,TRANSPARENT
                JE        PT3
                CMP       DX,BX
                JGE       PT3
                MOV       ES:[DI],AL
PT3:            INC       DI
                INC       DX
                LOOP      PT2

                POP       DX

PT4:            POP       CX
                POP       BX
                INC       BX
                LOOP      PT1

                POP       BP

                POP       ES
                POP       DS

                POP       DI
                POP       SI

                RET
PLACETILE       ENDP

;INCREMENT THE CELL COUNTER - THE CELL POINTER IS IN ES:DI
NEXTCELL        PROC      NEAR
                INC       WORD PTR ES:[DI+THISCELL]
                MOV       AX,ES:[DI+THISCELL]
                CMP       AX,ES:[DI+CELLCOUNT]
                JL        NC1
                MOV       WORD PTR ES:[DI+THISCELL],0000H
NC1:            RET
NEXTCELL        ENDP

;ADD ES:SI AND DX:AX
FARPTR_SI       PROC      NEAR

                MOV       BX,SI          ;SEGMENT += OFFSET / 16
```

```
                        MOV     CL,4
                        SHR     BX,CL
                        MOV     CX,DS
                        ADD     CX,BX
                        MOV     DS,CX

                        AND     SI,000FH        ;OFFSET &= 000FH

                        MOV     BX,AX           ;OFFSET += N & 000FH
                        AND     BX,000FH
                        ADD     SI,BX

                        MOV     CL,4            ;SEG += N / 16
                        SHR     AX,CL
                        MOV     BX,DX
                        AND     BX,000FH
                        MOV     CL,12
                        SHL     BX,CL
                        OR      AX,BX

                        MOV     BX,DS
                        ADD     BX,AX
                        MOV     DS,BX

                        RET
        FARPTR_SI       ENDP

        ;ADD ES:DI AND DX:AX
        FARPTR_DI       PROC    NEAR

                        MOV     BX,DI           ;SEGMENT += OFFSET / 16
                        MOV     CL,4
                        SHR     BX,CL
                        MOV     CX,ES
                        ADD     CX,BX
                        MOV     ES,CX

                        AND     DI,000FH        ;OFFSET &= 000FH

                        MOV     BX,AX           ;OFFSET += N & 000FH
                        AND     BX,000FH
                        ADD     DI,BX

                        MOV     CL,4            ;SEG += N / 16
                        SHR     AX,CL
                        MOV     BX,DX
                        AND     BX,000FH
                        MOV     CL,12
                        SHL     BX,CL
                        OR      AX,BX

                        MOV     BX,ES
                        ADD     BX,AX
                        MOV     ES,BX
                        RET
```

```
FARPTR_DI       ENDP

HANDLER         PROC    FAR
                PUSH    AX
                PUSH    BX
                PUSH    CX
                PUSH    DX
                PUSH    SI
                PUSH    DI
                PUSH    DS
                PUSH    ES

                CLI

                CALL    UPDATE

                STI

                POP     ES
                POP     DS
                POP     DI
                POP     SI
                POP     DX
                POP     CX
                POP     BX
                POP     AX
                IRET
HANDLER         ENDP

;RETURN THE CHARACTER ATTRIBUTES:
;               AX = THE CURRENT ACTION
;               BX = THE WIDTH OF THE CURRENT CELL
;               CX = THE DEPTH OF THE CURRENT CELL
;               DX = THE NUMBER OF THE CURRENT CELL
;               SI:DS = THE CHARACTER BITMAP
GETCHARACTER    PROC    NEAR
                PUSH    DI
                PUSH    ES

                MOV     DI,WORD PTR CS:[CHARACTER+0]
                MOV     ES,WORD PTR CS:[CHARACTER+2]

                MOV     AX,ES:[DI+ACTION]

                CMP     AX,DOWALKLEFT
                JNE     GC1

                MOV     BX,ES:[DI+LEFTFRAME+4]
                SUB     BX,ES:[DI+LEFTFRAME+0]

                MOV     CX,ES:[DI+LEFTFRAME+6]
                SUB     CX,ES:[DI+LEFTFRAME+2]

                MOV     DX,ES:[DI+THISCHARCELL]
```

```
                         PUSH    BX

                         MOV     BX,ES:[DI+THISCHARCELL]
                         SHL     BX,1
                         SHL     BX,1

                         MOV     SI,WORD PTR ES:[DI+WALKLEFT+0+BX]
                         MOV     DS,WORD PTR ES:[DI+WALKLEFT+2+BX]

                         POP     BX

                         JMP     GCX

                GC1:     CMP     AX,DOWALKRIGHT
                         JNE     GC2

                         MOV     BX,ES:[DI+RIGHTFRAME+4]
                         SUB     BX,ES:[DI+RIGHTFRAME+0]

                         MOV     CX,ES:[DI+RIGHTFRAME+6]
                         SUB     CX,ES:[DI+RIGHTFRAME+2]

                         MOV     DX,ES:[DI+THISCHARCELL]

                         PUSH    BX

                         MOV     BX,ES:[DI+THISCHARCELL]
                         SHL     BX,1
                         SHL     BX,1

                         MOV     SI,WORD PTR ES:[DI+WALKRIGHT+0+BX]
                         MOV     DS,WORD PTR ES:[DI+WALKRIGHT+2+BX]

                         POP     BX

                         JMP     GCX

                GC2:     CMP     AX,DOJUMPLEFT
                         JNE     GC3

                         MOV     BX,ES:[DI+LEFTJUMPFRAME+4]
                         SUB     BX,ES:[DI+LEFTJUMPFRAME+0]

                         MOV     CX,ES:[DI+LEFTJUMPFRAME+6]
                         SUB     CX,ES:[DI+LEFTJUMPFRAME+2]

                         MOV     DX,ES:[DI+THISCHARCELL]

                         MOV     SI,WORD PTR ES:[DI+JUMPLEFT+0]
                         MOV     DS,WORD PTR ES:[DI+JUMPLEFT+2]

                         JMP     GCX

                GC3:     CMP     AX,DOJUMPRIGHT
                         JNE     GC4
```

```
                    MOV       BX,ES:[DI+RIGHTJUMPFRAME+4]
                    SUB       BX,ES:[DI+RIGHTJUMPFRAME+0]

                    MOV       CX,ES:[DI+RIGHTJUMPFRAME+6]
                    SUB       CX,ES:[DI+RIGHTJUMPFRAME+2]

                    MOV       DX,ES:[DI+THISCHARCELL]

                    MOV       SI,WORD PTR ES:[DI+JUMPRIGHT+0]
                    MOV       DS,WORD PTR ES:[DI+JUMPRIGHT+2]

                    JMP       GCX

GC4:                MOV       AX,_DATA             ;THIS SETS UP NON-NASTY
                    MOV       DS,AX                ;VALUES IN THE EVENT OF
                    MOV       SI,OFFSET DUMMY_CELL ;A BAD VALUE IN THE CELL

                    MOV       BX,0000H
                    MOV       CX,0000H
                    MOV       DX,0000H

GCX:                POP       ES
                    POP       DI
                    RET
GETCHARACTER        ENDP

UPDATECOUNTERS      PROC      NEAR
                    PUSH      DI
                    PUSH      ES

                    MOV       DI,WORD PTR CS:[CHARACTER+0]
                    MOV       ES,WORD PTR CS:[CHARACTER+2]

                    MOV       AX,ES:[DI+ACTION]

                    CMP       AX,DOWALKLEFT
                    JNE       UPC1

                    INC       WORD PTR ES:[DI+THISCHARCELL]
                    MOV       AX,ES:[DI+THISCHARCELL]
                    CMP       AX,ES:[DI+MAXLEFT]
                    JL        UPC1
                    MOV       WORD PTR ES:[DI+THISCHARCELL],0000H
                    JMP       UPC2

UPC1:               CMP       AX,DOWALKRIGHT
                    JNE       UPC2

                    INC       WORD PTR ES:[DI+THISCHARCELL]
                    MOV       AX,ES:[DI+THISCHARCELL]
                    CMP       AX,ES:[DI+MAXRIGHT]
                    JL        UPC2
                    MOV       WORD PTR ES:[DI+THISCHARCELL],0000H

UPC2:               POP       ES
```

```
8-11              POP     DI
Continued.        RET
UPDATECOUNTERS    ENDP

PROCPOINTER       DD      0

LEVELPOINTER      DD      0
OLDTIMER          DD      0

THISCELLPTR       DD      0
THISCHARWIDE      DW      0
THISCHARDEEP      DW      0

SCREENTBL         LABEL   WORD
                  SCREENTABLE SCREENWIDE SCREENDEEP

WINDOWLEFT        DW      0
WINDOWTOP         DW      0
WINDOWRIGHT       DW      0
WINDOWBOTTOM      DW      0

LEFTOFFSET        DW      0
TOPOFFSET         DW      0

DOORPOINTER       DD      0

CHARACTER         DD      0

CHARACTER_X       DW      -1
CHARACTER_Y       DW      -1

TIMESLICE_TEXT    ENDS

DGROUP            GROUP   _DATA,_BSS
_DATA             SEGMENT WORD PUBLIC 'DATA'

DUMMY_CELL        DW      2 DUP (0)

_DATA             ENDS

_BSS              SEGMENT WORD PUBLIC 'BSS'

_BSS              ENDS

                  END
```

One of the important things to note about TIMESLIC.ASM is that it has STRUC equivalents to the data struct objects used in the C language programs that will call it. If you change one, make very certain you change the other, or all sorts of odd things may happen.

The TIMESLIC.ASM code handles the graphic manipulation and the time slice functions of Alice. The graphic functions are actually pretty elementary and are included in TIMESLIC.ASM simply because they can be performed more rapidly in assembly language. The time slice code is genuinely obtuse.

In making the indicator objects appear to move, for example, independent of Alice's peregrinations, it's essential that they be treated as a sort of background task. There's a very crude mechanism for doing this sort of thing on a PC. No matter what generation of PC you have, a hardware timer will cause an INT 1CH instruction to be executed by the processor about eighteen times per second. In most cases, the vector for this interrupt will point to a dummy return up in the BIOS, such that it does nothing. However, you can hook it to cause it to perform a periodic task behind the back of whatever software is running at the time. One common use for this facility is that of maintaining a screen clock.

There are several important considerations for using the clock interrupt like this. It must preserve the machine state, such that when it seizes control of the system for an instant, does what it wants to do, and returns control to the primary application running on your computer, nothing will appear to have changed. It must also be careful about how much work it undertakes to perform: if it hogs too much of the system's resources, the computer as a whole will seem to slow down or function erratically.

The time slicing for Alice is fairly elementary, and is abetted by the knowledge that the foreground task it will be interrupting will be the game itself. The processor requirements of the game are quite modest; most of the time Alice will be standing around doing nothing, waiting for a key press.

Time slicing is initiated by calling the StartTime function in TIMESLIC.ASM. This should be passed a pointer to the LEVEL object that defines the room to be played. Aside from storing the pointer, StartTime seizes the 1CH interrupt vector, storing the original vector so it can be replaced when the game concludes. The StopTime function, to be called when the room terminates, will replace the old vector.

It's very important to call StopTime before the game ends. If you don't, or if you break out of the program unexpectedly, the time slice function will continue to be called—even after its code in memory has been overwritten by something else.

When StartTime has run, the 1CH interrupt vector will point to the HANDLER function in TIMESLIC.ASM. This illustrates how the machine state is preserved. It calls the UPDATE code to handle the screen and bitmap manipulation involved in playing the game.

While it won't be quite as apparent in assembly language, UPDATE walks the OBJECT list of the current level, performing whatever graphic manipulations as are required along the way—just like its C language counterparts have done in the programs earlier in this chapter. This involves two sorts of objects: to wit, those with the attributes INDICATOR and DOOR. When it encounters an indicator, it will decrement the timeleft element of its OBJECT and, if the time between cells has run out, display the next cell in its list. The number of time slices between cells was set in the LVL file that defined the object.

Those objects with the attribute DOOR are handled a bit differently. Normally they're largely ignored by UPDATE. However, if the PLAYGAME code wants to open a door, it sets the DOORPOINTER element to point to the door in question by calling `OpenDoor`. On the next time slice, UPDATE will note that this pointer is no longer null and will cycle once through the door animation cells. Unlike indicator objects, which run continuously, a door only runs once, at which point UPDATE will reset the DOORPOINTER to NULL. It will also call the OBJECTPROC function in the OBJECT that defines the door, which tells PLAYGAME that the door has completed its travel.

Watch this code and the C language calling function carefully. Note that when PLAYGAME calls `OpenDoor`, the door will be closed and will remain closed for a substantial part of a second until the current time slice expires. Several more passes through the code in `PlayGame` can take place before the door completes its travel and the level ends. Multitasking—of which this game is a crude form—can be somewhat tricky to keep track of if you're used to thinking of programs as only doing one thing at a time.

The other fairly involved function in TIMESLIC.ASM is `PlaceCharacter`, which handles moving Alice around. In fact, it's nowhere near as complex as the time slicing code was. It does two things each time it's called: it replaces the area behind the existing cell and paints a new one.

The code in `PlaceCharacter` is vastly simplified—and greatly sped up—by the application of a bit of simple arithmetic. The bitmap that defines a room will usually be larger than 64K, which entails the use of pointer normalization to address it. There are assembly language versions of the `farPtr` function discussed earlier in this book included in TIMESLIC.ASM to handle this. However, for reasons of finite memory, a 256-color room bitmap can't be much larger than 640 by 480 pixels. Alice herself is 32 pixels high, which means that the area she occupies on the screen and in the bitmap can require no more than 32 lines. A 32-line band of the room bitmap will fit in 64K. As such, while a call to one of the FARPTR functions will be required to find the first line in the bitmap where Alice resides, the rest of the pointer manipulation as she's drawn or erased can be done with 16-bit numbers.

The first section of `PlaceCharacter` handles erasing the existing cell on the screen by copying the appropriate part of the room bitmap over it. This involves finding a pointer to the bitmap within the struct pointed to by LEVELPOINTER. Handling complex data structures is nowhere near as elegant in assembly language as it is in C. Once the location of the area of the bitmap has been calculated, moving its lines to the appropriate area of the screen is pretty elementary. The screen, at 320 by 200 pixels, can always be addressed using 16-bit arithmetic.

The second part of `PlaceCharacter`, starting at the label PC2, is even simpler. Neither the character cells nor the screen buffer require a call to FARPTR. The only important consideration is that pixels in the cells that are set to color 255—that is, transparent—not be drawn on the screen.

Note that `UpdateWindow` also performs the function of `PlaceCharacter`—at least, of the second half of it. In order to make the animation in `Alice` not appear to flicker as the playing window is repainted, it's essential that Alice be redrawn as the window is updated, rather than after the update is completed.

If you work your way through the functions in TIMESLIC.ASM you'll find the periodic use of BP in a somewhat uncommon application—that of a normal arithmetic register. While there's no reason why it can't be used as such, it's usually reserved for addressing arguments on the stack. Its use this way takes into account the fairly limited number of 8088 machine registers, and the significant speed penalty the processor imposes on instructions that have to address memory. Functions that work exclusively using values maintained in the machine registers will run quite a bit faster, an important consideration in graphic code for a game. In a pinch, you can press the BP register into service. In doing so, however, make sure that you either no longer require its services to address the stack or that you preserve it until it's required again.

It seems at times that the thing that impresses people about graphic adventure games is their scale: such games must be massive to be truly engaging. Massive games are typically implemented using massive amounts of code and data, often crowding the limits of the system hardware in the process.

The game's afoot

By their nature, books can offer a limited amount of source code. Aside from being largely unreadable, 1600-page books usually aren't all that popular among publishers. As was noted earlier, this chapter has provided an introduction to writing games; it certainly hasn't explored the subject in depth.

In her inception, Alice began amidst a single floppy disk worth of source code. Her graphics and code—including a world editor, sound effects files, and so on—now occupy most of a twenty megabyte floptical disk, with little end in sight.

You can apply the code and techniques explored in this chapter to games of your own devising. However, unlike the other aspects of this book, plan on having to expand it quite a lot. Impressively monumental games by their nature require a monumental effort to complete.

A Detecting super VGA cards

Because super VGA applications must be equipped with drivers specific to the hardware they'll be driving, it's important to know which super VGA card one has. This is complicated enormously by large numbers of third-party cards, in which the name of the card has nothing much to do with the name of the manufacturer of the card's chip set. Very often, low-cost super VGA cards—while quite capable and based on fairly advanced chips—have names no more illuminating than "VGA card 1024."

The Desktop Paint 256 application on the companion disk for this book is typical of software that must know the specific manufacturer of the super VGA chips set that it's to drive, lest it be reduced to little more than a pile of bites and a nice picture of a tree frog. It deals with this problem using a utility called VGACARD.COM, which seeks to analyze the nature of one's display hardware programmatically. While this is a process fraught with perils—it's not uncommon to find that the test for one type of chip set disables or confuses chips from other manufacturers—you can create a function to identify a respectably large number of chips. While hardly exhaustive, VGACARD will sort out all the card types covered in this book and is fairly reliable.

The appendix will present the source code for VGACARD, as well as briefly cover its function.

To start, let's test for the presence of a basic VGA BIOS. The most rudimentary check is to look for the existence of an extension BIOS at location C000:0000H. This can be identified by the bytes 55H and AAH at this location. As it turns out, however, this isn't really a very good test to rely on, as some unconventional systems don't locate their VGA BIOSs here (one such system being the IBM PS/2).

A better approach is to let the BIOS tell you about itself. This bit of code will indicate the existence of a VGA BIOS of some sort in your system:

```
MOV   AX,1B00H
MOV   BX,0000H
MOV   DI, OFFSET BUFFER
PUSH  CS
POP   ES
INT   10H
```

The nature of BUFFER is immaterial at the moment, so long as it's at least 64 bytes long. When this call returns, AL will contain the value 1BH if there's a VGA card in the system and something else—most likely, a 0—if not.

The information in the buffer filled in by this call will tell you a bewildering number of things about the display hardware in your system. For this application, the only thing of immediate interest is the list of supported modes. You can find this by creating a far pointer from the first four bytes of the buffer and testing bits where the pointer points. If ES:DI is the pointer, this will be true if mode 12H 640 by 480 16-color graphics are supported:

```
TEST BYTE PTR ES:[DI+2],04H
```

This will be true if mode 13H 320 by 200 by 256-color graphics are supported:

```
TEST BYTE PTR ES:[DI+2],08H
```

You might want to consult an IBM ROM BIOS reference book for a complete list of characteristics of this buffer. All VGA cards should pass forgoing three checks.

The next thing VGACARD checks for is the presence of a VESA BIOS. As was mentioned earlier in Chapter 3, it's pretty easy to do this and to work out which VESA modes are available.

The rest of VGACARD deals with the exceedingly tricky prospect of testing for specific chip sets and their attendant BIOSs. Because a super VGA chip set is always accompanied by its specific BIOS, testing for a specific BIOS is just as reliable as testing for a chip itself and is usually a good deal easier. Not all super VGA BIOSs can be identified, however.

The simplest BIOS to check for is that of Paradise cards. This includes all sorts of generic cards, Western Digital's own cards, and several third-party cards, such as the Diamond Speedstar 24X. If you look at location C000:007DH on a Paradise card, you'll find the string "VGA=".

Testing for ATI cards is equally effortless. You'll find the string "761295520" at location C000:0031H in all ATI BIOSs.

The Trident cards are a bit trickier. The Trident BIOS does not provide a signature string as the Paradise and ATI BIOSs do. You can, however, meddle with a Trident chip's registers to make it return a revision number, which is reasonably reliable. Note that if you read a register that doesn't exist, it will always return FFH; this is not one of the legal Trident revision numbers.

The Trident revision number can be read from port 03C4H, index 0BH. The source code for VGACARD illustrates which chips the various return values correspond to.

The Oak Technologies cards are a bit of a poser, especially as documentation about how their chip sets work is all but impossible to find. There does not seem to be a signature string in the Oak Technologies BIOS, but you can test the Oak chips themselves with a bit of register fiddling. It's illustrated in VGACARD.

Honesty bids me note that I have no idea what this code actually tests. I found the test by tracing through the first few instructions of the Oak Technologies VESA TSR. Inasmuch as the VESA TSR knew whether it was being loaded on a machine with an Oak card—and would refuse to load if one wasn't present—it seemed reasonable to assume that it included a test for the chip set. This turned out to be the case.

The Tseng Labs chips turn out to be the all-around nastiest of the chip sets covered in this book to test for. There's a fairly simple test described in the Tseng Labs documentation, which involves reading the miscellaneous functions register, flipping bit four, writing it back, and reading it again. If the bit remains flipped, the card is based on a Tseng Labs chip set.

Unfortunately, this test as it stands also blanks the card. You can prevent it from doing this by ORing the index to the miscellaneous functions register with 20H. The index to this register is 16H. If you use 36H instead, the screen doesn't blank. Thanks to Larry Lefkowitz at Tseng Labs for this one.

Figure A-1 illustrates the source code for VGACARD. This is exactly the same program that comes with Desktop Paint 256; you no doubt will want to modify it for your own uses. This should be assembled to produce a .COM file.

A-1
The source code for
VGACARD.

```
;
;                    VGA Card identifier
;                    Copyright (c) 1992 Alchemy Mindworks Inc.
;

CODE                 SEGMENT
                     ASSUME  CS:CODE,DS:CODE

OK                   EQU     0                    ;RETURNED ERROR LEVEL
                                                  ;CODES
ERROR                EQU     1

;THIS MACRO GETS BACK TO DOS
EXITPROGRAM          MACRO   ARG
                     MOV     AH,4CH
                     MOV     AL,ARG
                     INT     21H
                     ENDM

;THIS MACRO DISPLAYS A MESSAGE IN ARG
MESSAGE              MACRO   ARG
                     LOCAL   LAB1,LAB2
                     JMP     LAB2
```

```
LAB1:           DB        ARG
LAB2:           MOV       AX,4000H
                MOV       BX,0001H
                MOV       CX,LAB2-LAB1
                MOV       DX,OFFSET LAB1
                PUSH      CS
                POP       DS
                INT       21H
                ENDM


;DISPLAY MESSAGE ARG2 IF AX = ARG1
TESTMESSAGE     MACRO     ARG1,ARG2
                LOCAL     LAB1,LAB2,LAB3
                JMP       LAB2
LAB1:           DB        ARG2
LAB2:           CMP       AX,ARG1
                JNE       LAB3
                MOV       AX,4000H
                MOV       BX,0001H
                MOV       CX,LAB2-LAB1
                MOV       DX,OFFSET LAB1
                PUSH      CS
                POP       DS
                INT       21H
LAB3:
                ENDM


;DISPLAY THE MESSAGE POINTED TO BY DS:SI - A NULL TERMINATED STRING
PRINTSTRING     MACRO
                MOV       CX,0000H

                PUSH      SI

LAB1:           LODSB
                CMP       AL,00H
                JE        LAB2
                INC       CX
                JMP       LAB1

LAB2:           MOV       AX,4000H
                MOV       BX,0001H
                POP       DX
                INT       21H
                ENDM

;DO A LONG LOOP
LNGLOOP         MACRO     ARG1
                LOCAL     LAB1
                DEC       CX
                CMP       CX,0000H
                JE        LAB1
                JMP       ARG1
LAB1:
                ENDM
```

```
        ;DO A LONG JE
        LNGJE           MACRO   ARG1
                        LOCAL   LAB1
                        JNE     LAB1
                        JMP     ARG1
        LAB1:
                        ENDM


        ;DO A LONG JNE
        LNGJNE          MACRO   ARG1
                        LOCAL   LAB1
                        JE      LAB1
                        JMP     ARG1
        LAB1:
                        ENDM

                        ORG     100H

        VGACARD         PROC    FAR

        START:          MESSAGE <"Display card analyzer copyright (c) 1992 Alchemy Mindworks
                                Inc.",13,10>
                        MESSAGE <"                                      ",13,10,13,10>

                        ;GET THE VGA DISPLAY INFORMATION. IF IT'S NOT AVAILABLE,
                        ;THIS ISN'T A VGA CARD
                        MOV     AX,1B00H
                        MOV     BX,0000H
                        MOV     DI,OFFSET ENDPROGRAM
                        PUSH    CS
                        POP     ES
                        INT     10H

                        CMP     AL,1BH
                        JE      VGC1

                        MESSAGE <"No VGA BIOS was detected in this system.",13,10>

                        EXITPROGRAM ERROR

        VGC1:           MESSAGE <"A standard VGA BIOS was detected in this system.",13,10>

                        ;GET THE MODE TABLE POINTER
                        MOV     DI,WORD PTR [ENDPROGRAM+0]
                        MOV     ES,WORD PTR [ENDPROGRAM+2]

                        ;LOOK FOR THE 640 BY 480 16-COLOUR MODE
                        TEST    BYTE PTR ES:[DI+2],04H
                        JZ      VGC2

                        MESSAGE <"Mode 10H is supported - 640 by 480 pixels at 16 colours.",13,10>

        VGC2:           TEST    BYTE PTR ES:[DI+2],08H
                        JZ      VGC3
```

```
                    ;LOOK FOR THE 320 BY 200 256-COLOUR MODE
                    MESSAGE <"Mode 13H is supported - 320 by 200 pixels at 320 colours.",13,10>

                    MESSAGE <13,10>

                    ;SEE IF THERE'S A VESA BIOS
VGC3:               MOV     AX,4F00H
                    MOV     DI,OFFSET ENDPROGRAM
                    PUSH    CS
                    POP     ES
                    INT     10H

                    CMP     AX,004FH
                    LNGJNE  VGC5

                    ;IF THERE IS, USE VESA IF ALL ELSE FAILS
                    MOV     CS:[VESAFLAG],01H

                    MESSAGE <"                                        ",13,10>
                    MESSAGE <"A VESA BIOS has been detected.",13,10>
                    MESSAGE <"The manufacturer is ">

                    ;PRINT THE OEM STRING FROM THE VESA BLOCK
                    MOV     SI,WORD PTR [ENDPROGRAM+6]
                    MOV     DS,WORD PTR [ENDPROGRAM+8]
                    PRINTSTRING

                    MESSAGE <13,10>

                    ;GET A POINTER TO THE MODE LIST
                    MOV     SI,WORD PTR [ENDPROGRAM+14]
                    MOV     DS,WORD PTR [ENDPROGRAM+16]

                    ;WALK THE LIST AND SEE WHICH GRAPHIC MODES ARE SUPPORTED
VGC4:               LODSW
                    CMP     AX,0FFFFH
                    JE      VGC5

                    PUSH    SI
                    PUSH    DS
                    CALL    SHOWVESAMODE
                    POP     DS
                    POP     SI
                    JMP     VGC4

                    ;TEST FOR A PARADISE CARD
VGC5:               MESSAGE <13,10,                          ",13,10,13,10>
                    MOV     AX,0C000H
                    MOV     ES,AX
                    MOV     DI,007DH

                    MOV     SI,OFFSET PARADISE_ID
                    PUSH    CS
                    POP     DS
```

```
                    MOV     CX,4
                    CALL    MEMCMP
                    JNE     VGC6

        MESSAGE <"This appears to be a Paradise VGA card.",13,10>

        EXITPROGRAM OK

                    ;TEST FOR AN ATI CARD
VGC6:               MOV     AX,0C000H
                    MOV     ES,AX
                    MOV     DI,0031H

                    MOV     SI,OFFSET ATI_ID
                    PUSH    CS
                    POP     DS

                    MOV     CX,9
                    CALL    MEMCMP
                    JNE     VGC7

        MESSAGE <"This appears to be an ATI VGA card.",13,10>

        EXITPROGRAM OK

                    ;TEST FOR A TRIDENT CARD
VGC7:               MOV     DX,03C4H
                    MOV     AL,0BH
                    CALL    GETPORTBYTE

                    CMP     AL,02H
                    JNE     VGC7A

        MESSAGE <"This appears to be a Trident 8800 card (unsupported by Desktop Paint 256).",13,10>

        EXITPROGRAM OK

VGC7A:              CMP     AL,03H
                    JNE     VGC7B

        MESSAGE <"This appears to be a Trident 8900 card.",13,10>

        EXITPROGRAM OK

VGC7B:              CMP     AL,04H
                    JNE     VGC7C

        MESSAGE <"This appears to be a Trident 8900C card.",13,10>

        EXITPROGRAM OK

VGC7C:              CMP     AL,23H
                    JNE     VGC7D

        MESSAGE <"This appears to be a Trident 9000 card.",13,10>
```

```
                   EXITPROGRAM OK

VGC7D:             CMP      AL,13H
                   JNE      VGC7E

                   MESSAGE <"This appears to be a Trident 9000 card.",13,10>

                   EXITPROGRAM OK

VGC7E:             CMP      AL,83H
                   JNE      VGC7F

                   MESSAGE <"This appears to be a Trident 9200 card.",13,10>

                   EXITPROGRAM OK

VGC7F:             CMP      AL,93H
                   JNE      VGC8

                   MESSAGE <"This appears to be a Trident 9100 card.",13,10>

                   EXITPROGRAM OK

                   ;TEST FOR AN OAK CARD
VGC8:              MOV      DX,03DEH
                   MOV      AL,1AH
                   OUT      DX,AL
                   NOP
                   IN       AL,DX
                   CMP      AL,5AH
                   JE       VGC8A
                   CMP      AL,7AH
                   JE       VGC8A
                   JMP      VGC9

VGC8A:             MESSAGE <"This appears to be an Oak Technologies card.",13,10>

                   EXITPROGRAM OK

                   ;TEST FOR A VIDEO 7 CARD
VGC9:              MOV      BX,0000H
                   MOV      AX,6F00H
                   INT      10H
                   CMP      BX,5637H;'V7'
                   JNE      VGC10

                   MESSAGE <"This appears to be a Headland Video Seven card.",13,10>

                   EXITPROGRAM OK

                   ;TEST FOR A TSENG LABS CARD
VGC10:             MOV      CS:[TSENGKEY],03B8H
                   MOV      CS:[TSENGSTAT],03BAH

                   MOV      DX,03CCH         ;TEST FOR COLOUR OR MONOCHROME
```

```
                    IN      AL,DX

                    TEST    AL,01H
                    JZ      VGC10A

                    MOV     CS:[TSENGKEY],03D8H
                    MOV     CS:[TSENGSTAT],03DAH

        VGC10A:     MOV     DX,03BFH              ;SET THE KEY
                    MOV     AL,03H
                    OUT     DX,AL

                    MOV     DX,CS:[TSENGKEY]
                    MOV     AL,0A0H
                    OUT     DX,AL

                    MOV     DX,CS:[TSENGSTAT]     ;03DAH - SET TOGGLE TO INDEX
                    IN      AL,DX

                    MOV     DX,03C0H
                    IN      AX,DX

                    JMP     $+2                   ;PAUSE MOMENTARILY

                    MOV     DX,03C0H              ;SET THE INDEX TO 16H
                    MOV     AL,36H
                    OUT     DX,AL

                    MOV     DX,03C1H              ;READ THE PORT
                    IN      AL,DX

                    JMP     $+2                   ;PAUSE MOMENTARILY

                    MOV     BL,AL                 ;SAVE THE VALUE

                    XOR     AL,10H                ;CHANGE BIT 4
                    PUSH    AX

                    MOV     DX,CS:[TSENGSTAT]     ;03DAH - SET TOGGLE TO INDEX
                    IN      AL,DX

                    JMP     $+2                   ;PAUSE MOMENTARILY

                    MOV     DX,03C0H              ;SET THE INDEX
                    MOV     AL,36H
                    OUT     DX,AL

                    JMP     $+2                   ;PAUSE MOMENTARILY

                    MOV     DX,03C0H              ;WRITE THE NEW DATA
                    POP     AX
                    OUT     DX,AL

                    JMP     $+2                   ;PAUSE MOMENTARILY
```

```
          MOV     DX,CS:[TSENGSTAT]        ;03DAH - SET TOGGLE TO INDEX
          IN      AL,DX

          JMP     $+2                      ;PAUSE MOMENTARILY

          MOV     DX,03C0H                 ;SET THE INDEX
          MOV     AL,36H
          OUT     DX,AL

          JMP     $+2                      ;PAUSE MOMENTARILY

          MOV     DX,03C1H                 ;GET THE REGISTER BACK
          IN      AL,DX
          MOV     BH,AL

          JMP     $+2                      ;PAUSE MOMENTARILY

          MOV     DX,CS:[TSENGSTAT]        ;03DAH - SET TOGGLE TO INDEX
          IN      AL,DX

          MOV     DX,03C0H                 ;SET THE INDEX
          MOV     AL,36H
          OUT     DX,AL

          JMP     $+2                      ;PAUSE MOMENTARILY

          MOV     DX,03C0H                 ;PUT THE OLD VALUE BACK
          MOV     AL,BL
          OUT     DX,AL

          JMP     $+2                      ;PAUSE MOMENTARILY

          CMP     BL,BH                    ;SEE IF ANYTHING CHANGED
          LNGJE   VGC11

VGC10E:   MOV     CS:[TSENGKEY],03B0H

          MOV     DX,03CCH                 ;TEST FOR COLOUR OR MONOCHROME
          IN      AL,DX

          TEST    AL,01H
          JZ      VGC10F

          MOV     CS:[TSENGKEY],03D0H

VGC10F:   MOV     DX,CS:[TSENGKEY]
          ADD     DX,4
          MOV     AL,33H
          OUT     DX,AL

          JMP     $+2

          MOV     DX,CS:[TSENGKEY]
          ADD     DX,5
          IN      AL,DX
```

```
JMP       $+2

MOV       BL,AL

MOV       DX,CS:[TSENGKEY]
ADD       DX,5
XOR       AL,OFH
OUT       DX,AL

JMP       $+2

MOV       DX,CS:[TSENGKEY]
ADD       DX,5
IN        AL,DX

MOV       BH,AL

MOV       DX,CS:[TSENGKEY]
ADD       DX,5
MOV       AL,BL
OUT       DX,AL

AND       BL,OFH
AND       BH,OFH
CMP       BH,BL

JNE       VGC10G

MESSAGE <"This appears to be a Tseng Labs 3000 card (not supported
         by Desktop Paint 256).",13,10>

EXITPROGRAM OK
```

VGC10G:
```
MESSAGE <"This appears to be a Tseng Labs 4000 card.",13,10>

EXITPROGRAM OK

EXITPROGRAM OK
```

VGC11:
```
MESSAGE <"No recognizable super VGA card was detected.",13,10,13,10>

CMP       CS:[VESAFLAG],00H
LNGJE     VGCX1

MESSAGE  <"Use the VESA drivers supplied with Desktop Paint 256, Graphic",13,10>
MESSAGE <"Workshop and Image Gallery.",13,10>

JMP       VGCX2
```

VGCX1:
```
MESSAGE <"You can use Graphic Workshop and Image Gallery in the standard",13,10>
MESSAGE <"VGA graphic modes. You will not be able to use Desktop Paint 256",13,10>
MESSAGE <"with this display hardware.",13,10>
```

VGCX2:
```
EXITPROGRAM ERROR
```

```
VGACARD          ENDP

SHOWVESAMODE     PROC     NEAR

                 PUSH     AX
                 MESSAGE  <"Mode ">
                 POP      AX
                 PUSH     AX
                 CALL     ITOH
                 MESSAGE  <"H - ">
                 POP      AX

                 TESTMESSAGE 0100H "640 by 400, 256 colours."
                 TESTMESSAGE 0101H "640 by 480, 256 colours."
                 TESTMESSAGE 0102H "800 by 600, 16 colours."
                 TESTMESSAGE 0103H "800 by 600, 256 colours."
                 TESTMESSAGE 0104H "1024 by 768, 16 colours."
                 TESTMESSAGE 0105H "1024 by 768, 256 colours."
                 TESTMESSAGE 0106H "1280 by 1024, 16 colours."
                 TESTMESSAGE 0107H "1280 by 1024, 256 colours."
                 TESTMESSAGE 010dH "320 by 200, 32768 colours."
                 TESTMESSAGE 010eH "320 by 200, 65536 colours."
                 TESTMESSAGE 010fH "320 by 200, 16,777,216 colours."
                 TESTMESSAGE 0110H "640 by 480, 32768 colours."
                 TESTMESSAGE 0111H "640 by 480, 65536 colours."
                 TESTMESSAGE 0112H "640 by 480, 16,777,216 colours."
                 TESTMESSAGE 0113H "800 by 600, 32768 colours."
                 TESTMESSAGE 0114H "800 by 600, 65536 colours."
                 TESTMESSAGE 0115H "800 by 600, 16,777,216 colours."
                 TESTMESSAGE 0116H "1024 by 768, 32768 colours."
                 TESTMESSAGE 0117H "1024 by 768, 65536 colours."
                 TESTMESSAGE 0118H "1024 by 768, 16,777,216 colours."
                 TESTMESSAGE 0119H "1280 by 1024, 32768 colours."
                 TESTMESSAGE 011aH "1280 by 1024, 65536 colours."
                 TESTMESSAGE 011bH "1280 by 1024, 16,777,216 colours."

                 MESSAGE  <13,10>

                 RET
SHOWVESAMODE     ENDP

ITOH             PROC     NEAR

                 PUSH     AX
                 MOV      BX,AX
                 MOV      CL,12
                 SHR      BX,CL
                 AND      BX,000FH
                 MOV      AL,CS:[HEXTABLE+BX]
                 CALL     PUTCHAR
                 POP      AX

                 PUSH     AX
                 MOV      BX,AX
                 MOV      CL,8
```

```
                    SHR       BX,CL
                    AND       BX,000FH
                    MOV       AL,CS:[HEXTABLE+BX]
                    CALL      PUTCHAR
                    POP       AX

                    PUSH      AX
                    MOV       BX,AX
                    MOV       CL,4
                    SHR       BX,CL
                    AND       BX,000FH
                    MOV       AL,CS:[HEXTABLE+BX]
                    CALL      PUTCHAR
                    POP       AX

                    PUSH      AX
                    MOV       BX,AX
                    AND       BX,000FH
                    MOV       AL,CS:[HEXTABLE+BX]
                    CALL      PUTCHAR
                    POP       AX

                    RET
ITOH                ENDP

PUTCHAR             PROC      NEAR
                    MOV       DL,AL
                    MOV       AH,02H
                    INT       21H
                    RET
PUTCHAR             ENDP

;COMPARE THE STRINGS AT DS:SI AND ES:DI FOR CX BYTES, RETURN E=1 IF EQUAL
MEMCMP              PROC      NEAR

                    MOV       BX,0000H
MCM1:               MOV       AL,DS:[SI+BX]
                    MOV       AH,ES:[DI+BX]
                    INC       BX
                    CMP       AL,AH
                    JE        MCM2
                    RET
MCM2:               LOOP      MCM1
                    RET
MEMCMP              ENDP

GETPORTBYTE         PROC      NEAR
                    OUT       DX,AL
                    JMP       SHORT GPB1
GPB1:               INC       DX
                    IN        AL,DX
                    RET
GETPORTBYTE         ENDP

PARADISE_ID         DB        'VGA='
```

```
ATI_ID            DB        '761295520'

HEXTABLE          DB        '0123456789ABCDEF'
VESAFLAG          DB        0

TSENGSTAT         DW        0
TSENGKEY          DW        0

ENDPROGRAM        LABEL     BYTE

CODE              ENDS

                  END       START
```

As an aside, there are a number of inscrutable assembly language things going on in VGACARD.ASM. You might find the code a bit easier to understand if you know about them.

To begin with, the MESSAGE macro purports to print a message to the screen, but it actually appears to be using the DOS INT 21H call that writes to files. It does actually print to the screen; DOS maintains five permanent file handles, of which handle one is the screen. Anything written to it will appear on your monitor.

This rather odd bit of notation might prove confusing:

```
JMP  $+2
```

The dollar sign will be expanded by an assembler to be the current location in the program. This means, then, to jump two bytes further along—that is, to the next instruction. It does absolutely nothing, but it soaks up a few processor cycles, which is long enough to let the registers of a VGA card settle down after they've been written to. This is used when you want to write something to a register and then read it back immediately.

Finally, you might wonder about the label ENDPROGRAM. Various bits of the VGACARD.ASM code seem to treat this as a buffer of any size they require. Clearly, there's no more code after this point, but trying something like this in a C program would unquestionably crash your software in ways hitherto discussed only in whispers.

When you run a .COM program on a PC, DOS assumes that it owns all the memory above itself. As such, the space from ENDPROGRAM to the top of its segment is unquestionably the province of VGACARD, and it's free to use it as it sees fit.

Index

Order Form for Readers
Requiring a Single 5.25" Disk

This Windcrest/McGraw-Hill software product is also available on a 5.25"/1.2Mb disk.

If you need the software in 5.25" format, simply follow these instructions:

- Complete the order form below. Be sure to include the exact title of the Windcrest/McGraw-Hill book for which you are requesting a replacement disk.

- Make check or money order made payable to *Glossbrenner's Choice*. **The cost is $5.00 ($8.00 for shipments outside the U.S.) to cover media, postage, and handling. Pennsylvania residents, please add 6% sales tax.**

- Foreign orders: please send an international money order or a check drawn on a bank with a U.S. clearing branch. We cannot accept foreign checks.

- Mail order form and payment to:
  Glossbrenner's Choice
  Attn: Windcrest/McGraw-Hill Disk Replacement
  699 River Road
  Yardley, PA 19067-1965

Your disks will be shipped via First Class Mail. Please allow one to two weeks for delivery.

✂ ....

Windcrest/McGraw-Hill Disk Replacement

Please send me a replacement disk in 5.25"/1.2Mb format for the following Windcrest/McGraw-Hill book:

Book Title _____

Name _____

Address _____

City/State/ZIP_____

If you need help
with the enclosed disk

This supplementary disk contains codes and programs appearing in *Super VGA Graphics: Programming Secrets* (Book #4413), (C)1993 by Windcrest Books.

This disk should include the files:

DTPE10.ZIP   ALICEFRG.ZIP   SOURCE.ZIP
DTPV20.ZIP   RESTOOLS.ZIP   PKUNZIP.EXE
-READ.ME

You might find it more convenient to keep all of these files on your hard drive instead of having to access them from the floppy disk. To create a hard drive subdirectory to store these files in, type

```
MKDIR dirname
```

at your hard drive prompt (most likely C:\), where *dirname* is what you want to name the subdirectory.

To copy the files, place your disk in your floppy drive (probably drive B) and type

```
COPY  B:*.*  C:\dirname
```

The files on the disk will now be copied to your newly created subdirectory.

After copying the files, you must unzip the compacted ones (identified by the extension .ZIP); use the included PKUNZIP.EXE program to do this. The format for running PKUNZIP is

```
C:\dirname\PKUNZIP C:\dirname\zipfilename
```

where *zipfilename* is the .ZIP file that you want to unzip.

For more help, examine the -READ.ME file on the disk. One way to do this is to type

```
TYPE B:\-READ.ME | MORE
```

at the DOS prompt with your disk in Drive B.